NEW WEBSTER'S

WORD DIVIDER

AVENEL BOOKS · NEW YORK

ISBN: 0-517-37160X

h g f e d c b a

FOREWORD

This book is compiled with your convenience in mind. It is intended to give you the information you seek about dividing words simply and clearly. It is based on NEW WEBSTER'S DICTIONARY OF THE ENGLISH LANGUAGE, copyright 1975 by Consolidated Book Publishers.

A centered dot (•) is used throughout to indicate where words may be broken. Words should be broken only as indicated even though the word may have additional syllables. For example, "abra•sion" has three syllables, but it would be bad practice to break it after the initial "a."

The one exception to the above rule is the orthographic hyphen. This is a hyphen that is part of the spelling of a word: "about-face." This hyphen may never be eliminated and the word, except when absolutely necessary, should be broken only at the hyphen.

Some common proper names are included in this book. Generally, it is better practice not to break proper names but, when necessary, they may be broken as indicated.

aard·vark
Aa·ron
aback
ab·a·cus
  ab·a·cus·es
  ab·a·ci
abaft
ab·a·lo·ne
aban·don
  aban·doned
  aban·don·er
  aban·don·ment
abase
  abased
  abas·ing
  abase·ment
abash
  abash·ment
abate
  abat·ed
  abat·ing
  abat·a·ble
  abate·ment
ab·at·toir
ab·ba·cy
  ab·ba·tial
ab·bey
  ab·beys
ab·bre·vi·a·tion
  ab·bre·vi·ate
  ab·bre·vi·at·ed
  ab·bre·vi·at·ing
  ab·bre·vi·a·tor
ab·di·cate
  ab·di·cat·ed
  ab·di·cat·ing
  ab·di·ca·tion
ab·do·men
  ab·dom·i·nal
  ab·dom·i·nal·ly
ab·duct
  ab·duc·tion
  ab·duc·tor
abeam
abed
Ab·e·lard
Ab·er·deen
ab·er·rance
  ab·er·ran·cy
ab·er·rant
  ab·er·rant·ly
ab·er·ra·tion
  ab·er·ra·tion·al
abet
  abet·ted
  abet·ting
  abet·ment
  abet·tor
  abet·ter
abey·ance
ab·hor
  ab·horred
  ab·hor·ring
  ab·hor·rence
  ab·hor·er

ab·hor·rent
  ab·hor·rent·ly
abide
  abode
  abi·ded
  abid·ing
  abid·ance
  abid·ing
  abid·ing·ly
Abid·jan
Ab·i·gail
Ab·i·lene
abil·i·ty
  abil·i·ties
ab·ject
  ab·ject·ly
  ab·ject·ness
ab·jure
  ab·jured
  ab·jur·ing
  ab·ju·ra·tion
  ab·jur·er
ab·late
  ab·lat·ed
  ab·lat·ing
  ab·la·tion
  ab·la·tive
ablaze
able
ably
able-bod·ied
abloom
ab·lu·tion
  ab·lu·tion·ar·y
ab·ne·gate
  ab·ne·gat·ed
  ab·ne·gat·ing
ab·nor·mal
  ab·nor·mal·i·ty
  ab·nor·mal·i·ties
aboard
abode
abol·ish
  abol·ish·a·ble
  abol·ish·er
  abol·ish·ment
ab·o·li·tion
  ab·o·li·tion·ism
  ab·o·li·tion·ist
A-bomb
abom·i·na·ble
  abom·i·na·bly
abom·i·nate
  abom·i·nat·ed
  abom·i·nat·ing
  abom·i·na·tion
ab·o·rig·i·ne
  ab·o·rig·i·nal
abort
abor·tion
  abor·tion·ist
  abor·tive
abound
about
about-face

above
above-board
ab·ra·ca·dab·ra
abrade
  abrad·ed
  abrad·ing
Abra·ham
abra·sion
abra·sive
abreast
abridge
  abridged
  abridg·ing
  abridg·er
  abridg·a·ble
  abridge·a·ble
  abridg·ment
  abridge·ment
abroad
ab·ro·gate
  ab·ro·gat·ed
  ab·ro·gat·ing
  ab·ro·ga·tion
ab·rupt
Ab·sa·lom
ab·scess
  ab·scessed
ab·scis·sa
  ab·scis·sas
  ab·scis·sae
  ab·scis·sion
ab·scond
ab·sence
ab·sent
ab·sen·tee
  ab·sen·tee·ism
ab·sent-mind·ed
ab·sinthe
ab·so·lute
  ab·so·lute·ly
ab·so·lu·tion
ab·so·lut·ism
  ab·so·lut·ist
ab·solve
  ab·solved
  ab·solv·ing
  ab·solv·a·ble
  ab·solv·er
ab·sorb
  ab·sorb·a·bil·i·ty
  ab·sorb·a·ble
  ab·sorb·en·cy
  ab·sorb·ent
  ab·sorp·tion
  ab·sorp·tive
  ab·sorp·tiv·i·ty
  ab·sorb·ing
ab·stain
  ab·sten·tion
  ab·sti·nence
  ab·sti·nent
ab·ste·mi·ous
ab·stract
  ab·strac·tion
  ab·strac·tive

ab·stract·ed
  ab·stract·ed·ly
ab·struse
ab·surd
  ab·surd·i·ty
  ab·surd·i·ties
  ab·surd·ly
abun·dance
abun·dant
  abun·dant·ly
abuse
  abused
  abus·ing
  abus·er
abu·sive
  abu·sive·ly
  abu·sive·ness
abut
  abut·ted
  abut·ting
abut·ment
abysm
abys·mal
abyss
Ab·ys·sin·ia
aca·cia
ac·a·deme
ac·a·dem·ic
  ac·a·dem·i·cal·ly
  ac·a·dem·i·cal
acad·e·mi·cian
acad·e·my
  acad·e·mies
Aca·dia
acan·thus
  acan·thus·es
  acan·thi
a cap·pel·la
Aca·pul·co
ac·cede
  ac·ced·ed
  ac·ced·ing
ac·cel·er·ate
  ac·cel·er·at·ed
  ac·cel·er·at·ing
  ac·cel·er·a·tive
  ac·cel·er·a·tion
  ac·cel·er·a·tor
ac·cent
  ac·cen·tu·al
ac·cen·tu·ate
  ac·cen·tu·at·ed
  ac·cen·tu·at·ing
  ac·cen·tu·a·tion
ac·cept
  ac·cept·ance
  ac·cept·er
  ac·cept·or
ac·cept·a·ble
  ac·cept·a·bil·i·ty
ac·cept·ed
ac·cess
  ac·ces·si·ble
  ac·ces·si·bil·i·ty
ac·ces·sion

ac·ces·so·ry
  ac·ces·so·ri·ly
  ac·ces·so·ri·ness
ac·ci·dent
ac·ci·den·tal
  ac·ci·den·tal·ly
ac·claim
ac·cla·ma·tion
  ac·clam·a·to·ry
ac·cli·mate
  ac·cli·mat·ed
  ac·cli·mat·ing
  ac·cli·ma·tion
ac·cli·ma·tize
  ac·cli·ma·tized
  ac·cli·ma·tiz·ing
  ac·cli·ma·ti·za·tion
ac·cliv·i·ty
  ac·cliv·i·ties
ac·co·lade
ac·com·mo·date
  ac·com·mo·dat·ed
  ac·com·mo·dat·ing
  ac·com·mo·da·tive
  ac·com·mo·da·tion
ac·com·pa·ni·ment
ac·com·pa·nist
ac·com·pa·ny
  ac·com·pa·nied
  ac·com·pa·ny·ing
ac·com·plice
ac·com·plish
  ac·com·plish·a·ble
  ac·com·plish·ment
ac·com·plished
ac·cord
ac·cord·ance
ac·cord·ing
  ac·cord·ing·ly
ac·cor·di·on
  ac·cor·di·on·ist
ac·cost
ac·couche·ment
ac·count
ac·count·a·ble
  ac·count·a·bil·i·ty
  ac·count·a·bly
ac·count·an·cy
ac·count·ant
ac·count·ing
Ac·cra
ac·cred·it
ac·cre·tion
  ac·cre·tive
ac·cru·al
ac·crue
  ac·crued
  ac·cru·ing
ac·cum·u·late
  ac·cum·u·lat·ed
  ac·cum·u·lat·ing
ac·cum·u·la·tion
ac·cu·mu·la·tive
ac·cum·u·la·tor
ac·cu·ra·cy

ac·cu·rate
  ac·cu·rate·ly
  ac·cu·rate·ness
ac·curs·ed
ac·curst
ac·cu·sa·tive
ac·cuse
  ac·cused
  ac·cus·ing
ac·cu·sa·tion
ac·cu·sa·to·ry
  ac·cus·ing·ly
ac·cus·tom
ac·cus·tomed
acer·bi·ty
ac·e·tate
ace·tic
acet·i·fy
  acet·i·fied
  acet·i·fy·ing
ac·e·tone
acet·y·lene
ache
  ached
  ach·ing
achieve
  achieved
  achiev·ing
  achiev·a·ble
  achiev·er
  achieve·ment
Ach·il·le·an
Achil·les' heel
ach·ro·mat·ic
ac·id
acid·ic
acid·i·fy
  acid·i·fied
  acid·i·fy·ing
  acid·i·fi·ca·tion
  acid·i·fi·er
acid·i·ty
ac·i·do·sis
acid·u·late
  acid·u·lat·ed
  acid·u·lat·ing
  acid·u·la·tion
acid·u·lous
ac·knowl·edge
  ac·knowl·edged
  ac·knowl·edg·ing
  ac·knowl·edge·a·ble
  ac·knowl·edg·er
  ac·knowl·edg·ment
  ac·knowl·edge·ment
ac·me
ac·ne
ac·o·lyte
ac·o·nite
acorn
acous·tic
  acous·ti·cal
  acous·ti·cal·ly
acous·tics
ac·quaint

ac·quaint·ance
ac·quaint·ance·ship
ac·qui·esce
ac·qui·esced
ac·qui·esc·ing
ac·qui·es·cence
ac·qui·es·cent
ac·quire
ac·quired
ac·quir·ing
ac·quir·er
ac·quir·a·ble
ac·quire·ment
ac·qui·si·tion
ac·quit
ac·quit·ted
ac·quit·ting
ac·quit·tal
acre
acre·age
ac·rid
acrid·i·ty
ac·ri·mo·ni·ous
ac·ri·mo·ny
ac·ro·bat
ac·ro·bat·ic
ac·ro·nym
ac·ro·pho·bia
acrop·o·lis
across
acros·tic
acros·ti·cal·ly
acryl·ic
ac·ry·lo·ni·trile
act·ing
ac·tin·ic
ac·tin·ism
ac·tin·i·um
ac·ti·nom·e·ter
ac·ti·non
ac·ti·no·zo·an
ac·tion
ac·tion·a·ble
ac·tion·a·bly
ac·ti·vate
ac·ti·vat·ed
ac·ti·vat·ing
ac·ti·va·tion
ac·ti·va·tor
ac·tive
ac·tive·ly
ac·tive·ness
ac·tiv·ism
ac·tiv·ist
ac·tiv·i·ty
ac·tiv·i·ties
ac·tor
ac·tress
ac·tu·al
ac·tu·al·ly
ac·tu·al·i·ty
ac·tu·al·i·ties
ac·tu·al·ize
ac·tu·al·ized
ac·tu·al·iz·ing

ac·tu·al·i·za·tion
ac·tu·ary
ac·tu·ar·ies
ac·tu·ar·i·al
ac·tu·ate
ac·tu·at·ed
ac·tu·at·ing
ac·tu·a·tion
ac·tu·a·tor
acu·i·ty
acu·men
ac·u·punc·ture
acute
acute·ly
acute·ness
ad·age
ada·gio
Ad·am
Ad·ams
ad·a·mant
ad·a·mant·ly
ad·a·man·tine
adapt
adapt·er
adapt·a·ble
adapt·a·bil·i·ty
ad·ap·ta·tion
adap·tive
adap·tive·ly
add
add·a·ble
add·i·ble
ad·dend
ad·den·dum
ad·den·da
ad·der
ad·dict
ad·dic·tion
ad·dict·ed
ad·dic·tive
Ad·dis Ab·a·ba
Ad·di·son
ad·di·tion
ad·di·tion·al
ad·di·tion·al·ly
ad·di·tive
ad·dle
ad·dress
ad·dress·ee
ad·duce
ad·duct
ad·duc·tion
ad·duc·tive
ad·e·noid
ad·e·noi·dal
adept
adept·ly
adept·ness
ad·e·qua·cy
ad·e·quate
ad·e·quate·ly
ad·here
ad·hered
ad·her·ing
ad·her·ence

ad·her·ent
ad·he·sion
ad·he·sive
 ad·he·sive·ly
 ad·he·sive·ness
ad hoc
ad ho·mi·nem
ad·i·a·bat·ic
adieu
ad in·fi·ni·tum
adi·os
ad·i·pose
Ad·i·ron·dack
ad·ja·cen·cy
 ad·ja·cen·cies
ad·ja·cent
 ad·ja·cent·ly
ad·jec·tive
 ad·jec·ti·val
ad·join
 ad·join·ing
ad·journ
ad·journ·ment
ad·judge
 ad·judged
 ad·judg·ing
ad·ju·di·cate
 ad·ju·di·cat·ed
 ad·ju·di·cat·ing
 ad·ju·di·ca·tion
 ad·ju·di·ca·tor
ad·junct
 ad·junc·tive
ad·jure
 ad·jured
 ad·jur·ing
 ad·ju·ra·tion
 ad·ju·ra·to·ry
 ad·jur·er
ad·just
 ad·just·a·ble
 ad·just·er
 ad·just·or
 ad·just·ment
ad·ju·tan·cy
ad·ju·tant
ad-lib
 ad-libbed
 ad-lib·bing
ad·man
 ad·men
ad·min·is·ter
ad·min·is·trate
ad·min·is·tra·tion
 ad·min·is·tra·tive
 ad·min·is·tra·tor
ad·mi·ral
ad·mi·ral·ty
ad·mire
 ad·mired
 ad·mir·ing
 ad·mi·ra·ble
 ad·mi·ra·bly
 ad·mi·ra·tion
 ad·mir·er

ad·mir·ing·ly
ad·mis·si·ble
ad·mis·si·bil·i·ty
ad·mis·sion
ad·mit
 ad·mit·ted
 ad·mit·ting
 ad·mit·ted·ly
 ad·mit·tance
ad·mix
ad·mix·ture
ad·mon·ish
 ad·mon·ish·er
 ad·mo·ni·tion
 ad·mon·i·to·ry
ado
ado·be
ad·o·les·cence
ad·o·les·cent
Ad·olph
Adon·is
adopt
 adopt·a·ble
 adopt·er
 adop·tion
 adop·tive
adore
 adored
 ador·ing
 ador·a·ble
 ad·o·ra·tion
 ador·ing·ly
adorn
 adorn·ment
ad·re·nal
adren·a·line
Adri·an
adrift
adroit
 adroit·ly
 adroit·ness
ad·sorb
 ad·sor·bent
 ad·sorp·tion
ad·u·la·tion
ad·u·late
 ad·u·lat·ed
 ad·u·lat·ing
 ad·u·la·tor
 ad·u·la·to·ry
adult
 adult·hood
adul·ter·ate
 adul·ter·at·ed
 adul·ter·at·ing
 adul·ter·ant
 adul·ter·a·tion
adul·tery
adul·ter·er
 adul·ter·ess
 adul·ter·ous
ad·um·brate
 ad·um·brat·ed
 ad·um·brat·ing
ad va·lo·rem

ad·vance
  ad·vanced
  ad·vanc·ing
ad·vanced
  ad·vance·ment
ad·van·tage
  ad·van·taged
  ad·van·tag·ing
ad·van·ta·geous
  ad·van·ta·geous·ly
ad·vent
ad·ven·ti·tious
ad·ven·tive
ad·ven·ture
  ad·ven·tured
  ad·ven·tur·ing
  ad·ven·tur·er
  ad·ven·tur·ess
  ad·ven·tur·ous
  ad·ven·ture·some
ad·verb
  ad·ver·bi·al
ad·ver·sary
  ad·ver·sar·ies
ad·verse
  ad·verse·ly
  ad·verse·ness
ad·ver·si·ty
  ad·ver·si·ties
ad·vert
  ad·vert·ence
  ad·vert·ent
ad·ver·tise
  ad·ver·tised
  ad·ver·tis·ing
  ad·ver·tis·er
  ad·ver·tise·ment
ad·vice
ad·vise
  ad·vised
  ad·vis·ing
  ad·vis·a·bil·i·ty
  ad·vis·a·ble
  ad·vis·a·bly
  ad·vis·er
ad·vis·ed·ly
  ad·vise·ment
ad·vi·so·ry
ad·vo·ca·cy
  ad·vo·ca·cies
ad·vo·cate
  ad·vo·cat·ed
  ad·vo·cat·ing
  ad·vo·ca·tion
Ae·ge·an
Ae·gi·na
ae·gis
Ae·ne·as
Ae·ne·id
Ae·o·lus
ae·on
aer·ate
  aer·at·ed
  aer·at·ing
  aer·a·tion

aer·a·tor
aer·i·al
  aer·i·al·ly
  aer·i·al·ist
aer·ie
aer·i·fy
  aer·i·fi·ca·tion
aer·obe
aer·o·me·chan·ics
aer·o·naut·ics
  aer·o·nau·ti·cal
aer·o·plane
aer·o·sol
aer·o·space
Aes·chy·lus
Aes·cu·la·pi·us
Ae·sop
aes·thete
aes·thet·ic
  aes·thet·i·cal·ly
Aet·na
afar
af·fa·ble
  af·fa·bil·i·ty
  af·fa·bly
af·fair
af·fect
  af·fect·ing
  af·fect·ing·ly
af·fec·tive
af·fec·ta·tion
af·fect·ed
  af·fect·ed·ly
  af·fect·ed·ness
af·fec·tion
  af·fec·tion·ate
  af·fec·tion·ate·ly
  af·fec·tion·ate·ness
af·fer·ent
af·fi·ance
  af·fi·anced
  af·fi·anc·ing
af·fi·da·vit
af·fil·i·ate
  af·fil·i·at·ed
  af·fil·i·at·ing
af·fin·i·ty
  af·fin·i·ties
af·firm
  af·firm·a·ble
  af·firm·a·bly
  af·fir·ma·tion
  af·firm·a·tive
af·fix
af·fla·tus
af·flict
  af·flic·tion
af·flu·ence
  af·flu·ent
  af·flu·ent·ly
af·ford
af·fray
af·front
af·ghan
Af·ghan·i·stan

afield
afire
aflame
afloat
afoot
afore·men·tioned
afore·said
afore·thought
afoul
afraid
afresh
Af·ri·ca
Af·ri·can
Af·ri·kan·der
af·ter
af·ter·birth
af·ter·burn·er
af·ter·ef·fect
af·ter·glow
af·ter·life
af·ter·math
af·ter·noon
af·ter·taste
af·ter·thought
af·ter·ward
 af·ter·wards
again
against
Ag·a·mem·non
agape
agar
Ag·as·siz
ag·ate
aga·ve
age
 aged
 ag·ing
 age·ing
aged
age·less
age·long
agen·cy
 agen·cies
agen·da
agent
 agen·tial
ag·glom·er·ate
 ag·glom·er·at·ed
 ag·glom·er·at·ing
 ag·glom·er·a·tion
 ag·glom·er·a·tive
ag·glu·ti·nate
 ag·glu·ti·nat·ed
 ag·glu·ti·nat·ing
 ag·glu·ti·na·tion
 ag·glu·ti·na·tive
ag·gran·dize
 ag·gran·dized
 ag·gran·diz·ing
 ag·gran·dize·ment
 ag·gran·diz·er
ag·gra·vate
 ag·gra·vat·ed
 ag·gra·vat·ing
 ag·gra·va·tion

ag·gre·gate
 ag·gre·gat·ed
 ag·gre·gat·ing
 ag·gre·ga·tion
 ag·gre·ga·tive
ag·gress
 ag·gress·ive
 ag·gress·ive·ly
 ag·gress·ive·ness
 ag·gress·or
ag·gres·sion
ag·grieve
 ag·grieved
 ag·griev·ing
aghast
ag·ile
 ag·ile·ly
agil·i·ty
ag·i·tate
 ag·i·tat·ed
 ag·i·tat·ing
 ag·i·tat·ed·ly
 ag·i·ta·tion
 ag·i·ta·tor
agleam
aglow
ag·no·men
 ag·nom·i·na
ag·nos·tic
 ag·nos·ti·cism
ago
agog
agon·ic
ag·o·nize
 ag·o·nized
 ag·o·niz·ing
ag·o·ny
 ag·o·nies
ag·o·ra·pho·bia
agrar·i·an
 agrar·i·an·ism
agree
 agreed
 agree·ing
 agree·a·bil·i·ty
agree·a·ble
 agree·a·ble·ness
 agree·a·bly
agreed
agree·ment
ag·ri·cul·ture
 ag·ri·cul·tur·al
 ag·ri·cul·tur·ist
Agrip·pa
agron·o·my
 ag·ro·nom·ic
 ag·ro·nom·i·cal
 agron·o·mist
aground
Aguas·ca·lien·tes
ague
 agu·ish
aha
ahead
ahem

ahoy
Ai·da
aide-de-camp
ai·grette
ail
 ail·ing
ail·ment
ai·lan·thus
ai·ler·on
aim·less
air·less
air·borne
air·brush
air·con·di·tion
 air·con·di·tioned
air con·di·tion·er
air con·di·tion·ing
air·craft
air·craft car·ri·er
air·drome
air·drop
 air·dropped
 air·drop·ping
Aire·dale
air·field
air·foil
air·mail
air·man
 air·men
air·plane
air·port
air pres·sure
air·ship
air·sick·ness
air·space
air·speed
air·strip
air·tight
air·wave
air·way
airy
 air·i·er
 air·i·est
 air·i·ness
 air·i·ly
aisle
Aix-la-Cha·pelle
ajar
akim·bo
akin
Ak·ron
Al·a·bama
al·a·bas·ter
a la carte
alac·ri·ty
Alad·din
Al·a·me·da
Al·a·mo
Alar·cón
alarm
 alarm·ing
 alarm·ing·ly
alarm·ist
 alarm·ism
alas

Alas·ka
alate
 alat·ed
al·ba·core
Al·ba·nia
Al·ba·ny
al·ba·tross
al·be·it
Al·be·marle
Al·ber·ta
Al·bi·gen·ses
al·bi·no
 al·bi·nos
 al·bi·nism
Al·bi·on
al·bum
al·bu·men
al·bu·min
 al·bu·mi·nous
Al·bu·quer·que
Al·cae·us
Al·ca·traz
Al·ces·tis
al·che·my
 al·che·mist
Al·ci·bi·a·des
Al·ci·des
al·co·hol
al·co·hol·ic
al·co·hol·ism
Al·cott
al·cove
al·der
al·der·man
 al·der·man·ic
Al·der·ney
Al·drich
ale·a·to·ry
alee
alert
 alert·ness
Ales·san·dria
Aleu·tian
ale·wife
 ale·wives
Al·ex·an·der
Al·ex·an·dria
al·ex·an·drine
al·fal·fa
al·fres·co
al·ga
 al·gae
al·ge·bra
 al·ge·bra·ic
 al·ge·bra·ic·al
 al·ge·bra·ic·al·ly
Al·ge·ria
Al·giers
Al·gon·qui·an
Al·gon·quin
al·go·ri·thm
Al·ham·bra
ali·as
 ali·as·es
Ali Ba·ba

al·i·bi
al·ien
  al·ien·a·ble
  al·ien·a·bil·i·ty
al·ien·ate
  al·ien·at·ed
  al·ien·at·ing
al·ien·ist
  al·ien·ism
al·i·form
alight
  alight·ed
  alit
  alight·ing
align
align·ment
  aline·ment
alike
al·i·ment
  al·i·men·tal
  al·i·men·tal·ly
  al·i·men·ta·tion
al·i·men·ta·ry
  al·i·men·ta·ry ca·nal
al·i·mo·ny
al·i·quant
al·i·quot
Al·i·son
alive
al·ka·li
  al·ka·lies
  al·ka·lis
al·ka·line
  al·ka·lin·i·ty
al·ka·lize
  al·ka·lized
  al·ka·liz·ing
  al·ka·li·za·tion
al·ka·loid
  al·ka·loi·dal
Al·lah
all-A·mer·i·can
all-a·round
al·lay
  al·layed
  al·lay·ing
  al·lay·er
al·le·ga·tion
al·lege
  al·leged
  al·leg·ing
  al·lege·a·ble
Al·le·ghe·nies
Al·le·ghe·ny
al·le·giance
al·le·go·ry
  al·le·go·ries
  al·le·gor·ic
  al·le·gor·i·cal
  al·le·gor·i·cal·ly
  al·le·gor·ist
al·le·gret·to
al·le·gro
Al·len·town
al·ler·gen

al·ler·gy
  al·ler·gies
  al·ler·gic
  al·ler·gist
al·le·vi·ate
  al·le·vi·at·ed
  al·le·vi·at·ing
  al·le·vi·a·tion
  al·le·vi·a·tor
  al·le·vi·a·tive
  al·le·vi·a·to·ry
al·ley
  al·leys
All-hal·lows
al·li·ance
al·lied
al·li·ga·tor
al·lit·er·ate
  al·lit·er·at·ed
  al·lit·er·at·ing
  al·lit·er·a·tive
  al·lit·er·a·tive·ly
  al·lit·er·a·tive·ness
  al·lit·er·a·tion
al·lo·cate
  al·lo·cat·ed
  al·lo·cat·ing
  al·lo·ca·tion
al·lop·a·thy
  al·lo·path·ic
  al·lo·path·i·cal·ly
  al·lop·a·thist
al·lo·phone
al·lot
  al·lot·ted
  al·lot·ting
  al·lot·ment
  al·lot·ta·ble
  al·lot·ro·py
  al·lot·ro·pism
al·lo·trope
  al·lo·trop·ic
  al·lo·trop·i·cal·ly
al·low
  al·low·a·ble
  al·low·a·bly
  al·low·ed·ly
  al·low·ance
  al·low·anced
  al·low·anc·ing
al·loy
all right
all·spice
al·lude
  al·lud·ed
  al·lud·ing
al·lure
  al·lured
  al·lur·ing
  al·lure·ment
  al·lur·er
  al·lur·ing·ly
al·lu·sion
al·lu·sive
  al·lu·sive·ly

al·lu·sive·ness
al·lu·vi·al
al·lu·vi·um
al·lu·vi·ums
al·lu·via
al·ly
al·lied
al·ly·ing
al·ly
al·lies
al·ma ma·ter
al·ma·nac
al·mighty
al·mond
al·most
alms·giv·er
alms·giv·ing
alms·house
al·ni·co
al·oe
aloft
alo·ha
alone
alone·ness
along
along·shore
along·side
aloof
aloof·ly
aloof·ness
al·pen·stock
al·pha
al·pha·bet
al·pha·bet·ic
al·pha·bet·i·cal
al·pha·bet·i·cal·ly
al·pha·bet·i·za·tion
al·pha·bet·ize
al·pha·bet·ized
al·pha·bet·iz·ing
Al·phe·us
Al·phon·so
Al·pine
al·ready
Al·sace-Lor·raine
al·so
al·tar
al·ter
al·ter·a·bil·i·ty
al·ter·a·ble
al·ter·ant
al·ter·a·tion
al·ter·a·tive
al·ter·ca·tion
al·ter e·go
al·ter·nate
al·ter·nat·ed
al·ter·nat·ing
al·ter·nate·ly
al·ter·na·tion
al·ter·na·tive
al·ter·na·tive·ly
al·ter·na·tive·ness
al·ter·na·tor
al·though

al·tim·e·ter
al·tim·e·try
al·ti·pla·no
al·ti·tude
al·to
al·to·cu·mu·lus
al·to·gether
Al·too·na
al·to·re·lie·vo
al·to·stra·tus
al·tru·ism
al·tru·is·tic
al·lu·mi·na
alu·mi·nif·er·ous
alu·mi·nous
alu·mi·num
alum·na
alum·nae
alum·nus
alum·ni
al·ve·o·lar
al·ve·o·lus
al·ve·o·li
al·ways
amal·gam
amal·gam·a·ble
amal·gam·ate
amal·gam·at·ed
amal·gam·at·ing
amal·gam·a·tion
aman·u·en·sis
aman·u·en·ses
Am·a·ril·lo
am·a·ryl·lis
amass
amass·ment
am·a·teur
am·a·teur·ism
am·a·teur·ish
am·a·teur·ish·ly
am·a·teur·ish·ness
am·a·tive
am·a·tive·ness
am·a·to·ry
amaze
amazed
amaz·ing
amaz·ed·ly
amaz·ed·ness
amaze·ment
Am·a·zon
Am·a·zo·ni·an
am·bas·sa·dor
am·bas·sa·do·ri·al
am·ber
am·ber·gris
am·bi·dex·trous
am·bi·ance
am·bi·ence
am·bi·ent
am·big·u·ous
am·big·u·ous·ly
am·big·u·ous·ness
am·bi·gu·i·ty
am·bit

am·bi·tion
am·bi·tious
am·bi·tious·ly
am·bi·tious·ness
am·biv·a·lence
am·biv·a·lent
am·ble
am·bled
am·bling
am·bler
am·bro·sia
am·bro·sial
am·bro·sial·ly
am·bu·lance
am·bu·la·to·ry
am·bu·lant
am·bu·late
am·bu·lat·ed
am·bu·lat·ing
am·bus·cade
am·bus·cad·ed
am·bus·cad·ing
am·bush
am·bush·ment
ame·ba
amel·io·rate
amel·io·rat·ed
amel·io·rat·ing
amel·io·ra·ble
amel·io·ra·tion
amel·ior·a·tive
amel·io·ra·tor
amen
ame·na·ble
ame·na·bil·i·ty
ame·na·ble·ness
ame·na·bly
amend
amend·a·ble
amend·er
amend·ment
amends
amen·i·ty
amerce
amerced
amerc·ing
amerce·a·ble
amerce·ment
amerc·er
Amer·i·ca
Amer·i·can
Amer·i·cana
Amer·i·can·ism
am·e·thyst
am·e·thys·tine
Am·herst
ami·a·ble
ami·a·bil·i·ty
ami·a·bly
am·i·ca·ble
am·i·ca·bil·i·ty
am·i·ca·bly
am·ice
amid
amidst

am·ide
amid·ships
Am·i·ens
ami·go
amine
ami·no ac·id
amir
Amish
amiss
am·i·to·sis
am·i·tot·ic
am·i·tot·i·cal·ly
am·i·ty
Am·man
am·me·ter
Am·mon
am·mo·nia
am·mon·ic
am·mo·ni·ac
am·mo·ni·um
am·mo·ni·un chlo·ride
am·mo·ni·um hy·drox·ide
am·mu·ni·tion
am·ne·sia
am·ne·sic
am·nes·tic
am·nes·ty
am·ni·on
am·ni·ons
am·nia
am·ni·on·ic
am·ni·ot·ic
amoe·ba
amoe·bae
amoe·bas
amoe·bic
amoe·boid
amok
among
amongst
Amon·til·la·do
amor·al
am·o·rous
am·o·rous·ly
am·o·rous·ness
amor·phism
amor·phous
am·or·tize
am·or·tized
am·or·tiz·ing
am·or·ti·za·tion
amount
amour
am·per·age
am·pere
am·per·sand
am·phet·a·mine
Am·phib·ia
am·phib·i·an
am·phib·i·ous
am·phi·the·a·ter
am·phi·the·at·ric
am·pho·ra
am·pho·rae
am·pho·ras

am·ple
am·pler
am·plest
am·ple·ness
am·ply
am·pli·fy
am·pli·fied
am·pli·fy·ing
am·pli·fi·ca·tion
am·pli·fi·er
am·pli·tude
am·pul
am·pu·tate
am·pu·tat·ed
am·pu·tat·ing
am·pu·ta·tion
am·pu·tee
Am·ster·dam
Am·trak
amuck
am·u·let
amuse
amused
amus·ing
amuse·ment
am·yl·ase
An·a·bap·tist
anach·ro·nism
anach·ro·nis·tik
anach·ro·nis·ti·cal·ly
anach·ro·nous
an·a·con·da
an·aer·obe
an·aes·the·sia
an·aes·thet·ic
an·a·gram
an·a·gram·mat·ic
an·a·gram·mat·i·cal
ana·gram·ma·tize
ana·gram·ma·tized
ana·gram·ma·tiz·ing
anal
an·a·lects
an·al·ge·sia
an·al·ge·sic
an·a·log
an·a·log·i·cal
an·a·log·i·cal·ly
anal·o·gize
anal·o·gized
anal·o·giz·ing
anal·o·gy
anal·o·gies
anal·o·gous
anal·y·sis
anal·y·ses
an·a·lyst
an·a·lyt·ic
an·a·lyt·ics
an·a·lyze
an·a·lyzed
an·a·lyz·ing
an·a·lyz·a·ble
an·a·ly·za·tion
an·a·lyz·er

An·a·ni·as
an·a·pest
an·a·pes·tic
an·ar·chism
an·ar·chist
an·ar·chis·tic
an·ar·chy
an·ar·chic
an·ar·chi·cal
anath·e·ma
anath·e·mas
anath·e·ma·tize
anath·e·ma·tized
anath·e·ma·tiz·ing
anath·e·mat·iz·a·tion
An·a·to·lia
anat·o·mize
anat·o·mized
anat·o·mizing
anat·o·mi·za·tion
anat·o·my
anat·o·mies
an·a·tom·i·cal
an·a·tom·i·cal·ly
anat·o·mist
an·ces·tor
an·ces·tral
an·ces·tress
an·ces·try
An·chi·ses
an·chor
an·chor·age
an·cho·ress
an·cho·rite
an·cho·vy
an·cient
an·cient·ly
an·cient·ness
an·cil·lary
An·co·na
An·da·lu·sia
an·dan·te
An·de·an
An·der·son
An·des
and·i·ron
An·dor·ra
An·do·ver
an·dro·gen
an·drog·y·nous
an·drog·y·nal
an·drog·y·ny
An·drom·a·che
An·drom·e·da
An·dros
an·dros·ter·one
an·ec·dote
an·ec·dot·age
an·ec·do·tal
an·ec·dot·ist
ane·mia
ane·mic
an·e·mom·e·ter
an·e·mom·e·try
anem·o·ne

an·er·oid
an·es·the·sia
an·es·thet·ic
an·es·the·tist
an·es·the·tize
an·es·the·tized
an·es·the·tiz·ing
an·eu·rysm
an·eu·rism
an·eu·rys·mal
anew
an·ga·ry
an·gel
an·gel·ic
an·gel·i·cal
an·gel·i·cal·ly
an·gel·i·ca
An·ge·lus
an·ger
an·gi·na
an·gi·na pec·to·ris
an·gi·o·sperm
an·gi·o·sper·mous
Ang·kor
an·gle
an·gler
an·gle·worm
An·gli·can
An·gli·can·ism
An·gli·cism
An·gli·cize
An·gli·cized
An·gli·ciz·ing
An·gli·ci·za·tion
an·gling
An·glo·phile
An·glo·phobe
An·glo-Sax·on
An·go·la
an·go·ra
an·gos·tu·ra bark
an·gry
an·gri·ly
an·gri·ness
ang·strom unit
an·guish
an·gu·lar
an·gu·lar·i·ty
an·gu·lar·ly
an·gu·lar·ness
An·gus
an·hy·dride
an·hy·drous
an·i·line
an·i·mad·vert
an·i·mad·ver·sion
an·i·mal
an·i·mal·cule
an·i·mal·cu·lar
an·i·mal·ism
an·i·mal·i·ty
an·i·mal·ize
an·i·mal·ized
an·i·mal·iz·ing
an·i·mate

an·i·mat·ed
an·i·mat·ing
an·i·ma·tion
ani·ma·to
an·i·mism
an·i·mis·tic
an·i·mos·i·ty
an·i·mus
an·i·on
an·ise
an·i·seed
an·i·sette
An·jou
An·ka·ra
an·kle
an·kle·bone
an·klet
an·ky·lose
an·ky·losed
an·ky·los·ing
an·ky·lo·sis
an·ky·lot·ic
an·nal·ist
an·nal·is·tic
an·nals
An·nam
An·nap·o·lis
Ann Arbor
an·neal
an·ne·lid
an·nel·i·dan
an·nex
an·nex·a·tion
an·nex·a·tion·ist
an·ni·hi·late
an·ni·hi·lat·ed
an·ni·hi·lat·ing
an·ni·hi·la·tion
an·ni·hi·la·tor
An·nis·ton
an·ni·ver·sa·ry
an·ni·ver·sa·ries
an·no Dom·i·ni
an·no·tate
an·no·tat·ed
an·no·tat·ing
an·no·ta·tion
an·no·ta·tor
an·nounce
an·nounced
an·nounc·ing
an·nounce·ment
an·nounc·er
an·noy
an·noy·ance
an·noy·er
an·nu·al
an·nu·i·ty
an·nu·i·tant
an·nul
an·nulled
an·nul·ling
an·nul·ment
an·nu·lar
an·nu·lar·i·ty

an·nu·lar·ly
an·nu·late
an·nu·let
an·nu·lus
an·nu·lus·es
an·nun·ci·a·tion
an·nun·ci·ate
an·nun·ci·at·ed
an·nun·ci·at·ing
an·nun·ci·a·tor
an·ode
an·od·ic
an·o·dyne
anoint
anoint·er
anoint·ment
anom·a·ly
anom·a·lism
anom·a·lous
anom·a·lous·ly
anom·a·lous·ness
an·o·mie
an·o·my
an·o·nym
anon·y·mous
an·o·nym·i·ty
anon·y·mous·ly
anon·y·mous·ness
anoph·e·les
an·oth·er
an·ox·ia
An·schluss
an·ser·ine
an·swer
an·swer·a·ble
ant·ac·id
An·tae·us
an·tag·o·nist
an·tag·o·nism
an·tag·o·nis·tic
an·tag·o·nis·ti·cal·ly
an·tag·o·nize
an·tag·o·nized
an·tag·o·niz·ing
ant·arc·tic
Ant·arc·ti·ca
An·tar·es
an·te
an·ted
an·te·ing
ant·eat·er
an·te·bel·lum
an·te·ced·ence
an·te·ced·ent
an·te·cede
an·te·ced·ed
an·te·ced·ing
an·te·ce·dent·ly
an·te·cham·ber
an·te·choir
an·te·date
an·te·dat·ed
an·te·dat·ing
an·te·di·lu·vi·an
an·te·lope

an·te·lopes
an·te me·rid·i·em
an·ten·na
an·ten·nae
an·ten·nas
an·te·pe·nult
an·te·pe·nul·ti·mate
an·te·ri·or
an·te·room
an·them
an·ther
an·ther·id·i·um
an·thol·o·gy
an·thol·o·gies
an·thol·o·gist
an·thol·o·gize
an·thol·o·gized
an·thol·o·giz·ing
an·tho·zo·an
an·thra·cene
an·thra·cite
an·thra·cit·ic
an·thrax
an·thra·ces
an·thro·po·cen·tric
an·thro·po·gen·e·sis
an·thro·poid
an·thro·pol·o·gy
an·thro·po·log·ic
an·thro·po·log·i·cal
an·thro·pol·o·gist
an·thro·pom·e·try
an·thro·po·met·ric
an·thro·po·mor·phic
an·thro·po·mor·phi·cal·ly
an·thro·po·mor·phize
an·thro·po·mor·phized
an·thro·po·mor·phiz·ing
an·thro·po·mor·phism
an·thro·po·mor·phist
an·ti·air·craft
an·ti·bi·o·sis
an·ti·bi·ot·ic
an·ti·body
an·ti·bod·ies
an·tic
an·ti·christ
an·tic·i·pate
an·tic·i·pat·ed
an·tic·i·pat·ing
an·tic·i·pa·tion
an·tic·i·pa·tive
an·tic·i·pa·to·ry
an·ti·cler·i·cal
an·ti·cler·i·cal·ism
an·ti·cli·max
an·ti·cli·mac·tic
an·ti·cli·nal
an·ti·cline
an·ti·cy·clone
an·ti·dote
an·ti·dot·al
An·tie·tam
an·ti·fed·er·al
an·ti·fed·er·al·ist

an·ti·fed·er·al·ism
an·ti·freeze
an·ti·gen
An·tig·o·ne
An·tig·o·nus
An·ti·gua
an·ti·he·ro
an·ti·his·ta·mine
An·til·les
an·ti·log·a·rithm
an·ti·ma·cas·sar
an·ti·mis·sile
an·ti·mo·ny
An·ti·och
an·ti·pas·to
an·tip·a·thy
an·ti·phon
an·tiph·o·nal
an·ti·pode
an·ti·quar·i·an
an·ti·quary
an·ti·quar·ies
an·ti·quate
an·ti·quat·ed
an·ti·quat·ing
an·ti·quat·ed
an·tique
an·tiqued
an·tiq·uing
an·tique·ly
an·tique·ness
an·tiq·ui·ty
an·tiq·ui·ties
an·ti·Sem·i·tism
an·ti·sep·sis
an·ti·sep·tic
an·ti·se·rum
an·ti·slav·ery
an·ti·so·cial
an·tith·e·sis
an·tith·e·ses
an·ti·thet·i·cal
an·ti·tox·in
an·ti·tox·ic
an·ti·trust
ant·ler
ant·lefed
An·toi·nette
An·to·ny
an·to·nym
an·trum
an·tra
An·trim
Ant·werp
anus
an·vil
anx·i·e·ty
anx·i·e·ties
anx·ious
anx·ious·ness
any
an·y·body
an·y·bod·ies
an·y·how
an·y·more

an·y·one
an·y·place
an·y·thing
an·y·way
an·y·where
an·y·wise
aor·ta
aor·tas
aor·tae
aor·tal
aor·tic
apace
apache
apart
apart·heid
apart·ment
ap·a·thy
ap·a·thet·ic
ap·a·thet·i·cal·ly
ape
aped
ap·ing
Ap·en·nines
aper·ri·tif
ap·er·ture
apex
apex·es
api·ces
ap·i·cal
apha·sia
aphe·li·on
aphe·lia
aphid
aphis
aphi·des
aph·o·rism
aph·o·rist
aph·o·ris·tic
aph·ro·dis·i·ac
Aph·ro·di·te
api·an
api·ar·i·an
api·a·rist
api·ary
api·ar·ies
api·cul·ture
api·cul·tur·al
api·cul·tur·ist
apiece
ap·ish
ap·ish·ly
ap·ish·ness
aplomb
apoc·a·lypse
apoc·a·lyp·tic
apoc·o·pe
Apoc·ry·pha
apoc·ry·phal
Ap·o·des
ap·o·gee
apo·lit·i·cal
Apol·li·nar·is
Apol·lo
apol·o·get·ics
apol·o·gist

apol·o·gize
apol·o·gized
apol·o·giz·ing
apol·o·gy
apol·o·gies
apol·o·get·ic
apol·o·get·i·cal
Ap·o·lo·ni·us
ap·o·plec·tic
ap·o·plex·y
aport
apos·ta·sy
apos·ta·sies
apos·tate
apos·ta·tize
apos·ta·tized
apos·ta·tiz·ing
a pos·te·ri·o·ri
apos·tle
apos·tle·ship
apos·to·late
ap·os·tol·ic
ap·os·tol·i·cal
apos·tro·phe
apoth·e·cary
apoth·e·car·ies
ap·o·thegm
ap·o·phthegm
ap·o·theg·mat·ic
apoth·e·o·sis
apoth·e·o·ses
apoth·e·o·size
apoth·e·o·sized
apoth·e·o·siz·ing
Ap·pa·la·chi·an
ap·pall
ap·palled
ap·pal·ling
ap·pal·ling·ly
ap·pa·rat·us
ap·pa·rat·us
ap·pa·rat·us·es
ap·par·el
ap·par·ent
ap·pa·ri·tion
ap·pa·ri·tion·al
ap·peal
ap·peal·a·ble
ap·peal·er
ap·peal·ing·ly
ap·pear
ap·pear·ance
ap·pease
ap·peased
ap·peasing
ap·pease·ment
ap·peas·a·ble
ap·peas·er
ap·pel·lant
ap·pel·late
ap·pel·la·tion
ap·pel·la·tive
ap·pend
ad·pen·dage
ap·pend·ant

ap·pen·dec·to·my
ap·pen·di·ci·tis
ap·pen·dix
ap·pen·dix·es
ap·pen·di·ces
ap·per·cep·tion
ap·per·cep·tive
ap·per·tain
ap·pe·tite
ap·pe·tiz·er
ap·pe·tiz·ing
Ap·pi·an
ap·plaud
ap·plause
ap·ple
ap·ple·jack
Ap·ple·ton
ap·pli·ance
ap·pli·ca·ble
ap·pli·ca·bil·i·ty
ap·pli·ca·ble·ness
ap·pli·cant
ap·pli·ca·tion
ap·pli·ca·tive
ap·pli·ca·to·ry
ap·pli·ca·tor
ap·plied
ap·pli·qué
ap·ply
ap·plied
ap·ply·ing
ap·point
ap·point·a·ble
ap·point·er
ap·point·ee
ap·poin·tive
ap·point·ment
Ap·po·mat·tox
ap·por·tion
ap·por·tion·ment
ap·pose
ap·posed
ap·pos·ing
ap·po·site
ap·po·si·tion
ap·po·si·tion·al
ap·pos·i·tive
ap·praise
ap·praised
ap·prais·ing
ap·prais·er
ap·prais·al
ap·pre·ci·a·ble
ap·pre·ci·a·bly
ap·pre·ci·ate
ap·pre·ci·at·ed
ap·pre·ci·at·ing
ap·pre·ci·a·tion
ap·pre·ci·a·tive
ap·pre·hend
ap·pre·hen·si·ble
ap·pre·hen·si·bil·i·ty
ap·pre·hen·sion
ap·pre·hen·sive
ap·pre·hen·sive·ly

ap·pre·hen·sive·ness
ap·pren·tice
ap·pren·ticed
ap·pren·tic·ing
ap·pren·tice·ship
ap·prise
ap·prize
ap·prised
ap·pris·ing
ap·proach
ap·proach·a·bil·i·ty
ap·proach·a·ble
ap·pro·ba·tion
ap·pro·ba·tive
ap·pro·ba·to·ry
ap·pro·pri·ate
ap·pro·pri·at·ed
ap·pro·pri·at·ing
ap·pro·pri·ate·ly
ap·pro·pri·ate·ness
ap·pro·pri·a·tor
ap·pro·pri·a·tion
ap·pro·pri·a·tive
ap·prov·al
ap·prove
ap·proved
ap·prov·ing
ap·prov·a·ble
ap·prov·er
ap·prov·ing·ly
ap·prox·i·mate
ap·prox·i·mate·ly
ap·prox·i·ma·tion
ap·pur·te·nance
ap·pur·te·nant
ap·ri·cot
April
a pri·o·ri
apron
ap·ro·pos
apt
apt·ly
apt·ness
ap·ter·ous
ap·ti·tude
aq·ua
aq·uas
aq·uae
aqua·cul·ture
Aq·ua·lung
aq·ua·ma·rine
aq·ua·naut
aq·ua·plane
aquar·i·um
aquar·i·ums
aquar·ia
Aquar·i·us
aquat·ic
aq·ua·tint
aq·ue·duct
aque·ous
Aq·ui·la
aq·ui·line
Aqui·nas
Aq·ui·taine

Ar·ab
Ara·bia
Ara·bi·an
ar·a·besque
Ar·a·bic
Ar·ab·ist
ar·a·ble
Arach·ne
arach·nid
arach·ni·dan
Ar·a·gon
Ar·al
Ar·a·ma·ic
Ar·a·min·ta
Arap·a·ho
Ar·a·rat
Ar·as
ar·ba·lest
ar·ba·list
ar·ba·lest·er
ar·bi·ter
ar·bi·tral
ar·bit·ra·ment
ar·bi·trary
ar·bi·trar·i·ly
ar·bi·trar·i·ness
ar·bi·trate
ar·bi·trat·ed
ar·bi·trat·ing
ar·bi·tra·ble
ar·bi·tra·tor
ar·bi·tra·tion
ar·bor
ar·bo·re·al
ar·bo·res·cent
ar·bo·re·tum
ar·bo·re·tums
ar·bo·re·ta
ar·bor·vi·tae
ar·bu·tus
arc
arced
arcked
arc·ing
arck·ing
ar·cade
Ar·ca·dia
ar·cane
arch
arch·ly
arch·ness
ar·chae·ol·o·gy
ar·che·ol·o·gy
ar·chae·o·log·i·cal
ar·che·o·log·i·cal
ar·chae·ol·o·gist
ar·che·ol·o·gist
Ar·chae·o·zo·ic
Ar·che·o·zo·ic
ar·cha·ic
ar·cha·ism
ar·cha·ist
ar·cha·is·tic
arch·an·gel
arch·bish·op

arch·bish·op·ric
arch·dea·con
arch·di·o·cese
  arch·di·oc·e·san
arch·du·cal
arch·duch·ess
arch·duchy
  arch·duch·ies
arch·duke
Ar·che·an
arch·en·e·my
  arch·en·e·mies
arch·er
ar·chery
ar·che·type
  ar·che·typ·al
  ar·che·typ·i·cal
arch·fiend
ar·chi·e·pis·co·pate
  ar·chi·e·pis·co·pal
Ar·chi·me·de·an
Ar·chi·me·des
ar·chi·pel·a·go
  ar·chi·pel·a·goes
  ar·chi·pel·a·gos
ar·chi·tect
ar·chi·tec·ton·ic
ar·chi·tec·ture
  ar·chi·tec·tur·al
ar·chi·trave
ar·chive
  ar·chi·val
ar·chi·vist
ar·chon
arch·priest
arch·way
arc·tic
arc·tic cir·cle
Arc·tu·rus
ar·dent
  ar·dent·ly
ar·dor
ar·du·ous
  ar·du·ous·ly
  ar·du·ous·ness
ar·ea
  ar·e·al
  ar·e·a·way
are·na
are·o·la
  are·o·lae
  are·o·las
Ar·e·op·a·gus
Ar·e·thu·sa
ar·gent
Ar·gen·ti·na
ar·gen·tine
ar·gil
Ar·give
Ar·go·lis
ar·gon
Ar·go·naut
Ar·gonne
Ar·gos
ar·go·sy

ar·go·sies
ar·got
ar·got·ic
ar·gue
ar·gued
ar·gu·ing
ar·gu·a·ble
ar·gu·er
ar·gu·ment
ar·gu·men·ta·tion
ar·gu·men·ta·tive
Ar·gus
ar·gyle
  ar·gyll
aria
Ar·i·an
ar·id
arid·i·ty
Ar·i·el
A·ri·es
aright
arise
arose
aris·en
aris·ing
Ar·is·ti·des
ar·is·toc·ra·cy
  ar·is·toc·ra·cies
aris·to·crat
aris·to·crat·ic
Ar·is·toph·a·nes
Ar·is·tot·le
arith·me·tic
  ar·ith·met·i·cal
  ar·ith·met·i·cal·ly
arith·me·ti·cian
Ar·i·zo·na
Ar·kan·sas
Ar·ling·ton
ar·ma·da
ar·ma·dil·lo
Ar·ma·ged·don
ar·ma·ment
ar·ma·ture
arm·chair
armed forc·es
Ar·me·nia
Ar·men·tieres
arm·ful
arm·hole
ar·mi·stice
arm·let
ar·moire
ar·mor
ar·mored
ar·mor·er
ar·mory
  ar·mor·ies
arm·pit
Arm·strong
ar·my
  ar·mies
ar·ni·ca
Ar·nold
aro·ma

ar·o·mat·ic
ar·o·mat·i·cal
around
arouse
 aroused
 arous·ing
 arous·al
ar·peg·gio
 ar·peg·gi·os
ar·raign
 ar·raign·ment
ar·range
 ar·ranged
 ar·rang·ing
 ar·rang·er
 ar·range·ment
ar·rant
 ar·rant·ly
ar·ras
ar·ray
ar·rear
ar·rest
 ar·rest·er
 ar·rest·or
ar·ri·val
ar·rive
 ar·rived
 ar·riv·ing
ar·ro·gant
 ar·ro·gance
 ar·ro·gant·ly
ar·ro·gate
 ar·ro·gat·ed
 ar·ro·gat·ing
 ar·ro·ga·tion
ar·row
ar·row·head
ar·row·root
ar·royo
 ar·roy·os
ar·se·nal
ar·se·nate
ar·se·nic
ar·son
 ar·son·ist
Ar·te·mis
ar·te·ri·al
ar·te·ri·o·scle·ro·sis
ar·tery
 ar·te·ries
ar·te·sian well
art·ful
 art·ful·ly
 art·ful·ness
ar·thri·tis
 ar·thrit·ic
ar·thro·pod
 ar·throp·o·dal
 ar·throp·o·dous
Ar·thur
Ar·thu·ri·an
ar·ti·choke
ar·ti·cle
ar·tic·u·lar
ar·tic·u·late

ar·tic·u·lat·ed
ar·tic·u·lat·ing
ar·tic·u·late·ly
ar·tic·u·late·ness
ar·tic·u·la·tor
ar·tic·u·la·tion
ar·tic·u·la·to·ry
ar·ti·fact
 ar·te·fact
ar·ti·fice
 ar·tif·i·cer
ar·ti·fi·cial
 ar·ti·fi·ci·al·i·ty
 ar·ti·fi·cial·ly
 ar·ti·fi·cial·ness
 ar·ti·fi·cial res·pi·ra·tion
ar·til·lery
 ar·til·ler·ist
ar·ti·san
art·ist
ar·tiste
ar·tis·tic
 ar·tis·ti·cal·ly
art·ist·ry
art·less
 art·less·ly
 art·less·ness
arty
 ar·ti·ness
Ar·y·an
as·bes·tos
 as·bes·tus
As·bu·ry
as·cend
 as·cend·ance
 as·cend·ence
 as·cend·an·cy
 as·cend·en·cy
 as·cend·ant
 as·cend·ent
as·cen·sion
as·cent
as·cer·tain
 as·cer·tain·a·ble
 as·cer·tain·ment
as·cet·ic
 as·cet·ic·al
 as·cet·i·cism
As·cham
as·cot
as·cribe
 as·cribed
 as·crib·ing
 as·crib·a·ble
 as·crip·tion
asep·sis
asep·tic
asex·u·al
 asex·u·al·i·ty
 asex·u·al·ly
As·gard
ashamed
 asham·ed·ly
ash·en
Ashe·ville

ash·lar
ash·ler
ashore
ashy
Asi·at·ic
aside
as·i·nine
askance
askew
aslant
asleep
aslope
aso·cial
as·par·a·gus
as·pect
as·pen
as·per·i·ty
as·perse
as·persed
as·pers·ing
as·per·sion
as·phalt
as·phal·tic
as·pho·del
as·phyx·ia
as·phyx·i·ate
as·phyx·i·at·ed
as·phyx·i·at·ing
as·phyx·i·a·tion
as·pic
as·pi·dis·tra
as·pir·ant
as·pi·rate
as·pi·rat·ed
as·pi·rat·ing
as·pi·ra·tion
as·pi·ra·tor
as·pire
as·pired
as·pir·ing
as·pir·er
as·pi·rin
as·sail
as·sail·a·ble
as·sail·ant
As·sam
as·sas·sin
as·sas·si·nate
as·sas·si·nat·ed
as·sas·si·nat·ing
as·sas·si·na·tion
as·sas·si·na·tor
as·sault
as·say
as·say·er
as·sem·blage
as·sem·ble
as·sem·bled
as·sem·bling
as·sem·bler
as·sem·bly
as·sem·blies
as·sem·bly·man
as·sem·bly·men
as·sent

as·sent·er
as·sert
as·ser·tion
as·sert·er
as·ser·tive
as·ser·tive·ly
as·ser·tive·ness
as·sess
as·sess·a·ble
as·sess·ment
as·sess·or
as·set
as·sev·er·ate
as·sev·er·at·ed
as·sev·er·at·ing
as·sev·er·a·tion
as·si·du·i·ty
as·sid·u·ous
as·sid·u·ous·ly
as·sid·u·ous·ness
as·sign
as·sign·a·bil·i·ty
as·sign·a·ble
as·sign·a·bly
as·sig·na·tion
as·sign·ee
as·sign·ment
as·sim·i·late
as·sim·i·lat·ed
as·sim·i·lat·ing
as·sim·i·la·bil·i·ty
as·sim·i·la·ble
as·sim·i·la·tion
as·sim·i·la·tive
as·sim·i·la·tor
as·sist
as·sist·ance
as·sis·tant
as·size
as·so·ci·ate
as·so·ci·at·ed
as·so·ci·at·ing
as·so·ci·a·tion
as·so·ci·a·tive
as·so·nance
as·sort
as·sort·ed
as·sort·ment
as·suage
as·suaged
as·suag·ing
as·suage·ment
as·sume
as·sumed
as·sum·ing
as·sump·tion
as·sump·tive
as·sur·ance
as·sure
as·sured
as·sur·ing
as·sur·er
as·sur·ed·ly
as·sur·ed·ness
As·syr·ia

as·ter
as·ter·isk
astern
as·ter·oid
 as·ter·oi·dal
asth·ma
asth·mat·ic
astig·ma·tism
 as·tig·mat·ic
astir
as·ton·ish
 as·ton·ish·ing
 as·ton·ish·ing·ly
 as·ton·ish·ment
As·tor
As·to·ria
as·tound
 as·tound·ing
astrad·dle
as·tra·khan
as·tral
astray
astride
as·trin·gent
 as·trin·gen·cy
as·tro·dome
as·tro·labe
as·trol·o·gy
 as·trol·o·ger
 as·tro·log·ic
 as·tro·log·i·cal
 as·tro·log·i·cal·ly
as·tro·naut
as·tro·nau·tics
 as·tro·nau·ti·cal
as·tro·nom·ic
 as·tro·nom·i·cal·ly
as·tron·o·my
 as·tron·o·mer
as·tro·phys·ics
 as·tro·phys·i·cist
as·tute
 as·tute·ly
 as·tute·ness
asun·der
asy·lum
asym·me·try
 asym·met·ric
 asym·met·ri·cal
 asym·met·ri·cal·ly
at·a·vism
 at·a·vist
 at·a·vis·tic
atax·ia
 atax·ic
Atch·i·son
at·el·ier
Ath·a·na·si·us
athe·ism
 athe·ist
 athe·is·tic
 athe·is·ti·cal
 athe·is·ti·cal·ly
Athe·na
Ath·ens

ath·er·o·scle·ro·sis
athirst
ath·lete
ath·let·ic
ath·let·ics
Ath·os
athwart
atilt
At·lan·ta
At·lan·tic
at·las
 at·las·es
at·mos·phere
 at·mos·pher·ic
 at·mos·pher·i·cal
 at·mos·pher·i·cal·ly
 at·mos·pher·ics
at·oll
at·om
 atom·ic
 atom·i·cal
 atom·i·cal·ly
at·om·ize
 at·om·ized
 at·om·iz·ing
 at·om·iz·er
ato·nal·i·ty
ato·nal
 ato·nal·ly
atone
atoned
aton·ing
atone·ment
aton·er
atop
atri·um
atro·cious
 atro·cious·ly
 atro·cious·ness
atroc·i·ty
 atroc·i·ties
at·ro·phy
 at·ro·phies
 at·ro·phied
 at·ro·phy·ing
atroph·ic
at·ro·pine
At·ro·pos
at·tach
 at·tach·a·ble
 at·tach·ment
at·ta·ché
at·tack
at·tain
 at·tain·a·ble
 at·tain·a·bil·i·ty
 at·tain·a·ble·ness
 at·tain·ment
at·tain·der
at·taint
at·tar
at·tempt
 at·tempt·a·ble
at·tend
at·tend·ance

at·tend·ant
at·ten·tion
at·ten·tive
at·ten·u·ate
  at·ten·u·at·ed
  at·ten·u·at·ing
  at·ten·u·a·tion
at·test
  at·tes·ta·tion
at·tic
At·ti·ca
At·ti·la
at·tire
  at·tired
  at·tir·ing
at·ti·tude
at·ti·tu·di·nize
  at·ti·tu·di·nized
  at·ti·tu·di·niz·ing
at·tor·ney
  at·tor·neys
at·tor·ney gen·er·al
at·tract
  at·tract·a·ble
  at·trac·tive
  at·tract·or
at·trac·tion
at·tri·bute
  at·tri·but·ed
  at·tri·but·ing
  at·tri·but·a·ble
  at·tri·bu·tion
at·trib·u·tive
at·tri·tion
at·tune
  at·tuned
  at·tun·ing
atyp·i·cal
atyp·ic
atyp·i·cal·ly
au·burn
au cou·rant
auc·tion
auc·tion·eer
au·da·cious
  au·da·cious·ness
  au·dac·i·ty
au·di·ble
  au·di·ble·ness
  au·di·bly
au·di·ence
au·dio
au·di·o·vis·u·al
au·dit
au·di·tion
au·dit·or
au·di·to·ri·um
au·di·to·ry
Au·du·bon
au·ger
aug·ment
  aug·ment·a·ble
  aug·ment·er
  aug·men·ta·tion
  aug·ment·a·tive

au grat·in
Augs·burg
au·gur
au·gu·ry
  au·gu·ries
au·gust
  au·gust·ly
  au·gust·ness
Au·gust
Au·gus·ta
Au·gus·tine
Au·gus·tus
auk
auld lang syne
au na·tu·rel
aunt
au·ra
  au·ras
  au·rae
au·ral
  au·ral·ly
au·re·ate
au·re·ole
Au·re·o·my·cin
au re·voir
au·ri·cle
au·ric·u·lar
au·rif·er·ous
au·ro·ra
au·ro·ra bor·e·al·is
aus·cul·tate
  aus·cul·tat·ed
  aus·cul·tat·ing
  aus·cul·ta·tion
aus·pice
  aus·pic·es
aus·pi·cious
  aus·pi·cious·ly
  aus·pi·cious·ness
aus·tere
  aus·ter·i·ty
  aus·ter·i·ties
Aus·ter·litz
Aus·tin
aus·tral
Aus·tra·lia
Aus·tra·lian
Aus·tria
Aus·tri·an
au·then·tic
au·then·ti·cate
  au·then·ti·cat·ed
  au·then·ti·cat·ing
  au·then·ti·ca·tion
  au·then·tic·i·ty
  au·then·ti·ca·tor
au·thor
  au·thor·i·tar·i·an
  au·thor·i·tar·i·an·ism
  au·thor·i·ta·tive
  au·thor·i·ta·tive·ness
au·thor·i·ty
  au·thor·i·ties
au·thor·ize
  au·thor·ized

au·thor·iz·ing
au·thor·i·za·tion
au·thor·ship
au·to
au·to·bi·og·ra·phy
au·to·bi·og·ra·phies
au·to·bi·og·ra·pher
au·to·bi·o·graph·ic
au·to·bi·o·graph·i·cal
au·to·bi·o·graph·i·cal·ly
au·toc·ra·cy
au·toc·ra·cies
au·to·crat
au·to·crat·ic
au·to·crat·i·cal
au·to·crat·i·cal·ly
au·to·da·fé
au·tos·da·fé
au·to·graph
au·to·mat
au·to·mat·ic
au·to·ma·tion
au·to·mate
au·to·mat·ed
au·to·mat·ing
au·tom·a·tism
au·tom·a·ton
au·tom·a·tons
au·tom·a·ta
au·to·mo·bile
au·to·mo·tive
au·to·nom·ic
au·to·nom·i·cal·ly
au·ton·o·mous
au·ton·o·mous·ly
au·ton·o·my
au·ton·o·mies
au·ton·o·mist
au·top·sy
au·to·sug·ges·tion
au·tumn
au·tum·nal
Au·vergne
aux·il·ia·ry
aux·il·ia·ries
avail
avail·a·bil·i·ty
avail·a·ble
avail·a·ble·ness
avail·a·bly
av·a·lanche
av·a·lanched
av·a·lanch·ing
Av·a·lon
avant·garde
av·a·rice
av·a·ri·cious
av·a·ri·cious·ly
av·a·ri·cious·ness
avast
av·a·tar
ave
Ave Ma·ria
avenge
avenged

aveng·ing
aveng·er
Av·en·tine
av·e·nue
aver
averred
aver·ring
aver·ment
av·er·age
av·er·aged
av·er·ag·ing
averse
averse·ly
averse·ness
aver·sion
avert
avi·ary
avi·ar·ies
avi·a·rist
avi·a·tion
avi·a·tor
av·id
avid·i·ty
av·id·ly
Avi·gnon
avi·on·ics
av·o·ca·do
av·o·ca·dos
av·o·ca·tion
avoid
avoid·a·ble
avoid·ance
av·oir·du·pois
avouch
avow
avow·er
avow·al
avowed
avun·cu·lar
await
awake
awoke
awaked
awak·ing
awak·en
awak·en·ing
award
award·a·ble
award·er
aware
aware·ness
awash
away
awe
awed
aw·ing
aweigh
av·e·some
awe·some·ly
awe·some·ness
awe·strick·en
awe·struck
aw·ful
aw·ful·ly
aw·ful·ness

awhile
awk·ward
  awk·ward·ly
  awk·ward·ness
awn
  awned
  awn·less
awn·ing
awry
ax
  ax·es
ax·i·al
  ax·i·al·ly
ax·i·om
  ax·i·o·mat·ic
  ax·i·o·mat·i·cal
  ax·i·o·mat·i·cal·ly
ax·is
  ax·es
ax·le
Ayr·shire
azal·ea
az·i·muth
  az·i·muth·al
Az·tec
az·ure
Ba·al
bab·bitt
bab·ble
  bab·bled
  bab·bling
  bab·bler
ba·bel
ba·boon
ba·bush·ka
ba·by
  ba·bies
  ba·bied
  ba·by·ing
  ba·by·hood
  ba·by·ish
Bab·y·lon
Bab·y·lo·nia
ba·by·sit
  ba·by·sat
  ba·by·sit·ting
  ba·by·sit·ter
bac·ca·lau·re·ate
bac·ca·rat
bac·cha·nal
  bac·cha·na·li·an
bac·chant
bac·chan·te
Bac·chus
bach·e·lor
  bach·e·lor·hood
bac·il·lary
ba·cil·lus
  ba·cil·li
back·bite
  back·bit
  back·bit·ten
  back·bit·ing
  back·bit·er
back·board

back·bone
back·drop
back·er
back·field
back·fire
  back·fired
  back·fir·ing
back·gam·mon
back·ground
back·hand
  back·hand·ed
back·ing
back·lash
back·log
back·side
back·slide
  back·slid
  back·slid·den
  back·slid·ing
  back·slid·er
back·spin
back·stage
back·stairs
back·stay
back·stop
back·stretch
back·stroke
back·talk
back·track
back·up
back·ward
  back·wards
back·ward·ness
back·wash
back·wa·ter
back·woods
  back·woods·man
ba·con
bac·te·ria
  bac·ter·i·um
  bac·te·ri·al
  bac·te·ri·al·ly
bac·te·ri·cide
  bac·te·ri·ci·dal
bac·te·ri·ol·o·gy
  bac·te·ri·ol·o·gist
  bac·te·ri·o·log·i·cal
bac·te·ri·o·phage
bad
  worse
  worst
badge
  badged
  badg·ing
badg·er
bad·i·nage
bad·land
  bad·lands
bad·ly
bad·min·ton
Bae·de·ker
baf·fle
  baf·fled
  baf·fling
  baf·fler

bag
  bagged
  bag·ging
ba·gasse
bag·a·telle
Bag·dad
ba·gel
bag·gage
bag·gy
  bag·gi·er
  bag·gi·est
Bagh·dad
bag·man
ba·gnio
bag·pipe
  bag·pi·per
ba·guette
Ba·hai
Ba·ha·ma
Ba·hia
Bah·rain
bail·iff
bail·i·wick
bails·man
  bails·men
bake
  baked
  bak·ing
Ba·ke·lite
bak·er
bak·er·y
  bak·er·ies
bak·ing pow·der
bak·ing so·da
bak·sheesh
  bak·shish
Ba·laam
bal·a·lai·ka
bal·ance
  bal·anced
  bal·anc·ing
  bal·anc·er
Bal·boa
bal·brig·gan
bal·co·ny
  bal·co·nies
bald
  bald·ly
  bald·ness
bal·der·dash
bald·head
bal·dric
Bald·win
bale
  baled
  bal·ing
ba·leen
bale·ful
  bale·ful·ly
Bal·four
Ba·li
balk
  balk·er
Bal·kan
bal·kan·ize

bal·kan·ized
bal·kan·iz·ing
bal·kan·i·za·tion
balky
  balk·i·er
  balk·i·est
bal·lad
bal·lade
bal·lad·ry
bal·last
ball bear·ing
bal·le·ri·na
bal·let
Bal·li·ol
bal·lis·tic
  bal·lis·tics
  bal·lis·ti·cian
bal·loon
bal·lot
  bal·lot·ed
  bal·lot·ing
ball·room
bal·ly·hoo
balm
Bal·mor·al
balmy
  balm·i·er
  balm·i·est
  balm·i·ly
  balm·i·ness
ba·lo·ney
bal·sa
bal·sam
Bal·tic
Bal·ti·more
Ba·lu·chi·stan
bal·us·ter
bal·us·trade
Bal·zac
Ba·ma·ko
bam·bi·no
  bam·bi·nos
bam·boo
bam·boo·zle
  bam·boo·zled
  bam·boo·zling
  bam·boo·zler
ban
  banned
  ban·ning
ba·nal
  ba·nal·i·ty
ba·nana
band·age
  band·aged
  band·ag·ing
ban·dana
  ban·dan·na
ban·deau
  ban·deaux
ban·de·role
ban·dit
  ban·dits
  ban·dit·ti
  ban·dit·ry

band·mas·ter
ban·do·leer
 ban·do·lier
bands·man
 bands·men
band·stand
band·wag·on
ban·dy
 ban·died
 ban·dy·ing
ban·dy-leg·ged
bane·ful
 bane·ful·ness
Bang·kok
Ban·gla·desh
ban·gle
Ban·gor
Ban·gui
ban·ish
 ban·ish·ment
ban·is·ter
 ban·nis·ter
ban·jo
Ban·jul
bank
bank·book
bank·er
bank·ing
bank·roll
bank·rupt
 bank·rupt·cy
 bank·rupt·cies
ban·ner
ban·quet
 ban·quet·er
ban·quette
Ban·quo
ban·shee
ban·tam
ban·tam·weight
ban·ter
 ban·ter·er
 ban·ter·ing·ly
Ban·ting
Ban·tu
ban·yan
 ban·ian
ban·zal
ba·o·bab
bap·tism
 bap·tis·mal
bap·tist
bap·tis·tery
 bap·tis·ter·ies
bap·tize
 bap·tized
 bap·tiz·ing
bar
 barred
 bar·ring
Bar·ab·bas
Ba·raca
Bar·ba·dos
bar·bar·i·an
bar·bar·ic

bar·ba·rism
bar·bar·i·ty
 bar·bar·i·ties
bar·ba·rize
 bar·ba·rized
 bar·ba·riz·ing
Bar·ba·ros·sa
bar·ba·rous
Bar·ba·ry
bar·be·cue
 bar·be·cued
 bar·be·cu·ing
bar·ber
bar·ber·ry
 bar·ber·ries
bar·ber·shop
bar·bi·tal
bar·bi·tu·rate
bar·bi·tur·ic
Bar·bi·zon
Bar·busse
bar·ca·role
Bar·ce·lo·na
bare
 bar·er
 bar·est
 bare·ness
bare·back
bare·faced
bare·foot
bare·hand·ed
bare·head·ed
bare·ly
bar·gain
 bar·gain·er
barge
 barged
 barg·ing
bar·i·tone
bar·i·um
bar·keep·er
bar·ken·tine
bark·er
bar·ley
 bar·leys
bar·maid
bar·man
 bar·men
bar mitz·vah
barmy
Bar·na·bas
bar·na·cle
barn·storm
 barn·storm·er
 barn·storm·ing
Bar·num
barn·yard
bar·o·graph
ba·rom·et·er
 bar·o·met·ric
 bar·o·met·ric·al
bar·on
 ba·ro·ni·al
bar·on·age
bar·on·ess

bar·on·et
  bar·on·et·age
  bar·on·et·cy
bar·o·ny
  bar·o·nies
ba·roque
barque
bar·quen·tine
bar·rack
bar·ra·cu·da
  bar·ra·cu·das
bar·rage
  bar·raged
  bar·rag·ing
bar·ra·try
  bar·ra·tries
  bar·ra·tor
  bar·ra·trous
bar·rel
  bar·reled
  bar·relled
  bar·rel·ing
  bar·rel·ling
bar·ren
  bar·ren·ly
  bar·ren·ness
bar·rette
bar·ri·cade
  bar·ri·cad·ed
  bar·ri·cad·ing
bar·ri·er
bar·ring
bar·rio
  bar·ri·os
bar·ris·ter
bar·room
bar·row
bar·ten·der
bar·ter
  bar·ter·er
Bar·thol·o·mew
Bar·uch
ba·sal
  bas·al·ly
ba·salt
base
  based
  bas·ing
base·ball
base·board
base·born
Ba·sel
base·less
base·ment
bash·ful
  bash·ful·ly
  bash·ful·ness
ba·sic
  ba·si·cal·ly
ba·sil
ba·sil·i·ca
bas·i·lisk
ba·sin
ba·sis
  ba·ses

bas·ket
bas·ket·ball
bas·ket·ry
bas·re·lief
bas·si·net
bas·so
  bas·sos
bas·soon
bass·wood
bas·tard
  bas·tard·ize
  bas·tard·ized
  bas·tard·iz·ing
  bas·tard·ly
baste
  bast·ed
  bast·ing
bas·tille
bas·ti·on
  bas·ti·oned
Ba·su·to·land
bat
  bat·ted
  bat·ting
  bat·ter
Ba·ta·via
bate
  bat·ed
  bat·ing
bathe
  bathed
  bath·ing
  bath·er
bath·robe
Bath·she·ba
Bath·urst
bath·y·scaphe
bath·y·sphere
ba·tik
ba·tiste
bat·on
Bat·on Rouge
bat·tal·ion
bat·ten
bat·ter
bat·tery
bat·tle
  bat·tled
  bat·tling
bat·tle·field
bat·tle·ment
bat·ty
  bat·ti·er
  bat·ti·est
Bat·um
bau·ble
Bau·douin
baux·ite
Ba·var·ia
bawdy
  bawd·i·er
  bawd·i·est
Ba·yeux
bay·o·net
  bay·o·net·ed

bay·o·net·ing
Ba·yonne
bay·ou
Bay·reuth
ba·zaar
ba·zoo·ka
beach
beach·comb·er
beach·head
bea·con
bead
bead·ed
bead·like
beady
bead·i·er
bead·i·est
beak
beaked
beak·er
beam
beamed
bear
bore
borne
bear·ing
bear·a·ble
bear·a·bly
bear·er
beard
beard·ed
beard·less
bear·ing
bear·ish
bear·skin
beast
beast·li·ness
beast·ly
beast·li·er
beast·li·est
beat
beat·en
beat·ing
beat·er
be·a·tif·ic
be·at·i·fy
be·at·i·fied
be·at·i·fy·ing
be·at·i·fi·ca·tion
be·at·i·tude
beat·nik
beau
beaus
beaux
Beau·fort
beau geste
beaux gestes
Beau·mar·chais
Beau·mont
Beau·re·gard
beau·te·ous
beau·te·ous·ly
beau·ti·cian
beau·ti·fy
beau·ti·fied
beau·ti·fy·ing

beau·ti·fi·ca·tion
beau·ti·fi·er
beauty
beau·ti·ful
beau·ti·ful·ly
beaux-arts
bea·ver
be·calm
be·cause
Bech·u·an·a·land
Beck·et
beck·on
be·cloud
be·come
be·came
be·com·ing
be·com·ing·ly
bed
bed·ded
bed·ding
be·daub
be·daz·zle
be·daz·zled
be·daz·zling
be·daz·zle·ment
bed·bug
bed·clothes
be·deck
be·dev·il
be·dev·iled
be·dev·il·ing
be·dev·il·ment
be·dew
bed·fast
bed·fel·low
Bed·ford
be·dim
be·dimmed
be·dim·ming
bed·lam
Bed·ou·in
bed·pan
be·drag·gle
be·drag·gled
be·drag·gling
bed·rid·den
bed·rock
bed·room
bed·side
bed·sore
bed·spread
bed·spring
bed·stead
bed·time
bee·bread
beech
beef
beefs
beeves
beef·eat·er
beef·steak
beefy
beef·i·er
beef·i·est
bee·hive

bee·line
Beel·ze·bub
Beer·she·ba
beery
  beer·i·er
  beer·i·est
beest·ings
bees·wax
Bee·tho·ven
bee·tle
  bee·tled
  bee·tling
bee·tle-browed
be·fall
  be·fell
  be·fall·en
  be·fall·ing
be·fit
  be·fit·ted
  be·fit·ting
be·fog
  be·fogged
  be·fog·ging
be·fore
be·fore·hand
be·foul
be·friend
be·fud·dle
  be·fud·dled
  be·fud·dling
beg
  begged
  beg·ging
be·get
  be·got
  be·got·ten
  be·get·ter
beg·gar
  beg·gar·dom
  beg·gar·hood
beg·gar·ly
be·gin
  be·gan
  be·gun
  be·gin·ning
be·gin·ner
be·go·nia
be·grime
  be·grimed
  be·grim·ing
be·grudge
  be·grudged
  be·grudg·ing
  be·grudg·ing·ly
be·guile
  be·guiled
  be·guil·ing
  be·guil·er
be·half
be·have
  be·haved
  be·hav·ing
  be·hav·ior
  be·hav·ior·ism
  be·hav·ior·ist

be·hav·ior·is·tic
be·head
be·he·moth
be·hest
be·hind
be·hind·hand
be·hold
  be·held
  be·hold·ing
  be·hold·er
  be·hold·en
be·hoove
  be·hooved
  be·hoov·ing
Beh·ring
beige
be·ing
Bei·rut
be·la·bor
be·lat·ed
  be·lat·ed·ly
  be·lat·ed·ness
be·lay
  be·layed
  be·lay·ing
belch
be·lea·guer
Bel·fast
Bel·fort
bel·fry
  bel·fries
Bel·gian
Bel·gium
Bel·grade
be·lie
  be·lied
  be·ly·ing
be·lief
be·lieve
  be·lieved
  be·liev·ing
  be·liev·a·ble
  be·liev·er
be·lit·tle
  be·lit·tled
  be·lit·tling
bel·la·don·na
bell·boy
Bel·leau
belles let·tres
bell·hop
bel·li·cose
  bel·li·cos·i·ty
bel·lig·er·ence
bel·lig·er·en·cy
bel·lig·er·ent
  bel·lig·er·ent·ly
Bel·loc
bel·low
bel·lows
bell·weth·er
bel·ly
  bel·lies
  bel·lied
  bel·ly·ing

bel·ly·ache
  bel·ly·ached
  bel·ly·ach·ing
bel·ly·but·ton
Bel·mont
be·long
be·long·ings
be·loved
be·low
Bel·shaz·zar
belt
  belt·ed
belt·way
be·lu·ga
Be·midji
be·mire
  be·mired
  be·mir·ing
be·moan
be·muse
  be·mused
  be·mus·ing
  be·mused
Be·na·res
bench
bend
  bent
  bend·ing
bend·er
be·neath
ben·e·dict
Ben·e·dic·tine
ben·e·dic·tion
  ben·e·dic·to·ry
ben·e·fac·tion
ben·e·fac·tor
  ben·e·fac·tress
be·nef·ic
ben·e·fice
  ben·e·ficed
  ben·e·fic·ing
be·nef·i·cent
  be·nef·i·cence
ben·e·fi·cial
  ben·e·fi·cial·ly
ben·e·fi·ci·ar·y
  ben·e·fi·ci·ar·ies
ben·e·fit
  ben·e·fit·ed
  ben·e·fit·ing
Be·nes
be·nev·o·lence
  be·nev·o·lent
  be·nev·o·lent·ly
Ben·gal
Ben-Gu·rion
be·night·ed
be·nign
  be·nig·ni·ty
  be·nig·ni·ties
  be·nign·ly
be·nig·nant
  be·nig·nan·cy
  be·nig·nan·cies
ben·i·son

Ben·ja·min
Ben·ning·ton
ben·ny
  ben·nies
be·numb
Be·o·wulf
ben·zene
ben·zine
ben·zo·ate
ben·zo·in
ben·zol
be·queath
be·quest
be·rate
  be·rat·ed
  be·rat·ing
Ber·ber
ber·ceuse
be·reave
  be·reaved
  be·reft
  be·reav·ing
Ber·es·ford
be·ret
ber·ga·mot
Ber·gen
Ber·ge·rac
ber·i·beri
Ber·ing
Berke·ley
berke·li·um
Berk·ley
Berk·shire
Ber·lin
Ber·mu·das
Bern·hardt
ber·ry
  ber·ries
  ber·ried
  ber·ry·ing
ber·serk
berth
ber·tha
ber·yl
be·ryl·li·um
be·seech
  be·sought
  be·seeched
  be·seech·ing
  be·seech·ing·ly
be·set
  be·set·ting
be·side
be·sides
be·siege
  be·sieged
  be·sieg·ing
  be·sieg·er
be·smear
be·smirch
bes·om
be·sot
  be·sot·ted
  be·sot·ting
be·spat·ter

be·speak
be·spoke
be·spok·en
be·speak·ing
Bes·sa·ra·bia
Bes·se·mer
best
bes·tial
bes·tial·ly
bes·ti·al·i·ty
bes·ti·al·i·ties
be·stir
be·stirred
be·stir·ring
be·stow
be·stow·al
be·strew
be·stride
be·strode
be·strid·den
be·strid·ing
bet
bet·ted
bet·ting
be·ta
be·take
be·took
be·tak·en
be·tak·ing
be·ta·tron
be·tel
Be·tel·geuse
Beth·a·ny
beth·el
Be·thes·da
Beth·le·hem
Beth·sa·i·da
be·tide
be·tid·ed
be·tid·ing
be·to·ken
be·tray
be·tray·al
be·tray·er
be·troth
be·troth·al
be·trothed
bet·ter
bet·ter·ment
bet·tor
be·tween
be·twixt
bev·el
bev·eled
bev·el·ing
bev·er·age
bevy
bev·ies
be·wail
be·ware
be·wil·der
be·wil·der·ing·ly
be·wil·der·ment
be·witch
be·witch·er

be·witch·ery
be·witch·ing
be·witch·ing·ly
be·witch·ment
be·yond
be·zique
Bhu·tan
bi·an·nu·al
bi·as
bi·ased
bi·as·ing
bi·ax·i·al
bi·ax·i·al·ly
bi·be·lot
Bi·ble
Bib·li·cal
Bib·li·cal·ly
bib·li·og·ra·phy
bib·li·og·ra·phies
bib·li·og·ra·pher
bib·li·o·graph·ic
bib·li·o·ma·nia
bib·li·o·ma·ni·ac
bib·li·o·phile
bib·u·lous
bi·cam·er·al
bi·car·bo·nate
bi·cen·te·nary
bi·cen·te·nar·ies
bi·cen·ten·ni·al
bi·ceps
bi·chlo·ride
bick·er
bi·con·cave
bi·con·vex
bi·cus·pid
bi·cus·pi·dal
bi·cus·pi·date
bi·cy·cle
bi·cy·cled
bi·cy·cling
bi·cy·cler
bi·cy·clist
bid
bade
bid·den
bid·ding
bid·da·ble
bid·der
Bid·de·ford
bid·dy
bid·dies
bide
bid·ed
bid·ing
Bid·e·ford
bi·en·ni·al
bi·en·ni·al·ly
bier
bi·fid
bi·fo·cal
bi·fo·cals
bi·fur·cate
bi·fur·cat·ed
bi·fur·cat·ing

bi·fur·ca·tion
big
  big·ger
  big·gest
big·a·my
  big·a·mies
  big·a·mist
  big·a·mous
big-heart·ed
big·horn
big·no·nia
big·ot
  big·ot·ed
  big·ot·ed·ly
  big·ot·ry
  big·ot·ries
bi·jou
  bi·joux
bi·ju·gous
bi·ki·ni
bi·la·bi·al
bi·la·bi·ate
bi·lat·er·al
  bi·lat·er·al·ly
Bil·bao
bil·ber·ry
  bil·ber·ries
bil·i·ary
bi·lin·gual
bil·ious
bill
  billed
  bill·ing
bil·la·bong
bill·board
bil·let
bil·let-doux
bill·fold
bill·hook
bil·liards
bil·lings·gate
bil·lion
bil·lion·aire
bil·low
  bil·low·y
  bil·low·i·er
  bil·low·i·est
bi·met·al·lism
  bi·met·al·list
  bi·me·tal·lic
bi·month·ly
  bi·month·lies
bi·na·ry
bi·nate
bin·au·ral
bind
  bound
  bind·ing
bind·er
bind·ery
  bind·er·ies
Bi·net
binge
Bing·ham·ton
bin·go

bin·na·cle
bi·noc·u·lar
bi·no·mi·al
bi·o·chem·is·try
  bi·o·chem·i·cal
  bi·o·chem·ist
bi·o·e·col·o·gy
bi·o·en·gi·neer·ing
bi·o·gen·e·sis
  bi·o·ge·net·ic
bi·og·ra·phy
  bi·og·ra·pher
  bi·o·graph·ic
  bi·o·graph·i·cal
  bi·o·graph·i·cal·ly
bi·ol·o·gy
  bi·o·log·i·cal
  bi·ol·o·gist
bi·o·met·rics
bi·om·e·try
  bi·o·met·rics
bi·o·nom·ics
bi·o·phys·ics
  bi·o·phys·i·cal
  bi·o·phys·i·cist
bi·op·sy
  bi·op·sies
bi·o·sphere
bi·o·tin
bi·par·ti·san
bi·par·tite
bi·par·ti·tion
bi·ped
  bi·ped·al
bi·plane
bi·po·lar
  bi·po·lar·i·ty
birch
  birch·en
bird·bath
bird·brain
  bird·brained
bird·call
bird·ie
bird·lime
bird·man
bird's-eye
bi·ret·ta
Bir·ming·ham
birth·day
birth·mark
birth·place
birth·right
birth·stone
Bis·cay
bis·cuit
bi·sect
  bi·sec·tion
  bi·sec·tor
bi·sex·u·al
bish·op
bish·op·ric
Bis·marck
bis·muth
bi·son

bisque
Bis·sau
bis·ter
 bis·tered
bis·tro
 bis·tros
bi·sul·fide
bitch
bite
 bit
 bit·ten
 bit·ing
 bit·ing·ly
bit·stock
bit·ter
 bit·ter·ish
 bit·ter·ly
 bit·ter·ness
bit·tern
bit·ter·root
bit·ters
bit·ter·sweet
bi·tu·men
 bi·tu·mi·nous
bi·va·lent
 bi·va·lence
bi·valve
 bi·val·vu·lar
biv·ou·ac
 biv·ou·acked
 biv·ou·ack·ing
bi·week·ly
 bi·week·lies
bi·year·ly
bi·zarre
 bi·zarre·ly
 bi·zarre·ness
Bi·zet
blab
 blabbed
 blab·bing
 blab·ber
 blab·ber·mouth
black·ball
black·ber·ry
 black·ber·ries
black·bird
black·board
black·body
black·cap
black·en
black·eyed Su·san
Black·feet
Black·foot
black·guard
black·head
black·ing
black·jack
black·list
black·ly
black·mail
black·out
black·smith
black·snake
black·thorn

black·top
blad·der
blade
 blad·ed
blame
 blamed
 blam·ing
 blam·a·ble
 blame·a·ble
 blame·ful
 blame·less
 blame·less·ly
 blame·less·ness
blame·wor·thy
 blame·wor·thi·ness
blanch
 blanch·er
 blanch·ing
blanc·mange
bland
 bland·ly
 bland·ness
blan·dish
 blan·dish·er
 blan·dish·ment
blank
 blank·ly
 blank·ness
blan·ket
blare
 blared
 blar·ing
blar·ney
bla·sé
blas·pheme
 blas·phemed
 blas·phem·ing
 blas·phem·er
 blas·phem·ous
 blas·phemy
 blas·phem·ies
blast·ed
blas·tu·la
blat
 blat·ted
 blat·ting
bla·tant
 bla·tan·cy
 bla·tant·ly
blath·er·skite
blaze
 blazed
 blaz·ing
bla·zer
bleach
 bleach·er
bleak
 bleak·ly
 bleak·ness
blear
 bleary
 blear·i·ness
bleed
 bled
 bleed·ing

bleed·er
blem·ish
blend
  blend·ed
  blend·ing
  blend·er
Blen·heim
bless
  bless·ed
  blest
  bles·sing
  bless·ed·ness
blind
  blind·ing
  blind·ing·ly
  blind·ly
  blind·ness
blind·er
blind·fold
blind·man's buff
blink·er
bliss
  bliss·ful
  bliss·ful·ly
  bliss·ful·ness
blis·ter
  blis·tery
blithe
  blithe·ly
blithe·some
  blithe·some·ly
blitz·krieg
bliz·zard
block
  block·er
block·ade
  block·ad·ed
  block·ad·ing
  block·ad·er
block·bus·ter
block·head
block·house
block·ish
  block·ish·ly
blocky
blond
blond·ness
blood·curd·ling
blood·ed
blood·hound
blood·less
  blood·less·ly
  blood·less·ness
blood·let·ting
blood·shed
blood·shot
blood·stained
blood·stone
blood·suck·er
blood·thirsty
  blood·thirst·i·ly
bloody
  blood·i·er
  blood·i·est
  blood·ied

blood·y·ing
blood·i·ly
blood·i·ness
bloom·ers
bloom·ing
  bloom·ing·ly
bloop·er
blos·som
blot
  blot·ted
  blot·ting
blotch
  blotchy
blot·ter
blow
  blew
  blown
  blow·ing
  blow·er
blow·fly
  blow·flies
blow·gun
blow·hole
blow·out
blow·pipe
blow·torch
blow·up
blowy
blowzy
blub·ber
  blub·bery
bludg·eon
blue
  blu·er
  blu·est
  blu·ing
  blue·ness
Blue·beard
blue·bell
blue·ber·ry
  blue·ber·ries
blue·bird
blue-blood·ed
blue·bon·net
blue·coat
blue·col·lar
blue·fish
blue·grass
blue·gum
blue·jack·et
blue·nose
blue·pen·cil
blue·print
blue·stock·ing
blu·et
blu·ing
blun·der
  blun·der·er
  blun·der·ing·ly
  blun·der·buss
blunt
  blunt·ly
  blunt·ness
blur
  blurred

blur·ring
blur·ry
blush
blushed
blush·ing
blush·ing·ly
blus·ter
blus·ter·er
blus·ter·ing·ly
blus·ter·ous
blus·tery
boa
board·er
board·walk
boast
boas·ter
boast·ful
boast·ful·ness
boast·ing·ly
boat·house
boat·man
boat·men
boat·swain
bob
bobbed
bob·bing
bob·bin
bob·ble
bob·bled
bob·bling
bob·by pin
bob·cat
bob·o·link
bob·sled
bob·tail
bob·white
Boc·cac·cio
bode
bod·ed
bod·ing
bod·ice
bod·i·ly
bod·kin
bod·y
bod·ied
bod·y·ing
bod·y·guard
Bo·e·thi·us
bog
bog·gy
bog·ging
bo·gey
bog·gle
bog·gled
bog·gling
bog·gler
Bo·go·ta
bo·gus
bo·gy
Bo·he·mia
bo·he·mi·an
boil·er
Boi·se
bois·ter·ous
bois·ter·ous·ly

bois·ter·ous·ness
bo·la
bo·las
bold
bold·ly
bold·ness
bold·face
bo·le·ro
Bo·li·var
Bo·liv·ia
bol·lix
boll·worm
bo·lo
bo·lo·gna
bo·lo·ney
Bol·she·vik
Bol·she·vism
bol·ster
bol·ster·er
bolt
bolt·ed
bolt·er
bom·bard
bom·bard·ment
bom·bar·dier
bom·bast
bom·bas·tic
bom·bas·ti·cal·ly
Bom·bay
bomb·er
bomb·proof
bomb·shell
bomb·sight
bo·na fide
bo·nan·za
Bo·na·parte
Bo·na·ven·tu·ra
bon·bon
bond·age
bond·ed
bond·man
bond·men
bonds·man
bonds·men
bone
boned
bon·ing
bone·head
bon·er
bon·fire
bon·go
bon·gos
bon·goes
bon·ho·mie
Bon·i·face
bon·net
bon·ny
bo·nus
bo·nus·es
bon voy·age
bony
bon·i·er
bon·i·est
boo
booed

boo·ing
boo·by
 boo·bies
boo·by trap
boo·dle
boo·hoo
 boo·hooed
 boo·hoo·ing
book
 book·bind·er
book·case
book·end
book·ie
book·ish
 book·ish·ness
book·keep·ing
 book·keep·er
book·let
book·mak·er
book·mark
book·mo·bile
book·plate
book·sell·er
 book·sell·ing
book·stall
book·worm
boo·me·rang
boon·dog·gle
boor
 boor·ish
 boor·ish·ness
boost
 boost·er
boot·black
boot·ee
boot·jack
boot·leg
 boot·legged
 boot·leg·ging
 boot·leg·ger
boot·less
 boot·less·ly
 boot·less·ness
boot·lick
 boot·lick·er
boot·ty
 boo·ties
booze
 booz·er
 boozy
 booz·i·er
 booz·i·est
bo·rax
Bor·deaux
bor·der
 bor·dered
 bor·der·land
 bor·der·line
bore
 bored
 bor·ing
 bor·er
bo·re·al
bore·dom
Bor·gia

bo·ric
Bor·neo
bo·ron
bor·ough
bor·row
 bor·row·er
Bos·nia
bos·om
boss·ism
bossy
 boss·i·er
 boss·i·est
 boss·i·ness
Bos·ton
bo·sun
Bos·well
bot·a·ny
 bo·tan·i·cal
 bot·a·nist
 bot·a·nize
botch
 botchy
 botch·i·er
 botch·i·est
both·er
 both·er·some
Bot·swa·na
Bot·ti·cel·li
bot·tle
 bot·tled
 bot·tling
 bot·tle·ful
 bot·tler
bot·tle·neck
bot·tom
 bot·tom·less
bot·u·lism
bou·doir
bouf·fant
bough
bought
bouil·lon
boul·der
boul·e·vard
Bou·logne
bounce
 bounced
 bounc·ing
bound
bound·a·ry
 bound·a·ries
bound·less
 bound·less·ness
boun·te·ous
 boun·te·ous·ness
boun·ti·ful
boun·ty
 boun·ties
bou·quet
bour·bon
bour·geois
 bour·geoi·sie
bou·tique
bou·ton·niere
bo·vine

bow·el
bow·er
bow·ery
bow·ie
bow·ing
bow·knot
bowl
bow·leg
  bow·leg·ged
bowl·er
bow·line
bow·ling
bow·man
bow·men
bow·string
box
  box·ful
  box·fuls
box·car
box·er
box·ing
boy
  boy·hood
  boy·ish
  boy·ish·ly
  boy·ish·ness
boy·cott
boy·friend
boy·sen·ber·ry
boy·sen·ber·ries
brace
  braced
  brac·ing
brace·let
brac·er
bra·ces
brack·en
brack·et
brack·ish
  brack·ish·ness
brad
  brad·ded
  brad·ding
brag
  bragged
  brag·ging
brag·gart
Brah·ma
Brah·min
Brahms
braid
  braid·er
  braid·ing
braille
brain·child
brain·less
brain·pow·er
brain·storm
brain·storm·ing
brain·wash·ing
brainy
  brain·i·er
  brain·i·est
braise
  braised

brais·ing
brake
  braked
  brak·ing
brake·man
  brake·men
bram·ble
bram·bly
branch
  branch·ed
brand
  brand·er
Bran·deis
Bran·den·burg
bran·dish
brand-new
bran·dy
  bran·dies
  bran·died
  bran·dy·ing
Bran·dy·wine
bra·sier
Bra·si·lia
bras·se·rie
bras·se·ries
bras·siere
brassy
  brass·i·er
  brass·i·est
brat
  brat·tish
  brat·ty
bra·va·do
brave
  braved
  brav·ing
  brave·ness
brav·ery
  brav·er·ies
bra·vo
  bra·vos
bra·vu·ra
brawl
  brawl·er
brawn
  brawn·i·ness
  brawny
  brawn·i·er
  brawn·i·est
bra·zen
bra·zier
Bra·zil
Braz·za·ville
breach
bread
  bread·ed
breadth·ways
bread·win·ner
break
  broke
  bro·ken
  break·ing
  break·a·ble
break·age
break·a·way

break·down
break·er
break·fast
break·neck
break·out
break·through
break·up
break·wa·ter
breast·bone
breast·plate
breath
breathe
  breathed
  breath·ing
breath·er
breath·ing
breath·tak·ing
  breath·tak·ing·ly
breathy
  breath·i·er
  breath·i·est
breech·es
breech·load·er
breed
  bred
  breed·ing
breeze
breeze·way
breezy
  breez·i·er
  breez·i·est
  breez·i·ness
breth·ren
Bret·on
bre·vet
  bre·vet·ted
  bre·vet·ting
bre·vi·a·ry
  bre·vi·a·ries
brev·i·ty
brew
  brew·er
brew·ery
  brew·er·ies
Bri·and
bri·ar
  bri·ary
bribe
  bribed
  brib·ing
  brib·a·ble
brib·ery
  brib·er·ies
bric-a-brac
brick·lay·er
  brick·lay·ing
brick·work
brick·yard
bride
  brid·al
bride·groom
brides·maid
bridge
Bridge·port
Bridge·town

Bridge·wa·ter
bridge·work
bri·dle
  bri·dled
  bri·dling
brief
  brief·ly
  brief·ing
bri·er
bri·gade
brig·a·dier
brig·an·tine
bright
  bright·ly
  bright·ness
bright·en
Brigh·ton
bril·liance
  bril·lian·cy
  bril·liant
brim
  brimmed
  brim·ming
brim·stone
brine
  briny
bring
  brought
  bring·ing
brink
bri·oche
bri·quette
  bri·quet
brisk
  brisk·ly
  brisk·ness
bris·ket
bris·tle
  bris·tled
Bris·tol
Brit·ain
Bri·tan·nia
britch·es
Brit·ish
Brit·on
Brit·ta·ny
brit·tle
broach
  broached
  broach·ing
broad·cast
  broad·cast·ed
  broad·cast·ing
broad·cloth
broad-mind·ed
broad·side
Broad·way
bro·cade
  bro·cad·ed
  bro·cad·ing
broc·co·li
bro·chure
Brock·ton
broil·er
bro·ken

bro·ken-down
bro·ken-heart·ed
bro·ker
bro·ker·age
bro·mide
bro·mine
bron·chi
bron·chi·al
bron·chi·tis
bron·chus
bron·co
  bron·cos
Bron·te
bron·to·saur
bronze
  bronzed
  bronz·ing
brooch
brood
  brood·ing
brook
Brook·line
Brook·lyn
broom·stick
broth·el
broth·er
broth·er·hood
broth·er-in-law
  broth·ers-in-law
broth·er·ly
brow·beat
  brow·beat·en
  brow·beat·ing
brown
brown·ie
brown·out
brown·stone
Browns·ville
browse
  browsed
  brows·ing
bru·in
bruise
  bruised
  bruis·ing
bruis·er
brunch
bru·net
Bruns·wick
brush-off
brusque
Brus·sels
bru·tal
bru·tal·i·ty
bru·tal·ize
  bru·tal·ized
  bru·tal·iz·ing
  bru·tal·i·za·tion
brut·ish
Bru·tus
bub·ble
  bub·bled
  bub·bling
bub·bler
bu·bon·ic

buc·ca·neer
Bu·chan·an
Bu·cha·rest
buck·a·roo
buck·board
buck·et
  buck·et·ed
  buck·et·ing
buck·eye
Buck·ing·ham
buck·le
buck·ram
buck·saw
buck·shot
buck·skin
buck·tooth
  buck·teeth
  buck·toothed
buck·wheat
bu·col·ic
bud
  bud·ded
  bud·ding
Bu·da·pest
Bud·dha
Bud·dhism
  Bud·dhist
bud·dy
budge
budg·et
Bue·na Vis·ta
Bue·nos Ai·res
buf·fa·lo
  buf·fa·loes
  buf·fa·los
  buf·fa·loed
  buf·fa·lo·ing
buff·er
buf·fet
  buf·fet·ed
  buf·fet·ing
buf·foon
  buf·foon·ery
  buf·foon·er·ies
  buf·foon·ish
bug
  bugged
  bug·ging
bug·a·boo
bug·gy
  bug·gi·er
  bug·gi·est
bu·gle
  bu·gled
  bu·gling
  bu·gler
build
  build·er
  build·ing
build-up
built-in
built-up
Bu·jum·bu·ra
bulb
bul·ba·ceous

bul·bar
bul·bous
Bul·gar·ia
bulge
  bulged
  bulg·ing
  bulgy
bulk·head
bulky
  bulk·i·er
  bulk·i·est
  bulk·i·ly
  bulk·i·ness
bull·dog
bull·doze
  bull·dozed
  bull·doz·ing
  bull·doz·er
bul·let
bul·le·tin
bul·let·proof
bull·fight
  bull·fight·er
  bull·fight·ing
bull·finch
bull·frog
bull·head·ed
bull·horn
bul·lion
bull·ock
bull·pen
bull's-eye
bull·whip
bul·ly
  bul·lies
  bul·lied
  bul·ly·ing
bul·rush
bul·wark
bum
  bum·mer
  bum·mest
bum·ble·bee
bump·er
bump·kin
bump·tious
  bump·tious·ness
bumpy
  bump·i·er
  bump·i·est
  bump·i·ly
  bump·i·ness
bunch
  bunchy
  bunch·i·er
  bunch·i·est
bun·co
bun·combe
bun·dle
  bun·dled
  bun·dling
bun·ga·low
bun·gle
  bun·gled
  bun·gling

bun·gler
bun·ion
bunk·er
bunk·house
bun·ko
bun·kum
bun·ny
  bun·nies
Bun·sen
bun·ting
Bun·yan
bu·oy
buoy·an·cy
buoy·ant
buoy·ant·ly
Bur·bank
bur·ble
bur·den
bur·den·some
bur·dock
bu·reau
  bu·reaus
  bu·reaux
bu·reauc·ra·cy
  bu·reauc·ra·cies
  bu·reau·crat
  bu·reau·crat·ic
bu·rette
bur·geon
burg·er
bur·gess
bur·glar
  bur·glar·ize
    bur·glar·ized
    bur·glar·iz·ing
  bur·gla·ry
    bur·gla·ries
bur·gle
  bur·gled
  bur·gling
Bur·goyne
Bur·gun·dy
bur·i·al
bur·lap
Bur·leigh
bur·lesque
  bur·lesqued
  bur·les·quing
  bur·les·quer
Bur·ling·ton
bur·ly
  bur·li·er
  bur·li·est
  bur·li·ness
Bur·ma
burn
  burned
  burnt
  burn·ing
  burn·a·ble
burn·er
bur·nish
  bur·nish·er
bur·noose
burn·sides

burp
burr
  burred
  bur·ring
bur·ro
  bur·ros
Bur·roughs
bur·row
  bur·row·er
bur·sa
  bur·sae
  bur·sal
bur·sar
  bur·sa·ri·al
bur·sa·ry
  bur·sa·ries
bur·si·tis
burst
  burst·ing
  burst·er
Bu·run·di
bury
  bur·ied
  bur·y·ing
bus
  bus·es
  bused
  bus·ing
bus·boy
bus·by
  bus·bies
bushed
bush·el
bu·shi·do
bush·ing
bush·man
  bush·men
bush·mas·ter
bush·rang·er
bush·whack
  bush·whack·er
  bush·whack·ing
bushy
  bush·i·er
  bush·i·est
  bush·i·ness
bus·i·ly
busi·ness
busi·ness·like
busi·ness·man
  busi·ness·men
  busi·ness·wom·an
  busi·ness·wom·en
bus·kin
  bus·kined
bus·tard
bus·tle
  bus·tled
  bus·tling
  bus·tler
busy
  bus·i·er
  bus·i·est
  bus·ied
  bus·y·ing

bus·y·body
bu·ta·di·ene
bu·tane
butch·er
  butch·er·er
butch·er·bird
butch·er's-broom
butch·ery
  butch·er·ies
but·ler
  but·ler·ship
butte
but·ter
but·ter·cup
but·ter·fat
but·ter·fin·gered
  but·ter·fin·gers
but·ter·fish
but·ter·fly
  but·ter·flies
but·ter·milk
but·ter·nut
but·ter·scotch
but·tery
  but·ter·ies
but·tock
but·ton
but·ton·hole
  but·ton·holed
  but·ton·hol·ing
  but·ton·hol·er
but·ton·wood
but·tress
bu·ty·ric
bux·om
  bux·om·ly
  bux·om·ness
buy
  bought
  buy·ing
  buy·a·ble
  buy·er
buz·zard
buzz·er
by-e·lec·tion
by·gone
by·law
by·line
by·pass
by·path
by·play
by·prod·uct
by·road
By·ron
by·stand·er
byte
by·way
by·word
Byz·an·tine
By·zan·tium
ca·bal
  ca·balled
  ca·ball·ing
cab·a·la
  cab·a·lis·tic

cab·a·lis·ti·cal
ca·bal·le·ro
ca·ba·na
cab·a·ret
cab·bage
 cab·baged
 cab·bag·ing
cab·by
 cab·bies
ca·ber
cab·in
cab·i·net
cab·i·net·mak·er
 cab·i·net·mak·ing
cab·i·net·work
ca·ble
 ca·bled
 ca·bling
ca·ble·gram
cab·o·chon
ca·boo·dle
ca·boose
Cab·ot
cab·ri·o·let
cab·stand
ca·cao
cach·a·lot
cache
 cached
 cach·ing
ca·chet
ca·cique
cack·le
 cack·led
 cack·ling
 cack·ler
ca·coph·o·ny
 ca·coph·o·nies
cac·tus
 cac·tus·es
 cac·ti
cad
 cad·dish
ca·dav·er
 ca·dav·er·ous
cad·die
 cad·died
 cad·dy·ing
cad·dis fly
cad·dy
 cad·dies
ca·dence
ca·den·za
ca·det
cadge
 cadged
 cadg·ing
Cad·il·lac
Ca·diz
cad·mi·um
Cad·mus
ca·dre
ca·du·ce·us
 ca·du·cei
Cae·sar

Cae·sa·rea
Cae·sar·e·an
cae·su·ra
 cae·su·ras
 cae·su·rae
ca·fe
caf·e·te·ria
caf·feine
caf·tan
Ca·ga·yan
cage
 caged
 cag·ing
cai·man
cairn
Cai·ro
cais·son
cai·tiff
Ca·ius
ca·jole
 ca·joled
 ca·jol·ing
 ca·jol·ery
 ca·jol·ing·ly
Ca·jun
cake
 caked
 cak·ing
cake·walk
cal·a·bash
cal·a·boose
Ca·la·bria
Ca·lais
cal·a·mine
ca·lam·i·ty
 ca·lam·i·ties
 ca·lam·i·tous
cal·cic
cal·ci·fy
 cal·ci·fied
 cal·ci·fy·ing
 cal·ci·fi·ca·tion
cal·ci·mine
cal·cite
cal·ci·um
cal·cu·la·ble
 cal·cu·la·bil·i·ty
cal·cu·late
 cal·cu·lat·ed
 cal·cu·lat·ing
 cal·cu·la·tion
cal·cu·la·tor
cal·cu·lus
 cal·cu·lus·es
Cal·cut·ta
Cal·de·ron
cal·dron
Ca·leb
Cal·e·do·nia
cal·en·dar
cal·ends
calf
 calves
calf·skin
Cal·ga·ry

Cal·houn
cal·i·ber
cal·i·brate
  cal·i·brat·ed
  cal·i·brat·ing
  cal·i·bra·tion
cal·i·co
  cal·i·coes
Cal·i·for·nia
Ca·lig·u·la
cal·i·per
ca·liph
  cal·iph·ate
cal·is·then·ics
Cal·lao
Cal·les
cal·lig·ra·pher
cal·lig·ra·phy
call·ing
cal·li·o·pe
Cal·lis·to
cal·lous
  cal·loused
cal·low
cal·lus
  cal·lus·es
calm
ca·lor·ic
cal·o·rie
  cal·o·ries
cal·o·rif·ic
cal·u·met
cal·um·ny
  cal·um·nies
  ca·lum·ni·ate
  ca·lum·ni·at·ed
  ca·lum·ni·at·ing
  ca·lum·ni·a·tion
Cal·va·ry
calve
  calved
  calv·ing
Cal·vert
Cal·vin
Cal·vin·ism
Cal·y·don
ca·lyp·so
  ca·lyp·sos
ca·lyx
  ca·lyx·es
  cal·y·ces
ca·ma·ra·de·rie
cam·ber
cam·bi·um
Cam·bo·dia
Cam·bria
cam·bric
Cam·bridge
Cam·den
cam·el
ca·mel·lia
Cam·e·lot
Cam·em·bert
cam·eo
cam·era

cam·er·a·man
Cam·er·oon
cam·i·sole
cam·o·mile
Ca·mor·ra
cam·ou·flage
  cam·ou·flaged
  cam·ou·flag·ing
Cam·pa·gna
cam·paign
  cam·paign·er
cam·pa·ni·le
  cam·pa·ni·les
camp·er
camp·fire
cam·phor
cam·pus
  cam·pus·es
campy
  camp·i·er
  camp·i·est
cam·shaft
can
  canned
  can·ning
Ca·naan
Can·a·da
ca·nal
  ca·naled
  ca·nal·ing
can·a·pé
ca·nard
ca·nary
ca·nas·ta
Can·ber·ra
can·can
can·cel
  can·celed
  can·cel·ing
  can·cel·la·tion
can·cer
can·de·la·brum
  can·de·la·bra
  can·de·la·brums
can·did
can·di·da·cy
  can·di·da·cies
can·di·date
can·died
can·dle
  can·dled
  can·dling
can·dle·light
Can·dle·mas
can·dle·pow·er
can·dle·stick
can·dor
can·dy
  can·dies
  can·died
  can·dy·ing
cane
  caned
  can·ing
ca·nine

Ca·nis
can·is·ter
can·ker
 can·ker·ous
can·na·bis
canned
can·ner
can·nery
 can·ner·ies
Cannes
can·ni·bal
 can·ni·bal·ism
can·ni·bal·ize
 can·ni·bal·ized
 can·ni·bal·iz·ing
can·non
can·not
can·ny
 can·ni·er
 can·ni·est
 can·ni·ly
 can·ni·ness
ca·noe
 ca·noed
 ca·noe·ing
 ca·noe·ist
can·on
ca·non·i·cal
can·on·ize
 can·on·ized
 can·on·iz·ing
 can·on·i·za·tion
can·o·py
 can·o·pies
 can·o·pied
 can·o·py·ing
can·ta·loup
 can·ta·loupe
 can·ta·lope
can·tan·ker·ous
can·ta·ta
can·teen
can·ter
Can·ter·bury
can·ti·cle
Can·ti·gny
can·ti·lev·er
can·to
 can·tos
can·ton
can·tor
Ca·nuck
Ca·nute
can·vas
can·vass
 can·vass·er
can·yon
caou·tchouc
cap
 capped
 cap·ping
ca·pa·bil·i·ty
 ca·pa·bil·i·ties
ca·pa·ble
 ca·pa·bly

ca·pa·cious
ca·pac·i·tate
 ca·pac·i·tat·ed
 ca·pac·i·tat·ing
ca·pac·i·ty
 ca·pac·i·ties
Ca·pel·la
ca·per
Ca·per·na·um
Ca·pet
ca·pi·as
cap·il·lar·i·ty
cap·il·lary
 cap·il·lar·ies
cap·i·tal
cap·i·tal·ism
 cap·i·tal·is·tic
 cap·i·tal·ist
cap·i·tal·ize
 cap·i·tal·i·za·tion
 cap·i·tal·ly
cap·i·ta·tion
ca·pit·u·late
 ca·pit·u·lat·ed
 ca·pit·u·lat·ing
 ca·pit·u·la·tor
ca·pon
ca·pote
Cap·pa·do·cia
Ca·pri
ca·pric·cio
ca·price
 ca·pri·cious
 ca·pri·cious·ly
 ca·pri·cious·ness
Cap·ri·con
cap·ri·ole
 cap·ri·oled
 cap·ri·ol·ing
cap·size
 cap·sized
 cap·siz·ing
cap·stan
cap·stone
cap·sule
 cap·su·lar
cap·tain
 cap·tain·cy
 cap·tain·ship
cap·tion
cap·tious
 cap·tious·ness
cap·ti·vate
 cap·ti·vat·ed
 cap·ti·vat·ing
 cap·ti·vat·ing·ly
 cap·ti·va·tion
 cap·ti·va·tor
cap·tive
 cap·tiv·i·ty
 cap·tiv·i·ties
cap·tor
cap·ture
 cap·tured
 cap·tur·ing

cap·tur·er
Cap·u·let
Car·a·cal·la
Ca·ra·cas
car·a·cole
  car·a·coled
  car·a·col·ing
car·a·cul
ca·rafe
car·a·mel
car·a·pace
car·at
car·a·van
car·a·van·sa·ry
  car·a·van·sa·ries
car·a·vel
car·a·way
car·bide
car·bine
car·bo·hy·drate
car·bo·lat·ed
car·bol·ic
car·bon
car·bo·na·ceous
car·bo·nate
  car·bo·na·tion
car·bon di·ox·ide
car·bon·if·er·ous
car·bon·ize
  car·bon·ized
  car·bon·iz·ing
  car·bon·i·za·tion
car·bon mon·ox·ide
Car·bo·run·dum
car·boy
car·bun·cle
car·bu·re·tor
car·ca·jou
car·cass
car·cin·o·gen
  car·cin·o·gen·ic
car·ci·no·ma
  car·ci·no·mas
  car·ci·no·ma·ta
card
  card·er
car·da·mom
card·board
Car·de·nas
car·di·ac
Car·diff
car·di·gan
car·di·nal
car·di·o·graph
  car·di·og·ra·phy
card·sharp
care
  cared
  car·ing
ca·reen
ca·reer
care·free
care·ful
  care·ful·ly
  care·ful·ness

care·less
  care·less·ly
  care·less·ness
ca·ress
  ca·ress·ing·ly
car·et
care·tak·er
Ca·rew
care·worn
car·fare
car·go
  car·goes
  car·gos
car·hop
Car·ib·be·an
car·i·bou
car·i·ca·ture
  car·i·ca·tured
  car·i·ca·tur·ing
  car·i·ca·tur·ist
car·ies
car·il·lon
  car·il·lonned
  car·il·lon·ning
  car·il·lon·neur
car·load
Carls·bad
Car·mel
car·mine
car·nage
car·nal
  car·nal·i·ty
  car·nal·ly
car·na·tion
Car·ne·gie
car·nel·ian
car·ni·val
car·ni·vore
car·niv·o·rous
  car·niv·o·rous·ly
  car·niv·o·rous·ness
car·ol
  car·oled
  car·ol·ing
  car·ol·er
Car·o·li·na
car·om
ca·rot·id
ca·rous·al
ca·rouse
  ca·roused
  ca·rous·ing
  ca·rous·er
car·ou·sel
carp
car·pal
Car·pa·thi·an
car·pen·ter
  car·pen·try
car·pet
car·pet·bag·ger
car·pet·ing
car·port
car·pus
car·riage

car·ri·er
car·ri·ole
car·ri·on
car·rot
car·roty
car·ry
  car·ried
  car·ry·ing
car·ry·all
car·ry·o·ver
car·sick·ness
  car·sick
Car·son
cart
  car·ter
cart·age
Car·ta·ge·na
carte blanche
car·tel
Car·ter
Car·thage
Car·thu·sian
Car·tier
car·ti·lage
car·ti·lag·i·nous
car·tog·ra·phy
  car·tog·ra·pher
  car·to·graph·ic
car·ton
car·toon
  car·toon·ist
car·tridge
cart·wheel
Ca·ru·so
carve
  carved
  carv·ing
  carv·er
car·vel
car·y·at·id
  car·y·at·ids
  car·y·at·i·des
ca·sa·ba
Ca·sa·blan·ca
Ca·sals
Cas·a·no·va
cas·cade
  cas·cad·ed
  cas·cad·ing
case
  cased
  cas·ing
case·hard·en
ca·sein
case·mate
  case·mat·ed
case·ment
  case·ment·ed
case·work·er
  case·work
cash·book
cash·ew
cash·ier
cash·mere
cas·ing

ca·si·no
  ca·si·nos
cas·ket
Cas·pi·an
cas·sa·ba
Cas·san·dra
cas·sa·va
cas·se·role
cas·sette
cas·si·no
Cas·sius
cas·sock
  cas·socked
cas·so·wary
  cas·so·war·ies
cast
  cast·ing
cas·ta·net
cast·a·way
caste
cas·tel·lat·ed
cast·er
cas·ti·gate
  cas·ti·gat·ed
  cas·ti·gat·ing
  cas·ti·ga·tion
  cas·ti·ga·tor
Cas·tile
cast i·ron
cas·tle
  cas·tled
  cas·tling
cast·off
cas·tor
cas·trate
  cas·trat·ed
  cas·trat·ing
  cas·trat·er
  cas·tra·tion
Cas·tro
cas·u·al
  cas·u·al·ly
  cas·u·al·ness
cas·u·al·ty
  cas·u·al·ties
cas·u·ist
  cas·u·is·tic
  cas·u·ist·ry
  cas·u·ist·ries
cat
  cat·ted
  cat·ting
cat·a·clysm
  cat·a·clys·mal
cat·a·comb
cat·a·falque
cat·a·lep·sy
  cat·a·lep·tic
Cat·a·li·na
cat·a·log
  cat·a·loged
  cat·a·log·ing
  cat·a·log·er
  cat·a·log·ist
ca·tal·pa

ca·tal·y·sis
cat·al·y·ses
cat·a·lyt·ic
cat·a·lyst
cat·a·lyze
cat·a·lyzed
cat·a·lyz·ing
cat·a·ma·ran
cat·a·mount
cat·a·pult
cat·a·ract
ca·tarrh
ca·tas·tro·phe
cat·as·troph·ic
Ca·taw·ba
cat·bird
cat·boat
cat·call
catch
caught
catch·ing
catch·all
catch·er
catch·ing
catch·up
catch·word
catchy
catch·i·er
catch·i·est
cat·e·chism
cat·e·chis·mal
cat·e·chize
cat·e·chized
cat·e·chiz·ing
cat·e·chi·za·tion
cat·e·chist
cat·e·chiz·er
cat·e·chu·men
cat·e·gor·i·cal
cat·e·gor·i·cal·ly
cat·e·go·ry
cat·e·go·ries
cat·e·gor·ize
cat·e·gor·ized
cat·e·gor·iz·ing
ca·ter
ca·ter·er
cat·er·pil·lar
cat·er·waul
cat·fish
cat·fish·es
cat·gut
ca·thar·sis
ca·thar·ses
ca·thar·tic
Ca·thay
ca·the·dral
Cath·er
cath·e·ter
cath·ode
cath·o·lic
cath·o·lic·i·ty
ca·thol·i·cize
ca·thol·i·cized
ca·thol·i·ciz·ing

Ca·thol·i·cism
cat·i·on
cat·kin
cat·mint
cat·nap
cat·napped
cat·nap·ping
cat·nip
Ca·to
cat-o'-nine-tails
Cats·kill
cat's-paw
cat·sup
cat·tail
cat·tle
cat·tle·man
cat·ty
cat·ti·er
cat·ti·est
cat·ti·ly
cat·ti·ness
cat·ty-cor·ner
cat·ty-cor·nered
cat·walk
Cau·ca·sian
cau·cus
cau·cus·es
cau·cused
cau·cus·ing
cau·dal
cau·date
cau·dat·ed
cau·dle
caul·dron
cau·li·flow·er
caulk
caulk·er
caus·al
caus·al·ly
cau·sal·i·ty
cau·sal·i·ties
cause
caused
caus·ing
cau·sa·tion
caus·a·tive
cause·less
caus·er
cause·way
caus·tic
caus·ti·cal·ly
cau·ter·ize
cau·ter·ized
cau·ter·iz·ing
cau·ter·i·za·tion
cau·tery
cau·ter·ies
cau·tion
cau·tion·ary
cau·tious
cav·al·cade
cav·a·lier
cav·a·lier·ly
cav·al·ry
cav·al·ry·man

cav·al·ry·men
cave
  caved
  cav·ing
ca·ve·at
cave-in
cav·ern
  cav·ern·ous
cav·i·ar
cav·il
  cav·iled
  cav·il·ing
cav·i·ty
  cav·i·ties
ca·vort
cay·enne
cay·man
  cay·mans
cay·use
cease
  ceased
  ceas·ing
cease-fire
ce·cum
ce·dar
cede
  ced·ed
  ced·ing
ce·dil·la
ceil·ing
cel·an·dine
cel·e·brant
cel·e·brate
  cel·e·brat·ed
  cel·e·brat·ing
  cel·e·bra·tion
  cel·e·bra·tor
ce·leb·ri·ty
  ce·leb·ri·ties
ce·ler·i·ty
cel·ery
ce·les·tial
ce·li·ac
cel·i·ba·cy
  cel·i·bate
cel·lar
cel·lo
  cel·los
  cel·list
cel·lo·phane
cel·lu·lar
cel·lule
Cel·lu·loid
cel·lu·lose
Celt·ic
ce·ment
cem·e·tery
  cem·e·ter·ies
ce·no·bite
cen·o·taph
Ce·no·zo·ic
cen·ser
cen·sor
  cen·so·ri·al
  cen·sor·ship

cen·so·ri·ous
  cen·so·ri·ous·ly
  cen·so·ri·ous·ness
cen·sure
  cen·sured
  cen·sur·ing
  cen·sur·er
  cen·sur·a·ble
  cen·sur·a·bly
cen·sus
  cen·sus·es
  cen·sused
  cen·sus·ing
cen·tare
cen·taur
cen·te·nar·i·an
cen·te·na·ry
  cen·te·na·ries
cen·ten·ni·al
cen·ter
cen·ter·board
cen·ter·piece
cen·ti·are
cen·ti·grade
cen·ti·gram
cen·ti·li·ter
cen·ti·me·ter
cen·tral
cen·tral·ize
  cen·tral·ized
  cen·tral·iz·ing
cen·trif·u·gal
cen·tri·fuge
cen·trip·e·tal
cen·tu·ri·on
cen·tu·ry
  cen·tu·ries
ce·ram·ic
  ce·ram·ics
Cer·ber·us
ce·re·al
cer·e·bel·lum
cer·e·bral
cer·e·brum
cer·e·mo·ni·al
  cer·e·mo·ni·al·ism
cer·e·mo·ni·ous
cer·e·mo·ny
  cer·e·mo·nies
Ce·res
ce·rise
ce·ri·um
ce·ric
cer·tain
cer·tain·ly
cer·tain·ty
  cer·tain·ties
cer·tif·i·cate
cer·ti·fi·ca·tion
cer·ti·fy
  cer·ti·fied
  cer·ti·fy·ing
  cer·ti·fi·a·ble
  cer·ti·fi·a·bly
  cer·ti·fi·er

cer·ti·tude
ce·ru·le·an
Cer·van·tes
cer·vi·cal
cer·vix
  cer·vix·es
  cer·vi·ces
ces·sa·tion
ces·sion
cess·pool
ce·ta·cean
ce·ta·ceous
Cey·lon
Cha·blis
Cha·co
chafe
  chafed
  chaf·ing
chaf·er
chaff
  chaf·fer
  chaff·er·er
Cha·gall
Cha·gres
cha·grin
  cha·grined
  cha·grin·ing
chain re·ac·tion
chair·man
  chair·men
chair·man·ship
chair·per·son
chair·wom·an
  chair·wom·en
chaise longue
Chal·ce·don
Chal·dea
chal·et
chal·ice
chalk
  chalky
chal·lenge
  chal·lenged
  chal·leng·ing
cham·ber
cham·ber·maid
cha·me·le·on
cham·ois
cham·pagne
cham·pi·on
  cham·pi·on·ship
Cham·plain
Champs Ely·sées
chance·ful
chan·cel·lor
Chan·cel·lors·ville
chancy
  chanc·i·er
  chanc·i·est
chan·de·lier
change
  changed
  chang·ing
change·a·ble
change·ful

chan·nel
chan·ti·cleer
cha·os
cha·ot·ic
chap
  chapped
  chap·ping
cha·pa·re·jos
chap·ar·ral
cha·peau
  cha·peaux
chap·el
chap·e·ron
chap·fall·en
chap·lain
chap·let
Chap·lin
chap·ter
char
  charred
  char·ring
char·ac·ter
  char·ac·ter·is·tic
  char·ac·ter·is·ti·cal·ly
  char·ac·ter·ize
  char·ac·ter·ized
  char·ac·ter·iz·ing
  char·ac·ter·i·za·tion
  char·ac·ter·iz·er
cha·rade
char·coal
charge
  charged
  char·ging
char·gé d'af·faires
charg·er
char·i·ot
  char·i·ot·eer
cha·ris·ma
char·i·ta·ble
  char·i·ta·ble·ness
  char·i·ta·bly
char·i·ty
  char·i·ties
cha·riv·a·ri
char·la·tan
  char·la·tan·ism
Char·le·magne
Charles·ton
Charles·town
char·ley horse
Char·lotte
Char·lottes·ville
Char·lotte·town
charm·er
char·nel
char·ter
char·treuse
char·wom·an
chary
  char·i·er
  char·i·est
Cha·ryb·di·an
Cha·ryb·dis
chase

chased
chas·ing
chas·er
chasm
chas·sis
chaste
  chaste·ly
chas·ten
chas·tise
  chas·tised
  chas·tis·ing
  chas·tise·ment
  chas·tis·er
chas·ti·ty
chat
  chat·ted
  chat·ting
cha·teau
  cha·teaux
Cha·teau·bri·and
Châ·teau-Thier·ry
chat·e·laine
Chat·ham
Chat·ta·hoo·chee
Chat·ta·noo·ga
chat·tel
chat·ter
chat·ter·box
Chat·ter·ton
chat·ty
  chat·ti·er
  chat·ti·est
  chat·ti·ly
  chat·ti·ness
Chau·cer
chauf·feur
chau·vin·ist
  chau·vin·ism
  chau·vin·is·tic
cheap
  cheap·ly
  cheap·ness
cheap·en
cheap·skate
cheat
check·book
check·er
check·er·board
check·list
check·mate
  check·mat·ed
  check·mat·ing
check·out
check·point
check·room
check·up
ched·dar
cheek·bone
cheeky
  cheek·i·er
  cheek·i·est
  cheek·i·ly
  cheek·i·ness
cheer·ful
  cheer·ful·ly

cheer·ful·ness
cheer·lead·er
cheer·less
  cheer·less·ly
  cheer·less·ness
cheery
  cheer·i·er
  cheer·i·est
  cheer·i·ly
  cheer·i·ness
cheese·burg·er
cheese·cake
cheese·cloth
cheesy
  chees·i·er
  chees·i·est
  chees·i·ness
chee·tah
Chel·sea
chem·i·cal
  chem·i·cal·ly
che·mise
chem·ist
chem·is·try
chem·o·ther·a·py
che·nille
Cher·bourg
cher·ish
Cher·o·kee
che·root
cher·ry
  cher·ries
cher·ub
  cher·ubs
  cher·u·bim
  che·ru·bic
cher·vil
Ches·a·peake
Chesh·ire
chess·man
  chess·men
Ches·ter·field
Ches·ter·ton
chest·nut
chesty
  chest·i·er
  chest·i·est
Chev·ro·let
chev·ron
chew
  chew·er
Chey·enne
Chiang Kai·shek
Chi·an·ti
chi·a·ro·scu·ro
Chi·ca·go
chi·can·ery
  chi·can·er·ies
Chi·ca·no
chi·chi
chick·a·dee
Chick·a·hom·i·ny
Chick·a·mau·ga
Chick·a·saw
chic·ken

chic·ken·heart·ed
chic·le
chic·o·ry
  chic·o·ries
chide
  chid·ed
  chid·ing
chief
  chief·ly
chief·tain
chif·fon
chif·fo·nier
chi·gnon
Chi·hua·hua
chil·blain
chil·dren
child·bear·ing
child·birth
child·hood
child·ish
  child·ish·ly
child·like
chili
  chil·ies
chill
  chill·ing·ly
Chil·lon
chilly
  chill·i·er
  chill·i·est
  chill·i·ness
chi·me·ra
chi·mer·ic
  chi·mer·i·cal
  chi·mer·i·cal·ly
  chi·mer·i·cal·ness
chim·ney
chim·pan·zee
chin
  chinned
  chin·ning
chi·na
Chi·na·town
chin·chil·la
Chi·nese
Chin·kiang
chi·no
  chi·nos
chi·noi·se·rie
chintzy
  chintz·i·er
  chintz·i·est
chip
  chipped
  chip·ping
chip·munk
Chip·pen·dale
chip·per
Chip·pe·wa
chi·rog·ra·pher
chi·rog·ra·phy
chi·rop·o·dist
chi·ro·prac·tic
chi·ro·prac·tor
chis·el

chis·eled
chis·el·ing
chis·el·er
chit·chat
chi·tin
chit·ter·ling
chiv·al·ry
  chiv·al·ries
  chiv·al·ric
  chiv·al·rous
  chiv·al·rous·ly
  chiv·al·rous·ness
chlo·rine
chlo·ro·form
chlo·ro·phyll
chock-full
choc·o·late
Choc·taw
choice
  choice·ly
  choice·ness
choir·boy
choke
  choked
  chok·ing
chok·er
chol·er
chol·era
chol·er·ic
cho·les·te·rol
choose
  chose
  cho·sen
  choos·ing
choosy
  choos·i·er
  choos·i·est
chop
  chopped
  chop·ping
Cho·pin
chop·per
chop·pi·ness
chop·py
  chop·pi·er
  chop·pi·est
chop·sticks
chop su·ey
cho·ral
  cho·ral·ly
cho·rale
chord
  chord·al
cho·rea
cho·re·og·ra·phy
  cho·re·og·ra·pher
  cho·re·o·graph·ic
cho·ric
chor·is·ter
chor·tle
  chor·tled
  chor·tling
cho·rus
  cho·rus·es
  cho·rused

cho·rus·ing
chos·en
chow·der
chow mein
chrism
Christ
Chris·ta·bel
chris·ten
 chris·ten·ing
Chris·ten·dom
Chris·tian
Chris·ti·an·i·ty
 Chris·ti·an·i·ties
Chris·tian·ize
 Chris·tian·ized
 Chris·tian·iz·ing
Christ·like
Christ·mas
Christ·mas·tide
chro·mate
chro·mat·ic
 chro·mat·i·cal·ly
chro·mat·ics
chro·ma·tin
chro·mic
chro·mi·um
chro·mo
 chro·mos
chro·mo·lith·o·graph
 chro·mo·li·thog·ra·pher
 chro·mo·lith·o·graph·ic
chro·mo·some
chro·mo·sphere
chron·ic
 chron·i·cal·ly
chron·i·cle
 chron·i·cled
 chron·i·cling
 chron·i·cler
chron·o·log·i·cal
 chron·o·log·i·cal·ly
chro·nol·o·gy
 chro·nol·o·gies
 chro·nol·o·gist
chron·om·e·ter
 chron·o·met·ric
chrys·a·lis
 chrys·a·lis·es
 chry·sal·i·des
chry·san·the·mum
chrys·o·lite
chub·by
 chub·bi·er
 chub·bi·est
 chub·bi·ness
chuck-full
chuck·le
 chuck·led
 chuck·ling
chuk·ker
chum·my
 chum·mi·er
 chum·mi·est
Chung·king
chunk

chunky
 chunk·i·er
 chunk·i·est
church
 church·li·ness
church·ly
church·go·er
Church·ill
church·man
 church·men
church·war·den
church·yard
churl·ish
 churl·ish·ly
 churl·ish·ness
churn·er
chut·ney
chutz·pah
ci·bo·ri·um
 ci·bo·ria
ci·ca·da
 ci·ca·das
 ci·ca·dae
cic·a·trix
 cic·a·tri·ces
 cic·a·trize
 cic·a·trized
 cic·a·triz·ing
Cic·e·ro
cic·e·ro·ne
ci·der
ci·gar
cig·a·rette
cil·ia
cil·i·ar·y
cil·i·ate
Ci·li·cia
cin·cho·na
Cin·cin·nati
cinc·ture
cin·der
Cin·der·el·la
cin·e·ma
 cin·e·mas
 cin·e·mat·ic
 cin·e·mat·o·graph
 cin·e·ma·tog·ra·pher
 cin·e·ma·tog·ra·phy
cin·e·rar·i·um
cin·na·bar
cin·na·mon
cinque·foil
ci·on
ci·pher
cir·ca
cir·ca·di·an
Cir·ce
cir·cle
 cir·cled
 cir·cling
cir·clet
cir·cuit
cir·cu·i·tous
 cir·cu·i·tous·ly
 cir·cu·i·tous·ness

cir·cu·lar
cir·cu·lar·ize
  cir·cu·lar·ized
  cir·cu·lar·iz·ing
  cir·cu·lar·i·za·tion
cir·cu·la·tion
  cir·cu·late
  cir·cu·lat·ed
  cir·cu·lat·ing
  cir·cu·la·tive
  cir·cu·la·tor
  cir·cu·la·to·ry
cir·cum·am·bi·ent
cir·cum·cise
  cir·cum·cised
  cir·cum·cis·ing
  cir·cum·cis·er
  cir·cum·ci·sion
cir·cum·fer·ence
  cir·cum·fer·en·tial
cir·cum·flex
cir·cum·flu·ent
cir·cum·fuse
  cir·cum·fused
  cir·cum·fus·ing
  cir·cum·fu·sion
cir·cum·lo·cu·tion
  cir·cum·lo·cu·to·ry
cir·cum·nav·i·gate
  cir·cum·nav·i·gat·ed
  cir·cum·nav·i·gat·ing
  cir·cum·nav·i·ga·tion
  cir·cum·nav·i·ga·tor
cir·cum·scribe
  cir·cum·scribed
  cir·cum·scrib·ing
  cir·cum·scrib·er
  cir·cum·scrip·tion
  cir·cum·scrip·tive
cir·cum·spect
cir·cum·stance
cir·cum·stan·tial
  cir·cum·stan·ti·al·i·ty
  cir·cum·stan·ti·ate
  cir·cum·stan·ti·at·ed
  cir·cum·stan·ti·at·ing
  cir·cum·stan·ti·a·tion
cir·cum·vent
  cir·cum·ven·tion
  cir·cum·ven·tive
cir·cus
  cir·cus·es
cir·rho·sis
  cir·rhot·ic
cir·rus
Cis·ter·cian
cis·tern
cit·a·del
cite
  cit·ed
  cit·ing
  ci·ta·tion
cith·a·ra
cit·i·zen
  cit·i·zen·ship

cit·i·zen·ry
  cit·i·zen·ries
cit·rate
cit·ric
cit·ron
cit·ron·el·la
cit·rus
cit·tern
city
  cit·ies
ci·ty-state
civ·et
civ·ic
civ·ics
civ·il
ci·vil·ian
ci·vil·i·ty
  ci·vil·i·ties
civ·i·li·za·tion
civ·i·lize
  civ·i·lized
  civ·i·liz·ing
clab·ber
claim
  claim·a·ble
  claim·ant
  claim·er
clair·voy·ance
  clair·voy·ant
clam
  clammed
  clam·ming
clam·bake
clam·bar
clam·my
  clam·mi·er
  clam·mi·est
  clam·mi·ly
  clam·mi·ness
clam·or
  clam·or·ous
clan
  clan·nish
clan·des·tine
clang·or
  clang·or·ous
clans·man
  clans·men
clap
  clapped
  clap·ping
clap·board
clap·per
clap·trap
claque
clar·et
clar·i·fy
  clar·i·fied
  clar·i·fy·ing
  clar·i·fi·ca·tion
clar·i·net
  clar·i·net·ist
clar·i·on
clar·i·ty
class·a·ble

clas·sic
clas·si·cal
  clas·si·cal·ly
clas·si·cism
  clas·si·cist
clas·si·fied
clas·si·fy
  clas·si·fied
  clas·si·fy·ing
  clas·si·fi·er
  clas·si·fi·ca·tion
class·mate
class·room
classy
  class·i·er
  class·i·est
clat·ter
Clau·di·us
clause
  claus·al
claus·tro·pho·bia
clav·i·chord
clav·i·cle
cla·vier
clay
  clay·ey
clay·more
clean-cut
clean·er
clean·ly
  clean·li·er
  clean·li·est
  clean·li·ness
cleanse
  cleansed
  cleans·ing
  cleans·er
clean·up
clear
  clear·ly
  clear·ness
clear·ance
clear-cut
clear·ing
clear-sight·ed
cleav·age
cleave
  cleaved
  cleav·ing
cleav·er
clef
cleft
Cle·men·ceau
clem·en·cy
  clem·ent
Clem·ens
Cle·o·pat·ra
clere·sto·ry
  clere·sto·ries
cler·gy
  cler·gies
cler·gy·man
  cler·gy·men
cler·ic
cler·i·cal

cler·i·cal·ism
  cler·i·cal·ist
Cler·mont
Cleve·land
clev·er
  clev·er·ly
  clev·er·ness
clev·is
  clev·is·es
clew
cli·ché
cli·ent
cli·en·tele
cliff·hang·er
cli·mac·ter·ic
cli·mate
cli·mat·ic
cli·mat·i·cal
cli·max
cli·mac·tic
climb
  climb·a·ble
  climb·er
clinch·er
cling
  clung
  cling·ing
  cling·ing·ly
  cling·er
clin·ic
clin·i·cal
  clin·i·cal·ly
clink·er
Clin·ton
clip
  clipped
  clip·ping
  clip·per
clique
  cliqu·ey
  cliqu·ish
clit·o·ris
clo·a·ca
  clo·a·cae
  clo·a·cal
clob·ber
clock·wise
clock·work
clod
  clod·dish
  clod·dy
clog
  clogged
  clog·ging
clois·ter
  clois·tral
close
  closed
  clos·ing
  clos·er
  clos·est
  close·ly
  close·ness
close-fist·ed
close-mouthed

clos·et
  clos·et·ed
  clos·et·ing
close-up
clo·sure
clot
  clot·ted
  clot·ting
clothe
  clothed
  cloth·ing
clothes·horse
clothes·line
clothes·pin
cloth·ier
cloth·ing
clo·ture
cloud·burst
cloudy
  cloud·i·er
  cloud·i·est
  cloud·i·ly
  cloud·i·ness
clo·ven
clo·ver
clo·ver·leaf
Clo·vis
clown
  clown·ish
cloy
  cloy·ing·ly
club
  clubbed
  club·bing
club·foot
club·house
clump
  clumpy
clum·sy
  clum·si·er
  clum·si·est
  clum·si·ly
  clum·si·ness
Clu·ny
clus·ter
clut·ter
Clydes·dale
coach·man
  coach·men
co·ag·u·late
  co·ag·u·lat·ed
  co·ag·u·lat·ing
  co·ag·u·la·tion
co·a·lesce
  co·a·lesced
  co·a·les·cing
  co·a·les·cence
  co·a·les·cent
co·a·li·tion
coarse
  coars·er
  coars·est
  coars·en
  coarse·ly
coast·er

coast·line
coat·ing
co·au·thor
coax
  coax·ing·ly
co·balt
cob·ble
  cob·bled
  cob·bling
  cob·bler
cob·ble·stone
co·bra
cob·web
  cob·webbed
  cob·web·by
co·ca
co·caine
coc·cyx
  coc·cy·ges
  coc·cyg·e·al
coch·le·a
cock·ade
cock·a·too
cock·crow
cocker·er span·iel
cock·eyed
cock·fight
cock·le
  cock·le·bur
  cock·le·shell
cock·ney
  cock·neys
cock·pit
cock·roach
cocks·comb
cock·sure
cock·tail
cocky
  cock·i·er
  cock·i·est
  cock·i·ly
  cock·i·ness
co·coa
co·co·nut
co·coon
cod
  cod·fish
cod·dle
  cod·dled
  cod·dling
code
  cod·ed
  cod·ing
co·deine
codg·er
cod·i·cil
cod·i·fy
  cod·i·fied
  cod·i·fy·ing
  cod·i·fi·ca·tion
cod-liv·er oil
co·ed
co·ed·u·ca·tion
co·ef·fi·cient
coe·len·ter·ate

co·e·qual
co·erce
  co·erced
  co·er·cing
  co·er·ci·ble
  co·er·cion
  co·er·cive
co·ex·ist
  co·ex·ist·ence
  co·ex·ist·ent
cof·fee
cof·fee·house
cof·fee·pot
cof·fer
cof·fin
co·gent
  co·gen·cy
  co·gent·ly
cog·i·tate
  cog·i·tat·ed
  cog·i·tat·ing
  cog·i·ta·ble
  cog·i·ta·tive
cog·nac
cog·nate
cog·ni·tion
  cog·ni·tive
cog·ni·zance
cog·ni·zant
cog·wheel
co·hab·it
  co·hab·i·ta·tion
co·here
  co·hered
  co·her·ing
  co·her·ent
  co·her·ence
  co·her·en·cy
  co·her·ent·ly
co·he·sion
  co·he·sive
  co·he·sive·ly
  co·he·sive·ness
co·hort
coif·feur
coif·fure
  coif·fured
  coif·fur·ing
coin·age
co·in·cide
  co·in·cid·ed
  co·in·cid·ing
  co·in·ci·dence
  co·in·ci·dent
  co·in·ci·den·tal
  co·in·ci·den·tal·ly
co·i·tion
co·i·tus
  co·i·tal
coke
  coked
  cok·ing
co·la
col·an·der
Col·chis

cold·blood·ed
cole·slaw
col·ic
  col·icky
col·i·se·um
co·li·tis
col·lab·o·rate
  col·lab·o·rat·ed
  col·lab·o·rat·ing
  col·lab·o·ra·tion
  col·lab·o·ra·tor
col·lage
col·lapse
  col·lapsed
  col·laps·ing
  col·lap·si·ble
col·lar
col·lar·bone
col·late
  col·lat·ed
  col·lat·ing
  col·la·tion
  col·la·tor
col·lat·er·al
col·league
col·lect
  col·lect·i·ble
  col·lect·or
  col·lect·ed
  col·lec·tion
  col·lec·tive
  col·lec·tive·ly
  col·lec·tiv·i·ty
  col·lec·tiv·ism
  col·lec·tiv·ize
  col·lec·tiv·ized
  col·lec·tiv·iz·ing
  col·lec·tiv·i·za·tion
col·lege
  col·le·gi·al
  col·le·gian
  col·le·giate
col·lide
  col·lid·ed
  col·lid·ing
  col·li·sion
col·li·mate
  col·li·mat·ed
  col·li·mat·ing
  col·li·ma·tion
col·lo·cate
  col·lo·cat·ed
  col·lo·cat·ing
  col·lo·ca·tion
col·loid
col·lo·qui·al
  col·lo·qui·al·ly
  col·lo·qui·al·ism
col·lo·quy
  col·lo·quies
col·lu·sion
  col·lu·sive
co·logne
Co·lom·bia
Co·lom·bo

co·lon
colo·nel
co·lo·ni·al
co·lo·ni·al·ism
  co·lo·ni·al·ist
col·o·nist
col·on·nade
col·o·ny
  col·o·nies
  col·o·nize
  col·o·nized
  col·o·niz·ing
  col·o·niz·er
  col·o·ni·za·tion
col·or
  col·or·er
  col·or·less
Col·o·rado
col·or·a·tion
col·or-blind
  col·or-blind·ness
col·or·cast
col·ored
col·or·fast
col·or·ful
col·or·ing
co·los·sal
Col·os·se·um
Co·los·si·an
co·los·sus
  co·los·si
colt·ish
Co·lum·bia
col·um·bine
Co·lum·bus
col·umn
  co·lum·nar
  col·umned
col·um·nist
co·ma
  co·mas
  co·ma·tose
Co·man·che
com·bat
  com·bat·ed
  com·bat·ing
com·bat·ant
com·ba·tive
comb·er
com·bi·na·tion
  com·bi·na·tion·al
  com·bi·na·tive
com·bine
  com·bined
  com·bin·ing
  com·bin·a·ble
  com·bin·er
com·ic
  com·i·cal
com·ing
com·i·ty
  com·i·ties
com·ma
  com·mas
com·mand

com·man·dant
com·man·deer
com·mand·er
  com·mand·er·ship
com·mand·ment
com·man·do
  com·man·dos
com·mem·o·rate
  com·mem·o·rat·ed
  com·mem·o·rat·ing
  com·mem·o·ra·ble
  com·mem·o·ra·tion
  com·mem·o·ra·tive
  com·mem·o·ra·to·ry
com·mence
  com·menced
  com·menc·ing
com·mence·ment
com·mend
  com·mend·a·ble
  com·mend·a·bly
  com·men·da·tion
  com·mend·a·to·ry
com·men·su·rate
  com·men·su·rate·ly
  com·men·su·ra·tion
com·ment
com·men·tary
  com·men·tar·ies
  com·men·ta·tor
com·merce
com·mer·cial
  com·mer·cial·ism
  com·mer·cial·ize
  com·mer·cial·ized
  com·mer·cial·iz·ing
  com·mer·cial·i·za·tion
com·mie
com·mis·er·ate
  com·mis·er·at·ed
  com·mis·er·at·ing
  com·mis·er·a·tion
  com·mis·er·a·tive
com·mis·sar
com·mis·sary
  com·mis·sar·ies
com·mis·sion
  com·mis·sioned
com·mis·sion·er
com·bo
  com·bos
com·bus·ti·ble
  com·bus·ti·bil·i·ty
com·bus·tion
  com·bus·tive
come
  com·ing
come·back
co·me·di·an
  co·me·di·enne
come·down
com·e·dy
  com·e·dies
come·ly
  come·li·ness

come-on
com·er
com·et
come·up·pance
com·fort
com·fort·a·ble
  com·fort·a·bly
com·fort·er
com·fy
  com·fi·er
  com·fi·est
com·mit
  com·mit·ted
  com·mit·ting
com·mit·ment
com·mit·tee
  com·mit·tee·man
  com·mit·tee·wo·man
com·mode
com·mo·di·ous
com·mod·i·ty
  com·mod·i·ties
com·mo·dore
com·mon
com·mon·al·ty
  com·mon·al·ties
com·mon·place
com·mons
com·mon·weal
com·mon·wealth
com·mo·tion
com·mu·nal
  com·mu·nal·i·ty
com·mune
  com·muned
  com·mun·ing
com·mu·ni·cant
com·mu·ni·cate
  com·mu·ni·cat·ed
  com·mu·ni·cat·ing
  com·mu·ni·ca·ble
  com·mu·ni·ca·tive
com·mu·ni·ca·tion
com·mun·ion
com·mu·ni·qué
com·mun·ism
com·mun·ist
com·mu·ni·ty
  com·mu·ni·ties
com·mu·nize
  com·mu·nized
  com·mu·niz·ing
com·mu·ta·tion
com·mu·ta·tor
com·mute
  com·mut·ed
  com·mut·ing
  com·mut·a·ble
com·mut·er
Co·mo·ra
com·pact
com·pan·ion
com·pan·ion·a·ble
com·pan·ion·ship
com·pa·ny

com·pa·nies
com·pa·ra·ble
  com·pa·ra·bil·ity
com·par·a·tive
com·pare
  com·pared
  com·par·ing
  com·par·i·son
com·part·ment
  com·part·men·tal
  com·part·ment·ed
  com·part·men·tal·ize
com·pass
com·pas·sion
  com·pas·sion·ate
com·pat·i·ble
  com·pat·i·bly
  com·pat·i·bil·i·ty
com·pa·tri·ot
com·peer
com·pel
  com·pelled
  com·pel·ling
com·pen·di·ous
com·pen·di·um
com·pen·sate
  com·pen·sat·ed
  com·pen·sat·ing
  com·pen·sa·tive
  com·pen·sa·tor
  com·pen·sa·to·ry
com·pen·sa·tion
com·pete
  com·pet·ed
  com·pet·ing
  com·pet·i·tor
com·pe·tence
com·pe·ten·cy
com·pe·tent
com·pe·ti·tion
com·pet·i·tive
com·pile
  com·piled
  com·pil·ing
  com·pi·la·tion
com·pla·cence
  com·pla·cen·cy
  com·pla·cent
com·plain
  com·plain·ant
com·plaint
com·plai·sance
  com·plai·sant
com·plect·ed
com·ple·ment
  com·ple·men·tal
  com·ple·men·ta·ry
com·plete
  com·plet·ed
  com·plet·ing
  com·plet·a·ble
com·ple·tion
com·plex
com·plex·ion
  com·plex·ioned

com·plex·i·ty
com·plex·i·ties
com·pli·ance
com·pli·an·cy
com·pli·ant
com·pli·cate
com·pli·cat·ed
com·pli·cat·ing
com·pli·ca·tion
com·plic·i·ty
com·plic·i·ties
com·pli·ment
com·pli·men·ta·ry
com·pli·men·ta·ri·ly
com·ply
com·plied
com·ply·ing
com·po·nent
com·port
com·port·ment
com·pose
com·posed
com·pos·ing
com·pos·er
com·pos·ite
com·po·si·tion
com·post
com·po·sure
com·pote
com·pound
com·pre·hend
com·pre·hend·i·ble
com·pre·hen·si·ble
com·pre·hen·si·bil·i·ty
com·pre·hen·si·bly
com·pre·hen·sion
com·pre·hen·sive
com·press
com·pressed
com·press·i·ble
com·press·i·bil·i·ty
com·pres·sion
com·pres·sor
com·prise
com·prised
com·pris·ing
com·pro·mise
com·pro·mised
com·pro·mis·ing
comp·trol·ler
com·pul·sion
com·pul·sive
com·pul·so·ry
com·punc·tion
com·pute
com·put·ed
com·put·ing
com·put·a·ble
com·pu·ta·tion
com·put·er
com·put·er·ize
com·put·er·ized
com·put·er·iz·ing
com·put·er·i·za·tion
com·rade

com·rade·ship
com·sat
con
conned
con·ning
Co·na·kry
con·cave
con·ceal
con·ceal·a·ble
con·ceal·ment
con·cede
con·ced·ed
con·ced·ing
con·ceit
con·ceit·ed
con·ceive
con·ceived
con·ceiv·ing
con·ceiv·a·ble
con·ceiv·a·bly
con·cen·trate
con·cen·tra·ted
con·cen·trat·ing
con·cen·tra·tive
con·cen·tra·tor
con·cen·tra·tion
con·cen·tric
con·cen·tri·cal
con·cen·tric·i·ty
con·cept
con·cep·tu·al
con·cep·tion
con·cep·tive
con·cep·tu·al·ize
con·cep·tu·al·ized
con·cep·tu·al·iz·ing
con·cep·tu·al·i·za·tion
con·cern
con·cerned
con·cern·ing
con·cert
con·cert·ed
con·cer·ti·na
con·cert·mas·ter
con·cer·to
con·ces·sion
con·ces·sion·aire
conch
conchs
con·cil·i·ate
con·cil·i·at·ed
con·cil·i·at·ing
con·cil·i·a·tion
con·cil·i·a·to·ry
con·cise
con·cise·ness
con·cise·ly
con·clave
con·clude
con·clud·ed
con·clud·ing
con·clu·sion
con·clu·sive
con·coct
con·coc·tion

con·com·i·tant
con·com·i·tance
con·cord
con·cord·ance
con·cord·ant
con·course
con·crete
con·cret·ed
con·cret·ing
con·cre·tion
con·cre·tive
con·cu·bine
con·cur
con·curred
con·cur·ring
con·cur·rence
con·cur·rent
con·cus·sion
con·cus·sive
con·demn
con·dem·na·ble
con·dem·na·tion
con·dem·na·to·ry
con·dense
con·densed
con·dens·ing
con·den·sa·ble
con·den·sa·tion
con·dens·er
con·de·scend
con·de·scend·ing
con·de·scen·sion
con·di·ment
con·di·tion
con·di·tion·al
con·di·tion·er
con·di·tioned
con·dole
con·doled
con·dol·ing
con·do·la·to·ry
con·do·ler
con·do·lence
con·dom
con·do·min·i·um
con·done
con·doned
con·don·ing
con·do·na·tion
con·dor
con·duce
con·duced
con·duc·ing
con·du·cive
con·duct
con·duct·i·bil·i·ty
con·duct·i·ble
con·duct·ance
con·duc·tion
con·fer·ence
con·fer·en·tial
con·fess
con·fess·ed·ly
con·fes·sion
con·fes·sion·al

con·fes·sor
con·fet·ti
con·fi·dant
con·fi·dante
con·fide
con·fid·ed
con·fid·ing
con·fi·dence
con·fi·dent
con·fi·den·tial
con·fig·u·ra·tion
con·fig·u·ra·tion·al
con·fine
con·fined
con·fin·ing
con·fine·ment
con·firm
con·firm·a·ble
con·fir·ma·tion
con·fir·ma·tive
con·fir·ma·to·ry
con·firmed
con·firm·ed·ly
con·firm·ed·ness
con·fis·cate
con·fis·cat·ed
con·fis·cat·ing
con·fis·ca·tion
con·fis·ca·tor
con·fis·ca·to·ry
con·fla·gra·tion
con·flict
con·flict·ing
con·flic·tive
con·flic·tion
con·flu·ence
con·flu·ent
con·flux
con·form
con·form·ist
con·form·ism
con·form·a·ble
con·form·a·bly
con·form·ance
con·for·ma·tion
con·form·i·ty
con·form·i·ties
con·found
con·found·ed
con·found·ed·ly
con·front
con·fron·ta·tion
Con·fu·cius
con·fuse
con·fused
con·fus·ing
con·fus·ed·ly
con·fus·ed·ness
con·fu·sion
con·fute
con·fut·ed
con·fut·ing
con·fu·ta·tion
con·ga
con·gas

con·geal
  con·geal·ment
con·gen·ial
  con·ge·ni·al·i·ty
  con·gen·ial·ly
con·gen·i·tal
con·ger
con·ge·ries
con·gest
  con·ges·tion
  con·ges·tive
con·glom·er·ate
  con·glom·er·at·ed
  con·glom·er·at·ing
  con·glom·er·a·tion
Con·go
con·grat·u·late
  con·grat·u·lat·ed
  con·grat·u·lat·ing
  con·grat·u·la·tor
  con·grat·u·la·to·ry
  con·grat·u·la·tion
con·gre·gate
  con·gre·gat·ed
  con·gre·gat·ing
  con·gre·ga·tion
  con·gre·ga·tion·al
con·gress
  con·gres·sion·al
con·gress·man
  con·gress·men
  con·gress·wom·an
  con·gress·wom·en
con·gru·ent
  con·gru·ent·ly
  con·gru·ence
  con·gru·en·cy
  con·gru·en·cies
con·gru·ous
  con·gru·ous·ly
  con·gru·ous·ness
  con·gru·i·ty
  con·gru·i·ties
con·ic
  con·i·cal
co·ni·fer
con·jec·ture
  con·jec·tured
  con·jec·tur·ing
  con·jec·tur·al
con·join
con·joint
  con·joint·ly
con·ju·gal
  con·ju·gal·ly
con·ju·gate
  con·ju·gat·ed
  con·ju·gat·ing
  con·ju·ga·tion
  con·ju·ga·tive
con·junc·tion
con·junc·tive
con·jur·a·tion
con·jure
  con·jured

con·jur·ing
con·jur·er
con·nect
  con·nec·tor
Con·nect·i·cut
  con·nec·tion
  con·nec·tive
con·nip·tion
con·nive
  con·nived
  con·niv·ing
  con·niv·ance
con·nois·seur
con·note
  con·not·ed
  con·not·ing
  con·no·ta·tion
  con·no·ta·tive
con·nu·bi·al
  con·nu·bi·al·ly
con·quer
  con·quer·a·ble
  con·quer·or
con·quest
con·quis·ta·dor
  con·quis·ta·dors
  con·quis·ta·dor·es
con·san·guin·e·ous
  con·san·guin·i·ty
con·science
con·sci·en·tious
  con·sci·en·tious·ly
con·scious
  con·scious·ly
  con·scious·ness
con·script
  con·scrip·tion
con·se·crate
  con·se·crat·ed
  con·se·crat·ing
  con·se·cra·tive
  con·se·cra·tor
  con·se·cra·tion
con·sec·u·tive
  con·sec·u·tive·ly
con·sen·sus
con·sent
  con·sent·er
con·se·quence
con·se·quent
  con·se·quent·ly
con·se·quen·tial
  con·se·quen·ti·al·i·ty
  con·se·quen·tial·ly
con·ser·va·tion
  con·ser·va·tion·al
  con·ser·va·tion·ist
con·serv·a·tive
  con·serv·a·tism
  con·ser·va·tive·ly
con·serv·a·to·ry
  con·serv·a·to·ries
con·serve
  con·served
  con·serv·ing

con·serv·a·ble
con·serv·er
con·sid·er
con·sid·er·a·ble
con·sid·er·a·bly
con·sid·er·ate
con·sid·er·a·tion
con·sid·er·ing
con·sign
con·sign·er
con·sign·or
con·sign·ment
con·sign·ee
con·sist
con·sist·en·cy
con·sist·en·cies
con·sist·ence
con·sist·ent
con·sist·ent·ly
con·sis·to·ry
con·sis·to·ries
con·so·la·tion
con·sol·a·to·ry
con·sole
con·soled
con·sol·ing
con·sol·a·ble
con·sol·i·date
con·sol·i·dat·ed
con·sol·i·dat·ing
con·sol·i·da·tion
con·som·mé
con·so·nant
con·so·nance
con·so·nant·ly
con·so·nan·tal
con·sort
con·sor·ti·um
con·sor·tia
con·spic·u·ous
con·spic·u·ous·ly
con·spic·u·ous·ness
con·spire
con·spired
con·spir·ing
con·spir·a·cy
con·spir·a·cies
con·spir·a·tor
con·spir·a·to·ri·al
con·spir·er
con·spir·ing·ly
con·sta·ble
con·sta·ble·ship
con·stab·u·lary
con·stab·u·lar·ies
con·stant
con·stan·cy
Con·stan·tine
Con·stan·ti·no·ple
con·stant·ly
con·stel·la·tion
con·ster·na·tion
con·sti·pa·tion
con·sti·pate
con·stit·u·en·cy

con·stit·u·en·cies
con·stit·u·ent
con·sti·tute
con·sti·tu·tion
con·sti·tu·tion·al
con·sti·tu·tion·al·i·ty
con·sti·tu·tion·al·ly
con·strain
con·strain·a·ble
con·strained
con·straint
con·strict
con·stric·tive
con·stric·tion
con·stric·tor
con·struct
con·struc·tor
con·struc·tion
con·struc·tion·al
con·struc·tive
con·struc·tive·ly
con·struc·tive·ness
con·strue
con·strued
con·stru·ing
con·stru·a·ble
con·stru·er
con·sul
con·su·lar
con·sul·ship
con·su·late
con·sult
con·sul·ta·tion
con·sult·ant
con·sume
con·sumed
con·sum·ing
con·sum·a·ble
con·sum·er
con·sum·mate
con·sum·mat·ed
con·sum·mat·ing
con·sum·mate·ly
con·sum·ma·tion
con·sump·tion
con·sump·tive
con·tact
con·ta·gion
con·ta·gious
con·ta·gious·ness
con·tain
con·tain·a·ble
con·tain·er
con·tain·ment
con·tam·i·nate
con·tam·i·nat·ed
con·tam·i·nat·ing
con·tam·i·nant
con·tam·i·na·tion
con·tam·i·na·tive
con·tam·i·na·tor
con·tem·plate
con·tem·plat·ed
con·tem·plat·ing
con·tem·pla·tion

con·tem·pla·tive
con·tem·po·ra·ne·ous
con·tem·po·rary
con·tem·po·rar·ies
con·tempt
con·tempt·i·ble
con·tempt·i·bly
con·temp·tu·ous
con·temp·tu·ous·ly
con·tend
con·tend·er
con·tent
con·tent·ment
con·tent·ed
con·tent·ed·ly
con·tent·ed·ness
con·ten·tion
con·ten·tious
con·ten·tious·ly
con·ten·tious·ness
con·ter·mi·nous
con·test
con·test·a·ble
con·test·er
con·test·ant
con·text
con·tig·u·ous
con·ti·gu·i·ty
con·ti·gu·i·ties
con·tig·u·ous·ly
con·tig·u·ous·ness
con·ti·nence
con·ti·nen·cy
con·ti·nent
con·ti·nent·ly
con·ti·nent
con·ti·nen·tal
con·tin·gent
con·tin·gen·cy
con·tin·gen·cies
con·tin·gent·ly
con·tin·u·al
con·tin·u·al·ly
con·tin·u·ance
con·tin·ue
con·tin·ued
con·tin·u·ing
con·tin·u·a·tion
con·tin·u·er
con·ti·nu·i·ty
con·ti·nu·i·ties
con·tin·u·ous
con·tin·u·ous·ly
con·tin·u·um
con·tin·ua
con·tort
con·tor·tion
con·tor·tive
con·tor·tion·ist
con·tour
con·tra·band
con·tra·cep·tive
con·tra·cep·tion
con·tract
con·tract·ed

con·tract·i·ble
con·trac·tu·al
con·trac·tion
con·trac·tive
con·trac·tile
con·trac·tor
con·tra·dict
con·tra·dict·a·ble
con·tra·dic·tion
con·tra·dic·to·ry
con·tra·dis·tinc·tion
con·trail
con·tral·to
con·tral·tos
con·tral·ti
con·trap·tion
con·tra·pun·tal
con·tra·ri·wise
con·tra·ry
con·tra·ries
con·tra·ri·ly
con·tra·ri·ness
con·trast
con·trast·a·ble
con·trast·ing·ly
con·tra·vene
con·tra·vened
con·tra·ven·ing
con·tra·ven·er
con·tra·ven·tion
con·trib·ute
con·trib·ut·ed
con·trib·ut·ing
con·trib·ut·a·ble
con·trib·u·tor
con·trib·u·tory
con·tri·bu·tion
con·trite
con·trite·ly
con·trite·ness
con·tri·tion
con·trive
con·trived
con·triv·ing
con·triv·ance
con·trol
con·trolled
con·trol·ling
con·trol·la·ble
con·trol·ler
con·trol·ler·ship
con·tro·ver·sy
con·tro·ver·sies
con·tro·ver·sial
con·tro·ver·sial·ly
con·tro·vert
con·tu·me·ly
con·tu·me·lies
con·tuse
con·tused
con·tus·ing
con·tu·sion
co·nun·drum
con·va·lesce
con·va·lesced

con·va·les·cing
con·va·les·cence
con·va·les·cent
con·vec·tion
con·vene
con·vened
con·ven·ing
con·ven·er
con·ven·ience
con·ven·ient
con·ven·ient·ly
con·vent
con·ven·tion
con·ven·tion·al
con·ven·tion·al·ism
con·ven·tion·al·ist
con·ven·tion·al·i·ty
con·ven·tion·al·i·ties
con·ven·tion·al·ize
con·ven·tion·al·ized
con·ven·tion·al·iz·ing
con·verge
con·verged
con·verg·ing
con·ver·gence
con·ver·gen·cy
con·ver·gent
con·ver·sant
con·ver·sa·tion
con·ver·sa·tion·al
con·ver·sa·tion·al·ist
con·verse
con·versed
con·vers·ing
con·verse·ly
con·ver·sion
con·vert
con·vert·er
con·vert·i·ble
con·vert·i·bil·i·ty
con·vert·i·bly
con·vex
con·vex·ly
con·vex·i·ty
con·vey
con·vey·a·ble
con·vey·ance
con·vey·er
con·vey·or
con·vict
con·vic·tion
con·vic·tion·al
con·vince
con·vinced
con·vinc·ing
con·vinc·er
con·vinc·i·ble
con·viv·i·al
con·viv·i·al·i·ty
con·viv·i·al·ly
con·vo·ca·tion
con·vo·ca·tion·al
con·voke
con·voked
con·vok·ing

con·vok·er
con·vo·lute
con·vo·lut·ed
con·vo·lut·ing
con·vo·lute·ly
con·vo·lu·tion
con·voy
con·vulse
con·vulsed
con·vuls·ing
con·vul·sion
con·vul·sive
con·vul·sive·ly
co·ny
coo
cooed
coo·ing
coo·ing·ly
cook·book
cook·e·ry
cook·e·ries
cook·ie
cook·ies
cook·out
cool
cool·ish
cool·ly
cool·ness
cool·ant
cool·er
Coo·lidge
coo·lie
coo·lies
coon·skin
coop·er
coop·er·age
co·op·er·ate
co·op·er·at·ed
co·op·er·at·ing
co·op·er·a·tion
co·op·er·a·tive
co·op·er·a·tive·ly
co·opt
co·op·ta·tion
co·or·di·nate
co·or·di·nat·ed
co·or·di·nat·ing
co·or·di·nate·ly
co·or·di·na·tor
co·or·di·na·tion
coot·ie
cop
copped
cop·ping
co·pa·cet·ic
co·part·ner
co·part·ner·ship
cope
coped
cop·ing
Co·pen·ha·gen
Co·per·ni·cus
cope·stone
cop·i·er
co·pi·lot

co·pi·ous
co·pi·ous·ly
co·pi·ous·ness
cop-out
cop·per
cop·pery
cop·per·head
cop·per·plate
cop·pice
cop·ra
copse
Cop·tic
cop·u·la
cop·u·las
cop·u·lae
cop·u·lar
cop·u·late
cop·u·lat·ed
cop·u·lat·ing
cop·u·la·tion
cop·u·la·tive
cop·u·la·tive·ly
copy
cop·ies
cop·ied
cop·y·ing
cop·y·book
cop·y·cat
cop·y·ist
cop·y·right
co·quet
co·quet·ted
co·quet·ting
co·quet·ry
co·quet·ries
co·quette
co·quet·tish
co·quet·tish·ly
cor·a·cle
cor·al
cor·bel
cord·age
cor·date
cor·date·ly
cor·dial
cor·dial·i·ty
cor·dial·ness
cor·dial·ly
cor·dil·le·ra
cord·ite
Cor·do·ba
cor·don
cor·do·van
cor·du·roy
cord·wood
core
cored
cor·ing
co·re·la·tion
co·re·spond·ent
co·ri·an·der
Cor·inth
Co·rin·thi·an
cor·ker
cork·screw

corn·cob
cor·nea
cor·ne·al
cor·ner
cor·ner·stone
cor·net
cor·net·ist
corn·flow·er
cor·nice
Cor·nish
corn·starch
cor·nu·co·pia
Corn·wall
Corn·wal·lis
corny
corn·i·er
corn·i·est
co·rol·la
cor·ol·lary
cor·ol·lar·ies
co·ro·na
co·ro·nas
co·ro·nae
Cor·o·na·do
cor·o·nary
cor·o·na·tion
cor·o·ner
cor·o·ner·ship
cor·o·net
cor·o·net·ed
cor·po·ral
cor·po·rate
cor·po·rate·ly
cor·po·ra·tive
cor·po·ra·tion
cor·po·rat·ism
cor·po·re·al
cor·po·re·al·i·ty
cor·po·re·al·ness
corps
corpse
corps·man
corps·men
cor·pu·lent
cor·pu·lence
cor·pu·len·cy
cor·pus
Cor·pus Chris·ti
cor·pus·cle
cor·pus·cu·lar
cor·ral
cor·ralled
cor·ral·ling
cor·rect
cor·rect·a·ble
cor·rect·i·ble
cor·rect·ness
cor·rec·tor
cor·rec·tion
cor·rec·tion·al
cor·rec·tive
Cor·reg·i·dor
cor·re·late
cor·re·lat·ed
cor·re·lat·ing

cor·re·la·tion
cor·rel·a·tive
cor·re·spond
  cor·re·spond·ing
  cor·re·spond·ing·ly
cor·re·spond·ence
cor·re·spond·ent
cor·ri·dor
cor·ri·gi·ble
  cor·ri·gi·bil·i·ty
  cor·ri·gi·bly
cor·rob·o·rate
  cor·rob·o·rat·ed
  cor·rob·o·rat·ing
  cor·rob·o·ra·tion
  cor·rob·o·ra·tive
  cor·rob·o·ra·to·ry
cor·rode
  cor·rod·ed
  cor·rod·ing
  cor·rod·i·ble
cor·ro·sion
cor·ro·sive
cor·ru·gate
  cor·ru·gat·ed
  cor·ru·gat·ing
  cor·ru·ga·tion
cor·rupt
  cor·rupt·er
  cor·rupt·i·ble
  cor·rupt·i·bil·i·ty
  cor·rupt·ly
  cor·rupt·ness
cor·rup·tion
cor·sage
cor·sair
cor·set
  cor·set·ed
Cor·si·ca
cor·tex
  cor·ti·ces
cor·ti·cal
cor·ti·sone
co·run·dum
co·sig·na·to·ry
cos·met·ic
cos·mic
  cos·mi·cal·ly
cos·mog·o·ny
  cos·mog·o·nies
  cos·mo·gon·ic
  cos·mog·o·nist
cos·mog·ra·phy
  cos·mog·ra·phies
  cos·mog·ra·pher
  cos·mo·graph·ic
cos·mol·o·gy
  cos·mol·o·gies
  cos·mo·log·ic
  cos·mo·log·i·cal
  cos·mol·o·gist
cos·mo·naut
cos·mo·pol·i·tan
  cos·mo·pol·i·tan·ism
cos·mop·o·lite

cos·mos
Cos·sack
Cos·ta Ri·ca
cost·ly
  cost·li·er
  cost·li·est
  cost·li·ness
cost-plus
cos·tume
  cos·tumed
  cos·tum·ing
cos·tum·er
co·sy
  co·si·er
  co·si·est
co·te·rie
co·ter·mi·nous
co·til·lion
cot·tage
cot·ter
cot·ton
  cot·tony
cot·ton·mouth
cot·ton·seed
cot·ton·tail
cot·ton·wood
couch
cough
cou·lée
coun·cil
  coun·cil·or
  coun·cil·man
  coun·cil·lor·ship
coun·sel
  coun·seled
  coun·sel·ing
coun·se·lor
  coun·se·lor·ship
count
  count·a·ble
count·down
coun·te·nance
  coun·te·nanced
  coun·te·nanc·ing
  coun·te·nanc·er
count·er
coun·ter·act
  coun·ter·ac·tion
  coun·ter·ac·tive
coun·ter·at·tack
coun·ter·charge
  coun·ter·charged
  coun·ter·char·ging
coun·ter·claim
  coun·ter·claim·ant
coun·ter·clock·wise
coun·ter·cul·ture
coun·ter·es·pi·o·nage
coun·ter·feit
  coun·ter·feit·er
coun·ter·in·tel·li·gence
coun·ter·mand
coun·ter·meas·ure
coun·ter·of·fen·sive
coun·ter·pane

coun·ter·part
coun·ter·point
coun·ter·poise
  coun·ter·poised
  coun·ter·pois·ing
coun·ter·rev·o·lu·tion
coun·ter·sign
  coun·ter·sig·na·ture
coun·ter·sink
  coun·ter·sank
  coun·ter·sunk
coun·ter·spy
  coun·ter·spies
coun·ter·weight
coun·tess
count·less
coun·tri·fied
coun·try
  coun·tries
coun·try·man
  coun·try·men
  coun·try·wo·man
  coun·try·wo·men
coun·try·side
coun·ty
  coun·ties
coup
  coups
coupé
coup·le
  coup·led
  coup·ling
coup·ler
cou·pon
cour·age
  cou·ra·geous
cour·i·er
course
  coursed
  cours·ing
cours·er
cour·te·ous
  cour·te·ous·ly
cour·te·sy
  cour·te·sies
court·house
cour·ti·er
court·ly
  court·li·er
  court·li·est
  court·li·ness
court·mar·tial
  courts-mar·tial
  court-mar·tialed
  court-mar·tial·ing
court·room
court·ship
court·yard
cous·in
  cous·in·hood
  cous·in·ly
cou·tu·rier
cov·e·nant
  cov·e·nan·ter
  cov·e·nan·tor

Cov·en·try
cov·er
  cov·ered
  cov·er·ing
  cov·er·less
cov·er·age
cov·er·all
cov·er·let
cov·ert
  cov·ert·ly
  cov·ert·ness
cov·er·up
cov·et
  cov·et·a·ble
  cov·et·er
  cov·et·ous
  cov·et·ous·ly
cov·ey
cow·ard
  cow·ard·ly
  cow·ard·li·ness
cow·ard·ice
cow·boy
cow·er
  cow·er·ing·ly
cow·hide
cowl
  cowled
cow·lick
cowl·ing
cow·man
  cow·men
co-work·er
cow·poke
cow·pox
cow·ry
  cow·rie
  cow·ries
cox·swain
coy
  coy·ly
  coy·ness
coy·o·te
coz·en
  coz·en·age
  coz·en·er
co·zy
  co·zi·er
  co·zi·est
  co·zi·ly
  co·zi·ness
crab
  crabbed
  crab·bing
crab·by
  crab·bed·ly
  crab·bed·ness
crack·down
crack·er
crack·ing
crack·le
  crack·led
  crack·ling
crack-up
Cra·cow

cra·dle
  cra·dled
  cra·dling
crafts·man
  crafts·man·ship
crafty
  craft·i·er
  craft·i·est
  craft·i·ly
  craft·i·ness
crag
  crag·ged
  crag·gy
  crag·gi·ness
cram
  crammed
  cram·ming
  cram·mer
cran·ber·ry
  cran·ber·ries
crane
  craned
  cran·ing
cra·ni·um
  cra·ni·ums
  cra·nia
  cra·ni·al
  cra·ni·ate
  cra·ni·al·ly
crank·case
crank·shaft
cranky
  crank·i·er
  crank·i·est
  crank·i·ly
  crank·i·ness
Cran·mer
cran·ny
  cran·nies
  cran·nied
crash-land
crass
  crass·ly
  crass·ness
Cras·sus
crate
  crat·ed
  crat·ing
cra·ter
  cra·ter·al
  cra·tered
cra·vat
crave
  craved
  crav·ing
  crav·er
  crav·ing·ly
craw·fish
crawl
  crawly
  crawl·ing·ly
  crawl·er
cray·fish
cray·on
craze

crazed
craz·ing
cra·zy
  cra·zi·er
  cra·zi·est
  cra·zi·ly
  cra·zi·ness
creak
  creak·i·ly
  creak·i·ness
  creaky
  creak·i·er
  creak·i·est
cream
  cream·i·ly
  cream·i·ness
  creamy
  cream·i·er
  cream·i·est
  cream·er
  cream·ery
  cream·er·ies
crease
  creased
  creas·ing
  creasy
  creas·i·er
  creas·i·est
cre·ate
  cre·at·ed
  cre·at·ing
  cre·a·tion
  cre·a·tion·al
  cre·a·tive
  cre·a·tiv·i·ty
  cre·a·tor
cre·a·ture
cre·dence
cre·den·tial
cre·den·za
cred·i·ble
  cred·i·bil·i·ty
  cred·i·bly
cred·it
  cred·it·a·ble
  cred·it·a·bil·i·ty
  cred·it·a·bly
  cred·i·tor
cre·do
  cre·dos
cred·u·lous
creek
creel
creep
  crept
  creep·ing
  creepy
  creep·i·er
  creep·i·est
  creep·i·ness
  creep·er
cre·mate
  cre·mat·ed
  cre·mat·ing
  cre·ma·tion

cre·ma·ter
cre·ma·to·ry
cre·ma·to·ri·um
Cre·ole
cre·o·sote
crêpe
crepe
　creped
　crep·ing
cre·pus·cu·lar
cres·cen·do
　cres·cen·dos
cres·cent
crest
　crest·ed
　crest·less
　crest·fall·en
cre·ta·ceous
Cre·tan
cre·tin·ism
cre·tonne
cre·vasse
crev·ice
crew·el
crib
　cribbed
　crib·bing
　crib·ber
crib·bage
crick·et
cri·er
Cri·mea
crim·i·nal
　crim·i·nal·i·ty
　crim·i·nal·ly
crim·i·nol·o·gy
　crim·i·nol·o·gist
crimpy
　crimp·i·er
　crimp·i·est
crim·son
cringe
　cringed
　cring·ing
crin·kle
　crin·kled
　crin·kling
　crin·kly
　crin·kli·er
　crin·kli·est
crip·ple
　crip·pled
　crip·pling
cri·sis
　cri·ses
crisp
　crisp·er
　crisp·ness
　crispy
　crisp·i·er
　crisp·i·est
criss·cross
Cris·to·bal
cri·te·ri·on
　cri·te·ria

crit·ic
crit·i·cal
　crit·i·cal·ly
　crit·i·cal·ness
crit·i·cism
crit·i·cize
　crit·i·cized
　crit·i·ciz·ing
　crit·i·ciz·a·ble
cri·tique
crit·ter
croaky
　croak·i·er
　croak·i·est
croak·er
Cro·a·tia
cro·chet
　cro·cheted
　cro·chet·ing
　cro·chet·er
crock·ery
Crock·ett
croc·o·dile
cro·cus
　cro·cus·es
crois·sant
Cro-Mag·non
cro·ny
　cro·nies
crook·ed
croon·er
crop
　cropped
　crop·ping
crop·per
cro·quet
cro·quette
cross·bar
cross·bones
cross·bow
cross·bred
　cross·breed
　cross·breed·ing
cross-coun·try
cross·cut
cross-ex·am·ine
　cross-ex·am·ined
　cross-ex·am·in·ing
cross-fer·ti·li·za·tion
cross·hatch
cross·ing
cross-pol·li·na·tion
　cross-pol·li·nate
cross-pur·pose
cross-ref·er·ence
cross·road
cross-stitch
cross·tie
cross·walk
cross·wise
　cross·ways
crotch·ety
　crotch·et·i·ness
crouch
croup

croupy
crou·pi·er
crou·ton
crow·bar
crow's-foot
 crow's-feet
crow's-nest
cru·cial
 cru·ci·al·i·ty
 cru·cial·ly
cru·ci·ble
cru·ci·fix
cru·ci·fix·ion
cru·ci·form
cru·ci·fy
 cru·ci·fied
 cru·ci·fy·ing
crude
 crud·er
 crud·est
 crude·ly
 crude·ness
 cru·di·ty
 cru·di·ties
cru·el
 cru·el·ly
 cru·el·ness
 cru·el·ty
cru·et
cruise
 cruised
 cruis·ing
 cruis·er
crul·ler
crum·ble
 crum·bled
 crum·bling
 crum·bly
crum·my
 crum·mi·er
 crum·mi·est
crum·pet
crum·ple
 crum·pled
 crum·pling
 crum·pler
 crum·ply
 crum·pli·er
 crum·pli·est
crunchy
 crunch·i·er
 crunch·i·est
cru·sade
 cru·sad·er
crush·er
 crush·ing
 crush·ing·ly
Cru·soe
crus·ta·cean
crusty
 crust·i·er
 crust·i·est
 crust·i·ly
 crust·i·ness
crux

crux·es
cru·ces
cry
 cried
 cry·ing
cry·ba·by
cry·o·gen·ics
cry·o·sur·gery
crypt
 crypt·al
crypt·a·nal·y·sis
cryp·tic
 cryp·ti·cal
 cryp·ti·cal·ly
cryp·to·gram
cryp·to·graph
 cryp·tog·ra·phy
 cryp·to·graph·ic
 cryp·tog·ra·pher
crys·tal
 crys·tal·line
 crys·tal·lize
 crys·tal·lized
 crys·tal·liz·ing
 crys·tal·liz·er
 crys·tal·liz·a·ble
 crys·tal·li·za·tion
Cu·ba
cub·by
 cub·bies
cub·by·hole
cube
 cubed
 cub·ing
cu·bic
cu·bi·cle
cub·ism
cu·bit
cuck·old
 cuck·old·ry
cuck·oo
 cuck·oos
 cuck·ooed
 cuck·oo·ing
cu·cum·ber
cud·dle
 cud·dled
 cud·dling
 cud·dle·some
 cud·dly
 cud·dli·er
 cud·dli·est
cudg·el
 cudg·eled
 cudg·el·ing
cue
 cued
 cu·ing
cui·sine
cul-de-sac
 culs-de-sac
cu·li·nary
cul·mi·nant
cul·mi·nate
 cul·mi·nat·ed

cul·mi·nat·ing
cul·mi·na·tion
cu·lottes
cul·pa·ble
 cul·pa·bil·i·ty
 cul·pa·bly
cul·prit
cult
 cul·tic
cul·ti·vate
 cul·ti·vat·ed
 cul·ti·vat·ing
 cul·ti·va·tion
 cul·ti·va·ble
 cul·ti·vat·a·ble
cul·ti·va·tor
cul·tur·al
cul·ture
 cul·tured
 cul·tur·ing
cul·vert
cum·ber
 cum·ber·some
Cum·ber·land
cum·brance
cum lau·de
cum·mer·bund
cu·mu·late
 cu·mu·lat·ed
 cu·mu·lat·ing
 cu·mu·la·tion
 cu·mu·la·tive
 cu·mu·lo·nim·bus
 cu·mu·lo·nim·bus·es
 cu·mu·lus
 cu·mu·lous
cu·ne·i·form
cun·ni·lin·gus
cun·ning
 cun·ning·ly
 cun·ning·ness
cup
 cupped
 cup·ping
cup·board
cup·cake
cup·ful
 cup·fuls
Cu·pid
cu·pid·i·ty
cu·po·la
cur·a·ble
 cur·a·bil·i·ty
 cur·a·bly
Cu·ra·cao
cu·rate
cu·ra·tive
cu·ra·tor
 cu·ra·to·ri·al
 cu·ra·tor·ship
curb·ing
curb·stone
cur·dle
 cur·dled
 cur·dling

cure
 cured
 cur·ing
 cur·er
cure-all
cur·few
cu·ria
 cu·ri·ae
 cu·ri·al
cu·rie
cu·rio
 cu·ri·os
 cu·ri·os·i·ty
 cu·ri·os·i·ties
cu·ri·ous
cu·ri·um
curl
 curl·er
 curl·i·cue
 curl·ing
curly
 curl·i·er
 curl·i·est
 curl·i·ness
cur·rant
cur·ren·cy
 cur·ren·cies
cur·rent
cur·ric·u·lum
 cur·ric·u·lums
 cur·ric·u·la
 cur·ric·u·lar
cur·rish
cur·ry
 cur·ries
 cur·ried
 cur·ry·ing
 cur·ri·er
cur·ry·comb
curse
 cursed
 curs·ing
 curs·ed·ly
 curs·ed·ness
cur·sive
 cur·sive·ly
cur·so·ry
 cur·so·ri·ly
 cur·so·ri·ness
curt
 curt·ly
 curt·ness
cur·tail
 cur·tail·ment
cur·tain
curt·sy
 curt·sies
 curt·sied
 curt·sy·ing
cur·va·ceous
cur·va·ture
curve
 curved
 curv·ing
 curv·ed·ness

cur·vi·lin·e·ar
cush·ion
cushy
  cush·i·er
  cush·i·est
cus·pid
  cus·pi·dal
  cus·pi·date
  cus·pi·dor
cuss·ed
  cuss·ed·ly
  cuss·ed·ness
cus·tard
Cus·ter
cus·to·di·an
  cus·to·di·an·ship
cus·to·dy
  cus·to·dies
  cus·to·di·al
cus·tom
cus·tom·ary
  cus·tom·ar·ies
  cus·tom·ar·i·ly
  cus·tom·ar·i·ness
cus·tom-built
cus·tom·er
cus·tom·house
cus·tom·ize
  cus·tom·ized
  cus·tom·iz·ing
cus·tom-made
cu·ta·ne·ous
cut·back
cute
  cut·er
  cut·est
  cute·ly
  cute·ness
cu·ti·cle
cut·lass
cut·lery
cut·let
cut·off
cut·out
cut-rate
cut·ter
cut·throat
cut·ting
  cut·ting·ly
cut·tle
cut·tle·fish
cut·up
cut·worm
cy·an·ic
cy·a·nide
cy·a·no·sis
cy·ber·na·tion
cy·ber·net·ics
cyc·la·men
cy·cle
  cy·cled
  cy·cling
  cy·clist
cy·clic
  cy·cli·cal

cy·cli·cal·ly
cy·clom·e·ter
cy·clone
cy·clo·rama
cy·clo·ram·ic
cy·clo·tron
cyg·net
cyl·in·der
  cy·lin·dric
  cy·lin·dri·cal
cym·bal
  cym·bal·ist
cyn·ic
  cyn·i·cism
cyn·i·cal
  cyn·i·cal·ly
cy·no·sure
cy·pher
cy·press
Cy·prus
cyst
  cys·tic
cys·tic fi·bro·sis
cy·tol·o·gy
  cy·tol·o·gist
czar
czar·e·vitch
cza·ri·na
Czech·o·slo·va·kia
dab
  dabbed
  dab·bing
dab·ble
  dab·bled
  dab·bling
  dab·bler
Dac·ca
Da·cron
dac·tyl
  dac·tyl·ic
dad·dy-long·legs
daf·fo·dil
daf·fy
  daf·fi·er
  daf·fi·est
dag·ger
Da·guerre
da·guerre·o·type
dahl·ia
Da·ho·mey
dai·ly
  dai·lies
dain·ty
  dain·ti·er
  dain·ti·est
  dain·ties
  dain·ti·ly
  dain·ti·ness
dai·qui·ri
dairy
  dair·ies
  dair·y·man
  dair·y·men
da·is
dai·sy

dai·sies
Da·kar
Da·ko·ta
Dal·las
dal·ly
dal·lied
dal·ly·ing
dal·li·ance
Dal·ma·tia
dam
dammed
dam·ming
dam·age
dam·aged
dam·ag·ing
dam·age·a·ble
dam·a·scene
dam·a·scened
dam·a·scen·ing
Da·mas·cus
dam·ask
damn
dam·na·ble
dam·na·ble·ness
dam·na·bly
dam·na·tion
damned
damp·en
damp·er
dam·sel
dam·son
dance
danced
danc·ing
dan·cer
dan·de·li·on
dan·der
dan·dle
dan·dled
dan·dling
dan·druff
dan·dy
dan·dies
dan·di·er
dan·di·est
dan·dy·ism
dan·ger
dan·ger·ous
dan·ger·ous·ly
dan·ger·ous·ness
dan·gle
dan·gled
dan·gling
dan·gler
Dan·ish
dank
dank·ly
dank·ness
dan·seuse
dan·seus·es
Dan·te
Dan·ube
Dan·ville
Dan·zig
dap·per

dap·ple
dap·pled
dap·pling
Dar·da·nelles
dare
dared
dar·ing
dare·dev·il
Dar·i·en
dar·ing·ly
dark
dark·ish
dark·ly
dark·ness
Dark Ag·es
dark·en
dark·ling
dark·room
dar·ling
dar·ling·ly
dar·ling·ness
Darm·stadt
darn·er
dart·er
Dart·mouth
Dar·win
Dar·win·ism
Dar·win·ist
dash·board
dash·ing
das·tard
das·tard·li·ness
das·tard·ly
da·ta
date
dat·ed
dat·ing
dat·a·ble
dat·er
date·less
date·line
da·tive
da·tum
da·ta
daub
daub·er
daugh·ter
daugh·ter·ly
daugh·ter-in-law
daugh·ters-in-law
daunt·less
daunt·less·ly
daunt·less·ness
dau·phin
dav·en·port
Da·vid
dav·it
daw·dle
daw·dled
daw·dling
daw·dler
dawn
day·break
day·dream
day·dream·er

day·light
day·light-sav·ing time
day·time
Day·ton
Day·to·na
daze
  dazed
  daz·ing
  daz·ed·ly
daz·zle
  daz·zled
  daz·zling
  daz·zler
  daz·zling·ly
D-day
dea·con
  dea·con·ry
  dea·con·ship
  dea·con·ess
dead·beat
dead·en
  dead·en·er
dead-end
dead·line
dead·lock
dead·ly
  dead·li·er
  dead·li·est
  dead·li·ness
dead·pan
dead·wood
deaf
  deaf·ly
  deaf·ness
deaf·en
  deaf·en·ing·ly
deaf-mute
deal
  dealt
  deal·ing
  deal·er
dean·ship
dear
  dear·ly
  dear·ness
Dear·born
dearth
death
  death·less
  death·ly
death·blow
death's-head
death·trap
death·watch
de·ba·cle
de·bar
  de·barred
  de·bar·ring
  de·bar·ment
de·bark
  de·bar·ka·tion
de·base
  de·based
  de·bas·ing
  de·base·ment

de·bas·er
de·bate
  de·bat·ed
  de·bat·ing
  de·bat·a·ble
  de·bat·er
de·bauch
  de·bauch·er
  de·bauch·ment
  de·bauch·ery
  de·bauch·er·ies
deb·au·chee
de·ben·ture
de·bil·i·tate
  de·bil·i·tat·ed
  de·bil·i·tat·ing
  de·bil·i·ta·tion
de·bil·i·ty
  de·bil·i·ties
deb·it
deb·o·nair
Deb·o·rah
de·bris
debt·or
de·bunk
  de·bunk·er
de·but
deb·u·tante
de·cade
dec·a·dent
  dec·a·dence
  dec·a·dent·ly
dec·a·gon
dec·a·gram
dec·a·he·dron
  dec·a·he·drons
de·cal
Dec·a·logue
de·camp
  de·camp·ment
de·cant
  de·cant·er
de·cap·i·tate
  de·cap·i·tat·ed
  de·cap·i·tat·ing
  de·cap·i·ta·tion
dec·a·pod
De·cap·o·lis
de·cath·lon
De·ca·tur
de·cay
Dec·can
de·cease
  de·ceased
de·ceit
  de·ceit·ful
  de·ceit·ful·ly
  de·ceit·ful·ness
de·ceive
  de·ceived
  de·ceiv·ing
  de·ceiv·er
  de·ceiv·ing·ly
  de·ceiv·a·ble
de·cel·er·ate

de·cel·er·at·ed
de·cel·er·at·ing
de·cel·er·a·tion
De·cem·ber
de·cen·cy
de·cen·cies
de·cen·ni·al
de·cen·ni·al·ly
de·cent
de·cent·ly
de·cen·tral·ize
de·cen·tral·ized
de·cen·tral·iz·ing
de·cen·tral·i·za·tion
de·cep·tion
de·cep·tive
de·cep·tive·ly
de·cep·tive·ness
dec·i·bel
de·cide
de·cid·ed
de·cid·ing
de·cid·a·ble
de·cid·ed·ly
de·cid·ed·ness
de·cid·u·ous
de·cid·u·ous·ly
dec·i·mal
dec·i·mate
dec·i·mat·ed
dec·i·mat·ing
dec·i·ma·tion
de·ci·pher
de·ci·pher·a·ble
de·ci·sion
de·ci·sive
de·ci·sive·ly
de·ci·sive·ness
deck·le
de·claim
dec·la·ma·tion
de·clam·a·tory
de·clare
de·clared
de·clar·ing
de·clar·a·tive
de·clar·a·to·ry
de·clar·er
dec·la·ra·tion
de·clas·si·fy
de·clas·si·fied
de·clas·si·fy·ing
de·clen·sion
dec·li·na·tion
de·cline
de·clined
de·clin·ing
de·clin·a·ble
de·cliv·i·ty
de·cliv·i·ties
de·code
de·cod·ed
de·cod·ing
de·cod·er
dé·colle·tage

de·com·pose
de·com·posed
de·com·pos·ing
de·com·po·si·tion
de·com·press
de·com·pres·sion
de·con·tam·i·nate
de·con·tam·i·nat·ed
de·con·tam·i·nat·ing
de·con·tam·i·na·tion
de·con·trol
de·con·trolled
de·con·trol·ling
de·cor
dec·o·rate
dec·o·rat·ed
dec·o·rat·ing
dec·o·ra·tion
dec·o·ra·tive
dec·o·ra·tive·ly
dec·o·ra·tor
dec·o·rous
dec·o·rous·ly
de·co·rum
de·coy
de·crease
de·creased
de·creas·ing
de·creas·ing·ly
de·cree
de·creed
de·cree·ing
de·crep·it
de·crep·i·tude
de·crep·it·ly
de·cre·scen·do
de·cre·scen·dos
de·cry
de·cried
de·cry·ing
de·cri·al
ded·i·cate
ded·i·cat·ed
ded·i·cat·ing
ded·i·ca·to·ry
ded·i·ca·tive
ded·i·ca·tion
de·duce
de·duc·i·ble
de·duct
de·duct·i·ble
de·duc·tion
de·duc·tive
de·duc·tive·ly
deep
deep·ly
deep·ness
deep·en
deep-root·ed
deep-seat·ed
deer·skin
de-es·ca·late
de-es·ca·lat·ed
de-es·ca·lat·ing
de-es·ca·la·tion

de·face
 de·faced
 de·fac·ing
 de·face·ment
 de·fac·er
de fac·to
de·fame
 de·famed
 de·fam·ing
 def·a·ma·tion
 de·fam·a·to·ry
 de·fam·er
de·fault
 de·fault·er
de·feat
 de·feat·ism
 de·feat·ist
def·e·cate
 def·e·cat·ed
 def·e·cat·ing
 def·e·ca·tion
de·fect
 de·fec·tion
 de·fec·tor
 de·fec·tive
 de·fec·tive·ly
 de·fec·tive·ness
de·fend
 de·fend·er
 de·fend·ant
de·fense
 de·fense·less
 de·fense·less·ly
 de·fense·less·ness
 de·fen·si·ble
 de·fen·si·bil·i·ty
 de·fen·si·bly
de·fen·sive
 de·fen·sive·ly
de·fer
 de·ferred
 de·fer·ring
 de·fer·ment
def·er·ence
 def·er·en·tial
 def·er·en·tial·ly
de·fi·ance
 de·fi·ant
 de·fi·ant·ly
de·fi·cient
 de·fi·cien·cy
 de·fi·cien·cies
 de·fi·cient·ly
def·i·cit
de·file
 de·filed
 de·fil·ing
de·fine
 de·fined
 de·fin·ing
 de·fin·er
 de·fin·a·ble
 de·fin·a·bly
def·i·nite
 def·i·nite·ly

def·i·nite·ness
def·i·ni·tion
de·fin·i·tive
 de·fin·i·tive·ly
de·flate
 de·flat·ed
 de·flat·ing
 de·fla·tion
 de·fla·tion·ary
de·flect
 de·flec·tion
 de·flec·tive
 de·flec·tor
de·flow·er
De·foe
de·fo·li·ate
 de·fo·li·at·ed
 de·fo·li·at·ing
de·for·est
 de·for·est·a·tion
de·form
 de·for·ma·tion
 de·formed
 de·form·i·ty
 de·form·i·ties
de·fraud
de·fray
 de·fray·al
 de·fray·ment
 de·fray·a·ble
de·frost
 de·frost·er
deft
 deft·ly
 deft·ness
de·funct
de·fy
 de·fied
 de·fy·ing
 de·fi·er
de·gen·er·ate
 de·gen·er·at·ed
 de·gen·er·at·ing
 de·gen·er·ate·ly
 de·gen·er·a·cy
 de·gen·er·a·tion
 de·gen·er·a·tive
de·grade
 de·grad·ed
 de·grad·ing
 deg·ra·da·tion
de·gree
de·his·cence
 de·his·cent
de·hy·drate
 de·hy·drat·ed
 de·hy·drat·ing
 de·hy·dra·tion
de·i·fy
 de·i·fied
 de·i·fy·ing
 de·i·fi·ca·tion
 de·i·fi·er
deign
de·ist

de·ism
de·is·tic
de·is·ti·cal
de·i·ty
de·i·ties
de·ject·ed
de·jec·ted·ly
de·jec·tion
de ju·re
Del·a·ware
de·lay
de·lay·er
de·lec·ta·ble
de·lec·ta·ble·ness
de·lec·ta·bly
de·lec·ta·tion
del·e·gate
del·e·gat·ed
del·e·gat·ing
del·e·ga·tion
de·lete
de·let·ed
de·let·ing
de·le·tion
del·e·te·ri·ous
Del·hi
de·lib·er·ate
de·lib·er·at·ed
de·lib·er·at·ing
de·lib·er·ate·ly
de·lib·er·ate·ness
de·lib·er·a·tion
de·lib·er·a·tive
de·lib·er·a·tor
del·i·ca·cy
del·i·ca·cies
del·i·cate
del·i·cate·ly
del·i·cate·ness
del·i·ca·tes·sen
de·li·cious
de·li·cious·ly
de·li·cious·ness
de·light
de·light·ed
de·light·ed·ly
de·light·ful
de·light·ful·ly
de·light·ful·ness
De·li·lah
de·lim·it
de·lim·i·ta·tion
de·lin·e·ate
de·lin·e·at·ed
de·lin·e·at·ing
de·lin·e·a·tion
de·lin·e·a·tor
de·lin·quent
de·lin·quen·cy
de·lin·quen·cies
de·lir·i·um
de·lir·i·ums
de·lir·ia
de·lir·i·ous
de·lir·i·ous·ly

de·liv·er
de·liv·er·a·ble
de·liv·er·er
de·liv·er·ance
de·liv·ery
de·liv·er·ies
de·louse
de·loused
de·lous·ing
Del·phi
del·phin·i·um
del·ta
del·toid
de·lude
de·lud·ed
de·lud·ing
de·lud·er
de·lu·sive
de·lu·so·ry
de·lu·sive·ly
del·uge
del·uged
del·ug·ing
de·lu·sion
de·luxe
delve
delved
delv·ing
dem·a·gogue
dem·a·gogu·ery
dem·a·gog·ic
dem·a·gog·i·cal
de·mand
de·mand·er
de·mar·ca·tion
de·mean
de·mean·or
de·ment·ed
de·men·tia
de·mer·it
De·me·tri·us
dem·i·god
dem·i·john
de·mise
de·mised
de·mis·ing
dem·i·tasse
de·mo·bi·lize
de·mo·bi·lized
de·mo·bi·liz·ing
de·mo·bi·li·za·tion
de·moc·ra·cy
de·moc·ra·cies
dem·o·crat
dem·o·crat·ic
dem·o·crat·i·cal·ly
de·moc·ra·tize
de·moc·ra·tized
de·moc·ra·tiz·ing
de·moc·ra·ti·za·tion
De·moc·ri·tus
de·mog·ra·phy
de·mog·ra·pher
dem·o·graph·ic
de·mol·ish

de·mol·ish·er
dem·o·li·tion
de·mon
de·mon·ic
de·mon·e·tize
de·mon·e·tized
de·mon·e·tiz·ing
de·mon·e·ti·za·tion
de·mo·ni·ac
de·mo·ni·a·cal
de·mon·ol·o·gy
de·mon·ol·o·gist
dem·on·strate
dem·on·strat·ed
dem·on·strat·ing
de·mon·stra·ble
de·mon·stra·bly
dem·on·stra·tion
de·mon·stra·tive
de·mon·stra·tive·ly
de·mon·stra·tive·ness
dem·on·stra·tor
de·mor·al·ize
de·mor·al·ized
de·mor·al·iz·ing
de·mor·al·i·za·tion
de·mor·al·iz·er
De·mos·the·nes
de·mote
de·mot·ed
de·mot·ing
de·mo·tion
de·mur
de·murred
de·mur·ring
de·mur·ral
de·mur·er
de·mur·est
de·mure·ly
de·mure·ness
de·mur·rage
de·nat·u·ral·ize
de·nat·u·ral·ized
de·nat·u·ral·iz·ing
de·nat·u·ral·i·za·tion
de·na·ture
de·na·tured
de·na·tur·ing
den·drite
den·dro·lite
den·drol·o·gy
den·e·ga·tion
de·ni·al
de·ni·er
den·im
den·i·zen
Den·mark
de·nom·i·nate
de·nom·i·nat·ed
de·nom·i·nat·ing
de·nom·i·na·tion
de·nom·i·na·tion·al
de·nom·i·na·tion·al·ism
de·nom·i·na·tive
de·nom·i·na·tor

de·note
de·not·ed
de·not·ing
de·no·ta·tion
de·noue·ment
de·nounce
de·nounced
de·noun·cing
de·nounce·ment
de·nun·ci·a·tion
de·nun·ci·a·to·ry
dense
den·ser
den·sest
dense·ly
dense·ness
den·si·ty
den·si·ties
den·tal
den·tate
den·ti·frice
den·tin
den·tist
den·tist·ry
den·ti·tion
den·ture
de·nude
de·nud·ed
de·nud·ing
den·u·da·tion
de·nun·ci·ate
de·nun·ci·at·ed
de·nun·ci·at·ing
de·nun·ci·a·tion
de·nun·ci·a·to·ry
Den·ver
de·ny
de·nied
de·ny·ing
de·o·dor·ant
de·o·dor·ize
de·o·dor·ized
de·o·dor·iz·ing
de·part
de·part·ed
de·part·ment
de·part·men·tal
de·par·ture
de·pend
de·pend·ence
de·pend·a·ble
de·pend·a·bly
de·pend·a·bil·i·ty
de·pend·en·cy
de·pend·en·cies
de·pend·ent
de·pict
de·pic·tion
de·pil·a·to·ry
de·pil·a·to·ries
de·plete
de·plet·ed
de·plet·ing
de·ple·tion
de·plor·a·ble

de·plor·a·bly
de·plore
de·plored
de·plor·ing
de·ploy
de·ploy·ment
de·po·nent
de·pop·u·late
de·pop·u·lat·ed
de·pop·u·lat·ing
de·pop·u·la·tion
de·port
de·por·ta·tion
de·port·ment
de·pose
de·posed
de·pos·ing
de·pos·a·ble
de·pos·it
de·pos·i·tor
dep·o·si·tion
de·pos·i·to·ry
de·pot
de·prave
de·praved
de·prav·ing
de·prav·i·ty
dep·re·cate
dep·re·cat·ed
dep·re·cat·ing
dep·re·cat·ing·ly
dep·re·ca·tion
dep·re·ca·to·ry
de·pre·ci·ate
de·pre·ci·at·ed
de·pre·ci·at·ing
de·pre·ci·a·tion
de·pre·ci·a·to·ry
de·pre·ci·a·tor
dep·re·date
dep·re·dat·ed
dep·re·dat·ing
dep·re·da·tion
de·press
de·pres·sant
de·pressed
de·pres·sion
de·prive
de·prived
de·priv·ing
dep·ri·va·tion
depth
dep·u·ta·tion
de·pute
de·put·ed
de·put·ing
dep·u·tize
dep·u·tized
dep·u·tiz·ing
dep·u·ty
dep·u·ties
dep·u·ty·ship
de·rail
de·rail·ment
de·range

de·ranged
de·rang·ing
de·range·ment
Der·by
Der·bies
Der·by·shire
der·e·lict
der·e·lic·tion
de·ride
de·rid·ed
de·rid·ing
de·ri·sion
de·ri·sive
de·ri·sive·ly
de·ri·so·ry
der·i·va·tion
de·riv·a·tive
de·rive
de·rived
de·riv·ing
de·riv·a·ble
der·ma
der·mal
der·ma·tol·o·gy
der·ma·to·log·i·cal
der·ma·tol·o·gist
der·mis
der·o·gate
der·o·gat·ed
der·o·gat·ing
der·o·ga·tion
de·rog·a·to·ry
de·rog·a·to·ri·ly
der·rick
der·rin·ger
der·vish
des·cant
Des·cartes
de·scend
de·scend·a·ble
de·scend·ant
de·scent
de·scribe
de·scribed
de·scrib·ing
de·scrib·a·ble
de·scrib·er
de·scrip·tion
de·scrip·tive
de·scrip·tive·ly
de·scrip·tive·ness
de·scry
de·scried
de·scry·ing
des·e·crate
des·e·crat·ed
des·e·crat·ing
des·e·cra·tion
de·seg·re·gate
de·seg·re·gat·ed
de·seg·re·gat·ing
de·seg·re·ga·tion
des·ert
de·sert
de·sert·er

de·ser·tion
de·serve
  de·served
  de·serv·ing
  de·serv·ed·ly
des·ha·bille
des·ic·cate
  des·ic·cat·ed
  des·ic·cat·ing
  des·ic·ca·tion
  des·ic·ca·tive
de·sid·er·a·tum
de·sign
des·ig·nate
  des·ig·nat·ed
  des·ig·nat·ing
  des·ig·na·tion
  des·ig·na·tive
  des·ig·na·tor
de·sign·ed·ly
de·sign·er
de·sign·ing
de·sire
  de·sired
  de·sir·ing
  de·sir·a·ble
  de·sir·a·bil·i·ty
  de·sir·a·bly
  de·sir·ous
de·sist
Des Moines
des·o·late
  des·o·lat·ed
  des·o·lat·ing
  des·o·late·ly
  des·o·la·tion
De So·to
de·spair
  de·spair·ing
  de·spair·ing·ly
des·per·a·do
  des·per·a·does
des·per·ate
  des·per·ate·ly
  des·per·ate·ness
  des·per·a·tion
des·pi·ca·ble
  des·pi·ca·bly
de·spise
  de·spised
  de·spis·ing
de·spite
de·spoil
  de·spoil·er
  de·spo·li·a·tion
de·spond
  de·spond·en·cy
  de·spond·ence
  de·spond·ent
  de·spond·ent·ly
des·pot
  des·pot·ic
  des·pot·i·cal·ly
des·pot·ism
des·sert

des·ti·na·tion
des·tine
  des·tined
  des·tin·ing
des·ti·ny
  des·ti·nies
des·ti·tute
  des·ti·tu·tion
de·stroy
de·stroy·er
de·struc·tion
  de·struct·i·ble
  de·struct·i·bil·i·ty
de·struc·tive
  de·struc·tive·ly
  de·struc·tive·ness
des·ue·tude
des·ul·to·ry
  des·ul·to·ri·ly
de·tach
  de·tach·a·ble
  de·tached
  de·tach·ment
de·tail
  de·tailed
de·tain
  de·tain·ment
  de·tain·er
de·tect
  de·tect·a·ble
  de·tec·tion
  de·tec·tive
  de·tec·tor
dé·tente
  dé·tentes
de·ten·tion
de·ter
  de·terred
  de·ter·ring
de·ter·gent
de·te·ri·o·rate
  de·te·ri·o·rat·ed
  de·te·ri·o·rat·ing
  de·te·ri·o·ra·tion
de·ter·mi·na·ble
de·ter·mi·nant
de·ter·mi·nate
de·ter·mi·na·tion
  de·ter·mi·na·tive
de·ter·mine
  de·ter·mined
  de·ter·min·ing
  de·ter·min·er
  de·ter·mined
  de·ter·mined·ly
  de·ter·min·ism
  de·ter·min·ist
de·ter·rent
  de·ter·rence
de·test
  de·test·a·ble
  de·test·a·bly
  de·tes·ta·tion
de·throne
  de·throned

de·thron·ing
de·throne·ment
det·o·nate
  det·o·nat·ed
  det·o·nat·ing
  det·o·na·tion
  det·o·na·tor
de·tour
de·tract
  de·trac·tion
  de·trac·tor
det·ri·ment
  det·ri·men·tal
  det·ri·men·tal·ly
de·tri·tus
De·troit
deuce
deu·te·ri·um
Deu·ter·on·o·my
Deutsch·land
de·val·u·ate
  de·val·u·at·ed
  de·val·u·at·ing
  de·val·u·a·tion
dev·as·tate
  dev·as·tat·ed
  dev·as·tat·ing
  dev·as·ta·tion
de·vel·op
  de·vel·op·ment
  de·vel·op·er
de·vi·ate
  de·vi·at·ed
  de·vi·at·ing
  de·vi·ant
  de·vi·a·tion
de·vice
dev·il
  dev·il·ment
  dev·il·try
  dev·il·tries
  dev·il·ry
dev·il·ish
  dev·il·ish·ly
  dev·il·ish·ness
dev·il-may-care
de·vi·ous
  de·vi·ous·ly
  de·vi·ous·ness
de·vise
  de·vised
  de·vis·ing
  de·vis·a·ble
  de·vis·al
  de·vi·see
  de·vi·sor
de·void
de·volve
  de·volved
  de·volv·ing
  dev·o·lu·tion
Dev·on
Dev·on·shire
de·vote
  de·vot·ed

de·vot·ing
de·vot·ed
  de·vot·ed·ly
dev·o·tee
de·vo·tion
  de·vo·tion·al
de·vour
  de·vour·er
  de·vour·ing·ly
de·vout
  de·vout·ly
  de·vout·ness
dew·ber·ry
  dew·ber·ries
dew·drop
Dew·ey
dew·lap
dewy
  dew·i·er
  dew·i·est
  dew·i·ness
dew·y-eyed
dex·ter·ous
  dex·ter·i·ty
  dex·ter·ous·ly
dex·trose
di·a·be·tes
  di·a·bet·ic
di·a·bol·ic
  di·a·bol·i·cal
  di·a·bol·i·cal·ly
di·a·crit·ic
  di·a·crit·i·cal
  di·a·crit·i·cal·ly
di·a·dem
di·ag·nose
  di·ag·nosed
  di·ag·nos·ing
  di·ag·no·sis
  di·ag·no·ses
  di·ag·nos·tic
  di·ag·nos·ti·cian
di·ag·o·nal
  di·ag·o·nal·ly
di·a·gram
  di·a·gramed
  di·a·gram·ing
  di·a·gram·mat·ic
  di·a·gram·mat·i·cal
di·al
  di·aled
  di·al·ing
di·a·lect
  di·a·lec·tal
  di·a·lec·tic
  di·a·lec·ti·cal
  di·a·lec·ti·cian
di·a·logue
di·am·e·ter
di·a·met·ric
  di·a·met·ric·al
  di·a·met·ric·al·ly
dia·mond
Di·ana
dia·per

di·aph·a·nous
di·a·phragm
di·ar·rhea
di·a·ry
  di·a·ries
  di·a·rist
di·as·to·le
  di·as·tol·ic
di·a·ther·mic
di·a·ther·my
di·a·tom
di·a·ton·ic
di·a·tribe
Di·az
dib·ble
  dib·bled
  dib·bling
dice
  diced
  dic·ing
di·chot·o·my
  di·chot·o·mies
  di·chot·o·mous
  di·cho·tom·ic
dick·ens
dick·er
dick·ey
  dick·eys
Dick·in·son
Dic·ta·phone
dic·tate
  dic·tat·ed
  dic·tat·ing
  dic·ta·tion
dic·ta·tor
  dic·ta·tor·ship
  dic·ta·to·ri·al
  dic·ta·to·ri·al·ly
dic·tion
dic·tion·ar·y
  dic·tion·ar·ies
dic·tum
  dic·tums
  dic·ta
di·dac·tic
  di·dac·ti·cal
  di·dac·ti·cal·ly
did·dle
  did·dled
  did·dling
Di·de·rot
die
  died
  dy·ing
di·e·cious
Di·e·go
die·hard
di·e·lec·tric
di·er·e·sis
  di·er·e·ses
die·sel
die·sink·er
  die·sink·ing
di·et
  di·et·er

di·e·tary
  di·e·tar·ies
di·e·tet·ic
  di·e·tet·i·cal
  di·e·tet·i·cal·ly
  di·e·tet·ics
di·e·ti·cian
dif·fer
dif·fer·ence
  dif·fer·enced
  dif·fer·en·cing
dif·fer·ent
  dif·fer·ent·ly
dif·fer·en·tial
  dif·fer·en·tial·ly
  dif·fer·en·ti·ate
  dif·fer·en·ti·at·ed
  dif·fer·en·ti·at·ing
  dif·fer·en·ti·a·tion
dif·fi·cult
  dif·fi·cult·ly
  dif·fi·cul·ty
  dif·fi·cul·ties
dif·fi·dence
  dif·fi·dent
  dif·fi·dent·ly
dif·fuse
  dif·fused
  dif·fus·ing
  dif·fuse·ly
  dif·fuse·ness
  dif·fu·sion
  dif·fu·sive·ly
  dif·fu·sive·ness
dig
  dig·ging
di·gest
  di·gest·er
  di·gest·i·ble
  di·gest·i·bil·i·ty
  di·ges·tion
  di·ges·tive
dig·ger
dig·gings
dig·it
  dig·it·al
  dig·i·tal·is
dig·ni·fied
dig·ni·fy
  dig·ni·fied
  dig·ni·fy·ing
dig·ni·tary
  dig·ni·tar·ies
dig·ni·ty
  dig·ni·ties
di·graph
di·gress
  di·gres·sion
  di·gres·sive
  di·gres·sive·ly
di·he·dral
dike
  diked
  dik·ing
di·lap·i·dat·ed

di·lap·i·da·tion
dil·a·ta·tion
di·late
di·lat·ed
di·lat·ing
di·lat·a·bil·i·ty
di·lat·a·ble
di·la·tion
dil·a·to·ry
dil·a·to·ri·ly
di·lem·ma
dil·et·tan·te
dil·et·tan·tes
dil·i·gence
dil·i·gent
dil·i·gent·ly
dil·ly·dal·ly
dil·ly·dal·lied
dil·ly·dal·ly·ing
di·lute
di·lut·ed
di·lut·ing
di·lute·ness
di·lu·tion
dim
dim·mer
dim·mest
dimmed
dim·ming
dim·ly
dim·ness
di·men·sion
di·men·sion·less
di·men·sion·al
di·min·ish
di·min·ish·a·ble
di·min·u·en·do
di·min·u·en·dos
dim·i·nu·tion
di·min·u·tive
di·min·u·tive·ly
di·min·u·tive·ness
dim-out
dim·ple
dim·pled
dim·pling
dim·wit
dim·wit·ted
din
dinned
din·ning
dine
dined
din·ing
din·er
di·nette
ding-dong
din·ghy
din·ghies
din·gy
din·gi·er
din·gi·est
din·gi·ness
dinky
dink·i·er

dink·i·est
din·ner
di·no·saur
di·o·cese
di·oc·e·san
Di·o·cle·tian
Di·og·e·nes
Di·o·me·des
di·o·rama
dip
dipped
dip·ping
diph·the·ria
diph·thong
di·plo·ma
di·plo·ma·cy
di·plo·ma·cies
dip·lo·mat
dip·lo·mat·ic
dip·lo·mat·i·cal·ly
dip·per
dip·so·ma·nia
dip·so·ma·ni·ac
dip·stick
dire
dir·er
dir·est
dire·ly
dire·ness
di·rect
di·rect·ness
di·rec·tion
di·rec·tion·al
di·rec·tive
di·rect·ly
di·rec·tor
di·rec·to·ri·al
di·rec·tor·ship
di·rec·to·rate
di·rec·to·ry
di·rec·to·ries
dirge
dirty
dirt·i·er
dirt·i·est
dirt·ied
dirt·y·ing
dirt·i·ly
dirt·i·ness
dis·a·ble
dis·a·bled
dis·a·bling
dis·a·bil·i·ty
dis·a·bil·i·ties
dis·a·ble·ment
dis·a·buse
dis·a·bused
dis·a·bus·ing
dis·ad·van·tage
dis·ad·van·taged
dis·ad·van·tag·ing
dis·ad·van·ta·geous
dis·ad·van·ta·geous·ly
dis·af·fect
dis·af·fec·tion

dis·af·fect·ed
dis·a·gree
　dis·a·greed
　dis·a·gree·ing
dis·a·gree·a·ble
　dis·a·gree·a·ble·ness
　dis·a·gree·a·bly
dis·a·gree·ment
dis·al·low
　dis·al·low·ance
dis·ap·pear
　dis·ap·pear·ance
dis·ap·point
　dis·ap·point·ment
dis·ap·pro·ba·tion
dis·ap·prove
　dis·ap·proved
　dis·ap·prov·ing
　dis·ap·prov·al
　dis·ap·prov·ing·ly
dis·arm
dis·ar·ma·ment
dis·ar·range
　dis·ar·ranged
　dis·ar·rang·ing
　dis·ar·range·ment
dis·ar·ray
dis·as·sem·ble
dis·as·ter
　dis·as·trous
　dis·as·trous·ly
dis·a·vow
　dis·a·vow·al
dis·band
　dis·band·ment
dis·bar
　dis·barred
　dis·bar·ring
dis·be·lieve
　dis·be·lieved
　dis·be·liev·ing
　dis·be·lief
　dis·be·liev·er
dis·burse
　dis·bursed
　dis·burs·ing
　dis·burse·ment
　dis·burs·er
dis·card
dis·cern
　dis·cern·er
　dis·cern·i·ble
　dis·cern·i·bly
dis·cern·ing
　dis·cern·ing·ly
dis·cern·ment
dis·charge
　dis·charged
　dis·charg·ing
　dis·charge·a·ble
　dis·char·ger
dis·ci·ple
　dis·ci·ple·ship
dis·ci·pli·nar·i·an
dis·ci·pline

dis·ci·plined
dis·ci·plin·ing
dis·ci·pli·nary
dis·claim
dis·claim·er
dis·close
dis·closed
dis·clos·ing
dis·clos·er
dis·clo·sure
dis·coid
dis·col·or
　dis·col·or·a·tion
dis·com·fit
　dis·com·fi·ture
dis·com·fort
dis·com·mode
　dis·com·mod·ed
　dis·com·mod·ing
dis·com·pose
　dis·com·posed
　dis·com·pos·ing
　dis·com·po·sure
dis·con·cert
　dis·con·cert·ing
　dis·con·cert·ed
dis·con·nect
　dis·con·nec·tion
　dis·con·nect·ed
　dis·con·nect·ed·ness
dis·con·so·late
　dis·con·so·late·ly
dis·con·tent
　dis·con·tent·ment
　dis·con·tent·ed
　dis·con·tent·ed·ly
dis·con·tin·ue
　dis·con·tin·ued
　dis·con·tin·u·ing
　dis·con·tin·u·ance
　dis·con·tin·u·a·tion
　dis·con·tin·u·ous
　dis·con·ti·nu·i·ty
dis·cord
　dis·cord·ance
　dis·cor·dan·cy
　dis·cord·ant·ly
dis·co·thèque
dis·count
dis·cour·age
　dis·cour·aged
　dis·cour·ag·ing
　dis·cour·age·ment
　dis·cour·ag·ing
dis·course
　dis·coursed
　dis·cours·ing
dis·cour·te·ous
　dis·cour·te·ous·ly
　dis·cour·te·ous·ness
　dis·cour·te·sy
　dis·cour·te·sies
dis·cov·er
　dis·cov·er·a·ble
　dis·cov·er·er

dis·cov·ery
dis·cov·er·ies
dis·cred·it
dis·cred·it·a·ble
dis·cred·it·a·bly
dis·creet
dis·creet·ly
dis·crep·an·cy
dis·crep·an·cies
dis·crete
dis·cre·tion
dis·cre·tion·ary
dis·crim·i·nate
dis·crim·i·nat·ed
dis·crim·i·nat·ing
dis·crim·i·nate·ly
dis·crim·i·na·tion
dis·crim·i·na·tive
dis·crim·i·na·to·ry
dis·crim·i·na·tor
dis·cur·sive
dis·cur·sive·ly
dis·cur·sive·ness
dis·cus
dis·cus·es
dis·cuss
dis·cuss·i·ble
dis·cus·sion
dis·dain
dis·dain·ful
dis·dain·ful·ly
dis·ease
dis·eased
dis·eas·ing
dis·em·bark
dis·em·bar·ka·tion
dis·em·bark·ment
dis·em·body
dis·em·bod·ied
dis·em·bod·y·ing
dis·em·bod·i·ment
dis·em·bow·el
dis·em·bow·eled
dis·em·bow·el·ing
dis·em·bow·el·ment
dis·en·chant
dis·en·chant·ment
dis·en·cum·ber
dis·en·fran·chise
dis·en·fran·chised
dis·en·fran·chis·ing
dis·en·gage
dis·en·gaged
dis·en·gag·ing
dis·en·gage·ment
dis·en·tan·gle
dis·en·tan·gled
dis·en·tan·gling
dis·en·tan·gle·ment
dis·es·tab·lish
dis·es·tab·lish·ment
dis·fa·vor
dis·fig·ure
dis·fig·ured
dis·fig·ur·ing

dis·fig·ure·ment
dis·fran·chise
dis·fran·chised
dis·fran·chis·ing
dis·fran·chise·ment
dis·gorge
dis·gorged
dis·gorg·ing
dis·grace
dis·graced
dis·grac·ing
dis·grace·ful
dis·grace·ful·ly
dis·grace·ful·ness
dis·grun·tle
dis·grun·tled
dis·grun·tling
dis·guise
dis·guised
dis·guis·ing
dis·guis·er
dis·gust
dis·gust·ed
dis·gust·ing
dis·ha·bille
dis·har·mo·ny
dis·har·mo·nies
dis·heart·en
dis·heart·en·ing
di·shev·eled
dis·hon·est
dis·hon·est·ly
dis·hon·es·ty
dis·hon·es·ties
dis·hon·or
dis·hon·or·a·ble
dis·hon·or·a·bly
dis·il·lu·sion
dis·il·lu·sion·ment
dis·in·cline
dis·in·clined
dis·in·clin·ing
dis·in·cli·na·tion
dis·in·fect
dis·in·fect·ant
dis·in·fec·tion
dis·in·her·it
dis·in·her·i·tance
dis·in·te·grate
dis·in·te·grat·ed
dis·in·te·grat·ing
dis·in·te·gra·tion
dis·in·te·gra·tor
dis·in·ter
dis·in·terred
dis·in·ter·ring
dis·in·ter·ment
dis·in·ter·est
dis·in·ter·est·ed
dis·in·ter·est·ed·ly
dis·join
dis·joint
dis·joint·ed
dis·joint·ed·ness
dis·joint·ed·ly

dis·junc·tion
disk
  disk·like
dis·like
  dis·liked
  dis·lik·ing
  dis·lik·a·ble
dis·lo·cate
  dis·lo·cat·ed
  dis·lo·cat·ing
  dis·lo·ca·tion
dis·lodge
  dis·lodged
  dis·lodg·ing
dis·loy·al
  dis·loy·al·ly
  dis·loy·al·ty
  dis·loy·al·ties
dis·mal
  dis·mal·ly
dis·man·tle
  dis·man·tled
  dis·man·tling
dis·may
dis·mem·ber
  dis·mem·ber·ment
dis·miss
  dis·mis·sal
dis·mount
dis·o·be·di·ence
  dis·o·be·di·ent
  dis·o·be·di·ent·ly
dis·o·bey
  dis·o·bey·er
dis·or·der
  dis·or·dered
  dis·or·der·ly
  dis·or·der·li·ness
dis·or·gan·ize
  dis·or·gan·ized
  dis·or·gan·iz·ing
  dis·or·gan·i·za·tion
dis·o·ri·ent
  dis·o·ri·en·ta·tion
dis·own
dis·par·age
  dis·par·aged
  dis·par·ag·ing
  dis·par·age·ment
  dis·par·ag·ing·ly
dis·pa·rate
  dis·pa·rate·ly
  dis·pa·rate·ness
dis·par·i·ty
  dis·par·i·ties
dis·pas·sion
  dis·pas·sion·ate·ness
  dis·pas·sion·ate
  dis·pas·sion·ate·ly
dis·patch
dis·patch·er
dis·pel
  dis·pelled
  dis·pel·ling
dis·pen·sa·ble

dis·pen·sa·bil·i·ty
dis·pen·sa·ry
  dis·pen·sa·ries
dis·pen·sa·tion
dis·pense
  dis·pensed
  dis·pens·ing
dis·perse
  dis·persed
  dis·pers·ing
dis·place
  dis·placed
  dis·plac·ing
dis·play
dis·please
  dis·pleased
  dis·pleas·ing
  dis·pleas·ure
dis·port
dis·pos·a·ble
dis·pose
  dis·posed
  dis·pos·ing
dis·po·si·tion
dis·pro·por·tion
  dis·pro·por·tion·ate·ness
dis·prove
  dis·proved
  dis·prov·ing
dis·pute
  dis·put·ed
  dis·put·ing
  dis·put·a·ble
dis·qual·i·fy
  dis·qual·i·fied
  dis·qual·i·fy·ing
  dis·qual·i·fi·ca·tion
dis·qui·et
Dis·rae·li
dis·re·gard
dis·re·pair
dis·rep·u·ta·ble
dis·re·spect
  dis·re·spect·ful
  dis·re·spect·a·ble
dis·robe
  dis·robed
  dis·rob·ing
dis·rupt
dis·rup·tion
dis·rup·tive
  dis·rup·tive·ly
  dis·rup·tive·ness
dis·rupt·er
dis·sat·is·fac·tion
dis·sat·is·fac·to·ry
dis·sat·is·fy
  dis·sat·is·fied
  dis·sat·is·fy·ing
dis·sect
  dis·sect·ed
  dis·sec·tion
dis·sem·blance
dis·sem·ble
  dis·sem·bled

dis·sem·bling
dis·sem·bler
dis·sem·i·nate
dis·sem·i·nat·ed
dis·sem·i·nat·ing
dis·sem·i·na·tion
dis·sem·i·na·tive
dis·sem·i·na·tor
dis·sent
dis·sent·ing
dis·sen·sion
dis·sen·tious
dis·sent·er
dis·ser·tate
dis·ser·ta·ted
dis·ser·ta·ting
dis·ser·ta·tion
dis·ser·ta·tor
dis·serve
dis·served
dis·serv·ing
dis·serv·ice
dis·si·dence
dis·si·dent
dis·sim·i·lar
dis·sim·i·lar·i·ty
dis·sim·i·lar·ly
dis·sim·i·late
dis·sim·i·lat·ed
dis·sim·i·lat·ing
dis·sim·i·la·tion
dis·sim·i·la·tive
dis·sim·i·la·to·ry
dis·si·mil·i·tude
dis·sim·u·late
dis·sim·u·lat·ed
dis·sim·u·lat·ing
dis·sim·u·la·tion
dis·sim·u·la·tive
dis·sim·u·la·tor
dis·si·pate
dis·si·pat·ed
dis·si·pat·ing
dis·si·pat·ed
dis·si·pa·ted·ly
dis·si·pat·ed·ness
dis·si·pa·tive
dis·si·pa·tor
dis·si·pa·tion
dis·so·ci·ate
dis·so·ci·at·ed
dis·so·ci·at·ing
dis·so·ci·a·tive
dis·so·ci·a·tion
dis·so·lute
dis·so·lute·ly
dis·so·lu·tion
dis·solve
dis·solved
dis·solv·ing
dis·solv·er
dis·solv·a·ble
dis·so·nance
dis·so·nant
dis·so·nant·ly

dis·suade
dis·suad·ed
dis·suad·ing
dis·suad·er
dis·sua·sion
dis·sua·sive
dis·taff
dis·tal
dis·tance
dis·tant
dis·tant·ly
dis·taste
dis·taste·ful
dis·taste·ful·ly
dis·taste·ful·ness
dis·tem·per
dis·tend
dis·ten·sion
dis·ten·tion
dis·till
dis·tilled
dis·till·ing
dis·till·a·ble
dis·til·la·tion
dis·til·late
dis·till·er
dis·till·ery
dis·till·er·ies
dis·tinct
dis·tinct·ly
dis·tinct·ness
dis·tinc·tion
dis·tinc·tive
dis·tin·guish
dis·tin·guish·a·ble
dis·tin·guished
dis·tort
dis·tor·tion
dis·tor·tion·al
dis·tort·ed
dis·tract
dis·tract·ing
dis·tract·ing·ly
dis·tract·ed
dis·tract·ed·ly
dis·trac·tion
dis·trac·tive
dis·trait
dis·traught
dis·tress
dis·tress·ful
dis·tress·ful·ly
dis·tress·ful·ness
dis·tress·ing
dis·tress·ing·ly
dis·trib·ute
dis·trib·ut·ed
dis·trib·ut·ing
dis·trib·ut·a·ble
dis·tri·bu·tion
dis·trib·u·tor
dis·trict
dis·trict at·tor·ney
dis·trust
dis·trust·ful

dis·trust·ful·ly
dis·trust·ful·ness
dis·turb
dis·turb·ance
dis·turbed
dis·un·ion
dis·u·nite
dis·u·ni·ted
dis·u·ni·ting
dis·u·ni·ty
dis·u·ni·ties
dis·use
dis·used
dis·us·ing
ditch
ditch·er
dith·er
dit·to
dit·tos
dit·toed
dit·to·ing
dit·ty
dit·ties
di·u·ret·ic
di·ur·nal
di·ur·nal·ly
di·van
dive
dived
dove
div·ing
div·er
di·verge
di·verged
di·verg·ing
di·ver·gence
di·ver·gen·cy
di·ver·gent
di·vers
di·verse
di·ver·si·fi·ca·tion
di·ver·si·fy
di·ver·si·fied
di·ver·si·fy·ing
di·ver·sion
di·ver·sion·ary
di·ver·si·ty
di·ver·si·ties
di·vert
Di·ves
di·vide
di·vid·ed
di·vid·ing
div·i·dend
di·vine
di·vined
di·vin·ing
di·vin·i·ty
di·vin·i·ties
di·vis·i·ble
di·vis·i·bly
di·vi·sion
di·vi·sive
di·vi·sor
di·vorce

di·vorced
di·vorc·ing
di·vor·cé
di·vor·cee
di·vulge
di·vulged
di·vulg·ing
di·vul·gence
Dix·ie
Dix·on
diz·zy
diz·zi·er
diz·zi·est
diz·zied
diz·zy·ing
diz·zi·ly
diz·zi·ness
Dja·kar·ta
do·a·ble
Do·ber·man
doc·ile
dock·yard
doc·tor
doc·tor·al
doc·tor·ate
doc·trine
doc·tri·nal
doc·u·ment
doc·u·men·ta·ry
doc·u·men·ta·ries
doc·u·men·ta·ri·ly
doc·u·men·ta·tion
dod·der
dod·dered
dodge
dodged
dodg·ing
dodg·er
do·do
do·dos
do·er
doe·skin
doesn't
dog
dogged
dog·ging
dog-eared
dog·fight
dog·ged
dog·ged·ly
dog·ged·ness
dog·gone
dog·goned
dog·gon·ing
dog·house
dog·ma
dog·mas
dog·ma·ta
dog·mat·ic
dog·mat·i·cal
dog·mat·i·cal·ly
dog·ma·tism
dog·ma·tist
dog·ma·tize
dog·ma·tized

dog·ma·tiz·ing
do-good·er
dog·wood
Do·ha
doi·ly
  doi·lies
do·ing
do-it-your·self
dol·drums
dole
  doled
  dol·ing
dole·ful
dol·lar
dol·ly
  dol·lies
  dol·lied
  dol·ly·ing
dol·or·ous
dol·phin
dolt
  dolt·ish
do·main
dome
  domed
  dom·ing
Domes·day
do·mes·tic
  do·mes·ti·cal·ly
do·mes·ti·cate
  do·mes·ti·cat·ed
  do·mes·ti·cat·ing
  do·mes·ti·ca·ble
  do·mes·ti·ca·tion
do·mes·tic·i·ty
  do·mes·tic·i·ties
dom·i·cile
  dom·i·ciled
  dom·i·cil·ing
dom·i·nance
  dom·i·nan·cy
dom·i·nant
dom·i·nate
  dom·i·nat·ed
  dom·i·nat·ing
  dom·i·na·tion
  dom·i·na·tor
dom·i·neer
  dom·i·neer·ing
Do·min·i·can
do·min·ion
dom·i·no
  dom·i·noes
don
  donned
  don·ning
do·nate
  do·nat·ed
  do·nat·ing
  do·na·tor
do·na·tion
do·nee
Don·e·gal
don·key
  don·keys

do·nor
do-noth·ing
Don Qui·xo·te
don't
doo·dad
doo·dle
  doo·dled
  doo·dling
dooms·day
door·bell
door·jamb
door·knob
door·mat
door·step
door·way
dope
  doped
  dop·ing
dop·ey
  dop·i·er
  dop·i·est
  dop·i·ness
Dor·ches·ter
Dor·ic
dor·mant
  dor·man·cy
dor·mer
  dor·mered
dor·mi·to·ry
  dor·mi·to·ries
dor·sal
Dor·set·shire
dory
  dor·ies
dos·age
dose
  dosed
  dos·ing
dos·si·er
dot
  dot·ted
  dot·ting
dot·age
dot·ard
dote
  dot·ed
  dot·ing
  dot·er
  dot·ing·ly
dot·ty
  dot·ti·er
  dot·ti·est
dou·ble
  dou·bled
  dou·bling
  doub·ly
dou·ble-breast·ed
dou·ble-cross
dou·ble-deck·er
dou·ble-faced
dou·ble-head·er
dou·ble-joint·ed
dou·ble·take
dou·ble-time
  dou·ble-timed

dou·ble-tim·ing
doubt
doubt·a·ble
doubt·ful
  doubt·ful·ly
doubt·less
douche
  douched
  douch·ing
dough
dough·nut
dough·ty
  dough·ti·er
  dough·ti·est
  dough·ti·ly
  dough·ti·ness
dour
  dour·ly
  dour·ness
douse
  doused
  dous·ing
dove·cote
Do·ver
dove·tail
dow·a·ger
dow·dy
  dow·di·er
  dow·di·est
  dow·di·ness
dow·el
  dow·eled
  dow·el·ing
dow·er
down
  down·i·ness
  downy
down·cast
down·fall
  down·fall·en
down·grade
  down·grad·ed
  down·grad·ing
down·heart·ed
down·hill
down·pour
down·right
down·stairs
down·stream
down-to-earth
down·town
down·trod·den
down·ward
  down·ward·ly
down·wind
dow·ry
  dow·ries
dox·ol·o·gy
doze
  dozed
  doz·ing
doz·en
  doz·enth
drab
  drab·ber

drab·best
drab·ly
drab·ness
draft
  draft·er
  draft·ee
drafts·man
  drafts·men
  drafts·man·ship
drafty
  draft·i·er
  draft·i·est
  draft·i·ly
drag
  dragged
  drag·ging
  drag·ging·ly
drag·gle
drag·net
drag·on
drag·on·fly
  drag·on·flies
drain
  drain·a·ble
  drain·er
drain·age
drain·pipe
drake
dra·ma
  dra·mat·ic
  dra·mat·i·cal·ly
  dra·mat·ics
dram·a·tist
dram·a·tize
  dram·a·tized
  dram·a·tiz·ing
  dram·a·ti·za·tion
drape
  draped
  drap·ing
drap·er
dra·pery
  dra·per·ies
dras·tic
  drast·i·cal·ly
draught
draw
  drawn
  draw·ing
draw·back
draw·bridge
draw·er
draw·ers
draw·ing
drawl
drawn
dread
dread·ful
  dread·ful·ly
dream
  dreamed
  dreamt
  dream·ing
  dream·er
  dream·ful·ly

dream·like
dreamy
  dream·i·er
  dream·i·est
dreary
  drear·i·er
  drear·i·est
  drear·i·ly
  drear·i·ness
dredge
  dredged
  dredg·ing
  dredg·er
dreg
  dreg·gy
drench
Dres·den
dress
  dressed
  dres·sing
  dress·er
dress·mak·er
dressy
  dress·i·er
  dress·i·est
Drey·fus
drib·ble
  drib·bled
  drib·bling
  drib·bler
drib·let
dri·er
drift
  drift·age
  drift·er
drift·wood
drill·ing
dri·ly
drink
  drank
  drunk
  drink·ing
  drink·a·ble
  drink·er
Drink·wa·ter
drip
  dripped
  drip·ping
  drip·py
drip-dry
  drip-dried
  drip-dry·ing
drive
  drove
  driv·en
  driv·ing
driv·el
  driv·eled
  driv·el·ing
  driv·el·er
driv·er
drive·way
driz·zle
  driz·zled
  driz·zling

driz·zly
droll
  droll·ery
  droll·er·ies
drom·e·dary
  drom·e·dar·ies
drone
  droned
  dron·ing
drool
droop
  droop·ing·ly
  droop·y
  droop·i·er
  droop·i·est
drop
  dropped
  drop·ping
drop·let
drop·out
drop·per
drop·sy
dross
drought
droughty
  drought·i·er
  drought·i·est
drowned
drowse
  drowsed
  drows·ing
  drow·si·ly
  drow·si·ness
  drow·sy
  drow·si·er
  drow·si·est
drub
  drubbed
  drub·bing
drudge
  drudged
  drudg·ing
  drudg·ery
  drudg·er·ies
  drudg·ing·ly
drug
  drugged
  drug·ging
drug·gist
drug·store
dru·id
drum
  drummed
  drum·ming
drum·mer
drum·stick
drunk·ard
drunk·en
  drunk·en·ly
  drunk·en·ness
dry
  dri·er
  dri·est
  dried
  dry·ing

dry·ly
dry·ness
dry·ad
dry·ads
dry·a·des
dry goods
du·al
du·al·i·ty
du·al·ism
du·al·ist
du·al·is·tic
dub
dubbed
dub·bing
dub·ber
du·bi·ous
du·bi·e·ty
du·bi·ous·ly
du·bi·ous·ness
Dub·lin
Du·buque
du·cal
du·cal·ly
du·cat
duch·ess
duchy
duch·ies
duck·bill
duck·ling
ducky
duck·i·er
duck·i·est
duct·less
duc·tile
du·el
du·eled
du·el·ing
du·el·ist
du·en·na
du·et
duf·fel bag
duff·er
dug·out
duke·dom
dul·cet
dull
dull·ard
dull·ish
dull·ness
Dul·les
Du·luth
du·ly
dumb
dumb·ly
dumb·ness
dumb·bell
dumb·struck
dumb·wait·er
dum·dum
dum·found
dum·my
dum·mies
dump·i·ness
dump·ling
dumpy

dump·i·er
dump·i·est
dump·i·ness
dun
dunned
dun·ning
dunce
Dun·dee
dune
dung
dungy
dun·ga·ree
dun·geon
dung·hill
dunk·er
Dun·kirk
dun·nage
duo
du·o·dec·i·mal
du·o·de·num
du·o·de·na
du·o·de·nal
dupe
duped
dup·ing
du·plex
du·pli·cate
du·pli·cat·ed
du·pli·cat·ing
du·pli·ca·tion
du·pli·ca·tor
du·plic·i·ty
du·plic·i·ties
Du·quesne
du·ra·ble
du·ra·bil·i·ty
du·ra·bly
dur·ance
du·ra·tion
du·ress
Dur·ham
dur·ing
dusk
dusk·i·ly
dusk·i·ness
dusky
dusk·i·er
dusk·i·est
dust·er
dust·pan
dusty
dust·i·er
dust·i·est
dust·i·ly
dust·i·ness
Dutch·man
du·ti·a·ble
du·ti·ful
du·ti·ful·ly
du·ti·ful·ness
du·ty
du·ties
dwarf
dwarf·ish
dwell

dwelt
dwelled
dwell·ing
dwin·dle
dwin·dled
dwin·dling
dye
dyed
dye·ing
dyed-in-the-wool
dye·stuff
dy·ing
dyke
dy·nam·ic
dy·nam·i·cal
dy·nam·i·cal·ly
dy·na·mism
dy·nam·ics
dy·na·mite
dy·na·mo
dy·na·mos
dy·na·mo·e·lec·tric
dy·nas·ty
dy·nas·ties
dyne
dys·en·tery
dys·func·tion
dys·pep·sia
dys·pep·tic
dys·pep·ti·cal
dys·pep·ti·cal·ly
dys·tro·phy
ea·ger
ea·ger·ly
ea·ger·ness
ea·gle
ea·gle-eyed
ea·glet
ear·ache
ear·drum
Ear·hart
earl·dom
ear·ly
ear·li·er
ear·li·est
ear·li·ness
ear·mark
ear·muff
earn
earn·er
ear·nest
ear·nest·ly
ear·nest·ness
earn·ings
ear·phone
ear·ring
ear·shot
earth·bound
earth·en
earth·en·ware
earth·ly
earth·li·er
earth·li·est
earth·quake
earth·ward

earth·work
earth·worm
earthy
earth·i·er
earth·i·est
earth·i·ness
ear·wax
ease
eased
eas·ing
ea·sel
ease·ment
eas·i·ly
eas·i·ness
East·er
east·er·ly
east·ern
East·ern·er
east·ern·most
Eas·ter·tide
Eas·ton
east·ward
east·wards
easy
eas·i·er
eas·i·est
eas·y·go·ing
eat
ate
eat·en
eat·ing
eat·a·ble
eat·er
eau de co·logne
eaves·drop
eaves·dropped
eaves·drop·ping
eaves·drop·per
ebb
Eb·e·ne·zer
Eber·hart
eb·ony
eb·on·ies
ebul·lience
ebul·lient
eb·ul·li·tion
ec·cen·tric
ec·cen·tri·cal·ly
ec·cen·tric·i·ty
ec·cen·tric·i·ties
Ec·cle·si·as·tes
ec·cle·si·as·tic
ec·cle·si·as·ti·cal
ec·cle·si·as·ti·cal·ly
ech·e·lon
echi·no·derm
echo
ech·oes
ech·oed
ech·o·ing
ech·o·er
echo·ic
eclair
ec·lec·tic
ec·lec·ti·cal·ly

ec·lec·ti·cism
eclipse
  eclipsed
  eclips·ing
eclip·tic
ecol·o·gy
  ec·o·log·ic
  ec·o·log·i·cal
  ecol·o·gist
eco·nom·ic
eco·nom·i·cal
eco·nom·ics
econ·o·mist
econ·o·mize
  econ·o·mized
  econ·o·miz·ing
  econ·o·miz·er
econ·o·my
  econ·o·mies
ec·o·sys·tem
ec·ru
ec·sta·sy
  ec·sta·sies
ec·stat·ic
  ec·stat·i·cal
ec·to·morph
  ec·to·mor·phic
ec·to·plasm
Ec·ua·dor
ec·u·men·i·cal
  ec·u·men·ic
  ec·u·men·i·cal·ly
  ec·u·men·ism
ec·ze·ma
ed·dy
  ed·dies
  ed·died
  ed·dy·ing
ede·ma
  ede·ma·ta
Eden
eden·tate
edge
  edged
  edg·ing
edge·wise
Edge·worth
edgy
  edg·i·er
  edg·i·est
  edg·i·ness
ed·i·ble
edict
ed·i·fice
ed·i·fy
  ed·i·fied
  ed·i·fy·ing
  ed·i·fi·ca·tion
Ed·in·burgh
ed·it
edi·tion
ed·i·tor
  ed·i·tor·ship
ed·i·to·ri·al
  ed·i·to·ri·al·ly

ed·i·to·ri·al·ize
  ed·i·to·ri·al·ized
  ed·i·to·ri·al·iz·ing
ed·u·cate
  ed·u·cat·ed
  ed·u·cat·ing
  ed·u·ca·ble
  ed·u·ca·tive
  ed·u·ca·tor
ed·u·ca·tion
  ed·u·ca·tion·al
educe
  educed
  educ·ing
  educ·i·ble
  educ·tion
eel
  eel-like
  eely
ee·rie
  ee·ri·er
  ee·ri·est
  ee·ri·ly
  ee·ri·ness
ef·face
  ef·faced
  ef·fac·ing
  ef·face·ment
  ef·fac·er
ef·fect
ef·fec·tive
  ef·fec·tive·ness
  ef·fec·tive·ly
  ef·fec·tive·ness
ef·fec·tu·al
  ef·fec·tu·al·i·ty
  ef·fec·tu·ate
  ef·fec·tu·at·ed
  ef·fec·tu·at·ing
ef·fem·i·nate
  ef·fem·i·na·cy
  ef·fem·i·na·cies
  ef·fem·i·nate·ly
ef·fer·vesce
  ef·fer·vesced
  ef·fer·vesc·ing
  ef·fer·ves·cence
  ef·fer·ves·cent
ef·fete
ef·fi·ca·cious
ef·fi·ca·cy
  ef·fi·ca·cies
ef·fi·cien·cy
  ef·fi·cien·cies
ef·fi·cient
  ef·fi·cient·ly
ef·fi·gy
  ef·fi·gies
ef·flo·resce
  ef·flo·resced
  ef·flo·resc·ing
  ef·flo·res·cence
  ef·flo·res·cent
ef·flu·ent
ef·flu·ence

ef·flu·vi·um
ef·flu·via
ef·flu·vi·ums
ef·flu·vi·al
ef·fort
ef·fort·less
ef·fort·less·ly
ef·fort·less·ness
ef·fron·tery
ef·fron·ter·ies
ef·ful·gent
ef·ful·gence
ef·fuse
ef·fused
ef·fus·ing
ef·fu·sion
ef·fu·sive
ef·fu·sive·ly
ef·fu·sive·ness
egal·i·tar·i·an
egal·i·tar·i·an·ism
egg·head
egg·nog
egg·plant
egg·shell
ego
egos
ego·cen·tric
ego·ism
ego·ist
ego·is·tic
ego·tism
ego·tist
ego·tis·tic
ego·tis·ti·cal
egre·gious
egre·gious·ly
egress
egret
Egypt
Egyp·tian
ei·der·down
Eif·fel
eight
eighth
eight·ball
eight·een
eight·eenth
eight·fold
eighty
eight·ies
eight·i·eth
Ein·stein
Ei·sen·how·er
ei·ther
ejac·u·late
ejac·u·lat·ed
ejac·u·lat·ing
ejac·u·la·tion
ejac·u·la·to·ry
eject
ejec·tion
eject·ment
ejec·tor
eke

eked
ek·ing
elab·o·rate
elab·o·rat·ed
elab·o·rat·ing
elab·o·rate·ly
elab·o·rate·ness
elab·o·ra·tion
élan
elapse
elapsed
elaps·ing
elas·tic
elas·ti·cal·ly
elas·tic·i·ty
elate
elat·ed
elat·ing
ela·tion
El·ba
el·bow
el·bow·room
el·der
eld·er
eld·er·ship
el·der·ly
eld·er·li·ness
eld·est
El Do·ra·do
El·e·a·zar
elect
elec·tion
elec·tion·eer
elec·tive
elec·tor
elec·tor·al
elec·tor·ate
elec·tric
elec·tri·cal
elec·tri·cal·ly
elec·tri·cian
elec·tric·i·ty
elec·tri·fy
elec·tri·fied
elec·tri·fy·ing
elec·tri·fi·ca·tion
elec·tri·fi·er
elec·tro·car·di·o·graph
elec·tro·cute
elec·tro·cut·ed
elec·tro·cut·ing
elec·tro·cu·tion
elec·trode
elec·tro·dy·nam·ics
elec·trol·y·sis
elec·tro·lyze
elec·tro·lyzed
elec·tro·lyz·ing
elec·tro·lyte
elec·tro·lyt·ic
elec·tro·mag·net
elec·tro·mag·net·ism
elec·tro·mag·net·ic
elec·tron
elec·tron·ics

elec·tron·ic
elec·tron·i·cal·ly
elec·tro·plate
elec·tro·plat·ed
elec·tro·plat·ing
elec·tro·ther·a·py
elec·trum
el·ee·mos·y·nary
el·e·gant
el·e·gance
el·e·gan·cy
el·e·gant·ly
el·e·gy
el·e·gies
el·e·gi·ac
el·e·gist
el·e·gize
el·e·gized
el·e·giz·ing
el·e·ment
el·e·men·tal
el·e·men·tal·ly
el·e·men·ta·ry
el·e·men·ta·ri·ly
el·e·phant
el·e·phan·tine
el·e·vate
el·e·vat·ed
el·e·vat·ing
el·e·va·tion
el·e·va·tor
elev·en
elev·enth
elf
elves
elf·in
elf·ish
El·gin
Eli·as
elic·it
el·i·gi·ble
el·i·gi·bil·i·ty
el·i·gi·bly
Eli·jah
elim·i·nate
elim·i·nat·ed
elim·i·nat·ing
elim·i·na·tion
elim·i·na·tor
Eli·sha
elite
elit·ism
elit·ist
elix·ir
Eliz·a·beth·an
el·lipse
el·lip·sis
el·lip·ses
el·lip·ti·cal
el·lip·tic
el·lip·ti·cal·ly
El·mi·ra
el·o·cu·tion
el·o·cu·tion·ary
el·o·cu·tion·ist

elon·gate
elon·gat·ed
elon·gat·ing
elon·ga·tion
elope
eloped
elop·ing
elope·ment
elop·er
el·o·quence
el·o·quent
el·o·quent·ly
El Paso
else·where
elu·ci·date
elu·ci·dat·ed
elu·ci·dat·ing
elu·ci·da·tion
elu·ci·da·tor
elude
elud·ed
elud·ing
elu·sion
elu·sive
elu·so·ry
elu·sive·ly
elu·sive·ness
elv·ish
Ely·see
ema·ci·ate
ema·ci·at·ed
ema·ci·at·ing
ema·ci·a·tion
em·a·nate
em·a·nat·ed
em·a·nat·ing
em·a·na·tion
eman·ci·pate
eman·ci·pat·ed
eman·ci·pat·ing
eman·ci·pa·tor
emas·cu·late
emas·cu·lat·ed
emas·cu·lat·ing
emas·cu·la·tion
em·balm
em·balm·er
em·balm·ment
em·bank·ment
em·bar·go
em·bar·goes
em·bar·goed
em·bar·go·ing
em·bark
em·bar·ka·tion
em·bark·ment
em·bar·rass
em·bar·rass·ing·ly
em·bar·rass·ment
em·bas·sy
em·bas·sies
em·bat·tle
em·bat·tled
em·bat·tling
em·bat·tle·ment

em·bed
  em·bed·ded
  em·bed·ding
em·bel·lish
  em·bel·lish·ment
em·ber
em·bez·zle
  em·bez·zled
  em·bez·zling
  em·bez·zle·ment
  em·bez·zler
em·bit·ter
  em·bit·ter·ment
em·bla·zon
  em·bla·zon·er
  em·blaz·on·ment
  em·bla·zon·ry
em·blem
  em·blem·at·ic
  em·blem·at·i·cal
em·bod·y
  em·bod·ied
  em·bod·y·ing
  em·bod·i·ment
em·bold·en
em·bo·lism
em·bo·lus
em·bos·om
em·boss
  em·boss·ment
em·bou·chure
em·brace
  em·braced
  em·brac·ing
em·broi·der
  em·broi·dery
  em·broi·der·ies
em·broil
  em·broil·ment
em·bryo
  em·bry·os
  em·bry·on·ic
  em·bry·ol·o·gy
em·cee
  em·ceed
  em·cee·ing
emend
em·er·ald
emerge
  emerged
  emerg·ing
  emer·gence
  emer·gent
emer·gen·cy
  emer·gen·cies
emer·i·tus
Em·er·son
em·ery
emet·ic
em·i·grant
em·i·grate
  em·i·grat·ed
  em·i·grat·ing
  em·i·gra·tion
émi·gré

émi·grés
em·i·nence
em·i·nent
em·i·ent·ly
em·i·nent do·main
em·is·sary
  em·is·sar·ies
emis·sion
emis·sive
emit
  emit·ted
  emit·ting
  emit·ter
Em·man·u·el
emol·lient
emol·u·ment
emote
  emot·ed
  emot·ing
  emo·tive
emo·tion
  emo·tion·al
  emo·tion·al·ly
  emo·tion·al·ism
em·pan·el
em·pa·thize
  em·pa·thized
  em·pa·thiz·ing
em·pa·thy
  em·pa·thet·ic
  em·path·ic
em·per·or
em·pha·sis
  em·pha·ses
em·pha·size
  em·pha·sized
  em·pha·siz·ing
em·phat·ic
  em·phat·i·cal·ly
em·phy·se·ma
em·pire
em·pir·i·cal
  em·pir·i·cal·ly
  em·pir·i·cism
  em·pir·i·cist
em·place·ment
em·ploy
  em·ploy·a·ble
  em·ploy·ee
  em·ploy·er
  em·ploy·ment
em·po·ri·um
  em·po·ri·ums
  em·po·ria
em·pow·er
em·press
emp·ty
  emp·ti·er
  emp·ti·est
  emp·tied
  emp·ty·ing
  emp·ti·ly
  emp·ti·ness
emp·ty-hand·ed
emp·ty-head·ed

emu
em·u·late
  em·u·lat·ed
  em·u·lat·ing
  em·u·la·tion
emul·si·fy
  emul·si·fied
  emul·si·fy·ing
  emul·si·fi·ca·tion
  emul·si·fi·er
emul·sion
  emul·sive
en·a·ble
  en·a·bled
  en·a·bling
en·act
enam·el
  enam·eled
  enam·el·ing
  enam·el·er
  enam·el·ware
en·am·or
  en·am·ored·ness
en·camp
  en·camp·ment
en·cap·su·late
  en·cap·su·lat·ed
  en·cap·su·lat·ing
  en·cap·sule
en·case
  en·cased
  en·cas·ing
en·ceinte
en·ceph·a·li·tis
  en·ceph·a·lit·ic
en·ceph·a·lon
  en·ceph·a·la
en·chant
  en·chant·er
  en·chant·ress
  en·chant·ing
  en·chant·ing·ly
  en·chant·ment
en·chi·la·da
en·cir·cle
  en·cir·cled
  en·cir·cling
  en·cir·cle·ment
en·clave
en·close
  en·closed
  en·clos·ing
  en·clo·sure
en·code
  en·cod·ed
  en·cod·ing
en·co·mi·ast
en·com·pass
  en·com·pass·ment
en·core
en·coun·ter
en·cour·age
  en·cour·aged
  en·cour·ag·ing
  en·cour·ag·ing·ly

en·croach
  en·croach·er
  en·croach·ment
en·crust
  en·crus·ta·tion
en·cum·ber
  en·cum·brance
en·cy·clo·pe·dia
en·cy·clo·pe·dic
  en·cy·clo·pe·di·cal
  en·cy·clo·pe·di·cal·ly
en·cyst
en·dan·ger
  en·dan·ger·ment
en·dear
  en·dear·ment
en·deav·or
en·dem·ic
  en·dem·i·cal
  en·dem·i·cal·ly
end·ing
end·less
  end·less·ly
  end·less·ness
end·most
en·do·crine
  en·do·cri·nol·o·gy
  en·do·crin·o·log·ic
  en·do·crin·o·log·i·cal
  en·do·cri·nol·o·gist
en·dog·e·nous
en·dorse
  en·dorsed
  en·dors·ing
  en·dor·see
  en·dor·ser
  en·dorse·ment
en·do·sperm
en·dow
  en·dow·ment
en·due
  en·dued
  en·du·ing
en·dur·ance
en·dure
  en·dured
  en·dur·ing
  en·dur·a·ble
  en·dur·a·bly
  en·dur·ing·ness
end·ways
en·e·ma
en·e·my
  en·e·mies
en·er·get·ic
  en·er·get·i·cal
  en·er·get·i·cal·ly
en·er·gize
  en·er·gized
  en·er·giz·ing
  en·er·giz·er
en·er·gy
  en·er·gies
en·er·vate
  en·er·vat·ed

en·er·vat·ing
en·er·va·tion
en·fee·ble
en·fee·bled
en·fee·bling
en·fee·ble·ment
en·fi·lade
en·fi·lad·ed
en·fi·lad·ing
en·fold
en·force
en·forced
en·forc·ing
en·force·a·ble
en·force·ment
en·forc·er
en·fran·chise
en·fran·chised
en·fran·chis·ing
en·fran·chise·ment
en·gage
en·gaged
en·gag·ing
en·gage·ment
en·gen·der
en·gine
en·gi·neer
en·gi·neer·ing
En·gland
En·glish
en·gorge
en·gorged
en·gorg·ing
en·gorge·ment
en·grave
en·graved
en·grav·ing
en·grav·er
en·gross
en·grossed
en·gross·er
en·gross·ing
en·gross·ing·ly
en·gross·ment
en·gulf
en·gulf·ment
en·hance
en·hanced
en·hanc·ing
en·hance·ment
enig·ma
en·ig·mat·ic
en·ig·mat·i·cal
en·ig·mat·i·cal·ly
en·join
en·join·er
en·join·ment
en·joy
en·joy·a·ble
en·joy·a·ble·ness
en·joy·a·bly
en·joy·ment
en·large
en·larged
en·larg·ing

en·large·a·ble
en·larg·er
en·large·ment
en·light·en
en·light·en·ment
en·list
en·list·ed
en·list·ment
en·liv·en
en·liv·en·er
en·mesh
en·mi·ty
en·mi·ties
en·no·ble
en·no·bled
en·no·bling
en·no·ble·ment
en·no·bler
en·nui
enor·mi·ty
enor·mi·ties
enor·mous
enor·mous·ly
enor·mous·ness
enough
en·plane
en·planed
en·plan·ing
en·rage
en·raged
en·rag·ing
en·rap·ture
en·rap·tured
en·rap·tur·ing
en·rapt
en·rich
en·rich·er
en·rich·ment
en·roll
en·roll·ment
en route
en·sconce
en·sconced
en·sconc·ing
en·sem·ble
en·shrine
en·shrined
en·shrin·ing
en·shroud
en·sign
en·si·lage
en·si·laged
en·si·lag·ing
en·slave
en·slaved
en·slav·ing
en·slave·ment
en·slav·er
en·snare
en·snared
en·snar·ing
en·snare·ment
en·snar·er
en·snar·ing·ly
en·sue

en·sued
en·su·ing
en·su·ing·ly
en·sure
en·sured
en·sur·ing
en·sur·er
en·tail
en·tail·er
en·tail·ment
en·tan·gle
en·tan·gled
en·tan·gling
en·tan·gle·ment
en·tan·gler
en·tente
en·ter
en·ter·a·ble
en·ter·i·tis
en·ter·prise
en·ter·pris·ing
en·ter·pris·ing·ly
en·ter·tain
en·ter·tain·er
en·ter·tain·ing
en·ter·tain·ing·ly
en·ter·tain·ment
en·thrall
en·thralled
en·thrall·ing
en·thrall·ment
en·throne
en·throned
en·thron·ing
en·throne·ment
en·thuse
en·thused
en·thus·ing
en·thu·si·asm
en·thu·si·ast
en·thu·si·as·tic
en·thu·si·as·ti·cal·ly
en·tice
en·ticed
en·tic·ing
en·tice·ment
en·tic·er
en·tic·ing·ly
en·tire
en·tire·ly
en·tire·ness
en·tire·ty
en·tire·ties
en·ti·tle
en·ti·tled
en·ti·tling
en·ti·tle·ment
en·ti·ty
en·ti·ties
en·to·mol·o·gy
en·to·mol·o·gies
en·to·mo·log·ic
en·to·mo·log·i·cal
en·to·mo·log·i·cal·ly
en·to·mol·o·gist

en·tou·rage
en·trails
en·train
en·train·er
en·trance
en·trance·way
en·trance
en·tranced
en·tranc·ing
en·trance·ment
en·tranc·ing·ly
en·trant
en·trap
en·trapped
en·trap·ping
en·trap·ment
en·treat
en·treat·ing·ly
en·treat·ment
en·treaty
en·tree
en·trench
en·trench·ment
en·tre·pre·neur
en·tre·pre·neur·i·al
en·tre·pre·neur·ship
en·tro·py
en·trust
en·trust·ment
en·try
en·tries
en·twine
en·twined
en·twin·ing
enu·mer·ate
enu·mer·at·ed
enu·mer·at·ing
enu·mer·a·tion
enu·mer·a·tive
enu·mer·a·tor
enun·ci·ate
enun·ci·at·ed
enun·ci·at·ing
enun·ci·a·tion
enun·ci·a·tive
enun·ci·a·tor
en·u·re·sis
en·u·ret·ic
en·vel·op
en·vel·oped
en·vel·op·ing
en·ve·lope
en·vi·a·ble
en·vi·a·ble·ness
en·vi·a·bly
en·vi·ous
en·vi·ous·ly
en·vi·ous·ness
en·vi·ron
en·vi·ron·ment
en·vi·ron·men·tal
en·vi·ron·men·tal·ly
en·vi·rons
en·vis·age
en·vis·aged

en·vis·ag·ing
en·vi·sion
en·voy
en·vy
 en·vies
en·vied
en·vy·ing
en·vi·er
en·vy·ing·ly
en·zyme
 en·zy·mat·ic
 en·zy·mat·i·cal·ly
eon
ep·au·let
épée
 épée·ist
ephed·rine
ephem·er·al
 ephem·er·al·ness
 ephem·er·al·ly
Ephe·sian
Eph·e·sus
Ephra·im
Eph·ra·ta
ep·ic
 ep·i·cal
ep·i·cen·ter
ep·i·cure
 epi·cu·re·an
ep·i·dem·ic
 ep·i·dem·i·cal·ly
ep·i·der·mis
 ep·i·der·mal
 ep·i·der·mic
ep·i·glot·tis
ep·i·gram
 ep·i·gram·mat·ic
 ep·i·gram·mat·i·cal
 ep·i·gram·mat·i·cal·ly
 ep·i·gram·ma·tist
ep·i·gram·ma·tize
 ep·i·gram·ma·tized
 ep·i·gram·ma·tiz·ing
ep·i·lep·sy
ep·i·lep·tic
ep·i·logue
 ep·i·log
Epiph·a·ny
 Epiph·a·nies
epis·co·pa·cy
 epis·co·pa·cies
epis·co·pal
epis·co·pa·lian
 epis·co·pa·lian·ism
epis·co·pate
ep·i·sode
 ep·i·sod·ic
 ep·i·sod·i·cal
 ep·i·sod·i·cal·ly
epis·te·mol·o·gy
 epis·te·mo·log·i·cal
 epis·te·mol·o·gist
epis·tle
epis·to·lary
ep·i·taph

ep·i·taph·ic
ep·i·taph·ist
ep·i·thet
 ep·i·thet·ic
 ep·i·thet·i·cal
epit·o·me
epit·o·mize
 epit·o·mized
 epit·o·miz·ing
ep·och
 ep·och·al
ep·oxy
ep·oxy res·in
ep·si·lon
Ep·som
eq·ua·ble
 eq·ua·bil·i·ty
 eq·ua·ble·ness
 eq·ua·bly
equal
 equaled
 equal·ling
 equal·ly
 equal·ness
equal·i·tar·i·an
 equal·i·tar·i·an·ism
equal·i·ty
 equal·i·ties
equal·ize
 equal·ized
 equal·iz·ing
 equal·i·za·tion
 equal·iz·er
equa·nim·i·ty
equate
 equat·ed
 equat·ing
equa·tion
 equa·tion·al
 equa·tion·al·ly
equa·tor
equa·to·ri·al
 equa·to·ri·al·ly
eques·tri·an
 eques·tri·enne
equi·dis·tance
equi·dis·tant
 equi·dis·tant·ly
equi·lat·er·al
equi·li·brate
 equi·li·brat·ed
 equi·li·brat·ing
 equi·li·bra·tion
 equi·li·bra·tor
equi·lib·ri·um
 equi·lib·ri·ums
 equi·lib·ria
equine
equi·noc·tial
equi·nox
equip
 equipped
 equip·ping
 equip·per
eq·ui·page

equip·ment
equi·poise
eq·ui·ta·ble
  eq·ui·ta·ble·ness
  eq·ui·ta·bly
eq·ui·ty
  eq·ui·ties
equiv·a·lence
  equiv·a·len·cy
equiv·a·lent
  equiv·a·lent·ly
equiv·o·cal
  equiv·o·cal·ly
  equiv·o·cal·ness
equiv·o·cate
  equiv·o·cat·ed
  equiv·o·cat·ing
  equiv·o·ca·tor
  equiv·o·ca·tion
era
erad·i·cate
  erad·i·cat·ed
  erad·i·cat·ing
  erad·i·ca·ble
  erad·i·ca·tion
  erad·i·ca·tive
  erad·i·ca·tor
erase
  erased
  eras·ing
  eras·a·bil·i·ty
  eras·a·ble
eras·er
Eras·mus
eras·ure
Er·a·tos·the·nes
erect
  erect·a·ble
  erect·er
  erec·tive
  erect·ly
  erect·ness
erec·tile
  erec·til·i·ty
erec·tion
erec·tor
er·go
Er·hard
Er·ic·son
Er·in
Er·i·trea
er·mine
erode
  erod·ed
  erod·ing
erog·e·nous
Er·os
ero·sion
erot·ic
  erot·i·cal·ly
  erot·i·cism
err
  err·ing·ly
er·rand
er·rant

er·rant·ly
er·rat·ic
  er·rat·i·cal·ly
er·ra·tum
  er·ra·ta
er·ro·ne·ous
  er·ro·ne·ous·ly
  er·ro·ne·ous·ness
er·ror
  er·ror·less
er·satz
erst·while
er·u·dite
  er·u·dite·ly
  er·u·dite·ness
  er·u·di·tion
erupt
  erup·tion
  erup·tive
  erup·tive·ly
  erup·tive·ness
es·ca·lade
  es·ca·lad·ed
  es·ca·lad·ing
  es·ca·lad·er
es·ca·late
  es·ca·lat·ed
  es·ca·lat·ing
  es·ca·la·tion
  es·ca·la·tor
es·cal·lop
es·ca·pade
es·cape
  es·caped
  es·cap·ing
  es·cap·er
  es·ca·pee
  es·cap·ist
  es·cap·ism
es·carp·ment
es·chew
  es·chew·al
  es·chew·er
es·cort
es·cri·toire
es·crow
es·cutch·eon
  es·cutch·eoned
Es·ki·mo
  Es·ki·mos
esoph·a·gus
es·o·ter·ic
  es·o·ter·i·cal
  es·o·ter·i·cal·ly
es·pal·ier
es·pe·cial
  es·pe·cial·ly
  es·pe·cial·ness
Es·pe·ran·to
es·pi·o·nage
es·pla·nade
es·pouse
  es·poused
  es·pous·ing
  es·pous·er

es·pous·al
es·pres·so
es·prit
es·prit de corps
es·py
　es·pied
　es·py·ing
es·quire
　es·quired
　es·quir·ing
es·say
　es·say·er
　es·say·ist
es·sence
es·sen·tial
　es·sen·ti·al·i·ty
　es·sen·tial·ly
　es·sen·tial·ness
Es·sex
es·tab·lish
　es·tab·lish·er
　es·tab·lish·ment
es·tate
es·teem
es·thete
es·thet·ic
es·ti·ma·ble
　es·ti·ma·ble·ness
　es·ti·ma·bly
es·ti·mate
　es·ti·mat·ed
　es·ti·mat·ing
　es·ti·ma·tive
　es·ti·ma·tor
es·ti·ma·tion
Es·to·nia
es·trange
　es·tranged
　es·trang·ing
　es·trange·ment
　es·tran·ger
es·trus
es·tu·ary
　es·tu·ar·ies
　es·tu·ar·i·al
et cet·era
etch
　etch·er
etch·ing
eter·nal
　eter·nal·ly
eter·ni·ty
eter·nize
　eter·nized
　eter·niz·ing
　eter·ni·za·tion
eth·a·nol
ether
ethe·re·al
　ethe·re·al·i·ty
　ethe·re·al·ly
　ethe·re·al·ness
　ethe·re·al·ize
　ethe·re·al·ized
　ethe·re·al·iz·ing

ethe·re·al·i·za·tion
eth·ic
eth·i·cal
　eth·i·cal·ly
eth·ics
Ethi·o·pia
eth·nic
　eth·ni·cal
　eth·ni·cal·ly
eth·nol·o·gy
eth·yl
eti·ol·o·gy
　eti·o·lo·gist
　eti·o·log·i·cal
　eti·o·log·i·cal·ly
et·i·quette
Etrus·can
etude
et·y·mol·o·gy
　et·y·mol·o·gies
　et·y·mo·log·ic
　et·y·mo·log·i·cal
　et·y·mol·o·gist
eu·ca·lyp·tus
　eu·ca·lyp·tus·es
　eu·ca·lyp·ti
Eu·cha·rist
　Eu·cha·ris·tic
　Eu·cha·ris·ti·cal
Eu·clid
Eu·clid·e·an
eu·gen·ic
　eu·gen·i·cal·ly
eu·gen·ics
eu·lo·gize
　eu·lo·gized
　eu·lo·giz·ing
　eu·lo·giz·er
eu·lo·gy
　eu·lo·gies
　eu·lo·gist
　eu·lo·gis·tic
　eu·lo·gis·ti·cal·ly
eu·nuch
eu·phe·mism
　eu·phe·mist
　eu·phe·mis·tic
　eu·phe·mis·ti·cal
　eu·phe·mis·ti·cal·ly
eu·phe·mize
　eu·phe·mized
　eu·phe·miz·ing
eu·pho·ni·ous
　eu·pho·ni·ous·ly
　eu·pho·ni·ous·ness
eu·pho·ny
　eu·phon·ic
　eu·phon·i·cal
　eu·phon·i·cal·ly
eu·pho·ria
　eu·phor·ic
Eu·phra·tes
Eur·asia
Eur·a·sian
eu·re·ka

Eu·rip·i·des
Eu·rope
Eu·ro·pe·an
Eu·ro·pe·an·ize
  Eu·ro·pe·an·ized
  Eu·ro·pe·an·iz·ing
  Eu·ro·pe·an·i·za·tion
Eu·sta·chian
eu·tha·na·sia
evac·u·ate
  evac·u·at·ed
  evac·u·at·ing
  evac·u·a·tion
  evac·u·a·tive
  evac·u·a·tor
evac·u·ee
evade
  evad·ed
  evad·ing
  evad·a·ble
  evad·er
  evad·ing·ly
eval·u·ate
  eval·u·at·ed
  eval·u·at·ing
  eval·u·a·tion
  eval·u·a·tor
ev·a·nesce
  ev·a·nesced
  ev·a·nesc·ing
ev·a·nes·cent
  ev·a·nes·cence
  ev·a·nes·cent·ly
evan·gel
evan·gel·i·cal
  evan·gel·ic
  evan·gel·i·cal·ism
  evan·gel·i·cal·ly
  evan·gel·i·cal·ness
Evan·ge·line
evan·ge·lism
  evan·ge·lis·tic
  evan·ge·lis·ti·cal·ly
evan·ge·list
evan·ge·lize
  evan·ge·lized
  evan·ge·liz·ing
  evan·ge·li·za·tion
  evan·ge·liz·er
Ev·ans·ton
Ev·ans·ville
evap·o·rate
  evap·o·rat·ed
  evap·o·rat·ing
  evap·o·ra·ble
  evap·o·ra·tion
  evap·o·ra·tive
  evap·o·ra·tor
eva·sion
eva·sive
  eva·sive·ly
  eva·sive·ness
even
  even·ly
  even·ness

even-hand·ed
eve·ning
event
event·ful
  event·ful·ly
  event·ful·ness
even·tu·al
  even·tu·al·ly
  even·tu·al·i·ty
  even·tu·al·i·ties
even·tu·ate
  even·tu·at·ed
  even·tu·at·ing
ev·er
Ev·er·est
Ev·er·ett
Ev·er·glades
ev·er·green
ev·er·last·ing
  ev·er·last·ing·ly
  ev·er·last·ing·ness
ev·er·more
evert
  ever·si·ble
  ever·sion
ev·ery
ev·ery·body
ev·ery·day
ev·ery·one
ev·ery·thing
ev·ery·where
evict
evic·tion
evic·tor
ev·i·dence
  ev·i·denced
  ev·i·denc·ing
ev·i·dent
  ev·i·dent·ly
ev·i·den·tial
  ev·i·den·tial·ly
evil
  evil-do·er
  evil-do·ing
  evil·ly
  evil·ness
evil-mind·ed
  evil-mind·ed·ly
  evil-mind·ed·ness
evince
  evinced
  evinc·ing
  evin·ci·ble
evis·cer·ate
  evis·cer·at·ed
  evis·cer·at·ing
  evis·cer·a·tion
evoke
  evoked
  evok·ing
  ev·o·ca·tion
ev·o·lu·tion
  ev·o·lu·tion·al
  ev·o·lu·tion·ary
  ev·o·lu·tion·ism

ev·o·lu·tion·ist
evolve
  evolved
  evolv·ing
  evolv·a·ble
  evolve·ment
  evolv·er
ew·er
ex·ac·er·bate
  ex·ac·er·bat·ed
  ex·ac·er·bat·ing
  ex·ac·er·ba·tion
ex·act
  ex·act·a·ble
  ex·ac·tor
  ex·act·ing
  ex·act·ing·ly
  ex·act·ing·ness
  ex·act·i·tude
  ex·act·ly
ex·ag·ger·ate
  ex·ag·ger·at·ed
  ex·ag·ger·at·ing
  ex·ag·ger·a·tion
  ex·ag·ger·a·tor
ex·alt
  ex·alt·er
ex·al·ta·tion
  ex·alt·ed
  ex·alt·ed·ly
  ex·alt·ed·ness
ex·am
ex·am·i·na·tion
ex·am·ine
  ex·am·ined
  ex·am·in·ing
  ex·am·in·a·ble
  ex·am·i·nant
  ex·am·in·er
  ex·am·i·nee
ex·am·ple
  ex·am·pled
  ex·am·pling
ex·as·per·ate
  ex·as·per·at·ed
  ex·as·per·at·ing
  ex·as·per·a·tion
Ex·cal·i·bur
ex·ca·vate
  ex·ca·vat·ed
  ex·ca·vat·ing
  ex·ca·va·tion
  ex·ca·va·tor
ex·ceed
  ex·ceed·ing
  ex·ceed·ing·ly
ex·cel
  ex·celled
  ex·cel·ling
  ex·cel·lence
  ex·cel·len·cy
  ex·cel·len·cies
  ex·cel·lent
  ex·cel·lent·ly
  ex·cel·si·or

ex·cept
ex·cept·ing
ex·cep·tion
  ex·cep·tion·a·ble
  ex·cep·tion·al
ex·cerpt
ex·cess
ex·ces·sive
  ex·ces·sive·ly
  ex·ces·sive·ness
ex·change
  ex·changed
  ex·chang·ing
  ex·change·a·bil·i·ty
  ex·change·a·ble
  ex·chan·ger
ex·cheq·uer
ex·cise
  ex·cised
  ex·cis·ing
  ex·cis·a·ble
  ex·ci·sion
ex·cit·a·ble
  ex·cit·a·bil·i·ty
  ex·cit·a·bly
ex·ci·ta·tion
ex·cite
  ex·cit·ed
  ex·cit·ing
ex·cit·ed
  ex·cit·ed·ly
  ex·cit·ed·ness
ex·cite·ment
ex·cit·ing
  ex·cit·ing·ly
ex·claim
ex·cla·ma·tion
ex·clam·a·to·ry
  ex·clam·a·to·ri·ly
ex·clude
  ex·clud·ed
  ex·clud·ing
  ex·clud·a·bil·i·ty
  ex·clud·a·ble
  ex·clud·er
ex·clu·sion
ex·clu·sive
  ex·clu·sive·ly
  ex·clu·sive·ness
  ex·clu·siv·i·ty
ex·com·mu·ni·cate
  ex·com·mu·ni·cat·ed
  ex·com·mu·ni·cat·ing
  ex·com·mu·ni·cant
  ex·com·mu·ni·ca·ble
  ex·com·mu·ni·ca·tion
  ex·com·mu·ni·ca·tive
  ex·com·mu·ni·ca·to·ry
ex·co·ri·ate
  ex·co·ri·at·ed
  ex·co·ri·at·ing
  ex·co·ri·a·tion
ex·cre·ment
  ex·cre·men·tal
ex·cres·cence

ex·cres·cent
ex·cre·ta
 ex·cre·tal
ex·crete
 ex·cret·ed
 ex·cret·ing
ex·cre·tion
ex·cru·ci·ate
 ex·cru·ci·at·ed
 ex·cru·ci·at·ing
 ex·cru·ci·at·ing·ly
 ex·cru·ci·a·tion
ex·cul·pate
 ex·cul·pat·ed
 ex·cul·pat·ing
 ex·cul·pa·tion
 ex·cul·pa·to·ry
ex·cur·sion
 ex·cur·sion·al
 ex·cur·sion·ary
 ex·cur·sion·ist
ex·cur·sive
 ex·cur·sive·ly
 ex·cur·sive·ness
ex·cus·a·to·ry
ex·cuse
 ex·cused
 ex·cus·ing
 ex·cus·a·ble
 ex·cus·a·bly
 ex·cus·er
ex·cuse
 ex·cuse·less
 ex·cus·ing·ly
ex·e·cra·ble
 ex·e·cra·ble·ness
 ex·e·cra·bly
ex·e·crate
 ex·e·crat·ed
 ex·e·crat·ing
 ex·e·cra·tive
 ex·e·cra·tor
 ex·e·cra·tion
ex·e·cute
 ex·e·cut·ed
 ex·e·cut·ing
 ex·e·cut·a·ble
 ex·e·cut·er
ex·e·cu·tion
 ex·e·cu·tion·er
ex·ec·u·tive
 ex·ec·u·tive·ly
ex·ec·u·tor
 ex·ec·u·tor·ship
ex·e·ge·sis
 ex·e·ge·ses
ex·em·plar
ex·em·pla·ry
 ex·em·pla·ri·ly
 ex·em·pla·ri·ness
ex·em·pli·fy
 ex·em·pli·fied
 ex·em·pli·fy·ing
 ex·em·pli·fi·a·ble
 ex·em·pli·fi·ca·tion

ex·empt
ex·emp·tion
ex·er·cise
 ex·er·cised
 ex·er·cis·ing
 ex·er·cis·er
 ex·er·cis·a·ble
ex·ert
ex·er·tion
Ex·e·ter
ex·fo·li·ate
 ex·fo·li·at·ed
 ex·fo·li·at·ing
 ex·fo·li·a·tion
ex·ha·la·tion
ex·hale
 ex·haled
 ex·hal·ing
 ex·hal·ant
ex·haust
 ex·haust·er
 ex·haust·i·bil·i·ty
 ex·haust·i·ble
 ex·haust·ed
 ex·haust·ed·ly
 ex·haus·tion
 ex·haust·ing
 ex·haus·tive
 ex·haus·tive·ly
 ex·haus·tive·ness
ex·hib·it
 ex·hib·it·a·ble
 ex·hib·i·tor
 ex·hib·i·to·ry
ex·hi·bi·tion
 ex·hi·bi·tion·ism
 ex·hi·bi·tion·ist
 ex·hi·bi·tion·is·tic
ex·hil·a·rate
 ex·hil·a·rat·ed
 ex·hil·a·rat·ing
 ex·hil·a·ra·tion
 ex·hil·a·ra·tive
 ex·hil·a·ra·to·ry
ex·hort
 ex·hor·ta·tive
 ex·hor·ta·to·ry
 ex·hort·er
 ex·hort·ing·ly
 ex·hor·ta·tion
ex·hume
 ex·humed
 ex·hum·ing
ex·i·gen·cy
 ex·i·gen·cies
ex·i·gent
 ex·i·gent·ly
ex·ile
 ex·iled
 ex·il·ing
 ex·il·a·ble
 ex·il·er
ex·ist
 ex·ist·ence
 ex·ist·ent

ex·is·ten·tial
ex·is·ten·tial·ly
ex·it
ex li·bris
ex·o·dus
ex of·fi·cio
ex·og·a·my
ex·og·a·mous
ex·og·e·nous
ex·og·e·nous·ly
ex·on·er·ate
ex·on·er·at·ed
ex·on·er·at·ing
ex·on·er·a·tion
ex·on·er·a·tive
ex·or·bi·tant
ex·or·bi·tance
ex·or·bi·tant·ly
ex·or·cise
ex·or·cised
ex·or·cis·ing
ex·or·cism
ex·or·cist
ex·o·tic
ex·ot·i·cal·ly
ex·ot·i·cism
ex·pand
ex·pand·er
ex·panse
ex·pan·si·ble
ex·pan·si·bil·i·ty
ex·pan·sion
ex·pan·sion·ism
ex·pan·sion·ist
ex·pan·sive
ex·pan·sive·ly
ex·pan·sive·ness
ex·pa·ti·ate
ex·pa··ti·at·ed
ex·pa·ti·at·ing
ex·pa·ti·a·tion
ex·pa·tri·ate
ex·pa·tri·at·ed
ex·pa·tri·at·ing
ex·pa·tri·a·tion
ex·pect
ex·pect·a·ble
ex·pect·a·bly
ex·pect·ing·ly
ex·pect·an·cy
ex·pect·an·cies
ex·pect·ant
ex·pect·ant·ly
ex·pec·ta·tion
ex·pec·to·rate
ex·pec·to·rat·ed
ex·pec·to·rat·ing
ex·pec·to·ra·tion
ex·pe·di·en·cy
ex·pe·di·ent
ex·pe·di·ent·ly
ex·pe·dite
ex·pe·dit·ed
ex·pe·dit·ing
ex·pe·dit·er

ex·pe·di·tion
ex·pe·di·tion·ary
ex·pe·di·tious
ex·pe·di·tious·ly
ex·pe·di·tious·ness
ex·pel
ex·pelled
ex·pel·ling
ex·pend
ex·pend·a·ble
ex·pend·a·bil·i·ty
ex·pend·i·ture
ex·pense
ex·pen·sive
ex·pen·sive·ly
ex·pen·sive·ness
ex·pe·ri·ence
ex·pe·ri·enced
ex·pe·ri·enc·ing
ex·pe·ri·en·tial
ex·pe·ri·en·tial·ly
ex·per·i·ment
ex·per·i·men·ta·tion
ex·per·i·men·tal
ex·per·i·men·tal·ism
ex·per·i·men·tal·ist
ex·per·i·men·tal·ly
ex·pert
ex·pert·ly
ex·pert·ness
ex·per·tise
ex·pi·ate
ex·pi·at·ed
ex·pi·at·ing
ex·pi·a·ble
ex·pi·a·tion
ex·pi·a·tor
ex·pi·a·to·ry
ex·pi·ra·tion
ex·pir·a·to·ry
ex·pire
ex·pired
ex·pir·ing
ex·plain
ex·plain·a·ble
ex·plain·er
ex·pla·na·tion
ex·plan·a·to·ry
ex·plan·a·to·ri·ly
ex·ple·tive
ex·pli·ca·ble
ex·pli·cate
ex·pli·cat·ed
ex·pli·cat·ing
ex·pli·ca·tion
ex·pli·ca·tive
ex·pli·ca·tor
ex·plic·it
ex·plic·it·ly
ex·plic·it·ness
ex·plode
ex·plod·ed
ex·plod·ing
ex·plod·er
ex·ploit

ex·ploit·a·ble
ex·ploi·ta·tion
ex·ploit·er
ex·ploit·ive
ex·plore
ex·plo·ra·tion
ex·plor·a·to·ry
ex·plor·er
ex·plo·sion
ex·plo·sive
ex·plo·sive·ly
ex·plo·sive·ness
ex·po·nent
ex·po·nen·tial
ex·po·nen·tial·ly
ex·port
ex·port·a·ble
ex·por·ta·tion
ex·port·er
ex·pose
ex·posed
ex·pos·ing
ex·pos·er
ex·po·sé
ex·po·si·tion
ex·pos·i·tor
ex·pos·i·to·ry
ex post fac·to
ex·pos·tu·late
ex·pos·tu·lat·ed
ex·pos·tu·lat·ing
ex·pos·tu·la·tion
ex·pos·tu·la·tive
ex·pos·tu·la·to·ry
ex·po·sure
ex·pound
ex·pound·er
ex·press
ex·press·er
ex·press·i·ble
ex·pres·sion
ex·pres·sive
ex·pres·sive·ly
ex·pres·sive·ness
ex·press·ly
ex·press·way
ex·pro·pri·ate
ex·pro·pri·at·ed
ex·pro·pri·at·ing
ex·pro·pri·a·tor
ex·pro·pri·a·tion
ex·pul·sion
ex·pul·sive
ex·punge
ex·punged
ex·pung·ing
ex·pung·er
ex·pur·gate
ex·pur·gat·ed
ex·pur·gat·ing
ex·pur·ga·tion
ex·pur·ga·tor
ex·pur·ga·to·ry
ex·pur·ga·to·ri·al
ex·qui·site

ex·qui·site·ly
ex·qui·site·ness
ex·tant
ex·tem·po·ra·ne·ous
ex·tem·po·ra·ne·ous·ly
ex·tem·po·ra·ne·ous·ness
ex·tem·po·rize
ex·tem·po·rized
ex·tem·po·riz·ing
ex·tem·po·ri·za·tion
ex·tem·po·riz·er
ex·tend
ex·tend·i·bil·i·ty
ex·tend·i·ble
ex·tend·ed
ex·tend·ed·ly
ex·tend·ed·ness
ex·tend·er
ex·ten·si·ble
ex·ten·si·bil·i·ty
ex·ten·sion
ex·ten·sion·al
ex·ten·sive
ex·ten·sive·ly
ex·ten·sive·ness
ex·tent
ex·ten·u·ate
ex·ten·u·at·ed
ex·ten·u·at·ing
ex·ten·u·a·tion
ex·ten·u·a·tor
ex·te·ri·or
ex·te·ri·or·ly
ex·ter·mi·nate
ex·ter·mi·nat·ed
ex·ter·mi·nat·ing
ex·ter·mi·na·tion
ex·ter·mi·na·tor
ex·ter·mi·na·to·ry
ex·ter·nal
ex·ter·nal·ly
ex·tinct
ex·tinc·tion
ex·tin·guish
ex·tin·guish·a·ble
ex·tin·guish·er
ex·tin·guish·ment
ex·tir·pate
ex·tir·pat·ed
ex·tir·pat·ing
ex·tir·pa·tion
ex·tir·pa·tive
ex·tol
ex·tolled
ex·tol·ling
ex·tol·ler
ex·tol·ling·ly
ex·tol·ment
ex·tort
ex·tor·ter
ex·tor·tive
ex·tor·tion
ex·tor·tion·ary
ex·tor·tion·ate
ex·tor·tion·er

ex·tor·tion·ist
ex·tra
ex·tract
  ex·tract·a·ble
  ex·trac·tive
  ex·trac·tor
ex·trac·tion
ex·tra·cur·ric·u·lar
ex·tra·dite
  ex·tra·dit·ed
  ex·tra·dit·ing
  ex·tra·dit·a·ble
ex·tra·di·tion
ex·tra·ne·ous
  ex·tra·ne·ous·ly
  ex·tra·ne·ous·ness
ex·traor·di·nary
  ex·traor·di·nar·i·ly
ex·trap·o·late
  ex·trap·o·lat·ed
  ex·trap·o·lat·ing
  ex·trap·o·la·tion
ex·tra·sen·so·ry
ex·tra·ter·res·tri·al
ex·tra·ter·ri·to·ri·al
  ex·tra·ter·ri·to·ri·al·i·ty
ex·trav·a·gance
  ex·trav·a·gan·cy
ex·trav·a·gant
  ex·trav·a·gant·ly
ex·trav·a·gan·za
ex·treme
  ex·treme·ly
  ex·treme·ness
ex·trem·ist
  ex·trem·ism
ex·trem·i·ty
  ex·trem·i·ties
ex·tri·cate
  ex·tri·cat·ed
  ex·tri·cat·ing
  ex·tri·ca·ble
  ex·tri·ca·tion
ex·trin·sic
ex·tro·vert
  ex·tro·ver·sion
ex·trude
  ex·trud·ed
  ex·trud·ing
  ex·tru·sion
  ex·tru·sive
ex·u·ber·ance
ex·u·ber·ant
  ex·u·ber·ant·ly
ex·ude
  ex·ud·ed
  ex·ud·ing
  ex·u·da·tion
ex·ult
  ex·ult·ant
  ex·ult·ant·ly
  ex·ul·ta·tion
  ex·ult·ing·ly
ex·ur·ban·ite
eye

eyed
eye·ing
eye·ball
eye·bright
eye·brow
eye·cup
eye·ful
  eye·fuls
eye·glass
  eye·glass·es
eye·hole
eye·lash
eye·let
eye·lid
eye·o·pen·er
  eye·o·pen·ing
eye·piece
eye·shade
eye·sight
eye·sore
eye·strain
eye·tooth
  eye·teeth
eye·wash
eye·wa·ter
eye·wink
eye·wit·ness
ey·rie
ey·ry
  ey·ries
Eze·ki·el
Ez·ra
Fa·bi·an
Fa·bi·us
fa·ble
  fa·bled
fab·ric
fab·ri·cate
  fab·ri·cat·ed
  fab·ri·cat·ing
  fab·ri·ca·tion
  fab·ri·ca·tive
  fab·ri·ca·tor
fab·u·lous
  fab·u·lous·ly
  fab·u·lous·ness
fa·cade
  fa·cades
face
  faced
  fac·ing
fac·et
fa·ce·tious
  fa·ce·tious·ly
  fa·ce·tious·ness
fa·cial
  fa·cial·ly
fac·ile
  fac·ile·ly
  fac·ile·ness
fa·cil·i·tate
  fa·cil·i·tat·ed
  fa·cil·i·tat·ing
fa·cil·i·ty
  fa·cil·i·ties

fac·sim·i·le
fac·tion
  fac·tion·al
  fac·tion·al·ism
  fac·tion·al·ly
fac·ti·tious
  fac·ti·tious·ly
  fac·ti·tious·ness
fac·tor
fac·to·ry
  fac·to·ries
fac·to·tum
fac·tu·al
  fac·tu·al·ly
fac·ul·ty
fad
  fad·dish
  fad·dism
  fad·dist
fade
  fad·ed
  fad·ing
fa·er·ie
  fa·ery
  fa·er·ies
fag
  fagged
  fag·ging
fag·got
Fa·gin
Fahr·en·heit
fail·ing
  fail·ing·ly
fail·safe
fail·ure
faint
  faint·ly
  faint·ness
faint·heart·ed
  faint·heart·ed·ly
  faint·heart·ed·ness
fair
  fair·ness
Fair·fax
fair·ground
fair·ly
fair·mind·ed
  fair·mind·ed·ness
fairy
  fair·ies
  fair·y·like
faith·ful
faith·less
  faith·less·ly
  faith·less·ness
fake
  faked
  fak·ing
  fak·er
fal·con
fal·con·ry
Falk·land
fall
  fall·en
  fall·ing

fal·la·cious
  fal·la·cious·ly
  fal·la·cious·ness
fal·la·cy
fal·li·ble
  fal·li·bil·i·ty
  fal·li·bly
Fal·lo·pi·an
fall·out
fal·low
  fal·low·ness
false
  fals·er
  fals·est
  false·ly
  false·ness
false·hood
fal·si·fy
  fal·si·fied
  fal·si·fy·ing
  fal·si·fi·ca·tion
  fal·si··fi·er
fal·si·ty
Fal·staff
fal·ter
  fal·ter·er
  fal·ter·ing·ly
famed
fa·mil·ial
fa·mil·iar
  fa·mil·iar·ly
  fa·mil·i·ar·i·ty
  fa·mil·i·ar·i·ties
fa·mil·iar·ize
  fa·mil·iar·ized
  fa·mil·iar·iz·ing
  fa·mil·iar·i·za·tion
fam·i·ly
  fam·i·lies
fam·ine
fam·ish
  fam·ished
fa·mous
  fa·mous·ly
fan
  fan·like
  fan·ner
  fanned
  fan·ning
fa·nat·ic
  fa·nat·i·cal
  fa·nat·i·cal·ly
  fa·nat·i·cism
  fa·nat·i·cize
  fa·nat·i·cized
  fa·nat·i·ciz·ing
fan·ci·er
fan·ci·ful
  fan·ci·ful·ly
  fan·ci·ful·ness
fan·cy
  fan·cies
  fan·ci·er
  fan·ci·est
  fan·cied

fan·cy·ing
fan·ci·ly
fan·ci·ness
fan·cy·work
Fan·euil
fan·fare
fanged
fan·light
fan·tas·tic
fan·tas·ti·cal
fan·tas·ti·cal·ly
fan·tas·ti·cal·i·ty
fan·tas·ti·cal·ness
fan·ta·sy
fan·ta·sies
far
far·ther
far·thest
Far·a·day
far·a·way
farce
farced
farc·ing
far·ci·cal
far·ci·cal·i·ty
far·ci·cal·ly
fare
fared
far·ing
far·er
fare·well
far-fetched
far-flung
Far·go
farm·er
farm·hand
farm·house
farm·ing
farm·yard
far-off
Fa·rouk
Far·ra·gut
far-reach·ing
far-reach·ing·ly
far-reach·ing·ness
far-see·ing
far-sight·ed
far-sight·ed·ly
far-sight·ed·ness
far·ther·most
fas·cia
fas·ci·ae
fas·ci·as
fas·ci·al
fas·ci·cle
fas·ci·cled
fas·ci·nate
fas·ci·nat·ed
fas·ci·nat·ing
fas·ci·nat·ing·ly
fas·ci·na·tion
fas·cism
fas·cist
fa·scis·tic
fa·scis·ti·cal·ly

fash·ion
fash·ion·a·ble
fash·ion·a·ble·ness
fash·ion·a·bly
fas·ten
fas·ten·er
fas·ten·ing
fas·tid·i·ous
fas·tid·i·ous·ly
fas·tid·i·ous·ness
fat
fat·ter
fat·test
fat·ted
fat·ting
fat·ly
fat·ness
fa·tal
fa·tal·ly
fa·tal·ism
fa·tal·ist
fa·tal·is·tic
fa·tal·is·ti·cal·ly
fa·tal·i·ty
fa·tal·i·ties
fate
fat·ed
fat·ing
fate·ful
fate·ful·ly
fate·ful·ness
fa·ther
fa·ther·hood
fa·ther·li·ness
fa·ther·ly
fa·ther-in-law
fa·thers-in-law
fa·ther·land
fath·om
fath·om·a·ble
fath·om·less
fa·tigue
fa·tigued
fa·tig·uing
fat·i·ga·ble
fat·i·ga·bil·i·ty
Fat·i·ma
fat·ten
fat·ten·er
fat·ty
fat·ti·er
fat·ti·est
fat·ti·ness
fat·tish
fa·tu·i·ty
fa·tu·i·ties
fat·u·ous
fat·u·ous·ly
fat·u·ous·ness
fau·cet
Faulk·ner
fault
fault·find·er
fault·find·ing
fault·less

fault·less·ly
fault·less·ness
faulty
  fault·i·er
  fault·i·est
  fault·i·ly
  fault·i·ness
fau·na
  fau·nas
  fau·nae
faux pas
fa·vor
  fa·vor·ing·ly
fa·vor·a·ble
  fa·vor·a·ble·ness
  fa·vor·a·bly
fa·vored
  fa·vored·ly
  fa·vored·ness
fa·vor·ite
fa·vor·it·ism
fawn
faze
  fazed
  faz·ing
fe·al·ty
fear·ful
  fear·ful·ly
  fear·ful·ness
fear·less
  fear·less·ly
  fear·less·ness
fear·some
  fear·some·ly
  fear·some·ness
fea·si·ble
  fea·si·bil·i·ty
  fea·si·ble·ness
  fea·si·bly
feath·er
  feath·ered
  feath·er·ed·ding
fea·ture
  fea·tured
  fea·tur·ing
  fea·ture·less
fe·brile
Feb·ru·ary
  Feb·ru·ar·ies
fe·ces
  fe·cal
feck·less
fe·cund
  fe·cun·di·ty
fe·cun·date
  fe·cun·dat·ed
  fe·cun·dat·ing
  fe·cun·da·tion
fed·er·al
fed·er·al·ism
fed·er·al·ist
fed·er·al·ize
  fed·er·al·ized
  fed·er·al·iz·ing
  fed·er·al·i·za·tion

fed·er·al·ly
fed·er·ate
  fed·er·at·ed
  fed·er·at·ing
fee·ble
  fee·bler
  fee·blest
  fee·bly
fee·ble·mind·ed
  fee·ble·mind·ed·ness
feed
  fed
  feed·ing
  feed·er
feed·back
feel
  felt
  feel·ing
  feel·er
feel·ing
  feel·ing·ly
  feel·ing·ness
feign
  feigned
  feign·ed·ly
  feign·er
  feign·ing·ly
feint
feisty
  feist·i·er
  feist·i·est
fe·lic·i·tate
  fe·lic·i·tat·ed
  fe·lic·i·tat·ing
  fe·lic·i·ta·tion
fe·lic·i·tous
  fe·lic·i·tous·ly
  fe·lic·i·tous·ness
fe·lic·i·ty
  fe·lic·i·ties
fe·line
  fe·line·ly
  fe·lin·i·ty
fel·la·tio
fel·low
  fel·low·ship
fel·on
fel·o·ny
  fel·o·nies
  fe·lo·ni·ous
  fe·lo·ni·ous·ly
  fe·lo·ni·ous·ness
fe·male
fem·i·nine
  fem·i·nine·ly
  fem·i·nine·ness
  fem·i·nin·i·ty
fem·i·nism
fem·i·nist
  fem·i·nis·tic
fem·i·nize
  fem·i·nized
  fem·i·niz·ing
  fem·i·ni·za·tion
fe·mur

fe·murs
fem·o·ra
fem·o·ral
fen
  fen·ny
  fen·ni·er
  fen·ni·est
fence
  fenced
  fenc·ing
  fenc·er
fen·der
fe·ral
Fer·di·nand
fer·ment
  fer·ment·a·ble
  fer·men·ta·tion
Fer·nan·dez
fern·ery
  fern·er·ies
fe·ro·cious
  fe·ro·cious·ness
  fe·ro·cious·ly
  fe·ro·ci·ty
fer·ret
  fer·ret·er
Fer·ris wheel
fer·ro·con·crete
fer·ro·mag·net·ic
fer·ru·gi·nous
fer·rule
fer·ry
  fer·ries
  fer·ry·boat
  fer·ry·man
fer·tile
  fer·tile·ly
  fer·tile·ness
  fer·til·i·ty
  fer·ti·li·za·tion
    fer·ti·li·za·tion·al
  fer·ti·lize
  fer·ti·lized
  fer·ti·liz·ing
  fer·ti·liz·a·ble
  fer·ti·liz·er
fer·vent
  fer·ven·cy
  fer·vent·ly
fer·vid
  fer·vid·ly
  fer·vid·ness
fer·vor
fes·ter
fes·ti·val
fes·tive
  fes·tive·ly
  fes·tive·ness
  fes·tiv·i·ty
fes·toon
  fes·toon·ery
  fes·toon·er·ies
fe·tal
fetch
  fetch·er

fetch·ing
  fetch·ing·ly
fete
fet·id
  fet·id·ly
  fet·id·ness
fet·ish
  fet·ish·ism
  fet·ish·ist
  fet·ish·is·tic
fet·lock
fet·ter
fet·tle
fe·tus
  fe·tus·es
feud
  feud·ist
feu·dal
feu·dal·ism
feu·dal·ist
  feu·dal·is·tic
feu·dal·i·za·tion
feu·dal·ize
  feu·dal·ized
  feu·dal·iz·ing
fe·ver
fe·ver·ish
  fe·ver·ish·ly
  fe·ver·ish·ness
fe·ver·ous
  fe·ver·ous·ly
few·ness
fez·zes
fi·an·cé
fi·an·cée
fi·as·co
  fi·as·cos
  fi·as·coes
fi·at
fib
  fib·ber
  fib·ster
fi·ber
  fi·bered
fi·ber·board
fi·ber·glass
fi·bril
fi·bril·la·tion
fi·broid
fi·brous
fib·u·la
  fib·u·las
  fib·u·lae
  fib·u·lar
fick·le
  fick·le·ness
fic·tion
  fic·tion·al
  fic·tion·al·ly
fic·ti·tious
  fic·ti·tious·ly
  fic·ti·tious·ness
fid·dle
  fid·dler
  fid·dled

fid·dling
fi·del·i·ty
fidg·et
  fidg·ety
  fidg·et·i·er
  fidg·et·i·est
fi·du·ci·ary
fief
field day
field·er
field·er's choice
field glass
field house
field mar·shal
field·work
fiend
  fiend·ish
  fiend·ish·ly
  fiend·ish·ness
fierce
  fierce·ly
  fierce·ness
fiery
  fier·i·er
  fier·i·est
  fier·i·ly
  fier·i·ness
fif·teen
fif·teenth
fif·ti·eth
fif·ty
  fif·ties
Fig·a·ro
fight·er
fig·ment
fig·u·ra·tion
fig·u·ra·tive
  fig·ur·a·tive·ly
  fig·ur·a·tive·ness
fig·ure
  fig·ured
  fig·ur·ing
  fig·ure·less
  fig·ur·er
fig·ure·head
fig·ur·ine
Fi·ji
fil·a·ment
  fil·a·men·ta·ry
  fil·a·ment·ed
  fil·a·men·tous
filch·er
file
  filed
  fil·ing
fi·let
fi·let mi·gnon
fil·i·al
  fil·i·al·ly
fil·i·bus·ter
fil·i·gree
  fil·i·greed
  fil·i·gree·ing
fil·lings
Fil·i·pi·no

fill·er
fil·let
fill·ing
fil·lip
fil·ly
  fil·lies
film·strip
filmy
  film·i·er
  film·i·est
  film·i·ness
fil·ter
filth
  filth·i·ness
filthy
  filth·i·er
  filth·i·est
fin
  finned
  fin·ning
fin·less
fin·like
fi·na·gle
  fi·na·gled
  fi·na·gling
  fi·na·gler
fi·nal
  fi·na·le
  fi·nal·ist
  fi·nal·i·ty
    fi·nal·i·ties
  fi·nal·ize
    fi·nal·ized
    fi·nal·iz·ing
  fi·nal·ly
fi·nance
  fi·nanced
  fi·nanc·ing
  fi·nan·cial
    fi·nan·cial·ly
fin·an·cier
finch
find
  found
  find·ing
find·er
fine
  fin·er
  fin·est
  fine·ly
  fine·ness
fin·ery
  fin·er·ies
fi·nesse
  fi·nessed
  fi·nes·sing
Fin·gal
fin·ger
fin·ger·bowl
fin·ger·ing
fin·ger·nail
fin·ger·print
fin·i·al
fin·i·cal
  fin·i·cal·ly

fin·icky
  fin·ick·ing
fin·is
  fin·is·es
fin·ish
  fin·ished
  fin·ish·er
fi·nite
  fi·nite·ly
  fi·nite·ness
Fin·land
Finn·ish
fire
  fired
  fir·ing
  fir·er
fire·arm
fire·ball
fire·brand
fire·bug
fire·crack·er
fire·fight·er
fire·fly
  fire·flies
fire·man
fire·place
fire·plug
fire·pow·er
fire·proof
fire·side
fire·trap
fire·wa·ter
fire·wood
fire·works
fir·ing squad
firm
  firm·ly
  firm·ness
fir·ma·ment
first-born
first·hand
first·ling
first·ly
first-rate
first-string
fis·cal
  fis·cal·ly
fish·er
fish·er·man
  fish·er·men
fish·ery
  fish·er·ies
fish·hook
fish·ing
fish·wife
  fish·wives
fishy
  fish·i·er
  fish·i·est
fis·sile
fis·sion
fis·sure
  fis·sured
  fis·sur·ing
fist·ic

fist·i·cuff
fit
  fit·ter
  fit·test
  fit·ted
  fit·ting
  fit·ly
  fit·ness
fit·ful
  fit·ful·ly
  fit·ful·ness
fit·ting
  fit·ting·ly
  fit·ting·ness
five·fold
five-and-ten
fix
  fix·a·ble
  fixed
  fix·ed·ly
  fix·er
fix·a·tion
fix·a·tive
fix·ings
fix·i·ty
  fix·i·ties
fix·ture
fiz·zle
  fiz·zled
  fiz·zling
fiz·zy
  fiz·zi·er
  fiz·zi·est
flab·ber·gast
flab·by
  flab·bi·er
  flab·bi·est
  flab·bi·ly
  flab·bi·ness
flac·cid
flag
  flagged
  flag·ging
flag·el·lant
flag·el·late
  flag·el·lat·ed
  flag·el·lat·ing
  flag·el·la·tion
fla·gi·tious
  fla·gi·tious·ly
flag·on
flag·pole
flag·rank
fla·grant
  fla·grant·ly
flag·ship
flag·stone
flail
flair
flake
  flaked
  flak·ing
flaky
  flak·i·er
  flak·i·est

flak·i·ness
flam·boy·ant
flam·boy·ance
flam·boy·an·cy
flam·boy·ant·ly
flame
flamed
flam·ing
flam·ing·ly
flam·ma·ble
Flan·a·gan
Flan·ders
flange
flank
flank·er
flan·nel·ette
flap
flapped
flap·ping
flap·per
flap·jack
flare
flared
flar·ing
flare-up
flash·back
flash·light
flashy
flash·i·er
flash·i·est
flash·i·ly
flash·i·ness
flask
flat
flat·ly
flat·ted
flat·ting
flat·ness
flat·car
flat·foot
flat·foot·ed
flat·foot·ed·ly
flat·foot·ed·ness
flat·ten
flat·ten·er
flat·ter
flat·ter·er
flat·ter·ing·ly
flat·tery
flat·ter·ies
flat·u·lent
flat·u·lence
flat·u·len·cy
flat·u·lent·ly
flat·ware
flaunt
flaunt·er
flaunt·ing·ly
flaunty
flaunt·i·er
flaunt·i·est
flau·tist
fla·vor
fla·vored
fla·vor·less

fla·vor·ing
flaw·less
flax·en
flax·seed
flay·er
flea·bite
flea-bit·ten
fleck
flec·tion
fledge
fledged
fledg·ing
fledg·ling
flee
fled
flee·ing
fleece
fleeced
fleec·ing
fleecy
fleec·i·er
fleec·i·est
fleec·i·ness
fleet
fleet·ly
fleet·ness
fleet·ing
fleet·ing·ly
fleet·ing·ness
Flem·ish
flesh·ly
flesh·li·er
flesh·li·est
flesh·pots
fleshy
flesh·i·er
flesh·i·est
flesh·i·ness
Fleu·ry
flex·i·ble
flex·i·bil·i·ty
flex·i·bly
flex·ion
flex·or
flex·ure
fib·ber·ti·gib·bet
flick·er
flick·er·ing
fli·er
flight
flight·less
flighty
flight·i·er
flight·i·est
flight·i·ly
flight·i·ness
flim·flam
flim·flammed
flim·flam·ming
flim·sy
flim·si·er
flim·si·est
flim·si·ly
flim·si·ness
flinch

flinch·er
flinch·ing·ly
flin·ders
fling
  flung
  fling·ing
flinty
  flint·i·er
  flint·i·est
  flint·i·ness
flip
  flipped
  flip·ping
flip-flop
flip·pant
  flip·pan·cy
  flip·pant·ly
flip·per
flirt·er
flir·ta·tion
  flir·ta·tious
flit
  flit·ted
  flit·ting
  flit·ter
float·a·ble
float·a·tion
float·er
float·ing
floc·cu·lent
  floc·cu·lence
flocked
flocky
flog
  flogged
  flog·ging
  flog·ger
flood·gate
flood·light
  flood·light·ed
  flood·lit
  flood·light·ing
floor·ing
floor·walk·er
floo·zy
  floo·zies
flop
  flopped
  flop·ping
  flop·per
flop·house
flop·py
  flop·pi·er
  flop·pi·est
  flop·pi·ly
  flop·pi·ness
flo·ra
  flo·ras
  flo·rae
flo·ral
Flor·ence
Flor·en·tine
flo·res·cence
  flo·res·cent
flo·ret

flo·ri·cul·ture
  flo·ri·cul·tur·al
  flo·ri·cul·tur·ist
flor·id
  flo·rid·i·ty
  flor·id·ly
  flor·id·ness
Flor·i·da
flo·rist
floss
flossy
  floss·i·er
  floss·i·est
flo·ta·tion
flo·til·la
flot·sam
flounce
  flounced
  flounc·ing
floun·der
floury
  flour·i·er
  flour·i·est
flour·ish
  flour·ish·ing
flout·er
flow·er
  flow·ered
  flow·er·ing
flow·ery
  flow·er·i·ness
flub
  flubbed
  flub·bing
fluc·tu·ate
  fluc·tu·at·ed
  fluc·tu·at·ing
  fluc·tu·a·tion
flue
flu·ent
  flu·en·cy
  flu·ent·ly
fluff
  fluff·i·ness
fluffy
  fluff·i·er
  fluff·i·est
flu·id
  flu·id·ly
  flu·id·ness
fluke
fluky
  fluk·i·er
  fluk·i·est
flum·mery
  flum·mer·ies
flun·ky
  flun·kies
flu·o·resce
  flu·o·resced
  flu·o·resc·ing
  flu·o·res·cence
  flu·o·res·cent
fluor·i·da·tion
  fluor·i·date

fluor·i·dat·ed
fluor·i·dat·ing
fluor·o·scope
flur·ry
flur·ries
flur·ried
flur·ry·ing
Flush·ing
flus·ter
flute
flut·ed
flut·ing
flut·ist
flut·ter
flut·ter·er
flut·ter·ing·ly
flut·tery
flut·ter·i·er
flut·ter·i·est
flux·ion
fly·blown
fly-by-night
fly·er
fly·ing
fly·leaf
fly·leaves
fly·pa·per
fly·speck
fly·wheel
foal
foam
foam·i·ness
foamy
foam·i·er
foam·i·est
fob
fobbed
fob·bing
fo·cal
fo·cal·ly
fo·cal·ize
fo·cal·ized
fo·cal·iz·ing
fo·cus
fo·cus·es
fo·cused
fo·cus·ing
fo·cus·er
fod·der
foe·tus
foe·tal
fog
fogged
fog·ging
fog·gy
fog·gi·er
fog·gi·est
fog·gi·ly
fog·gi·ness
fog·horn
fo·gy
fo·gies
fo·gy·ish
foi·ble
fold·er

fol·de·rol
fo·li·a·ceous
fo·li·age
fo·li·ate
fo·li·at·ed
fo·li·at·ing
fo·li·a·tion
fo·lio
fo·li·os
fo·li·oed
fo·li·o·ing
folk·lore
folk·lor·ist
folk·sy
folk·si·er
folk·si·est
folk·si·ness
folk·ways
fol·li·cle
fol·lic·u·lar
fol·low
fol·low·er
fol·low·ing
fol·ly
fol·lies
fo·ment
fo·men·ta·tion
fo·ment·er
fon·dant
fon·dle
fon·dled
fon·dling
fon·dler
fond·ly
fond·ness
fon·due
Fon·taine·bleau
Foo·chow
food·stuff
fool·ery
fool·er·ies
fool·har·dy
fool·har·di·ness
fool·proof
fools·cap
foot·age
foot·ball
foot·board
foot·can·dle
foot·ed
foot·fall
foot·hill
foot·hold
foot·ing
foot·lights
foot·loose
foot·note
foot·not·ed
foot·not·ing
foot·path
foot·print
foot·sore
foot·step
foot·stool
foot·wear

foot·work
foo·zle
  foo·zled
  foo·zling
fop
  fop·pery
  fop·per·ies
  fop·pish
  fop·pish·ly
  fop·pish·ness
for·age
  for·aged
  for·ag·ing
for·ay
for·bear
  for·bore
  for·borne
  for·bear·ing
  for·bear·ance
  for·bear·ing·ly
for·bid
  for·bade
  for·bid·den
  for·bid·ding
  for·bid·dance
for·bid·ding
  for·bid·ding·ly
  for·bid·ding·ness
force
  forced
  forc·ing
  force·a·ble
  force·less
  forc·er
force·ful
  force·ful·ly
  force·ful·ness
for·ceps
for·ci·ble
  for·ci·bly
ford·a·ble
fore·arm
fore·bear
fore·bode
  fore·bod·ed
  fore·bod·ing
  fore·bod·er
  fore·bod·ing
fore·brain
fore·cast
  fore·cast·ed
  fore·cast·ing
  fore·cast·er
fore·close
  fore·closed
  fore·clos·ing
  fore·clo·sure
fore·fa·ther
fore·fin·ger
fore·foot
  fore·feet
fore·front
fore·gath·er
fore·go
  fore·went

fore·gone
  fore·go·ing
fore·gone
fore·ground
fore·hand
fore·hand·ed
  fore·hand·ed·ness
fore·head
for·eign
  for·eign·er
  for·eign·ness
fore·know
  fore·knew
  fore·known
  fore·know·ing
  fore·knowl·edge
fore·leg
fore·lock
fore·man
  fore·men
fore·most
fore·noon
fo·ren·sic
fore·or·dain
fore·quar·ter
fore·run
  fore·ran
  fore·run·ning
  fore·run·ner
fore·see
  fore·saw
  fore·seen
  fore·see·ing
  fore·see·a·ble
  fore·se·er
fore·shad·ow
  fore·shad·ow·er
fore·short·en
fore·sight
  fore·sight·ed
  fore·sight·ed·ness
fore·skin
for·est
fore·stall
for·est·a·tion
for·es·ter
for·est·ry
fore·taste
  fore·tast·ed
  fore·tast·ing
fore·tell
  fore·told
  fore·tell·ing
  fore·tell·er
fore·thought
for·ev·er
  for·ev·er·more
fore·warn
fore·word
for·feit
  for·feit·er
  for·fei·ture
for·gath·er
forge
  forged

forg·ing
forg·er
for·gery
 for·ger·ies
for·get
 for·got
 for·got·ten
 for·get·ting
 for·get·ta·ble
 for·get·ter
for·get·ful
 for·get·ful·ly
 for·get·ful·ness
for·give
 for·gave
 for·giv·en
 for·giv·ing
 for·giv·a·ble
 for·give·ness
 for·giv·er
for·go
 for·went
 for·gone
 for·go·ing
 for·go·er
fork·lift
for·lorn
 for·lorn·ly
 for·lorn·ness
for·mal
 for·mal·ly
 for·mal·ism
 for·mal·i·ty
 for·mal·i·ties
 for·mal·ize
 for·mal·ized
 for·mal·iz·ing
 for·mal·i·za·tion
for·mat
for·ma·tion
form·a·tive
for·mer
 for·mer·ly
For·mi·ca
for·mi·da·ble
 for·mi·da·ble·ness
 for·mi·da·bly
form·less
 form·less·ly
 form·less·ness
For·mo·sa
for·mu·la
 for·mu·las
 for·mu·lae
for·mu·lary
 for·mu·lar·ies
for·mu·late
 for·mu·lat·ed
 for·mu·lat·ing
 for·mu·la·tion
 for·mu·la·tor
for·ni·cate
 for·ni·cat·ed
 for·ni·cat·ing
 for·ni·cat·or

for·ni·ca·tion
for·sake
 for·sook
 for·sak·en
 for·sak·ing
 for·sak·en
 for·sak·en·ly
for·swear
 for·swore
 for·sworn
 for·swear·ing
 for·swear·er
fort
forte
for·te
forth·com·ing
forth·right
 forth·right·ness
forth·with
for·ti·fi·ca·tion
for·ti·fy
 for·ti·fied
 for·ti·fy·ing
 for·ti·fi·er
for·tis·si·mo
for·ti·tude
fort·night
 fort·night·ly
 fort·night·lies
for·tress
for·tu·i·tous
 for·tu·i·tous·ly
 for·tu·i·tous·ness
for·tu·nate
 for·tu·nate·ly
for·tune
 for·tune·tell·er
 for·tune·tell·ing
for·ty
 for·ties
 for·ty·nin·er
fo·rum
 fo·rums
 fo·ra
for·ward
 for·ward·er
 for·ward·ly
 for·ward·ness
fos·sil
fos·sil·ize
 fos·sil·ized
 fos·sil·iz·ing
 fos·sil·i·za·tion
fos·ter
 fos·tered
 fos·ter·ing
fought
fou·lard
found
 foun·da·tion
 foun·da·tion·al
 found·er
 found·ling
 found·ry
 found·ries

foun·tain
foun·tain·head
four·flush·er
four·fold
four-post·er
four·score
four·some
four·square
four·teen
  four·teenth
fourth
  fourth·ly
fowl
  fowl·er
fox·hole
fox·hound
fox·tail
foxy
  fox·i·er
  fox·i·est
  fox·i·ly
  fox·i·ness
foy·er
fra·cas
  fra·cas·es
frac·tion
  frac·tion·al
frac·tious
  frac·tious·ly
frac·ture
  frac·tured
  frac·tur·ing
frag·ile
  fra·gil·i·ty
frag·ment
  frag·men·tal
  frag·men·tar·i·ness
  frag·men·tary
  frag·men·ta·tion
  frag·ment·ize
  frag·ment·ized
  frag·ment·iz·ing
fra·grance
fra·grant
  fra·grant·ly
frail
  frail·ty
frail·ness
frail·ty
  frail·ties
frame
  framed
  fram·ing
  fram·er
frame-up
frame·work
franc
fran·chise
  fran·chised
  fran·chis·ing
  fran·chise·ment
Fran·cis·can
Fran·co·phile
Fran·co·pho·bia
fran·gi·ble

frank
  frank·er
  frank·ly
  frank·ness
Frank·en·stein
Frank·fort
  frank·furt·er
  frank·in·cense
Frank·lin
fran·tic
  fran·ti·cal·ly
fra·ter·nal
  fra·ter·nal·ly
fra·ter·ni·ty
  fra·ter·ni·ties
frat·er·nize
  frat·er·nized
  frat·er·niz·ing
  frat·er·niz·er
frat·ri·cide
  frat·ri·cid·al
fraud·u·lent
  fraud·u·lence
  fraud·u·lent·ly
fraught
Fra·zer
fraz·zle
  fraz·zled
  fraz·zling
freak
  freak·ish
  freak·ish·ness
freaky
  freak·i·er
  freak·i·est
freck·le
  freck·led
  freck·ling
  freck·led
  freck·ly
  freck·li·er
  freck·li·est
Fred·er·ick
Fred·er·icks·burg
free
  fre·er
  fre·est
  free·ly
free·bie
free·boot·er
free·dom
free·hand
  free·hand·ed
free·lance
  free·lanced
  free·lanc·ing
Free·ma·son
  Free·ma·son·ry
free·spo·ken
  free·spo·ken·ness
free·stone
free·think·er
  free·think·ing
Free·town
free·way

free·wheel
freeze
  froze
  fro·zen
  freez·ing
freeze-dry
  freeze-dried
  freeze-dry·ing
freez·er
freight·age
freight·er
Fre·mont
French·man
Fre·neau
fre·net·ic
  fre·net·i·cal·ly
fren·zy
  fren·zies
  fren·zied
  fren·zy·ing
Fre·on
fre·quen·cy
  fre·quen·cies
fre·quent
  fre·quent·er
  fre·quent·ly
fre·quen·ta·tive
fres·co
  fres·coes
  fres·cos
  fres·coed
  fres·co·ing
fresh
  fresh·ly
  fresh·ness
fresh·en
  fresh·en·er
fresh·et
fresh·man
  fresh·men
Fres·no
fret
  fret·ted
  fret·ting
  fret·ful
  fret·ful·ly
fret·work
Freud·i·an
fri·a·ble
fri·ar
fri·ary
  fri·ar·ies
Fri·bourg
fric·as·see
  fric·as·seed
  fric·as·see·ing
fric·tion
fric·tion·al
  fric·tion·less
Fri·day
friend
  friend·less
  friend·less·ness
  friend·ship
  friend·ly

friend·li·er
friend·li·est
friend·li·ly
friend·li·ness
Fries·land
frieze
fright·en
  fright·en·ing·ly
fright·ful
  fright·ful·ly
  fright·ful·ness
frig·id
  fri·gid·i·ty
  frig·id·ly
  frig·id·ness
Frig·i·daire
frilly
  frill·i·er
  frill·i·est
fringe
  fringed
  fring·ing
frip·pery
  frip·per·ies
Fris·co
frisky
  frisk·i·er
  frisk·i·est
  frisk·i·ly
  frisk·i·ness
frit·ter
friv·o·lous
  fri·vol·i·ty
  fri·vol·i·ties
  friv·o·lous·ly
frizz
  friz·zi·ness
  friz·zy
  friz·zi·er
  friz·zi·est
friz·zle
  friz·zled
  friz·zling
  friz·zly
  friz·zli·er
  friz·zli·est
Fro·bish·er
frog
  frogged
  frog·ging
  frog·man
frol·ic
  frol·icked
  frol·ick·ing
  frol·ic·some
front·age
fron·tal
  fron·tal·ly
fron·tier
  fron·tiers·man
  fron·tiers·men
fron·tis·piece
frost
  frost·ed
  frost·bite

frost·bit
frost·bit·ten
frost·bit·ing
frost·ing
frosty
  frost·i·er
  frost·i·est
  frost·i·ly
  frost·i·ness
froth
  froth·i·ness
frothy
  froth·i·er
  froth·i·est
frou·frou
fro·ward
frown
  frown·ing·ly
frow·zy
  frow·zi·er
  frow·zi·est
fro·zen
  fro·zen·ly
  fro·zen·ness
fruc·ti·fy
  fruc·ti·fied
  fruc·ti·fy·ing
  fruc·ti·fi·ca·tion
fru·gal
  fru·gal·i·ty
  fru·gal·i·ties
  fru·gal·ly
fruit·ful
  fruit·ful·ly
  fruit·ful·ness
fru·i·tion
fruit·less
  fruit·less·ly
  fruit·less·ness
fruity
frump
  frump·ish
frumpy
  frump·i·er
  frump·i·est
frus·trate
  frus·trat·ed
  frus·trat·ing
  frus·tra·tion
fry
  fried
  fry·ing
fry·er
fud·dle
  fud·dled
  fud·dling
fud·dy-dud·dy
  fud·dy-dud·dies
fudge
  fudged
  fudg·ing
fu·el
  fu·eled
  fu·el·ing
fu·gi·tive

fu·gi·tive·ly
Füh·rer
Fu·ji·ya·ma
ful·crum
  ful·crums
  ful·cra
ful·fill
  ful·filled
  ful·fil·ling
  ful·fill·ment
full
  full·ness
  ful·ly
full·back
full-blood·ed
full-blown
Ful·ler
full-fledged
full-scale
ful·mi·nate
  ful·mi·nat·ed
  ful·mi·nat·ing
  ful·mi·na·tion
ful·some
  ful·some·ly
Ful·ton
fum·ble
  fum·bled
  fum·bling
  fum·bler
fume
  fumed
  fum·ing
  fum·ing·ly
fu·mi·gate
  fu·mi·gat·ed
  fu·mi·gat·ing
  fu·mi·ga·tion
  fu·mi·ga·tor
func·tion
  func·tion·less
  func·tion·al
  func·tion·al·ly
  func·tion·ary
  func·tion·ar·ies
fun·da·men·tal
  fun·da·men·tal·ly
  fun·da·men·tal·ism
  fun·da·men·tal·ist
Fun·dy
fu·ner·al
fu·ne·re·al
fun·gi·cide
  fun·gi·cid·al
  fun·gi·cid·al·ly
fun·gous
fun·gus
  fun·gi
  fun·gus·es
fu·nic·u·lar
funky
  funk·i·er
  funk·i·est
fun·nel
  fun·neled

fun·nel·ing
fun·ny
fun·ni·er
fun·ni·est
fun·nies
fun·ni·ly
fun·ni·ness
fur
furred
fur·ring
fur·bish
fu·ri·ous
fu·ri·ous·ly
fur·long
fur·lough
fur·nace
fur·nish
fur·nish·ings
fur·ni·ture
fu·ror
fur·ri·er
fur·row
fur·ry
 fur·ri·er
 fur·ri·est
fur·ther
fur·ther·more
fur·ther·most
fur·thest
fur·tive
 fur·tive·ly
fu·ry
 fu·ries
fuse
fused
 fus·ing
fu·see
fu·se·lage
fu·si·bil·i·ty
fu·si·ble
fu·si·form
fu·sil·lade
 fu·sil·lad·ed
 fu·sil·lad·ing
fu·sion
fussy
 fuss·i·er
 fuss·i·est
 fuss·i·ly
 fuss·i·ness
fus·tian
fus·ty
 fus·ti·er
 fus·ti·est
 fus·ti·ly
 fus·ti·ness
fu·tile
fu·til·i·ty
 fu·til·i·ties
fu·ture
fu·tur·ism
fu·tur·is·tic
fu·tu·ri·ty
 fu·tu·ri·ties
fu·zee

fuzzy
 fuzz·i·er
 fuzz·i·est
 fuzz·i·ly
 fuzz·i·ness
gab
 gabbed
 gab·bing
 gab·ber
gab·ar·dine
gab·ble
 gab·bled
 gab·bling
 gab·bler
gab·by
 gab·bi·er
 gab·bi·est
ga·ble
 ga·bled
 ga·bling
Ga·bon
Ga·bri·el
gad
 gad·ded
 gad·ding
gad·a·bout
gad·fly
 gad·flies
gad·get
 gad·get·ry
Gad·ite
Gads·den
Gael·ic
gaffe
gaf·fer
gag
 gagged
 gag·ging
ga·ga
gai·e·ty
 gai·e·ties
gai·ly
gain·er
gain·ful
gain·say
 gain·said
 gain·say·ing
Gains·bor·ough
gait
Ga·ius
ga·la
ga·lac·tic
Gal·a·had
Ga·la·pa·gos
Gal·a·tea
Ga·la·tia
gal·axy
 gal·ax·ies
Gal·i·lee
Gal·i·leo
gal·lant
gal·lant·ry
 gal·lant·ries
gal·lery
 gal·ler·ies

gal·ley
Gal·lic
gal·li·cism
Gal·li·e·nus
gal·li·mau·fry
  gal·li·mau·fries
gall·ing
gal·li·vant
gal·lon
gal·lop
gal·lows
  gal·lows·es
gall·stone
ga·loot
ga·losh
ga·lumph
gal·van·ic
gal·va·nism
gal·va·nize
  gal·va·nized
  gal·va·niz·ing
gal·va·nom·e·ter
Gal·ves·ton
Gal·way
Gam·bia
gam·bit
gam·ble
  gam·bled
  gam·bling
gam·bol
gam·brel
game
  gam·er
  gam·est
  gamed
  gam·ing
game·keep·er
games·man·ship
game·some
game·ster
gam·ete
  ga·met·ic
gam·in
gam·ma
gam·ma glob·u·lin
gam·mon
gam·ut
gamy
  gam·i·er
  gam·i·est
  gam·i·ly
  gam·i·ness
gan·der
Gan·dha·ra
Gan·dhi
Gan·ges
gang·land
gang·gling
gan·gli·on
  gan·glia
  gan·gli·ons
gan·gly
  gan·gli·er
  gan·gli·est

gang·plank
gan·grene
  gan·grened
  gan·gren·ing
  gan·gre·nous
gang·ster
gang·way
gant·let
gan·try
  gan·tries
gaol
gap
  gapped
  gap·ping
ga·rage
  ga·raged
  ga·rag·ing
gar·bage
gar·ble
  gar·bled
  gar·bling
gar·den
Gar·di·ner
Gard·ner
Gar·field
Gar·gan·tua
gar·gan·tu·an
gar·gle
  gar·gled
  gar·gling
gar·goyle
Gar·i·bal·di
gar·ish
gar·land
gar·ment
gar·ner
gar·net
gar·nish
gar·nish·ee
  gar·nish·eed
  gar·nish·ee·ing
gar·nish·ment
gar·ni·ture
gar·ret
gar·ri·son
gar·rote
  gar·rot·ed
  gar·rot·ing
  gar·rot·er
gar·ru·lous
gar·ter
gas
  gassed
  gas·sing
Gas·co·ny
gas·e·ous
gas·i·fy
  gas·i·fied
  gas·i·fy·ing
  gas·i·fi·ca·tion
  gas·i·fi·er
gas·ket
gas·light
gas·lit
gas·o·line

gas·ser
gas·sy
 gas·si·er
 gas·si·est
 gas·si·ness
gas·tric
gas·tri·tis
gas·tro·in·tes·ti·nal
gas·tron·o·my
 gas·tro·nom·ic
 gas·tro·nom·i·cal
 gas·tro·nom·i·cal·ly
gas·works
gate·crash·er
 gate·crash·ing
gate·house
gate·keep·er
gate·post
gate·way
gath·er
gath·er·ing
Gat·ling
Ga·tun
gauche
gau·cho
gaudy
 gaud·i·er
 gaud·i·est
 gaud·i·ly
 gaud·i·ness
gauge
 gauged
 gaug·ing
Gau·guin
Gaull·ist
gaunt·let
gauze
 gauz·i·ness
 gauzy
 gauz·i·er
 gauz·i·est
gav·el
Ga·wain
gawky
 gawk·i·er
 gawk·i·est
 gawk·i·ly
 gawk·i·ness
gay·e·ty
gay·ly
Ga·za
gaze
 gazed
 gaz·ing
 gaz·er
ga·ze·bo
 ga·ze·bos
 ga·ze·boes
ga·zelle
ga·zette
gaz·et·teer
gear·box
gear·ing
gear·shift
gear·wheel

gee
 geed
 gee·ing
 gee·zer
Ge·hen·na
Gei·ger count·er
gei·sha
Geiss·ler
gel
 gelled
 gel·ling
gel·a·tin
ge·lat·i·nous
ge·la·tion
geld
 geld·ed
 gelt
 geld·ing
gel·id
gem
 gemmed
 gem·ming
gem·i·nate
 gem·i·nat·ed
 gem·i·nat·ing
 gem·i·nate·ly
 gem·i·na·tion
Gem·i·ni
gem·ol·o·gy
 gem·o·log·i·cal
 gem·o·lo·gist
gem·stone
gen·darme
gen·der
gene
ge·ne·al·o·gy
 ge·ne·a·log·i·cal
 ge·ne·al·o·gist
gen·er·al
 gen·er·al·is·si·mo
 gen·er·al·is·si·mos
 gen·er·al·ist
 gen·er·al·i·ty
 gen·er·al·i·ties
 gen·er·al·ize
 gen·er·al·ized
 gen·er·al·iz·ing
 gen·er·al·i·za·tion
 gen·er·al·iz·er
gen·er·ate
 gen·er·at·ed
 gen·er·at·ing
 gen·er·a·tive
 gen·er·a·tive·ly
 gen·er·a·tion
 gen·er·a·tor
ge·ner·ic
 ge·ner·i·cal
 ge·ner·i·cal·ly
gen·er·ous
 gen·er·os·i·ty
 gen·er·os·i·ties
gen·e·sis
 gen·e·ses
ge·net·ic

ge·net·i·cal·ly
ge·net·ics
ge·net·i·cist
Ge·ne·va
Gen·ghis Khan
gen·ial
ge·ni·al·i·ty
ge·nie
ge·nies
ge·nii
gen·i·tal
gen·i·ta·lia
gen·i·tals
gen·ius
gen·ius·es
Gen·oa
gen·o·cide
gen·o·ci·dal
gen·re
gen·teel
gen·tian
gen·tile
gen·til·i·ty
gen·til·i·ties
gen·tle
gen·tler
gen·tlest
gen·tly
gen·tle·folk
gen·tle·man
gen·tle·men
gen·tle·wom·an
gen·tle·wom·en
gen·try
gen·u·flect
gen·u·flec·tion
gen·u·flec·tor
gen·u·ine
ge·nus
gen·e·ra
ge·nus·es
ge·o·cen·tric
ge·o·cen·tri·cal·ly
ge·o·chem·is·try
ge·o·chem·i·cal
ge·o·chem·ist
ge·ode
ge·o·des·ic
ge·o·gra·phy
ge·o·gra·phies
ge·o·gra·pher
ge·o·gra·phic
ge·o·graph·i·cal
ge·ol·o·gy
ge·ol·o·gies
ge·o·log·ic
ge·o·log·i·cal
ge·o·log·i·cal·ly
ge·ol·o·gist
ge·o·mag·net·ic
ge·o·mag·ne·tism
ge·o·met·ric
ge·om·e·try
ge·om·e·tries
ge·o·phys·ics

ge·o·phys·i·cal
ge·o·phys·i·cist
ge·o·pol·i·tics
ge·o·pol·i·tic
ge·o·po·lit·i·cal
ge·o·po·lit·i·cal·ly
George·town
Geor·gia
ge·o·ther·mal
ger·bil
Ger·hard
ger·i·at·rics
ger·i·at·ric
ger·i·a·tri·cian
ger·i·at·rist
ger·mane
Ger·man
Ger·ma·ny
ger·mi·cide
ger·mi·cid·al
ger·mi·nate
ger·mi·nat·ed
ger·mi·nat·ing
ger·mi·na·tion
Ge·ron·i·mo
ger·on·tol·o·gy
ger·on·tol·o·gist
ger·ry·man·der
Gersh·win
ger·und
ges·so
Ge·stalt
ges·tate
ges·tat·ed
ges·tat·ing
ges·ta·tion
ges·tic·u·late
ges·tic·u·lat·ed
ges·tic·u·lat·ing
ges·tic·u·la·tion
ges·tic·u·la·tive
ges·tic·u·la·to·ry
ges·tic·u·la·tor
ges·ture
ges·tured
ges·tur·ing
ges·tur·er
ge·sund·heit
get·a·way
Geth·sem·a·ne
get·to·geth·er
Get·tys·burg
get·up
gew·gaw
gey·ser
Gha·na
ghast·ly
ghast·li·er
ghast·li·est
ghast·li·ness
gher·kin
ghet·to
ghet·tos
ghet·toes
Ghi·ber·ti

ghost·ly
  ghost·li·er
  ghost·li·est
  ghost·li·ness
ghost·write
  ghost·wrote
  ghost·writ·ten
  ghost·writ·ing
ghoul
gi·ant
gib·ber·ish
gib·bon
gibe
  gib·er
  gib·ing·ly
Gib·e·on·ite
gib·let
Gi·bral·tar
Gib·son
gid·dy
  gid·di·er
  gid·di·est
  gid·di·ly
  gid·di·ness
Gid·e·on
gi·gan·tic
gi·gan·tism
gig·gle
  gig·gled
  gig·gling
  gig·gler
  gig·gly
  gig·gli·er
  gig·gli·est
gig·o·lo
Gi·la
Gil·bert
gild·ed
Gil·e·ad
gilt-edged
gim·crack
gim·let
gim·mick
gin·ger
gin·ger·bread
gin·ger·ly
  gin·ger·li·ness
gin·ger·snap
gin·ger·y
ging·ham
Giot·to
Gio·van·ni
Gip·sy
  gip·sy
  gip·sies
Gi·rard
gird·er
gir·dle
  gir·dled
  gir·dling
girl·hood
girl·ish
girth
gist
give

gave
giv·en
giv·ing
give-and-take
give·a·way
giz·zard
gla·cial
gla·cier
glad
  glad·der
  glad·dest
  glad·ly
  glad·ness
glad·den
glad·i·a·tor
  glad·i·a·to·ri·al
glad·i·o·lus
  glad·i·o·lus·es
  glad·i·o·la
glad·some
Glad·stone
glam·or·ize
  glam·or·ized
  glam·or·iz·ing
  glam·or·i·za·tion
  glam·or·iz·er
glam·or·ous
  glam·or·ous·ly
  glam·or·ous·ness
glam·our
glance
  glanced
  glanc·ing
glan·du·lar
glare
  glared
  glar·ing
  glar·i·ness
  glary
  glar·i·er
  glar·i·est
Glas·gow
glass·blow·ing
  glass·blow·er
glass·ful
glass·ware
glassy
  glass·i·er
  glass·i·est
  glass·i·ly
  glass·i·ness
glau·co·ma
glaze
  glazed
  glaz·ing
gla·zier
gleam
  gleam·ing
  gleamy
glean
  glean·er
  glean·ing
glee
  glee·ful
  gleee·ful·ly

glee·ful·ness
Gleich·schal·tung
Glen·gar·ry
glib
  glib·ber
  glib·best
  glib·ly
  glib·ness
glide
  glid·ed
  glid·ing
glim·mer
glimpse
  glimpsed
  glimps·ing
glis·san·do
  glis·san·di
  glis·san·dos
glis·ten
glit·ter
gloam·ing
gloat
  gloat·er
  gloat·ing
glob
glob·al
  glob·al·ly
globe·trot·ter
  globe·trot·ting
glob·u·lar
glob·ule
glock·en·spiel
gloomy
  gloom·i·er
  gloom·i·est
  gloom·i·ly
  gloom·i·ness
glo·ri·fy
  glo·ri·fied
  glo·ri·fy·ing
  glo·ri·fi·ca·tion
  glo·ri·fi·er
glo·ri·ous
  glo·ri·ous·ly
  glo·ri·ous·ness
glo·ry
  glo·ries
  glo·ried
  glo·ry·ing
glos·sa·ry
  glos·sa·ries
glossy
  gloss·i·er
  gloss·i·est
  gloss·i·ly
  gloss·i·ness
glot·tis
  glot·tis·es
  glot·ti·des
Glouces·ter
Glouces·ter·shire
glove
  gloved
  glov·ing
glow

glow·er
glow·ing
glow·worm
glu·cose
glue
  glued
  glu·ing
glum
  glum·mer
  glum·mest
glut
  glut·ted
  glut·ting
glu·ten
glu·ti·nous
glut·ton
  glut·ton·ous
  glut·tony
glyc·er·in
  glyc·er·ine
glyc·er·ol
gnarl
  gnarled
  gnarly
  gnarl·i·er
  gnarl·i·est
gnash
gnat
gnaw
  gnawed
  gnaw·ing
gneiss
gnome
gnu
  gnus
goad·ed
go·a·head
goal·keep·er
goat·ee
goat·herd
goat·skin
gob·ble
  gob·bled
  gob·bling
  gob·ble·dy·gook
gob·bler
go·be·tween
Go·bi
gob·let
gob·lin
go·cart
god·child
  god·chil·dren
  god·daugh·ter
  god·son
god·dess
god·fa·ther
god·head
Go·di·va
god·less
  god·less·ness
god·like
god·ly
  god·li·er
  god·li·est

god·li·ness
god·moth·er
god·par·ent
god·send
God·speed
Goeb·bels
Goe·thals
Goe·the
go-get·ter
gog·gle
  gog·gled
  gog·gling
gog·gle-eyed
gog·gles
go·ing
goi·ter
gold·brick
gold·en
gold·smith
Gol·go·tha
Go·li·ath
Go·mor·rah
Gom·pers
go·nad
gon·do·la
gon·do·lier
gon·er
gon·or·rhea
goo·ber
good-by
  good-bye
good-for-noth·ing
good-heart·ed
good·ish
good-look·ing
good·ly
  good·li·er
  good·li·est
good-na·tured
good·ness
Good·rich
good-tem·pered
goody
  good·ies
Good·year
goof-off
goofy
  goof·i·er
  goof·i·est
  goof·i·ness
goose·ber·ry
  goose·ber·ries
gore
  gored
  gor·ing
gorge
  gorged
  gorg·ing
gor·geous
  gor·geous·ly
  gor·geous·ness
gory
  gor·i·er
  gor·i·est
Go·shen

gos·ling
gos·pel
gos·sa·mer
  gos·sa·mery
  gos·sa·mer·i·er
  gos·sa·mer·i·est
gos·sip
  gos·sip·ing
  gos·sipy
Goth·am
Goth·ic
gouge
  gouged
  goug·ing
  goug·er
gou·lash
gourd
gour·mand
gour·met
  gour·mets
gout
gouty
  gout·i·er
  gout·i·est
gov·ern
  gov·ern·a·ble
  gov·ern·ess
  gov·ern·ment
  gov·ern·men·tal
  gov·er·nor
  gov·er·nor·ship
gow·and
gowned
grab
  grabbed
  grab·bing
  grab·ber
grace
  graced
  grac·ing
grace·ful
  grace·ful·ly
  grace·ful·ness
grace·less
gra·cious
gra·da·tion
grade
  grad·ed
  grad·ing
  grad·er
gra·di·ent
grad·u·al
  grad·u·al·ly
  grad·u·al·ness
grad·u·ate
  grad·u·at·ed
  grad·u·at·ing
grad·u·a·tion
graf·fi·to
  graf·fi·ti
graft
  graft·age
  graft·er
  graft·ing
gra·ham

Grail
grain
grainy
grain·i·er
grain·i·est
grain·i·ness
gram
gram·mar
gram·mar·i·an
gram·mat·i·cal
gram·mat·i·cal·ly
Gra·na·da
gra·na·ry
gra·na·ries
grand
grand·ly
grand·child
grand·daugh·ter
gran·dee
gran·deur
grand·fa·ther
gran·dil·o·quence
gran·dil·o·quent
gran·di·ose
gran·di·ose·ly
grand·moth·er
grand·par·ent
Grand Rap·ids
grand·son
grand·stand
grange
grang·er
gran·ite
gra·nit·ic
gran·ny
gran·nies
gran·u·lar
gran·u·lar·i·ty
gran·u·late
gran·u·lat·ed
gran·u·lat·ing
gran·u·la·tion
gran·ule
grape·fruit
grape·vine
graph·ic
graph·i·cal
graph·i·cal·ly
graph·ite
graph·ol·o·gy
graph·ol·o·gist
grap·nel
grap·ple
grap·pled
grap·pling
grap·pler
grasp·ing
grass
grassy
grass·i·er
grass·i·est
grass·hop·per
grass·land
grate
grat·ed

grat·ing
grate·ful
grate·ful·ly
grate·ful·ness
grat·i·fy
grat·i·fied
grat·i·fy·ing
grat·i·fi·ca·tion
grat·ing
gra·tis
grat·i·tude
gra·tu·i·tous
gra·tu·i·tous·ly
gra·tu·i·ty
gra·tu·i·ties
grave
graved
grav·en
grav·ing
grav·er
grav·est
grave·ly
grave·ness
grav·el
grav·eled
grav·el·ing
grav·el·ly
grav·en
grave·stone
grave·yard
grav·i·tate
grav·i·tat·ed
grav·i·tat·ing
grav·i·ta·tion
grav·i·ta·tion·al
grav·i·ty
grav·i·ties
grav·i·ta·tion
gra·vy
gra·vies
gray
gray·ly
gray·ness
gray·ling
graze
grazed
graz·ing
grease
greased
greas·ing
greasy
greas·i·er
greas·i·est
greas·i·ly
greas·i·ness
great
great·ly
great·ness
Great Brit·ain
great·coat
great-heart·ed
Gre·cian
greedy
greed·i·er
greed·i·est

greed·i·ly
greed·i·ness
Greek
Gree·ley
green·back
green·ery
 green·er·ies
green·gro·cer
 green·gro·cery
 green·gro·cer·ies
green·horn
green·house
 green·hous·es
green·ing
green·ish
 green·ish·ness
Green·land
green·sward
Green·wich
greet
 greet·er
greet·ing
gre·gar·i·ous
 gre·gar·i·ous·ly
 gre·gar·i·ous·ness
Gre·go·ri·an
grem·lin
Gre·na·da
gren·a·dier
gren·a·dine
Gre·no·ble
grey
 grey·ly
 grey·ness
grid·dle
grid·dle·cake
grid·i·ron
grief
griev·ance
grieve
 grieved
 griev·ing
griev·ous
 griev·ous·ly
grif·fin
grif·fon
grill
gril·lage
grille
grill·room
grim
 grim·mer
 grim·mest
 grim·ly
 grim·ness
grim·ace
 grim·aced
 grim·ac·ing
grime
 grimed
 grim·ing
grimy
 grim·i·er
 grim·i·est
 grim·i·ly

grim·i·ness
grin
 grinned
 grin·ning
 grin·ner
grind
 ground
 grind·ing
 grind·er
grind·stone
grin·go
 grin·gos
grip
 gripped
 grip·ping
gripe
 griped
 grip·ing
 grip·er
grippe
Gri·sel·da
gris·ly
 gris·li·er
 gris·li·est
 gris·li·ness
gris·tle
gris·tly
 gris·tli·er
 gris·tli·est
grit
 grit·ted
 grit·ting
grit·ty
 grit·ti·er
 grit·ti·est
 grit·ti·ly
 grit·ti·ness
griz·zled
griz·zly
 griz·zli·er
 griz·zli·est
 griz·zlies
groan
 groan·er
gro·cer
gro·cery
 gro·cer·ies
grog·gy
 grog·gi·er
 grog·gi·est
 grog·gi·ly
 grog·gi·ness
groin
Gro·li·er
grom·met
groom
groove
 grooved
 groov·ing
 groov·er
groovy
 groov·i·er
 groov·i·est
grope
 groped

grop·ing
gros·grain
gross
  gross·es
  gross·ly
  gross·ness
gro·tesque
  gro·tesque·ly
  gro·tesque·ness
grot·to
  grot·toes
  grot·tos
grouch
  grouchy
  grouch·i·er
  grouch·i·est
ground·er
ground·less
  ground·less·ly
  ground·less·ness
ground·ling
ground·nut
ground·work
group·ie
grouse
  groused
  grous·ing
  grous·er
grov·el
  grov·eled
  grov·el·ing
  grov·el·er
grow
  grew
  grown
  grow·ing
  grow·er
growl
  growl·er
grown·up
growth
grub
  grubbed
  grub·bing
  grub·ber
grub·by
  grub·bi·er
  grub·bi·est
grub·stake
  grub·staked
  grub·stak·ing
grudge
  grudged
  grudg·ing
  grudg·ing·ly
gru·el
  gru·el·ing
grue·some
  grue·some·ly
gruff
  gruff·ly
  gruff·ness
grum·ble
  grum·bled
  grum·bling

grum·bler
grumpy
  grump·i·er
  grump·i·est
  grump·i·ly
  grump·i·ness
Grun·dy
grunt
  grunt·er
  grunt·ing
Gua·dal·ca·nal
Gua·dal·qui·vir
Gua·de·loupe
gua·no
  gua·nos
Gua·ra·ni
guar·an·tee
  guar·an·teed
  guar·an·tee·ing
guar·an·tor
guar·an·ty
  guar·an·ties
  guar·an·tied
  guar·an·ty·ing
guard·ed
  guard·ed·ly
  guard·house
  guard·i·an
  guards·man
  guards·men
Gua·te·ma·la
gua·va
gu·ber·na·to·ri·al
gudg·eon
Guern·sey
guer·ril·la
  gue·ril·la
guess
  guess·er
  guess·work
guest
guf·faw
Gui·ana
guid·ance
guide
  guid·ed
  guid·ing
  guide·book
  guide·post
gui·don
guild·hall
guile
  guile·ful
  guile·ful·ly
  guile·less
  guile·less·ly
Guil·ford
guil·lo·tine
  guil·lo·tined
  guil·lo·tin·ing
guilt
  guilt·less
  guilt·less·ly
guilty
  guilt·i·er

guilt·i·est
guilt·i·ly
guilt·i·ness
guin·ea
Guin·e·vere
guise
gui·tar
gui·tar·ist
gul·let
gul·li·ble
gul·li·bil·i·ty
gul·li·bly
Gul·li·ver
gul·ly
gul·lies
gul·lied
gul·ly·ing
gum
gummed
gum·ming
gum·bo
gum·bos
gum·drop
gum·my
gum·mi·er
gum·mi·est
gum·mi·ness
gump·tion
gum·shoe
gum·shoed
gum·shoe·ing
gun
gunned
gun·ning
gun·boat
gun·fight
gun·fight·er
gun·fire
gun·man
gun·men
gun·ner
gun·nery
gun·ny
gun·nies
gun·ny·bag
gun·pow·der
gun·shot
gun·smith
gun·stock
Gun·ther
gun·wale
gup·py
gup·pies
gur·gle
gur·gled
gur·gling
gu·ru
gush·er
gush·ing
gushy
gush·i·er
gush·i·est
gush·i·ness
gus·set
gus·ta·to·ry

gus·to
gusty
gust·i·er
gust·i·est
gust·i·ly
gust·i·ness
gut
gut·ted
gut·ting
Gu·ten·berg
Gut·ten·berg
gut·ter
gut·tur·al
gut·tur·al·ly
Guy·a·na
guz·zle
guz·zled
guz·zling
guz·zler
gym·na·si·um
gym·na·si·ums
gym·na·sia
gym·nast
gym·nas·tic
gym·nas·tics
gy·ne·col·o·gy
gy·ne·co·log·ic
gy·ne·co·log·i·cal
gy·ne·col·o·gist
gyp
gypped
gyp·ping
gyp·sum
gyp·sy
gyp·sies
gy·ral
gy·rate
gy·rat·ed
gy·rat·ing
gy·ra·tion
gy·ra·tor
gy·ra·to·ry
gyr·fal·con
gy·ro·com·pass
gy·roi·dal
gy·rom·e·ter
gy·ro·plane
gy·ro·scope
gy·ro·scop·ic
gy·ro·scop·i·cal·ly
gy·rose
gy·ro·sta·bi·liz·er
gy·ro·sta·tics
gy·rus
gyve
gyved
gyv·ing
Haar·lem
Hab·ak·kuk
ha·be·as cor·pus
hab·er·dash·er
hab·er·dash·ery
hab·er·dash·er·ies
ha·bil·i·ment
hab·it

hab·it·a·ble
hab·i·tat
hab·i·ta·tion
ha·bit·u·al
  ha·bit·u·al·ly
  ha·bit·u·al·ness
ha·bit·u·ate
  ha·bit·u·at·ed
  ha·bit·u·at·ing
  ha·bit·u·a·tion
ha·bit·ué
  ha·bit·u·és
ha·ci·en·da
  ha·ci·en·das
hack·le
  hack·led
  hack·ling
hack·ney
hack·neyed
hack·saw
Ha·des
had·n't
hae·mo·glo·bin
hae·mo·phil·ia
Ha·ga·nah
Ha·gen
hag·gard
  hag·gard·ly
hag·gle
  hag·gled
  hag·gling
  hag·gler
hag·i·ol·o·gy
  hag·i·ol·o·gies
  hag·i·ol·o·gist
hag·rid·den
Hai·fa
hai·ku
hail·stone
hail·storm
hair·breadth
hair·brush
hair·cut
hair·do
hair·dress·er
hair·line
hair·pin
hair·rais·ing
hair·split·ter
  hair·split·ting
hair·spring
hairy
  hair·i·er
  hair·i·est
Hai·ti
Ha·la·kah
hal·cy·on
hale
  haled
  hal·ing
half·back
half·baked
half·breed
half·caste
half-heart·ed

half-heart·ed·ly
half-hour
half·life
half-lives
half-mast
half-moon
half note
half step
half·tone
half-track
half-truth
half·way
half·wit
  half·wit·ted
hal·i·but
Hal·i·fax
hal·i·to·sis
Hal·low·een
hal·le·lu·jah
hall·mark
hal·lo
hal·low
  hal·lowed
Hal·low·een
hal·lu·ci·nate
  hal·lu·ci·nat·ed
  hal·lu·ci·nat·ing
  hal·lu·ci·na·tion
  hal·lu·ci·na·to·ry
  hal·lu·cin·o·gen
  hal·lu·cin·o·gen·ic
hall·way
ha·lo
  ha·los
  ha·loes
halt
  halt·ing
  halt·ing·ly
hal·ter
halve
  halved
  halv·ing
  halves
hal·yard
Ham·burg
ham·burg·er
Ham·e·lin
Ham·il·ton
ham·let
Ham·mar·skjöld
ham·mer
ham·mer·head
ham·mer·less
Ham·mer·stein
ham·mock
Ham·mond
Ham·mu·ra·bi
ham·my
  ham·mi·er
  ham·mi·est
Hamp·den
ham·per
Hamp·shire
Hamp·ton
ham·ster

ham·string
  ham·strung
  ham·string·ing
Ham·tramck
Han·cock
hand·bag
hand·ball
hand·bill
hand·book
hand·cuff
hand·ed
Han·del
hand·ful
  hand·fuls
hand·i·cap
  hand·i·capped
  hand·i·cap·ping
  hand·i·cap·per
hand·i·craft
hand·i·ly
  hand·i·ness
hand·i·work
hand·ker·chief
han·dle
  han·dled
  han·dling
  han·dler
han·dle·bar
hand·made
hand·maid·en
hand·me-down
hand·out
hand·pick
  hand-picked
hand·rail
hand·shake
hand·some
  hand·som·er
  hand·som·est
  hand·some·ly
  hand·some·ness
hand·spring
hand-to-hand
hand-to-mouth
hand·work
hand·writ·ing
handy
  hand·i·er
  hand·i·est
hand·y·man
  hand·y·men
hang
  hung
  hanged
  hang·ing
hang·ar
hang·dog
hang·er
hang·er-on
hang·man
  hang·men
hang·nail
hang·out
hang·o·ver
hang-up

hank·er
Han·kow
Han·ni·bal
Ha·noi
Han·o·ver
han·som
Ha·nuk·kah
hap·haz·ard
  hap·haz·ard·ly
  hap·haz·ard·ness
hap·less
  hap·less·ly
hap·ly
hap·pen
hap·pen·ing
hap·pen·stance
hap·pi·ness
hap·py
  hap·pi·er
  hap·pi·est
  hap·pi·ly
hap·py-go-lucky
Haps·burg
ha·ra·ki·ri
ha·rangue
  ha·rangued
  ha·rang·uing
har·ass
  har·ass·ment
har·bin·ger
har·bor
hard-bit·ten
hard-boiled
hard-core
hard·en
  hard·en·er
hard-hat
hard·head·ed
hard·heart·ed
har·di·hood
har·di·ness
Har·ding
hard·ly
hard·pan
hard·ship
hard·tack
hard·top
hard·ware
hard·wood
har·dy
  har·di·er
  har·di·est
  har·di·ly
hare·brained
hare·lip
har·em
har·ken
Har·lem
har·le·quin
har·lot
  har·lot·ry
harm·ful
  harm·ful·ly
  harm·ful·ness
harm·less

harm·less·ly
harm·less·ness
har·mon·ic
har·mon·i·cal·ly
har·mon·i·ca
har·mon·ics
har·mo·ni·ous
har·mo·ni·ous·ly
har·mo·nize
har·mo·nized
har·mo·niz·ing
har·mo·ny
har·mo·nies
har·ness
harp·ist
har·poon
harp·si·chord
har·py
har·pies
har·ri·dan
Har·ri·man
Har·ris·burg
Har·ri·son
har·row
har·row·ing
har·ry
har·ried
har·ry·ing
harsh
harsh·ly
harsh·ness
Hart·ford
har·um-scar·um
Har·vard
har·vest
har·ves·ter
Har·vey
has-been
hash·ish
hash·eesh
has·n't
has·sle
has·sled
has·sling
has·sock
has·ten
Has·tings
hast·y
hast·i·er
hast·i·est
hast·i·ness
hatch·ery
hatch·er·ies
hatch·et
hatch·way
hate
hat·ed
hat·ing
hat·er
hate·ful
hate·ful·ly
hate·ful·ness
ha·tred
hat·ter
haugh·ty

haugh·ti·er
haugh·ti·est
haugh·ti·ly
haugh·ti·ness
haul
haul·age
haunch
haunch·es
haunt·ed
haunt·ing
Haupt·mann
Hau·sa
hau·teur
Ha·va·na
ha·ven
have-nots
have·n't
Ha·ver·hill
hav·er·sack
haves
hav·oc
Ha·waii
hawk
hawk·ish
haw·ser
Haw·thorne
Hay·dn
hay·loft
hay·mak·er
Hay·mar·ket
hay·mow
hay·seed
hay·stack
hay·wire
haz·ard
haz·ard·ous
haz·ard·ous·ly
haz·ard·ous·ness
haze
hazed
haz·ing
ha·zel
ha·zel·nut
ha·zy
ha·zi·er
ha·zi·est
ha·zi·ly
ha·zi·ness
head·ache
head·band
head·dress
head·er
head·first
head·fore·most
head·gear
head·hunt·er
head·ing
head·land
head·less
head·light
head·line
head·lined
head·lin·ing
head·long
head·mas·ter

head·mis·tress
head·most
head-on
head·piece
head·quar·ters
head·set
head·stone
head·strong
head·wait·er
head·wa·ters
head·way
head·wind
heady
  head·i·er
  head·i·est
  head·i·ly
  head·i·ness
heal·er
health·ful
  health·ful·ly
healthy
  health·i·er
  health·i·est
  health·i·ly
  health·i·ness
heaped
hear
  heard
  hear·ing
  hear·er
hark·en
hear·say
hearse
heart·ache
heart·break
  heart·break·ing
heart·brok·en
heart·burn
heart·en
heart·felt
hearth·stone
heart·less
  heart·less·ly
  heart·less·ness
heart·rend·ing
heart·sick
heart·strings
heart-to-heart
hearty
  heart·i·er
  heart·i·est
  heart·i·ly
  heart·i·ness
heat·ed
heat·er
heath
hea·then
heave
  heaved
  heav·ing
heav·en
heav·en·ly
heav·en·ward
  heav·en·wards
heavy

heav·i·er
heav·i·est
heav·i·ly
heav·i·ness
heav·y-du·ty
heav·y-hand·ed
heav·y-heart·ed
heav·y·weight
Hebe
He·brew
  He·bra·ic
  He·bra·i·cal·ly
Heb·ri·des
He·bron
heck·le
  heck·led
  heck·ling
  heck·ler
hec·tare
hec·tic
  hec·ti·cal·ly
hec·to·gram
hec·to·li·ter
hec·to·me·ter
hedge
  hedged
  hedg·ing
  hedg·er
he·don·ism
he·don·ist
  he·do·nis·tic
hee-haw
hefty
  heft·i·er
  heft·i·est
He·gel
he·gem·o·ny
  he·gem·o·nies
  heg·e·mon·ic
he·gi·ra
Hei·del·berg
heif·er
height·en
  height·en·er
hei·nous
  hei·nous·ly
  hei·nous·ness
heir·ess
heir·loom
Hei·sen·berg
heist
Hel·e·na
hel·i·cop·ter
He·li·op·o·lis
He·li·os
he·li·um
he·lix
  hel·i·ces
  he·lix·es
hell-bent
hell·cat
Hel·len·ic
Hel·les·pont
hell·ion
hell·ish

hell·ish·ly
hell·ish·ness
hel·lo
hel·los
helm
helm·less
hel·met
hel·met·ed
helms·man
helms·men
help·er
help·ful
help·ful·ly
help·ful·ness
help·ing
help·less
help·less·ly
help·less·ness
help·mate
Hel·sin·ki
hel·ter-skel·ter
Hel·ve·tia
hem
hemmed
hem·ming
he-man
he-men
Hem·ing·way
hem·i·sphere
hem·i·spher·ic
hem·i·spher·i·cal
hem·lock
he·mo·glo·bin
he·mo·phil·ia
hem·or·rhage
hem·or·rhaged
hem·or·rhag·ing
hem·or·rhag·ic
hem·or·rhoid
hem·or·rhoi·dal
hemp·en
hem·stitch
hence·forth
hench·man
hench·men
hench·man·ship
Hen·der·son
hen·na
hen·peck
hep·a·ti·tis
her·ald
he·ral·dic
her·ald·ry
her·ald·ries
herb
her·ba·ceous
her·bage
her·biv·o·rous
her·cu·le·an
Her·cu·les
herd·er
herds·man
herds·men
here·af·ter
he·red·i·tary

he·red·i·tar·i·ly
he·red·i·tar·i·ness
he·red·i·ty
he·red·i·ties
Her·e·ford
here·in
here·of
her·e·sy
her·e·sies
her·e·tic
he·ret·i·cal
he·ret·i·cal·ly
here·to
here·to·fore
here·up·on
here·with
her·it·a·ble
her·it·a·bil·i·ty
her·it·a·bly
her·it·age
her·maph·ro·dite
her·maph·ro·dit·ic
her·maph· o·dit·i·cal·ly
her·maph·ro·dit·ism
Her·mes
her·met·ic
her·met·i·cal
her·met·i·cal·ly
her·mit
her·mit·age
her·nia
her·ni·al
her·ni·a·tion
he·ro
he·roes
Her·od
He·ro·di·as
he·ro·ic
he·ro·i·cal
he·ro·i·cal·ly
her·o·in
her·o·ine
her·o·ism
her·on
her·ring·bone
her·ring·boned
her·ring·bon·ing
her·self
Hert·ford
Hert·ford·shire
hes·i·tant
hes·i·tan·cy
hes·i·tan·cies
hes·i·tance
hes·i·tant·ly
hes·i·tate
hes·i·tat·ed
hes·i·tat·ing
hes·i·tat·er
hes·i·ta·tor
hes·i·ta·tor
hes·i·tat·ing·ly
hes·i·ta·tion
Hes·per·i·des
Hes·per·us

Hes·sian
het·er·o·dox
  het·er·o·doxy
het·er·o·ge·ne·ous
  het·er·o·ge·ne·i·ty
  het·er·o·ge·ne·ous·ness
  het·er·o·ge·ne·ous·ly
het·er·o·sex·u·al
  het·er·o·sex·u·al·i·ty
hew
  hewed
  hewn
  hew·ing
  hew·er
hex·a·gon
  hex·ag·o·nal
  hex·ag·o·nal·ly
hey·day
  hey·dey
Hez·e·ki·ah
hi·a·tus
  hi·a·tus·es
hi·ba·chi
hi·ber·nate
  hi·ber·nat·ed
  hi·ber·nat·ing
  hi·ber·na·tion
Hi·ber·nia
hi·bis·cus
hic·cup
  hic·cuped
  hic·cup·ing
hid·den
  hid·den·ness
hide
  hid
  hid·den
  hid·ing
  hid·er
hide·bound
hid·e·ous
  hid·e·ous·ly
  hid·e·ous·ness
hide·out
hi·er·ar·chy
  hi·er·ar·chies
  hi·er·ar·chal
  hi·er·ar·chic
  hi·er·ar·chi·cal
  hi·er·ar·chi·cal·ly
hi·er·o·glyph·ic
  hi·er·o·glyph·i·cal
  hi·er·o·glyph
  hi·er·o·glyph·i·cal·ly
hi-fi
high·ball
high·born
high·boy
high·brow
  high·browed
  high·brow·ism
high·er-up
high·fa·lu·tin
  high·fa·lu·ting
high·flown

high-grade
high-hand·ed
  high-hand·ed·ly
  high-hand·ed·ness
high-hat
high·land
High·land·er
high·light
high-mind·ed
  high·mind·ed·ly
  high·mind·ed·ness
high·ness
high-pres·sure
  high-pres·sured
  high-pres·sur·ing
high school
high seas
high-spir·it·ed
  high-spir·it·ed·ly
  high-spir·it·ed·ness
high-strung
high·tail
high-ten·sion
high-toned
high·way
high·way·man
  high·way·men
hi·jack
  hi·jack·er
  hi·jack·ing
hike
  hiked
  hik·ing
  hik·er
hi·lar·i·ous
  hi·lar·i·ous·ly
  hi·lar·i·ous·ness
  hi·lar·i·ty
hill·bil·ly
  hill·bil·lies
hill·ock
hill·side
hill·top
hilly
  hill·i·er
  hill·i·est
Him·a·laya
him·self
Hin·den·burg
hin·der
  hind·er·er
hind·most
hind·quar·ter
hin·drance
hind·sight
Hin·du
Hin·du·ism
Hin·du·stan
hinge
  hinged
  hing·ing
hint·er
  hint·ing·ly
hin·ter·land
hipped

hip·pie
hip·po
 hip·pos
Hip·poc·ra·tes
hip·po·drome
Hip·pol·y·tus
hip·po·pot·a·mus
 hip·po·pot·a·mus·es
 hip·po·pot·a·mi
hire·ling
Hi·ro·hi·to
Hi·ro·shi·ma
hir·sute
 hir·sute·ness
His·pa·nia
His·pan·ic
His·pan·i·o·la
hiss
 hiss·er
his·ta·mine
 his·ta·min·ic
his·to·ri·an
his·tor·ic
his·tor·i·cal
 his·tor·i·cal·ly
 his·tor·i·cal·ness
his·to·ry
 his·to·ries
his·tri·on·ic
 his·tri·on·i·cal
 his·tri·on·i·cal·ly
his·tri·on·ics
hit
 hit·ting
hit-and-run
hitch·er
hitch·hike
 hitch·hiked
 hitch·hik·ing
 hitch·hik·er
hith·er
hith·er·to
Hit·ler
Hit·tite
hive
 hived
 hiv·ing
hoary
 hoar·i·er
 hoar·i·est
 hoar·i·ness
hoard
 hoard·er
 hoard·ing
hoar·frost
hoarse
 hoarse·ly
hoars·en
 hoarse·ness
hoax
 hoax·er
hob·ble
 hob·bled
 hob·bling
hob·by

hob·bies
hob·by-horse
hob·gob·lin
hob·nail
 hob·nailed
hob·nob
 hob·nobbed
 hob·nob·bing
ho·bo
 ho·boes
 ho·bos
ho·bo·ism
Ho·bo·ken
hock·er
hock·ey
ho·cus-po·cus
hodge·podge
Hodg·kin's
hoe
 hoed
 hoe·ing
hoe·down
Hoff·mann
hog
 hogged
 hog·ging
hog·gish
 hog·gish·ly
 hog·gish·ness
hogs·head
hog·tie
 hog·tied
 hog·ty·ing
hog·wash
Ho·hen·stau·fen
Ho·hen·zol·lern
hoi poi·loi
hoist·er
ho·kum
hol·der
hold·ing
hold·out
hold·o·ver
hold·up
hole
 holed
 hol·ing
 holey
hol·i·day
ho·li·ness
Hol·land
hol·ler
hol·low
 hol·low·ly
 hol·low·ness
hol·ly
 hol·lies
hol·ly·hock
Hol·ly·wood
hol·mi·um
hol·o·caust
ho·lo·gram
hol·o·graph
Hol·stein
hol·ster

ho·ly
ho·li·er
ho·li·est
ho·lies
hom·age
hom·bre
hom·bres
Hom·burg
home·com·ing
home·less
home·less·ness
home·ly
home·li·er
home·li·est
home·li·ness
home·made
hom·er
home·sick
home·sick·ness
home·spun
home·stead
home·stead·er
home·ward
home·wards
home·work
homey
hom·i·er
hom·i·est
hom·i·ness
hom·i·cide
hom·i·let·ics
hom·i·ly
hom·i·lies
hom·ing pi·geon
hom·i·ny
Ho·mo
ho·mo·ge·ne·ous
ho·mo·ge·ne·i·ty
ho·mo·ge·ne·ous·ly
ho·mo·ge·ne·ous·ness
ho·mog·e·nize
ho·mog·e·nized
ho·mog·e·niz·ing
hom·o·graph
ho·mol·o·gous
ho·mol·o·gy
ho·mol·o·gies
hom·o·nym
hom·o·nym·ic
hom·o·phone
hom·o·phon·ic
Ho·mo sa·pi·ens
ho·mo·sex·u·al
ho·mo·sex·u·al·i·ty
Hon·du·ras
hone
honed
hon·ing
hon·est
hon·est·ly
hon·es·ty
hon·es·ties
hon·ey
hon·eys
hon·eyed

hon·ied
hon·ey·ing
hon·ey·bee
hon·ey·comb
hon·ey·moon
hon·ey·moon·er
hon·ey·suck·le
hon·ey·suck·led
honk·y·tonk
Hon·o·lu·lu
hon·or
hon·or·a·ble
hon·or·a·bly
hon·o·rar·i·um
hon·o·rar·i·ums
hon·o·rar·ia
hon·or·ary
hon·or·if·ic
hood·ed
hood·lum
hoo·doo
hoo·doo·ism
hood·wink
hood·wink·er
hoo·ey
hoof
hoofs
hooves
hoofed
hooked
hook·er
hook·up
hoo·li·gan
hoo·li·gan·ism
hoop
hooped
hoop·like
hoop·la
hoo·ray
hoose·gow
Hoo·sier
hoot
hoot·er
hoot·ing·ly
Hoo·ver
hop
hopped
hop·ping
hope
hoped
hop·ing
hop·er
hope·ful
hope·ful·ly
hope·ful·ness
hope·less
hope·less·ly
hope·less·ness
hop·head
Hop·kins
hop·per
hop·scotch
Hor·ace
Ho·ra·tius
horde

hord·ed
hord·ing
Ho·reb
ho·ri·zon
hor·i·zon·tal
hor·i·zon·tal·ly
hor·mone
hor·mo·nal
horn
horned
horn·like
horny
horn·i·er
horn·i·est
hor·net
horn·swog·gle
horn·swog·gled
horn·swog·gling
ho·rol·o·gy
ho·rol·o·ger
ho·rol·o·gist
hor·o·scope
hor·ren·dous
hor·ren·dous·ly
hor·ri·ble
hor·ri·bly
hor·rid
hor·rid·ly
hor·rid·ness
hor·ri·fy
hor·ri·fied
hor·ri·fy·ing
hor·ri·fi·ca·tion
hor·ror
hors d'oeu·vre
hors d'oeu·vres
horse
hors·es
horsed
hors·ing
horse·back
horse·fly
horse·flies
horse·hair
horse·laugh
horse·man
horse·men
horse·man·ship
horse·wom·an
horse·wom·en
horse op·era
horse·play
horse·pow·er
horse·rad·ish
horse·shoe
horse·sho·er
horse·whip
horse·whipped
horse·whip·ping
hors·ey
horsy
hors·i·er
hors·i·est
hors·i·ly
hors·i·ness

hor·ta·to·ry
hor·ti·cul·ture
hor·ti·cul·tur·al
hor·ti·cul·tur·ist
ho·san·na
hose
hos·es
hosed
hos·ing
Ho·sea
ho·siery
hos·pice
hos·pi·ta·ble
hos·pi·ta·bly
hos·pi·tal
hos·pi·tal·i·ty
hos·pi·tal·i·ties
hos·pi·tal·i·za·tion
hos·pi·tal·ize
hos·pi·tal·ized
hos·pi·tal·iz·ing
hos·tage
hos·tel
hos·tel·ry
hos·tel·ries
host·ess
hos·tile
hos·tile·ly
hos·til·i·ty
hos·til·i·ties
hos·tler
hot
hot·ter
hot·test
hot·ly
hot·bed
hot-blood·ed
ho·tel
hot·head
hot·head·ed
hot·head·ed·ness
hot·house
hot·shot
Hot·ten·tot
Hou·di·ni
hound
hound·er
hour·glass
hour·ly
house
hous·es
housed
hous·ing
house·boat
house·bro·ken
house·break
house·broke
house·break·ing
house·fly
house·hold
house·hold·er
house·keep·er
house·keep·ing
house·maid
house·warm·ing

house·wife
house·wives
house·wife·ly
house·wif·ery
house·work
hous·ing
Hous·ton
hov·el
hov·eled
hov·el·ing
hov·er
hov·er·er
hov·er·ing
how·ev·er
how·itz·er
howl·er
how·so·ev·er
hoy·den
hoy·den·ish
hub·bub
huck·le·ber·ry
huck·le·ber·ries
huck·ster
hud·dle
hud·dled
hud·dling
hud·dler
Hud·son
Huer·ta
huffy
huff·i·er
huff·i·est
huff·i·ly
huff·i·ness
hug
hugged
hug·ging
hug·ger
huge
hug·er
hug·est
huge·ly
huge·ness
Hu·gue·not
hu·la
hulk·ing
hul·la·ba·loo
hum
hummed
hum·ming
hum·mer
hu·man
hu·man·ness
hu·mane
hu·mane·ly
hu·mane·ness
hu·man·ism
hu·man·ist
hu·man·is·tic
hu·man·i·tar·i·an
hu·man·i·tar·i·an·ism
hu·man·i·ty
hu·man·i·ties
hu·man·ize
hu·man·ized

hu·man·iz·ing
hu·man·i·za·tion
hu·man·iz·er
hu·man·kind
hu·man·ly
hum·ble
hum·bler
hum·blest
hum·bled
hum·bling
hum·ble·ness
hum·bly
Hum·boldt
hum·bug
hum·bugged
hum·bug·ging
hum·bug·ger
hum·bug·ger·y
hum·ding·er
hum·drum
hu·mer·us
hu·mid
hu·mid·ly
hu·mid·i·fy
hu·mid·i·fied
hu·mid·i·fy·ing
hu·mid·i·fi·er
hu·mid·i·ty
hu·mi·dor
hu·mil·i·ate
hu·mil·i·at·ed
hu·mil·i·at·ing
hu·mil·i·a·tion
hu·mil·i·ty
hum·ming bird
hum·mock
hum·mocky
hum·mock·i·er
hum·mock·i·est
hu·mor
hu·mor·ist
hu·mor·is·tic
hu·mor·ous
hu·mor·ous·ly
hu·mor·ous·ness
hump
humped
humpy
hump·i·er
hump·i·est
hump·back
hu·mus
hunch·back
hunch·backed
hun·dred
hun·dredth
hun·dred·weight
Hun·ga·ry
hun·ger
hun·gry
hun·gri·er
hun·gri·est
hun·gri·ly
hun·gri·ness
Hun·nish

Hun·nish·ness
hunt
  hunt·er
  hunt·ing
  hunt·ress
  hunts·man
  hunts·men
Hun·ting·ton
hur·dle
  hur·dled
  hur·dling
  hur·dler
hur·dy-gur·dy
  hur·dy-gur·dies
hurl·er
hurl·y-burly
  hurl·y-burl·ies
Hu·ron
hur·rah
hur·ri·cane
hur·ry
  hur·ried
  hur·ry·ing
  hur·ried·ly
  hur·ry·ing·ly
hurt·ful
  hurt·ful·ly
hurt·ing
hur·tle
  hur·tled
  hur·tling
hus·band
  hus·band·less
hus·band·ry
husk·er
husky
  husk·i·er
  husk·i·est
  husk·i·ly
  husk·i·ness
  husk·ies
hus·sar
Huss·ite
hus·sy
  huss·ies
hus·tings
hus·tle
  hus·tled
  hus·tling
  hus·tler
hutch
Hux·ley
huz·zah
  huz·za
hy·a·cinth
hy·brid
  hy·brid·ism
hy·brid·ize
  hy·brid·ized
  hy·brid·iz·ing
  hy·brid·i·za·tion
hy·dra
  hy·dras
  hy·drae
hy·dran·gea

hy·drant
hy·drate
  hy·dra·ted
  hy·dra·ting
  hy·dra·tion
  hy·dra·tor
hy·drau·lic
  hy·drau·li·cal·ly
hy·drau·lics
hy·dro·car·bon
hy·dro·chlo·ric·ac·id
hy·dro·dy·nam·ics
  hy·dro·dy·nam·ic
hy·dro·e·lec·tric
hy·dro·gen
  hy·drog·e·nous
hy·drol·y·sis
  hy·drol·y·ses
hy·drom·e·ter
  hy·dro·met·ric
  hy·dro·met·ri·cal
hy·drom·e·try
hy·dro·pho·bia
hy·dro·plane
  hy·dro·planed
  hy·dro·plan·ing
hy·dro·pon·ics
  hy·dro·pon·ic
hy·dro·ther·a·py
  hy·dro·ther·a·pist
hy·drous
hy·drox·ide
hy·drox·yl
hy·dro·zo·an
hy·e·na
hy·giene
  hy·gi·en·ic
  hy·gi·en·i·cal·ly
  hy·gien·ist
hy·men
hy·me·ne·al
  hy·me·ne·al·ly
hym·nal
hy·per·bo·la
hy·per·bo·le
  hy·per·bo·lize
  hy·per·bo·lized
  hy·per·bo·liz·ing
hy·per·bol·ic
hy·per·crit·i·cal
  hy·per·crit·i·cal·ly
hy·per·sen·si·tive
  hy·per·sen·si·tive·ness
  hy·per·sen·si·tiv·i·ty
hy·per·ten·sion
hy·per·thy·roid·ism
hy·phen
hy·phen·ate
  hy·phen·at·ed
  hy·phen·at·ing
hyp·no·sis
hyp·not·ic
hyp·no·tism
  hyp·no·tist
hyp·no·tize

hyp·no·tized
hyp·no·tiz·ing
hy·po
hy·po·chon·dria
hy·po·chon·dri·ac
hy·poc·ri·sy
hyp·oc·ri·sies
hyp·o·crite
hy·po·der·mic
hy·po·der·mic in·jec·tion
hy·po·sen·si·tize
hy·po·sen·si·tized
hy·po·sen·si·tiz·ing
hy·po·ten·sion
hy·pot·e·nuse
hy·poth·e·cate
hy·poth·e·cat·ed
hy·poth·e·cat·ing
hy·poth·e·ca·tion
hy·poth·e·ca·tor
hy·poth·e·sis
hy·poth·e·ses
hy·poth·e·size
hy·poth·e·sized
hy·poth·e·siz·ing
hy·po·thet·i·cal
hy·po·thet·i·cal·ly
hy·pox·e·mia
hy·pox·ia
hyp·sog·ra·phy
hyp·som·e·ter
hyp·som·e·try
hy·son
hys·sop
hys·ter·ec·to·my
hys·ter·ec·to·mies
hys·ter·e·sis
hys·te·ria
hys·ter·ic
hys·ter·i·cal
hys·ter·i·cal·ly
hys·ter·ics
iamb
iambs
iam·bus
iam·bus·es
iam·bi
iam·bic
iat·ric
Ibe·ria
ibid
ibi·dem
ibis
ibis·es
ice
iced
ic·ing
ice·bag
ice·berg
ice·boat
ice·box
ice·cap
ice·cold
ice cream
Ice·land

ice·man
ice·men
ice-skate
ice-skat·ed
ice-skat·ing
ice-skat·er
Ich·a·bod
ich·nol·o·gy
ich·no·log·i·cal
ich·thy·ol·o·gy
ich·thy·o·log·i·cal
ich·thy·ol·o·gist
ici·cle
ici·ly
ici·ness
icon
icon·o·clasm
icon·o·clas·tic
icon·o·clast
icy
ici·er
ici·est
Ida·ho
idea
ide·al
ide·al·ness
ide·al·ism
ide·al·ist
ide·al·is·tic
ide·al·ize
ide·al·ized
ide·al·iz·ing
ide·al·i·za·tion
ide·al·ly
idem
iden·ti·cal
iden·ti·cal·ly
iden·ti·cal·ness
iden·ti·fi·a·ble
iden·ti·fi·a·bly
iden·ti·fi·ca·tion
iden·ti·fy
iden·ti·fied
iden·ti·fy·ing
iden·ti·fi·er
iden·ti·ty
iden·ti·ties
ide·ol·o·gist
ide·ol·o·gy
ide·ol·o·gies
ides
id·i·o·cy
id·i·o·cies
id·i·om
id·i·o·mat·ic
id·i·o·mat·i·cal·ly
id·i·o·syn·cra·sy
id·i·o·syn·cra·sies
id·i·o·syn·crat·ic
id·i·o·syn·crat·i·cal·ly
id·i·ot
id·i·ot·ic
id·i·ot·i·cal·ly
idle
idler

idlest
idled
idling
idle·ness
idler
idly
idol
idol·a·try
idol·a·tries
idol·a·ter
idol·a·trous
idol·ize
idol·ized
idol·iz·ing
idol·i·za·tion
idol·iz·er
idyll
idyl·lic
idyl·lic·al·ly
if·fy
ig·loo
ig·loos
ig·ne·ous
ig·nite
ig·nit·ed
ig·nit·ing
ig·nit·er
ig·nit·a·ble
ig·nit·a·bil·i·ty
ig·ni·tion
ig·no·ble
ig·no·bil·i·ty
ig·no·ble·ness
ig·no·bly
ig·no·miny
ig·no·min·ies
ig·no·min·i·ous
ig·no·min·i·ous·ly
ig·no·min·i·ous·ness
ig·no·ra·mus
ig·no·rant
ig·no·rance
ig·no·rant·ly
ig·nore
ig·nored
ig·nor·ing
i·gua·na
Il·i·ad
ill-ad·vised
ill-ad·vis·ed·ly
ill-bred
il·le·gal
il·le·gal·i·ty
il·le·gal·ly
il·leg·i·ble
il·leg·i·bil·i·ty
il·leg·i·ble·ness
il·leg·i·bly
il·le·git·i·mate
il·le·git·i·ma·cy
il·le·git·i·ma·cies
il·le·git·i·mate·ly
ill-fat·ed
ill-fa·vored
ill-got·ten

il·lib·er·al
il·lic·it
il·lim·it·a·ble
Il·li·nois
il·lit·er·ate
il·lit·er·a·cy
il·lit·er·a·cies
ill·ness
il·log·i·cal
ill-starred
ill-tem·pered
ill-tem·pered·ly
ill-tem·pered·ness
ill-timed
il·lu·mi·nate
il·lu·mi·nat·ed
il·lu·mi·nat·ing
il·lu·mi·na·tor
il·lu·mi·na·tion
il·lu·mine
il·lu·mined
il·lu·min·ing
ill-use
ill-used
ill-us·ing
ill-us·age
il·lu·sion
il·lu·sive
il·lu·sive·ly
il·lu·sive·ness
il·lu·so·ry
il·lu·so·ri·ly
il·lu·so·ri·ness
il·lus·trate
il·lus·trat·ed
il·lus·trat·ing
il·lus·tra·tion
il·lus·tra·tive
il·lus·tra·tive·ly
il·lus·tra·tor
il·lus·tri·ous
il·lus·tri·ous·ly
il·lus·tri·ous·ness
Il·lyr·ia
im·age
im·aged
im·ag·ing
im·age·a·ble
im·ag·er
im·age·ry
im·age·ries
im·a·ge·ri·al
im·ag·i·na·ble
imag·i·na·ble·ness
imag·i·na·bly
im·ag·i·nary
im·ag·i·nar·ies
imag·i·nar·i·ly
imag·i·nar·i·ness
im·ag·i·na·tion
imag·i·na·tion·al
im·ag·i·na·tive
imag·i·na·tive·ly
imag·i·na·tive·ness
im·ag·ine

im·ag·ined
im·ag·in·ing
im·bal·ance
im·be·cile
im·be·cil·ic
im·be·cile·ly
im·be·cil·i·ty
im·bed
im·bed·ded
im·bed·ding
im·bibe
im·bibed
im·bib·ing
im·bib·er
im·bro·glio
im·bue
im·bued
im·bu·ing
im·i·ta·ble
im·i·tate
im·i·tat·ed
im·i·tat·ing
im·i·ta·tor
im·i·ta·tion
im·i·ta·tive
im·mac·u·late
im·mac·u·la·cy
im·mac·u·late·ness
im·mac·u·late·ly
im·ma·nent
im·ma·nence
im·ma·nen·cy
im·ma·nent·ly
im·ma·te·ri·al
im·ma·te·ri·al·ness
im·ma·te·ri·al·i·ty
im·ma·ture
im·ma·ture·ly
im·ma·ture·ness
im·ma·tu·ri·ty
im·meas·ur·a·ble
im·meas·ur·a·ble·ness
im·meas·ur·a·bly
im·me·di·a·cy
im·me·di·a·cies
im·me·di·ate
im·me·di·ate·ly
im·me·di·ate·ness
im·me·mo·ri·al
im·me·mo·ri·al·ly
im·mense
im·mense·ly
im·mense·ness
im·men·si·ty
im·merge
im·merged
im·merg·ing
im·mer·gence
im·merse
im·mersed
im·mers·ing
im·mer·sion
im·mi·grant
im·mi·grate
im·mi·grat·ed

im·mi·grat·ing
im·mi·gra·tion
im·mi·gra·tor
im·mi·nent
im·mi·nence
im·mo·bile
im·mo·bil·i·ty
im·mo·bi·lize
im·mo·bi·lized
im·mo·bi·liz·ing
im·mod·er·ate
im·mod·er·ate·ly
im·mod·er·ate·ness
im·mod·est
im·mod·est·ly
im·mod·es·ty
im·mo·late
im·mo·lat·ed
im·mo·lat·ing
im·mo·la·tion
im·mo·la·tor
im·mor·al
im·mor·al·ist
im·mo·ral·i·ty
im·mo·ral·i·ties
im·mor·al·ly
im·mor·tal
im·mor·tal·i·ty
im·mor·tal·ize
im·mor·tal·ized
im·mor·tal·iz·ing
im·mor·tal·ly
im·mov·a·ble
im·mov·a·bil·i·ty
im·mov·a·bly
im·mune
im·mu·ni·ty
im·mu·ni·ties
im·mu·nize
im·mu·nized
im·mu·niz·ing
im·mu·ni·za·tion
im·mu·nol·o·gy
im·mure
im·mured
im·mur·ing
im·mu·ta·ble
im·mu·ta·bil·i·ty
im·mu·ta·ble·ness
im·mu·ta·bly
im·pact
im·pac·tion
im·pact·ed
im·pair
im·pair·er
im·pair·ment
im·pala
im·pal·as
im·pal·ae
im·pale
im·paled
im·pal·ing
im·pale·ment
im·pal·er
im·pal·pa·ble

im·pal·pa·bil·i·ty
im·pal·pa·bly
im·pan·el
im·pan·eled
im·pan·el·ing
im·part
im·par·tial
im·par·ti·al·i·ty
im·par·tial·ness
im·par·tial·ly
im·pass·a·ble
im·pass·a·bil·i·ty
im·pass·a·ble·ness
im·pass·a·bly
im·passe
im·pas·si·ble
im·pas·si·bil·i·ty
im·pas·si·ble·ness
im·pas·si·bly
im·pas·sion
im·pas·sioned
im·pas·sioned·ly
im·pas·sioned·ness
im·pas·sive
im·pas·sive·ly
im·pas·sive·ness
im·pas·siv·i·ty
im·pa·tient
im·pa·tience
im·pa·tient·ly
im·peach
im·peach·a·ble
im·peach·ment
im·pec·ca·ble
im·pec·ca·bil·i·ty
im·pec·ca·bly
im·pe·cu·ni·ous
im·pe·cu·ni·ous·ly
im·pe·cu·ni·ous·ness
im·pede
im·ped·ed
im·ped·ing
im·ped·i·ment
im·pel
im·pelled
im·pel·ling
im·pend
im·pend·ing
im·pen·e·tra·bil·i·ty
im·pen·e·tra·ble
im·pen·e·tra·ble·ness
im·pen·e·tra·bly
im·pen·i·tent
im·pen·i·tence
im·pen·i·tent·ly
im·per·a·tive
im·per·a·tive·ly
im·per·a·tive·ness
im·per·cep·ti·ble
im·per·cep·ti·bil·i·ty
im·per·cep·ti·bly
im·per·cep·tive
im·per·cep·tive·ness
im·per·fect
im·per·fect·ly

im·per·fect·ness
im·per·fec·tion
im·pe·ri·al
im·pe·ri·al·ly
im·pe·ri·al·ism
im·pe·ri·al·ist
im·pe·ri·al·is·tic
im·pe·ri·al·is·ti·cal·ly
im·per·il
im·per·iled
im·per·il·ing
im·per·il·ment
im·pe·ri·ous
im·pe·ri·ous·ly
im·pe·ri·ous·ness
im·per·ish·a·ble
im·per·ish·a·bil·i·ty
im·per·ish·a·ble·ness
im·per·ish·a·bly
im·per·ma·nent
im·per·ma·nence
im·per·ma·nen·cy
im·per·ma·nent·ly
im·per·me·a·ble
im·per·me·a·bil·i·ty
im·per·me·a·ble·ness
im·per·me·a·bly
im·per·son·al
im·per·son·al·i·ty
im·per·son·al·i·ties
im·per·son·al·ly
im·per·son·ate
im·per·son·at·ed
im·per·son·at·ing
im·per·son·a·tion
im·per·son·a·tor
im·per·ti·nent
im·per·ti·nence
im·per·ti·nent·ly
im·per·turb·a·ble
im·per·turb·a·bly
im·per·vi·ous
im·per·vi·ous·ly
im·per·vi·ous·ness
im·pe·ti·go
im·pet·u·ous
im·pet·u·os·i·ty
im·pet·u·ous·ly
im·pet·u·ous·ness
im·pe·tus
im·pe·tus·es
im·pi·e·ty
im·pi·e·ties
im·pinge
im·pinged
im·ping·ing
im·pinge·ment
im·ping·er
im·pi·ous
im·pi·ous·ly
im·pi·ous·ness
im·plac·a·ble
im·plac·a·bil·i·ty
im·plac·a·ble·ness
im·plac·a·bly

im·plant
 im·plan·ta·tion
 im·plant·er
im·plau·si·ble
 im·plau·si·bly
 im·plau·si·bil·i·ty
im·ple·ment
 im·ple·men·tal
 im·ple·men·ta·tion
im·pli·cate
 im·pli·cat·ed
 im·pli·cat·ing
im·pli·ca·tion
im·plic·it
 im·plic·it·ly
 im·plic·it·ness
im·plode
 im·plod·ed
 im·plod·ing
 im·plo·sion
 im·plo·sive
im·plore
 im·plored
 im·plor·ing
 im·plo·ra·tion
im·ply
 im·plied
 im·ply·ing
im·po·lite
 im·po·lite·ly
 im·po·lite·ness
im·pol·i·tic
 im·pol·i·tic·ly
im·pon·der·a·ble
 im·pon·der·a·bil·i·ty
 im·pon·der·a·ble·ness
 im·pon·der·a·bly
im·port
 im·port·a·ble
 im·port·er
 im·por·tance
 im·por·tant
 im·por·tant·ly
 im·por·ta·tion
 im·por·tu·nate
 im·por·tu·nate·ly
 im·por·tune
 im·por·tuned
 im·por·tun·ing
im·pose
 im·posed
 im·pos·ing
 im·pos·ter
 im·po·si·tion
im·pos·si·ble
 im·pos·si·bil·i·ty
 im·pos·si·bil·i·ties
 im·pos·si·bly
im·post
im·pos·tor
im·pos·ture
im·po·tent
 im·po·tence
 im·po·ten·cy
 im·po·tent·ly

im·pound
 im·pound·age
im·pov·er·ish
 im·pov·er·ish·ment
im·prac·ti·ca·ble
 im·prac·ti·ca·bil·i·ty
 im·prac·ti·ca·ble·ness
 im·prac·ti·ca·bly
im·prac·ti·cal
im·pre·cate
 im·pre·cat·ed
 im·pre·cat·ing
 im·pre·ca·tion
im·preg·na·ble
 im·preg·na·bil·i·ty
 im·preg·na·ble·ness
 im·preg·na·bly
im·preg·nate
 im·preg·nat·ed
 im·preg·nat·ing
 im·preg·na·tion
 im·preg·na·tor
im·pre·sa·rio
 im·pre·sa·ri·os
im·press
 im·press·er
 im·press·i·ble
 im·press·ment
im·pres·sion
 im·pres·sion·ist
 im·pres·sion·a·ble
 im·pres·sion·a·bly
 im·pres·sion·ism
 im·pres·sion·ist
 im·pres·sion·is·tic
im·pres·sive
 im·pres·sive·ly
 im·pres·sive·ness
im·pri·ma·tur
im·print
 im·prin·ter
im·pris·on
 im·pris·on·ment
im·prob·a·ble
 im·prob·a·bil·i·ty
 im·prob·a·ble·ness
 im·prob·a·bly
im·promp·tu
im·prop·er
 im·prop·er·ly
 im·prop·er·ness
im·pro·pri·e·ty
 im·pro·pri·e·ties
im·prove
 im·proved
 im·prov·ing
 im·prov·a·bil·i·ty
 im·prov·a·ble
im·prove·ment
im·prov·i·dent
 im·prov·i·dence
 im·prov·i·dent·ly
im·prov·i·sa·tion
 im·prov·i·sa·tion·al
im·pro·vise

im·pro·vised
im·pro·vis·ing
im·pro·vi·ser
im·pru·dent
im·pru·dence
im·pru·dent·ly
im·pugn
im·pugn·er
im·pulse
im·pul·sion
im·pul·sive
im·pu·ni·ty
im·pure
im·pure·ly
im·pure·ness
im·pu·ri·ty
im·pu·ri·ties
im·pute
im·put·ed
im·put·ing
im·pu·ta·ble
im·pu·ta·tion
im·put·a·tive
im·put·er
in·a·bil·i·ty
in·ac·ces·si·ble
in·ac·ces·si·bil·i·ty
in·ac·ces·si·ble·ness
in·ac·ces·si·bly
in·ac·cu·rate
in·ac·cu·rate·ly
in·ac·cu·ra·cy
in·ac·cu·ra·cies
in·ac·tion
in·ac·tive
in·ac·tive·ly
in·ac·tiv·i·ty
in·ad·e·quate
in·ad·e·qua·cy
in·ad·e·qua·cies
in·ad·e·quate·ly
in·ad·mis·si·ble
in·ad·mis·si·bly
in·ad·vert·ent
in·ad·vert·ence
in·ad·vert·en·cy
in·ad·vert·ent·ly
in·al·ien·a·ble
in·al·ien·a·bly
in·am·o·ra·ta
in·am·o·ra·tas
in·ane
in·ane·ly
in·ane·ness
in·an·i·ty
in·an·i·ties
in·an·i·mate
in·ap·pro·pri·ate
in·ap·pro·pri·ate·ly
in·ap·pro·pri·ate·ness
in·apt
in·ap·ti·tude
in·apt·ly
in·apt·ness
in·ar·tic·u·late

in·ar·tic·u·late·ly
in·ar·tic·u·late·ness
in·as·much as
in·at·ten·tion
in·at·ten·tive
in·at·ten·tive·ly
in·au·gu·ral
in·au·gu·rate
in·au·gu·rat·ed
in·au·gu·rat·ing
in·au·gu·ra·tion
in·aus·pi·cious
in·aus·pi·cious·ly
in·board
in·born
in·bred
in·breed
in·breed·ing
In·ca
in·cal·cu·la·ble
in·cal·cu·la·bly
in·can·des·cent
in·can·des·cence
in·can·des·cent·ly
in·can·ta·tion
in·ca·pa·ble
in·ca·pa·bly
in·ca·pac·i·tate
in·ca·pac·i·tat·ed
in·ca·pac·i·tat·ing
in·ca·pac·i·ty
in·ca·pac·i·ties
in·car·cer·ate
in·car·cer·at·ed
in·car·cer·at·ing
in·car·cer·a·tion
in·car·nate
in·car·nat·ed
in·car·nat·ing
in·car·na·tion
in·cen·di·a·ry
in·cen·di·a·ries
in·cense
in·censed
in·cens·ing
in·cen·tive
in·cep·tion
in·ces·sant
in·ces·sant·ly
in·cest
in·ces·tu·ous
in·ces·tu·ous·ly
in·ces·tu·ous·ness
in·cho·ate
in·cho·ate·ly
in·cho·ate·ness
in·ci·dence
in·ci·dent
in·ci·den·tal
in·ci·den·tal·ly
in·cin·er·ate
in·cin·er·at·ed
in·cin·er·at·ing
in·cin·er·a·tion
in·cin·er·a·tor

in·cip·i·ent
in·cip·i·ent·ly
in·cise
in·cised
in·cis·ing
in·ci·sion
in·ci·sive
in·ci·sive·ly
in·ci·sive·ness
in·ci·sor
in·cite
in·cit·ed
in·cit·ing
in·cite·ment
in·cit·er
in·clem·ent
in·clem·en·cy
in·clem·ent·ly
in·cli·na·tion
in·cline
in·clined
in·clin·ing
in·clin·er
in·clude
in·clud·ed
in·clud·ing
in·clud·a·ble
in·clu·sion
in·clu·sive
in·clu·sive·ly
in·clu·sive·ness
in·cog·ni·to
in·cog·ni·tos
in·co·her·ent
in·co·her·ence
in·co·her·ent·ly
in·come
in·com·ing
in·com·men·su·ra·ble
in·com·men·su·ra·bly
in·com·men·su·rate
in·com·men·su·rate·ly
in·com·mo·di·ous
in·com·pa·ra·ble
in·com·pa·ra·bly
in·com·pat·i·ble
in·com·pat·i·bil·i·ty
in·com·pat·i·bly
in·com·pe·tent
in·com·pe·tence
in·com·pe·ten·cy
in·com·pe·tent·ly
in·com·plete
in·com·plete·ly
in·com·plete·ness
in·com·ple·tion
in·com·pre·hen·si·ble
in·com·pre·hen·si·bly
in·com·pre·hen·sion
in·con·ceiv·a·ble
in·con·ceiv·a·bly
in·con·clu·sive
in·con·clu·sive·ly
in·con·clu·sive·ness
in·con·gru·ous

in·con·gru·ous·iy
in·con·gru·ous·ness
in·con·gru·i·ty
in·con·gru·i·ties
in·con·se·quen·tial
in·con·se·quen·tial·ly
in·con·sid·er·a·ble
in·con·sid·er·a·bly
in·con·sid·er·ate
in·con·sid·er·ate·ly
in·con·sid·er·ate·ness
in·con·sis·tent
in·con·sist·ent·ly
in·con·sol·a·ble
in·con·sol·a·ble·ness
in·con·sol·a·bly
in·con·spic·u·ous
in·con·spic·u·ous·ly
in·con·spic·u·ous·ness
in·con·stant
in·con·stan·cy
in·con·stan·cies
in·con·stant·ly
in·con·test·a·ble
in·con·test·a·bly
in·con·ti·nent
in·con·ti·nence
in·con·ti·nen·cy
in·con·ti·nent·ly
in·con·tro·vert·i·ble
in·con·ven·ience
in·con·ven·ien·cy
in·con·ven·ienced
in·con·ven·ienc·ing
in·con·ven·ient
in·con·ven·ient·ly
in·cor·po·rate
in·cor·po·rat·ed
in·cor·po·rat·ing
in·cor·po·ra·tion
in·cor·po·ra·tor
in·cor·po·re·al
in·cor·rect
in·cor·rect·ly
in·cor·ri·gi·ble
in·cor·ri·gi·bil·i·ty
in·cor·ri·gi·ble·ness
in·cor·ri·gi·bly
in·cor·rupt·i·ble
in·cor·rupt·i·bil·i·ty
in·cor·rupt·i·ble·ness
in·cor·rupt·i·bly
in·crease
in·creased
in·creas·ing
in·creas·a·ble
in·creas·ing·ly
in·cred·i·ble
in·cred·i·bil·i·ty
in·cred·i·ble·ness
in·cred·i·bly
in·cred·u·lous
in·cre·du·li·ty
in·cred·u·lous·ness
in·cred·u·lous·ly

in·cre·ment
in·cre·men·tal
in·crim·i·nate
in·crim·i·nat·ed
in·crim·i·nat·ing
in·crim·i·na·tion
in·crim·i·na·tor
in·crim·i·na·to·ry
in·crust
in·crus·ta·tion
in·cu·bate
in·cu·bat·ed
in·cu·bat·ing
in·cu·ba·tion
in·cu·ba·tor
in·cu·bus
in·cu·bus·es
in·cul·cate
in·cul·cat·ed
in·cul·cat·ing
in·cul·ca·tion
in·cul·ca·tor
in·cul·pate
in·cul·pat·ed
in·cul·pat·ing
in·cul·pa·tion
in·cum·bent
in·cum·ben·cy
in·cum·ben·cies
in·cum·bent·ly
in·cur
in·curred
in·cur·ring
in·cur·a·ble
in·cur·a·bil·i·ty
in·cur·a·ble·ness
in·cur·a·bly
in·cur·sion
in·cur·sive
in·debt·ed
in·debt·ed·ness
in·de·cent
in·de·cen·cy
in·de·cen·cies
in·de·cent·ly
in·de·ci·sion
in·de·ci·sive
in·de·ci·sive·ly
in·de·ci·sive·ness
in·deed
in·de·fat·i·ga·ble
in·de·fat·i·ga·bil·i·ty
in·de·fat·i·ga·ble·ness
in·de·fat·i·ga·bly
in·de·fen·si·ble
in·de·fen·si·bil·i·ty
in·de·fen·si·bly
in·def·i·nite
in·def·i·nite·ly
in·def·i·nite·ness
in·del·i·ble
in·del·i·bil·i·ty
in·del·i·ble·ness
in·del·i·bly
in·del·i·cate

in·del·i·ca·cy
in·del·i·cate·ness
in·del·i·cate·ly
in·dem·ni·fy
in·dem·ni·fied
in·dem·ni·fy·ing
in·dem·ni·fi·ca·tion
in·dem·ni·fi·er
in·dem·ni·ty
in·dem·ni·ties
in·dent
in·den·ta·tion
in·dent·ed
in·den·ture
in·den·tured
in·den·tur·ing
in·de·pend·ence
in·de·pend·en·cy
in·de·pend·ent
in·de·pend·ent·ly
in·de·scrib·a·ble
in·de·scrib·a·bil·i·ty
in·de·scrib·a·ble·ness
in·de·scrib·a·bly
in·de·struct·i·ble
in·de·struct·i·bil·i·ty
in·de·struct·i·ble·ness
in·de·struct·i·bly
in·de·ter·mi·nate
in·de·ter·mi·nate·ly
in·de·ter·mi·nate·ness
in·de·ter·mi·na·cy
in·de·ter·mi·na·tion
in·dex
in·dex·es
in·di·ces
in·dex·er
In·dia
In·di·an
In·di·ana
In·di·an·ap·o·lis
in·di·cate
in·di·cat·ed
in·di·cat·ing
in·di·ca·tion
in·dic·a·tive
in·dic·a·tive·ly
in·dic·a·tor
in·dic·a·tory
in·dict
in·dict·a·ble
in·dict·er
in·dict·or
in·dict·ment
In·dies
in·dif·fer·ent
in·dif·fer·ence
in·dif·fer·ent·ist
in·dif·fer·ent·ly
in·dig·e·nous
in·dig·e·nous·ly
in·dig·e·nous·ness
in·di·gent
in·di·gence
in·di·gent·ly

in·di·gest·i·ble
in·di·gest·i·bil·i·ty
in·di·gest·i·ble·ness
in·di·ges·tion
in·di·ges·tive
in·dig·nant
in·dig·nant·ly
in·dig·na·tion
in·dig·ni·ty
in·dig·ni·ties
in·di·go
in·di·gos
in·di·goes
in·di·rect
in·di·rec·tion
in·di·rect·ly
in·di·rect·ness
in·dis·creet
in·dis·creet·ly
in·dis·creet·ness
in·dis·crete
in·dis·cre·tion
in·dis·crim·i·nate
in·dis·crim·i·nate·ly
in·dis·crim·i·nate·ness
in·dis·crim·i·nat·ing
in·dis·crim·i·na·tion
in·dis·pen·sa·ble
in·dis·pen·sa·bil·i·ty
in·dis·pen·sa·ble·ness
in·dis·pen·sa·bly
in·dis·pose
in·dis·posed
in·dis·pos·ing
in·dis·po·si·tion
in·dis·sol·u·ble
in·dis·sol·u·bil·i·ty
in·dis·sol·u·ble·ness
in·dis·sol·u·bly
in·di·um
in·di·vid·u·al
in·di·vid·u·al·ly
in·di·vid·u·al·ism
in·di·vid·u·al·ist
in·di·vid·u·al·is·tic
in·di·vid·u·al·is·ti·cal·ly
in·di·vid·u·al·i·ty
in·di·vid·u·al·i·ties
in·di·vid·u·al·ize
in·di·vid·u·al·ized
in·di·vid·u·al·iz·ing
in·di·vid·u·al·i·za·tion
In·do-Chi·na
in·doc·tri·nate
in·doc·tri·nat·ed
in·doc·tri·nat·ing
in·doc·tri·na·tion
in·doc·tri·na·tor
in·do·lent
in·do·lence
in·do·lent·ly
in·dom·i·ta·ble
in·dom·i·ta·bil·i·ty
in·dom·i·ta·ble·ness
in·dom·i·ta·bly

In·do·ne·sia
in·door
in·doors
in·du·bi·ta·ble
in·du·bi·ta·ble·ness
in·du·bi·ta·bil·i·ty
in·du·bi·tab·ly
in·duce
in·duced
in·duc·ing
in·duce·ment
in·duc·er
in·duc·i·ble
in·duct
in·duct·ee
in·duc·tion
in·duc·tive
in·dulge
in·dulged
in·dulg·ing
in·dul·gence
in·dul·gent
in·dul·gent·ly
In·dus
in·dus·tri·al
in·dus·tri·al·ly
in·dus·tri·al·ness
in·dus·tri·al·ism
in·dus·tri·al·ize
in·dus·tri·al·ized
in·dus·tri·al·iz·ing
in·dus·tri·al·i·za·tion
in·dus·tri·al·ist
in·dus·tri·ous
in·dus·tri·ous·ly
in·dus·try
in·dus·tries
in·e·bri·ate
in·e·bri·at·ed
in·e·bri·at·ing
in·e·bri·a·tion
in·e·bri·e·ty
in·ed·u·ca·ble
in·ef·fa·ble
in·ef·fa·bil·i·ty
in·ef·fa·ble·ness
in·ef·fa·bly
in·ef·fec·tive
in·ef·fec·tive·ly
in·ef·fec·tive·ness
in·ef·fec·tu·al
in·ef·fec·tu·al·i·ty
in·ef·fec·tu·al·ness
in·ef·fec·tu·al·ly
in·ef·fi·cient
in·ef·fi·cien·cy
in·ef·fi·cien·cies
in·ef·fi·cient·ly
in·el·i·gi·ble
in·el·i·gi·bil·i·ty
in·el·i·gi·bly
in·e·luc·ta·ble
in·ept
in·ept·i·tude
in·ept·ly

in·ept·ness
in·e·qual·i·ty
in·eq·ui·ta·ble
in·eq·ui·ty
in·eq·ui·ties
in·ert
in·ert·ly
in·ert·ness
in·er·tia
in·er·tial
in·es·cap·a·ble
in·es·ti·ma·ble
in·es·ti·ma·bly
in·ev·i·ta·ble
in·ev·i·ta·bil·i·ty
in·ev·i·ta·ble·ness
in·ev·i·ta·bly
in·ex·haust·i·ble
in·ex·haust·i·bil·i·ty
in·ex·haust·i·ble·ness
in·ex·haust·i·bly
in·ex·o·ra·ble
in·ex·o·ra·bil·i·ty
in·ex·o·ra·ble·ness
in·ex·o·ra·bly
in·ex·pe·ri·ence
in·ex·pe·ri·enced
in·ex·pert
in·ex·pert·ly
in·ex·pert·ness
in·ex·pi·a·ble
in·ex·pi·a·ble·ness
in·ex·pi·a·bly
in·ex·pli·ca·ble
in·ex·pli·ca·bil·i·ty
in·ex·pli·ca·ble·ness
in·ex·pli·ca·bly
in·ex·press·i·ble
in·ex·press·i·bil·i·ty
in·ex·press·i·ble·ness
in·ex·press·i·bly
in·ex·tin·guish·a·ble
in·ex·tin·guish·a·bly
in·ex·tri·ca·ble
in·ex·tri·ca·bil·i·ty
in·ex·tri·ca·ble·ness
in·ex·tri·ca·bly
in·fal·li·ble
in·fal·li·bil·i·ty
in·fal·li·ble·ness
in·fal·li·bly
in·fa·mous
in·fa·mous·ly
in·fa·mous·ness
in·fa·my
in·fa·mies
in·fan·cy
in·fan·cies
in·fant
in·fant·hood
in·fant·like
in·fan·tile
in·fan·tine
in·fan·til·i·ty
in·fan·try

in·fan·tries
in·fan·try·man
in·fan·try·men
in·fat·u·ate
in·fat·u·at·ed
in·fat·u·at·ing
in·fat·u·at·ed·ly
in·fat·u·a·tion
in·fect
in·fect·ed·ness
in·fect·er
in·fect·or
in·fec·tion
in·fec·tious
in·fec·tious·ly
in·fec·tious·ness
in·fec·tive
in·fer
in·ferred
in·fer·ring
in·fer·a·ble
in·fer·a·bly
in·fer·ence
in·fer·er
in·fe·ri·or
in·fe·ri·or·i·ty
in·fe·ri·or·ly
in·fer·nal
in·fer·no
in·fer·nos
in·fest
in·fes·ta·tion
in·fest·er
in·fi·del
in·fi·del·i·ty
in·fi·del·i·ties
in·field
in·field·er
in·fight·ing
in·fight·er
in·fil·trate
in·fil·trat·ed
in·fil·trat·ing
in·fil·tra·tion
in·fil·tra·tive
in·fil·tra·tor
in·fi·nite
in·fi·nite·ly
in·fi·nite·ness
in·fin·i·tude
in·fin·i·tes·i·mal
in·fin·i·tes·i·mal·ly
in·fin·i·tive
in·fin·i·tive·ly
in·fin·i·ty
in·fin·i·ties
in·firm
in·firm·ly
in·firm·ness
in·fir·ma·ry
in·fir·ma·ries
in·fir·mi·ty
in·fir·mi·ties
in·flame
in·flamed

in·flam·ing
in·flam·er
in·flam·ma·ble
in·flam·ma·bil·i·ty
in·flam·ma·ble·ness
in·flam·ma·bly
in·flam·ma·tion
in·flam·ma·to·ry
in·flate
in·flat·ed
in·flat·ing
in·flat·a·ble
in·flat·ed·ness
in·fla·tor
in·flat·er
in·fla·tion
in·fla·tion·ary
in·fla·tion·ism
in·fla·tion·ist
in·flect
in·flec·tion
in·flec·tion·al
in·flec·tion·al·ly
in·flec·tion·less
in·flec·tive
in·flec·tor
in·flex·i·ble
in·flex·i·bil·i·ty
in·flex·i·ble·ness
in·flex·i·bly
in·flict
in·flict·a·ble
in·flict·er
in·flict·or
in·flic·tion
in·flic·tive
in·flu·ence
in·flu·enced
in·flu·enc·ing
in·flu·ence·a·ble
in·flu·enc·er
in·flu·en·tial
in·flu·en·tial·ly
in·flu·en·za
in·flu·en·zal
in·flu·en·za·like
in·flux
in·form
in·formed
in·for·mer
in·for·mal
in·for·mal·i·ty
in·for·mal·ly
in·form·ant
in·for·ma·tion
in·for·ma·tion·al
in·for·ma·tive
in·for·ma·tive·ly
in·for·ma·tive·ness
in·for·ma·to·ry
in·frac·tion
in·fran·gi·ble
in·fran·gi·bil·i·ty
in·fran·gi·ble·ness
in·fran·gi·bly

in·fra·red
in·fra·struc·ture
in·fre·quent
in·fre·quen·cy
in·fre·quent·ly
in·fringe
in·fringed
in·fring·ing
in·fringe·ment
in·fring·er
in·fu·ri·ate
in·fu·ri·at·ed
in·fu·ri·at·ing
in·fu·ri·at·ing·ly
in·fu·ri·a·tion
in·fuse
in·fused
in·fus·ing
in·fus·er
in·fus·i·bil·i·ty
in·fus·i·ble
in·fu·sion
in·fu·sive
in·gen·ious
in·gen·ious·ly
in·gen·ious·ness
in·gé·nue
in·gé·nues
in·ge·nu·i·ty
in·gen·u·ous
in·gen·u·ous·ly
in·gen·u·ous·ness
In·ger·soll
in·gest
in·ges·tion
in·ges·tive
in·glo·ri·ous
in·glo·ri·ous·ly
in·glo·ri·ous·ness
in·got
in·grain
in·grained
in·grate
in·gra·ti·ate
in·gra·ti·at·ed
in·gra·ti·at·ing
in·gra·ti·a·tion
in·grat·i·tude
in·gre·di·ent
in·group
in·grow·ing
in·grown
in·growth
in·gulf
in·hab·it
in·hab·it·a·ble
in·hab·i·ta·tion
in·hab·it·er
in·hab·it·ed
in·hab·it·ant
in·hal·ant
in·ha·la·tion
in·ha·la·tor
in·hale
in·haled

in·hal·ing
in·hal·er
in·here
in·hered
in·her·ing
in·her·ence
in·her·ent
in·her·ent·ly
in·he·sion
in·her·it
in·her·i·tor
in·her·i·tance
in·hib·it
in·hib·i·tive
in·hib·i·to·ry
in·hib·i·ter
in·hib·it·or
in·hi·bi·tion
in·hos·pi·ta·ble
in·hos·pi·tal·i·ty
in·hu·man
in·hu·man·i·ty
in·hu·mane
in·im·i·cal
in·im·i·ta·ble
in·iq·ui·ty
in·iq·ui·ties
in·iq·ui·tous
in·i·tial
in·i·tialed
in·i·tial·ing
in·i·tial·ly
in·i·ti·ate
in·i·ti·at·ed
in·i·ti·at·ing
in·i·ti·a·tion
in·i·ti·a·tor
in·i·ti·a·tive
in·ject
in·jec·tion
in·jec·tor
in·ju·di·cious
in·junc·tion
in·junc·tive
in·jure
in·jured
in·jur·ing
in·ju·ri·ous
in·ju·ry
in·ju·ries
in·jus·tice
ink·blot
ink·ling
inky
ink·i·er
ink·i·est
in·laid
in·land
in·law
in·lay
in·laid
in·lay·ing
in·let
in·mate
in me·mo·ri·am

in·most
in·nards
in·nate
in·ner
in·ner·most
in·ner·sole
in·ner·vate
in·ner·vat·ed
in·ner·vat·ing
in·ner·va·tion
in·nerve
in·nerved
in·nerv·ing
in·ning
inn·keep·er
in·no·cence
in·no·cent
in·no·cent·ly
in·noc·u·ous
in·no·vate
in·no·vat·ed
in·no·vat·ing
in·no·va·tion
in·no·va·tive
in·no·va·tor
in·nu·en·do
in·nu·en·dos
in·nu·en·does
in·nu·mer·a·ble
in·nu·mer·ous
in·nu·mer·a·bly
in·ob·serv·ance
in·ob·serv·ant
in·ob·serv·ant·ly
in·oc·u·lant
in·oc·u·late
in·oc·u·lat·ed
in·oc·u·lat·ing
in·oc·u·la·tion
in·oc·u·la·tor
in·oc·u·lum
in·of·fen·sive
in·op·er·a·ble
in·op·er·a·tive
in·op·por·tune
in·op·por·tu·ni·ty
in·or·di·nate
in·pa·tient
in·pour
in·put
in·quest
in·qui·e·tude
in·quire
in·quired
in·quir·ing
in·quir·er
in·quiry
in·quir·ies
in·qui·si·tion
in·quis·i·tive
in·quis·i·tor
in·road
in·rush
in·sane
in·san·i·ty

in·san·i·ties
in·sa·tia·ble
in·sa·tia·bil·i·ty
in·sa·tia·bly
in·sa·ti·ate
in·scribe
in·scribed
in·scrib·ing
in·scrip·tion
in·scrip·tive
in·scru·ta·ble
in·scru·ta·bil·i·ty
in·scru·ta·bly
in·seam
in·sect
in·sec·ti·cide
in·sec·ti·cid·al
in·se·cure
in·se·cu·ri·ty
in·sem·i·nate
in·sem·i·nat·ed
in·sem·i·nat·ing
in·sem·i·na·tion
in·sen·sate
in·sen·si·ble
in·sen·si·tive
in·sen·si·tiv·i·ty
in·sen·ti·ent
in·sep·a·ra·ble
in·sep·a·ra·bil·i·ty
in·sep·a·ra·bly
in·sert
in·sert·er
in·ser·tion
in·set
in·set·ting
in·shore
in·side
in·sid·er
in·sid·i·ous
in·sight
in·sight·ful
in·sig·nia
in·sig·nif·i·cant
in·sig·nif·i·cance
in·sin·cere
in·sin·cer·i·ty
in·sin·cer·i·ties
in·sin·u·ate
in·sin·u·at·ed
in·sin·u·at·ing
in·sin·u·a·tor
in·sin·u·a·tion
in·sip·id
in·si·pid·i·ty
in·sip·id·ness
in·sist
in·sist·ence
in·sist·ent
in·sist·ent·ly
in·sist·ing·ly
in·so·bri·e·ty
in·so·cia·ble
in·so·cia·bil·i·ty
in·so·cia·bly

in·so·far
in·sole
in·so·lent
in·so·lence
in·sol·u·ble
in·sol·u·bil·i·ty
in·sol·u·bly
in·solv·a·ble
in·sol·vent
in·sol·ven·cy
in·som·nia
in·som·ni·ac
in·so·much
in·spect
in·spec·tion
in·spec·tor
in·spi·ra·tion
in·spi·ra·tion·al
in·spire
in·spired
in·spir·ing
in·spir·it
in·sta·ble
in·sta·bil·i·ty
in·stall
in·stall·er
in·stal·la·tion
in·stall·ment
in·stance
in·stant
in·stan·ta·ne·ous
in·stant·ly
in·state
in·stat·ed
in·stat·ing
in·state·ment
in·stead
in·step
in·sti·gate
in·sti·gat·ed
in·sti·gat·ing
in·sti·ga·tion
in·sti·ga·tor
in·still
in·stilled
in·stil·ling
in·stil·la·tion
in·stinct
in·stinc·tive
in·stinc·tu·al
in·stinc·tive·ly
in·sti·tute
in·sti·tut·ed
in·sti·tut·ing
in·sti·tut·er
in·sti·tu·tor
in·sti·tu·tion
in·sti·tu·tion·al
in·sti·tu·tion·al·ism
in·sti·tu·tion·al·ize
in·sti·tu·tion·al·ized
in·sti·tu·tion·al·iz·ing
in·struct
in·struc·tion
in·struc·tive

in·struc·tor
in·stru·ment
in·stru·men·tal
in·stru·men·ta·list
in·stru·men·ta·tion
in·sub·or·di·nate
in·sub·or·di·na·tion
in·sub·stan·tial
in·sub·stan·ti·al·i·ty
in·suf·fer·a·ble
in·suf·fer·a·bly
in·suf·fi·cient
in·suf·fi·cience
in·suf·fi·cien·cy
in·su·lar
in·su·lar·i·ty
in·su·late
in·su·lat·ed
in·su·lat·ing
in·su·la·tion
in·su·la·tor
in·su·lin
in·sult
in·sup·port·a·ble
in·sup·press·i·ble
in·sur·ance
in·sure
in·sured
in·sur·ing
in·sur·er
in·sur·gent
in·sur·gence
in·sur·gen·cy
in·sur·mount·a·ble
in·sur·rec·tion
in·sur·rec·tion·ary
in·sus·cep·ti·ble
in·tact
in·take
in·tan·gi·ble
in·tan·gi·bil·i·ty
in·tan·gi·ble·ness
in·tan·gi·bly
in·te·ger
in·te·gral
in·te·gral·ly
in·te·grate
in·te·grat·ed
in·te·grat·ing
in·te·gra·tion
in·te·gra·tion·ist
in·teg·ri·ty
in·tel·lect
in·tel·lec·tu·al
in·tel·lec·tu·al·ism
in·tel·lec·tu·al·ize
in·tel·lec·tu·al·ized
in·tel·lec·tu·al·iz·ing
in·tel·li·gence
in·tel·li·gent
in·tel·li·gent·ly
in·tel·li·gent·sia
in·tel·li·gi·ble
in·tel·li·gi·bil·i·ty
in·tel·li·bi·bly

in·tem·per·ance
in·tem·per·ate
in·tend
in·tend·er
in·tend·ed
in·tense
in·tense·ly
in·tense·ness
in·ten·si·fy
in·ten·si·fied
in·ten·si·fy·ing
in·ten·si·fi·ca·tion
in·ten·si·fi·er
in·ten·sion
in·ten·si·ty
in·ten·si·ties
in·ten·sive
in·ten·sive·ly
in·ten·sive·ness
in·tent
in·ten·tion
in·ten·tion·al
in·ten·tion·al·ly
in·ten·tioned
in·ter
in·terred
in·ter·ring
in·ter·ment
in·ter·act
in·ter·ac·tion
in·ter·ac·tive
in·ter·breed
in·ter·bred
in·ter·breed·ing
in·ter·cede
in·ter·ced·ed
in·ter·ced·ing
in·ter·ced·er
in·ter·cept
in·ter·cep·ter
in·ter·cept·or
in·ter·cep·tion
in·ter·cep·tive
in·ter·ces·sion
in·ter·change
in·ter·changed
in·ter·chang·ing
in·ter·change·a·ble
in·ter·change·a·bil·i·ty
in·ter·change·a·ble·ness
in·ter·change·a·bly
in·ter·col·le·gi·ate
in·ter·com
in·ter·com·mu·ni·cate
in·ter·com·mu·ni·cat·ed
in·ter·com·mu·ni·cat·ing
in·ter·com·mu·ni·ca·tion
in·ter·con·nect
in·ter·con·nec·tion
in·ter·con·ti·nen·tal
in·ter·course
in·ter·cul·tur·al
in·ter·cur·rent
in·ter·de·nom·i·na·tion·al
in·ter·de·nom·i·na·tion·al·ism

in·ter·de·part·men·tal
in·ter·de·pend·ent
in·ter·de·pend
in·ter·de·pend·ence
in·ter·de·pend·en·cy
in·ter·dict
in·ter·dic·tion
in·ter·dis·ci·pli·nary
in·ter·est
in·ter·est·ed
in·ter·est·ed·ly
in·ter·est·ing
in·ter·face
in·ter·fa·cial
in·ter·faith
in·ter·fere
in·ter·fered
in·ter·fer·ing
in·ter·fer·ence
in·ter·fer·er
in·ter·fer·ing·ly
in·ter·ga·lac·tic
in·ter·im
in·te·ri·or
in·ter·ject
in·ter·jec·tion
in·ter·jec·tion·al·ly
in·ter·jec·to·ry
In·ter·la·ken
in·ter·lay·er
in·ter·leaf
in·ter·leaves
in·ter·leave
in·ter·leaved
in·ter·leav·ing
in·ter·line
in·ter·lined
in·ter·lin·ing
in·ter·link
in·ter·lock
in·ter·lo·cu·tion
in·ter·loc·u·tor
in·ter·loc·u·to·ry
in·ter·lope
in·ter·loped
in·ter·lop·ing
in·ter·lop·er
in·ter·lude
in·ter·lu·nar
in·ter·lu·na·ry
in·ter·mar·ry
in·ter·mar·ried
in·ter·mar·ry·ing
in·ter·mar·riage
in·ter·me·di·ary
in·ter·me·di·ar·ies
in·ter·me·di·ate
in·ter·me·di·at·ed
in·ter·me·di·at·ing
in·ter·me·di·a·tion
in·ter·me·di·a·tor
in·ter·me·di·a·to·ry
in·ter·mi·na·ble
in·ter·min·gle
in·ter·min·gled

in·ter·min·gling
in·ter·mis·sion
in·ter·mis·sive
in·ter·mit
in·ter·mit·ted
in·ter·mit·ting
in·ter·mit·tence
in·ter·mit·ten·cy
in·ter·mit·tent
in·ter·mit·tent·ly
in·ter·mit·ting·ly
in·ter·mix
in·ter·mix·ture
in·tern
in·tern·ship
in·ter·nal
in·ter·nal·ly
in·ter·nal·ize
in·ter·nal·ized
in·ter·nal·iz·ing
in·ter·nal·i·za·tion
in·ter·na·tion·al
in·ter·na·tion·al·i·ty
in·ter·na·tion·al·ly
in·ter·na·tion·al·ize
in·ter·na·tion·al·ized
in·ter·na·tion·al·iz·ing
in·ter·na·tion·al·i·za·tion
in·ter·na·tion·al·ism
in·tern·ee
in·tern·ist
in·tern·ment
in·ter·of·fice
in·ter·pen·e·trate
in·ter·pen·e·tra·tion
in·ter·plan·e·tary
in·ter·play
in·ter·po·late
in·ter·po·lat·ed
in·ter·po·lat·ing
in·ter·po·la·tion
in·ter·po·la·tive
in·ter·po·la·tor
in·ter·pose
in·ter·posed
in·ter·pos·ing
in·ter·pos·er
in·ter·po·si·tion
in·ter·pret
in·ter·pret·a·ble
in·ter·pret·er
in·ter·pre·tive
in·ter·pre·ta·tion
in·ter·pre·ta·tion·al
in·ter·pre·ta·tive
in·ter·ra·cial
in·ter·re·late
in·ter·re·lat·ed
in·ter·re·lat·ing
in·ter·ro·gate
in·ter·ro·gat·ed
in·ter·ro·gat·ing
in·ter·ro·ga·tion
in·ter·ro·ga·tion·al
in·ter·rog·a·tive

in·ter·ro·ga·tor
in·ter·rupt
  in·ter·rup·tion
  in·ter·rup·tive
in·ter·rupt·er
in·ter·rupt·or
in·ter·scho·las·tic
in·ter·sect
in·ter·sec·tion
in·ter·space
  in·ter·spaced
  in·ter·spac·ing
in·ter·sperse
  in·ter·spersed
  in·ter·spers·ing
  in·ter·sper·sion
in·ter·state
in·ter·stel·lar
in·ter·tid·al
in·ter·twine
  in·ter·twined
  in·ter·twin·ing
in·ter·ur·ban
in·ter·val
in·ter·vene
  in·ter·vened
  in·ter·ven·ing
  in·ter·ven·er
  in·ter·ve·nor
  in·ter·ven·tion
in·ter·view
  in·ter·view·er
in·ter·weave
  in·ter·wove
  in·ter·weav·ing
  in·ter·wo·ven
in·tes·tate
in·tes·tine
  in·tes·ti·nal
in·ti·mate
  in·ti·mat·ed
  in·ti·mat·ing
  in·ti·mate·ly
  in·ti·ma·tion
in·tim·i·date
  in·tim·i·dat·ed
  in·tim·i·dat·ing
  in·tim·i·da·tion
  in·tim·i·da·tor
in·ti·tle
  in·ti·tled
  in·ti·tling
in·to
in·tol·er·a·ble
  in·tol·er·a·bly
in·tol·er·ant
  in·tol·er·ance
in·tomb
in·to·mate
  in·to·nat·ed
  in·to·nat·ing
in·to·na·tion
in·tone
  in·toned
  in·ton·ing

in·ton·er
in·tox·i·cant
in·tox·i·cate
  in·tox·i·cat·ed
  in·tox·i·cat·ing
  in·tox·i·ca·tion
in·trac·ta·ble
  in·trac·ta·bil·i·ty
in·tra·mu·ral
  in·tra·mu·ral·ly
in·tran·si·gent
  in·tran·si·gence
  in·tran·si·gen·cy
in·tran·si·tive
in·tra·state
in·tra·u·ter·ine
in·tra·ve·nous
in·trench
in·trep·id
  in·tre·pid·i·ty
in·tri·cate
  in·tri·ca·cy
  in·tri·ca·cies
  in·tri·cate·ly
  in·tri·cate·ness
in·trigue
  in·trigued
  in·tri·guing
  in·tri·guer
in·trin·sic
  in·trin·si·cal
  in·trin·si·cal·ly
in·tro·duce
  in·tro·duced
  in·tro·duc·ing
  in·tro·duc·er
  in·tro·duc·tion
  in·tro·duc·to·ry
in·tro·spect
  in·tro·spec·tion
  in·tro·spec·tive
in·tro·ver·sion
  in·tro·ver·sive
in·tro·vert
  in·tro·vert·ed
in·trude
  in·trud·ed
  in·trud·ing
  in·trud·er
in·tru·sion
in·tru·sive
in·trust
in·tu·it
in·tu·i·tion
  in·tu·i·tion·al
in·tu·i·tive
in·un·date
  in·un·dat·ed
  in·un·dat·ing
  in·un·da·tion
  in·un·da·tor
in·ure
  in·ured
  in·ur·ing
in·vade

in·vad·ed
in·vad·ing
in·vad·er
in·va·lid
in·val·id
in·va·lid·i·ty
in·val·i·date
in·val·i·dat·ed
in·val·i·dat·ing
in·val·i·da·tion
in·val·i·da·tor
in·va·lid·ism
in·val·u·a·ble
in·var·i·a·ble
in·var·i·a·bil·i·ty
in·var·i·a·ble·ness
in·var·i·ant
in·var·i·ance
in·va·sion
in·va·sive
in·vec·tive
in·veigh
in·veigh·er
in·vent
in·vent·a·ble
in·ven·tor
in·ven·tion
in·ven·tive
in·ven·tive·ness
in·ven·to·ry
in·ven·to·ries
in·ven·to·ried
in·ven·to·ry·ing
In·ver·ness
in·verse
in·ver·sion
in·vert
in·ver·te·brate
in·vert·ed
in·vest
in·ves·tor
in·ves·ti·gate
in·ves·ti·gat·ed
in·ves·ti·gat·ing
in·ves·ti·ga·tion
in·ves·ti·ga·tive
in·ves·ti·ga·tor
in·ves·ti·ture
in·vest·ment
in·vet·er·ate
in·vid·i·ous
in·vig·or·ate
in·vig·or·at·ed
in·vig·or·at·ing
in·vig·or·ant
in·vig·or·a·tion
in·vig·or·a·tor
in·vin·ci·ble
in·vin·ci·bil·i·ty
in·vin·ci·ble·ness
in·vin·ci·bly
in·vi·o·la·ble
in·vi·o·la·bil·i·ty
in·vi·o·la·bly
in·vi·o·late

in·vis·i·ble
in·vis·i·bil·i·ty
in·vis·i·bly
in·vi·ta·tion
in·vi·ta·tion·al
in·vite
in·vit·ed
in·vit·ing
in·vit·er
in·vo·ca·tion
in·voice
in·voke
in·voked
in·vok·ing
in·vol·un·tary
in·vol·un·tar·i·ly
in·vol·un·tar·i·ness
in·vo·lute
in·vo·lu·tion
in·volve
in·volved
in·volv·ing
in·volve·ment
in·volv·er
in·vul·ner·a·ble
in·ward
in·wards
in·ward·ly
in·ward·ness
in·weave
in·wove
in·weaved
in·wov·en
in·weav·ing
in·wrought
io·dine
ion
ion·ic
ion·ize
ion·ized
ion·iz·ing
ion·i·za·tion
ion·iz·er
ion·o·sphere
io·ta
Io·wa
ip·so fac·to
Ips·wich
Ira·ni·an
iras·ci·ble
iras·ci·bil·i·ty
iras·ci·ble·ness
iras·ci·bly
irate
Ire·land
ir·i·des·cent
ir·i·des·cence
irid·i·um
iris
iris·es
ir·i·des
Irish
Irish·man
irk·some
iron

iron·er
iron·clad
iron·hand·ed
iron·heart·ed
iron·ic
  iron·i·cal
Iron·sides
iron·smith
iron·stone
iron·ware
iron·work
  iron·work·er
iro·ny
  iro·nies
Ir·o·quois
ir·ra·di·ate
  ir·ra·di·at·ed
  ir·ra·di·at·ing
  ir·ra·di·a·tion
  ir·ra·di·a·ter
ir·rad·i·ca·ble
ir·ra·tion·al
  ir·ra·tion·al·i·ty
ir·re·claim·a·ble
ir·rec·on·cil·a·ble
  ir·rec·on·cil·a·bil·i·ty
ir·re·cov·er·a·ble
ir·re·duc·i·ble
ir·ref·u·ta·ble
ir·re·gard·less
ir·reg·u·lar
  ir·reg·u·lar·i·ty
ir·rel·e·vant
  ir·rel·e·vance
  ir·rel·e·van·cy
ir·re·li·gion
ir·re·li·gious
ir·re·mis·si·ble
ir·re·mov·a·ble
ir·rep·a·ra·ble
ir·re·place·a·ble
ir·re·press·i·ble
  ir·re·press·i·bil·i·ty
  ir·re·press·i·bly
ir·re·proach·a·ble
ir·re·sist·i·ble
  ir·re·sist·i·bil·i·ty
ir·res·o·lute
  ir·res·o·lu·tion
ir·re·spec·tive
ir·re·spon·si·ble
  ir·re·spon·si·bil·i·ty
ir·re·spon·sive
  ir·re·spon·sive·ness
ir·re·triev·a·ble
  ir·re·triev·a·bil·i·ty
ir·rev·er·ence
  ir·rev·er·ent
ir·re·vers·i·ble
  ir·re·vers·i·bil·i·ty
  ir·re·vers·i·bly
ir·rev·o·ca·ble
  ir·rev·o·ca·bil·i·ty
ir·ri·gate
  ir·ri·gat·ed

ir·ri·gat·ing
ir·ri·ga·tion
ir·ri·ga·tor
ir·ri·ta·ble
  ir·ri·ta·bil·i·ty
  ir·ri·ta·ble·ness
ir·ri·tant
ir·ri·tate
  ir·ri·tat·ed
  ir·ri·tat·ing
  ir·ri·ta·tion
ir·rupt
Ir·ving
Is·a·bel
Isa·iah
Is·car·i·ot
Ish·ma·el
Is·lam
  Is·lam·ic
  Is·lam·ism
Is·lam·a·bad
is·land
is·land·er
isle
is·let
iso·bar
iso·bar·ic
Isoc·ra·tes
iso·gloss
iso·late
  iso·lat·ed
  iso·lat·ing
  iso·la·tion
iso·la·tion·ism
  iso·la·tion·ist
iso·met·ric
  iso·met·ri·cal
ison·o·my
isos·ce·les
iso·therm
iso·ton·ic
iso·tope
  iso·top·ic
Is·ra·el
Is·rae·li
  Is·rae·lis
is·su·ance
is·sue
  is·sued
  is·su·ing
Is·tan·bul
isth·mus
Ital·ian
ital·ic
ital·i·cize
  ital·i·cized
  ital·i·ciz·ing
  ital·i·ci·za·tion
It·a·ly
itch
  itch·i·ness
itchy
item
item·ize
  item·ized

item·iz·ing
it·er·ate
it·er·at·ed
it·er·at·ing
it·er·a·tion
it·er·a·tive
Ith·a·ca
itin·er·ant
itin·er·ary
itin·er·ar·ies
itin·er·ate
itin·er·at·ed
itin·er·at·ing
itin·er·a·tion
it'll
its
it's
Ivan
I've
ivied
ivo·ry
ivo·ries
ivy
ivies
Iz·mir
jab
jabbed
jab·bing
jab·ber
jab·ber·er
jack·al
jack·ass
jack·boot
jack·et
jack·et·ed
jack·ham·mer
jack-in-the-box
jack-in-the-box·es
jack·knife
jack·knives
jack·knifed
jack·knif·ing
jack-of-all-trades
jack-o'-lan·tern
jack·pot
jack rab·bit
jail·bird
jail·break
jail·er
Jai·pur
Ja·i·rus

ja·lopy
ja·lop·ies
jal·ou·sie
jam
jammed
jam·ming
jam·mer
Ja·mai·ca
jamb
jam·bo·ree
James·town
jan·gle
jan·gled
jan·gling
jan·gler
jan·gly
jan·i·tor
jan·i·to·ri·al
Jan·sen
Jan·u·ary
Ja·nus
Ja·pan
Jap·a·nese
Jap·a·nese bee·tle
Ja·pheth
jar
jar·ful
jarred
jar·ring
jar·di·niere
Ja·red
jar·gon
jas·mine
Ja·son
jaun·dice
jaun·diced
jaun·dic·ing
jaunt
jaun·ty
jaun·ti·er
jaun·ti·est
jaun·ti·ly
jaun·ti·ness
Ja·va
jave·lin
jaw·bone
jaw·break·er
Jay·cee
jay·walk
jay·walk·er
jazz
jazz·ist
jazz·man
jazzy
jazz·i·er
jazz·i·est
jazz·i·ly
jazz·i·ness
jeal·ous
jeal·ousy
jeal·ous·ies
jeer·er
Jef·fer·son
Je·ho·vah
Je·hu

Jek·yll
jel·li·fy
 jel·li·fied
 jel·li·fy·ing
Jell·o
jel·ly
 jel·lies
 jel·lied
 jel·ly·ing
 jel·ly·like
 jel·ly·bean
 jel·ly·fish
Je·mi·mah
jen·ny
 jen·nies
jeop·ar·dy
 jeop·ar·dize
 jeop·ar·dized
 jeop·ar·diz·ing
Jeph·thah
Jer·e·mi·ah
Jer·i·cho
jerk
 jerk·er
 jerk·i·ly
 jerk·i·ness
 jerky
 jerk·i·er
 jerk·i·est
jer·kin
Jer·o·bo·am
Je·rome
jer·ry·build
 jer·ry·built
 jer·ry·build·ing
 jer·ry·build·er
jer·sey
Je·ru·sa·lem
jes·sa·mine
Jes·se
jest·er
 jest·ing
Jes·u·it
Je·sus
jet
 jet·ted
 jet·ting
jet·lin·er
jet·port
jet-pro·pelled
jet·sam
jet·ti·son
jet·ty
 jet·ties
jew·el
 jew·eled
 jew·el·ing
jew·el·er
jew·el·ry
Jew·ish
Jew·ry
jew's-harp
 jews'-harp
Jez·e·bel
jibe

jibed
jib·ing
jif·fy
 jif·fies
jig
 jigged
 jig·ging
jig·ger
jig·gle
 jig·gled
 jig·gling
 jig·gly
jig·saw
jilt·er
Jim Crow·ism
jim-dan·dy
jim·my
 jim·mies
 jim·mied
 jim·my·ing
jin·gle
 jin·gled
 jin·gling
jinx
jit·ney
 jit·neys
jit·ter
 jit·ters
 jit·tery
jit·ter·bug
 jit·ter·bugged
 jit·ter·bug·ging
Jo·ab
Jo·a·chim
job
 jobbed
 job·bing
job·ber
job·hold·er
jock·ey
 jock·eys
 jock·eyed
 jock·ey·ing
jock·strap
jo·cose
jo·cos·i·ty
joc·u·lar
joc·u·lar·i·ty
joc·und
jo·cun·di·ty
jodh·pur
Jo·el
jog
 jogged
 jog·ging
 jog·ger
jog·gle
 jog·gled
 jog·gling
Jo·han·nes·burg
John·son
John·ston
Johns·town
join·a·ble
join·er

joint
joint·ed
joint·ly
joist
joke
joked
jok·ing
joke·ster
jok·ing·ly
jok·er
Jo·li·et
jol·ly
jol·li·er
jol·li·est
jol·lied
jol·ly·ing
jolt
jolt·er
jolt·ing·ly
jolty
Jo·nah
Jon·a·than
jon·quil
Jop·lin
Jop·pa
Jor·dan
Jo·seph
Jo·se·phus
Josh·ua
Jo·si·ah
jos·tle
jos·tled
jos·tling
jos·tler
jot
jot·ted
jot·ting
joule
jour·nal
jour·nal·ism
jour·nal·ist
jour·nal·is·tic
jour·ney
jour·ney·man
jour·ney·men
joust
jo·vi·al
jo·vi·al·i·ty
jowl
jowled
jowly
joy·ful
joy·less
joy·ous
joy·ride
Jua·rez
ju·bi·lant
ju·bi·lance
ju·bi·lan·cy
ju·bi·la·tion
ju·bi·late
ju·bi·lat·ed
ju·bi·lat·ing
ju·bi·lee
Ju·dah

Ju·da·ism
Ju·da·ic
Ju·da·i·cal
Ju·das
Ju·dea
judge
judged
judg·ing
Judg·es
judg·ment
judg·men·tal
ju·di·cial
ju·di·ci·ary
ju·di·cious
Ju·dith
ju·do
jug
jugged
jug·ging
jug·ful
jug·ger·naut
jug·gle
jug·gled
jug·gling
jug·gler
Ju·go·sla·via
jug·u·lar
juice
juice·less
juic·er
juicy
juic·i·er
juic·i·est
juic·i·ly
juic·i·ness
ju·jit·su
juke·box
ju·lep
ju·li·enne
Ju·lius
Ju·ly
jum·ble
jum·bled
jum·bling
jum·bo
jum·bos
jump
jump·ing
jump·i·ness
jumpy
jump·er
jump-off
junc·tion
junc·ture
Ju·neau
jun·gle
jun·ior
ju·ni·per
junk
junk·man
junky
jun·ket
junk·ie
jun·ta
Ju·pi·ter

ju·ris·dic·tion
  ju·ris·dic·tion·al
ju·ris·pru·dence
  ju·ris·pru·dent
  ju·ris·pru·den·tial
ju·rist
  ju·ris·tic
ju·ror
ju·ry
  ju·ries
  ju·ry·man
just
  just·ly
  just·ness
jus·tice
  jus·tice·less
  jus·tice·like
jus·ti·fi·ca·tion
jus·ti·fy
  jus·ti·fied
  jus·ti·fy·ing
  jus·ti·fi·a·ble
  jus·tif·i·ca·to·ry
jut
  jut·ted
  jut·ting
jute
Jut·land
ju·ve·nes·cence
  ju·ve·nes·cent
ju·ve·nile
  ju·ve·nil·i·ty
jux·ta·pose
  jux·ta·posed
  jux·ta·pos·ing
  jux·ta·po·si·tion
Kaa·ba
ka·bob
Ka·bul
Ka·byle
Kaf·fir
Kaf·ka
kai·ser
Kal·a·ma·zoo
ka·lei·do·scope
  ka·lei·do·scop·ic
  ka·lei·do·scop·i·cal
ka·mi·ka·ze
Ka·naka
kan·ga·roo
Kan·sas
ka·o·lin
  ka·o·line
ka·pok
ka·put
Ka·ra·chi
kar·at
ka·ra·te
kar·ma
  kar·mic
Kar·nak
Kash·mir
Ka·tan·ga
Kat·man·du
ka·ty·did

Ka·u·ai
kay·ak
kayo
  kay·os
kedge
  kedged
  kedg·ing
keel·haul
keel·son
keen·ly
  keen·ness
keep·ing
keep·sake
keg·ler
kelp
Ken·il·worth
Ken·ne·bec
Ken·ne·dy
ken·nel
  ken·neled
  ken·nel·ing
Ken·ny
ke·no
Ken·sing·ton
Kent·ish
Ken·tucky
Ke·nya
Ken·yon
Ke·o·kuk
Kep·ler
ker·a·tin
ker·chief
ker·mis
ker·nel
ker·o·sene
Ker·ry
kes·trel
ketch·up
ke·tone
ket·tle
ket·tle·drum
Ke·wee·naw·an
key
  keyed
key·board
key·hole
key·note
  key·not·ed
  key·not·ing
key·stone
khaki
  khak·is
kha·lif
khan
Khar·toum
Khru·shchev
Khy·ber
kib·butz
  kib·but·zim
kib·itz·er
ki·bosh
kick·back
kick·off
kid
  kid·dish

kid·dish·ness
kid·ded
kid·ding
kid·der
kid·nap
kid·naped
kid·napped
kid·nap·ing
kid·nap·ping
kid·nap·er
kid·nap·per
kid·ney
kid·neys
Kier·ke·gaard
Ki·ga·la
Kil·i·man·ja·ro
Kil·ken·ny
Kil·lar·ney
kill·deer
kill·ing
kill·joy
kiln
kilo
kil·os
kil·o·cy·cle
kil·o·gram
kil·o·me·ter
kil·o·ton
kil·o·watt
Kil·pat·rick
kilt
kilt·er
Kim·ber·ley
ki·mo·no
kin·der·gar·ten
kind·heart·ed
kind·heart·ed·ness
kin·dle
kin·dled
kin·dling
kind·ly
kind·li·er
kind·li·est
kind·li·ness
kin·dred
kin·e·mat·ics
kin·e·mat·ic
kin·e·mat·i·cal
kin·e·scope
ki·net·ic
ki·net·ics
kin·folk
king·bird
king·bolt
king·dom
king·fish
king·fish·er
king·ly
king·li·er
king·li·est
king·li·ness
king·pin
king·size
king·sized
Kings·ley

Kings·ton
kinky
kink·i·er
kink·i·est
kins·folk
Kin·sha·sa
kin·ship
kins·man
kins·men
kins·wom·an
ki·osk
Kip·ling
kip·per
Kirch·hoff
kir·mess
kis·met
kiss·a·ble
kiss·er
kitch·en
kitch·en·ette
kitch·en·ware
kite
kit·ed
kit·ing
kitsch
kit·ten
kit·ten·ish
kit·ten·ish·ly
kit·ty
kit·ties
kit·ty-cor·ner
Kit·ty·hawk
Ki·wa·nis
ki·wi
klatch
klatsch
Kleen·ex
klep·to·ma·nia
klep·to·ma·ni·ac
Klon·dike
knack
knap·sack
knave
knav·ery
knav·ish
knav·ish·ly
knead
knee
kneed
knee·ing
knee-cap
knee-deep
kneel
knelt
kneeled
kneel·ing
kneel·er
knee·pan
knell
knick·ers
knick·er·bock·ers
knick·knack
knife
knives
knifed

knif·ing
knife·like
knight
  knight·hood
  knight·ly
knight-er·rant
  knights-er·rant
knight-er·rant·ry
knit
  knit·ted
  knit·ting
  knit·ter
knob
  knobbed
  knob·by
  knob·bi·er
  knob·bi·est
knock
  knock·a·bout
  knock·down
  knock·er
  knock-knee
    knock-kneed
  knock·out
knoll
knot
  knot·ted
  knot·ting
  knot·less
  knot·like
  knot·ty
knot·hole
knout
know
  knew
  known
  know·ing
  know·a·ble
  know·er
  know-how
  know·ing·ly
  knowl·edge
  knowl·edge·a·ble
  know-noth·ing
Knox·ville
knuck·le
  knuck·led
  knuck·ling
knurl
  knurled
  knurly
ko·a·la
ko·bold
Ko·dak
Ko·di·ak
ko·el
ko·gas·in
kohl·ra·bi
  kohl·ra·bies
ko·la
ko·lin·sky
  ko·lin·skies
kook
  kooky
  kook·i·er

kook·i·est
kook·a·bur·ra
ko·peck
Ko·ran
Ko·rea
Kor·sa·koff
ko·ru·na
ko·sher
kou·mis
kow·tow
kra·ken
Krem·lin
kreu·zer
krim·mer
Krish·na
kro·na
kro·ne
kryp·ton
Kua·la Lum·per
Ku·blai Khan
ku·dos
ku·miss
küm·mel
kum·quat
Kuo·min·tang
Ku·wait
Kwa·ja·lein
la·bel
  la·beled
  la·bel·ing
  la·bel·er
la·bi·al
  la·bi·al·ly
la·bi·ate
la·bi·o·den·tal
la·bi·um
la·bia
la·bor
  la·bor·er
lab·o·ra·to·ry
la·bored
la·bo·ri·ous
  la·bo·ri·ous·ly
  la·bo·ri·ous·ness
la·bor-sav·ing
Lab·ra·dor
La Bru·yère
la·bur·num
lab·y·rinth
  lab·y·rin·thine
  lab·y·rin·thi·an
lace
  laced
  lace·like
  lac·er
  lacy
  lac·i·er
  lac·i·est
Lac·e·de·mo·ni·an
lac·er·ate
  lac·er·at·ed
  lac·er·at·ing
  lac·er·a·tion
lace·wing
lach·es

lach·ry·mal
lach·ry·mose
 lach·ry·mose·ly
lac·ing
lack·a·dai·si·cal
 lack·a·dai·si·cal·ly
Lack·a·wan·na
lack·ey
 lack·eyed
 lack·ey·ing
lack·lus·ter
La·co·nia
la·con·ic
 la·con·i·cal·ly
lac·quer
 lac·quer·er
la·crosse
lac·tate
 lac·tat·ed
 lac·tat·ing
lac·ta·tion
lac·te·al
lac·tic
lac·tose
la·cu·na
 la·cu·nas
 la·cu·nae
lad·der
lad·die
lade
 lad·ed
 lad·en
 lad·ing
la·di·da
La·di·no
la·dle
 la·dled
 la·dling
la·dy
 la·dy·bug
 la·dy·fin·ger
 la·dy-in-wait·ing
 la·dy-kil·ler
 la·dy·like
 la·dy·love
 la·dy·ship
 la·dy's-slip·per
La·fay·ette
Laf·fite
La Fol·lette
La Fon·taine
lag
 lagged
 lag·ging
la·ger
lag·gard
la·gniappe
la·goon
La·gos
La Guar·dia
La·hore
la·ic
 la·i·cal
 la·i·cal·ly
lair

laird
lais·sez faire
la·i·ty
 la·i·ties
lake·side
lal·la·tion
la·lop·a·thy
lam
 lammed
 lam·ming
la·ma
La·ma·ism
 La·ma·ist
 la·ma·sery
 la·ma·ser·ies
lam·baste
 lam·bast·ed
 lam·bast·ing
lam·bent
 lam·ben·cy
 lam·bent·ly
Lam·beth
lam·bre·quin
lamb·skin
lame
 lam·er
 lam·est
 lamed
 lam·ing
 lame·ly
 lame·ness
la·mé
la·mel·la
 la·mel·las
 la·mel·lae
 la·mel·lar
 lam·el·late
la·ment
 lam·en·ta·ble
 lam·en·ta·bly
 lam·en·ta·tion
lam·i·na
 lam·i·nae
 lam·i·nas
lam·i·nate
 lam·i·nat·ed
 lam·i·nat·ing
 lam·i·na·tion
lamp·black
lam·poon
lam·prey
 lam·preys
Lan·ark
Lan·ca·shire
Lan·cas·ter
lance
 lanced
 lanc·ing
 lance·like
Lan·ce·lot
lan·ce·o·late
lanc·er
lan·cet
lance·wood
lan·dau

land·ed
land·fall
land·hold·er
land·ing
land·la·dy
  land·la·dies
land·locked
land·lord
land·lub·ber
land·mark
land·own·er
  land·own·ing
  land·own·er·ship
land·scape
  land·scaped
  land·scap·ing
  land·scap·er
land·slide
lands·man
Land·sturm
land·ward
  land·wards
lang·syne
lan·guage
lan·guid
  lan·guid·ly
lan·guish
  lan·guish·ing
  lan·guish·ing·ly
lan·guor
  lan·guor·ous
  lan·guor·ous·ly
La·nier
lank·ness
lanky
  lank·i·er
  lank·i·est
  lank·i·ness
lan·o·lin
Lan·sing
Lan·ston
lan·tern
lan·tha·num
lan·yard
La·os
lap
  lapped
  lap·ping
  lap·per
la·pel
lap·ful
  lap·fuls
  laps·ful
lap·i·dary
  lap·i·dar·ies
lap·in
lap·is laz·u·li
La·place
Lap·land
lap·pet
lapse
  lapsed
  laps·ing
La·pu·ta
Lar·a·mie

lar·board
lar·ce·ny
  lar·ce·nies
  lar·ce·nous
larch
lar·der
La·res
large
  larg·er
  larg·est
  large·ness
large·ly
large-scale
lar·gess
lar·ghet·to
  lar·ghet·tos
larg·ish
lar·go
  lar·gos
lar·i·at
lark·spur
La Roche·fou·cauld
lar·rup
lar·va
  lar·vae
  lar·val
lar·yn·gi·tis
lar·ynx
  lar·ynx·es
la·ryn·ges
la·ryn·ge·al
las·civ·i·ous
  las·civ·i·ous·ly
  las·civ·i·ous·ness
la·ser
lash
  lash·ing
  lash·er
las·sie
las·si·tude
las·so
  las·sos
  las·soes
  las·so·er
last·ing
  last·ing·ly
last·ly
Las Ve·gas
latch·key
late
  lat·er
  lat·est
  late·ness
la·teen sail
late·ly
la·tent
  la·ten·cy
  la·tent·ly
lat·er·al
  lat·er·al·ly
la·tex
  la·tex·es
  lat·i·ces
lathe
lath·er

lath·er·er
lath·ery
lath·ing
Lat·in
Lat·in-A·mer·i·can
lat·i·tude
lat·i·tu·di·nal
lat·i·tu·di·nar·i·an
La·ti·um
La·to·na
la·trine
lat·ter
Lat·ter-day Saint
lat·tice
lat·ticed
lat·tic·ing
lat·tice·work
Lat·via
laud·a·ble
laud·a·bly
lau·da·num
laud·a·to·ry
laud·a·tive
Lau·der
laugh
laugh·er
laugh·ing·ly
laugh·a·ble
laugh·a·bly
laugh·ter
launch
launch·er
laun·der
laun·der·er
laun·dress
laun·der·ette
Laun·dro·mat
laun·dry
laun·dries
laun·dry·man
laun·dry·men
laun·dry·wom·an
laun·dry·wom·en
lau·re·ate
lau·rel
Lau·ren·tian
Lau·ri·er
Lau·sanne
la·va
lav·a·liere
lav·a·to·ry
lav·a·to·ries
lave
laved
lav·ing
lav·en·der
lav·ish
lav·ish·ly
lav·ish·ness
La·voi·sier
law-a·bid·ing
law·break·er
law·break·ing
law·ful
law·ful·ly

law·ful·ness
law·giv·er
law·giv·ing
law·less
law·less·ly
law·less·ness
law·mak·er
law·mak·ing
lawn
Law·rence
law·ren·ci·um
law·suit
law·yer
lax
lax·i·ty
lax·ly
lax·ness
lax·a·tive
lay·er
lay·ette
lay·man
lay·men
lay·off
lay·out
lay·o·ver
Laz·a·rus
laze
lazed
laz·ing
la·zy
la·zi·er
la·zi·est
la·zi·ly
la·zi·ness
la·zy·bones
lea
leach
lead
led
lead·ing
lead·en
lead·en·ly
lead·en·ness
lead·er
lead·er·less
lead·er·ship
leaf·age
leaf·less
leaf·stalk
leafy
leaf·i·er
leaf·i·est
leaf·i·ness
league
leagued
lea·guing
leak
leak·age
leak·i·ness
leaky
leak·i·er
leak·i·est
lean
lean·ly
lean·ness

lean·ing
lean-to
  lean-tos
leap
  leaped
  leapt
  leap·ing
  leap·er
leap·frog
learn
  learned
  learnt
  learn·ing
  learn·er
learn·ed·ly
learn·ed·ness
lease
  leased
  leas·ing
leash
least·wize
  least·ways
leath·er
leath·er·neck
leath·ery
leave
  left
  leav·ing
  leav·er
leav·en
Leav·en·worth
leaves
leave-tak·ing
Leb·a·nese
Leb·a·non
lech·er
  lech·er·ous
  lech·er·ous·ly
  lech·ery
  lech·er·ies
lec·tern
lec·ture
  lec·tured
  lec·tur·ing
  lec·tur·er
ledge
ledg·er
leech
leek
leer·ing·ly
leery
lee·ward
lee·way
left-hand·ed
  left-hand·ed·ly
  left-hand·ed·ness
left·ist
left·o·ver
left-wing
  left-wing·er
leg
  legged
  leg·ging
leg·a·cy
  leg·a·cies

le·gal
le·gal·ly
le·gal·ism
  le·gal·ist
  le·gal·is·tic
le·gal·i·ty
  le·gal·i·ties
le·gal·ize
  le·gal·ized
  le·gal·iz·ing
  le·gal·i·za·tion
leg·ate
leg·a·tee
le·ga·tion
le·ga·to
leg·end
leg·end·ary
leg·er·de·main
leg·gy
  leg·gi·er
  leg·gi·est
leg·horn
leg·i·ble
  leg·i·bil·i·ty
  leg·i·bly
le·gion
  le·gion·ary
  le·gion·ar·ies
  le·gion·naire
leg·is·late
  leg·is·lat·ed
  leg·is·lat·ing
  leg·is·la·tive
  leg·is·la·tor
leg·is·la·tion
leg·is·la·ture
le·git
le·git·i·mate
  le·git·i·mat·ed
  le·git·i·mat·ing
  le·git·i·ma·cy
  le·git·i·mate·ly
  le·git·i·mist
  le·git·i·mize
  le·git·i·mized
  le·git·i·miz·ing
leg·ume
le·gu·mi·nous
Le·high
lei
  leis
Leib·nitz
Leices·ter
Leip·zig
lei·sure
  lei·sure·ly
  lei·sure·li·ness
leit·mo·tif
lem·ming
lem·on
lem·on·ade
le·mur
lend
  lent
  lend·ing

lend·er
length
length·en
length·wise
lengthy
  length·i·er
  length·i·est
  length·i·ly
  length·i·ness
le·ni·ent
  le·ni·ence
  le·ni·en·cy
  le·ni·ent·ly
Len·in
Len·in·grad
len·i·tive
len·i·ty
Len·ox
lens
Lent·en
len·til
len·to
Leo
Leom·in·ster
le·o·nine
leop·ard
  leop·ard·ess
le·o·tard
Le·pan·to
lep·er
lep·i·dop·ter·ous
lep·re·chaun
lep·ro·sy
lep·rous
les·bi·an
  les·bi·an·ism
le·sion
Le·sot·ho
les·see
less·en
less·er
les·son
les·sor
least
let·down
le·thal
  le·thal·ly
leth·ar·gy
  leth·ar·gies
  le·thar·gic
  le·thar·gi·cal
Le·the
let·ter
  let·ter·er
let·tered
let·ter·head
let·ter·ing
let·ter-per·fect
let·ter·press
let·tuce
let·up
leu·ke·mia
leu·ko·cyte
Le·vant
  Le·van·tine

lev·ee
lev·el
  lev·eled
  lev·el·ing
  lev·el·er
  lev·el·ly
  lev·el·ness
lev·el-head·ed
  lev·el-head·ed·ness
lev·er
  lev·er·age
le·vi·a·than
Le·vi
Le·vis
lev·i·tate
  lev·i·tat·ed
  lev·i·tat·ing
  lev·i·ta·tion
Le·vite
Le·vit·i·cus
lev·i·ty
levy
  lev·ies
  lev·ied
  lev·y·ing
lewd
  lewd·ly
  lewd·ness
Lew·is
Lew·i·sohn
Lew·is·ton
Lew·is·town
lex·i·cog·ra·phy
  lex·i·cog·ra·pher
  lex·i·co·graph·ic
  lex·i·co·graph·i·cal
lex·i·con
Lex·ing·ton
Ley·den
li·a·bil·i·ty
  li·a·bil·i·ties
li·a·ble
li·ai·son
li·ar
li·ba·tion
li·bel
  li·beled
  li·bel·ing
  li·bel·er
  li·bel·ous
  li·bel·ous·ly
lib·er·al
  lib·er·al·ly
  lib·er·al·ness
lib·er·al·ism
lib·er·al·i·ty
  lib·er·al·i·ties
lib·er·al·ize
  lib·er·al·ized
  lib·er·al·iz·ing
  lib·er·al·i·za·tion
lib·er·ate
  lib·er·at·ed
  lib·er·at·ing
  lib·er·a·tion

lib·er·a·tor
Li·be·ria
lib·er·tar·i·an
lib·er·tine
lib·er·tin·ism
lib·er·ty
lib·er·ties
li·bid·i·nous
li·bid·i·nous·ly
li·bid·i·nous·ness
li·bi·do
li·bid·in·al
Li·bra
li·brar·i·an
li·brary
li·brar·ies
li·bret·to
li·bret·tos
li·bret·ist
Li·bre·ville
Lib·ya
li·cense
li·censed
li·cens·ing
li·cen·see
li·cens·er
li·cen·ti·ate
li·cen·tious
li·cen·tious·ly
li·cen·tious·ness
li·chee
li·chen
lic·it
lick·e·ty-split
lick·spit·tle
lic·o·rice
lid·ded
Lieb·frau·milch
Liech·ten·stein
Lie·der·kranz
lief
liege
lien
lieu
lieu·ten·an·cy
lieu·ten·an·cies
lieu·ten·ant
life·blood
life·boat
life·guard
life·less
life·less·ly
life·less·ness
life·like
life·line
lif·er
life·sav·er
life·size
life·style
life·time
life·work
lift-off
lig·a·ment
lig·a·ture
lig·a·tured

lig·a·tur·ing
light·en
light·er
light-fin·gered
light·foot·ed
light·foot·ed·ly
light·foot·ed·ness
light-head·ed
light-head·ed·ly
light-head·ed·ness
light·heart·ed
light·heart·ed·ly
light·heart·ed·ness
light·house
light·ing
light·ly
light-mind·ed
light-mind·ed·ly
light-mind·ed·ness
light·ning
light·weight
light-year
lig·nite
lig·nit·ic
like
liked
lik·ing
lik·a·ble
like·a·ble
lik·a·ble·ness
like·a·ble·ness
like·li·hood
like·ly
like·li·er
like·li·est
like-mind·ed
lik·en
like·ness
like·wise
lik·ing
li·lac
Lil·li·put
Lil·li·pu·tian
lilt·ing
lily
lil·ies
lil·y-liv·ered
li·ma
limb
lim·ber
lim·ber·ness
lim·bo
Lim·burg·er
lime
limed
lim·ing
limy
lim·i·er
lim·i·est
lime·like
lime·light
lime·light·er
lim·er·ick
lime·stone
lim·it

lim·it·a·ble
lim·i·ta·tive
lim·it·er
lim·it·less
lim·i·ta·tion
lim·it·ed
lim·it·ed·ly
lim·it·ed·ness
Li·moges
lim·ou·sine
limp
limp·er
limp·ing·ly
limp·ly
limp·ness
lim·pet
lim·pid
lim·pid·i·ty
lim·pid·ly
lim·pid·ness
lin·age
Lin·coln
Lind·bergh
lin·den
line
lined
lin·ing
lin·e·age
lin·e·al
lin·e·a·ment
lin·e·ar
lin·e·ar·ly
line·back·er
line·back·ing
line·man
line·men
lin·en
lin·er
line·up
lin·ger
lin·ger·er
lin·ger·ing·ly
lin·ge·rie
lin·go
lin·goes
lin·gua fran·ca
lin·gual
lin·gual·ly
lin·guist
lin·guis·tics
lin·guis·tic
lin·guis·ti·cal
lin·guis·ti·cal·ly
lin·i·ment
lin·ing
link
linked
link·er
link·age
lin·net
li·no·le·um
lin·seed
lint
linty
lint·i·er

lint·i·est
lin·tel
li·on
li·on·ess
li·on·like
Li·o·nel
li·on·heart·ed
li·on·ize
li·on·ized
li·on·iz·ing
li·on·i·za·tion
li·on·iz·er
Lip·pi
lip·py
lip·pi·er
lip·pi·est
lip·stick
liq·ue·fy
liq·ue·fied
liq·ue·fy·ing
liq·ue·fac·tion
liq·ue·fi·a·ble
liq·ue·fi·er
li·queur
liq·uid
li·quid·i·ty
liq·uid·ness
liq·uid·ly
liq·ui·date
liq·ui·dat·ed
liq·ui·dat·ing
liq·ui·da·tion
liq·ui·da·tor
liq·uor
Lis·bon
lisle
lisp
lisp·ing·ly
lis·some
lis·some·ly
lis·some·ness
list
list·ed
lis·ter
list·ing
lis·ten
lis·ten·er
Lis·ter
list·less
list·less·ly
list·less·ness
lit·a·ny
lit·a·nies
li·tchi
li·tchis
li·ter
lit·er·a·cy
lit·er·al
lit·er·al·i·ty
lit·er·al·ness
lit·er·al·ly
lit·er·ary
lit·er·ar·i·ly
lit·er·ar·i·ness
lit·er·ate

lit·er·ate·ly
lit·e·ra·ti
lit·er·a·ture
lithe
  lithe·some
  lithe·ly
  lithe·ness
lith·i·um
lith·o·graph
  li·thog·ra·pher
  lith·o·graph·ic
  lith·o·graph·i·cal·ly
li·thog·ra·phy
Lith·u·a·nia
lit·i·gate
  lit·i·gat·ed
  lit·i·gat·ing
  lit·i·ga·tion
  lit·i·ga·tor
lit·mus
lit·ter
  lit·ter·bug
lit·tle
  lit·tler
  lit·tlest
lit·to·ral
lit·ur·gy
  lit·ur·gies
  lit·ur·gist
li·tur·gic
li·tur·gi·cal
liv·a·ble
  live·a·ble
  liv·a·ble·ness
  live·a·ble·ness
live·li·hood
live·long
live·ly
  live·li·er
  live·li·est
  live·li·ness
liv·en
  liv·en·er
liv·er
Liv·er·pool
liv·er·wurst
liv·ery
  liv·er·ies
  liv·er·ied
  liv·er·y·man
  liv·er·y·men
live·stock
liv·id
  li·vid·i·ty
  liv·id·ness
  liv·id·ly
liv·ing
  liv·ing·ly
  liv·ing·ness
Liv·ing·ston
liz·ard
lla·ma
lla·no
  lla·nos
load

load·ed
load·er
loaf
loaves
loaf·er
loamy
loath
  loath·ness
loathe
  loathed
  loath·ing
  loath·ing·ly
loath·some
  loath·some·ly
  loath·some·ness
lob
  lobbed
  lob·bing
lob·by
  lob·bies
  lob·by·ist
lobe
lo·bar
lo·bate
lobed
lob·ster
lo·cal
  lo·cal·ly
lo·cale
  lo·cal·i·ty
  lo·cal·i·ties
lo·cal·ize
  lo·cal·ized
  lo·cal·iz·ing
  lo·cal·i·za·tion
lo·cate
  lo·cat·ed
  lo·cat·ing
  lo·ca·tor
lo·ca·tion
loch
Loch·in·var
lock·a·ble
lock·er
lock·et
lock·jaw
lock·out
lock·smith
lock·up
lo·co
  lo·co·mo·tion
  lo·co·mo·tive
  lo·co·weed
lo·cus
  lo·ci
lo·cust
lo·cu·tion
lode·star
lode·stone
lodge
  lodged
  lodg·ing
  lodg·er
  lodg·ment
lofty

loft·i·er
loft·i·est
loft·i·ly
loft·i·ness
lo·gan·ber·ry
lo·gan·ber·ries
log·a·rithm
log·a·rith·mic
log·a·rith·mi·cal
log·a·rith·mi·cal·ly
log·book
loge
log·ger
log·ger·head
log·ic
lo·gi·cian
log·i·cal
log·i·cal·i·ty
log·i·cal·ly
log·i·cal·ness
lo·gis·tics
lo·gis·tic
lo·gis·ti·cal
log·jam
Lo·gos
log·roll·ing
log·roll
lo·gy
lo·gi·er
lo·gi·est
Lo·hen·grin
loin·cloth
loi·ter
loi·ter·er
lol·li·pop
Lom·bard
Lo·me
Lo·mond
Lon·don
Lon·don·der·ry
lone·ly
lone·li·er
lone·li·est
lone·li·ly
lone·li·ness
lon·er
lone·some
lone·some·ly
lone·some·ness
lon·gev·i·ty
Long·fel·low
long·hair
long·hand
long·ing
long·ing·ly
Lon·gi·nus
lon·gi·tude
lon·gi·tu·di·nal
lon·gi·tu·di·nal·ly
long-lived
long-lived·ness
long-play·ing
long-range
long·shore·man
long·shore·men

long-suf·fer·ing
long-suf·fer·ing·ly
long-term
long-wind·ed
long-wind·ed·ly
long-wind·ed·ness
long·wise
look·er-on
look·ers-on
look·out
loony
loon·i·er
loon·i·est
loon·ies
loon·i·ness
loop·hole
loop·holed
loop·hol·ing
loose
loos·er
loos·est
loosed
loos·ing
loose·ly
loose·ness
loos·en
loot·er
lop
lopped
lop·ping
lope
loped
lop·ing
lop·er
Lo·pez
lop·sid·ed
lop·sid·ed·ly
lop·sid·ed·ness
lo·qua·cious
lo·qua·cious·ly
lo·qua·cious·ness
lo·quac·i·ty
lo·quac·i·ties
lord·ly
lord·li·er
lord·li·est
lord·li·ness
lord·ship
lor·gnette
Lor·raine
lor·ry
lor·ries
Los An·ge·les
lose
lost
los·ing
los·a·ble
los·er
Los·sen
lot
lot·ted
lot·ting
Lo·thar·io
Lo·thar·i·os
lo·tion

lot·tery
  lot·ter·ies
lot·to
lo·tus
  lo·tus·es
  lo·tus-eat·er
loud
  loud·ly
  loud·ness
loud-mouthed
loud·speak·er
Lou·i·si·ana
Lou·is·ville
lounge
  lounged
  loung·ing
  loung·er
louse
  lice
lousy
  lous·i·er
  lous·i·est
  lous·i·ly
  lous·i·ness
lout
  lout·ish
  lout·ish·ly
  lout·ish·ness
lou·ver
  lou·vered
Lou·vre
love
  loved
  lov·ing
  lov·a·ble
  love·a·ble
  lov·a·bil·i·ty
  lov·a·ble·ness
  lov·a·bly
  love·less
love·bird
love·lorn
love·ly
  love·li·er
  love·li·est
  love·li·ness
lov·er
lov·ing
  lov·ing·ly
  lov·ing·ness
low-born
low-boy
low·brow
low-down
Low·ell
low·er
low·er-case
low·er·ing
  low·er·ing·ly
low·ery
low-key
  low-keyed
low·land
  low·land·er
low·ly

low·li·er
low·li·est
low·li·ness
low-mind·ed
low-mind·ed·ly
low-mind·ed·ness
loy·al
loy·al·ist
loy·al·ly
loy·al·ty
loy·al·ties
Loy·o·la
loz·enge
Lu·an·da
lu·au
lub·ber
  lub·ber·li·ness
  lub·ber·ly
Lub·bock
Lu·beck
lu·bri·cant
lu·bri·cate
  lu·bri·cat·ed
  lu·bri·cat·ing
  lu·bri·ca·tion
  lu·bri·ca·tive
  lu·bri·ca·tor
Lu·cerne
lu·cid
  lu·cid·i·ty
  lu·cid·ness
  lu·cid·ly
Lu·cite
luck
  luck·i·ly
  luck·i·ness
lucky
  luck·i·er
  luck·i·est
lu·cra·tive
  lu·cra·tive·ly
  lu·cra·tive·ness
lu·cre
lu·cu·brate
  lu·cu·brat·ed
  lu·cu·brat·ing
  lu·cu·bra·tion
  lu·cu·bra·tor
lu·di·crous
  lu·di·crous·ly
  lu·di·crous·ness
Lud·wig
Luft·waf·fe
lug
  lugged
  lug·ging
lug·gage
lug·ger
lug·sail
lu·gu·bri·ous
  lu·gu·bri·ous·ly
  lu·gu·bri·ous·ness
luke·warm
  luke·warm·ly
  luke·warm·ness

lull·a·by
  lull·a·bies
lum·ba·go
lum·bar
lum·ber
  lum·ber·ing·ly
  lum·ber·er
lum·ber·ing
lum·ber·jack
lum·ber·man
  lum·ber·men
lu·men
  lu·mens
  lu·mi·na
lu·mi·nary
  lu·mi·nar·ies
lu·mi·nes·cence
  lu·mi·nes·cent
lu·mi·nous
  lu·mi·nos·i·ty
  lu·mi·nous·ly
  lu·mi·nous·ness
lum·mox
lumpy
  lump·i·er
  lump·i·est
  lump·i·ly
  lump·i·ness
lu·na·cy
  lu·na·cies
lu·nar
lu·nate
lu·na·tic
lunch
  lunch·er
lunch·eon
lunch·room
lunge
  lunged
  lung·ing
lunk·head
  lunk·head·ed
Lu·per·ca·lia
lu·pine
lurch
lure
  lured
  lur·ing
lu·rid
  lu·rid·ly
  lu·rid·ness
lurk
  lurk·er
  lurk·ing·ly
Lu·sa·ka
lus·cious
  lus·cious·ly
  lus·cious·ness
lush
  lush·ly
  lush·ness
Lu·si·ta·nia
lust
  lust·ful
  lust·ful·ly

lust·ful·ness
lus·ter
  lus·ter·less
lus·trous
  lus·trous·ly
  lus·trous·ness
lusty
  lust·i·er
  lust·i·est
  lust·i·ly
  lust·i·ness
lu·te·ti·um
Lu·ther
  Lu·ther·an
lut·ist
Lux·em·bourg
lux·u·ri·ant
  lux·u·ri·ance
  lux·u·ri·an·cy
  lux·u·ri·ant·ly
lux·u·ri·ate
  lux·u·ri·at·ed
  lux·u·ri·at·ing
  lux·u·ri·a·tion
lux·u·ri·ous
  lux·u·ri·ous·ly
  lux·u·ri·ous·ness
lux·u·ry
  lux·u·ries
ly·cée
ly·ce·um
ly·ing
ly·ing-in
lymph
  lym·phoid
  lym·phat·ic
lynch
  lynch·er
  lynch·ing
lynx
  lynx·es
  lynx·eyed
Ly·ons
lyre
ly·ric
  lyr·i·cal
  lyr·i·cal·ly
  lyr·i·cal·ness
  lyr·i·cism
  lyr·i·cist
ly·ser·gic
ly·sine
Ly·sol
ma·ca·bre
  ma·ca·bre·ly
mac·ad·am
mac·ad·am·ize
  mac·ad·am·ized
  mac·ad·am·iz·ing
  mac·ad·am·i·za·tion
Ma·cao
ma·caque
mac·a·ro·ni
mac·a·roon
Mac·Ar·thur

ma·caw
Mac·beth
mace
 maced
 mac·ing
Mac·e·do·nia
mac·er·ate
 mac·er·at·ed
 mac·er·at·ing
 mac·er·a·tion
 mac·er·a·tor
Mach
ma·chete
Ma·chia·vel·li
Mach·i·a·vel·li·an
 Mach·i·a·vel·li·an·ism
mach·i·nate
 mach·i·nat·ed
 mach·i·nat·ing
 mach·i·na·tion
 mach·i·na·tor
ma·chine
 ma·chined
 ma·chin·ing
 ma·chin·a·bil·i·ty
 ma·chin·a·ble
 ma·chine·like
ma·chin·ery
 ma·chin·er·ies
ma·chin·ist
Mac·ken·zie
mack·er·el
Mack·i·nac
mack·i·naw
mack·in·tosh
mac·in·tosh
MacMil·lan
Ma·con
mac·ra·mé
mac·ro·cosm
 mac·ro·cos·mic
 mac·ro·cos·mi·cal·ly
ma·cron
mad
 mad·der
 mad·dest
 mad·ly
 mad·ness
Mad·a·gas·car
mad·am
 mes·dames
mad·ame
 mes·dames
Ma·da·ria·ga
mad·cap
mad·den
 mad·den·ing
 mad·den·ing·ly
Ma·dei·ra
mad·e·moi·selle
 mad·e·moi·selles
 mes·de·moi·selles
made-up
mad·house
Mad·i·son

mad·man
mad·men
Ma·don·na
mad·ras
Ma·drid
mad·ri·gal
 mad·ri·gal·ist
Mae·ce·nas
mael·strom
maes·tro
Mae·ter·linck
Maf·e·king
Ma·fia
mag·a·zine
Mag·da·len
Mag·de·burg
Ma·gel·lan
ma·gen·ta
Mag·gio·re
mag·got
 mag·goty
Ma·gi
 Ma·gus
mag·ic
 mag·i·cal
 mag·i·cal·ly
ma·gi·cian
Ma·gi·not
mag·is·te·ri·al
 mag·is·te·ri·al·ly
 mag·is·te·ri·al·ness
mag·is·tra·cy
 mag·is·tra·cies
mag·is·trate
mag·ma
 mag·mas
 mag·ma·ta
 mag·mat·ic
Mag·na Car·ta
mag·nan·i·mous
 mag·nan·i·mous·ly
 mag·nan·i·mous·ness
 mag·na·nim·i·ty
 mag·na·nim·i·ties
mag·nate
mag·ne·sia
 mag·ne·sian
mag·ne·si·um
mag·net
 mag·net·ic
 mag·net·i·cal·ly
mag·net·ism
mag·net·ize
 mag·net·ized
 mag·net·iz·ing
 mag·net·iz·a·ble
 mag·net·i·za·tion
 mag·net·iz·er
mag·ne·to
 mag·ne·tos
mag·ne·tom·e·ter
 mag·ne·to·met·ric
 mag·ne·tom·e·try
Mag·nif·i·cat
mag·nif·i·cent

mag·nif·i·cence
mag·nif·i·cent·ly
mag·ni·fy
mag·ni·fied
mag·ni·fy·ing
mag·ni·fi·a·ble
mag·ni·fi·ca·tion
mag·ni·fi·er
mag·ni·tude
mag·no·lia
mag·num
mag·pie
mag·uey
Mag·yar
Ma·ha·bha·ra·ta
Ma·han
ma·ha·ra·jah
ma·ha·ra·ni
ma·hat·ma
ma·hat·ma·ism
mah-jongg
ma·hog·a·ny
ma·hog·a·nies
Ma·hom·et
ma·hout
Mah·rat·ta
maid·en
maid·en·hair
maid·en·head
maid·ser·vant
mail·a·ble
mail·box
mail·man
mail·men
maim
maim·er
Mai·mon·i·des
Main·er
main·land
main·land·er
main·ly
main·mast
main·sail
main·spring
main·stream
main·tain
main·tain·a·ble
main·te·nance
mai·tre d'hô·tel
mai·tres d'hô·tel
maize
maj·es·ty
maj·es·ties
ma·jes·tic
ma·jes·ti·cal
ma·jes·ti·cal·ly
ma·jol·i·ca
ma·jor
Ma·jor·ka
ma·jor-do·mo
ma·jor-do·mos
ma·jor·i·ty
ma·jor·i·ties
Ma·kas·sar
make

mak·a·ble
ma·ker
mak·ing
make-be·lieve
make-shift
make-up
Mal·a·bar
Ma·lac·ca
Mal·a·chi
mal·a·dapt·ed
mal·ad·just·ment
mal·ad·just·ed
mal·ad·min·is·ter
mal·ad·min·is·tra·tion
mal·a·droit
mal·a·droit·ly
mal·a·droit·ness
mal·a·dy
mal·a·dies
Mal·a·ga
Mal·a·gasy
ma·laise
mal·a·prop
mal·a·prop·ism
ma·lar·ia
ma·lar·i·al
ma·lar·i·an
ma·lar·i·ous
ma·lar·key
Mal·a·wi
Ma·laya
Ma·lay·sia
Mal·colm
mal·con·tent
Mal·dive
mal·e·dict
mal·e·dic·tion
mal·e·dic·to·ry
mal·e·fac·tion
mal·e·fac·tor
ma·lev·o·lent
ma·lev·o·lence
ma·lev·o·lent·ly
mal·fea·sance
mal·fea·sant
mal·for·ma·tion
mal·formed
mal·func·tion
Ma·li
mal·ice
ma·li·cious
ma·li·cious·ly
ma·li·cious·ness
ma·lign
ma·lign·er
ma·lign·ly
ma·lig·nant
ma·lig·nan·cy
ma·lig·nan·cies
ma·lig·nant·ly
Ma·lines
ma·lin·ger
ma·lin·ger·er
mal·lard
mal·le·a·ble

mal·le·a·bil·i·ty
mal·le·a·ble·ness
mal·let
mal·low
mal·nour·ished
mal·nu·tri·tion
mal·oc·clu·sion
mal·o·dor
 mal·o·dor·ous
 mal·o·dor·ous·ly
 mal·o·dor·ous·ness
mal·prac·tice
 mal·prac·ti·tion·er
malt
 malty
 malt·i·er
 malt·i·est
Mal·ta
Mal·tese
mal·treat
 mal·treat·ment
Mam·e·luke
mam·ma
 ma·ma
mam·mal
 mam·ma·li·an
mam·ma·ry
 mam·ma·ries
mam·mon
mam·moth
mam·my
 mam·mies
man
 manned
 man·ning
man·a·cle
 man·a·cled
 man·a·cling
man·age
 man·aged
 man·ag·ing
 man·age·a·ble
 man·age·a·bil·i·ty
 man·age·a·ble·ness
 man·age·a·bly
man·age·ment
man·ag·er
 man·ag·er·ship
man·a·ge·ri·al
 man·a·ge·ri·al·ly
Ma·na·gua
ma·ña·na
Ma·nas·sas
Ma·nas·seh
man·a·tee
Man·ches·ter
Man·chu·ko
Man·chu·ria
man·da·la
Man·da·lay
man·da·rin
man·date
 man·dat·ed
 man·dat·ing
man·da·to·ry

man·da·to·ries
 man·da·to·ri·ly
Man·de·ville
man·di·ble
 man·dib·u·lar
 man·dib·u·lary
 man·dib·u·late
man·do·lin
 man·do·lin·ist
man·drake
man·drill
man·eat·er
 man·eat·ing
Ma·net
ma·neu·ver
 ma·neu·ver·a·bil·i·ty
 ma·neu·ver·a·ble
 ma·neu·ver·er
man·ful
 man·ful·ly
 man·ful·ness
man·ga·nese
mange
man·ger
man·gle
 man·gled
 man·gling
man·go
man·goes
man·gos
man·grove
man·gy
 man·gi·er
 man·gi·est
 man·gi·ly
 man·gi·ness
man·han·dle
 man·han·dled
 man·han·dling
Man·hat·tan
man·hole
man·hood
man·hour
man·hunt
 man·hunt·er
ma·nia
man·ic
ma·ni·ac
 ma·ni·a·cal
 ma·ni·a·cal·ly
man·ic-de·pres·sive
Man·i·che·an
man·i·cure
 man·i·cured
 man·i·cur·ing
 man·i·cur·ist
man·i·fest
 man·i·fest·er
 man·i·fest·ly
 man·i·fes·ta·tion
man·i·fes·to
 man·i·fes·tos
 man·i·fes·toes
man·i·fold
 man·i·fold·er

man·i·fold·ly
man·i·fold·ness
man·i·kin
man·a·kin
man·ni·kin
ma·nila
ma·nil·la
ma·nip·u·late
ma·nip·u·lat·ed
ma·nip·u·lat·ing
ma·nip·u·la·ble
ma·nip·u·la·tion
ma·nip·u·la·tive
ma·nip·u·la·tor
ma·nip·u·la·to·ry
Man·i·to·ba
man·kind
man·like
man·ly
man·li·er
man·li·est
man·li·ness
man·made
man·na
man·ne·quin
man·ner
man·nered
man·ner·ism
man·ner·ly
man·ner·li·ness
man·nish
man-of-war
men-of-war
ma·nom·e·ter
man·or
ma·no·ri·al
man·pow·er
man·sard
man·serv·ant
man·sion
man-sized
man·slaugh·ter
man·slay·er
man·slay·ing
man·tel
man·tle
man·til·la
man·tle
man·tled
man·tling
man-trap
Man·tua
man·u·al
man·u·al·ly
man·u·fac·ture
man·u·fac·tured
man·u·fac·tur·ing
man·u·fac·tur·a·ble
man·u·fac·tur·al
man·u·fac·tur·er
ma·nure
man·u·script
many
man·y-sid·ed
Mao Tse-tung

map
mapped
map·ping
map·per
ma·ple
mar
marred
mar·ring
ma·ra·ca
Mar·a·cai·bo
mar·a·schi·no
Ma·ra·tha
mar·a·thon
ma·raud
ma·raud·er
mar·ble
mar·bled
mar·bling
mar·ble·ize
mar·ble·ized
mar·ble·iz·ing
mar·bly
Mar·ble·head
Mar·burg
mar·cel
mar·celled
mar·cel·ling
march·er
mar·chion·ess
Mar·co·ni
Mar·co Po·lo
Mar·di gras
Ma·ren·go
mare's-tail
mar·ga·rine
mar·gin
mar·gi·nal
mar·gi·na·lia
mar·gin·al·i·ty
mar·gin·al·ly
mar·gin·ate
mar·gin·at·ed
mar·gin·at·ing
mar·gin·a·tion
Mar·got
mar·gue·rite
Ma·ria
Mar·i·co·pa
mar·i·cul·ture
mar·i·gold
ma·ri·jua·na
ma·rim·ba
ma·ri·na
mar·i·nade
mar·i·nad·ed
mar·i·nad·ing
mar·i·nate
mar·i·nat·ed
mar·i·nat·ing
mar·i·na·tion
ma·rine
mar·i·ner
Ma·ri·nist
mar·i·on·ette
Ma·ri·tain

mar·i·tal
mar·i·time
mar·jo·ram
marked
 mark·ed·ly
mark·er
mar·ket
 mar·ket·er
mar·ket·a·ble
 mar·ket·a·bil·i·ty
mar·ket·ing
mar·ket·place
Mark·ham
mark·ing
marks·man
 marks·men
 marks·man·ship
Marl·bor·ough
mar·lin
Mar·lowe
mar·ma·lade
Mar·mi·on
mar·mo·set
mar·mot
ma·roon
mar·quee
Mar·quette
mar·quis
 mar·quis·es
 mar·quess
mar·quise
 mar·quis·es
mar·riage
 mar·riage·a·ble
 mar·riage·a·bil·i·ty
mar·ried
mar·row
 mar·rowy
mar·row·bone
mar·ry
 mar·ried
 mar·ry·ing
Mar·seilles
mar·shal
 mar·shaled
 mar·shal·ing
marsh·mal·low
marshy
 marsh·i·er
 marsh·i·est
 marsh·i·ness
mar·su·pi·al
mar·tial
Mar·tian
mar·tin
Mar·ti·neau
mar·ti·ni
 mar·ti·nis
Mar·ti·nique
mar·tyr
 mar·tyr·ize
 mar·tyr·ized
 mar·tyr·iz·ing
 mar·tyr·dom
mar·vel

mar·veled
 mar·vel·ing
mar·vel·ous
 mar·vel·ous·ly
Marx·ism
 Marx·ist
 Marx·i·an
Mary
Mary·land
mar·zi·pan
Ma·sa·ryk
mas·cara
mas·cot
mas·cu·line
 mas·cu·line·ness
 mas·cu·lin·i·ty
mas·cu·lin·ize
 mas·cu·lin·ized
 mas·cu·lin·iz·ing
Mas·eru
mash·er
mask
 mask·like
masked
mas·och·ism
 mas·och·ist
 mas·och·is·tic
ma·son
 ma·son·ic
Ma·son·ite
ma·son·ry
 ma·son·ries
masque
mas·quer·ade
 mas·quer·ad·ed
 mas·quer·ad·ing
 mas·quer·ad·er
Mas·sa·chu·setts
mas·sa·cre
 mas·sa·cred
 mas·sa·cring
 mas·sa·crer
mas·sage
 mas·saged
 mas·sag·ing
 mas·sag·er
 mas·sag·ist
mas·seur
mas·seuse
 mas·seus·es
mas·sive
mass-pro·duce
 mass-pro·duced
 mass-pro·duc·ing
 mass-pro·duc·er
 mass-pro·duc·tion
massy
 mass·i·er
 mass·i·est
 mass·i·ness
mas·tec·to·my
 mas·tec·to·mies
mas·ter
 mas·ter·ful
mas·ter·mind

mas·ter·piece
mas·tery
  mas·ter·ies
mast·head
mas·tic
mas·ti·cate
  mas·ti·ca·ted
  mas·ti·ca·ting
  mas·ti·ca·ble
  mas·ti·ca·tion
  mas·ti·ca·tor
mas·tiff
mas·to·don
mas·toid
mas·tur·bate
  mas·tur·bat·ed
  mas·tur·bat·ing
  mas·tur·ba·tion
mat
  mat·ted
  mat·ting
mat·a·dor
match·book
match·mak·er
  match·mak·ing
mate
  mat·ed
  mat·ing
  mate·less
ma·te·ri·al
  ma·te·ri·al·ly
  ma·te·ri·al·ism
  ma·te·ri·al·ist
  ma·te·ri·al·is·tic
  ma·te·ri·al·is·ti·cal·ly
  ma·te·ri·al·ize
  ma·te·ri·al·ized
  ma·te·ri·al·iz·ing
ma·té·ri·el
ma·ter·nal
  ma·ter·nal·ism
  ma·ter·nal·is·tic
  ma·ter·nal·ly
ma·ter·ni·ty
  ma·ter·ni·ties
math·e·mat·i·cal
  math·e·mat·ic
  math·e·mat·i·cal·ly
math·e·ma·ti·cian
math·e·mat·ics
Math·er
ma·tin
  mat·in·al
mat·i·nee
ma·tri·arch
  ma·tri·ar·chal·ism
  ma·tri·ar·chy
  ma·tri·ar·chies
mat·ri·cide
ma·tric·u·lant
ma·tric·u·late
  ma·tric·u·lat·ed
  ma·tric·u·lat·ing
  ma·tric·u·la·tion
ma·tri·lin·e·al

mat·ri·mo·ny
  mat·ri·mo·nies
  mat·ri·mo·ni·al
ma·trix
  ma·tri·ces
  ma·trix·es
ma·tron
  ma·tron·ly
mat·ter
Mat·ter·horn
mat·ter-of-course
mat·ter-of-fact
  mat·ter-of-fact·ly
  mat·ter-of-fact·ness
Mat·thew
Mat·thi·as
mat·ting
mat·tress
mat·u·rate
  mat·u·rat·ed
  mat·u·rat·ing
  mat·u·ra·tion
ma·ture
ma·tu·ri·ty
mat·zo
  mat·zoth
  mat·zos
maud·lin
Ma·ui
Mau·re·ta·nia
Mau·ri·ti·us
mau·so·le·um
  mau·so·le·ums
  mau·so·lea
mauve
mav·er·ick
mawk·ish
max·im
max·i·mal
  max·i·mal·ly
Max·i·mil·ian
max·i·mize
  max·i·mized
  max·i·miz·ing
max·i·mum
  max·i·mums
  max·i·ma
Ma·ya
may·be
May·day
may·flow·er
may·fly
  may·flies
may·hem
may·on·naise
may·or
  may·or·al
  may·or·al·ty
  may·or·al·ties
May·time
maze
  mazed
  maz·ing
ma·zy
  ma·zi·er

ma·zi·est
ma·zi·ly
ma·zi·ness
Mba·ba·ne
Mc·Coy
McKin·ley
mead·ow
mead·ow·lark
mea·ger
mea·ger·ly
mea·ger·ness
meal·time
meal·worm
mealy
meal·i·er
meal·i·est
meal·i·ness
meal·y-mouthed
mean
mean·ing
mean·ly
mean·ness
me·an·der
mean·ing·ful
mean·ing·ful·ly
mean·ing·less
mean·ing·less·ly
mean·ing·less·ness
meant
mean·time
mean·while
mea·sles
mea·sly
mea·sli·er
mea·sli·est
meas·ur·a·ble
meas·ur·a·bil·i·ty
meas·ur·a·bly
meas·ure
meas·ur·er
meas·ured
meas·ure·ment
meat-and-po·ta·toes
meaty
meat·i·er
meat·i·est
meat·i·ness
mec·ca
me·chan·ic
me·chan·i·cal
me·chan·i·cal·ly
me·chan·ics
mech·an·ism
mech·a·nis·tic
mech·a·nis·ti·cal·ly
mech·a·nize
mech·a·nized
mech·a·niz·ing
mech·a·ni·za·tion
mech·a·niz·er
med·al
med·aled
med·al·ing
me·dal·lic
me·dal·lion

med·dle
med·dled
med·dling
med·dler
med·dle·some
Me·dea
me·dia
me·di·al
me·di·an
me·di·an·ly
me·di·ate
me·di·at·ed
me·di·at·ing
me·di·a·tion
me·di·a·tive
me·di·a·to·ry
me·di·a·tor
med·ic
med·i·ca·ble
med·i·ca·bly
Med·i·caid
med·i·cal
med·i·cal·ly
me·dic·a·ment
Med·i·care
med·i·cate
med·i·cat·ed
med·i·cat·ing
med·i·ca·tion
Med·i·ci
me·dic·i·nal
me·dic·i·nal·ly
med·i·cine
med·i·cined
med·i·cin·ing
med·i·co
me·di·e·val
me·di·e·val·ism
Me·di·na
me·di·o·cre
me·di·oc·ri·ty
me·di·oc·ri·ties
med·i·tate
med·i·tat·ed
med·i·tat·ing
med·i·tat·ing·ly
med·i·ta·tor
med·i·ta·tion
med·i·ta·tive
med·i·ter·ra·ne·an
me·di·um
me·dia
me·di·ums
med·ley
med·leys
meet·ing
meet·ing·house
meg·a·city
meg·a·cit·ies
meg·a·cy·cle
meg·a·lo·ma·nia
meg·a·lo·ma·ni·ac
meg·a·lo·ma·ni·a·cal
meg·a·lop·o·lis
meg·a·lo·pol·i·tan

meg·a·phone
meg·a·phoned
meg·a·phon·ing
meg·a·ton
meg·a·watt
mei·o·sis
mei·ot·ic
mel·a·mine
mel·an·cho·lia
mel·an·cho·li·ac
mel·an·choly
mel·an·chol·ies
mel·an·chol·ic
mel·an·chol·i·cal·ly
mel·an·chol·i·ty
mel·an·chol·i·ness
Mel·a·ne·sia
mé·lange
mel·a·nin
mel·a·no·ma
mel·a·no·mas
mel·a·no·ma·ta
Mel·ba
Mel·bourne
Mel·chi·or
me·lee
mel·io·rate
mel·io·rat·ed
mel·io·rat·ing
mel·io·ra·ble
mel·io·ra·tion
mel·io·ra·tor
mel·lif·lu·ous
mel·lif·lu·ent
mel·lif·lu·ous·ly
mel·low
me·lo·de·on
mel·o·dra·ma
mel·o·dra·mat·ic
mel·o·dra·mat·i·cal·ly
mel·o·dra·mat·ics
mel·o·dy
mel·o·dies
me·lod·ic
me·lod·i·cal·ly
me·lo·di·ous
me·lo·di·ous·ness
mel·on
Mel·rose
melt
melt·ed
melt·ing
melt·a·bil·i·ty
melt·a·ble
melt·er
Mel·ville
mem·ber
mem·bered
mem·ber·less
mem·ber·ship
mem·brane
mem·bra·nous
me·men·to
me·men·tos
me·men·toes

Mem·non
memo
mem·oir
mem·o·ra·bil·ia
mem·o·ra·ble
mem·o·ra·bly
mem·o·ran·dum
mem·o·ran·dums
mem·o·ran·da
me·mo·ri·al
me·mo·ri·al·ly
me·mo·ri·al·ize
me·mo·ri·al·ized
me·mo·ri·al·iz·ing
me·mo·ri·al·iza·tion
me·mo·ri·al·iz·er
me·mo·ri·al·ly
mem·o·rize
mem·o·rized
mem·o·riz·ing
mem·o·riz·a·ble
mem·o·ri·za·tion
mem·o·ry
mem·o·ries
Mem·phis
men·ace
men·aced
men·ac·ing
mé·nage
me·nag·er·ie
mend
mend·a·ble
men·da·cious
men·da·cious·ly
men·da·cious·ness
men·dac·i·ty
Men·del
men·de·le·vi·um
men·di·cant
me·ni·al
me·ni·al·ly
me·nin·ges
men·in·gi·tis
me·nis·cus
me·nis·cus·es
me·nis·ci
Men·no·nite
men·o·pause
men·o·pau·sal
me·nor·ah
men·sal
men·ses
men·stru·al
men·stru·a·tion
men·stru·ate
men·stru·at·ed
men·stru·at·ing
men·sur·a·ble
men·tal
men·tal·ly
men·tal·i·ty
men·tal·i·ties
men·thol
men·tho·lat·ed
men·tion

men·tion·a·ble
men·tion·er
men·tor
menu
me·ow
me·pro·ba·mate
mer·can·tile
mer·can·til·ism
mer·can·til·ist
mer·ce·nary
mer·ce·nar·ies
mer·ce·nar·i·ly
mer·cer·ize
mer·cer·ized
mer·cer·iz·ing
mer·chan·dise
mer·chan·dised
mer·chan·dis·ing
mer·chan·dis·er
mer·chant
mer·chant·man
mer·chant·men
mer·cu·ri·al
Mer·cu·ro·chrome
mer·cu·ry
mer·cu·ries
mer·cy
mer·cies
mer·ci·ful
mer·ci·ful·ly
mer·ci·less
mere·ly
mer·e·tri·cious
mer·e·tri·cious·ly
mer·e·tri·cious·ness
merge
merged
merg·ing
mer·gence
merg·er
Mer·i·den
me·rid·i·an
me·rid·i·o·nal
me·ringue
mer·it
mer·it·ed
mer·it·ed·ly
mer·it·less
mer·i·to·ri·ous
mer·maid
mer·man
mer·men
Mer·ri·mac
mer·ri·ment
mer·ry
mer·ri·er
mer·ri·est
mer·ri·ness
mer·ry-go-round
mer·ry·mak·er
mer·ry·mak·ing
me·sa
mes·cal
mes·dames
mes·de·moi·selles

mesh·work
me·si·al
mes·mer·ism
mes·mer·ic
mes·mer·i·cal·ly
mes·mer·ist
mes·mer·ize
mes·mer·ized
mes·mer·iz·ing
mes·mer·i·za·tion
mes·mer·iz·er
mes·o·morph
mes·o·mor·phic
mes·o·mor·phism
mes·o·mor·phy
me·son
Mes·o·po·ta·mia
mes·o·sphere
Meso·zo·ic
mes·quite
mess
mess·i·ly
mess·i·ness
messy
mess·i·er
mess·i·est
mes·sage
mes·sen·ger
Mes·si·ah
Mes·si·an·ic
mes·ti·zo
me·tab·o·lism
met·a·bol·ic
met·a·bol·i·cal
me·tab·o·lize
me·tab·o·lized
me·tab·o·liz·ing
met·al
met·aled
met·al·ing
met·al·ize
met·al·ized
met·al·iz·ing
me·tal·lic
me·tal·li·cal·ly
met·al·loid
met·al·lur·gy
met·al·lur·gic
met·al·lur·gi·cal
met·al·lur·gi·cal·ly
met·al·lur·gist
met·al·work
met·al·work·er
met·al·work·ing
met·a·mor·phism
met·a·mor·phic
met·a·mor·phose
met·a·mor·phosed
met·a·mor·phos·ing
met·a·mor·pho·sis
met·a·mor·pho·ses
met·a·phor
met·a·phor·ic
met·a·phor·i·cal
met·a·phys·ic

met·a·phys·ics
met·a·phys·i·cal
met·a·tar·sus
met·a·tar·si
met·a·tar·sal
met·a·zo·an
met·a·zo·al
met·a·zo·ic
mete
met·ed
met·ing
me·te·or
me·te·or·ic
me·te·or·ite
me·te·or·it·ic
me·te·or·oid
me·te·or·ol·o·gy
me·te·or·o·log·i·cal
me·te·or·o·log·i·cal·ly
me·te·or·ol·o·gist
me·ter
me·tre
me·ter-kil·o·gram-sec·ond
meth·a·done
meth·ane
meth·a·nol
meth·od
me·thod·i·cal
me·thod·i·cal·ly
Meth·od·ist
meth·od·ize
meth·od·ized
meth·od·iz·ing
meth·od·iz·er
meth·od·ol·o·gy
meth·od·ol·o·gies
meth·od·o·log·i·cal
meth·od·ol·o·gist
Me·thu·se·lah
me·tic·u·lous
me·tic·u·los·i·ty
me·tic·u·lous·ly
mé·tier
mé·tis
met·ric
met·ri·cal
met·ri·cal·ly
met·ri·fi·ca·tion
met·ro
met·ro·nome
met·ro·nom·ic
me·trop·o·lis
met·ro·pol·i·tan
met·ro·pol·i·tan·ism
Met·ter·nich
met·tle
met·tle·some
Mex·i·can
Mex·i·co
Mey·er·beer
mez·za·nine
mez·zo
Mi·ami
mi·as·ma
mi·as·mas

mi·as·ma·ta
mi·as·mal
mi·as·mat·ic
mi·as·mic
mi·ca
Mi·chel·an·ge·lo
Mich·i·gan
mi·crobe
mi·cro·bi·al
mi·cro·bi·an
mi·cro·bic
mi·cro·bi·ol·o·gy
mi·cro·bi·o·log·i·cal
mi·cro·bi·ol·o·gist
mi·cro·copy
mi·cro·cop·ies
mi·cro·cosm
mi·cro·cos·mos
mi·cro·cos·mic
mi·cro·cos·mi·cal
mi·cro·film
mi·cro·gram
mi·cro·groove
mi·crom·e·ter
mi·crom·e·try
mi·cro·mi·cron
mi·cro·mil·li·me·ter
mi·cron
mi·crons
mi·cra
mi·cro·or·gan·ism
mi·cro·phone
mi·cro·phon·ic
mi·cro·pho·to·graph
mi·cro·pho·to·graph·ic
mi·cro·pho·tog·ra·phy
mi·cro·read·er
mi·cro·scope
mi·cro·scop·ic
mi·cro·scop·i·cal
mi·cro·scop·i·cal·ly
mi·cros·co·py
mi·cros·co·pist
mi·cro·sec·ond
mi·cro·wave
Mi·das
mid·day
mid·dle
mid·dled
mid·dling
mid·dle-aged
mid·dle·man
mid·dle·men
mid·dle·most
mid·dle·weight
mid·dy
mid·dies
midg·et
Mid·i·an
mid·land
mid·line
Mid·lo·thi·an
mid·most
mid·night
mid·point

mid·riff
mid·sec·tion
mid·ship
mid·ship·man
 mid·ship·men
midst
mid·sum·mer
mid·term
mid·way
mid·wife
 mid·wives
mid·wife·ry
mid·year
mien
mighty
 might·i·er
 might·i·est
 might·i·ly
 might·i·ness
mi·graine
mi·grant
mi·grate
 mi·grat·ed
 mi·grat·ing
 mi·gra·tion
 mi·gra·tor
 mi·gra·to·ry
mi·la·dy
 mi·la·dies
Mi·lan
mild
 mild·ly
 mild·ness
mil·dew
 mil·dewy
mile·age
mil·er
mile·stone
mi·lieu
 mi·lieus
mil·i·tant
 mil·i·tan·cy
 mil·i·tant·ness
mil·i·ta·rism
 mil·i·ta·ris·tic
 mil·i·ta·ris·ti·cal·ly
 mil·i·ta·rize
 mil·i·ta·rized
 mil·i·ta·riz·ing
 mil·i·ta·ri·za·tion
mil·i·tary
 mil·i·tar·i·ly
mi·li·tia
milk
 milk·er
 milky
 milk·i·er
 milk·i·est
milk·maid
milk·man
 milk·men
milk·weed
Mil·lay
mill·board
mil·len·ni·um

mil·len·nia
mil·len·ni·al
mill·er
mil·let
mil·li·am·pere
mil·li·bar
mil·li·gram
mil·li·li·ter
mil·li·me·ter
mil·li·mi·cron
mil·li·ner
mil·li·nery
mill·ing
mil·lion
 mil·lionth
mil·lion·aire
mil·li·sec·ond
mill·pond
mill·run
mill·stone
mill·stream
mi·lord
milt
Mil·wau·kee
mime
 mimed
 mim·ing
 mim·er
mim·e·o·graph
mim·ic
 mim·icked
 mim·ick·ing
 mim·i·cal
 mim·ick·er
mim·ic·ry
 mim·ic·ries
min·a·ble
mine·a·ble
min·a·ret
mince
 minced
 minc·ing
 minc·er
 minc·ing·ly
mince·meat
mind·ed
mind·less
 mind·less·ly
 mind·less·ness
min·er
mine·field
min·er·al
min·er·al·ize
 min·er·al·ized
 min·er·al·iz·ing
 min·er·al·i·za·tion
min·er·al·o·gy
 min·er·al·og·i·cal
 min·er·al·o·gist
min·e·stro·ne
mine·sweep·er
 mine·sweep·ing
min·gle
 min·gled
 min·gling

min·i·a·ture
min·i·a·tur·ize
min·i·a·tur·ized
min·i·a·tur·iz·ing
min·i·a·tur·i·za·tion
min·im
min·i·mal
min·i·mal·ly
min·i·mize
min·i·mized
min·i·miz·ing
min·i·mi·za·tion
min·i·miz·er
min·i·mum
min·i·mums
min·i·ma
min·ing
min·ion
min·is·ter
min·is·te·ri·al
min·is·trant
min·is·tra·tion
min·is·try
min·is·tries
Min·ne·ap·o·lis
Min·ne·so·ta
min·now
mi·nor
mi·nor·i·ty
mi·nor·i·ties
min·strel
mint·age
mint·er
min·u·end
mi·nus
mi·nus·cule
min·ute
min·ut·ed
min·ut·ing
mi·nute
mi·nut·er
mi·nut·est
min·ute·man
min·ute·men
mi·nu·tia
mi·nu·ti·ae
minx
mir·a·cle
mi·rac·u·lous
mi·rage
mire
mired
mir·ing
mir·ror
mirth
mirth·ful
mirth·ful·ly
mirth·ful·ness
mirth·less
mis·ad·ven·ture
mis·ad·vise
mis·ad·vised
mis·ad·vis·ing
mis·al·li·ance
mis·an·thrope

mis·an·thro·pist
mis·an·throp·ic
mis·an·throp·i·cal
mis·an·thro·py
mis·ap·ply
mis·ap·plied
mis·ap·ply·ing
mis·ap·pli·ca·tion
mis·ap·pre·hend
mis·ap·pre·hen·sion
mis·ap·pro·pri·ate
mis·ap·pro·pri·at·ed
mis·ap·pro·pri·at·ing
mis·ap·pro·pri·a·tion
mis·be·have
mis·be·haved
mis·be·hav·ing
mis·be·hav·er
mis·be·ha·vior
mis·cal·cu·late
mis·cal·cu·lat·ed
mis·cal·cu·lat·ing
mis·cal·cu·la·tion
mis·cal·cu·la·tor
mis·call
mis·car·riage
mis·car·ry
mis·car·ried
mis·car·ry·ing
mis·ce·ge·na·tion
mis·ce·ge·net·ic
mis·cel·la·ne·ous
mis·cel·la·ny
mis·cel·la·nies
mis·chance
mis·chief
mis·chie·vous
mis·chie·vous·ly
mis·chie·vous·ness
mis·ci·ble
mis·ci·bil·i·ty
mis·con·ceive
mis·con·ceived
mis·con·ceiv·ing
mis·con·ceiv·er
mis·con·cep·tion
mis·con·duct
mis·con·strue
mis·con·strued
mis·con·stru·ing
mis·con·struc·tion
mis·count
mis·cre·ant
mis·cue
mis·cued
mis·cu·ing
mis·deal
mis·dealt
mis·deal·ing
mis·deed
mis·de·mean·or
mis·di·rect
mis·di·rec·tion
mis·do
mis·did

mis·done
mis·do·ing
mis·em·ploy
mis·em·ploy·ment
mi·ser
mi·ser·li·ness
mi·ser·ly
mis·er·a·ble
mis·er·a·ble·ness
mis·er·a·bly
mis·ery
mis·er·ies
mis·fea·sance
mis·fire
mis·fired
mis·fir·ing
mis·fit
mis·fit·ted
mis·fit·ting
mis·for·tune
mis·giv·ing
mis·gov·ern
mis·gov·ern·ment
mis·guide
mis·guid·ed
mis·guid·ing
mis·guid·ance
mis·han·dle
mis·han·dled
mis·han·dling
mis·hap
mish·mash
mis·in·form
mis·in·form·ant
mis·in·form·er
mis·in·for·ma·tion
mis·in·ter·pret
mis·in·ter·pre·ta·tion
mis·in·ter·pret·er
mis·judge
mis·judged
mis·judg·ing
mis·judg·ment
mis·lay
mis·laid
mis·lay·ing
mis·lead
mis·led
mis·lead·ing
mis·lead·er
mis·man·age
mis·man·aged
mis·man·ag·ing
mis·man·age·ment
mis·match
mis·mate
mis·mat·ed
mis·mat·ing
mis·name
mis·named
mis·nam·ing
mis·no·mer
mi·sog·a·my
mi·sog·y·ny
mi·sog·y·nist

mi·sog·y·nous
mis·place
mis·placed
mis·plac·ing
mis·place·ment
mis·play
mis·print
mis·pri·sion
mis·prize
mis·prized
mis·priz·ing
mis·pro·nounce
mis·pro·nounced
mis·pro·nounc·ing
mis·pro·nun·ci·a·tion
mis·quote
mis·quot·ed
mis·quot·ing
mis·quo·ta·tion
mis·read
mis·read·ing
mis·rep·re·sent
mis·rep·re·sen·ta·tion
mis·rep·re·sen·ta·tive
mis·rule
mis·ruled
mis·rul·ing
mis·sal
mis·shape
mis·shaped
mis·shap·ing
mis·shap·en
mis·sile
miss·ing
mis·sion
mis·sion·ary
mis·sion·ar·ies
Mis·sis·sip·pi
mis·sive
Mis·sou·ri
mis·spell
mis·spelled
mis·spelt
mis·spel·ling
mis·spend
mis·spent
mis·spend·ing
mis·state
mis·stat·ed
mis·stat·ing
mis·state·ment
mis·step
mist
mist·i·ly
mist·i·ness
mis·tak·a·ble
mis·take
mis·took
mis·tak·en
mis·tak·ing
mis·tak·en·ly
mis·tak·en·ness
mis·tak·er
Mis·ter
mis·tle·toe

mis·tral
mis·treat
  mis·treat·ment
mis·tress
mis·tri·al
mis·trust
  mis·trust·ful
  mis·trust·ful·ly
  mis·trust·ing·ly
  mis·trust·ful·ness
misty
  mist·i·er
  mist·i·est
mis·un·der·stand
  mis·un·der·stood
  mis·un·der·stand·ing
mis·us·age
mis·use
  mis·used
  mis·us·ing
  mis·us·er
mis·val·ue
  mis·val·ued
  mis·val·u·ing
mi·ter
  mi·tre
mit·i·cide
  mit·i·cid·al
mit·i·gate
  mit·i·gat·ed
  mit·i·gat·ing
  mit·i·ga·tion
  mit·i·ga·tive
  mit·i·ga·tor
  mit·i·ga·to·ry
mi·to·sis
mi·tral
mit·ten
mix
  mixed
  mix·ing
mix·er
mix·ture
mix-up
Miz·pah
miz·zen
mne·mon·ic
mne·mon·ics
moa
Mo·ab·ite
mob
  mobbed
  mob·bing
  mob·bish
mo·bile
  mo·bil·i·ty
  mo·bi·lize
  mo·bi·lized
  mo·bi·liz·ing
  mo·bi·li·za·tion
mob·ster
moc·ca·sin
mo·cha
mock
  mock·er

mock·ing·ly
mock·ery
  mock·er·ies
mock·ing·bird
mock-up
mod·al
  mo·dal·i·ty
  mod·al·ly
mod·el
  mod·eled
  mod·el·ing
  mod·el·er
mod·er·ate
  mod·er·at·ed
  mod·er·at·ing
  mod·er·ate·ly
  mod·er·ate·ness
  mod·er·a·tion
  mod·er·a·tor
  mod·er·a·tor·ship
mod·ern
  mod·ern·ism
  mod·ern·ist
  mod·ern·ist·ic
  mod·ern·ize
  mod·ern·ized
  mod·ern·iz·ing
  mod·ern·iz·er
  mod·ern·i·za·tion
mod·est
  mod·est·ly
  mod·es·ty
  mod·es·ties
mod·i·cum
mod·i·fi·ca·tion
mod·i·fy
  mod·i·fied
  mod·i·fy·ing
  mod·i·fi·a·ble
  mod·i·fi·er
mod·ish
  mod·ish·ly
  mod·ish·ness
mo·diste
mod·u·late
  mod·u·lat·ed
  mod·u·lat·ing
  mod·u·la·tion
  mod·u·la·tor
  mod·u·la·to·ry
mod·ule
mod·u·lar
mo·dus o·pe·ran·di
mo·dus vi·ven·di
mo·gul
mo·hair
Mo·ham·med
Mo·ham·med·an
  Mo·ham·med·an·ism
Mo·ha·ve
Mo·hawk
Mo·hi·can
moi·e·ty
  moi·e·ties
moil

moil·er
moil·ing·ly
moi·ré
mois·ten
moist·en·er
mois·ture
mois·tur·ize
mois·tur·ized
mois·tur·iz·ing
mois·tur·iz·er
mo·lar
mo·las·ses
mold
mold·a·ble
mold·er
mold·board
mold·ing
moldy
mold·i·er
mold·i·est
mold·i·ness
mol·e·cule
mole·hill
mole·skin
mo·lest
mo·les·ta·tion
mo·lest·er
Mo·li·na
mol·li·fy
mol·li·fied
mol·li·fy·ing
mol·li·fi·ca·tion
mol·li·fi·er
mol·li·fy·ing·ly
mol·lusk
mol·ly·cod·dle
mol·ly·cod·dled
mol·ly·cod·dling
Mo·lo·kai
Mo·lo·tov
molt
moult
molt·er
mol·ten
mol·ten·ly
Mo·luc·ca
mo·lyb·de·num
mo·ment
mo·men·tary
mo·men·tar·i·ly
mo·men·tar·i·ness
mo·men·tous
mo·men·tous·ly
mo·men·tous·ness
mo·men·tum
Mon·a·co
mon·ad
mo·nad·ic
mo·nad·i·cal
mo·nad·al
mo·nad·i·cal·ly
mon·arch
mo·nar·chal
mo·nar·chal·ly
mo·nar·chi·cal

mo·nar·chic
mo·nar·chi·cal·ly
mon·ar·chism
mon·ar·chist
mon·ar·chist·ic
mon·ar·chy
mon·ar·chies
mon·as·tery
mon·as·ter·ies
mon·as·te·ri·al
mo·nas·tic
mo·nas·ti·cal
mo·nas·ti·cal·ly
mo·nas·ti·cism
mon·au·ral
mon·au·ral·ly
Mon·day
Mo·net
mon·e·tary
mon·e·tar·i·ly
mon·e·tize
mon·e·tized
mon·e·tiz·ing
mon·e·ti·za·tion
mon·ey
mon·ey·chang·er
mon·eyed
mon·ied
mon·ey·mak·er
mon·ey·mak·ing
mon·ger
Mon·go·lia
Mon·gol·ism
mon·gol·oid
mon·goose
mon·goos·es
mon·grel
mon·i·ker
mon·ism
mon·ist
mo·nis·tic
mo·nis·ti·cal
mo·nis·ti·cal·ly
mo·ni·tion
mon·i·tor
mon·i·to·ri·al
monk
monk·ish
monk·ish·ly
mon·key
mon·keys
mon·keyed
mon·key·ing
mon·key·shines
Mon·mouth
mon·o·chro·mat·ic
mon·o·chro·mat·i·cal·ly
mon·o·chrome
mon·o·chro·mic
mon·o·chro·mi·cal
mon·o·chro·mi·cal·ly
mon·o·chrom·ist
mon·o·cle
mon·o·cled
mon·o·cli·nal

mon·o·cline
  mon·o·cli·nal·ly
mon·o·cli·nous
mon·o·dist
mon·o·dy
  mon·o·dies
  mo·nod·ic
mo·noe·cious
  mo·noe·cious·ly
mo·nog·a·my
  mo·nog·a·mist
  mo·nog·a·mous
mon·o·gram
  mon·o·grammed
  mon·o·gram·ming
  mon·o·gram·mat·ic
mon·o·graph
  mo·nog·ra·pher
  mon·o·graph·ic
mon·o·lith
mon·o·logue
  mon·o·log
  mon·o·logu·ist
  mon·o·log·ist
mon·o·ma·nia
  mon·o·ma·ni·ac
  mon·o·ma·ni·a·cal
mon·o·met·al·lism
  mon·o·me·tal·lic
mo·no·mi·al
Mo·non·ga·he·la
mon·o·nu·cle·o·sis
mon·o·phon·ic
mon·o·plane
mo·nop·o·lize
  mo·nop·o·lized
  mo·nop·o·liz·ing
  mo·nop·o·li·za·tion
  mo·nop·o·liz·er
mo·nop·o·ly
  mo·nop·o·lies
mon·o·rail
mon·o·so·di·um glu·ta·mate
mon·o·syl·lab·ic
  mon·o·syl·lab·i·cal·ly
mon·o·syl·la·ble
mon·o·the·ism
  mon·o·the·ist
  mon·o·the·is·tic
  mon·o·the·is·ti·cal·ly
mon·o·tone
mo·not·o·nous
  mo·not·o·nous·ly
  mo·not·o·nous·ness
mo·not·o·ny
mon·o·treme
mon·o·type
  mon·o·typ·er
  mon·o·typ·ic
mon·o·va·lent
  mon·o·va·lence
  mon·o·va·len·cy
mon·ox·ide
Mon·roe Doc·trine
Mon·ro·via

mon·sei·gneur
mes·sei·gneurs
mon·sieur
mes·sieurs
Mon·si·gnor
  mon·si·gnors
  mon·si·gno·ri
mon·soon
mon·ster
mon·stros·i·ty
  mon·stros·i·ties
mon·strous
  mon·strous·ly
  mon·strous·ness
mon·tage
Mon·taigne
Mon·tana
Mon·te Car·lo
Mon·te·ne·grin
Mon·te·ne·gro
Mon·te·rey
Mon·ter·rey
Mon·tes·quieu
Mon·tes·so·ri
Mon·te·vi·deo
Mon·te·zu·ma
Mont·gol·fier
Mont·gom·ery
month·ly
month·lies
Mon·ti·cel·lo
Mont·mar·tre
Mont·pe·lier
Mon·tre·al
mon·u·ment
mon·u·men·tal
  mon·u·men·tal·ly
mooch
mooch·er
moody
mood·i·er
mood·i·est
mood·i·ly
mood·i·ness
moon·beam
moon·light
moon·light·er
  moon·light·ing
moon·scape
moon·shine
moon·shin·er
moon·stone
moon·struck
moony
moon·i·er
moon·i·est
moor·ing
Moor·ish
moot·ness
mop
mopped
mop·ping
mope
moped
mop·ing

mop·er
mop·ish
mop·pet
mo·raine
  mo·rain·al
  mo·rain·ic
mor·al
  mor·al·ly
mo·rale
mor·al·ist
  mor·al·is·tic
mo·ral·i·ty
  mo·ral·i·ties
mor·al·ize
  mor·al·ized
  mor·al·iz·ing
  mor·al·i·za·tion
  mor·al·iz·er
mo·rass
mor·a·to·ri·um
  mor·a·to·ri·ums
  mor·a·to·ria
Mo·ra·vi·an
mo·ray
mor·bid
  mor·bid·ly
  mor·bid·i·ty
  mor·bid·ness
mor·dant
  mor·dan·cy
  mor·dant·ly
Mor·de·cai
more·o·ver
mo·res
mor·ga·nat·ic
  mor·ga·nat·i·cal·ly
Mor·gan·ton
Mor·gan·town
Mor·gen·thau
morgue
mor·i·bund
mo·ri·on
Mor·mon
  Mor·mon·ism
morn·ing
morn·ing-glo·ry
  morn·ing-glo·ries
Mo·ro
mo·roc·co
mo·ron
  mo·ron·ic
  mo·ron·i·cal·ly
Mo·roni
mo·rose
  mo·rose·ly
  mo·rose·ness
mor·pheme
Mor·phe·us
mor·phine
mor·phol·o·gy
  mor·pho·log·ic
  mor·pho·log·i·cal
  mor·phol·o·gist
Mor·ris·town
mor·row

mor·sel
mor·tal
  mor·tal·ly
  mor·tal·i·ty
  mor·tal·i·ties
mor·tar
mor·tar·board
mort·gage
  mort·gaged
  mort·gag·ing
  mort·ga·gee
  mort·ga·ger
mor·ti·cian
mor·ti·fy
  mor·ti·fied
  mor·ti·fy·ing
  mor·ti·fi·ca·tion
mor·tise
  mor·tised
  mor·tis·ing
mort·main
mor·tu·ary
  mor·tu·ar·ies
mo·sa·ic
Mos·cow
Mo·ses
mo·sey
  mo·seyed
  mo·sey·ing
Mos·lem
mosque
mos·qui·to
  mos·qui·toes
  mos·qui·tos
moss
  moss·like
  mossy
  moss·i·er
  moss·i·est
moss·back
most·ly
mo·tel
mo·tet
moth·ball
moth-eat·en
moth·er
  moth·er·less
  moth·er·hood
Moth·er Hub·bard
moth·er-in-law
  moth·ers-in-law
moth·er·land
moth·er·ly
  moth·er·li·ness
moth·er-of-pearl
mo·tif
mo·tile
  mo·til·i·ty
mo·tion
  mo·tion·less
  mo·tion·less·ly
  mo·tion·less·ness
mo·ti·vate
  mo·ti·vat·ed
  mo·ti·vat·ing

mo·ti·va·tion
mo·ti·va·tion·al
mo·tive
mot·ley
mo·tor
mo·tor·bike
mo·tor·boat
mo·tor·bus
mo·tor·cade
mo·tor·car
mo·tor court
mo·tor·cy·cle
  mo·tor·cy·cled
  mo·tor·cy·cling
  mo·tor·cy·clist
mo·tor·ist
mo·tor·ize
  mo·tor·ized
  mo·tor·iz·ing
  mo·tor·i·za·tion
mo·tor·man
mo·tor·men
mot·tle
  mot·tled
  mot·tling
  mot·tler
mound
mount
  mount·a·ble
  mount·er
moun·tain
  moun·tain·eer
  moun·tain·ous
moun·te·bank
mount·ing
Mount Ver·non
mourn
  mourn·er
mourn·ful
  mourn·ful·ly
  mourn·ful·ness
mourn·ing
  mourn·ing·ly
mouse
  moused
  mous·ing
mous·er
Mous·sorg·sky
mous·tache
mousy
  mous·i·er
  mous·i·est
mouth
  mouthed
  mouth·er
mouth·ful
  mouth·fuls
mouth·piece
mouthy
  mouth·i·er
  mouth·i·est
  mouth·i·ness
mou·ton
mov·a·ble
  mov·a·ble·ness

mov·a·bil·i·ty
mov·a·bly
move
  moved
  mov·ing
  mov·er
move·ment
mov·ie
mow
  mowed
  mow·ing
  mow·er
mox·ie
Mo·zam·bique
Mo·zart
mu·ci·lage
  mu·ci·lag·i·nous
muck
  mucky
muck·rake
  muck·raked
  muck·rak·ing
  muck·rak·er
mu·cous
  mu·cos·i·ty
mu·cus
mud
  mud·ded
  mud·ding
mud·dle
  mud·dled
  mud·dling
  mud·dler
mud·dy
  mud·di·er
  mud·di·est
  mud·di·ly
  mud·di·ness
mu·ez·zin
muf·fin
muf·fle
  muf·fled
  muf·fling
  muf·fler
muf·ti
mug
  mugged
  mug·ging
  mug·ger
mug·gy
  mug·gi·er
  mug·gi·est
  mug·gi·ness
mu·lat·to
  mu·lat·toes
mul·ber·ry
  mul·ber·ries
mulch
mu·le·teer
mul·ish
  mul·ish·ly
  mul·ish·ness
mul·let
mul·li·gan
mul·li·ga·taw·ny

mul·lion
 mul·lioned
mul·ti·far·i·ous
 mul·ti·far·i·ous·ly
 mul·ti·far·i·ous·ness
mul·ti·lat·er·al
mul·ti·mil·lion·aire
mul·ti·ple
mul·ti·ple scle·ro·sis
mul·ti·pli·cand
mul·ti·pli·ca·tion
mul·ti·plic·i·ty
mul·ti·pli·er
mul·ti·ply
 mul·ti·plied
 mul·ti·ply·ing
 mul·ti·pli·a·ble
mul·ti·tude
mul·ti·tu·di·nous
 mul·ti·tu·di·nous·ly
 mul·ti·tu·di·nous·ness
mum·ble
 mum·bled
 mum·bling
 mum·bler
 mum·bling·ly
Mum·bo Jum·bo
mum·mer
mum·mery
mum·mi·fy
 mum·mi·fied
 mum·mi·fy·ing
 mum·mi·fi·ca·tion
mum·my
 mum·mies
 mum·mied
 mum·my·ing
munch
 munch·er
mun·dane
 mun·dane·ly
Mu·nich
mu·nic·i·pal
 mu·nic·i·pal·ly
 mu·nic·i·pal·i·ty
mu·nif·i·cent
 mu·nif·i·cence
 mu·nif·i·cent·ly
mu·ni·tion
mu·ral
 mu·ral·ist
mur·der
 mur·der·er
 mur·der·ess
mur·der·ous
 mur·der·ous·ly
 mur·der·ous·ness
mu·ri·at·ic ac·id
Mu·ril·lo
murky
 murk·i·er
 murk·i·est
 murk·i·ly
 murk·i·ness
mur·mur

mur·mur·er
mur·mur·ing
mur·mur·ing·ly
mur·rain
mus·cat
 mus·ca·tel
mus·cle
 mus·cled
 mus·cling
mus·cle-bound
Mus·co·vite
mus·cu·lar
 mus·cu·lar·i·ty
 mus·cu·lar·ly
mus·cu·lar dys·tro·phy
mus·cu·la·ture
muse
 mused
 mus·ing
 mus·er
 mus·ing·ly
mu·se·um
mush
 mushy
 mush·i·er
 mush·i·est
 mush·i·ly
 mush·i·ness
mush·room
mu·sic
mu·si·cal
 mu·si·cal·ly
 mu·si·cal·i·ty
 mu·si·cal·ness
mu·si·cale
mu·si·cian
 mu·si·cian·ship
musk
 musky
 musk·i·er
 musk·i·est
 musk·i·ness
mus·kel·lunge
mus·ket
 mus·ket·eer
 mus·ket·ry
musk·mel·on
Mus·ko·gee
musk·rat
mus·lin
muss
 mussy
 muss·i·er
 muss·i·est
mus·sel
Mus·so·li·ni
mus·tache
mus·tang
mus·tard
mus·ter
mus·ty
 mus·ti·er
 mus·ti·est
 mus·ti·ly
 mus·ti·ness

mu·ta·ble
  mu·ta·bil·i·ty
  mu·ta·ble·ness
  mu·ta·bly
mu·tant
mu·ta·tion
  mu·tate
  mu·tat·ed
  mu·tat·ing
  mu·ta·tion·al
mute
  mut·ed
  mut·ing
  mute·ly
  mute·ness
mu·ti·late
  mu·ti·lat·ed
  mu·ti·lat·ing
  mu·ti·la·tion
  mu·ti·la·tor
mu·ti·neer
mu·ti·ny
  mu·ti·nies
  mu·ti·nied
  mu·ti·ny·ing
  mu·ti·nous
mut·ter
  mut·ter·er
  mut·ter·ing·ly
mut·ton
mu·tu·al
  mu·tu·al·i·ty
  mu·tu·al·ly
muz·zle
  muz·zled
  muz·zling
  muz·zler
My·ce·nae
my·col·o·gy
  my·col·o·gist
my·na
  my·nah
my·o·pia
  my·op·ic
myr·i·ad
myr·mi·don
myrrh
myr·tle
my·self
mys·te·ri·ous
  mys·te·ri·ous·ly
  mys·te·ri·ous·ness
mys·tery
  mys·ter·ies
mys·tic
mys·ti·cal
  mys·ti·cal·ly
  mys·ti·cal·ness
mys·ti·cism
mys·ti·fy
  mys·ti·fied
  mys·ti·fy·ing
  mys·ti·fy·ing·ly
  mys·ti·fi·ca·tion
mys·tique

myth
  myth·ic
  myth·i·cal
  myth·i·cal·ly
  myth·i·cist
  myth·i·cize
my·thol·o·gy
  my·thol·o·gies
  myth·o·log·ic
  myth·o·log·i·cal
  my·thol·o·gist
nab
  nabbed
  nab·bing
na·bob
na·cre
  na·cre·ous
na·dir
nag
  nagged
  nag·ging
  nag·ger
  nag·ging·ly
Na·ga·sa·ki
Na·go·ya
Na·hum
nail·er
Nai·ro·bi
na·ive
  na·ive·ly
  na·ive·ness
  na·ive·te
na·ked
  na·ked·ly
  na·ked·ness
nam·by-pam·by
name
  named
  nam·ing
  name·less
  name·less·ly
  name·less·ness
  name·ly
  name·sake
Na·mur
Na·nai·mo
nan·keen
  nan·kin
Nan·king
nan·ny
  nan·nies
Nan·tuck·et
Na·o·mi
nap
  napped
  nap·ping
  nap·per
na·palm
nape
naph·tha
  naph·tha·lene
Na·pi·er
nap·kin
Na·ples
Na·po·leon

nar·cis·sism
nar·cism
nar·cis·sist
nar·cis·sis·tic
nar·cis·sus
nar·cis·sus·es
nar·cis·si
nar·co·sis
nar·cot·ic
nar·cot·i·cal·ly
nar·co·tize
nar·co·tized
nar·co·tiz·ing
nar·is
nar·es
Nar·ra·gan·sett
nar·rate
nar·ra·ted
nar·ra·ting
nar·ra·tor
nar·ra·tion
nar·ra·tion·al
nar·ra·tive
nar·ra·tive·ly
nar·row
nar·row·ly
nar·row·ness
nar·row-mind·ed
nar·row-mind·ed·ly
nar·row-mind·ed·ness
Nar·va·ez
nary
na·sal
na·sal·i·ty
na·sal·ize
na·sal·ized
na·sal·iz·ing
na·sal·ly
nas·cent
nas·cence
nas·cen·cy
Nash·ville
Nas·sau
Nas·ser
na·stur·tium
nas·ty
nas·ti·er
nas·ti·est
nas·ti·ly
nas·ti·ness
na·tal
Natch·ez
na·tion
na·tion·hood
na·tion·al
na·tion·al·ly
na·tion·al·ism
na·tion·al·ist
na·tion·al·is·tic
na·tion·al·i·ty
na·tion·al·i·ties
na·tion·al·ize
na·tion·al·ized
na·tion·al·iz·ing
na·tion·al·i·za·tion

na·tion-wide
na·tive
na·tive·ly
na·tive·ness
na·tiv·i·ty
na·tiv·i·ties
nat·ty
nat·ti·er
nat·ti·est
nat·ti·ly
nat·ti·ness
nat·u·ral
nat·u·ral·ly
nat·u·ral·ness
nat·u·ral·ism
nat·u·ral·ist
nat·u·ral·is·tic
nat·u·ral·ize
nat·u·ral·ized
nat·u·ral·iz·ing
nat·u·ral·i·za·tion
na·ture
naught
naugh·ty
naugh·ti·er
naugh·ti·est
naugh·ti·ly
naugh·ti·ness
Nau·ru
nau·sea
nau·se·ate
nau·se·at·ed
nau·se·at·ing
nau·seous
nau·seous·ly
nau·seous·ness
nau·ti·cal
nau·ti·cal·ly
nau·ti·lus
nau·ti·lus·es
nau·ti·li
Nav·a·jo
na·val
Na·varre
na·vel
nav·i·ga·ble
nav·i·ga·bil·i·ty
nav·i·ga·ble·ness
nav·i·ga·bly
nav·i·gate
nav·i·gat·ed
nav·i·gat·ing
nav·i·ga·tion
nav·i·ga·tion·al
nav·i·ga·tor
na·vy
na·vies
Naz·a·rene
Naz·a·reth
Na·zi
Na·zis
Na·zism
Na·zi·ism
Ne·an·der·thal
Ne·a·pol·i·tan

near
near·ly
near·ness
near·by
Ne·arc·tic
near-sight·ed
near-sight·ed·ly
near-sight·ed·ness
neat
neat·ly
neat·ness
neb·bish
Ne·bo
Ne·bras·ka
Neb·u·chad·nez·zar
neb·u·la
neb·u·las
neb·u·lae
neb·u·lous
neb·u·lar
neb·u·lous·ly
neb·u·lous·ness
nec·es·sary
nec·es·sar·ies
nec·es·sar·i·ly
ne·ces·si·tate
ne·ces·si·ta·ted
ne·ces·si·ta·ting
ne·ces·si·ty
ne·ces·si·ties
neck·er·chief
neck·ing
neck·lace
neck·tie
ne·crol·o·gy
ne·crol·o·gies
nec·ro·man·cy
nec·ro·man·cer
ne·cro·sis
ne·crot·ic
nec·tar
nec·tar·ine
need·ful
need·ful·ly
need·ful·ness
nee·dle
nee·dled
nee·dling
nee·dle·like
nee·dler
nee·dle·point
need·less
need·less·ly
need·less·ness
nee·dle·work
nee·dle·work·er
needy
need·i·er
need·i·est
need·i·ness
ne'er-do-well
ne·far·i·ous
ne·far·i·ous·ly
ne·far·i·ous·ness
ne·gate

ne·ga·ted
ne·ga·ting
ne·ga·tion
neg·a·tive
neg·a·tive·ly
neg·a·tive·ness
neg·a·tiv·i·ty
neg·a·tiv·ism
ne·glect
ne·glec·ter
ne·glec·tor
ne·glect·ful·ness
ne·glect·ful
ne·glect·ful·ly
neg·li·gee
neg·li·gent
neg·li·gence
neg·li·gent·ly
neg·li·gi·ble
neg·li·gi·bly
neg·li·gi·bil·i·ty
ne·go·ti·a·ble
ne·go·ti·a·bil·i·ty
ne·go·ti·ate
ne·go·ti·at·ed
ne·go·ti·at·ing
ne·go·ti·a·tion
ne·go·ti·a·tor
Ne·gro
Ne·groes
Ne·groid
Ne·he·mi·ah
Neh·ru
neigh·bor
neigh·bor·ing
neigh·bor·ly
neigh·bor·li·ness
neigh·bor·hood
nei·ther
Nel·son
Nem·bu·tal
nem·e·sis
nem·e·ses
ne·o·clas·sic
ne·o·clas·si·cal
ne·o·clas·si·cism
ne·o·lith·ic
ne·ol·o·gism
ne·ol·o·gy
ne·on
ne·o·phyte
Ne·pal
ne·pen·the
ne·pen·the·an
neph·ew
ne·phri·tis
ne·phrit·ic
nep·o·tism
nep·o·tist
Nep·tune
Nep·tu·ni·an
nep·tu·ni·um
nerve
nerved
nerv·ing

nerve·less
 nerve·less·ly
 nerve·less·ness
nerve-rack·ing
 nerve-wrack·ing
nerv·ous
 nerv·ous·ly
 nerv·ous·ness
nervy
 nerv·i·er
 nerv·i·est
 nerv·i·ness
nes·tle
 nes·tled
 nes·tling
 nes·tler
net
 net·ted
 net·ting
neth·er
Neth·er·lands
neth·er·most
net·tle
 net·tled
 net·tling
net·work
neu·ral
 neu·ral·ly
 neu·ral·gia
 neu·ral·gic
neu·ras·the·nia
 neu·ras·then·ic
neu·ri·tis
 neu·rit·ic
neu·rol·o·gy
 neu·ro·log·i·cal
 neu·rol·o·gist
neu·ron
 neu·ron·ic
neu·ro·sis
 neu·ro·ses
neu·rot·ic
 neu·rot·i·cal·ly
neu·ter
neu·tral
 neu·tral·i·ty
 neu·tral·ly
 neu·tral·ism
 neu·tral·ist
neu·tral·ize
 neu·tral·ized
 neu·tral·iz·ing
 neu·tral·i·za·tion
 neu·tral·iz·er
neu·tri·no
neu·tron
Ne·vada
nev·er
nev·er·more
nev·er·the·less
new
 new·ish
 new·ness
New·ark
new·born

New·burgh
New·cas·tle
new·com·er
New Del·hi
new·el
new·fan·gled
New·found·land
New·gate
New Guin·ea
New Hamp·shire
New Ha·ven
New Jer·sey
new·ly
new·ly·wed
New Mex·i·co
New Or·leans
New·port
news·boy
news·cast
 news·cast·er
news·pa·per
 news·pa·per·man
news·print
news·reel
news·stand
newsy
 news·i·er
 news·i·est
newt
New·ton
New Zea·land
nex·us
ni·a·cin
Ni·ag·a·ra
Ni·a·my
nib·ble
 nib·bled
 nib·bling
 nib·bler
nib·lick
Nic·a·ra·gua
nice
 nic·er
 nic·est
 nice·iy
 nice·ness
Ni·cene
ni·ce·ty
 ni·ce·ties
niche
Nich·o·las
nick·el
nick·el·o·de·on
nick·name
 nick·named
 nick·nam·ing
Ni·co·sia
nic·o·tine
 nic·o·tin·ic
Nie·buhr
niece
Nietz·sche
nif·ty
 nif·ti·er
 nif·ti·est

Ni·ger
Ni·ge·ria
nig·gard
  nig·gard·li·ness
  nig·gard·ly
nigh
  nigh·er
  nigh·est
night·cap
night·dress
night·fall
night·gown
night·hawk
night·in·gale
night·ly
night·mare
  night·mar·ish
night·shade
night·shirt
night·time
ni·hil·ism
  ni·hil·ist
  ni·hil·is·tic
Ni·ke
nim·ble
  nim·bler
  nim·blest
  nim·ble·ness
  nim·bly
nim·bus
Nim·rod
nin·com·poop
nine·pins
nine·teen
  nine·teenth
nine·ty
  nine·ties
  nine·ti·eth
Nin·e·vah
nin·ny
  nin·nies
ninth
Ni·o·be
nip
  nipped
  nip·ping
nip·per
nip·ple
Nip·pon
nip·py
  nip·pi·er
  nip·pi·est
nir·va·na
Ni·sei
Nis·sen
nit
  nit·ty
  nit·ti·er
  nit·ti·est
ni·ter
nit-pick
ni·trate
  ni·trat·ed
  ni·trat·ing
  ni·tra·tion

ni·tra·tor
ni·tric
ni·tro·gen
ni·trog·e·nous
ni·tro·glyc·er·in
ni·trous ox·ide
nit·ty-grit·ty
nit·wit
No·a·chi·an
No·ah
No·bel
no·be·li·um
no·bil·i·ty
no·bil·i·ties
no·ble
  no·bler
  no·blest
  no·ble·man
  no·ble·men
  no·ble·ness
  no·ble·wom·an
  no·ble·wom·en
  no·bly
no·body
noc·tur·nal
noc·turne
nod
  nod·ded
  nod·ding
  nod·der
node
nod·al
nod·ule
  nod·u·lar
no·el
nog·gin
No·gu·chi
noise
  noised
  nois·ing
noise·less
  noise·less·ly
  noise·less·ness
noi·some
  noi·some·ly
  noi·some·ness
noisy
  nois·i·er
  nois·i·est
  nois·i·ly
  nois·i·ness
No·ko·mis
no·mad
  no·mad·ic
  no·mad·i·cal·ly
  no·mad·ism
nom de plume
noms de plume
no·men·cla·ture
nom·i·nal
  nom·i·nal·ly
nom·i·nate
  nom·i·nat·ed
  nom·i·nat·ing
  nom·i·na·tion

nom·i·na·tor
nom·i·na·tive
nom·i·nee
non·age
nonce
non·cha·lant
  non·cha·lance
  non·cha·lant·ly
non·com
non·com·bat·ant
non·com·mit·tal
  non·com·mit·tal·ly
non·con·duc·tor
  non·con·duc·ting
non·con·form·ist
  non·con·form·i·ty
non·de·script
non·en·ti·ty
  non·en·ti·ties
none·the·less
rfon·in·ter·ven·tion
  non·in·ter·ven·tion·ist
non·met·al
  non·me·tal·lic
non·pa·reil
non·par·ti·san
  non·par·ti·san·ship
non·plus
  non·plused
  non·plus·ing
non·prof·it
non·res·i·dent
  non·res·i·dence
  non·res·i·den·cy
  non·res·i·den·cies
non·re·stric·tive
non·sec·tar·i·an
non·sense
  non·sen·si·cal
  non·sen·si·cal·ly
non se·qui·tur
non·stop
non·sup·port
non·un·ion
  non·un·ion·ism
  non·un·ion·ist
non·vi·o·lence
  non·vi·o·lent
  non·vi·o·lent·ly
noo·dle
noon
  noon·day
  noon·time
noose
  noosed
  noos·ing
Nor·dic
Nor·folk
nor·mal
  nor·mal·cy
  nor·mal·i·ty
  nor·mal·ly
nor·mal·ize
  nor·mal·ized
  nor·mal·iz·ing

nor·mal·i·za·tion
Nor·man·dy
Norse·man
North Amer·i·ca
North·amp·ton
North Car·o·li·na
North Da·ko·ta
north·east
  north·east·ern
  north·east·er
  north·east·er·ly
  north·east·ward
  north·east·ward·ly
north·er
nor·ther·ly
  north·er·li·ness
north·ern
  north·ern·most
north·ern·er
North·um·ber·land
North·um·bri·an
north·ward
  north·wards
  north·ward·ly
north·west
  north·west·ern
  north·west·er
  north·west·ward
  north·west·ward·ly
Nor·way
Nor·wich
nose
  nosed
  nos·ing
nose·gay
nos·tal·gia
  nos·tal·gic
nos·tril
nos·trum
nosy
  nos·i·er
  nos·i·est
  nos·i·ly
  nos·i·ness
no·ta·ble
  no·ta·ble·ness
  no·ta·bil·i·ty
  no·ta·bly
no·ta·rize
  no·ta·rized
  no·ta·riz·ing
  no·ta·ri·za·tion
no·ta·ry
  no·ta·ries
no·ta·tion
  no·ta·tion·al
notch
  notched
note
  not·ed
  not·ing
  not·er
note·book
not·ed
  not·ed·ly

not·ed·ness
note·wor·thy
  note·wor·thi·ness
noth·ing
noth·ing·ness
no·tice
  no·ticed
  no·tic·ing
  no·tice·a·ble
  no·tice·a·bly
no·ti·fy
  no·ti·fied
  no·ti·fy·ing
  no·ti·fi·ca·tion
  no·ti·fi·er
no·tion
no·to·ri·ous
  no·to·ri·ous·ly
  no·to·ri·ous·ness
  no·to·ri·e·ty
no-trump
Not·ting·ham
Not·ting·ham·shire
not·with·stand·ing
Nou·ak·chott
nought
nour·ish
  nour·ish·er
  nour·ish·ing
  nour·ish·ment
no·va
  no·vas
  no·vae
No·va Sco·tia
nov·el
  nov·el·ist
  nov·el·is·tic
nov·el·ette
nov·el·ty
  nov·el·ties
No·vem·ber
no·ve·na
  no·ve·nae
nov·ice
no·vi·ti·ate
No·vo·cain
now·a·days
no·where
no·wise
nox·ious
  nox·ious·ly
  nox·ious·ness
noz·zle
nu·ance
nub·bin
nu·bile
nu·cle·ar
nu·cle·us
  nu·cle·us·es
  nu·clei
nude
  nude·ly
  nude·ness
  nu·di·ty
nudge

nudged
nudg·ing
nudg·er
nud·ism
nud·ist
nug·get
nui·sance
null
nul·li·ty
nul·li·ties
nul·li·fy
  nul·li·fied
  nul·li·fy·ing
  nul·li·fi·ca·tion
  nul·li·fi·er
numb
  numb·ly
  numb·ness
  numb·ing
  numb·ing·ly
num·ber
  num·ber·er
  num·ber·less
numb·skull
nu·mer·al
  num·er·al·ly
nu·mer·ate
  nu·mer·at·ed
  nu·mer·at·ing
  nu·mer·a·tion
  nu·mer·a·tor
nu·mer·i·cal
  nu·mer·i·cal·ly
nu·mer·ous
  nu·mer·ous·ly
  nu·mer·ous·ness
nu·mis·mat·ics
  nu·mis·mat·ic
  nu·mis·mat·i·cal
  nu·mis·ma·tist
num·skull
nun·cio
  nun·ci·os
nun·nery
  nun·ner·ies
nup·tial
  nup·tial·ly
Nur·em·berg
nurse
  nursed
  nurs·ing
  nurs·er
nurse·maid
nurs·ery
  nurs·er·ies
nur·ture
  nur·tured
  nur·tur·ing
  nur·tur·er
nut
  nut·ted
  nut·ting
nut·crack·er
nut·hatch
nut·meg

nu·tri·ent
nu·tri·ment
nu·tri·tion
nu·tri·tion·al
nu·tri·tion·al·ly
nu·tri·tion·ist
nu·tri·tious
nu·tri·tious·ly
nu·tri·tious·ness
nu·tri·tive
nu·tri·tive·ly
nu·tri·tive·ness
nut·shell
nut·ty
nut·ti·er
nut·ti·est
nut·ti·ness
nuz·zle
nuz·zled
nuz·zling
Ny·an·za
ny·lon
nymph
nym·phal
nym·pho·ma·nia
nym·pho·ma·ni·ac
oaf
oaf·ish
oaf·ish·ly
oaf·ish·ness
Oa·hu
oak·en
Oak·land
oa·kum
oar
oared
oars·man
oars·men
oar·lock
oa·sis
oa·ses
oat·en
oath
oat·meal
Oba·di·ah
ob·bli·ga·to
ob·bli·ga·tos
ob·du·rate
ob·du·ra·cy
ob·du·rate·ly
ob·du·rate·ness
Obe·ah
obe·di·ence
obe·di·ent
obe·di·ent·ly
obei·sance
obei·sant
ob·e·lisk
Ober·am·mer·gau
Ober·lin
Ober·on
obese
obese·ness
obes·i·ty
obey

obey·er
ob·fus·cate
ob·fus·ca·ted
ob·fus·ca·ting
ob·fus·ca·tion
obit
obit·u·ary
obit·u·ar·ies
ob·ject
ob·ject·less
ob·ject·or
ob·jec·tion
ob·jec·tion·a·ble
ob·jec·tion·a·ble·ness
ob·jec·tion·a·bly
ob·jec·tive
ob·jec·tive·ly
ob·jec·tive·ness
ob·jec·tiv·i·ty
ob·jur·gate
ob·jur·gat·ed
ob·jur·gat·ing
ob·jur·ga·tion
ob·jur·ga·to·ry
ob·late
ob·late·ly
ob·late·ness
ob·li·gate
ob·li·gat·ed
ob·li·gat·ing
ob·li·ga·tion
ob·lig·a·to·ry
oblige
obliged
oblig·ing
oblig·er
oblig·ing
oblig·ing·ly
oblig·ing·ness
ob·lique
ob·liqued
ob·liqu·ing
ob·lique·ly
ob·lique·ness
ob·liq·ui·ty
ob·lit·er·ate
ob·lit·er·at·ed
ob·lit·er·at·ing
ob·lit·er·a·tion
ob·lit·er·a·tive
ob·liv·i·on
ob·liv·i·ous
ob·liv·i·ous·ly
ob·liv·i·ous·ness
ob·long
ob·lo·quy
ob·lo·quies
ob·nox·ious
ob·nox·ious·ly
ob·nox·ious·ness
oboe
obo·ist
ob·scene
ob·scene·ly
ob·scene·ness

ob·scen·i·ty
ob·scen·i·ties
ob·scure
ob·scur·er
ob·scur·est
ob·scured
ob·scur·ing
ob·scure·ly
ob·scure·ness
ob·scu·ri·ty
ob·scu·ri·ties
ob·se·qui·ous
ob·se·qui·ous·ly
ob·se·qui·ous·ness
ob·se·quy
ob·se·quies
ob·serv·a·ble
ob·serv·a·ble·ness
ob·serv·a·bly
ob·ser·vance
ob·ser·vant
ob·ser·vant·ly
ob·ser·va·tion
ob·ser·va·tion·al
ob·ser·va·to·ry
ob·ser·va·to·ries
ob·serve
ob·served
ob·serv·ing
ob·serv·ed·ly
ob·serv·er
ob·serv·ing·ly
ob·sess
ob·ses·sive
ob·ses·sive·ly
ob·ses·sion
ob·sid·i·an
ob·so·les·cent
ob·so·les·cence
ob·so·les·cent·ly
ob·so·lete
ob·so·lete·ness
ob·sta·cle
ob·ste·tri·cian
ob·stet·rics
ob·stet·ric
ob·stet·ri·cal
ob·stet·ri·cal·ly
ob·sti·nate
ob·sti·na·cy
ob·sti·na·cies
ob·sti·nate·ly
ob·sti·nate·ness
ob·strep·er·ous
ob·strep·er·ous·ly
ob·strep·er·ous·ness
ob·struct
ob·struc·tive
ob·struc·tor
ob·struc·tion
ob·struc·tion·ism
ob·struc·tion·ist
ob·tain
ob·tain·a·ble
ob·tain·er

ob·tain·ment
ob·trude
ob·trud·ed
ob·trud·ing
ob·trud·er
ob·tru·sion
ob·tru·sive
ob·tru·sive·ness
ob·tuse
ob·tuse·ly
ob·tuse·ness
ob·verse
ob·verse·ly
ob·vi·ate
ob·vi·at·ed
ob·vi·at·ing
ob·vi·a·tion
ob·vi·a·tor
ob·vi·ous
ob·vi·ous·ly
ob·vi·ous·ness
oc·ca·sion
oc·ca·sion·al
oc·ca·sion·al·ly
oc·ci·dent
oc·ci·den·tal
oc·clude
oc·clud·ed
oc·clud·ing
oc·clu·sive
oc·clu·sion
oc·cult
oc·cult·ly
oc·cult·ness
oc·cult·ism
oc·cult·ist
oc·cu·pan·cy
oc·cu·pan·cies
oc·cu·pant
oc·cu·pa·tion
oc·cu·pa·tion·al
oc·cu·pa·tion·al·ly
oc·cu·py
oc·cu·pied
oc·cu·py·ing
oc·cu·pi·er
oc·cur
oc·curred
oc·cur·ring
oc·cur·rence
oc·cur·rent
ocean
oce·an·ic
Oce·an·ia
oce·a·nog·ra·phy
oce·a·nog·ra·pher
oce·a·no·graph·ic
oce·a·no·graph·i·cal
oce·lot
ocher
ocher·ous
ochery
Ock·ham
o'clock
oc·ta·gon

oc·tag·o·nal
oc·tag·o·nal·ly
oc·ta·he·dron
oc·ta·he·drons
oc·ta·he·dra
oc·ta·he·dral
oc·tane
oc·tave
Oc·ta·vi·us
oc·ta·vo
oc·tet
Oc·to·ber
oc·to·ge·nar·i·an
oc·tog·e·nary
Oc·top·o·da
oc·to·pus
oc·u·lar
oc·u·lar·ly
oc·u·list
odd
odd·ly
odd·ness
odd·ball
odd·i·ty
odd·i·ties
Odes·sa
od·ic
odi·ous
odi·ous·ly
odi·ous·ness
odi·um
odom·e·ter
odor
odored
odor·less
odor·ous
odor·ous·ly
odor·ous·ness
odor·if·er·ous
odor·if·er·ous·ly
Odys·seus
od·ys·sey
Oed·i·pus com·plex
oed·i·pal
of·fal
off·beat
off·col·or
of·fend
of·fend·er
of·fense
of·fense·less
of·fen·sive
of·fen·sive·ly
of·fen·sive·ness
of·fer
of·fer·er
of·fer·ing
of·fer·to·ry
of·fer·to·ries
of·fer·to·ri·al
off·hand
off·hand·ed·ly
off·hand·ed·ness
of·fice
of·fice·hold·er

of·fic·er
of·fi·cial
of·fi·cial·ism
of·fi·cial·ly
of·fi·cial·dom
of·fi·ci·ate
of·fi·ci·at·ed
of·fi·ci·at·ing
of·fi·ci·a·tion
of·fi·ci·a·tor
of·fi·cious
of·fi·cious·ly
of·fi·cious·ness
off·ing
off·set
off·set·ting
off·shoot
off·shore
off·side
off·spring
off·stage
off-the-cuff
of·ten
of·ten·times
Ogal·la·la
Og·den
ogle
ogled
ogling
ogler
Ogle·thorpe
ogre
ogre·ish
Ohio
ohm
ohm·age
ohm·ic
ohm·me·ter
oil·cloth
oil·er
oil·skin
oily
oil·i·er
oil·i·est
oil·i·ness
oint·ment
Ojib·wa
Oke·fe·no·kee
Okie
Oki·na·wa
Okla·ho·ma
okra
old
old·er
old·est
old·en
old·ish
old·ness
old-fash·ioned
old·ster
old-time
old-tim·er
old-world
ole·ag·i·nous
ole·ag·i·nous·ly

ole·ag·i·nous·ness
oleo
ole·o·mar·ga·rine
ol·fac·tion
  ol·fac·to·ry
  ol·fac·to·ries
ol·i·gar·chy
  ol·i·gar·chies
  ol·i·gar·chic
  ol·i·gar·chi·cal
  ol·i·garch
ol·i·gop·o·ly
ol·ive
Ol·i·ver
Ol·i·vet
Olym·pia
Olym·pi·an
O·lym·pic
Olym·pus
Oma·ha
Omar Khay·yam
om·buds·man
  om·buds·men
om·e·let
omen
om·i·nous
  om·i·nous·ly
  om·i·nous·ness
omis·sion
omit
  omit·ted
  omit·ting
om·ni·bus
  om·ni·bus·es
om·nip·o·tence
  om·nip·o·tent·ly
om·ni·pres·ent
  om·ni·pres·ence
  om·ni·pres·ent·ly
om·nis·cience
  om·nis·cient
  om·nis·cient·ly
om·niv·or·ous
  om·niv·o·rous·ly
  om·niv·o·rous·ness
onan·ism
  onan·ist
  onan·is·tic
once-o·ver
on·com·ing
Onei·da
on·er·ous
  on·er·ous·ly
  on·er·ous·ness
one·self
one-sid·ed
  one-sid·ed·ly
  one-sid·ed·ness
one-time
one-track
one-up·man·ship
one-way
on·go·ing
on·ion

on·ion·like
on·iony
on·ion·skin
on-line
on·look·er
  on·look·ing
on·ly
on·o·mat·o·poe·ia
  on·o·mat·o·poe·ic
  on·o·mat·o·po·et·ic
  on·o·mat·o·poe·i·cal·ly
  on·o·mat·o·po·et·i·cal·ly
On·on·da·ga
on·rush
  on·rush·ing
on·set
on·shore
on·slaught
On·tar·io
on·to
onus
on·ward
on·yx
oo·dles
ooze
  oozed
  ooz·ing
  oo·zi·ness
  oo·zy
  oo·zi·er
  oo·zi·est
opac·i·ty
  opac·i·ties
opal
opal·es·cence
  opal·es·cent
opaque
  opaque·ly
  opaque·ness
open
  open·er
  open·ly
  open·ness
open-air
open-door
open-end
open-eyed
open-hand·ed
  open-hand·ed·ly
  open-hand·ed·ness
open house
open·ing
open-mind·ed
  open-mind·ed·ly
open-mouthed
open ses·a·me
open·work
opera
op·er·at·ic
  op·er·at·i·cal·ly
op·er·a·ble
  op·er·a·bil·i·ty
  op·er·a·bly
op·er·a glass·es
op·er·a house

op·er·ate
op·er·at·ed
op·er·at·ing
op·er·a·tion
op·er·a·tive
op·er·a·tive·ly
op·er·a·tive·ness
op·er·a·tor
op·er·et·ta
oph·thal·mic
oph·thal·mol·o·gist
oph·thal·mol·o·gy
oph·thal·mo·log·ic
opi·ate
opine
opined
opin·ing
opin·ion
opin·ion·at·ed
opin·ion·at·ed·ly
opin·ion·at·ed·ness
opi·um
opos·sum
Op·pen·hei·mer
op·po·nent
op·por·tune
op·por·tune·ly
op·por·tune·ness
op·por·tun·ism
op·por·tun·ist
op·por·tun·is·tic
op·por·tu·ni·ty
op·por·tu·ni·ties
op·pos·a·ble
op·pos·a·bil·i·ty
op·pose
op·posed
op·pos·ing
op·pos·er
op·pos·ing·ly
op·po·site
op·po·site·ly
op·po·site·ness
op·po·si·tion
op·po·si·tion·al
op·press
op·pres·si·ble
op·pres·sor
op·pres·sion
op·pres·sive
op·pres·sive·ly
op·pres·sive·ness
op·pro·bri·ous
op·pro·bri·ous·ly
op·pro·bri·ous·ness
op·pro·bri·um
op·tic
op·ti·cal
op·ti·cal·ly
op·ti·cian
op·tics
op·ti·mal
op·ti·mism
op·ti·mist
op·ti·mis·tic

op·ti·mis·ti·cal·ly
op·ti·mize
op·ti·mized
op·ti·miz·ing
op·ti·mi·za·tion
op·ti·mum
op·ti·ma
op·tion
op·tion·al
op·tion·al·ly
op·tom·e·trist
op·tom·e·try
op·to·met·ric
op·to·met·ri·cal
op·u·lent
op·u·lence
op·u·lent·ly
opus
ope·ra
opus·es
or·a·cle
orac·u·lar
orac·u·lar·i·ty
orac·u·lar·ly
oral
oral·ly
or·ange
or·ange·ade
or·ange·wood
orang·u·tan
orate
orat·ed
orat·ing
ora·tion
or·a·tor
or·a·tor·i·cal
or·a·tor·i·cal·ly
or·a·to·rio
or·a·to·ri·os
or·a·to·ry
or·bic·u·lar
or·bic·u·late
or·bic·u·lar·i·ty
or·bic·u·lar·ly
or·bit
or·bit·al
or·bit·er
or·chard
or·ches·tra
or·ches·tral
or·ches·tral·ly
or·ches·trate
or·ches·trat·ed
or·ches·trat·ing
or·ches·tra·tion
or·chid
or·dain
or·dain·er
or·dain·ment
or·deal
or·der
or·dered
or·der·ly
or·der·li·ness
or·di·nal

or·di·nance
or·di·nar·i·ly
or·di·nary
 or·di·nar·i·ness
or·di·na·tion
ord·nance
or·dure
oreg·a·no
Ore·gon
Ores·tes
or·gan
or·gan·dy
or·gan·ic
 or·gan·i·cal·ly
or·gan·ism
 or·gan·is·mal
 or·gan·is·mic
or·gan·ist
or·gan·i·za·tion
 or·gan·i·za·tion·al
 or·gan·i·za·tion·al·ly
or·gan·ize
 or·gan·ized
 or·gan·iz·ing
 or·gan·iz·a·ble
 or·gan·iz·er
or·gasm
 or·gas·mic
or·gi·as·tic
 or·gi·as·ti·cal·ly
or·gy
 or·gies
ori·ent
Ori·en·tal
 ori·en·tal·ism
 ori·en·tal·ist
 ori·en·tal·ly
ori·en·tate
 ori·en·tat·ed
 ori·en·tat·ing
ori·en·ta·tion
or·i·fice
ori·ga·mi
Or·i·gen
orig·i·nal
 orig·i·nal·i·ty
 orig·i·nal·ly
orig·i·nate
 orig·i·nat·ed
 orig·i·nat·ing
 orig·i·na·tion
 orig·i·na·tor
 orig·i·na·tive
 orig·i·na·tive·ly
Ori·no·co
or·i·son
Or·lan·do
Or·leans
Or·lon
or·na·ment
 or·na·men·tal
 or·na·men·ta·tion
or·nate
 or·nate·ly
 or·nate·ness

or·nery
 or·ner·i·ness
or·ni·thol·o·gy
 or·ni·tho·log·ic
 or·ni·tho·log·i·cal
 or·ni·tho·log·i·cal·ly
 or·ni·thol·o·gist
oro·tund
 oro·tun·di·ty
or·phan
 or·phan·hood
or·phan·age
or·tho·don·tics
 or·tho·don·tic
 or·tho·don·tist
or·tho·dox
 or·tho·dox·ly
 or·tho·dox·ness
or·tho·doxy
 or·tho·dox·ies
or·tho·gen·ic
or·thog·o·nal
 or·thog·o·nal·ly
or·thog·ra·phy
 or·thog·ra·phies
 or·thog·ra·pher
or·tho·graph·ic
 or·tho·graph·i·cal
 or·tho·graph·i·cal·ly
or·tho·pe·dics
 or·tho·pe·dic
 or·tho·pe·dist
Osa·ka
Os·car
os·cil·late
 os·cil·lat·ed
 os·cil·lat·ing
 os·cil·la·tion
 os·cil·la·tor
 os·cil·la·to·ry
os·cil·lo·scope
os·cu·late
 os·cu·lat·ed
 os·cu·lat·ing
 os·cu·la·tion
 os·cu·la·to·ry
Osh·kosh
Os·lo
os·mi·um
os·mose
 os·mosed
 os·mos·ing
os·mo·sis
 os·mot·ic
 os·mot·i·cal·ly
os·prey
os·si·fy
 os·si·fied
 os·si·fy·ing
 os·si·fi·er
Os·si·ning
os·ten·si·ble
 os·ten·si·bly
os·ten·sive
 os·ten·sive·ly

os·ten·ta·tion
os·ten·ta·tious
os·ten·ta·tious·ly
os·ten·ta·tious·ness
os·te·op·a·thy
os·te·o·path
os·te·o·path·ic
os·te·o·path·i·cal·ly
os·tra·cism
os·tra·cize
os·tra·cized
os·tra·ciz·ing
os·trich
Os·we·go
Othel·lo
oth·er
oth·er·ness
oth·er·wise
oth·er world
oth·er·world·ly
oth·er·world·li·ness
oti·ose
oti·ose·ly
oti·os·i·ty
Ot·ta·wa
ot·ter
ot·to·man
Oua·ga·dou·gou
ought
Oui·da
Oui·ja
ounce
our·self
our·selves
oust·er
out·bid
out·bid·den
out·bid·ding
out·bid·der
out·board
out·bound
out·brave
out·braved
out·brav·ing
out·break
out·build·ing
out·burst
out·cast
out·come
out·cry
out·cries
out·dat·ed
out·dis·tance
out·dis·tanced
out·dis·tanc·ing
out·do
out·did
out·done
out·do·ing
out·door
out·er
out·er·most
out·er space
out·face
out·faced

out·fac·ing
out·field
out·field·er
out·fit
out·fit·ted
out·fit·ting
out·fit·ter
out·flank
out·fox
out·go
out·went
out·gone
out·go·ing
out·grow
out·grew
out·grown
out·grow·ing
out·growth
out·guess
out·ing
out·land·ish
out·land·ish·ly
out·land·ish·ness
out·last
out·law
out·law·ry
out·lay
out·laid
out·lay·ing
out·let
out·line
out·lined
out·lin·ing
out·live
out·lived
out·liv·ing
out·look
out·ly·ing
out·mod·ed
out·num·ber
out-of-date
out-of-date·ness
out·post
out·put
out·rage
out·raged
out·rag·ing
out·ra·geous
out·ra·geous·ly
out·ra·geous·ness
out·range
out·ranged
out·rang·ing
out·rank
out·rig·ger
out·right
out·run
out·ran
out·run·ning
out·sell
out·sold
out·sell·ing
out·set
out·shine
out·shone

out·shin·ing
out·side
out·sid·er
out·skirts
out·smart
out·spo·ken
out·spo·ken·ly
out·spo·ken·ness
out·stand·ing
out·stand·ing·ly
out·stand·ing·ness
out·strip
out·stripped
out·strip·ping
out·ward
out·wards
out·ward·ly
out·ward·ness
out·wear
out·wore
out·worn
out·wear·ing
out·weigh
out·wit
out·wit·ted
out·wit·ting
ova
oval
oval·ly
oval·ness
ova·ry
ova·ries
ovar·i·an
ovate
ova·tion
ov·en
over
over·act
over·age
over·all
over·alls
over·awe
over·awed
over·aw·ing
over·bear·ing
over·bear·ing·ly
over·blown
over·board
over·build
over·built
over·build·ing
over·cast
over·charge
over·charged
over·charg·ing
over·coat
over·come
over·came
over·com·ing
over·com·er
over·com·pen·sa·tion
over·com·pen·sate
over·com·pen·sat·ed
over·com·pen·sat·ing
over·con·fi·dence

over·con·fi·dent
over·do
over·did
over·done
over·do·ing
over·dose
over·dos·age
over·dosed
over·dos·ing
over·draft
over·draw
over·drew
over·drawn
over·draw·ing
over·drive
over·due
over·em·pha·sis
over·em·pha·size
over·em·pha·sized
over·em·pha·sizing
over·es·ti·mate
over·es·ti·mat·ed
over·es·ti·mat·ing
over·es·ti·ma·tion
over·flow
over·flowed
over·flown
over·flowing
over·gen·er·ous
over·gen·er·ous·ness
over·grow
over·grew
over·grown
over·grow·ing
over·growth
over·hand
over·hand·ed
over·hang
over·hung
over·hang·ing
over·haul
over·haul·ing
over·head
over·hear
over·heard
over·hear·ing
over·joy
over·joyed
over·kill
over·land
over·lap
over·lapped
over·lap·ping
over·lay
over·laid
over·lay·ing
over·look
over·lord
over·lord·ship
over·ly
over·much
over·night
over·pass
over·play
over·pow·er

over·pow·er·ing
over·pow·er·ing·ly
over·rate
over·rat·ed
over·rat·ing
over·reach
over·ride
over·rode
over·rid·den
over·rid·ing
over·rule
over·ruled
over·rul·ing
over·run
over·ran
over·run·ning
over·seas
over·see
over·saw
over·seen
over·see·ing
over·se·er
over·sexed
over·shad·ow
over·shoe
over·shoot
over·shot
over·shoot·ing
over·sight
over·sim·pli·fy
over·sim·pli·fied
over·sim·pli·fy·ing
over·sim·pli·fi·ca·tion
over·size
over·sleep
over·slept
over·sleep·ing
over·spread
over·spread·ing
over·state
over·stat·ed
over·stat·ing
over·state·ment
over·stay
over·step
over·stepped
over·step·ping
over·strung
over·stuff
overt
overt·ly
over·take
over·took
over·tak·en
over·tak·ing
over·tax
over-the-coun·ter
over·throw
over·threw
over·thrown
over·throw·ing
over·time
over·tone
over·ture
over·turn

over·view
over·ween·ing
over·ween·ing·ly
over·ween·ing·ness
over·weight
over·whelm
over·whelm·ing
over·whelm·ing·ly
over·work
over·worked
over·work·ing
over·wrought
ovi·duct
ovip·a·rous
ovip·ar·ous·ly
ovip·ar·ous·ness
ovoid
ovoi·dal
ovu·late
ovu·lat·ed
ovu·lat·ing
ovu·la·tion
ovule
ovu·lar
ovum
ova
owe
owed
ow·ing
owl·ish
own·er
ox·al·ic ac·id
ox·bow
ox·en
ox·ford
ox·i·da·tion
ox·i·da·tive
ox·i·dant
ox·ide
ox·i·dize
ox·i·dized
ox·i·diz·ing
ox·y·a·cet·y·lene
ox·y·gen
ox·y·gen·ate
ox·y·gen·at·ed
ox·y·gen·at·ing
ox·y·gen·a·tion
oys·ter
ozone
pab·u·lum
pace
paced
pac·ing
pac·er
pace·mak·er
pa·cif·ic
pa·cif·i·ca·tion
pa·cif·i·ca·tor
pa·cif·i·ca·to·ry
pac·i·fi·er
pac·i·fism
pac·i·fist
pac·i·fy
pac·i·fied

pac·i·fy·ing
pack·age
  pack·ag·er
pack·er
pack·et
pack·ing
pad
  pad·ded
  pad·ding
pad·dle
  pad·dled
  pad·dling
  pad·dler
pad·dock
pad·dy
  pad·dies
pad·lock
pae·an
  pe·an
pa·gan
  pa·gan·ism
page
  paged
  pag·ing
pag·eant
  pag·eant·ry
pag·i·nate
  pag·i·nat·ed
  pag·i·nat·ing
pa·go·da
pain
  pain·ful
  pain·less
  pain·less·ness
pain·kil·ler
pains·tak·ing
  pains·tak·ing·ly
paint·er
paint·ing
pais·ley
pa·jam·as
Pak·i·stan
pal·ace
pal·at·a·ble
  pal·at·a·bil·i·ty
  pal·at·a·bly
pal·ate
pa·la·tial
  pa·la·tial·ly
pal·a·tine
  pa·lat·i·nate
pa·lav·er
pale
  paled
  pal·ing
  pale·ly
  pale·ness
Pa·le·o·lith·ic
pa·le·on·tol·o·gy
  pa·le·on·to·log·ic
  pa·le·on·to·log·i·cal
  pa·le·on·tol·o·gist
Pa·ler·mo
Pal·es·tine
pal·ette

pal·imp·sest
pal·in·drome
pal·ing
pal·i·sade
  pal·i·sad·ed
  pal·i·sad·ing
pal·la·di·um
pall·bear·er
pal·let
pal·li·ate
  pal·li·at·ed
  pal·li·at·ing
  pal·li·a·tion
pal·lid
pal·lor
palm
pal·ma·ceous
pal·mate
  pal·mate·ly
palm·er
palm·is·try
palm·ist
palmy
  palm·i·er
  palm·i·est
pal·o·mi·no
  pal·o·mi·nos
Pa·los
pal·pa·ble
  pal·pa·bil·i·ty
  pal·pa·bly
pal·pate
  pal·pat·ed
  pal·pat·ing
  pal·pa·tion
pal·pi·tate
  pal·pi·tat·ed
  pal·pi·tat·ing
  pal·pi·ta·tion
pal·sy
  pal·sied
  pal·sy·ing
pal·ter
  pal·ter·er
pal·try
  pal·tri·er
  pal·tri·est
  pal·tri·ness
pam·pas
pam·pe·an
pam·per
  pam·per·er
pam·phlet
pan
  panned
  pan·ning
pan·a·ce·a
  pan·a·ce·an
pa·nache
Pan·a·ma
Pan-Amer·i·can
pan·cake
  pan·caked
  pan·cak·ing
pan·cre·as

pan·cre·at·ic
pan·dem·ic
pan·de·mo·ni·um
pan·der
Pan·do·ra
pan·el
 pan·eled
 pan·el·ing
pan·el·ist
pang
pan·han·dle
 pan·han·dled
 pan·han·dling
pan·ic
 pan·icked
 pan·ick·ing
pan·nier
 pan·ier
pan·o·ply
 pan·o·plies
 pan·o·plied
pan·o·rama
 pan·o·ram·ic
 pan·o·ram·i·cal·ly
pan·sy
 pan·sies
pan·ta·loon
pan·the·ism
 pan·the·ist
 pan·the·is·tic
pan·the·on
pan·ther
pan·ties
pan·to·mime
 pan·to·mimed
 pan·to·mim·ing
 pan·to·mim·ic
 pan·to·mim·ist
pan·try
 pan·tries
pant·suit
pant·y·hose
pa·pa
pa·pa·cy
 pa·pa·cies
pa·pal
pa·per
 pa·per·er
 pa·pery
pa·per·back
pa·per·weight
pa·per·work
pa·pier·mâ·ché
pa·pil·la
 pa·pil·lae
pa·poose
pap·ri·ka
Pap·ua
pa·py·rus
par·a·ble
par·a·chute
 par·a·chut·ed
 par·a·chut·ing
 par·a·chut·ist
Par·a·clete

pa·rade
 pa·rad·ed
 pa·rad·ing
par·a·digm
 par·a·dig·mat·ic
par·a·dise
 par·a·di·si·a·cal
par·a·dox
 par·a·dox·i·cal
par·af·fin
par·a·gon
par·a·graph
 par·a·graph·er
Par·a·guay
par·a·keet
par·al·lax
 par·al·lac·tic
par·al·lel
 par·al·leled
 par·a·lel·ing
par·al·lel·o·gram
pa·ral·y·sis
 pa·ral·y·ses
 par·a·lyt·ic
par·a·lyze
 par·a·lyzed
 par·a·lyz·ing
Par·a·mar·i·bo
par·a·me·ci·um
par·a·med·ic
pa·ram·e·ter
par·a·mount
 par·a·mount·cy
 par·a·mount·ly
par·a·mour
par·a·noia
 par·a·noid
par·a·pet
par·a·pher·nal·ia
par·a·phrase
 par·a·phrased
 par·a·phras·ing
 par·a·phras·er
 par·a·phras·tic
par·a·ple·gia
 par·a·ple·gic
par·a·psy·chol·o·gy
par·a·site
 par·a·sit·ic
 par·a·sit·i·cal·ly
 par·a·sit·ism
par·a·sol
par·a·sym·pa·thet·ic
par·a·thi·on
par·a·troop·er
par·a·ty·phoid
par·boil
par·cel
 par·celed
 par·cel·ling
parch·ment
par·don
 par·don·a·able
 par·don·a·bly
pare

pared
par·ing
par·e·gor·ic
par·ent
pa·ren·tal
par·ent·age
pa·ren·the·sis
pa·ren·the·ses
par·en·thet·ic
par·en·thet·i·cal
pa·re·sis
pa·ret·ic
par·fait
pa·ri·ah
par·i·mu·tu·el
Par·is
par·ish
pa·rish·ion·er
par·i·ty
par·ka
Par·kin·son
park·way
par·lance
par·lay
par·layed
par·lay·ing
par·ley
par·leyed
par·ley·ing
par·lia·ment
par·lia·men·tar·i·an
par·lia·men·ta·ry
par·lor
Par·ma
Par·me·san
pa·ro·chi·al
par·o·dy
par·o·dies
par·o·died
par·o·dy·ing
pa·rod·ic
par·o·dist
pa·role
pa·roled
pa·rol·ing
pa·rot·id
par·ox·ysm
par·ox·ys·mal
par·quet
par·queted
par·quet·ing
par·quet·ry
par·rot
par·rot·like
par·roty
par·ry
par·ried
par·ry·ing
parse
par·si·mo·ny
par·si·mo·ni·ous
par·si·mo·ni·ous·ly
par·si·mo·ni·ous·ness
par·sley
pars·nip

par·son
par·son·age
par·take
par·took
par·tak·en
par·tak·ing
par·ta·ker
part·ed
par·the·no·gen·e·sis
Par·the·non
par·tial
par·tial·ly
par·ti·al·i·ty
par·ti·al·i·ties
par·tic·i·pant
par·tic·i·pate
par·tic·i·pat·ed
par·tic·i·pat·ing
par·tic·i·pa·tion
par·tic·i·pa·tive
par·ti·cip·i·al
par·ti·ci·ple
par·ti·cle
par·ti·col·ored
par·tic·u·lar
par·tic·u·lar·ly
par·tic·u·lar·i·ty
par·tic·u·lar·i·ties
par·tic·u·lar·ize
par·tic·u·lar·ized
par·tic·u·lar·iz·ing
par·tic·u·late
part·ing
par·ti·san
par·ti·san·ship
par·tite
par·ti·tion
par·ti·tive
part·ly
part·ner
part·ner·ship
par·tridge
par·tridg·es
part-time
par·tu·ri·ent
par·tu·ri·tion
par·ty
par·ties
par·ve·nu
Pas·a·de·na
pas·chal
pa·sha
pass·a·ble
pass·a·bly
pas·sage
pas·sage·way
Pas·sa·ic
pass·book
pas·sé
pas·sen·ger
pass·er-by
pass·ers-by
pass·ing
pas·sion
pas·sion·less

pas·sion·ate
  pas·sion·ate·ly
  pas·sion·ate·ness
pas·sive
pass·key
Pass·o·ver
pass·port
pass·word
pas·ta
paste
  pas·ted
  pas·ting
paste·board
pas·tel
Pas·teur
pas·teur·ize
  pas·teur·ized
  pas·teur·iz·ing
  pas·teur·i·za·tion
pas·tille
pas·time
pas·tor
pas·to·ral
pas·tor·ate
pas·tra·mi
pas·try
  pas·tries
pas·ture
  pas·tured
  pas·tur·ing
  pas·tur·age
pasty
  past·i·er
  past·i·est
pat
  pat·ted
  pat·ting
Pat·a·go·nia
Pa·taps·co
patch·work
patchy
  patch·i·er
  patch·i·est
pâ·té
  pâ·tés
pat·ent
  pa·ten·cy
  pat·ent·ly
pat·ent·ee
pat·er·nal
  pat·er·nal·ly
pa·ter·nal·ism
pa·ter·ni·ty
Pat·er·son
pa·thet·ic
path·find·er
pa·thol·o·gy
  pa·thol·o·gies
  path·o·log·ic
  path·o·log·i·cal
  path·o·log·i·cal·ly
  pa·thol·o·gist
pa·thos
path·way
pa·tience

pa·tient
  pa·tient·ly
pat·i·na
pa·tio
  pa·ti·os
pat·ois
pa·tri·arch
pa·tri·ar·chy
  pa·tri·ar·chies
pa·tri·cian
pat·ri·mo·ny
  pat·ri·mo·nies
pa·tri·ot
  pa·tri·ot·ic
  pa·tri·ot·i·cal·ly
  pa·tri·ot·ism
pa·trol
  pa·trolled
  pa·trol·ling
  pa·trol·ler
  pa·trol·man
  pa·trol·men
pa·tron
  pa·tron·ess
  pa·tron·age
  pa·tron·ize
  pa·tron·ized
  pa·tron·iz·ing
  pa·tron·iz·ing·ly
pat·ro·nym·ic
pat·sy
  pat·sies
pat·ter
pat·tern
  pat·terned
Pat·ton
pat·ty
  pat·ties
pau·ci·ty
Paul·ist
paunch
  paunch·i·ness
  paunchy
  paunch·i·er
  paunch·i·est
pau·per
  pau·per·ism
pause
  paused
  paus·ing
  paus·er
pave
  paved
  pav·ing
  pav·er
pave·ment
pa·vil·ion
Pav·lov
pawn
  pawn·er
pawn·bro·ker
Paw·nee
pawn·shop
Paw·tuck·et
pay

paid
pay·ing
pay·ee
pay·er
pay·a·ble
pay·check
pay·load
pay·ment
pay·off
pay·roll
Pea·body
peace
peace·a·ble
  peace·a·bly
peace·ful
  peace·ful·ly
  peace·ful·ness
peace·mak·er
peace·time
peach
pea·cock
peak·ed
pea·nut
pearl
  pearly
Pear·son
Pea·ry
peas·ant
  peas·ant·ry
peaty
peb·ble
  peb·bled
  peb·bling
  peb·bly
pe·can
pec·ca·dil·lo
  pec·ca·dil·loes
  pec·ca·dil·los
peck·er
pec·tin
pec·to·ral
pec·u·late
  pec·u·lat·ed
  pec·u·lat·ing
  pec·u·la·tion
  pec·u·la·tor
pe·cu·liar
  pe·cu·liar·ly
  pe·cu·li·ar·i·ty
  pe·cu·li·ar·i·ties
pe·cu·ni·ary
ped·a·gogue
  ped·a·gog
  ped·a·gog·ic
  ped·a·gog·i·cal
  ped·a·gog·i·cal·ly
  ped·a·go·gy
ped·al
  ped·aled
  ped·al·ing
ped·ant
  pe·dan·tic
  pe·dan·ti·cal·ly
  ped·ant·ry
ped·dle

ped·dled
ped·dling
ped·dler
ped·ler
ped·lar
ped·es·tal
pe·des·tri·an
  pe·des·tri·an·ism
pe·di·at·rics
pe·di·at·ric
pe·di·a·tri·cian
pe·di·at·rist
ped·ic·ure
  ped·i·cur·ist
ped·i·gree
  ped·i·greed
ped·i·ment
  ped·i·men·tal
  ped·i·ment·ed
pe·dom·e·ter
peep·hole
peer
  peer·age
  peer·ess
  peer·less
  peer·less·ly
peeve
  peeved
  peev·ing
peev·ish
  pee·vish·ly
  pee·vish·ness
pee·wee
peg
  pegged
  peg·ging
Peg·a·sus
Pei·ping
pe·jo·ra·tive
  pe·jo·ra·tive·ly
Pe·king·ese
Pe·ki·nese
pe·koe
Pe·la·gian
pel·i·can
pel·la·gra
pel·let
pell-mell
pel·lu·cid
  pel·lu·cid·i·ty
  pel·lu·cid·ness
  pel·lu·cid·ly
pelt·er
pelt·ry
pel·vis
  pel·vis·es
  pel·ves
  pel·vic
pem·mi·can
  pem·i·can
pen
  penned
  pen·ning
  pen·ner
pe·nal

pe·nal·ize
 pe·nal·ized
 pe·nal·iz·ing
 pe·nal·i·za·tion
 pe·nal·ly
pen·al·ty
 pen·al·ties
pen·ance
pen·chant
pen·cil
 pen·ciled
 pen·cil·ing
pend·ant
pend·ent
 pend·en·cy
 pend·ent·ly
pend·ing
pen·du·lous
 pen·du·lous·ly
 pen·du·lous·ness
pen·du·lum
pen·e·tra·ble
 pen·e·tra·bil·i·ty
 pen·e·tra·ble·ness
 pen·e·tra·bly
pen·e·trate
 pen·e·trat·ed
 pen·e·trat·ing
 pen·e·tra·tive
pen·e·tra·tion
pen·i·cil·lin
pen·in·su·la
 pen·in·su·lar
pe·nis
 pe·nes
 pe·nis·es
 pe·nile
 pe·ni·al
pen·i·tent
 pen·i·tence
 pen·i·ten·tial
 pen·i·ten·tial·ly
 pen·i·tent·ly
pen·i·ten·tia·ry
 pen·i·ten·tia·ries
pen·knife
 pen·knives
pen·man·ship
pen·nant
pen·ni·less
pen·non
Penn·syl·va·nia
pen·ny
 pen·nies
pen·ny an·te
pen·ny pinch·er
 pen·ny pinch·ing
pen·ny·weight
pen·ny-wise
Pe·nob·scot
pe·nol·o·gy
 pe·no·log·i·cal
 pe·nol·o·gist
Pen·sa·co·la
pen·sion

pen·sion·a·ble
pen·sion·ary
pen·sion·ar·ies
pen·sion·er
pen·sive
 pen·sive·ly
 pen·sive·ness
pen·ta·gon
 pen·tag·o·nal
 pen·tag·o·nal·ly
pen·tam·e·ter
Pen·ta·teuch
pen·tath·lon
Pen·te·cost
 Pen·te·cos·tal
pent·house
pent-up
pe·nult
 pe·nul·ti·ma
 pe·nul·ti·mate
pe·num·bra
 pe·num·bras
 pe·num·brae
 pe·num·bral
pe·nu·ri·ous
 pe·nu·ri·ous·ly
 pe·nu·ri·ous·ness
pen·u·ry
Pen·zance
pe·on
 pe·on·age
pe·o·ny
 pe·o·nies
peo·ple
 peo·pled
 peo·pling
 peo·pler
Pe·o·ria
pep
 pepped
 pep·ping
pep·per
 pep·per·corn
 pep·per·mint
 pep·pery
 pep·per·i·ness
pep·py
 pep·pi·er
 pep·pi·est
 pep·pi·ness
pep·sin
pep·tic
per·am·bu·late
 per·am·bu·lat·ed
 per·am·bu·lat·ing
 per·am·bu·la·tion
 per·am·bu·la·to·ry
 per·am·bu·la·tor
per an·num
per·cale
per cap·i·ta
per·ceive
 per·ceived
 per·ceiv·ing
 per·ceiv·a·ble

per·ceiv·a·bly
per·cent
  per·cent·age
per·cen·tile
per·cep·ti·ble
  per·cep·ti·bil·i·ty
  per·cep·ti·bly
per·cep·tion
  per·cep·tion·al
per·cep·tu·al
  per·cep·tu·al·ly
perch
perch·es
per·chance
per·co·late
  per·co·lat·ed
  per·co·lat·ing
  per·co·la·tion
per·co·la·tor
per·cus·sion
  per·cus·sion·ist
per di·em
per·di·tion
per·e·gri·nate
  per·e·gri·nat·ed
  per·e·gri·nat·ing
  per·e·gri·na·tion
  per·e·grine
per·emp·to·ry
  per·emp·to·ri·ly
  per·emp·to·ri·ness
per·en·ni·al
  per·en·ni·al·ly
per·fect
  per·fect·er
  per·fect·ness
per·fect·i·ble
  per·fect·i·bil·i·ty
per·fec·tive
  per·fec·tive·ness
per·fec·tion
  per·fec·tion·ist
per·fect·ly
per·fi·dy
  per·fid·i·ous
  per·fid·i·ous·ly
  per·fid·i·ous·ness
per·fo·rate
  per·fo·rat·ed
  per·fo·rat·ing
  per·fo·ra·tor
  per·fo·ra·tion
per·force
per·form
  per·form·a·ble
  per·form·er
per·for·mance
per·fume
  per·fumed
  per·fum·ing
  per·fum·er
  per·fum·ery
  per·fum·er·ies
per·func·to·ry
  per·func·to·ri·ly

per·func·to·ri·ness
per·haps
Per·i·cles
per·i·gee
  per·i·ge·al
  per·i·ge·an
per·i·he·li·on
  per·i·he·lia
per·il
  per·iled
  per·il·ing
  per·il·ous
  per·il·ous·ly
  per·il·ous·ness
pe·rim·e·ter
  per·i·met·ric
  per·i·met·ri·cal
  per·i·met·ri·cal·ly
pe·ri·od
pe·ri·od·ic
  pe·ri·o·dic·i·ty
pe·ri·od·i·cal
  pe·ri·od·i·cal·ly
per·i·pa·tet·ic
  per·i·pa·tet·i·cal·ly
pe·riph·ery
  pe·riph·er·ies
pe·riph·er·al
  pe·riph·er·al·ly
per·i·phrase
per·i·scope
  per·i·scopic
  per·i·scop·i·cal
per·ish
per·ish·a·ble
  per·ish·a·bil·i·ty
  per·ish·a·ble·ness
  per·ish·a·bly
per·i·stal·sis
  per·i·stal·ses
  per·i·stal·tic
per·i·style
per·i·to·ne·um
  per·i·to·ne·ums
  per·i·to·nea
  per·i·to·ne·al
  per·i·to·ni·tis
per·i·wig
per·i·win·kle
per·jure
  per·jured
  per·jur·ing
  per·jur·er
per·ju·ry
  per·ju·ries
perky
  perk·i·er
  perk·i·est
per·ma·nent
per·me·a·ble
  per·me·a·bil·i·ty
  per·me·a·bly
per·me·ate
  per·me·at·ed
  per·me·at·ing

per·me·a·tion
per·me·a·tive
per·mis·si·ble
  per·mis·si·bil·i·ty
  per·mis·si·bly
per·mis·sion
per·mis·sive
  per·mis·sive·ly
  per·mis·sive·ness
per·mit
  per·mit·ted
  per·mit·ting
  per·mit·ter
per·mu·ta·tion
per·ni·cious
  per·ni·cious·ly
  per·ni·cious·ness
Pe·ron
per·o·ra·tion
per·ox·ide
  per·ox·id·ed
  per·ox·id·ing
per·pen·dic·u·lar
  per·pen·dic·u·lar·i·ty
  per·pen·dic·u·lar·ly
per·pe·trate
  per·pe·trat·ed
  per·pe·trat·ing
  per·pe·tra·tion
  per·pe·tra·tor
per·pet·u·al
  per·pet·u·al·ly
per·pet·u·ate
  per·pet·u·at·ed
  per·pet·u·at·ing
  per·pet·u·a·tion
  per·pet·u·a·tor
per·pe·tu·i·ty
  per·pe·tu·i·ties
per·plex
  per·plexed
  per·plex·ing
  per·plex·ing·ly
  per·plex·ed·ly
  per·plex·i·ty
  per·plex·i·ties
per·qui·site
Per·ry·ville
per se
per·se·cute
  per·se·cut·ed
  per·se·cut·ing
  per·se·cu·tive
  per·se·cu·tor
  per·se·cu·tion
per·se·vere
  per·se·vered
  per·se·ver·ing
  per·se·ver·ance
  per·se·ver·ing·ly
Per·shing
Per·sia
per·si·flage
per·sim·mon
per·sist

per·sist·ence
per·sis·ten·cy
per·sist·ent
  per·sist·ent·ly
per·snick·ety
per·son
per·son·u·ble
per·son·age
per·son·al
per·son·al·i·ty
  per·son·al·i·ties
per·son·al·ize
  per·son·al·ized
  per·son·al·iz·ing
  per·son·al·ly
per·so·na non gra·ta
per·son·ate
  per·son·at·ed
  per·son·at·ing
  per·son·a·tion
  per·son·a·tor
per·son·i·fy
  per·son·i·fied
  per·son·i·fy·ing
  per·son·i·fi·ca·tion
  per·son·i·fi·er
per·son·nel
per·spec·tive
  per·spec·tive·ly
per·spi·ca·cious
  per·spi·ca·cious·ly
  per·spi·ca·cious·ness
  per·spi·cac·i·ty
per·spi·cu·i·ty
  per·spic·u·ous
  per·spic·u·ous·ly
per·spi·ra·tion
per·spire
  per·spired
  per·spir·ing
per·suade
  per·suad·ed
  per·suad·ing
  per·suad·a·ble
  per·suad·er
per·sua·sion
per·sua·sive
  per·sua·sive·ly
  per·sua·sive·ness
pert
  pert·ly
  pert·ness
per·tain
Perth·shire
per·ti·na·cious
  per·ti·na·cious·ly
  per·ti·na·cious·ness
  per·ti·nac·i·ty
per·ti·nent
  per·ti·nence
  per·ti·nen·cy
  per·ti·nent·ly
per·turb
  per·turb·a·ble
  per·tur·ba·tion

pe·ruke
pe·ruse
  pe·rused
  pe·rus·ing
  pe·rus·al
  pe·rus·er
per·vade
  per·vad·ed
  per·vad·ing
  per·vad·er
  per·va·sion
  per·va·sive
  per·va·sive·ly
  per·va·sive·ness
per·verse
  per·verse·ly
  per·verse·ness
  per·ver·si·ty
per·ver·sion
per·vert
  per·vert·ed
  per·vert·ed·ly
  per·vert·er
  per·vert·i·ble
per·vi·ous
  per·vi·ous·ness
pes·ky
  pes·ki·er
  pes·ki·est
  pesk·i·ly
  pesk·i·ness
pes·si·mism
  pes·si·mist
  pes·si·mis·tic
  pes·si·mis·ti·cal·ly
pes·ter
pest·hole
pest·i·cide
pes·tif·er·ous
  pes·tif·er·ous·ly
  pes·tif·er·ous·ness
pes·ti·lence
  pes·ti·len·tial
pes·ti·lent
  pes·ti·lent·ly
pes·tle
  pes·tled
  pes·tling
pet
  pet·ted
  pet·ting
  pet·ter
pet·al
  pet·aled
pet·cock
pe·ter
Pe·ters·burg
pet·i·ole
pe·tite
  pe·tite·ness
pet·it four
pe·ti·tion
  pe·ti·tion·ary
  pe·ti·tion·er
Pe·trarch

pet·rel
pet·ri·fy
  pet·ri·fied
  pet·ri·fy·ing
  pet·ri·fac·tion
pe·tro·chem·is·try
  pe·tro·chem·i·cal
Pet·ro·grad
pet·rol
pet·ro·la·tum
pe·trol·le·um
pet·ti·coat
pet·ti·fog
  pet·ti·fogged
  pet·ti·fog·ging
  pet·ti·fog·ger
  pet·ti·fog·gery
pet·tish
  pet·tish·ly
  pet·tish·ness
pet·ty
  pet·ti·er
  pet·ti·est
  pet·ti·ly
  pet·ti·ness
pet·u·lant
  pet·u·lance
  pet·u·lan·cy
  pet·u·lant·ly
pe·tu·nia
pew·ter
pe·yo·te
  pe·yo·tes
pha·e·ton
pha·lanx
  pha·lanx·es
  pha·lang·es
phal·lus
  phal·li
  phal·lus·es
  phal·lic
phan·tasm
  phan·tas·ma
  phan·tas·mal
  phan·tas·mic
phan·tas·ma·go·ria
  phan·tas·ma·go·ri·al
  phan·tas·ma·gor·ic
phan·ta·sy
  phan·ta·sies
phan·tom
phar·aoh
Phar·i·see
  phar·i·sa·ic
  phar·i·sa·i·cal
  phar·i·sa·ism
  phar·i·see·ism
phar·ma·ceu·ti·cal
  phar·ma·ceu·tic
  phar·ma·ceu·ti·cal·ly
  phar·ma·ceu·tics
phar·ma·cist
phar·ma·col·o·gy
  phar·ma·co·log·ic
  phar·ma·co·log·i·cal

phar·ma·col·o·gist
phar·ma·co·poe·ia
phar·ma·co·poe·ial
phar·ma·cy
phar·ma·cies
Pha·ros
phar·ynx
phar·yn·ges
pha·ryn·ge·al
pha·ryn·gal
phase
phased
phas·ing
pha·sic
pheas·ant
phe·no·bar·bi·tal
phe·nol
phe·nol·ic
phe·nom·e·non
phe·nom·e·na
phe·nom·e·nons
phe·nom·e·nal
phe·nom·e·nal·ly
phi·al
Phi Be·ta Kap·pa
Phil·a·del·phia
phi·lan·der
phi·lan·der·er
phi·lan·thro·py
phi·lan·thro·pies
phil·an·throp·ic
phil·an·throp·i·cal
phil·an·throp·i·cal·ly
phi·lan·thro·pist
phi·lat·e·ly
phil·a·tel·ic
phil·a·tel·i·cal
phil·lat·e·list
phil·har·mon·ic
Phil·ip
Phi·lip·pi·ans
Phil·ip·pine
Phi·lis·tine
Phi·lis·tin·ism
phil·o·den·dron
phil·o·den·drons
phil·o·den·dra
phi·lol·o·gy
phi·lol·o·gist
phi·lol·o·ger
phil·o·lo·gi·an
phil·o·log·i·cal
phil·o·log·ic
phil·o·log·i·cal·ly
phi·los·o·pher
phil·o·soph·i·cal
phil·o·soph·ic
phil·o·soph·i·cal·ly
phi·los·o·phize
phi·los·o·phized
phi·los·o·phiz·ing
phi·los·o·phiz·er
phi·los·o·phy
phi·los·o·phies
phil·ter

phil·tered
phil·ter·ing
phle·bi·tis
phle·bit·ic
phle·bot·o·my
phle·bot·o·mist
phlegm
phleg·mat·ic
phleg·mat·i·cal
phleg·mat·i·cal·ly
phlox
pho·bia
pho·bic
phoe·be
Phoe·ni·cia
phoe·nix
phone
phoned
phon·ing
pho·neme
pho·ne·mic
pho·net·ics
pho·net·ic
pho·net·i·cal
pho·net·i·cal·ly
phon·ic
phon·ics
pho·no·graph
pho·no·graph·ic
pho·no·graph·i·cal·ly
pho·nol·o·gy
pho·nol·o·gies
pho·no·log·ic
pho·no·log·i·cal
pho·no·log·i·cal·ly
pho·nol·o·gist
pho·ny
pho·ni·er
pho·ni·est
pho·nies
pho·ni·ness
phos·phate
phos·pho·res·cence
phos·pho·resce
phos·pho·resced
phos·pho·resc·ing
phos·pho·res·cent
phos·pho·res·cent·ly
phos·pho·rus
pho·to
pho·tos
pho·to·copy
pho·to·cop·ies
pho·to·cop·ied
pho·to·cop·y·ing
pho·to·e·lec·tric
pho·to·en·grav·ing
pho·to·en·grave
pho·to·en·graved
pho·to·en·grav·er
pho·to·flash
pho·to·gen·ic
pho·to·graph
pho·tog·ra·pher
pho·tog·ra·phy

pho·to·graph·ic
pho·to·graph·i·cal
pho·to·graph·i·cal·ly
pho·to·gra·vure
pho·to·off·set
Pho·to·stat
pho·to·stat·ed
pho·to·stat·ing
pho·to·stat·ic
pho·to·syn·the·sis
phrase
  phrased
  phras·ing
  phras·al
phra·se·ol·o·gy
phre·net·ic
phre·nol·o·gy
  phre·nol·o·gist
Phryg·i·an
phy·lac·ter·y
  phy·lac·ter·ies
phy·log·e·ny
  phy·lo·gen·e·sis
  phy·lo·ge·net·ic
  phy·lo·gen·ic
  phy·log·e·nist
phy·lum
phys·ic
  phys·icked
  phys·ick·ing
  phys·i·cal
  phys·i·cal·ly
phy·si·cian
phys·ics
  phys·i·cist
phys·i·og·no·my
  phys·i·og·no·mies
  phys·i·og·nom·ic
  phys·i·og·nom·i·cal
  phys·i·og·no·mist
phys·i·og·ra·phy
  phys·i·og·ra·pher
  phys·i·o·graph·ic
  phys·i·o·graph·i·cal
phys·i·ol·o·gy
  phys·i·o·log·ic
  phys·i·o·log·i·cal
  phys·i·o·log·i·cal·ly
  phys·i·ol·o·gist
phys·i·o·ther·a·py
phy·sique
pi·a·nis·si·mo
pi·an·ist
pi·ano
  pi·an·os
pi·an·o·for·te
pi·az·za
pi·ca
pic·a·dor
Pic·ar·dy
pic·a·resque
Pi·cas·so
pic·a·yune
  pic·a·yun·ish
Pic·ca·dil·ly

pic·ca·lil·li
pic·co·lo
  pic·co·los
pic·co·lo·ist
pick·ax
picked
pick·er·el
pick·et
  pick·et·er
pick·ing
pick·le
  pick·led
  pick·ling
pick·pock·et
pick·up
Pick·wick
picky
  pick·i·er
  pick·i·est
pic·nic
  pic·nicked
  pic·nick·ing
  pic·nick·er
pic·to·ri·al
  pic·to·ri·al·ly
pic·ture
  pic·tured
  pic·tur·ing
pic·tur·esque
  pic·tur·esque·ly
  pic·tur·esque·ness
pid·dle
  pid·dled
  pid·dling
pidg·in
pie·bald
piece
  piec·er
piece·meal
piece·work
  piece·work·er
pied
Pied·mont
pier
pierce
  pierced
  pierc·ing
  pierc·ing·ly
Pier·rot
pi·e·tism
  pi·e·tis·tic
  pi·e·tis·ti·cal
pi·e·ty
  pi·e·ties
pif·fle
pig
  pigged
  pig·ging
pi·geon
pi·geon·hole
  pi·geon·holed
  pi·geon·hol·ing
pi·geon·toed
pig·gish
  pig·gish·ly

pig·gish·ness
pig·gy·back
pig·head·ed
 pig·head·ed·ly
 pig·head·ed·ness
pig·ment
 pig·men·tary
pig·men·ta·tion
pig·pen
pig·skin
pig·sty
 pig·sties
pig·tail
pike
 piked
 pik·ing
pik·er
pi·las·ter
Pi·late
pil·chard
pile
 piled
 pil·ing
pil·fer
 pil·fer·age
 pil·fer·er
pil·grim
pil·grim·age
 pil·grim·aged
 pil·grim·ag·ing
pil·lage
 pil·laged
 pil·lag·ing
 pil·lag·er
pil·lar
pill·box
pil·lion
pil·lo·ry
 pil·lo·ries
 pil·lo·ried
 pil·lo·ry·ing
pil·low
pill·low·case
pi·lot
 pi·lot·age
 pi·lot·less
pi·lot·house
pi·men·to
 pi·men·tos
pim·ple
 pim·pled
 pim·ply
pin
 pinned
 pin·ning
pin·a·fore
pi·ña·ta
pince-nez
pin·cers
pinch
 pinch·er
pinch·beck
pin·cush·ion
Pin·dar
pine

pine·like
piney
pined
 pin·ing
pin·e·al
pine·ap·aple
pin·feath·er
 pin·feath·ered
 pin·feath·ery
pin·fold
pin·head
 pin·head·ed
pin·hole
pin·ion
pink·eye
pink·ie
pinko
 pink·os
 pink·oes
pin·na
 pin·nas
 pin·nae
 pin·nal
pin·na·cle
 pin·na·cled
 pin·na·cling
pin·nate
 pin·nate·ly
 pin·na·tion
pi·noch·le
 pi·noc·le
pin·point
pin·prick
pin·set·ter
pin·tail
 pin·tailed
pin·tle
pin·to
 pin·tos
pin-up
pin·wheel
pin·worm
pi·o·neer
pi·ous
 pi·ous·ly
 pi·ous·ness
pip
 pipped
 pip·ping
pipe·line
 pipe·lined
 pipe·lin·ing
pip·er
 pip·ing
pip·it
pip·pin
pip-squeak
pi·quant
 pi·quan·cy
 pi·quant·ness
 pi·quant·ly
pique
 piqued
 pi·quing
pi·qué

pi·ra·cy
  pi·ra·cies
Pi·rae·us
pi·ra·nha
pi·rate
  pi·rat·ed
  pi·rat·ing
  pi·rat·i·cal
  pi·rat·i·cal·ly
pi·rogue
pir·ou·ette
  pir·ou·et·ted
  pir·ou·et·ting
Pi·sa
Pis·ces
pis·ci·cul·ture
pis·ta·chio
  pis·ta·chi·os
pis·til
pis·til·late
pis·tol
  pis·toled
  pis·tol·ing
pis·ton
pit
  pit·ted
  pit·ting
pitch-black
pitch-blende
pitch·er
pitch·fork
pitchy
  pitch·i·er
  pitch·i·est
pit·e·ous
  pit·e·ous·ly
  pit·e·ous·ness
pit·fall
pith
pithy
  pith·i·er
  pith·i·est
  pith·i·ly
  pith·i·ness
pit·i·a·ble
  pit·i·a·ble·ness
  pit·i·a·bly
pit·i·ful
  pit·i·ful·ly
  pit·i·ful·ness
pit·i·less
  pit·i·less·ly
  pit·i·less·ness
pit·man
  pit·men
pit·tance
Pitts·burgh
pi·tu·i·tar·y
  pi·tu·i·tar·ies
Pi·us
pity
  pit·ies
  pit·ied
  pit·y·ing
  pit·y·ing·ly

piv·ot
  piv·ot·al
  piv·ot·al·ly
pix·i·lat·ed
pixy
  pix·ie
  pix·ies
piz·za
Pi·zar·ro
piz·ze·ri·a
piz·zi·ca·to
plac·a·ble
  plac·a·bil·i·ty
  plac·a·bly
plac·ard
pla·cate
  pla·cat·ed
  pla·cat·ing
  pla·cat·er
  pla·ca·tion
  pla·ca·tive
  pla·ca·to·ry
place
  placed
  plac·ing
pla·ce·bo
  pla·ce·bos
  pla·ce·boes
place·ment
pla·cen·ta
  pla·cen·tas
  pla·cen·tae
  pla·cen·tal
plac·er
plac·id
  pla·cid·i·ty
  plac·id·ness
  plac·id·ly
plack·et
pla·gia·rism
  pla·gia·rist
  pla·gia·ris·tic
pla·gia·rize
  pla·gia·rized
  pla·gia·riz·ing
  pla·gia·riz·er
pla·gia·ry
  pla·gia·ries
plague
  plagued
  pla·guing
  pla·guer
pla·guy
  pla·guey
  pla·gui·ly
plaid
plain
  plain·ly
  plain·ness
plain-clothes man
plain·song
plain-spo·ken
plain·tiff
plain·tive
  plain·tive·ly

plain·tive·ness
plait
  plait·ing
plan
  planned
  plan·ning
  plan·less
  plan·ner
plane
  planed
  plan·ing
plan·er
plan·et
plan·e·tar·i·um
  plan·e·tar·i·ums
  plan·e·tar·ia
plan·e·tary
plan·e·toid
plan·ish
  plan·ish·er
plank·ing
plank·ton
  plank·ton·ic
plant
  plant·a·ble
  plant·like
Plan·tag·e·net
plan·tain
plan·ta·tion
plant·er
plaque
plasm
plas·ma
  plas·mic
  plas·mat·ic
plas·ter
  plas·ter·er
  plas·ter·ing
  plas·ter·work
plas·ter·board
plas·tered
plas·tic
  plas·ti·cal·ly
  plas·tic·i·ty
  plas·ti·ciz·er
plat
  plat·ted
  plat·ting
plate
  plat·ed
  plat·ing
  plat·er
pla·teau
  pla·teaus
  pla·teaux
plate·ful
  plate·fuls
plate·let
plat·form
plat·i·num
plat·i·tude
  plat·i·tu·di·nal
  plat·i·tu·di·nous
  plat·i·tu·di·nize
  plat·i·tu·di·nized

plat·i·tu·di·niz·ing
Pla·to
pla·ton·ic
  pla·ton·i·cal·ly
pla·toon
plat·ter
plat·y·pus
  plat·y·pus·es
  plat·y·pi
plau·dit
plau·si·ble
  plau·si·bil·i·ty
  plau·si·ble·ness
  plau·si·bly
play·act
  play·act·ing
play·back
play·bill
play·boy
play·er
play·ful
  play·ful·ly
  play·ful·ness
play·go·er
play·ground
play·house
  play·hous·es
play·let
play·mate
play·off
play·pen
play·thing
play·time
play·wright
pla·za
plea
plead
  plead·ed
  plead·ing
  plead·a·ble
  plead·er
pleas·ant
  pleas·ant·ly
  pleas·ant·ness
  pleas·ant·ry
  pleas·ant·ries
please
  pleased
  pleas·ing
  pleas·ing·ly
  pleas·ing·ness
pleas·ur·a·ble
  pleas·ur·a·ble·ness
  pleas·ur·a·bly
pleas·ure
pleat
  pleat·ed
  pleat·er
plebe
ple·be·ian
pleb·i·scite
pledge
  pledged
  pledg·ing
  pledg·ee

pledg·er
ple·na·ry
plen·i·po·ten·ti·ar·y
plen·i·po·ten·ti·ar·ies
plen·i·tude
plen·te·ous
plen·te·ous·ly
plen·ti·ful
plen·ti·ful·ly
plen·ty
pleth·o·ra
ple·thor·ic
pleu·ra
pleu·rae
pleu·ral
pleu·ri·sy
pleu·rit·ic
plex·us
plex·us·es
pli·a·ble
pli·a·bil·i·ty
pli·a·ble·ness
pli·a·bly
pli·ant
pli·an·cy
pli·ant·ness
pli·ant·ly
pli·ca·tion
pli·ers
plight
plink
plod
plod·ded
plod·ding
plod·der
plop
plopped
plop·ping
plot
plot·ted
plot·ting
plot·ter
plow
plow·a·ble
plow·er
plow·man
plow·share
pluck
pluck·er
plucky
pluck·i·er
pluck·i·est
pluck·i·ly
pluck·i·ness
plug
plugged
plug·ging
plug·ger
plum·age
plumb·er
plumb·ing
plume
plumed
plum·ing
plume·like

plumy
plum·i·er
plum·i·est
plum·met
plump
plump·er
plump·ly
plump·ness
plun·der
plun·der·er
plun·der·ous
plunge
plunged
plung·ing
plung·er
plunk·er
plu·ral
plu·ral·ly
plu·ral·ize
plu·ral·ized
plu·ral·iz·ing
plu·ral·ism
plu·ral·ist
plu·ral·is·tic
plu·ral·i·ty
plu·ral·i·ties
plush
plush·i·ness
plushy
plush·i·er
plush·i·est
Plu·tarch
Plu·to
plu·toc·ra·cy
plu·toc·ra·cies
plu·to·crat
plu·to·crat·ic
plu·to·ni·um
plu·vi·al
ply
plied
ply·ing
Plym·outh
ply·wood
pneu·mat·ic
pneu·mat·i·cal·ly
pneu·mat·ics
pneu·mo·nia
pneu·mon·ic
poach
poach·er
Po·ca·hon·tas
pock·et
pock·et·book
pock·et·ful
pock·et·knife
pock·et·knives
pock·mark
pock·marked
pod
pod·ded
pod·ding
pod·like
podgy
podg·i·er

podg·i·est
po·di·a·trist
po·di·a·try
po·di·um
po·dia
po·di·ums
Po·dunk
po·em
po·et·ic
po·et·i·cal
po·et·i·cal·ly
po·e·sy
po·e·sies
po·et
po·et·ess
po·et·ize
po·et·ized
po·et·iz·ing
po·et·iz·er
po·et lau·re·ate
po·ets lau·re·ate
po·et·ry
po·go
po·grom
poign·ant
poign·an·cy
poig·nant·ly
poin·set·tia
point-blank
point·ed
point·ed·ly
point·ed·ness
point·er
poin·til·lism
poin·til·list
point·less
Poi·ret
poise
poised
pois·ing
poi·son
poi·son·er
poi·son·ing
poi·son·ous
poi·son-pen
Poi·tiers
poke
poked
pok·ing
pok·er
poky
pok·i·er
pok·i·est
pok·i·ly
pok·i·ness
Po·land
po·lar
Po·lar·is
po·lar·i·ty
po·lar·i·ties
po·lar·i·za·tion
po·lar·ize
po·lar·ized
po·lar·iz·ing
po·lar·iz·a·ble

po·lar·iz·er
Po·lar·oid
pole
poled
pol·ing
pole·less
pole·cat
po·lem·ic
po·lem·i·cal
po·lem·i·cal·ly
po·lem·i·cist
po·lem·ics
pole·star
po·lice
po·liced
po·lic·ing
pol·i·cy
pol·i·cies
pol·i·cy·hold·er
po·lio
pol·i·o·my·e·li·tis
pol·ish
pol·ish·er
po·lite
po·lite·ly
po·lite·ness
pol·i·tic
po·lit·i·cal
po·lit·i·cal·ly
pol·i·ti·cian
po·lit·i·cize
po·lit·i·cized
po·lit·i·ciz·ing
pol·i·tick
pol·i·tick·er
pol·i·tics
pol·i·ty
pol·i·ties
pol·ka
pol·kaed
pol·ka·ing
poll
poll·ee
poll·er
pol·len
pol·li·nate
pol·li·nat·ed
pol·li·nat·ing
pol·li·na·tion
pol·li·na·tor
pol·li·wog
poll·ster
pol·lu·tant
pol·lute
pol·lut·ed
pol·lut·ing
pol·lu·ter
pol·lu·tion
Pol·ly·an·na
po·lo
po·lo·ist
pol·o·naise
po·lo·ni·um
pol·ter·geist
pol·y·an·dry

pol·y·an·drous
pol·y·chro·mat·ic
pol·y·chrome
pol·y·es·ter
pol·y·eth·yl·ene
po·lyg·a·mist
po·lyg·a·my
po·lyg·a·mous
pol·y·glot
pol·y·gon
po·lyg·o·nal
po·lyg·o·nal·ly
pol·y·graph
pol·y·graph·ic
po·lyg·y·ny
po·lyg·y·nous
pol·y·he·dron
pol·y·he·drons
pol·y·he·dra
pol·y·he·dral
pol·y·mer
pol·y·mer·ize
pol·y·mer·ized
pol·y·mer·iz·ing
po·lym·er·ism
po·lym·er·i·za·tion
pol·y·mor·phism
pol·y·mor·phic
pol·y·mor·phous
Poly·ne·sia
pol·y·no·mi·al
pol·yp
pol·y·phon·ic
po·lyph·o·ny
pol·y·sty·rene
pol·y·syl·lab·ic
pol·y·syl·lab·i·cal·ly
pol·y·syl·la·ble
pol·y·tech·nic
pol·y·the·ism
po·y·the·ist
pol·y·the·is·tic
pol·y·the·is·ti·cal
pol·y·un·sat·u·rat·ed
pom·ace
po·made
po·mad·ed
po·mad·ing
pome·gran·ate
Pom·er·a·nia
pom·mel
pom·meled
pom·mel·ing
pom·pa·dour
Pom·peii
Pom·pey
pom·pon
pomp·ous
pom·pos·i·ty
pom·pous·ly
pom·pous·ness
Pon·ce
Pon·ce de Le·ón
pon·cho
pon·der

pon·der·a·ble
pon·der·er
pon·der·ous
pon·der·ous·ly
pon·der·ous·ness
pon·iard
Pon·ti·ac
pon·tiff
pon·tif·i·cal
pon·tif·i·cal·ly
pon·tif·i·cate
pon·tif·i·cat·ed
pon·tif·i·cat·ing
Pon·tius
pon·toon
po·ny
po·nies
po·nied
po·ny·ing
po·ny·tail
poo·dle
pool·room
poor
poor·ish
poor·ly
poor·ness
pop·corn
pop·ery
pop·ish
pop·eyed
pop·gun
pop·in·jay
pop·lar
pop·lin
Po·po·ca·te·petl
pop·per
pop·py
pop·pies
pop·pied
pop·py·cock
pop·u·lace
pop·u·lar
pop·u·lar·ly
pop·u·lar·i·ty
pop·u·lar·ize
pop·u·lar·ized
pop·u·lar·iz·ing
pop·u·lar·i·za·tion
pop·u·lar·iz·er
pop·u·late
pop·u·lat·ed
pop·u·lat·ing
pop·u·la·tion
pop·u·lism
pop·u·list
pop·u·lous
pop·u·lous·ly
por·ce·lain
por·cine
por·cu·pine
pore
pored
por·ing
pork·er
por·nog·ra·phy

por·nog·ra·pher
por·no·graph·ic
por·no·graph·i·cal·ly
po·rous
  po·ros·i·ty
  po·rous·ly
  po·rous·ness
por·poise
  por·pois·es
por·ridge
port·a·ble
  port·a·bil·i·ty
  port·a·bly
por·tage
  por·taged
  por·tag·ing
por·tal
Port-au-Prince
por·tend
por·tent
  por·ten·tous
por·ter
por·ter·house
port·fo·lio
  port·fo·li·os
port·hole
Por·tia
por·ti·co
  por·ti·coes
  por·ti·cos
por·tion
  por·tion·less
Port·land
port·ly
  port·li·er
  port·li·est
  port·li·ness
por·trait
  por·trait·ist
por·trai·ture
por·tray
  por·tray·er
  por·tray·al
Ports·mouth
Por·tu·gal
Por·tu·guese
pose
  posed
  pos·ing
Po·sei·don
pos·er
po·seur
pos·it
po·si·tion
  po·si·tion·al
  po·si·tion·er
pos·i·tive
  pos·i·tive·ly
  pos·i·tive·ness
pos·i·tiv·ism
pos·i·tron
pos·se
pos·sess
  pos·ses·sor
  pos·sessed

pos·ses·sion
pos·ses·sive
  pos·ses·sive·ly
  pos·ses·sive·ness
pos·si·bil·i·ty
pos·si·ble
pos·si·bly
pos·sum
post·age
post·box
post·date
  post·dat·ed
  post·dat·ing
post·er
pos·te·ri·or
  pos·te·ri·or·i·ty
pos·ter·i·ty
post·grad·u·ate
post·haste
post·hu·mous
  post·hu·mous·ly
post·lude
post·man
post·men
post·mark
post·mas·ter
  post·mis·tress
post me·rid·i·em
post-mor·tem
post·na·sal
post·na·tal
  post·na·tal·ly
post·paid
post·par·tum
post·pone
  post·poned
  post·pon·ing
  post·pon·a·ble
  post·pone·ment
  post·pon·er
post·script
pos·tu·lant
pos·tu·late
  pos·tu·lat·ed
  pos·tu·lat·ing
  pos·tu·la·tion
  pos·tu·la·tor
pos·ture
  pos·tured
  pos·tur·ing
  pos·tur·al
  pos·tur·er
post·war
po·sy
  po·sies
pot
  pot·ted
  pot·ting
po·ta·ble
pot·ash
po·tas·si·um
po·ta·to
  po·ta·toes
pot·bel·ly
  pot·bel·lied

pot·boil·er
po·tent
  po·ten·cy
  po·tent·ly
po·ten·tate
po·ten·tial
  po·ten·ti·al·i·ty
  po·ten·tial·ly
pot·hole
po·tion
pot·luck
Po·to·mac
pot·pour·ri
Pots·dam
pot·sherd
pot·tage
pot·ter
pot·tery
  pot·ter·ies
pot·ty
  pot·ties
pot·ty-chair
pouch
  pouched
  pouchy
  pouch·i·er
  pouch·i·est
Pough·keep·sie
poul·tice
  poul·ticed
  poul·tic·ing
poul·try
pounce
  pounced
  pounc·ing
pound·age
pound-fool·ish
pour
  pour·a·ble
  pour·er
pout
pov·er·ty
pov·er·ty-strick·en
pow·der
  pow·dery
Pow·ell
pow·er
pow·er·boat
pow·er·ful
  pow·er·ful·ly
  pow·er·ful·ness
pow·er·house
pow·er·less
Pow·ha·tan
pow·wow
prac·ti·ca·ble
  prac·ti·ca·bil·i·ty
  prac·ti·ca·ble·ness
  prac·ti·ca·bly
prac·ti·cal
  prac·ti·cal·i·ty
  prac·ti·cal·ly
prac·tice
prac·ticed
prac·ti·tion·er

prae·di·al
pre·di·al
prag·mat·ic
  prag·mat·i·cal
  prag·mat·i·cal·ly
  prag·mat·i·cal·ness
prag·ma·tism
prag·ma·tist
prag·ma·tis·tic
prai·rie
praise
  praised
  prais·ing
  prais·er
praise·wor·thy
  praise·wor·thi·ly
  praise·wor·thi·ness
pra·line
prance
  pranced
  pranc·ing
  pranc·er
prank
  prank·ish
  prank·ster
prate
  prat·ed
  prat·ing
  prat·er
  prat·ing·ly
prat·fall
prat·tle
  prat·tled
  prat·tling
  prat·tler
  prat·tling·ly
prawn
  prawn·er
prayer
pray·er
  prayer·ful
preach
  preach·er
preach·i·fy
  preach·i·fied
  preach·i·fy·ing
preach·ment
preachy
  preach·i·er
  preach·i·est
pre·ad·o·les·cence
  pre·ad·o·les·cent
pre·am·ble
pre·ar·range
  pre·ar·ranged
  pre·ar·rang·ing
  pre·ar·range·ment
pre·as·signed
pre·can·cel
  pre·can·celed
  pre·can·cel·ing
  pre·can·cel·la·tion
pre·car·i·ous
  pre·car·i·ous·ly
  pre·car·i·ous·ness

pre·cau·tion
  pre·cau·tion·ary
pre·cede
  pre·ced·ed
  pre·ced·ing
prec·e·dence
prec·e·dent
pre·cept
pre·cep·tive
pre·cep·tor
  pre·cep·to·ri·al
pre·ces·sion
  pre·ces·sion·al
pre·cinct
pre·cious
  pre·ci·os·i·ty
  pre·cious·ness
prec·i·pice
pre·cip·i·tant
  pre·cip·i·tant·ly
  pre·cip·i·tant·ness
pre·cip·i·tate
  pre·cip·i·tat·ed
  pre·cip·i·tat·ing
  pre·cip·i·ta·tive
  pre·cip·i·ta·tor
  pre·cip·i·ta·tion
pre·cip·i·tous
  pre·cip·i·tous·ly
  pre·cip·i·tous·ness
pré·cis
pre·cise
  pre·cise·ness
pre·ci·sion
  pre·ci·sion·ist
pre·clude
  pre·clud·ed
  pre·clud·ing
  pre·clu·sion
  pre·clu·sive
pre·co·cious
  pre·co·cious·ly
  pre·co·cious·ness
  pre·coc·i·ty
pre·cog·ni·tion
  pre·cog·ni·tive
pre·con·ceive
  pre·con·ceived
  pre·con·ceiv·ing
  pre·con·cep·tion
pre·cook
pre·cur·sor
  pre·cur·so·ry
pre·date
pred·a·tor
pred·a·to·ry
  pred·a·to·ri·ly
pre·dawn
pred·e·ces·sor
pre·des·ti·nate
  pre·des·ti·nat·ed
  pre·des·ti·nat·ing
  pre·des·ti·na·tion
pre·des·tine

pre·des·tined
pre·des·tin·ing
pre·de·ter·mine
  pre·de·ter·mined
  pre·de·ter·min·ing
  pre·de·ter·mi·na·tion
pred·i·ca·ble
  pred·i·ca·bil·i·ty
pre·dic·a·ment
pred·i·cate
  pred·i·cat·ed
  pred·i·cat·ing
  pred·i·ca·tion
  pred·i·ca·tive
pre·dict
  pre·dict·a·ble
  pre·dict·a·bly
  pre·dict·a·bil·i·ty
  pre·dic·tion
  pre·dic·tive
pre·di·lec·tion
pre·dis·po·si·tion
  pre·dis·pose
  pre·dis·posed
  pre·dis·pos·ing
pre·dom·i·nant
  pre·dom·i·nance
  pre·dom·i·nan·cy
pre·dom·i·nate
  pre·dom·i·nat·ed
  pre·dom·i·nat·ing
  pre·dom·i·na·tion
pre·em·i·nent
  pre·em·i·nence
pre·empt
  pre·emp·tor
  pre·emp·tion
  pre·emp·tive
preen·er
pre·ex·ist
  pre·ex·ist·ence
  pre·ex·ist·ent
pre·fab·ri·cate
  pre·fab·ri·cat·ed
  pre·fab·ri·cat·ing
  pre·fab·ri·ca·tion
pref·ace
  pref·aced
  pref·ac·ing
  pref·a·to·ry
pre·fer
  per·ferred
  pre·fer·ring
  pre·fer·rer
pref·er·a·ble
  pref·er·a·ble·ness
  pre·fer·a·bil·i·ty
  pref·er·a·bly
pref·er·ence
pref·er·en·tial
  pref·er·en·tial·ly
pre·fer·ment
pre·fix
pre·flight
pre·form

preg·na·ble
  preg·na·bil·i·ty
preg·nan·cy
  preg·nan·cies
preg·nant
pre·heat
pre·hen·sile
  pre·hen·sil·i·ty
pre·his·tor·ic
pre·his·to·ry
pre·judge
  pre·judged
  pre·judg·ing
  pre·judg·er
  pre·judg·ment
prej·u·dice
  prej·u·diced
  prej·u·dic·ing
prej·u·di·cial
  prej·u·di·cial·ly
  prej·u·di·cial·ness
prel·ate
  prel·ate·ship
  prel·a·ture
pre·lim·i·nary
  pre·lim·i·nar·ies
  pre·lim·i·nar·i·ly
prel·ude
  prel·ud·ed
  prel·ud·ing
pre·ma·ture
  pre·ma·ture·ness
  pre·ma·tu·ri·ty
pre·med·i·cal
pre·med·i·tate
  pre·med·i·tat·ed
  pre·med·i·tat·ing
  pre·med·i·ta·tor
  pre·med·i·tat·ed·ly
  pre·med·i·ta·tive
  pre·med·i·ta·tion
pre·men·stru·al
pre·mier
  pre·mier·ship
pre·miere
prem·ise
  prem·ised
  prem·is·ing
pre·mi·um
pre·mo·ni·tion
  pre·mon·i·to·ry
  pre·mon·i·to·ri·ly
pre·na·tal
  pre·na·tal·ly
pre·oc·cu·pa·tion
pre·oc·cu·py
  pre·oc·cu·pied
  pre·oc·cu·py·ing
prep·a·ra·tion
pre·par·a·to·ry
  pre·par·a·to·ri·ly
pre·pare
  pre·pared
  pre·par·ing
  pre·par·er

pre·par·ed·ness
pre·pay
  pre·paid
  pre·pay·ing
  pre·pay·ment
pre·plan
  pre·planned
  pre·plan·ning
pre·pon·der·ant
  pre·pon·der·ance
  pre·pon·der·an·cy
  pre·pon·der·ant·ly
pre·pon·der·ate
  pre·pon·der·at·ed
  pre·pon·der·at·ing
  pre·pon·der·at·ing·ly
  pre·pon·der·a·tion
prep·o·si·tion
  prep·o·si·tion·al
pre·pos·sess
  pre·pos·sess·ing
  pre·pos·sess·ing·ly
pre·pos·ter·ous
pre·puce
  pre·pu·tial
pre·re·cord
pre·req·ui·site
pre·rog·a·tive
pres·age
  pres·aged
  pres·ag·ing
  pres·ag·er
Pres·by·te·ri·an
  Pres·by·te·ri·an·ism
pres·by·tery
  pres·by·ter·ies
pre·school
pre·scribe
  pre·scribed
  pre·scrib·ing
  pre·scrib·er
pre·script
  pre·scrip·tion
  pre·scrip·tive
pre·sea·son
pres·ence
pre·sent
  pre·sent·er
pres·ent
  pre·sent·a·ble
  pre·sent·a·bil·i·ty
  pre·sent·a·ble·ness
  pre·sent·a·bly
pres·en·ta·tion
pres·ent-day
pres·ent·ly
pre·serv·a·tive
pre·serve
  pre·served
  pre·serv·ing
  pre·serv·a·ble
  pres·er·va·tion
  pre·serv·er
pre·side
  pre·sid·ed

pre·sid·ing
pre·sid·er
pres·i·den·cy
pres·i·den·cies
pres·i·dent
pres·i·den·tial
press·board
press·ing
pres·sure
pres·sured
pres·sur·ing
pres·su·rize
pres·su·rized
pres·su·riz·ing
pres·su·riz·er
pres·sur·i·za·tion
press·work
pres·ti·dig·i·ta·tion
pres·ti·dig·i·ta·tor
pres·tige
pres·tig·ious
pres·to
pre·sum·a·ble
pre·sum·a·bly
pre·sume
pre·sumed
pre·sum·ing
pre·sum·er
pre·sump·tion
pre·sump·tive
pre·sump·tu·ous
pre·sup·pose
pre·sup·posed
pre·sup·pos·ing
pre·sup·po·si·tion
pre·tend
pre·tend·ed
pre·tend·er
pre·tense
pre·ten·sion
pre·ten·tious
pre·ten·tious·ness
pre·test
pre·text
Pre·to·ria
pret·ti·fy
pret·ti·fied
pret·ti·fy·ing
pret·ti·fi·ca·tion
pret·ty
pret·ties
pret·tied
pret·ty·ing
pret·ti·ly
pret·ti·ness
pret·ty·ish
pret·zel
pre·vail
pre·vail·ing
prev·a·lent
prev·a·lence
pre·vent
pre·vent·a·ble
pre·vent·a·bil·i·ty
pre·vent·er

pre·ven·tion
pre·view
pre·vi·ous
pre·war
prey
prey·er
price·less
prick·er
prick·le
prick·ly
prick·li·er
prick·li·est
prick·li·ness
pride
prid·ed
prid·ing
pride·ful
pri·er
priest
priest·ess
priest·hood
priest·ly
priest·li·er
priest·li·est
priest·li·ness
prig
prig·gish
prim
prim·mer
prim·mest
primmed
prim·ming
prim·ness
pri·ma·cy
pri·ma·cies
pri·ma don·na
pri·ma don·nas
pri·mal
pri·ma·ri·ly
pri·ma·ry
pri·mar·ies
pri·mate
prime
primed
prim·ing
prime me·rid·i·an
prim·er
pri·me·val
prim·i·tive
pri·mo·gen·i·tor
pri·mo·gen·i·ture
pri·mor·di·al
pri·mor·di·al·ly
primp
prim·rose
prince·ly
prince·li·er
prince·li·est
prince·li·ness
prin·cess
Prince·ton
prin·ci·pal
prin·ci·pal·ly
prin·ci·pal·i·ty
prin·ci·pal·i·ties

prin·ci·ple
prin·ci·pled
print·a·ble
print·ing
print-out
pri·or
 pri·or·ate
pri·or·ess
pri·or·i·ty
 pri·or·i·ties
pri·ory
 pri·or·ies
prism
 pris·mat·ic
 pris·mat·i·cal·ly
pris·on
 pris·on·er
pris·sy
 pris·si·er
 pris·si·est
 pris·si·ly
 pris·si·ness
pris·tine
pri·va·cy
pri·vate
pri·va·tion
priv·et
priv·i·lege
 priv·i·leged
 priv·i·leg·ing
privy
 priv·ies
 priv·i·ly
prize
 prized
 priz·ing
prize·fight
 prize·fight·er
 prize·fight·ing
prob·a·bil·i·ty
 prob·a·bil·i·ties
prob·a·ble
 prob·a·bly
pro·bate
 pro·bat·ed
 pro·bat·ing
pro·ba·tion
 pro·ba·tion·al
 pro·ba·tion·ary
 pro·ba·tion·al·ly
pro·ba·tion·er
pro·ba·tive
probe
 probed
 prob·ing
 prob·er
prob·lem
prob·lem·at·ic
 prob·lem·at·i·cal
pro·bos·cis
 pro·bos·cis·es
 pro·bos·ci·des
pro·ce·dure
 pro·ce·dur·al
 pro·ce·dur·al·ly

pro·ceed
pro·ceed·ing
pro·ceeds
proc·ess
pro·ces·sion
pro·ces·sion·al
pro·claim
 pro·claim·er
proc·la·ma·tion
pro·cliv·i·ty
 pro·cliv·i·ties
pro·cras·ti·nate
 pro·cras·ti·nat·ed
 pro·cras·ti·nat·ing
 pro·cras·ti·na·tion
 pro·cras·ti·na·tor
pro·cre·ate
 pro·cre·at·ed
 pro·cre·at·ing
 pro·cre·a·tion
 pro·cre·a·tive
 pro·cre·a·tor
Pro·crus·tes
proc·tor
 proc·to·ri·al
proc·u·ra·tor
 proc·u·ra·to·ri·al
 proc·u·ra·tor·ship
pro·cure
 pro·cured
 pro·cur·ing
 pro·cur·a·ble
 pro·cur·ance
 pro·cure·ment
 pro·cur·er
prod
 prod·ded
 prod·ding
 prod·der
prod·i·gal
 prod·i·gal·i·ty
 prod·i·gal·ly
pro·di·gious
 pro·di·gious·ness
prod·i·gy
 prod·i·gies
pro·duce
 pro·duced
 pro·duc·ing
 pro·duc·er
prod·uct
pro·duc·tion
pro·duc·tive
 pro·duc·tive·ness
 pro·duc·tiv·i·ty
pro·fane
 pro·faned
 pro·fan·ing
 pro·fan·a·to·ry
 pro·fane·ness
 pro·fan·er
 pro·fan·i·ty
pro·fess
 pro·fessed
 pro·fess·ed·ly

pro·fes·sion
pro·fes·sion·al
  pro·fes·sion·al·ism
  pro·fes·sion·al·ize
  pro·fes·sion·al·ized
  pro·fes·sion·al·iz·ing
pro·fes·sor
  pro·fes·so·ri·al
  pro·fes·so·ri·al·ly
  pro·fes·sor·ship
prof·fer
  prof·fer·er
pro·fi·cien·cy
pro·fi·cient
pro·file
  pro·filed
  pro·fil·ing
prof·it
  prof·it·less
prof·it·a·ble
  prof·it·a·bil·i·ty
  prof·it·a·ble·ness
  prof·it·a·bly
prof·it·eer
prof·li·gate
  prof·li·ga·cy
pro·found
pro·fun·di·ty
  pro·fun·di·ties
pro·fuse
pro·fu·sion
pro·gen·i·tor
prog·e·ny
  prog·e·nies
pro·ges·ter·one
prog·no·sis
  prog·no·ses
prog·nos·tic
prog·nos·ti·cate
  prog·nos·ti·cat·ed
  prog·nos·ti·cat·ing
  prog·nos·ti·ca·tion
  prog·nos·ti·ca·tive
  prog·nos·ti·ca·tor
pro·gram
  pro·grammed
  pro·gram·ming
  pro·gramed
  pro·gram·ing
  pro·gram·mer
  pro·gram·er
prog·ress
pro·gres·sion
pro·gres·sive
  pro·gres·siv·ism
pro·hib·it
pro·hi·bi·tion
  pro·hi·bi·tion·ist
pro·hib·i·tive
pro·ject
pro·jec·tile
pro·jec·tion
  pro·jec·tion·ist
pro·jec·tive
  pro·jec·tive·ly

pro·jec·tiv·i·ty
pro·jec·tor
pro·le·tar·i·at
  pro·le·tar·i·an
pro·lif·er·ate
  pro·lif·er·at·ed
  pro·lif·er·at·ing
  pro·lif·er·a·tion
  pro·lif·er·a·tive
pro·lif·ic
  pro·lif·i·ca·cy
  pro·lif·ic·ness
  pro·lif·i·cal·ly
pro·lix
  pro·lix·i·ty
  pro·lix·ly
  pro·lix·ness
pro·logue
  pro·logued
  pro·log·uing
pro·long
  pro·lon·ga·tion
  pro·long·er
prom·e·nade
  prom·e·nad·ed
  prom·e·nad·ing
  prom·e·nad·er
Pro·me·theus
prom·i·nence
prom·i·nent
  prom·i·nent·ly
pro·mis·cu·i·ty
  pro·mis·cu·i·ties
pro·mis·cu·ous
  pro·mis·cu·ous·ly
  pro·mis·cu·ous·ness
prom·ise
  prom·ised
  prom·is·ing
  prom·is·a·ble
  prom·is·er
  prom·ise·ful
  prom·is·so·ry
prom·on·to·ry
  prom·on·to·ries
pro·mote
  pro·mot·ed
  pro·mot·ing
  pro·mot·a·ble
pro·mot·er
pro·mo·tion
pro·mo·tive
prompt
  prompt·er
  prompt·ly
  prompt·ness
prom·ul·gate
  prom·ul·gat·ed
  prom·ul·gat·ing
  prom·ul·ga·tion
prone
prong
pro·noun
pro·nounce
  pro·nounced

pro·nounc·ing
pro·nounce·a·ble
pro·nounce·er
pro·nounce·ment
pron·to
pro·nun·ci·a·tion
proof
proof·read
 proof·read·ing
 proof·read·er
prop
 propped
 prop·ping
prop·a·gan·da
 prop·a·gan·dist
 prop·a·gan·dis·tic
 prop·a·gan·dis·ti·cal·ly
 prop·a·gan·dism
 prop·a·gan·dize
 prop·a·gan·dized
 prop·a·gan·diz·ing
prop·a·gate
 prop·a·gat·ed
 prop·a·gat·ing
 prop·a·ga·tive
 prop·a·ga·tor
prop·a·ga·tion
 prop·a·ga·tion·al
pro·pane
pro·pel
 pro·pelled
 pro·pel·ling
 pro·pel·lant
 pro·pel·ler
pro·pen·si·ty
 pro·pen·si·ties
prop·er
 prop·er·ly
 prop·er·ness
prop·er·ty
 prop·er·ties
 prop·er·tied
 prop·er·ty·less
proph·e·cy
 proph·e·cies
proph·e·sy
 proph·e·sied
 proph·e·sy·ing
 proph·e·si·er
proph·et
pro·phet·ic
 pro·phet·i·cal
 pro·phet·i·cal·ly
pro·phy·lax·is
pro·pin·qui·ty
pro·pi·ti·ate
 pro·pi·ti·at·ed
 pro·pi·ti·at·ing
 pro·pi·ti·a·tion
 pro·pi·ti·a·to·ry
pro·pi·tious
 pro·pi·tious·ly
pro·po·nent
pro·por·tion
 pro·por·tion·a·ble

pro·por·tion·a·bly
pro·por·tion·al
 pro·por·tion·al·i·ty
pro·por·tion·ate
 pro·por·tion·at·ed
 pro·por·tion·at·ing
pro·pos·al
pro·pose
 pro·posed
 pro·pos·ing
 pro·pos·er
prop·o·si·tion
 pro·o·si·tion·al
pro·pound
 pro·pound·er
pro·pri·e·tary
 pro·pri·e·tar·ies
pro·pri·e·tor
 pro·pri·e·tor·ship
pro·pri·e·ty
 pro·pri·e·ties
pro·pul·sion
 pro·pul·sive
pro·rate
 pro·rat·ed
 pro·rat·ing
 pro·ra·tion
pro·sa·ic
 pro·sa·i·cal·ly
 pro·sa·ic·ness
pro·scribe
 pro·scribed
 pro·scrib·ing
 pro·scrib·er
pro·scrip·tion
 pro·scrip·tive
prose
 prosed
 pros·ing
pros·e·cute
 pros·e·cut·a·ble
 pros·e·cu·tion
 pros·e·cu·tor
pros·pect
 pros·pec·tor
 pro·spec·tive
 pro·spec·tus
pros·per
 pros·per·i·ty
 pros·per·ous
pros·tate
pros·the·sis
 pros·the·ses
 pros·thet·ic
 pros·thet·i·cal·ly
 pros·thet·ics
 pros·the·tist
pros·tho·don·tics
 pros·tho·don·tist
pros·ti·tute
 pros·ti·tut·ed
 pros·ti·tut·ing
 pros·ti·tu·tion
 pros·ti·tu·tor
pros·trate

pros·trat·ed
pros·trat·ing
pros·tra·tion
pros·tra·tor
pros·tra·tive
prosy
pros·i·er
pros·i·est
pros·i·ly
pros·i·ness
pro·tag·o·nist
pro·te·an
pro·tect
pro·tect·ing
pro·tec·tive
pro·tec·tive·ly
pro·tec·tive·ness
pro·tec·tor
pro·tec·tion
pro·tec·tion·ism
pro·tec·tion·ist
pro·tec·tor·ate
pro·té·gé
pro·tein
pro·test
Prot·es·tant
Prot·es·tant·ism
prot·es·ta·tion
pro·tist
pro·tis·tan
pro·to·col
pro·ton
pro·to·plasm
pro·to·plas·mic
pro·to·type
pro·to·ty·pal
pro·to·typ·ic
pro·to·zo·an
pro·to·zo·ic
pro·tract
pro·trac·tion
pro·trac·tive
pro·trac·tile
pro·trac·tor
pro·trude
pro·trud·ed
pro·trud·ing
pro·trud·ent
pro·tru·si·ble
pro·tru·sion
pro·tru·sive
pro·tu·ber·ance
pro·tu·ber·ant
proud
proud·ly
proud·ness
prove
proved
prov·en
prov·ing
prov·a·ble
prov·a·bly
prov·er
Pro·ven·cal
Prov·ence

prov·erb
pro·ver·bi·al
pro·ver·bi·al·ly
pro·vide
pro·vid·ed
pro·vid·ing
pro·vid·a·ble
pro·vid·er
prov·i·dence
prov·i·den·tial
prov·i·dent
prov·ince
Prov·ince·town
pro·vin·cial
pro·vin·ci·al·i·ty
pro·vin·cial·ly
pro·vin·cial·ist
pro·vin·cial·ize
pro·vin·cial·ized
pro·vin·cial·iz·ing
pro·vin·cial·ism
pro·vi·sion
pro·vi·sion·er
pro·vi·sion·al
pro·vi·sion·ary
prov·o·ca·tion
pro·voc·a·tive
pro·voc·a·tive·ly
pro·voc·a·tive·ness
pro·voke
pro·voked
pro·vok·ing
pro·vok·ing·ly
prov·ost
prow·ess
prowl
prowl·er
prox·i·mal
prox·i·mate
prox·i·mate·ly
prox·im·i·ty
proxy
prox·ies
prude
pru·dence
pru·dent
pru·den·tial
prud·ery
prud·er·ies
prud·ish
prune
pruned
prun·ing
prun·er
pru·ri·ent
pru·ri·ence
pru·ri·en·cy
Prus·sia
Prus·sian
pry
pried
pry·ing
pry·er
pri·er
psalm·book

psalm·ist
Psal·ter
pseu·do
pseu·do·nym
 pseu·don·y·mous
pseu·do·preg·nan·cy
 pseu·do·preg·nant
pseu·do·sci·ence
 pseu·do·sci·en·tif·ic
pshaw
psil·o·cy·bin
pso·ri·a·sis
 pso·ri·at·ic
psych
 psyched
 psych·ing
Psy·che
psych·e·del·ic
psy·chi·a·trist
psy·chi·a·try
 psy·chi·at·ric
 psy·chi·at·ri·cal·ly
psy·chic
 psy·chi·cal
 psy·chi·cal·ly
psy·cho
psy·cho·a·nal·y·sis
 psy·cho·an·a·lyt·ic
 psy·cho·an·a·lyt·i·cal
psy·cho·an·a·lyst
 psy·cho·an·a·lyze
 psy·cho·an·a·lyzed
 psy·cho·an·a·lyz·ing
psy·cho·bi·ol·o·gy
 psy·cho·bi·o·log·ic
 psy·cho·bi·o·log·i·cal
 psy·cho·bi·ol·o·gist
psy·cho·dra·ma
psy·cho·dy·nam·ic
 psy·cho·dy·nam·i·cal·ly
 psy·cho·dy·nam·ics
psy·cho·gen·e·sis
 pry·cho·ge·net·ic
 psy·cho·ge·net·i·cal·ly
psy·cho·gen·ic
 psy·cho·gen·i·cal·ly
psy·cho·log·i·cal
 psy·cho·log·ic
 psy·cho·log·i·cal·ly
psy·chol·o·gist
psy·chol·o·gy
psy·cho·mo·tor
psy·cho·neu·ro·sis
 psy·cho·neu·ro·ses
 psy·cho·neu·rot·ic
psy·cho·path
psy·cho·pa·thol·o·gy
 psy·cho·pa·thol·o·gist
 psy·cho·path·o·log·ic
 psy·cho·path·o·log·i·cal
psy·chop·a·thy
 psy·cho·path·ic
 psy·cho·path·i·cal·ly
psy·cho·sis
 psy·cho·ses

psy·chot·ic
 psy·chot·i·cal·ly
psy·cho·so·mat·ic
 psy·cho·so·mat·i·cal·ly
psy·cho·ther·a·py
 psy·cho·ther·a·peu·tics
 psy·cho·ther·a·peu·tic
 psy·cho·ther·a·peu·ti·cal·ly
 psy·cho·ther·a·pist
Ptol·e·my
pto·maine
pu·ber·ty
pu·bes·cence
 pu·bes·cen·cy
 pu·bes·cent
pu·bic
pub·lic
 pub·lic·ly
 pub·lic·ness
pub·li·ca·tion
 pub·li·cist
 pub·lic·i·ty
 pub·li·cize
 pub·li·cized
 pub·li·ciz·ing
pub·lish
 pub·lish·a·ble
 pub·lish·er
Puc·ci·ni
puce
puck·er
pud·ding
pud·dle
 pud·dled
 pud·dling
pudgy
 pudg·i·er
 pudg·i·est
 pudg·i·ness
pueb·lo
 pueb·los
pu·er·ile
 pu·er·il·i·ty
Puer·to Ri·co
puff
 puff·i·ness
puffy
 puff·i·er
 puff·i·est
puff·er
pu·gil·ism
 pu·gil·ist
 pu·gil·is·tic
pug·na·cious
 pug·na·cious·ness
 pug·nac·i·ty
puke
 puked
 puk·ing
Pu·las·ki
Pul·itz·er
pull·back
pul·let
pul·ley
Pull·man

pull·out
pull·o·ver
pul·mo·nary
pulp
  pulp·i·ness
  pulpy
  pulp·i·er
  pulp·i·est
pul·pit
pulp·wood
pul·sate
  pul·sat·ed
  pul·sat·ing
pul·sa·tion
pul·sa·tor
  pul·sa·to·ry
pulse
  pulsed
  puls·ing
pul·ver·ize
  pul·ver·ized
  pul·ver·iz·ing
  pul·ver·iz·a·ble
  pul·ver·i·za·tion
  pul·ver·iz·er
pu·ma
  pu·mas
pum·ice
  pu·mi·ceous
pum·mel
  pum·meled
  pum·melled
  pum·mel·ing
  pum·mel·ling
pump
  pump·a·ble
  pump·er
pum·per·nick·el
pump·kin
pun
  punned
  pun·ning
punch
  punch·er
punch-drunk
punchy
  punch·i·er
  punch·i·est
punc·tu·al
  punc·tu·al·i·ty
  punc·tu·al·ly
  punc·tu·al·ness
punc·tu·ate
  punc·tu·at·ed
  punc·tu·at·ing
  punc·tu·a·tor
punc·tu·a·tion
punc·ture
  punc·tured
  punc·tur·ing
  punc·tur·a·ble
pun·dit
pun·gent
  pun·gen·cy
  pun·gent·ly

Pu·nic
pun·ish
  pun·ish·a·ble
pun·ish·ment
pu·ni·tive
pun·ster
punt·er
pu·ny
  pu·ni·er
  pu·ni·est
  pu·ni·ness
pup
  pupped
  pup·ping
pu·pa
  pu·pae
  pu·pas
  pu·pal
pu·pate
  pu·pat·ed
  pu·pat·ing
  pu·pa·tion
pu·pil
  pu·pil·ar
  pu·pil·lary
Pu·pin
pup·pet
  pup·pet·eer
  pup·pet·ry
  pup·pet·ries
pup·py
  pup·pies
  pup·py·ish
pur·chase
  pur·chased
  pur·chas·ing
  pur·chas·a·ble
  pur·chas·er
Pur·due
pure
  pure·ly
  pure·ness
pu·rée
  pu·réed
  pu·rée·ing
pur·ga·tive
pur·ga·to·ry
  pur·ga·to·ries
  pur·ga·to·ri·al
purge
  purged
  purg·ing
  purg·er
pu·ri·fy
  pu·ri·fied
  pu·ri·fy·ing
  pu·ri·fi·ca·tion
  pu·ri·fi·er
Pu·rim
pur·ism
pur·ist
  pu·ris·tic
pu·ri·tan
  pu·ri·tan·i·cal
  pu·ri·tan·i·cal·ly

pu·ri·ty
purl
pur·loin
  pur·loin·er
pur·ple
  pur·pled
  pur·pling
  pur·plish
pur·port
  pur·port·ed
  pur·port·ed·ly
pur·pose
  pur·posed
  pur·pos·ing
  pur·pose·ful
  pur·pose·ful·ly
  pur·pose·ly
  pur·pos·ive
purse
  pursed
  purs·ing
purs·er
pur·su·ant
pur·sue
  pur·sued
  pur·su·ing
  pur·su·er
pur·suit
pur·sy
  pur·si·er
  pur·si·est
  pur·si·ness
pu·ru·lent
  pu·ru·lence
  pu·ru·len·cy
  pu·ru·lent·ly
pur·vey
  pur·vey·or
pur·vey·ance
pur·view
pushy
  push·i·er
  push·i·est
  push·i·ly
  push·i·ness
push·cart
push·o·ver
pu·sil·lan·i·mous
  pu·sil·la·nim·i·ty
  pu·sil·lan·i·mous·ly
pussy
  puss·ies
puss·y·foot
puss·y·wil·low
pus·tule
  pus·tu·lar
  pus·tu·late
put
  put·ting
pu·ta·tive
  pu·ta·tive·ly
put-on
pu·tre·fac·tion
pu·tre·fy
  pu·tre·fied

pu·tre·fy·ing
pu·trid
  pu·trid·i·ty
  pu·trid·ness
putt
  putt·ed
  putt·ing
put·ter
  put·ter·er
put·ty
  put·tied
  put·ty·ing
put-up
puz·zle
  puz·zled
  puz·zling
  puz·zler
puz·zle·ment
Pyg·ma·lion
Pyg·my
  Pyg·mies
py·lon
P'yong·yang
pyr·a·mid
  py·ram·i·dal
Pyr·a·mus
pyre
Pyr·e·nees
Py·rex
py·ric
py·ro·ma·nia
  py·ro·ma·ni·ac
  py·ro·ma·ni·a·cal
py·rom·e·ter
  py·rom·e·try
py·ro·tech·nics
  py·ro·tech·nic
  py·ro·tech·ni·cal
Pyr·rhic
Pyr·rhus
Py·thag·o·ras
py·thon
Qa·ter
quack·ery
  quack·er·ies
Quad·ra·ges·i·ma
quad·ran·gle
  quad·ran·gu·lar
quad·rant
  quad·ran·tal
quad·ra·phon·ic
quad·rate
  quad·rat·ed
  quad·rat·ing
quad·rat·ic
  quad·rat·i·cal·ly
  quad·rat·ics
quad·ra·ture
quad·ri·lat·er·al
qua·drille
quad·ril·lion
  quad·ril·lionth
quad·roon
quad·ru·ped
  quad·ru·pe·dal

quad·ru·ple
  quad·ru·pled
  quad·ru·pling
  quad·ru·plet
quad·ru·pli·cate
  quad·ru·pli·cat·ed
  quad·ru·pli·cat·ing
quaff
  quaff·er
quag·mire
  quag·mired
  quag·miry
quail
  quail·like
quaint
quake
  quaked
  quak·ing
Quak·er
qual·i·fi·ca·tion
qual·i·fied
qual·i·fied·ly
qual·i·fy
  qual·i·fy·ing
  qual·i·fi·a·ble
  qual·i·fi·er
qual·i·ta·tive
qual·i·ty
  qual·i·ties
qualm
  qualm·ish
quan·da·ry
  quan·da·ries
quan·ti·fi·er
quan·ti·fy
  quan·ti·fied
  quan·ti·fy·ing
  quan·ti·fi·a·ble
  quan·ti·fi·ca·tion
quan·ti·ta·tive
quan·ti·ty
  quan·ti·ties
quan·tum
  quan·ta
quar·an·tine
  quar·an·tin·a·ble
quar·rel
  quar·reled
  quar·rel·ing
  quar·rel·er
quar·rel·some
quar·ri·er
quar·ry
  quar·ries
  quar·ried
  quar·ry·ing
quart
quar·ter
quar·ter·back
quar·ter·deck
quar·ter·ing
quar·ter·ly
  quar·ter·lies
quar·ter·mas·ter
quar·tet

quartz
quash
qua·si
qua·ter·nary
quat·rain
qua·ver
  quav·er·ing·ly
qua·very
quay
quea·sy
  quea·si·er
  quea·si·est
  quea·si·ly
  quea·si·ness
Que·bec
queen
  queen·li·ness
  queen·ly
Queens·ber·ry
Queens·land
queer
quell
  quell·er
Que·moy
quench
  quench·a·ble
  quench·er
Quen·tin
quer·u·lous
que·ry
  que·ries
  que·ried
  que·ry·ing
quest
  quest·er
  quest·ing·ly
ques·tion
  ques·tion·er
  ques·tion·a·ble
  ques·tion·a·ble·ness
  ques·tion·a·bil·i·ty
  ques·tion·a·bly
ques·tion·naire
queue
  queued
  queu·ing
Que·zon
quib·ble
  quib·bled
  quib·bling
  quib·bler
quick
quick·en
  quick·en·er
quick-freeze
  quick-froze
  quick-fro·zen
  quick-freez·ing
quick·ie
quick·lime
quick·sand
quick·sil·ver
quick-tem·pered
quick-wit·ted
  quick-wit·ted·ly

quick-wit·ted·ness
qui·es·cent
qui·es·cence
qui·et
qui·et·ly
qui·et·ness
qui·et·er
qui·e·tude
quill
quilt
quilt·er
quilt·ing
quince
Quin·cy
qui·nine
Quin·qua·ges·i·ma
Quin·ta·na
quin·tes·sence
quin·tes·sen·tial
quin·tet
quin·til·lion
quin·til·lionth
quin·tu·ple
quin·tu·pled
quin·tu·pling
quin·tu·plet
quip
quipped
quip·ping
quip·pish
quip·ster
quirk
quirk·i·ly
quirk·i·ness
quirky
quirk·i·er
quirk·i·est
quis·ling
quit
quit·ted
quit·ting
quit·claim
quite
Qui·to
quits
quit·ter
quiv·er
quix·ot·ic
quix·ot·i·cal
quix·ot·i·cal·ly
quiz
quiz·zes
quizzed
quiz·zing
quiz·zer
quiz·zi·cal
quiz·zi·cal·ly
quoin
quoit
quon·dam
Quon·set
quo·rum
quo·ta
quot·a·ble
quot·a·bil·i·ty

quo·ta·tion
quote
quot·ed
quot·ing
quo·tid·i·an
quo·tient
Ra·bat
rab·bet
rab·bet·ed
rab·bet·ing
rab·bi
rab·bis
rab·bin·i·cal
rab·bin·i·cal·ly
rab·bit
rab·ble
rab·bled
rab·bling
Rab·e·lais
rab·id
rab·id·ly
ra·bies
Ra·bin·o·witz
race
raced
rac·ing
race·course
race·horse
ra·ceme
rac·er
race·track
ra·chis
ra·chis·es
rach·i·des
ra·cial
ra·cial·ly
Ra·cine
rac·ism
ra·cial·ism
rac·ist
rack·et
rack·et·eer
rac·on·teur
racy
rac·i·er
rac·i·est
rac·i·ly
rac·i·ness
ra·dar
Rad·cliffe
ra·di·al
ra·di·al·ly
ra·di·ance
ra·di·an·cy
ra·di·ant
ra·di·ant·ly
ra·di·ate
ra·di·at·ed
ra·di·at·ing
ra·di·a·tion
ra·di·a·tor
rad·i·cal
rad·i·cal·ly
rad·i·cal·ism
ra·dio

ra·di·os
ra·di·oed
ra·di·o·ing
ra·di·o·ac·tive
ra·di·o·ac·tiv·i·ty
ra·di·o·fre·quen·cy
ra·di·o·gram
ra·di·o·graph
ra·di·og·ra·phy
ra·di·ol·o·gy
ra·di·ol·o·gist
rad·ish
ra·di·um
ra·di·us
ra·di·us·es
ra·don
raf·fia
raf·fish
raf·fle
raf·fled
raf·fling
raft·er
rag
ragged
rag·ging
rag·a·muf·fin
rage
raged
rag·ing
rag·ing·ly
rag·ged
rag·ged·ly
rag·ged·ness
rag·man
rag·time
rag·weed
raid·er
rail·ing
rail·lery
rail·ler·ies
rail·road
rail·road·er
rail·road·ing
rail·way
rai·ment
rain·bow
rain·coat
rain·drop
rain·fall
Rai·nier
rainy
rain·i·er
rain·i·est
rain·i·ly
rain·i·ness
raise
raised
rais·ing
rais·er
rai·sin
Raj·put
rake
raked
rak·ing
rak·er

rake-off
rak·ish
rak·ish·ly
rak·ish·ness
Ra·leigh
ral·ly
ral·lied
ral·ly·ing
ral·lies
ram
rammed
ram·ming
ram·mer
Ram·a·dan
ram·ble
ram·bled
ram·bling
ram·bler
ram·bunc·tious
ram·i·fi·ca·tion
ram·i·fy
ram·i·fied
ram·i·fy·ing
ram·page
ram·paged
ram·pag·ing
ramp·ant
ram·pan·cy
ram·pant·ly
ram·part
ram·rod
ram·shack·le
ranch·er
ran·cid
ran·cid·i·ty
ran·cid·ness
ran·cor
ran·cor·ous
Ran·dolph
ran·dom
ran·dom·ly
ran·dom·ness
range
ranged
rang·ing
rang·er
Ran·goon
rangy
rang·i·er
rang·i·est
rang·i·ness
ran·kle
ran·kled
ran·kling
ran·sack
ran·som
rant·er
rap
rapped
rap·ping
ra·pa·cious
ra·pa·cious·ly
ra·pac·i·ty
rape
rap·ist

Raph·a·el
rap·id
  ra·pid·i·ty
  rap·id·ly
  rap·id·ness
rap·id-fire
ra·pi·er
rap·ine
Rap·pa·han·nock
rap·port
rap·proche·ment
rap·scal·lion
rap·ture
  rap·tur·ous
  rap·tur·ous·ly
  rap·tur·ous·ness
rare
  rar·er
  rar·est
rare·bit
rar·e·fy
  rar·e·fied
  rar·e·fy·ing
  rar·e·fac·tion
  rar·e·fied
rare·ly
rar·i·ty
  rar·i·ties
ras·cal
  ras·cal·i·ty
  ras·cal·ly
rash
  rash·ly
  rash·ness
rasp
  rasp·ing·ly
raspy
  rasp·i·er
  rasp·i·est
rasp·ber·ry
Ras·pu·tin
rat
  rat·ted
  rat·ting
rat·a·ble
ratch·et
rate
  rat·ed
  rat·ing
rath·er
rat·i·fy
  rat·i·fied
  rat·i·fy·ing
  rat·i·fi·ca·tion
  rat·i·fi·er
ra·tio
  ra·tios
ra·ti·oc·i·na·tion
ra·tion
ra·tion·al
  ra·tion·al·i·ty
  ra·tion·al·ly
  ra·tion·ale
  ra·tion·al·ism
  ra·tion·al·ist

ra·tion·al·is·tic
ra·tion·al·is·ti·cal·ly
ra·tion·al·ize
ra·tion·al·ized
ra·tion·al·iz·ing
ra·tion·al·i·za·tion
ra·tion·al·iz·er
rat·line
rat·tan
rat·tle
  rat·tled
  rat·tling
rat·tle·brain
rat·tler
rat·tle·snake
rat·tle·trap
rat·ty
  rat·ti·er
  rat·ti·est
rau·cous
  rau·cous·ly
raun·chy
  raun·chi·er
  raun·chi·est
rav·age
  rav·aged
  rav·ag·ing
  rav·ag·er
rave
  raved
  rav·ing
  rav·er
rav·el
  rav·eled
  rav·el·ing
  rav·el·er
ra·ven
Ra·ven·na
rav·en·ous
  rav·en·ous·ly
ra·vine
ra·vi·o·li
rav·ish
  rav·ish·ment
  rav·ish·ing
raw
  raw·ness
raw·boned
raw·hide
ray·on
raze
  razed
  raz·ing
  raz·er
ra·zor
raz·zle-daz·zle
re·act
  re·ac·tive
  re·ac·tion
  re·ac·tion·ary
  re·ac·tion·ar·ies
  re·ac·ti·vate
  re·ac·ti·vat·ed
  re·ac·ti·vat·ing
  re·ac·tor

read·a·ble
  read·a·bil·i·ty
  read·a·ble·ness
  read·a·bly
read·er
read·ing
re·ad·just
  re·ad·just·ment
ready
  read·i·er
  read·i·est
  read·ied
  read·y·ing
  read·i·ly
  read·i·ness
read·y·made
re·a·gent
re·al
re·al·ism
  re·al·ist
  re·al·is·tic
  re·al·is·ti·cal·ly
re·al·i·ty
  re·al·i·ties
re·al·ize
  re·al·ized
  re·al·iz·ing
  re·al·iz·a·ble
  re·al·i·za·tion
re·al·ly
realm
Re·al·tor
re·al·ty
ream·er
re·an·i·mate
  re·an·i·mat·ed
  re·an·i·mat·ing
  re·an·i·ma·tion
reap·er
re·ap·pear
  re·ap·pear·ance
  re·ap·por·tion·ment
  re·ap·por·tion
rear ad·mir·ral
re·arm
  re·ar·ma·ment
re·ar·range
  re·ar·ranged
  re·ar·rang·ing
  re·ar·range·ment
rear·ward
rea·son
  rea·son·er
rea·son·a·ble
  rea·son·a·bil·i·ty
  rea·son·a·ble·ness
  rea·son·a·bly
rea·son·ing
re·as·sem·ble
  re·as·sem·bled
  re·as·sem·bling
  re·as·sem·bly
re·as·sume
  re·as·sump·tion
re·as·sure

re·as·sured
re·as·sur·ing
re·as·sur·ance
re·as·sur·ing·ly
re·bate
  re·bat·ed
  re·bat·ing
  re·bat·er
Re·bec·ca
reb·el
re·bel
  re·belled
  re·bel·ling
  re·bel·lion
  re·bel·lious
  re·bel·lious·ly
  re·bel·lious·ness
re·birth
re·born
re·bound
re·buff
re·build
  re·built
  re·build·ing
re·buke
  re·buked
  re·buk·ing
  re·buk·er
re·bus
  re·bus·es
re·but
  re·but·ted
  re·but·ting
  re·but·ter
  re·but·tal
re·cal·ci·trant
  re·cal·ci·trance
  re·cal·ci·tran·cy
re·call
re·cant
  re·can·ta·tion
re·ca·pit·u·late
  re·ca·pit·u·lat·ed
  re·ca·pit·u·lat·ing
  re·ca·pit·u·la·tion
re·cap·ture
  re·cap·tured
  re·cap·tur·ing
re·cede
  re·ced·ed
  re·ced·ing
re·ceipt
re·ceiv·a·ble
re·ceive
  re·ceived
  re·ceiv·ing
  re·ceiv·er
  re·ceiv·er·ship
re·cent
  re·cent·ly
  re·cen·cy
  re·cent·ness
re·cep·ta·cle
re·cep·tion
  re·cep·tion·ist

re·cep·tive
 re·cep·tive·ly
 re·cep·tive·ness
 re·cep·tiv·i·ty
re·cess
re·ces·sion
 re·ces·sion·ary
re·ces·sion·al
re·ces·sive
re·charge
 re·charged
 re·charg·ing
Re·ci·fe
rec·i·pe
re·cip·i·ent
 re·cip·i·ence
 re·cip·i·en·cy
re·cip·ro·cal
 re·cip·ro·cal·ly
re·cip·ro·cate
 re·cip·ro·cat·ed
 re·cip·ro·cat·ing
 re·cip·ro·ca·tion
 re·cip·ro·ca·tive
rec·i·proc·i·ty
re·cit·al
rec·i·ta·tion
rec·i·ta·tive
re·cite
 re·cit·ed
 re·cit·ing
reck·less
 reck·less·ly
 reck·less·ness
reck·on
reck·on·ing
re·claim
rec·la·ma·tion
re·cline
 re·clined
 re·clin·ing
 re·clin·er
rec·luse
rec·og·ni·tion
re·cog·ni·zance
rec·og·nize
 rec·og·nized
 rec·og·niz·ing
 rec·og·niz·a·ble
 rec·og·niz·a·bly
re·coil
 re·coil·less
re·col·lect
rec·ol·lect
 rec·ol·lec·tion
rec·om·mend
 rec·om·mend·a·ble
 rec·om·mend·er
 rec·om·men·da·tion
rec·om·pense
 rec·om·pensed
 rec·om·pens·ing
rec·on·cile
 rec·on·ciled
 rec·on·cil·ing

rec·on·cil·a·ble
rec·on·cil·a·bly
rec·on·cil·er
rec·on·cil·i·a·tion
rec·on·cile·ment
rec·on·dite
re·con·di·tion
re·con·firm
re·con·nais·sance
re·con·noi·ter
 re·con·noi·tered
 re·con·noi·ter·ing
re·con·sid·er
 re·con·sid·er·a·tion
re·con·struct
 re·con·struc·tion
re·cord
re·cord·er
re·cord·ing
re·count
re·count
re·coup
re·course
re·cov·er
re·cov·ery
 re·cov·er·ies
rec·re·ant
re·cre·ate
 re·cre·at·ed
 re·cre·at·ing
 re·cre·a·tion
rec·re·a·tion
 rec·re·a·tion·al
re·crim·i·nate
 re·crim·i·nat·ed
 re·crim·i·nat·ing
 re·crim·i·na·tion
 re·crim·i·na·tive
 re·crim·i·na·to·ry
re·cruit
 re·cruit·er
 re·cruit·ment
rec·tal
rec·tan·gle
 rec·tan·gu·lar
rec·ti·fi·er
rec·ti·fy
 rec·ti·fied
 rec·ti·fy·ing
 rec·ti·fi·a·ble
 rec·ti·fi·ca·tion
rec·ti·lin·e·ar
rec·ti·tude
rec·tor
rec·to·ry
 rec·to·ries
rec·tum
 rec·tums
 rec·ta
re·cum·bent
 re·cum·ben·cy
 re·cum·bent·ly
re·cu·per·ate
 re·cu·per·at·ed
 re·cu·per·at·ing

re·cu·per·a·tion
re·cu·per·a·tive
re·cur
re·curred
re·cur·ring
re·cur·rence
re·cur·rent
red
red·der
red·dest
red·ness
red·bird
red·blood·ed
red·breast
red·den
red·dish
re·dec·o·rate
re·dec·o·rat·ed
re·dec·o·rat·ing
re·dec·o·ra·tion
re·ded·i·cate
re·ded·i·cat·ed
re·ded·i·cat·ing
re·ded·i·ca·tion
re·deem
re·deem·a·ble
re·deem·er
re·demp·tion
re·demp·tive
red·hand·ed
red·hot
re·di·rect
re·di·rec·tion
red·let·ter
red·neck
re·do
re·did
re·done
re·do·ing
red·o·lent
red·o·lence
red·o·len·cy
re·dou·ble
re·dou·bled
re·dou·bling
re·doubt·a·ble
re·doubt·a·bly
re·dound
re·dress
red·start
re·duce
re·duced
re·duc·ing
re·duc·er
re·duc·i·ble
re·duc·tion
re·dun·dant
re·dun·dance
re·dun·dan·cy
re·dun·dan·cies
re·dun·dant·ly
re·du·pli·cate
re·du·pli·cat·ed
re·du·pli·cat·ing
re·dup·li·ca·tion

red·wood
re·echo
re·ech·oed
re·ech·o·ing
re·ech·oes
reedy
reed·i·er
reed·i·est
reed·i·ness
reef·er
re·e·lect
re·e·lec·tion
re·em·pha·size
re·em·pha·sized
re·em·pha·siz·ing
re·en·force
re·en·forced
re·en·forc·ing
re·en·force·ment
re·en·list
re·en·list·ment
re·en·ter
re·en·trance
re·en·try
re·en·tries
re·es·tab·lish
re·es·tab·lish·ment
re·ex·am·ine
re·ex·am·ined
re·ex·am·in·ing
re·ex·am·i·na·tion
re·fec·to·ry
re·fec·to·ries
re·fer
re·ferred
re·fer·ring
re·fer·a·ble
re·fer·ral
ref·er·ee
ref·er·eed
ref·er·ee·ing
ref·er·ence
ref·er·enced
ref·er·enc·ing
ref·er·en·dum
ref·er·en·dums
ref·er·en·da
ref·er·ent
re·fill
re·fill·a·ble
re·fine
re·fined
re·fin·ing
re·fine·ment
re·fin·ery
re·fin·er·ies
re·fin·ish
re·fit
re·fit·ted
re·fit·ting
re·flect
re·flec·tion
re·flec·tive
re·flec·tive·ly
re·flec·tive·ness

re·flec·tor
re·flex
re·flex·ive
re·for·est
  re·for·est·a·tion
re·form
  re·formed
  re·form·er
  re·form·ist
Ref·or·ma·tion
re·form·a·to·ry
  re·form·a·to·ries
  re·form·a·tive
re·fract
  re·frac·tive
re·frac·tion
re·frac·to·ry
  re·frac·to·ri·ly
  re·frac·to·ri·ness
re·frain
re·fresh
  re·fresh·ing
re·fresh·er
re·fresh·ment
re·frig·er·ant
re·frig·er·ate
  re·frig·er·at·ed
  re·frig·er·at·ing
  re·frig·er·a·tion
re·frig·er·a·tor
re·fu·el
ref·uge
ref·u·gee
re·ful·gent
  re·ful·gence
re·fund
re·fur·bish
re·fus·al
re·fuse
  re·fused
  re·fus·ing
ref·use
re·fute
  re·fut·ed
  re·fut·ing
  re·fut·a·ble
ref·u·ta·tion
re·gain
re·gal
  re·gal·ly
re·gale
  re·galed
  re·gal·ing
re·ga·lia
re·gard
re·gard·ful
re·gard·ing
re·gard·less
  re·gard·less·ly
re·gat·ta
re·gen·cy
  re·gen·cies
re·gen·er·ate
  re·gen·er·at·ed
  re·gen·er·at·ing

re·gen·er·a·cy
re·gen·er·a·tion
re·gen·er·a·tive
re·gent
re·gime
reg·i·men
reg·i·ment
  reg·i·men·tal
  reg·i·men·ta·tion
re·gion
  re·gion·al
  re·gion·al·ly
reg·is·ter
  reg·is·tered
  reg·is·trant
reg·is·trar
reg·is·tra·tion
reg·is·try
  reg·is·tries
Re·gnault
re·gress
  re·gres·sion
  re·gres·sor
re·gret
  re·gret·ted
  re·gret·ting
  re·gret·ta·ble
  re·gret·ta·bly
  re·gret·ter
re·gret·ful
  re·gret·ful·ly
  re·gret·ful·ness
reg·u·lar
  reg·u·lar·i·ty
reg·u·late
  reg·u·lat·ed
  reg·u·lat·ing
  reg·u·la·tive
  reg·u·la·tor
  reg·u·la·to·ry
reg·u·la·tion
re·gur·gi·tate
  re·gur·gi·tat·ed
  re·gur·gi·tat·ing
  re·gur·gi·ta·tion
re·ha·bil·i·tate
  re·ha·bil·i·tat·ed
  re·ha·bil·i·tat·ing
  re·ha·bil·i·ta·tion
  re·ha·bil·i·ta·tive
re·hash
re·hears·al
re·hearse
  re·hearsed
  re·hears·ing
  re·hears·er
Re·ho·bo·am
Re·ho·both
Reichs·tag
reign
re·im·burse
  re·im·bursed
  re·im·burs·ing
  re·im·burse·ment
rein

re·in·car·na·tion
rein·deer
re·in·force
  re·in·forced
  re·in·forc·ing
re·in·force·ment
re·in·state
  re·in·stat·ed
  re·in·stat·ing
  re·in·state·ment
re·it·er·ate
  re·it·er·at·ed
  re·it·er·at·ing
  re·it·er·a·tion
re·ject
  re·jec·tion
re·joice
  re·joiced
  re·joic·ing
  re·joic·er
  re·joic·ing·ly
re·join
re·join·der
re·ju·ve·nate
  re·ju·ve·nat·ed
  re·ju·ve·nat·ing
  re·ju·ve·na·tion
  re·ju·ve·na·tor
re·kin·dle
  re·kin·dled
  re·kin·dling
re·lapse
  re·lapsed
  re·laps·ing
  re·laps·er
re·late
  re·lat·ed
  re·lat·ing
  re·lat·er
  re·lat·or
re·la·tion
  re·la·tion·al
  re·la·tion·ship
rel·a·tive
  rel·a·tive·ly
rel·a·tiv·i·ty
re·lax
re·lax·a·tion
re·lay
  re·laid
  re·lay·ing
re·lay
  re·layed
  re·lay·ing
re·lease
  re·leased
  re·leas·ing
  re·leas·a·ble
  re·leas·er
rel·e·gate
  rel·e·gat·ed
  rel·e·gat·ing
  rel·e·ga·tion
re·lent
re·lent·less

rel·e·vant
rel·e·vance
rel·e·van·cy
rel·e·vant·ly
re·li·a·ble
re·li·a·bil·i·ty
re·li·a·ble·ness
re·li·a·bly
re·li·ance
re·li·ant
rel·ic
re·lief
re·lieve
  re·lieved
  re·liev·ing
  re·liev·a·ble
  re·liev·er
re·li·gion
re·li·gi·os·i·ty
re·li·gious
re·lin·quish
rel·ish
re·live
  re·lived
  re·liv·ing
re·lo·cate
  re·lo·cat·ed
  re·lo·cat·ing
  re·lo·ca·tion
re·luc·tance
re·luc·tant
re·ly
  re·lied
  re·ly·ing
re·main
re·main·der
re·mand
re·mark
re·mark·a·ble
  re·mark·a·ble·ness
  re·mark·a·bly
Re·marque
Rem·brandt
re·me·di·a·ble
re·me·di·al
rem·e·dy
  rem·e·dies
  rem·e·died
  rem·e·dy·ing
re·mem·ber
re·mem·brance
re·mind
re·mind·er
Rem·ing·ton
rem·i·nisce
  rem·i·nisced
  rem·i·nisc·ing
  rem·i·nis·cence
  rem·i·nis·cent
re·miss
re·mis·sion
re·mit
  re·mit·ted
  re·mit·ting
  re·mit·tance

rem·nant
re·mod·el
re·mon·strance
re·mon·strate
  re·mon·strat·ed
  re·mon·strat·ing
re·morse
  re·morse·ful
  re·morse·ful·ly
  re·morse·less
re·mote
  re·mot·er
  re·mot·est
re·mount
re·mov·a·ble
re·mov·al
re·move
  re·moved
  re·mov·ing
re·mu·ner·ate
  re·mu·ner·at·ed
  re·mu·ner·at·ing
  re·mu·ner·a·tion
  re·mu·ner·a·tive
Re·mus
ren·ais·sance
Re·nan
re·nas·cence
  re·nas·cent
rend
  rend·ed
  rend·ing
ren·der
ren·dez·vous
  ren·dez·voused
  ren·dez·vous·ing
ren·di·tion
ren·e·gade
re·nege
  re·neged
  re·neg·ing
re·new
re·new·al
ren·net
Re·no
Re·noir
re·nounce
  re·nounced
  re·nounc·ing
ren·o·vate
  ren·o·vat·ed
  ren·o·vat·ing
  ren·o·va·tion
re·nown
re·nowned
rent·al
re·nun·ci·a·tion
re·or·gan·i·za·tion
re·or·gan·ize
  re·or·gan·ized
  re·or·gan·iz·ing
re·pair
re·pair·man
  re·pair·men
rep·a·ra·ble

rep·a·ra·tion
rep·ar·tee
re·past
re·pa·tri·ate
  re·pa·tri·at·ed
  re·pa·tri·at·ing
  re·pa·tri·a·tion
re·pay
  re·paid
  re·pay·ing
  re·pay·ment
re·peal
re·peat
  re·peat·a·ble
  re·peat·ed
  re·peat·er
re·pel
  re·pelled
  re·pel·ling
  re·pel·lent
re·pent
  re·pent·ance
  re·pent·ant
re·per·cus·sion
rep·er·toire
rep·er·to·ry
  rep·er·to·ries
rep·e·ti·tion
  rep·e·ti·tious
  re·pet·i·tive
re·place
  re·placed
  re·plac·ing
  re·place·a·ble
  re·place·ment
re·plen·ish
re·plete
  re·ple·tion
rep·li·ca
re·ply
  re·plied
  re·ply·ing
  re·plies
re·port
  re·port·ed·ly
  re·port·er
  rep·or·to·ri·al
re·pose
  re·posed
  re·pos·ing
  re·pose·ful
re·pos·i·tory
  re·pos·i·tor·ies
re·pos·sess
  re·pos·ses·sion
rep·re·hend
  rep·re·hen·si·ble
rep·re·sent
  rep·re·sen·ta·tion
  rep·re·sent·a·tive
re·press
  re·pres·sion
re·prieve
  re·prieved
  re·priev·ing

rep·ri·mand
re·print
re·pris·al
re·proach
re·proach·ful
rep·ro·bate
rep·ro·ba·tion
re·pro·duce
re·pro·duced
re·pro·duc·ing
re·pro·duc·tion
re·pro·duc·tive
re·proof
re·prove
re·proved
re·prov·ing
rep·tile
rep·til·i·an
re·pub·lic
re·pub·li·can
re·pub·li·can·ism
re·pu·di·ate
re·pu·di·at·ed
re·pu·di·at·ing
re·pu·di·a·tion
re·pug·nance
re·pug·nan·cy
re·pug·nant
re·pulse
re·pulsed
re·puls·ing
re·pul·sion
re·pul·sive
rep·u·ta·ble
rep·u·ta·bly
rep·u·ta·bil·i·ty
rep·u·ta·tion
re·pute
re·put·ed
re·put·ing
re·put·ed·ly
re·quest
req·ui·em
re·quire
re·quired
re·quir·ing
re·quire·ment
req·ui·site
req·ui·si·tion
re·quit·al
re·quite
re·quit·ed
re·quit·ing
re·run
re·run·ning
re·sale
re·scind
res·cue
res·cued
res·cu·ing
res·cu·er
re·search
re·search·er
re·sem·blance
re·sem·ble

re·sem·bled
re·sem·bling
re·sent
re·sent·ful
re·sent·ment
res·er·va·tion
re·serve
re·served
re·serv·ing
re·serv·ist
res·er·voir
re·set
re·set·ting
re·side
re·sid·ed
re·sid·ing
res·i·dence
res·i·den·cy
res·i·den·cies
res·i·dent
res·i·den·tial
re·sid·u·al
res·i·due
re·sign
res·ig·na·tion
re·signed
re·sil·ient
re·sil·ience
re·sil·ien·cy
res·in
res·in·ous
re·sist
re·sist·er
re·sist·i·ble
re·sist·ance
re·sist·ant
re·sist·less
re·sis·tor
res·o·lute
res·o·lu·tion
re·solve
re·solved
re·solv·ing
res·o·nance
res·o·nant
res·o·nate
res·o·nat·ed
res·o·nat·ing
res·o·na·tor
re·sort
re·sound
re·sound·ing
re·sound·ing·ly
re·source
re·source·ful
re·source·ful·ly
re·source·ful·ness
re·spect
re·spect·ful
re·spect·ful·ly
re·spect·ful·ness
re·spect·a·ble
re·spect·a·bil·i·ty
re·spect·ing
re·spec·tive

re·spec·tive·ly
res·pi·ra·tion
res·pi·ra·to·ry
res·pi·ra·tor
re·spire
 re·spired
 re·spir·ing
res·pite
re·splend·ent
 re·splend·ence
re·spond
re·spond·ent
re·sponse
re·spon·si·bil·i·ty
 re·spon·si·bil·i·ties
re·spon·si·ble
re·spon·sive
res·tau·rant
rest·ful
res·ti·tu·tion
res·tive
rest·less
res·to·ra·tion
re·stor·a·tive
re·store
 re·stored
 re·stor·ing
re·strain
re·straint
re·strict
 re·strict·ed
 re·strict·ed·ly
re·stric·tion
re·stric·tive
re·sult
re·sult·ant
re·sume
 re·sumed
 re·sum·ing
ré·su·mé
re·sump·tion
re·sur·gent
 re·sur·gence
res·ur·rect
res·ur·rec·tion
re·sus·ci·tate
 re·sus·ci·tat·ed
 re·sus·ci·tat·ing
 re·sus·ci·ta·tion
 re·sus·ci·ta·tor
re·tail
 re·tail·er
re·tain
 re·tain·er
re·take
 re·took
 re·tak·en
 re·tak·ing
re·tal·i·ate
 re·tal·i·at·ed
 re·tal·i·at·ing
 re·tal·i·a·tion
 re·tal·i·a·to·ry
re·tard
 re·tard·ant

re·tar·da·tion
re·tard·ed
re·ten·tion
re·ten·tive
ret·i·cent
 ret·i·cence
ret·i·na
 ret·i·nas
 ret·i·nae
 ret·i·nal
ret·i·nue
re·tire
 re·tired
 re·tir·ing
 re·tire·ment
re·tool
re·tort
re·touch
re·trace
 re·traced
 re·trac·ing
re·tract
 re·trac·tion
 re·trac·tor
 re·trac·tile
re·tread
re·treat
re·trench
 re·trench·ment
re·tri·al
ret·ri·bu·tion
re·trieve
 re·trieved
 re·triev·ing
 re·triev·er
ret·ro·ac·tive
ret·ro·grade
 ret·ro·grad·ed
 ret·ro·grad·ing
ret·ro·gress
 ret·ro·gres·sion
 ret·ro·gres·sive
ret·ro·rock·et
ret·ro·spect
 ret·ro·spec·tion
 ret·ro·spec·tive
re·turn
 re·turn·a·ble
 re·turn·ee
Reu·ben
re·un·ion
re·u·nite
 re·u·nit·ed
 re·u·nit·ing
rev
 revved
 rev·ving
re·vamp
re·veal
rev·eil·le
rev·el
 rev·el·er
 rev·e·la·tion
 rev·el·ry
 rev·el·ries

re·venge
re·venged
re·veng·ing
re·venge·ful
rev·e·nue
rev·e·nu·er
re·ver·ber·ate
re·ver·ber·at·ed
re·ber·ver·at·ing
re·ver·ber·a·tion
re·vere
re·vered
re·ver·ing
rev·er·ence
rev·er·enced
rev·er·enc·ing
rev·er·end
rev·er·ent
rev·er·en·tial
rev·er·ie
re·ver·sal
re·verse
re·versed
re·vers·ing
re·vers·i·ble
re·ver·sion
re·vert
re·view
re·view·er
re·vile
re·viled
re·vil·ing
re·vise
re·vised
re·vis·ing
re·vi·sion
re·vi·sion·ist
re·vi·sion·ism
re·viv·al
re·viv·al·ist
re·vive
re·vived
re·viv·ing
rev·o·ca·ble
rev·o·ca·tion
re·voke
re·voked
re·vok·ing
re·volt
rev·o·lu·tion
rev·o·lu·tion·ary
rev·o·lu·tion·ar·ies
rev·o·lu·tion·ist
rev·o·lu·tion·ize
rev·o·lu·tion·ized
rev·o·lu·tion·iz·ing
rev·o·lu·tion·iz·er
re·volve
re·volved
re·volv·ing
re·volv·er
re·vue
re·vul·sion
re·ward
re·write

re·wrote
re·writ·ten
re·writ·ing
Rey·kja·vik
Rey·nard
Reyn·olds
rhap·sod·ic
rhap·sod·i·cal
rhap·sod·i·cal·ly
rhap·so·dize
rhap·so·dized
rhap·so·diz·ing
rhap·so·dy
rhap·so·dies
rhap·so·dist
rhea
Rhen·ish
rhe·ni·um
rhe·o·stat
rhe·sus
rhet·o·ric
rhe·tor·i·cal
rhet·o·ri·cian
rheum
rheu·mat·ic
rheu·mat·i·cal·ly
rheu·ma·tism
rhine·stone
rhi·no
rhi·noc·er·os
rhi·noc·er·os·es
rhi·zome
Rhode Is·land
Rho·de·sia
rho·di·um
rho·do·den·dron
rhom·bic
rhom·boid
rhom·boi·dal
rhom·bus
rhom·bus·es
rhom·bi
rhu·barb
rhyme
rhymed
rhym·ing
rhyme·ster
rhythm
rhyth·mic
rhyth·mi·cal
rhyth·mi·cal·ly
rib
ribbed
rib·bing
rib·ald
rib·ald·ry
rib·ald·ries
rib·bon
ri·bo·fla·vin
rib·bo·nu·cle·ic
rice
riced
ric·ing
Riche·lieu
rich·es

Rich·mond
rich·ness
Rich·ter
rick·ets
rick·et·y
  rick·et·i·er
  rick·et·i·est
  rick·et·i·ness
rick·shaw
ric·o·chet
rid
  rid·ded
  rid·ding
rid·dance
rid·dle
  rid·dled
  rid·dling
ride
  rode
  rid·den
  rid·ing
rid·er
ridge
  ridged
  ridg·ing
ridge·pole
rid·i·cule
  rid·i·culed
  rid·i·cul·ing
ri·dic·u·lous
rif·fle
  rif·fled
  rif·fling
riff·raff
ri·fle
  ri·fled
  ri·fling
rig
  rigged
  rig·ging
Ri·ga
rig·ger
right·eous
right·ful
right-hand
right-hand·ed
right·ism
right of way
rig·id
  ri·gid·i·ty
rig·ma·role
rig·or
rig·or·ous
rile
  riled
  ril·ing
rim
  rimmed
  rim·ming
rime
  rimed
  rim·ing
  rim·er
ring·er
ring·lead·er

ring·let
ring·mas·ter
ring·side
ring·worm
rinse
  rinsed
  rins·ing
Rio de Ja·nei·ro
Rio Grande
ri·ot
ri·ot·ous
rip
  ripped
  rip·ping
rip·per
ri·par·i·an
rip·en
rip-off
rip·ple
  rip·pled
  rip·pling
rip·saw
rip·tide
rise
  rose
  ris·en
  ris·ing
ris·er
ris·i·ble
  ris·i·bil·i·ty
risky
  risk·i·er
  risk·i·est
  risk·i·ness
ris·qué
rit·u·al
rit·u·al·ism
  rit·u·al·ist
  rit·u·al·is·tic
  rit·u·al·is·ti·cal·ly
ritzy
  ritz·i·er
  ritz·i·est
ri·val
ri·val·ry
  ri·val·ries
riv·er
riv·er·side
riv·et
  riv·et·er
riv·i·er·a
riv·u·let
Ri·yadh
roach·es
road·bed
road·block
road·run·ner
road·side
road·ster
road·way
Ro·a·noke
roast·er
rob
  robbed
  rob·bing

rob·ber
rob·bery
rob·ber·ies
robe
robed
rob·ing
Robes·pierre
rob·in
Rob·in·son Cru·soe
ro·bot
ro·bust
Ro·cham·beau
Ro·chelle
Roch·es·ter
rock-and-roll
rock-bound
Rock·e·fel·ler
rock·er
rock·et
rock·et·ry
Rock·ford
Rock·ies
rock-ribbed
rocky
rock·i·er
rock·i·est
rock·i·ness
ro·co·co
ro·dent
ro·deo
ro·de·os
Ro·din
roe·buck
roent·gen
rog·er
rogue
ro·guish
ro·guish·ly
ro·guish·ness
ro·guery
ro·guer·ies
roist·er
roll·er
roll·er bear·ing
roll·er coast·er
roll·er-skate
roll·er-skat·ed
roll·er-skat·ing
roll·er-skat·er
rol·lick
rol·lick·ing
roll·ing mill
roll·ing pin
Röl·vaag
ro·ly-po·ly
ro·ly-po·lies
ro·maine
Ro·man
ro·mance
ro·manced
ro·manc·ing
Ro·man·esque
Ro·ma·nia
ro·man·tic
ro·man·ti·cism

ro·man·ti·cist
ro·man·ti·cize
ro·man·ti·cized
ro·man·ti·ciz·ing
Rom·a·ny
Ro·meo
romp·er
roof·ing
roof·tree
rook·ery
rook·er·ies
rook·ie
room·er
room·ful
room·mate
roomy
room·i·er
room·i·est
room·i·ly
room·i·ness
Roo·se·velt
roost·er
root·stock
rope
roped
rop·ing
ropy
rop·i·er
rop·i·est
rop·i·ness
Roque·fort
Ror·schach
Ro·sa·rio
ro·sa·ry
ro·sa·ries
ro·se·ate
rose·bud
rose-col·ored
rose·mary
rose·mar·ies
Ro·set·ta
ro·sette
rose·wood
Rosh Ha·sha·nah
ros·in
Ros·set·ti
ros·ter
ros·trum
ros·tra
ros·trums
rosy
ros·i·er
ros·i·est
ros·i·ly
ros·i·ness
rot
rot·ted
rot·ting
ro·ta·ry
ro·ta·ries
ro·tate
ro·tat·ed
ro·tat·ing
ro·ta·tion
ro·tis·ser·ie

ro·tor
rot·ten
Rot·ter·dam
ro·tund
  ro·tun·di·ty
  ro·tun·di·ties
ro·tun·da
rou·é
Rou·en
rouge
  rouged
  roug·ing
rough·age
rough-and-tum·ble
rough·en
rough-hew
  rough-hewed
  rough-hewn
  rough-hew·ing
rough·house
rough·neck
rough·rid·er
rough·shod
rou·lette
round·a·bout
round·ed
round·er
Round·head
round·ish
round-shoul·dered
round·up
rouse
  roused
  rous·ing
  rous·er
roust
roust·a·bout
rout
route
  rout·ed
  rout·ing
rout·er
rou·tine
rou·tin·ize
  rou·tin·ized
  rou·tin·iz·ing
rove
  roved
  rov·ing
  rov·er
row·boat
row·dy
  row·dies
  row·di·er
  row·di·est
  row·di·ly
  row·di·ness
row·lock
roy·al
  roy·al·ly
  roy·al·ist
  roy·al·ty
  roy·al·ties
rub
  rubbed

rub·bing
rub·ber
  rub·bery
rub·ber·ize
  rub·ber·ized
  rub·ber·iz·ing
rub·ber·neck
rub·bish
  rub·bishy
rub·ble
rub·bly
  rub·bli·er
  rub·bli·est
rub·down
ru·bel·la
Ru·bens
ru·be·o·la
Ru·bi·con
ru·bi·cund
ru·bid·i·um
Ru·bin·stein
ru·bric
ru·by
  ru·bies
ruck·sack
ruck·us
rud·der
rud·dy
  rud·di·er
  rud·di·est
  rud·di·ly
  rud·di·ness
rude
  rud·er
  rud·est
  rude·ly
  rude·ness
ru·di·ment
ru·di·men·tal
ru·di·men·ta·ry
rue
  rued
  ru·ing
rue·ful
  rue·ful·ly
  rue·ful·ness
ruff
  ruffed
ruf·fi·an
ruf·fle
  ruf·fled
  ruf·fling
Rug·by
rug·ged
  rug·ged·ly
  rug·ged·ness
ru·in
ru·in·a·tion
ru·in·ous
rule
  ruled
  rul·ing
rul·er
Ru·ma·nia
rum·ba

rum·baed
rum·ba·ing
rum·ble
rum·bled
rum·bling
rum·bler
rum·bly
ru·mi·nant
ru·mi·nate
ru·mi·nat·ed
ru·mi·nat·ing
ru·mi·na·tion
ru·mi·na·tor
rum·mage
rum·maged
rum·mag·ing
rum·mag·er
rum·my
rum·mies
ru·mor
ru·mor·mon·ger
rum·ple
rum·pled
rum·pling
rum·pus
run
run·ning
run·a·bout
run·a·round
run·a·way
run·down
run·in
run·ner
run·ner-up
run·ny
run·ni·er
run·ni·est
run·off
run-of-the-mill
run-on
runt
runty
runt·i·er
runt·i·est
run-through
run·way
rup·ture
rup·tured
rup·tur·ing
ru·ral
ru·ral·ly
ru·ral·ize
ru·ral·ized
ru·ral·iz·ing
ru·ral·i·za·tion
rus·set
Rus·sia
Rus·sian rou·lette
rus·tic
rus·ti·cate
rus·ti·cat·ed
rus·ti·cat·ing
rus·ti·ca·tion
rus·ti·ca·tor
rus·tic·i·ty

rus·tic·i·ties
rus·tle
rus·tled
rus·tling
rus·tler
rust·proof
rusty
rust·i·er
rust·i·est
rust·i·ly
rust·i·ness
rut
rut·ted
rut·ting
ru·ta·ba·ga
ru·the·ni·um
ruth·less
ruth·less·ly
ruth·less·ness
Rut·land
rut·ty
rut·ti·er
rut·ti·est
Rwan·da
Sab·a·oth
Sab·bath
Sab·bat·i·cal
sa·ber
sa·ber-toothed
sa·ble
sab·o·tage
sab·o·taged
sab·o·tag·ing
sab·o·teur
sa·bra
Sac·a·ga·wea
sac·cha·rine
sac·er·do·tal
sa·chet
sack·cloth
sack·ful
sack·fuls
sack·ing
sac·ra·ment
sac·ra·men·tal
Sac·ra·men·to
sa·cred
sa·cred·ly
sa·cred·ness
sac·ri·fice
sac·ri·ficed
sac·ri·fic·ing
sac·ri·fic·er
sac·ri·fi·cial
sac·ri·lege
sac·ri·le·gious
sac·ro·il·i·ac
sac·ro·sanct
sac·ro·sanc·ti·ty
sac·ro·sanct·ness
sac·rum
sac·rums
sac·ra
sa·cral
sad

sad·der
sad·dest
sad·ly
sad·ness
sad·den
sad·dle
sad·dled
sad·dling
sad·dle-backed
sad·dle-bag
Sad·du·cee
sad·ism
sad·ist
sa·dis·tic
sa·dis·ti·cal·ly
sad·o·mas·o·chism
sad·o·mas·o·chist
sa·fa·ri
sa·fa·ris
safe
saf·er
saf·est
safe-con·duct
safe·crack·er
safe·crack·ing
safe-de·pos·it
safe·guard
safe·keep·ing
safe·ty
safe·ties
safe·ty match
safe·ty pin
safe·ty valve
safe·ty zone
saf·flow·er
saf·fron
sag
sagged
sag·ging
sa·ga
sa·ga·cious
sa·gac·i·ty
sage
sag·er
sag·est
sage·ly
sage·ness
sage·brush
Sag·i·naw
Sag·it·ta·ri·us
Sag·ue·nay
Sai·gon
sail·boat
sail·cloth
sail·er
sail·fish
sail·ing
sail·or
saint
saint·hood
saint·ship
Saint Ber·nard
saint·ed
saint·ly
saint·li·er

saint·li·est
saint·li·ness
Sai·pan
sa·ke
Sa·kha·lin
sal·a·ble
sale·a·ble
sal·a·bil·i·ty
sal·a·bly
sa·la·cious
sal·ad
Sal·a·man·ca
sal·a·man·der
sa·la·mi
Sal·a·mis
sal·a·ry
sal·a·ries
Sa·lem
Sa·ler·no
sales·man
sales·men
sales·man·ship
sales·per·son
sales·peo·ple
sales·room
sa·li·ent
sa·li·ence
sa·li·en·cy
sa·li·ent·ly
sa·li·ent·ness
sa·line
sa·lin·i·ty
Salis·bury
sa·li·va
sal·i·vary
sal·i·vate
sal·i·vat·ed
sal·i·vat·ing
sal·i·va·tion
sal·low
sal·low·ish
sal·ly
sal·lies
sal·lied
sal·ly·ing
salm·on
Sa·lo·me
sa·lon
Sa·lon·i·ka
sa·loon
salt·cel·lar
salt·ed
sal·tine
salt·shak·er
salt·wa·ter
salt·wort
salty
salt·i·er
salt·i·est
salt·i·ness
sa·lu·bri·ous
Sa·lu·ki
sal·u·tary
sal·u·ta·tion
sa·lu·ta·to·ry

sa·lu·ta·to·ries
sa·lute
  sa·lut·ed
  sa·lut·ing
  sa·lut·er
Sal·va·dor
sal·vage
  sal·vaged
  sal·vag·ing
  sal·vage·a·ble
  sal·vag·er
sal·va·tion
Sal·va·tion Ar·my
salve
  salved
  salv·ing
sal·vor
sal·vo
  sal·vos
  sal·voes
Salz·burg
Sa·mar·i·a
Sa·mar·i·tan
Samar·kand
sam·ba
  sam·baed
  sam·ba·ing
same·ness
Sa·moa
sam·o·var
sam·ple
  sam·pled
  sam·pling
sam·pler
sam·pling
Sam·son
San·aa
San An·to·nio
san·a·to·ri·um
San·cho
sanc·ti·fy
  sanc·ti·fied
  sanc·ti·fy·ing
  sanc·ti·fi·ca·tion
  sanc·ti·fi·er
sanc·ti·mo·ny
  sanc·ti·mo·ni·ous
sanc·tion
  sanc·tion·a·ble
  sanc·tion·er
sanc·ti·ty
  sanc·ti·ties
sanc·tu·ary
  sanc·tu·ar·ies
sanc·tum
  sanc·ta
san·dal
san·dal·wood
sand·bag
  sand·bagged
  sand·bag·ging
  sand·bag·ger
sand·bank
sand·blast
sand·box

Sand·burg
sand·cast
  sand·cast·ed
  sand·cast·ing
San Di·e·go
sand·lot
sand·man
  sand·men
San Do·min·go
sand·pa·per
sand·pi·per
sand·stone
sand·storm
sand·wich
sandy
  sand·i·er
  sand·i·est
  sand·i·ness
sane
  san·er
  san·est
  sane·ly
  sane·ness
San·for·ize
  san·for·ized
  san·for·iz·ing
San Fran·cis·co
sang·froid
san·gui·nary
san·guine
  san·guine·ly
  san·guine·ness
San·he·drin
san·i·tar·i·um
  san·i·tar·i·ums
  san·i·tar·i·a
san·i·tary
  san·i·tar·i·ly
san·i·ta·tion
san·i·tize
  san·tized
  san·i·tiz·ing
san·i·ty
San Joa·quin
San Mar·i·no
San Sal·va·dor
San Se·bas·tian
San·skrit
San·ta An·na
San·ta Bar·ba·ra
San·ta Claus
San·ta Fe
San·ta Ma·ria
San·ta·ya·na
San·ti·a·go
San·to Do·min·go
São Pau·lo
sap
  sapped
  sap·ping
sap·head
  sap·head·ed
sa·pi·ent
  sa·pi·ence
  sa·pi·en·cy

sap·less
sap·ling
sa·pon·i·fy
  sa·pon·i·fied
  sa·pon·i·fy·ing
sap·per
sap·phire
sap·phism
sap·py
  sap·pi·er
  sap·pi·est
  sap·pi·ness
sap·suck·er
sap·wood
Sar·a·cen
Sa·ra·je·vo
sa·ran
Sar·a·so·ta
Sar·a·to·ga
sar·casm
  sar·cas·tic
  sar·cas·ti·cal·ly
sar·co·ma
  sar·co·mas
  sar·co·ma·ta
sar·coph·a·gus
  sar·coph·a·gi
  sar·coph·a·gus·es
sar·dine
Sar·din·ia
sar·don·ic
  sar·don·i·cal·ly
sar·gas·sum
sa·ri
  sa·ris
sa·rong
sar·sa·pa·ril·la
sar·to·ri·al
sa·shay
Sas·katch·e·wan
sas·sa·fras
sas·sy
  sas·si·er
  sas·si·est
Sa·tan
sa·tan·ic
  sa·tan·i·cal
sa·tan·ism
  sa·tan·ist
satch·el
sate
  sat·ed
  sat·ing
sa·teen
sat·el·lite
sa·ti·a·ble
  sa·ti·a·bly
  sa·ti·a·bil·i·ty
  sa·ti·a·ble·ness
sa·ti·ate
  sa·ti·at·ed
  sa·ti·at·ing
  sa·ti·a·tion
sa·ti·e·ty
sat·in

sat·iny
sat·ire
sa·tir·i·cal
  sa·tir·i·cal·ly
sat·i·rist
sat·i·rize
  sat·i·rized
  sat·i·riz·ing
  sat·i·riz·er
sat·is·fac·tion
sat·is·fac·to·ry
  sat·is·fac·to·ri·ly
sat·is·fy
  sat·is·fied
  sat·is·fy·ing
  sat·is·fi·a·ble
  sat·is·fi·er
  sat·is·fy·ing·ly
sat·u·ra·ble
sat·u·rate
  sat·u·rat·ed
  sat·u·rat·ing
  sat·u·ra·tion
Sat·ur·day
Sat·urn
sat·ur·na·lia
sat·ur·nine
sa·tyr
  sa·tyr·ic
sauce
  sauced
  sauc·ing
sau·cer
sau·cy
  sau·ci·er
  sau·ci·est
  sau·ci·ly
  sau·ci·ness
Sau·di
sau·er·bra·ten
sau·er·kraut
Sault Sainte Ma·rie
sau·na
saun·ter
  saun·ter·er
sau·sage
  sau·sage·like
sau·té
  sau·téed
  sau·tée·ing
sav·age
  sav·age·ness
  sav·age·ry
  sav·age·ries
sa·van·na
Sa·van·nah
sa·vant
save
  saved
  sav·ing
  sav·er
sav·ior
sa·vior-faire
sa·vor
  sa·vor·er

sa·vory
sa·vor·i·er
sa·vor·i·est
sa·vor·i·ly
sa·vor·i·ness
sav·vy
sav·vied
sav·vy·ing
sav·vi·er
sav·vi·est
saw·buck
saw·dust
sawed-off
saw·horse
saw·mill
saw-toothed
saw·yer
Sax·on
Sax·o·ny
sax·o·phone
sax·o·phon·ist
say
said
say·ing
say·a·ble
say·er
say-so
scab
scabbed
scab·bing
scab·bard
scab·by
scab·bi·er
scab·bi·est
scab·bi·ness
sca·bies
scaf·fold
scaf·fold·ing
sca·lar
scal·a·wag
scald
scald·ing
scale
scaled
scal·ing
scale·less
scale·like
scal·i·ness
scal·lion
scal·lop
scal·lop·er
scalp
scalp·er
scal·pel
scaly
scal·i·er
scal·i·est
scal·i·ness
scamp
scamp·er
scan
scanned
scan·ning
scan·ner
scan·dal

scan·dal·ize
scan·dal·ized
scan·dal·iz·ing
scan·dal·iz·er
scan·dal·i·za·tion
scan·dal·mon·ger
scan·dal·ous
Scan·di·na·via
Scan·di·na·vi·an
scan·sion
scant
scant·ness
scan·ties
scanty
scant·i·er
scant·i·est
scant·i·ly
scant·i·ness
scape·goat
scape·grace
scap·u·la
scap·u·las
scap·u·lae
scar
scarred
scar·ring
scarce
scarce·ness
scar·ci·ty
scare
scared
scar·ing
scar·er
scare·crow
scare·mon·ger
scarf
scarfs
scarves
scarf·less
scarf·like
scarf·skin
scar·i·fy
scar·i·fied
scar·i·fy·ing
scar·i·fi·ca·tion
scar·let
scarp
scary
scar·i·er
scar·i·est
scat
scat·ted
scat·ting
scathe
scathed
scath·ing
scathe·less
scat·o·log·i·cal
scat·ter
scat·ter·a·ble
scat·ter·er
scat·ter·brain
scat·ter·brained
scav·enge
scav·enged

scav·eng·ing
scav·en·ger
sce·nar·io
sce·nar·i·os
sce·nar·ist
scen·ery
scen·er·ies
sce·nic
sce·ni·cal
scent
scent·ed
scep·ter
scep·tered
scep·ter·ing
sched·ule
sched·uled
sched·ul·ing
sched·u·lar
sche·ma
sche·ma·ta
sche·mat·i·cal·ly
sche·ma·tize
sche·ma·tized
sche·ma·tiz·ing
scheme
schem·er
schem·ing
scher·zo
scher·zos
scher·zi
schism
schis·mat·ic
schis·mat·i·cal
schist
schizo
schiz·os
schiz·oid
schiz·o·phre·nia
schiz·o·phren·ic
schle·miel
schamltz
schmaltzy
schmo
schnapps
schnau·zer
schnit·zel
Schnitz·ler
schnook
schnor·kel
schnoz·zle
schol·ar
schol·ar·ly
schol·ar·li·ness
schol·ar·ship
scho·las·tic
scho·las·ti·cal
scho·las·ti·cism
school board
school·boy
school bus
school·child
school·chil·dren
school·girl
school·house
school·ing

school·marm
school·mas·ter
school·mate
school·mis·tress
school·room
school·teach·er
school·teach·ing
school·work
schoon·er
Scho·pen·hauer
Schu·bert
Schu·mann
schuss
schwa
Schweit·zer
sci·at·ic
sci·at·i·ca
sci·ence
sci·en·tif·ic
sci·en·tif·i·cal·ly
sci·en·tist
scim·i·tar
scin·tig·ra·phy
scin·til·la
scin·til·lant
scin·til·late
scin·til·lat·ed
scin·til·lat·ing
scin·til·la·tion
sci·on
scis·sor
scis·sors
scle·ra
scle·rot·i·ca
scle·ro·sis
scle·ro·ses
scle·rot·ic
scle·rous
scoff
scoff·er
scoff·ing·ly
scold
scold·er
scold·ing
scol·lop
sconce
scone
scoop
scoop·er
scoop·ful
scoot·er
scope
scorch
scorched
scorch·ing
scorch·er
score
scored
scor·ing
score·less
scor·er
score·board
score·keep·er
scorn
scorn·er

scorn·ful
scorn·ful·ness
Scor·pio
scor·pi·on
Scotch
Scotch-I·rish
Scotch·man
Scotch·men
scot-free
Scot·land Yard
Scots·man
Scots·men
scot·tie
Scot·tish
Scot·tish ter·ri·er
scoundrel
scoun·drel·ly
scour
scour·er
scourge
scourged
scourg·ing
scourg·er
scour·ings
scout·ing
scout·mas·ter
scowl
scowl·er
scrab·ble
scrab·bled
scrab·bling
scrab·bler
scrag
scragged
scrag·ging
scrag·gly
scrag·gli·er
scrag·gli·est
scrag·gy
scrag·gi·er
scrag·gi·est
scram
scrammed
scram·ming
scram·ble
scram·bled
scram·bling
scram·bler
Scran·ton
scrap
scrapped
scrap·ping
scrap·book
scrape
scraped
scrap·ing
scrap·a·ble
scrap·er
scrap·per
scrap·py
scrap·pi·er
scrap·pi·est
scrap·pi·ly
scrap·pi·ness
scratch

scratch·a·ble
scratch·er
scratchy
scratch·i·er
scratch·i·est
scratch·i·ly
scratch·i·ness
scrawl
scrawl·er
scrawly
scrawl·i·er
scrawl·i·est
scrawny
scrawn·i·er
scrawn·i·est
scrawn·i·ness
scream·er
scream·ing·ly
screech
screech·er
screen
screen·a·ble
screen·er
screen·ing
screen·play
screw
screw·ball
screw·driv·er
screwy
screw·i·er
screw·i·est
scrib·ble
scrib·bled
scrib·bling
scrib·bler
scribe
scribed
scrib·ing
scrib·al
scrim
scrim·mage
scrim·maged
scrim·mag·ing
scrim·mag·er
scrimpy
scrimp·i·er
scrimp·i·est
script
scrip·tur·al
scrip·ture
script·writ·er
scroll-work
scrooge
scro·tum
scro·ta
scro·tums
scro·tal
scrounge
scroung·er
scrub
scrubbed
scrub·bing
scrub·ber
scrub·by
scrub·bi·er

scrub·bi·est
scrub·wom·an
scrub·wom·en
scruffy
scruff·i·er
scruff·i·est
scrump·tious
scru·ple
scru·pled
scru·pling
scru·pu·lous
scru·pu·los·i·ty
scru·pu·lous·ness
scru·pu·lous·ly
scru·ta·ble
scru·ti·nize
scru·ti·nized
scru·ti·niz·ing
scru·ti·niz·er
scru·ti·niz·ing·ly
scru·ti·ny
scru·ti·nies
scu·ba
scud
scud·ded
scud·ding
scuf·fle
scuf·fled
scuf·fling
scul·lery
scul·ler·ies
sculp·tor
sculp·tress
sculp·ture
sculp·tured
sculp·tur·ing
sculp·tur·al
scum
scummed
scum·ming
scur·ri·lous
scur·ril·i·ty
scur·ril·i·ties
scur·ry
scur·ried
scur·ry·ing
scur·ries
scur·vy
scur·vi·er
scur·vi·est
scur·vi·ly
scur·vi·ness
scut·tle
scut·tled
scut·tling
scut·tle·butt
Scyl·la
scythe
scythed
scyth·ing
sea·bed
Sea·bee
sea·board
sea·coast
sea·drome

sea·far·ing
sea·far·er
sea·food
sea·fowl
sea·go·ing
sea·go·er
sea·green
sea gull
sea horse
seal
seal·er
sea lam·prey
sea legs
sea lev·el
seal·ing wax
sea li·on
seal·skin
seam
seam·er
seam·like
sea·maid
sea·man
sea·men
sea·man·ship
seam·stress
seamy
seam·i·er
seam·i·est
seam·i·ness
sé·ance
sea ot·ter
sea·plane
sea·port
sea·quake
search
search·a·ble
search·er
search·ing
search·light
search war·rant
sea·scape
sea ser·pent
sea·shell
sea·shore
sea·sick·ness
sea·sick
sea·side
sea·son
sea·son·er
sea·son·a·ble
sea·son·al
sea·son·al·ly
sea·son·ing
seat·ing
Se·at·tle
sea ur·chin
sea wall
sea·ward
sea·way
sea·weed
sea·wor·thy
sea·wor·thi·ness
se·ba·ceous
se·cant
se·cede

se·ced·ed
se·ced·ing
se·ced·er
se·ces·sion
se·ces·sion·ist
se·clude
se·clud·ed
se·clud·ing
se·clud·ed·ly
se·clud·ed·ness
se·clu·sion
se·clu·sive
sec·ond
sec·ond·ary
sec·ond·ar·i·ly
sec·ond-best
sec·ond-class
sec·ond-guess
sec·ond·hand
sec·ond-rate
sec·ond-sto·ry man
se·cre·cy
se·cre·cies
se·cret
sec·re·tar·i·at
sec·re·tary
sec·re·tar·ies
sec·re·tar·i·al
se·crete
se·cret·ed
se·cret·ing
se·cre·tion
se·cre·tive
se·cre·to·ry
se·cre·to·ries
sec·tar·i·an
sec·tar·i·an·ism
sec·tion
sec·tion·al
sec·tor
sec·to·ri·al
sec·u·lar
sec·u·lar·ism
sec·u·lar·ize
sec·u·lar·ized
sec·u·lar·iz·ing
sec·u·lar·i·za·tion
sec·u·lar·iz·er
se·cure
se·cured
se·cur·ing
se·cur·a·ble
se·cure·ness
se·cur·er
se·cu·ri·ty
se·cu·ri·ties
se·dan
se·date
se·dat·ed
se·dat·ing
se·date·ness
se·da·tion
sed·a·tive
sed·en·tary
sed·en·tar·i·ness

sedge
sed·i·ment
sed·i·men·tal
sed·i·men·ta·ry
sed·i·men·ta·tion
se·di·tion
se·di·tion·ary
se·di·tious
se·duce
se·duced
se·duc·ing
se·duc·er
se·duc·i·ble
se·duce·a·ble
se·duc·tion
se·duce·ment
se·duc·tive
se·duc·tive·ness
sed·u·lous
se·du·li·ty
sed·u·lous·ness
seed·bed
seed·case
seed·ling
seed·pod
seedy
seed·i·er
seed·i·est
seed·i·ly
seed·i·ness
see·ing
seek
sought
seek·ing
seem·ing
seem·ing·ness
seem·ly
seem·li·er
seem·li·est
seem·li·ness
seep
seepy
seep·i·er
seep·i·est
seep·age
se·er
seer·ess
seer·suck·er
see·saw
seethe
seethed
seeth·ing
seg·ment
seg·men·tal
seg·men·tary
seg·men·ta·tion
seg·re·gate
seg·re·gat·ed
seg·re·gat·ing
seg·re·ga·tion
seg·re·ga·tion·ist
sei·gneur
seine
seined
sein·ing

seis·mic
seis·mal
seis·mi·cal
seis·mi·cal·ly
seis·mo·graph
seis·mog·ra·pher
seis·mo·graph·ic
seis·mog·ra·phy
seis·mol·o·gy
seis·mo·log·ic
seis·mo·log·i·cal
seis·mol·o·gist
seize
seized
seiz·ing
seiz·er
sei·zure
sel·dom
se·lect
se·lect·ed
se·lec·tor
se·lec·tion
se·lec·tive
se·lec·tiv·i·ty
se·le·ni·um
self-a·base·ment
self-ab·ne·ga·tion
self-a·buse
self-ad·dressed
self-ag·gran·dize·ment
self-ag·gran·diz·ing
self-as·sur·ance
self-as·sured
self-cen·tered
self-cen·tered·ness
self-col·lect·ed
self-com·mand
self-com·posed
self-con·fessed
self-con·fi·dence
self-con·fi·dent
self-con·scious
self-con·scious·ness
self-con·tained
self-con·trol
self-con·trolled
self-cor·rect·ing
self-crit·i·cism
self-crit·i·cal
self-de·cep·tion
self-de·cep·tive
self-de·fense
self-de·ni·al
self-de·ny·ing
self-de·ter·mi·na·tion
self-de·ter·min·ing
self-dis·ci·pline
self-dis·ci·plined
self-ed·u·cat·ed
self-ed·u·ca·tion
self-ef·fac·ing
self-em·ployed
self-em·ploy·ment
self-es·teem
self-ev·i·dent

self-ev·i·dence
self-ex·plan·a·to·ry
self-ex·pres·sion
self-ex·pres·sive
self-ful·fill·ment
self-ful·fill·ing
self-gov·ern·ment
self-gov·erned
self-gov·ern·ing
self-help
self·hood
self-im·age
self-im·por·tance
self-im·por·tant
self-im·posed
self-im·prove·ment
self-in·duced
self-in·dul·gence
self-in·dul·gent
self-in·flict·ed
self-in·ter·est
self-in·ter·est·ed
self·ish
self·ish·ness
self-know·ledge
self·less
self·less·ness
self-love
self-lov·ing
self-made
self-per·pet·u·at·ing
self-per·pet·u·a·tion
self-pity
self-pit·y·ing
self-pol·li·na·tion
self-pos·sessed
self-pos·sessed·ly
self-pos·ses·sion
self-pres·er·va·tion
self-pro·pelled
self-pro·pel·ling
self-re·al·i·za·tion
self-re·li·ance
self-re·li·ant
self-re·spect
self-re·spect·ing
self-re·straint
self-re·strain·ing
self-right·eous
self-right·eous·ness
self-sac·ri·fice
self-sac·ri·fic·ing
self-same
self-sat·is·fied
self-sat·is·fac·tion
self-sat·is·fy·ing
self-serv·ice
self-serv·ing
self-start·er
self-start·ing
self-styled
self-suf·fi·cient
self-suf·fic·ing
self-suf·fi·cien·cy
self-sup·port

self-sup·port·ing
self-taught
self-will
self-willed
sell
sold
sell·ing
sell·er
sell·out
Selt·zer
sel·vage
sel·vaged
se·man·tics
se·man·tic
se·man·ti·cal
se·man·ti·cal·ly
sem·a·phore
sem·a·phored
sem·a·phor·ing
sem·blance
se·men
se·mes·ter
sem·i·an·nu·al
sem·i·an·nu·al·ly
sem·i·ar·id
sem·i·au·to·mat·ic
sem·i·cir·cle
sem·i·cir·cu·lar
sem·i·clas·si·cal
sem·i·clas·sic
sem·i·co·lon
sem·i·con·duc·tor
sem·i·con·duct·ing
sem·i·con·scious
sem·i·con·scious·ness
sem·i·de·tached
sem·i·fi·nal
sem·i·fi·nal·ist
sem·i·flu·id
sem·i·for·mal
sem·i·gloss
sem·i·liq·uid
sem·i·month·ly
sem·i·nal
sem·i·nal·ly
sem·i·nar
sem·i·nary
sem·i·nar·ies
sem·i·nar·i·an
Sem·i·nole
sem·i·of·fi·cial
sem·i·of·fi·cial·ly
sem·i·per·ma·nent
sem·i·per·me·a·ble
sem·i·pre·cious
sem·i·pri·vate
sem·i·pro·fes·sion·al
sem·i·pro
sem·i·pub·lic
sem·i·skilled
sem·i·sol·id
Sem·ite
Se·mit·ic
Sem·i·tism
sem·i·trail·er

sem·i·trop·ics
sem·i·trop·ic
sem·i·trop·i·cal
sem·i·vow·el
sem·i·week·ly
sem·i·week·lies
sem·i·year·ly
sen·a·ry
sen·ate
sen·a·tor
sen·a·tor·ship
sen·a·to·ri·al
sen·a·to·ri·al·ly
send-off
Sen·e·ca
Sen·e·gal
se·nile
se·nil·i·ty
se·nior
se·nior·i·ty
sen·na
Sen·nach·er·ib
se·ñor
se·ñors
se·ño·ra
se·ño·ri·ta
sen·sate
sen·sa·tion
sen·sa·tion·al
sen·sa·tion·al·ly
sen·sa·tion·al·ism
sense
sensed
sens·ing
sense·less
sense·less·ness
sen·si·bil·i·ty
sen·si·bil·i·ties
sen·si·ble
sen·si·ble·ness
sen·si·bly
sen·si·tive
sen·si·tiv·i·ty
sen·si·tiv·i·ties
sen·si·tize
sen·si·tized
sen·si·tiz·ing
sen·si·ti·za·tion
sen·si·tiz·er
sen·sor
sen·so·ry
sen·so·ri·al
sen·su·al
sen·su·al·i·ty
sen·su·al·ly
sen·su·al·ism
sen·su·al·ist
sen·su·al·ize
sen·su·al·ized
sen·su·al·iz·ing
sen·su·al·i·za·tion
sen·su·ous
sen·tence
sen·tenced
sen·tenc·ing

sen·tient
sen·ti·ment
sen·ti·men·tal
 sen·ti·men·tal·ly
sen·ti·men·tal·i·ty
sen·ti·men·tal·i·ties
sen·ti·men·tal·ist
sen·ti·men·tal·ize
sen·ti·men·tal·ized
sen·ti·men·tal·iz·ing
sen·ti·men·ta·li·za·tion
sen·ti·nel
 sen·ti·neled
 sen·ti·nel·ing
sen·try
 sen·tries
se·pal
 se·paled
 se·palled
sep·a·ra·ble
 sep·a·ra·bil·i·ty
 sep·a·ra·bly
sep·a·rate
 sep·a·rat·ed
 sep·a·rat·ing
 sep·a·rate·ness
sep·a·ra·tion
sep·a·ra·tist
 sep·a·ra·tism
sep·a·ra·tive
sep·a·ra·tor
se·pia
sep·sis
 sep·ses
Sep·tem·ber
sep·ten·ni·al
sep·tet
sep·tic
 sep·ti·cal·ly
 sep·tic·i·ty
sep·ti·ce·mia
 sep·ti·ce·mic
sep·tu·a·ge·nar·i·an
Sep·tu·a·gint
sep·tum
 sep·ta
sep·tu·ple
 sep·tu·pled
 sep·tu·pling
se·pul·cher
 se·pul·chered
 se·pul·cher·ing
 se·pul·chral
se·quel
se·quence
se·quent
se·quen·tial
 se·quen·tial·ly
se·ques·ter
 se·ques·tered
 se·ques·tra·ble
 se·ques·tra·tion
se·quin
 se·quined
se·quoia

se·ra·pe
ser·aph
 ser·aphs
 ser·a·phim
 se·raph·ic
Ser·bia
ser·e·nade
 ser·e·nad·ed
 ser·e·nad·ing
 ser·e·nad·er
ser·en·dip·i·ty
 ser·en·dip·i·tous
se·rene
 se·rene·ness
se·ren·i·ty
 se·ren·i·ties
serf
serge
ser·geant
 ser·geant at arms
 ser·geant ma·jor
se·ri·al
 se·ri·al·ly
 se·ri·al·ist
 se·ri·al·i·za·tion
 se·ri·al·ize
 se·ri·al·ized
 se·ri·al·iz·ing
se·ries
se·ri·ous
 se·ri·ous·ly
 se·ri·ous·ness
 se·ri·ous-mind·ed
 se·ri·ous-mind·ed·ly
ser·mon
 ser·mon·ize
 ser·mon·ized
 ser·mon·iz·ing
 ser·mon·iz·er
se·rol·o·gy
 se·ro·log·ic
 se·ro·log·i·cal
 se·rol·o·gist
se·rous
ser·pent
 ser·pen·tine
ser·rate
 ser·rat·ed
 ser·rat·ing
ser·ra·tion
se·rum
 se·rums
 se·ra
serv·ant
serve
 served
 serv·ing
 serv·er
serv·ice
 serv·iced
 serv·ic·ing
serv·ice·a·ble
 serv·ice·a·bil·i·ty
 serv·ice·a·ble·ness
 serv·ice·a·bly

serv·ice·man
ser·vil·i·ty
ser·vile·ness
ser·vi·tude
ser·vo·mech·an·ism
ses·a·me
ses·qui·cen·ten·ni·al
ses·sion
set·back
set-in
set·off
set·tee
set·ter
set·ting
set·tle
set·tled
set·tling
set·tle·ment
set·tler
set-to
set·up
sev·en
sev·enth
sev·en·teen
sev·en·teenth
sev·en·ty
sev·en·ti·eth
sev·er
sev·er·a·bil·i·ty
sev·er·a·ble
sev·er·al
sev·er·al·ly
sev·er·al·fold
sev·er·ance
se·vere
se·ver·er
se·ver·est
se·vere·ness
se·ver·i·ty
se·ver·i·ties
Se·ville
sew·age
Sew·ard
sew·er
sew·er·age
sew·ing
sew·ing ma·chine
sex·less
sex·less·ness
sex·ol·o·gy
sex·o·log·i·cal
sex·ol·o·gist
sex·tant
sex·tet
sex·ton
sex·tu·ple
sex·tu·pled
sex·tu·pling
sex·tu·plet
sex·u·al
sex·u·al·ly
sex·u·al·i·ty
sexy
sex·i·er

sex·i·est
sex·i·ness
shab·by
shab·bi·er
shab·bi·est
shab·bi·ly
shab·bi·ness
shack·le
shack·led
shack·ling
shack·ler
shade
shad·ed
shad·ing
shade·less
shad·ow
shad·ow·er
shad·ow·like
shad·ow·box
shad·owy
shady
shad·i·er
shad·i·est
shad·i·ly
shad·i·ness
shaft·ing
shag
shagged
shag·ging
shag·ged
shag·like
shag·bark
shag·gy
shag·gi·er
shag·gi·est
shag·gi·ly
shag·gi·ness
shake
shak·en
shak·ing
shake·down
shak·er
Shake·speare
Shake·spear·e·an
shake-up
shaky
shak·i·er
shak·i·est
shak·i·ly
shak·i·ness
shal·lot
shal·low
shal·low·ness
sham
shammed
sham·ming
sha·man
sha·man·ism
sha·man·ist
sham·bles
shame
shamed
sham·ing
shame·faced
shame·fac·ed·ly

shame·fac·ed·ness
shame·ful
  shame·ful·ly
shame·less
  shame·less·ly
  shame·less·ness
sham·mer
sham·my
sham·poo
  sham·pooed
  sham·poo·ing
  sham·poo·er
sham·rock
shang·hai
  shang·haied
  shang·hai·ing
Shan·gri-la
Shan·non
shan·tey
  shan·teys
shan·ty
  shan·ties
shan·ty·town
shape
  shaped
  shap·ing
  shap·a·ble
  shap·er
shape·less
shape·ly
  shape·li·er
  shape·li·est
  shape·li·ness
share
  shared
  shar·ing
  shar·er
share·crop·per
  share·crop
  share·cropped
  share·crop·ping
share·hold·er
shark·skin
Shar·on
sharp·en
  sharp·en·er
sharp·er
sharp·eyed
sharp·ie
sharp·shoot·er
  sharp·shoot·ing
sharp·tongued
sharp·wit·ted
  sharp·wit·ted·ly
  sharp·wit·ted·ness
Shas·ta
shat·ter
shat·ter·proof
shave
  shaved
  shav·en
  shav·ing
shav·er
shawl
Shaw·nee

sheaf
sheaves
shear
  sheared
  shear·ing
  shear·er
sheath
  sheath·less
  sheath·like
sheathe
  sheathed
  sheath·ing
  sheath·er
sheave
  sheaved
  sheav·ing
She·ba
she·bang
shed
  shed·ding
sheen
  sheeny
  sheen·i·er
  sheen·i·est
sheep·dog
sheep·herd·er
  sheep·herd·ing
sheep·ish
sheep·shear·ing
  sheep·shear·er
sheep·skin
sheer
  sheer·ly
  sheer·ness
sheet·ing
Shef·field
sheik
shelf
  shelves
shell
  shelled
  shell-like
  shel·ly
  shel·ler
shel·lac
  shel·lacked
  shel·lack·ing
shell·fire
shell·fish
shell·shocked
shel·ter
  shel·ter·er
shelve
  shelved
  shelv·ing
Shen·an·do·ah
she·nan·i·gan
shep·herd
  shep·herd·ess
Sher·a·ton
sher·bet
Sher·i·dan
sher·iff
Sher·lock
Sher·man

sher·ry
 sher·ries
Sher·wood
Shet·land
shib·bo·leth
shield
 shield·er
shift
 shift·er
 shift·ing·ness
shift·less
shifty
 shift·i·er
 shift·i·est
 shift·i·ly
 shift·i·ness
shi·ly-shal·ly
 shil·ly-shal·lied
 shil·ly-shal·ly·ing
Shi·loh
shim·mer
 shim·mery
 shim·mer·i·er
 shim·mer·i·est
shim·my
 shim·mies
 shim·mied
 shim·my·ing
shin
 shinned
 shin·ning
shin·bone
shin·dig
shine
 shined
 shone
 shin·ing
shin·er
shin·gle
 shin·gled
 shin·gling
 shin·gler
 shin·gles
shin·ing
 shin·ing·ly
shin·ny
 shin·nied
 shin·ny·ing
shiny
 shin·i·er
 shin·i·est
 shin·i·ness
ship
 shipped
 ship·ping
 ship·pa·ble
ship·board
ship·build·er
 ship·build·ing
ship·mate
ship·ment
ship·per
ship·shape
ship·wreck
ship·yard

shirk
 shirk·er
shirt·tail
shirt·waist
shish ke·bab
shiv·er
 shiv·ery
 shiv·er·i·er
 shiv·er·i·est
shoal
shock·er
shock·ing
shod·dy
 shod·dies
 shod·di·er
 shod·di·est
 shod·di·ly
 shod·di·ness
shoe·horn
shoe·lace
shoe·mak·er
sho·er
shoe·string
shoo-in
shoot
 shot
 shoot·ing
 shoot·er
shop
 shopped
 shop·ping
shop·keep·er
shop·lift·er
 shop·lift·ing
shop·per
shop·talk
shop·worn
shore
 shore·line
short
 short·ly
 short·ness
short·age
short-change
 short-changed
 short-chang·ing
 short-chang·er
short·com·ing
short·cut
 short-cut·ting
short·en
 short·en·er
 short·en·ing
short·hand
short-hand·ed
 short-hand·ed·ly
 short-hand·ed·ness
short-lived
short-sight·ed
 short-sight·ed·ly
 short-sight·ed·ness
short-tem·pered
short-term
short·wave
short-wind·ed

Sho·sho·ne
shot·gun
  shot·gunned
  shot·gun·ning
shoul·der
shoul·der blade
shout·er
shout·ing
shove
  shoved
  shov·ing
  shov·er
shov·el
  shov·eled
  shov·el·ing
  shov·el·er
  shov·el·ful
show
  showed
  shown
  show·ing
show·bill
show·boat
show·case
  show·cased
  show·cas·ing
show·down
show·er
  show·ery
show·man
  show·men
  show·man·ship
show·off
show·piece
show·place
show·room
showy
  show·i·er
  show·i·est
  show·i·ly
  show·i·ness
shrap·nel
shred
  shred·ded
  shred·ding
  shred·der
Shreve·port
shrew
  shrew·like
shrewd
  shrewd·ly
  shrewd·ness
shrew·ish
Shrews·bury
shriek
shrill
  shril·ly
  shrill·ness
shrimp
shrine
  shrined
  shrin·ing
shrink
  shrunk·en
  shrink·a·ble

shrink·er
shrink·age
shriv·el
  shriv·eled
  shriv·el·ing
Shrop·shire
shroud
Shrove·tide
shrub·bery
  shrub·ber·ies
shrub·by
  shrub·bi·er
  shrub·bi·est
shrug
  shrugged
  shrug·ging
shuck·er
shud·der
  shud·dery
shuf·fle
  shuf·fled
  shuf·fling
  shuf·fler
shuf·fle·board
shun
  shunned
  shun·ning
  shun·ner
shunt
  shunt·er
shut·down
shut·eye
shut·in
shut·off
shut·out
shut·ter
shut·tle
  shut·tled
  shut·tling
  shut·tle·like
shy
  shi·er
  shi·est
  shy·er
  shy·est
  shied
  shy·ing
  shy·ness
Shy·lock
shy·ster
Si·am
Si·a·mese
Si·be·ria
sib·i·lant
  sib·i·lance
sib·ling
sic
  sicked
  sick·ing
sick·bed
sick·en
  sick·en·ing
sick·ish
sick·le
sick·ly

sick·li·er
sick·li·est
sick·li·ness
sick·ness
sick·room
side·arm
side·board
side·burns
side·car
sid·ed
side·kick
side·light
side·line
side·lined
side·lin·ing
side·long
side·show
side·split·ting
side·step
side·stepped
side·step·ping
side·swipe
side·swiped
side·swip·ing
side·track
side·walk
side·wall
side·ward
side·ways
sid·ing
si·dle
si·dled
si·dling
siege
Si·ena
si·en·na
si·er·ra
Si·er·ra Le·one
Si·er·ra Ma·dre
Si·er·ra Ne·vad·as
si·es·ta
sieve
sieved
siev·ing
sift·er
sift·ings
sigh·er
sight·ed
sight·less
sight·ly
sight-read
sight-read·ing
sight·see·ing
sight·see·er
sig·nal
sig·naled
sig·nal·ing
sig·nal·er
sig·nal·man
sig·nal·men
sig·na·to·ry
sig·na·to·ries
sig·na·ture
sign·board
sig·net

sig·nif·i·cance
sig·nif·i·cant
sig·ni·fi·ca·tion
sig·ni·fy
sig·ni·fied
sig·ni·fy·ing
sig·ni·fi·a·ble
sig·ni·fi·er
sign·post
si·lage
si·lence
si·lenced
si·lenc·ing
si·lenc·er
si·lent
Si·le·sia
sil·hou·ette
sil·hou·et·ted
sil·hou·et·ting
sil·ica
sil·i·con
sil·i·cone
silk·en
silk·like
silk·weed
silk·worm
silky
silk·i·er
silk·i·est
silk·i·ly
silk·i·ness
sil·ly
sil·li·er
sil·li·est
sil·li·ly
sil·li·ness
si·lo
si·los
si·loed
si·lo·ing
silt
sil·ta·tion
silty
silt·i·er
silt·i·est
sil·ver
sil·ver·fish
sil·ver·smith
sil·ver-tongued
sil·ver·ware
sil·very
sil·ver·i·ness
Sim·e·on
sim·i·an
sim·i·lar
sim·i·lar·i·ty
sim·i·lar·i·ties
sim·i·le
si·mil·i·tude
sim·mer
si·mon·ize
si·mon·ized
si·mon·iz·ing
Si·mon Le·gree
sim·pa·ti·co

sim·per
  sim·per·er
  sim·per·ing·ly
sim·ple
  sim·pler
  sim·plest
  sim·ple·ness
sim·ple-mind·ed
  sim·ple-mind·ed·ness
sim·ple·ton
sim·plex
sim·plic·i·ty
  sim·plic·i·ties
sim·pli·fy
  sim·pli·fied
  sim·pli·fy·ing
  sim·pli·fi·ca·tion
  sim·pli·fi·er
sim·plism
  sim·plis·tic
  sim·plis·ti·cal·ly
sim·ply
sim·u·late
  sim·u·lat·ed
  sim·u·lat·ing
  sim·u·la·tion
  sim·u·la·tive
  sim·u·la·tor
si·mul·cast
  si·mul·cast·ing
si·mul·ta·ne·ous
  si·mul·ta·ne·ous·ness
  si·mul·ta·ne·i·ty
sin
  sinned
  sin·ning
Si·nai
Sin·bad
sin·cere
sin·cer·i·ty
si·ne·cure
si·ne qua non
sin·ew
sin·ewy
sin·ful
  sin·ful·ly
  sin·ful·ness
sing
  sing·ing
  sing·a·ble
Sing·a·pore
singe
  singed
  singe·ing
sing·er
sin·gle
  sin·gled
  sin·gling
  sin·gle·ness
sin·gle-breast·ed
sin·gle-hand·ed
  sin·gle-hand·ed·ly
  sin·gle-hand·ed·ness
sin·gle-mind·ed
  sin·gle-mind·ed·ly

sin·gle-mind·ed·ness
sin·gle-space
  sin·gle-spaced
  sin·gle-spac·ing
sin·gle·ton
sin·gle-track
sin·gly
sing·song
sin·gu·lar
  sin·gu·lar·i·ty
  sin·gu·lar·i·ties
sin·is·ter
  sin·is·ter·ness
sink·a·ble
sink·er
sink·hole
sin·less
sin·ner
sin·u·ate
  sin·u·at·ed
  sin·u·at·ing
sin·u·ous
  sin·u·os·i·ty
  sin·u·ous·ness
si·nus
si·nus·i·tis
sip
  sipped
  sip·ping
sip·per
si·phon
sire
  sired
  sir·ing
si·ren
sir·loin
sis·sy
  sis·sies
  sis·si·fied
  sis·sy·ish
sis·ter
  sis·ter·li·ness
  sis·ter·ly
sis·ter·hood
sis·ter-in-law
  sis·ters-in-law
si·tar
sit-in
Sit·ka
sit·ter
sit·ting
sit·u·ate
  sit·u·at·ed
  sit·u·at·ing
sit·u·a·tion
six-pack
six-shoot·er
six·teen
six·teenth
sixth
six·ty
six·ti·eth
siz·a·ble
  siz·a·ble·ness
  siz·a·bly

size
sized
siz·ing
siz·zle
siz·zled
siz·zling
siz·zler
skate
skat·ed
skat·ing
skat·er
ske·dad·dle
ske·dad·dled
ske·dad·dling
skein
skel·e·ton
skel·e·tal
skep·tic
skep·ti·cal
skep·ti·cism
sketch
sketch·er
sketch·book
sketchy
sketch·i·er
sketch·i·est
sketch·i·ly
sketch·i·ness
skew·er
skew·ness
ski
skied
ski·ing
ski·er
skid
skid·ded
skid·ding
skid·der
skilled
skil·let
skill·ful
skill·ful·ly
skill·ful·ness
skim
skimmed
skim·ming
skim·mer
skimp
skimp·i·ly
skimp·i·ness
skimp·ing·ly
skimp·y
skimp·i·er
skimp·i·est
skin
skinned
skin·ning
skin-deep
skin-dive
skin-dived
skin-div·ing
skin-div·er
skin·flint
skin·less
skin·ner

skin·ny
skin·ni·er
skin·ni·est
skin·tight
skip·per
skir·mish
skir·mish·er
skirt·er
skirt·ing
skit·ter
skit·tish
skiv·vy
skiv·vies
skoal
skul·dug·ger·y
skulk·er
skull·cap
skunk
sky
skies
skied
sky·ing
sky-blue
sky·cap
sky·div·ing
sky-high
sky·lark
sky·light
sky·line
sky·rock·et
sky·scrap·er
sky·ward
sky·way
sky·writ·ing
sky·writ·er
slab
slabbed
slab·bing
slack
slack·ness
slack·en
slack·er
slack-jawed
slake
slaked
slak·ing
sla·lom
slam
slammed
slam·ming
slam-bang
slan·der
slan·der·er
slan·der·ous
slang
slang·i·ly
slang·i·ness
slangy
slang·i·er
slang·i·est
slant
slant·ways
slant·wise
slap
slapped

slap·ping
slap·per
slap·dash
slap·hap·py
  slap·hap·pi·er
  slap·hap·pi·est
slap·stick
slasher
slash·ing
slat
  slat·ted
  slat·ting
slate
  slat·ed
  slat·ing
  slate·like
  slaty
  slat·i·er
  slat·i·est
slath·er
slat·tern
  slat·tern·li·ness
  slat·tern·ly
slaugh·ter
  slaugh·ter·er
  slaugh·ter·house
slave
  slaved
  slav·ing
slav·er
slav·ery
Slav·ic
slav·ish
  sla·vish·ly
  sla·vish·ness
slay
  slain
  slay·ing
  slay·er
slea·zy
  slea·zi·er
  slea·zi·est
  slea·zi·ly
  slea·zi·ness
sled
  sled·ded
  sled·ding
  sled·der
sledge
  sledged
  sledg·ing
sleek
  sleek·er
  sleek·ness
sleep·er
sleep·less
  sleep·less·ness
sleep·walk
  sleep·walk·er
  sleep·walk·ing
sleepy
  sleep·i·er
  sleep·i·est
  sleep·i·ly
  sleep·i·ness

sleep·y·head
sleet
  sleety
  sleet·i·ness
sleeve
  sleeved
  sleev·ing
  sleeve·less
sleigh
  sleigh·er
sleight
slen·der
  slen·der·ness
  slen·der·ize
  slen·der·ized
  slen·der·iz·ing
sleuth
slice
  sliced
  slic·ing
  slic·er
slick·er
slick·ness
slide
  slid
  slid·ing
  slid·er
slight
  slight·er
  slight·ing
slim
  slim·mer
  slim·mest
  slimmed
  slim·ming
  slim·ness
slime
  slimed
  slim·ing
  slimy
  slim·i·er
  slim·i·est
  slim·i·ly
  slim·i·ness
sling·er
sling-shot
slinky
  slink·i·er
  slink·i·est
slip
  slipped
  slip·ping
slip·cov·er
slip·knot
slip·on
slip·o·ver
slip·page
slip·per
slip·pery
  slip·per·i·er
  slip·per·i·est
  slip·per·i·ness
slip·py
slip·shod
slip·stick

slip-up
slit
  slit·ting
  slit·ter
slith·er
  slith·ery
sliv·er
  sliv·er·er
  sliv·er·like
slob·ber
  slob·ber·er
  slob·ber·ing·ly
sloe-eyed
slo·gan
  slo·gan·eer
slop
  slopped
  slop·ping
slope
  sloped
  slop·ing
  slop·er
slop·py
  slop·pi·er
  slop·pi·est
  slop·pi·ly
  slop·pi·ness
sloshy
  slosh·i·er
  slosh·i·est
slot
  slot·ted
  slot·ting
sloth
  sloth·ful
  sloth·ful·ly
  sloth·ful·ness
slouch
  slouch·er
  slouch·i·ly
  slouch·i·ness
  slouchy
  slouch·i·er
  slouch·i·est
slough
  sloughy
  slough·i·er
  slough·i·est
  slough·i·ness
Slo·vak
Slo·vak·ia
slov·en
slov·en·ly
  slov·en·li·ness
slow·down
slow-mo·tion
slow·poke
slow-wit·ted
sludge
  sludgy
  sludg·i·er
  sludg·i·est
slug
  slugged
  slug·ging

slug·ger
slug·gard
  slug·gard·li·ness
slug·gish
  slug·gish·ness
sluice
  sluiced
  sluic·ing
slum
  slummed
  slum·ming
  slum·mer
slum·ber
  slum·ber·er
  slum·ber·ous
slur
  slurred
  slur·ring
slush
  slush·i·ness
  slushy
  slush·i·er
  slush·i·est
slut
  slut·tish
sly
  sli·er
  sly·er
  sli·est
  sly·est
  sly·ly
  sli·ly
  sly·ness
smack·er
smack·ing
small-mind·ed
  small-mind·ed·ness
small·pox
small-time
  small-tim·er
smart
  smart·ness
smart al·eck
  smart-al·ecky
  smart·en
smarty
smash·er
smash·ing
smash-up
smat·ter
  smat·ter·er
  smat·ter·ing
smear
  smear·er
  smeary
  smear·i·er
  smear·i·est
  smear·i·ness
smell
  smelled
  smel·ling
  smell·er
  smelly
  smell·i·er
  smell·i·est

smelt
smelt·er
  smelt·ery
  smid·gen
smile
  smil·er
  smil·ing·ly
smirch
smirk
  smirk·er
  smirk·ing·ly
smite
  smote
  smit·ten
  smit·ing
  smit·er
smith·er·eens
Smith·so·ni·an
smit·ten
smock·ing
smog·gy
  smog·gi·er
  smog·gi·est
smoke
  smoked
  smok·ing
  smoke·less
smoke·house
smok·er
smoke·stack
smok·ing jack·et
smoky
  smok·i·er
  smok·i·est
  smok·i·ly
  smok·i·ness
smol·der
smooth
  smooth·er
  smooth·ness
smooth·en
smooth·ie
smoth·er
  smoth·ery
  smoth·er·i·er
  smoth·er·i·est
smudge
  smudged
  smudg·ing
  smudg·i·ly
  smudg·i·ness
  smudgy
  smudg·i·er
  smudg·i·est
smug
  smug·ger
  smug·gest
  smug·ly
  smug·ness
smug·gle
  smug·gled
  smug·gling
  smug·gler
smut
  smut·ted

smut·ting
smut·ty
  smut·ti·er
  smut·ti·est
  smut·ti·ly
  smut·ti·ness
Smyr·na
sna·fu
  sna·fued
  sna·fu·ing
snag
  snagged
  snag·ging
  snag·gy
  snag·gi·er
  snag·gi·est
snag·gle·tooth
  snag·gle·teeth
  snag·gle·toothed
snail
  snail·like
  snail-paced
snake
  snaked
  snak·ing
  snake·like
  snak·i·ly
snake·bite
snake·skin
snaky
  snak·i·er
  snak·i·est
  snak·i·ness
snap
  snapped
  snap·ping
snap·back
snap·drag·on
snap·per
snap·pish
  snap·pish·ness
snap·py
  snap·pi·er
  snap·pi·est
  snap·pi·ly
  snap·pi·ness
snap·shot
snare
  snared
  snar·ing
  snar·er
snarl
  snarl·er
  snarly
  snarl·i·er
  snarl·i·est
snatch
  snatch·er
  snatchy
  snatch·i·er
  snatch·i·est
  snatch·i·ly
snaz·zy
  snaz·zi·er
  snaz·zi·est

sneak·er
sneak·ing
sneaky
  sneak·i·er
  sneak·i·est
  sneak·i·ly
  sneak·i·ness
sneer
  sneer·er
  sneer·ing·ly
sneeze
  sneezed
  sneez·ing
  sneez·er
  sneezy
  sneez·i·er
  sneez·i·est
snick·er
snif·fle
  snif·fled
  snif·fling
  snif·fler
snif·fy
  snif·fi·er
  snif·fi·est
  snif·fi·ly
  snif·fi·ness
  sniff·ish
snif·ter
snip
  snipped
  snip·ping
  snip·per
snipe
  sniped
  snip·ing
  snip·er
snip·py
  snip·pi·er
  snip·pi·est
  snip·pi·ly
  snip·pi·ness
snitch·er
sniv·el
  sniv·eled
  sniv·el·ing
  sniv·el·er
snob
  snob·bery
  snob·bish
  snob·bish·ness
snoop
  snoopy
  snoop·i·er
  snoop·i·est
  snoop·er
snooty
  snoot·i·er
  snoot·i·est
  snoot·i·ly
  snoot·i·ness
snooze
  snoozed
  snooz·ing
  snooz·er

snore
snored
snor·ing
snor·er
snor·kel
snort
snort·er
snot·ty
  snot·ti·er
  snot·ti·est
snout
  snout·ed
  snouty
  snout·i·er
  snout·i·est
snow·ball
snow·blow·er
snow·bound
snow·cap
snow·drift
snow·fall
snow·flake
snow·man
  snow·men
snow·mo·bile
snow·plow
snow·shoe
  snow·shoed
  snow·shoe·ing
snow·suit
snow-white
snowy
  snow·i·er
  snow·i·est
  snow·i·ly
  snow·i·ness
snub
  snubbed
  snub·bing
  snub·ber
  snub·by
  snub·bi·er
  snub·bi·est
  snub·bi·ness
snub-nosed
snuf·fle
  snuf·fled
  snuf·fling
  snuf·fler
snuf·fly
  snuf·fli·er
  snuf·fli·est
snuffy
  snuff·i·er
  snuff·i·est
  snuff·i·ness
snug
  snug·ger
  snug·gest
  snugged
  snug·ging
  snug·ly
  snug·ness
snug·gle
  snug·gled

snug·gling
soak
  soak·age
  soak·er
  soak·ing·ly
so-and-so
soap·box
soap·suds
soapy
  soap·i·er
  soap·i·est
  soap·i·ly
  soap·i·ness
soar·er
sob
  sobbed
  sob·bing
  sob·ber
so·ber
  so·ber·ing·ly
  so·ber·ness
so·bri·e·ty
so·bri·quet
so-called
soc·cer
so·cia·ble
  so·cia·bil·i·ty
  so·cia·ble·ness
  so·cia·bly
so·cial
  so·ci·al·i·ty
  so·cial·ly
so·cial·ism
so·cial·ist
  so·cial·is·tic
  so·cial·is·ti·cal·ly
so·cial·ite
so·cial·ize
  so·cial·ized
  so·cial·iz·ing
  so·cial·i·za·tion
  so·cial·iz·er
so·ci·e·ty
  so·ci·e·ties
  so·ci·e·tal
so·ci·o·ec·o·nom·ic
so·ci·ol·o·gy
  so·ci·o·log·i·cal
  so·ci·ol·o·gist
so·ci·o·po·lit·i·cal
sock·et
Soc·ra·tes
sod
  sod·ded
  sod·ding
so·da
so·dal·i·ty
  so·dal·i·ties
sod·den
  sod·den·ness
so·di·um
Sod·om
sod·omy
so·ev·er
so·fa

So·fia
soft
  soft·ness
soft·ball
soft-boiled
sof·ten
  sof·ten·er
soft-head·ed
soft-heart·ed
  soft-heart·ed·ness
soft-ped·al
  soft-ped·aled
  soft-ped·al·ing
soft-shell
soft-shoe
soft-spo·ken
soft·ware
soft·wood
softy
  sof·ties
sog·gy
  sog·gi·er
  sog·gi·est
  sog·gi·ly
  sog·gi·ness
soi·rée
so·journ
  so·journ·er
sol·ace
  sol·aced
  sol·ac·ing
  sol·ac·er
so·lar
  so·lar·i·um
  so·lar·i·ums
  so·lar·ia
so·lar·ize
  so·lar·ized
  so·lar·iz·ing
  so·lar·i·za·tion
sol·der
  sol·der·er
sol·dier
  sol·diery
sol·e·cism
sole·ly
sol·emn
  sol·emn·ly
  sol·emn·ness
so·lem·ni·ty
  so·lem·ni·ties
sol·em·nize
  sol·em·nized
  sol·em·niz·ing
  sol·em·ni·za·tion
sole·ness
so·lic·it
  so·lic·i·ta·tion
so·lic·i·tor
so·lic·i·tous
  so·lic·i·tous·ness
so·lic·i·tude
sol·id
  so·lid·i·ty
  sol·id·ness

sol·i·dar·i·ty
sol·i·dar·i·ties
so·lid·i·fy
so·lid·i·fied
so·lid·i·fy·ing
so·lid·i·fi·ca·tion
so·lil·o·quize
so·lil·o·quized
so·lil·o·quiz·ing
so·lil·o·quist
so·lil·o·quy
so·lil·o·quies
sol·i·taire
sol·i·tary
sol·i·tar·ies
sol·i·tar·i·ly
sol·i·tar·i·ness
sol·i·tude
so·lo
so·loed
so·lo·ing
so·lo·ist
Sol·o·mon
So·lon
sol·stice
sol·u·ble
sol·u·bil·i·ty
sol·u·ble·ness
sol·u·bly
sol·ute
so·lu·tion
solve
solved
solv·ing
solv·a·ble
solv·a·bil·i·ty
solv·a·ble·ness
solv·er
sol·vent
sol·ven·cy
So·ma·li
so·mat·ic
so·ma·to·type
som·ber
som·ber·ly
som·ber·ness
som·bre·ro
som·bre·ros
some·body
some·bod·ies
some·day
some·how
some·one
some·place
som·er·sault
Som·er·set
Som·er·ville
some·thing
some·time
some·times
some·way
some·what
some·where
som·nam·bu·late
som·nam·bu·lat·ed

som·nam·bu·lat·ing
som·nam·bu·lant
som·nam·bu·la·tion
som·nam·bu·lism
som·nam·bu·list
som·no·lent
som·no·lence
som·no·len·cy
so·nar
so·na·ta
song·bird
song·fest
song·ster
song·stress
song·writ·er
son·ic
son-in-law
sons-in-law
son·net
son·net·eer
son·ny
son·nies
So·no·ra
so·no·rous
so·nor·i·ty
so·no·rous·ness
soon·er
soothe
soothed
sooth·ing
sooth·er
sooth·say·er
sooth·say·ing
sooty
soot·i·er
soot·i·est
soot·i·ly
soot·i·ness
sop
sopped
sop·ping
So·phia
soph·ist
soph·ism
so·phis·tic
so·phis·ti·cal
so·phis·ti·cate
so·phis·ti·cat·ed
so·phis·ti·cat·ing
so·phis·ti·ca·tion
so·phis·ti·ca·tor
soph·ist·ry
soph·ist·ries
Soph·o·cles
soph·o·more
soph·o·mor·ic
soph·o·mor·i·cal
soph·o·mor·i·cal·ly
sop·o·rif·ic
sop·py
sop·pi·er
sop·pi·est
so·prano
so·pran·os
Sor·bonne

sor·cer·er
 sor·cer·ess
sor·cery
 sor·cer·ies
 sor·cer·ous
sor·did
 sor·did·ness
sore
 sor·er
 sor·est
 sore·ly
 sore·ness
sore·head
 sore·head·ed
sor·ghum
so·ror·i·ty
 so·ror·i·ties
sor·rel
sor·row
 sor·row·er
 sor·row·ful
sor·ry
 sor·ri·er
 sor·ri·est
 sor·ri·ly
 sor·ri·ness
sort·a·ble
sort·er
sor·tie
so-so
sot
 sot·ted
 sot·tish
 sot·tish·ness
sot·to vo·ce
sou·bri·quet
souf·flé
 souf·fléed
sought
soul·ful
 soul·ful·ly
 soul·ful·ness
soul·less
soul·search·ing
sound
 sound·a·ble
 sound·ly
 sound·ness
sound·box
sound·er
sound·ing
sound·less
 sound·less·ly
 sound·less·ness
sound·proof
soupy
 soup·i·er
 soup·i·est
sour
 sour·ish
 sour·ness
sour·ball
source
souse
 soused

sous·ing
South·amp·ton
south·bound
South Car·o·li·na
South Da·ko·ta
south·east
south·east·er
south·east·er·ly
south·east·ern
south·east·ward
 south·east·ward·ly
south·er
south·er·ly
south·ern
 south·ern·most
 south·ern·er
South·ern Hem·i·sphere
south·paw
south·ward
 south·ward·ly
South·wark
south·west
south·west·er
south·west·er·ly
south·west·ern
 south·west·ern·er
south·west·ward
 south·west·ward·ly
sou·ve·nir
sov·er·eign
sov·er·eign·ty
 sov·er·eign·ties
so·vi·et
sow·er
soy·bean
space
 spaced
 spac·ing
 space·less
 spac·er
Space·Age
space·craft
space·man
 space·men
space·ship
space·walk
spa·cious
 spa·cious·ness
Spack·le
 spack·led
 spack·ling
spade
 spad·ed
 spad·ing
 spade·ful
 spad·er
spade·work
spa·ghet·ti
span
 spanned
 span·ning
span·gle
 span·gled
 span·gling
Span·iard

span·iel
Span·ish
spank·er
spank·ing
spar
 sparred
 spar·ring
spare
 spared
 spar·ing
 spar·er
 spar·est
 spare·a·ble
 spare·ness
 spar·er
spare·rib
spar·ing
 spar·ing·ness
spark·er
spar·kle
 spark·led
 spar·kling
spar·kler
spar·row
spar·row·grass
sparse
 spars·er
 spars·est
 sparse·ness
Spar·ta
Spar·tan
spasm
spas·mod·ic
 spas·mod·i·cal
 spas·mod·i·cal·ly
spas·tic
 spas·ti·cal·ly
spat
 spat·ted
 spat·ting
spa·tial
 spa·cial
 spa·ti·al·i·ty
 spa·tial·ly
spat·ter
spat·u·la
spawn
speak
 spok·en
 speak·ing
 speak·a·ble
speak·eas·y
 speak·eas·ies
speak·er
 speak·er·ship
spear·er
spear·head
spear·mint
spe·cial
 spe·cial·ly
 spe·cial·ist
spe·cial·ize
 spe·cial·ized
 spe·cial·iz·ing
 spe·cial·i·za·tion

spe·cial·ty
 spe·cial·ties
spe·cie
spe·cies
spec·i·fi·a·ble
spe·cif·ic
 spe·cif·i·cal·ly
 spec·i·fic·i·ty
spec·i·fi·ca·tion
spec·i·fy
 spec·i·fied
 spec·i·fy·ing
 spec·i·fi·er
spec·i·men
spe·cious
 spe·ci·os·i·ty
 spe·ci·os·i·ties
 spe·cious·ness
speck·le
 speck·led
 speck·ling
spec·ta·cle
 spec·ta·cled
spec·tac·u·lar
 spec·tac·u·lar·ly
spec·ta·tor
spec·ter
spec·tral
spec·tro·scope
 spec·tro·scop·ic
 spec·tro·scop·i·cal
 spec·tros·co·py
spec·trum
 spec·tra
 spec·trums
spec·u·late
 spec·u·lat·ed
 spec·u·lat·ing
 spec·u·la·tion
 spec·u·la·tor
 spec·u·la·tive
speech·i·fy
 speech·i·fied
 speech·i·fy·ing
speech·less
 speech·less·ness
speed
 speed·ed
 speed·ing
 speed·er
 speed·ster
speed·boat
 speed·boat·ing
speed·om·e·ter
speed-up
speed·way
speedy
 speed·i·er
 speed·i·est
 speed·i·ly
 speed·i·ness
spe·le·ol·o·gy
 spe·le·ol·o·gist
spell
 spelled

spell·ing
spell·bind
spell·bound
spell·bind·ing
spell·bind·er
spell·er
spe·lun·ker
spend
spent
spend·ing
spend·a·ble
spend·er
spend·thrift
sper·ma·ce·ti
sper·mat·ic
sper·ma·to·zo·on
sper·ma·to·zo·a
sper·ma·to·zo·ic
spew·er
sphag·num
sphere
sphered
spher·ing
spher·ic
sphe·ric·i·ty
spher·i·cal
spher·i·cal·ly
sphe·roid
sphe·roi·dal
sphinc·ter
sphinc·ter·al
sphinc·ter·ic
sphinx
sphinx·es
sphin·ges
spice
spiced
spic·ing
spi·cule
spic·u·lar
spic·u·late
spicy
spic·i·er
spic·i·est
spic·i·ly
spic·i·ness
spi·der
spi·dery
spiel
spiel·er
spi·er
spiffy
spiff·i·er
spiff·i·est
spiff·i·ness
spig·ot
spike
spiked
spik·ing
spiky
spik·i·er
spik·i·est
spill
spilled
spill·ing

spil·lage
spill·way
spin
spun
spin·ning
spin·ach
spi·nal
spi·nal·ly
spin·dle
spin·dled
spin·dling
spin·dle·legs
spin·dle·leg·ged
spin·dly
spin·dli·er
spin·dli·est
spine·less
spin·et
spin·na·ker
spin·ner
spin·ning wheel
spin-off
spi·nose
spi·nous
Spi·no·za
spin·ster
spiny
spin·i·ness
spi·ra·cle
spi·ral
spi·raled
spi·ral·ing
spi·ral·ly
spire
spired
spir·ing
spir·it
spir·it·ed
spir·it·ism
spir·it·ist
spir·it·less
spir·it·less·ness
spir·i·tous
spir·it·u·al
spir·it·u·al·ly
spir·it·u·al·ism
spir·it·u·al·ist
spir·it·u·al·is·tic
spir·it·u·al·i·ty
spir·it·u·al·i·ties
spir·it·u·al·ize
spir·it·u·al·ized
spir·it·u·al·iz·ing
spir·it·u·al·i·za·tion
spir·it·u·ous
spir·it·u·os·i·ty
spi·ro·chete
spit
spat
spit·ting
spit·ter
spite
spit·ed
spit·ing
spite·ful

spit·fire
spit·tle
spit·toon
splash
  splash·er
  splashy
  splash·i·er
  splash·i·est
  splash·i·ly
  splash·i·ness
splash·board
splash·down
splat·ter
splay·foot
  splay·feet
  splay·foot·ed
spleen
  spleen·ful
splen·did
splen·dif·er·ous
sple·net·ic
splice
  spliced
  splic·ing
  splic·er
splin·ter
  splin·tery
split
  split·ting
  split·a·ble
  split·ter
split-lev·el
split-sec·ond
splotch
  splotchy
  splotch·i·er
  splotch·i·est
splurge
  splurged
  splurg·ing
splut·ter
  splut·ter·er
spoil
  spoiled
  spoil·ing
  spoil·age
  spoil·er
spoil·sport
Spo·kane
spoke
  spoked
  spok·ing
spo·ken
spokes·man
  spokes·men
  spokes·wom·an
  spokes·wom·en
sponge
  sponged
  spong·ing
  spong·er
spon·gy
  spon·gi·er
  spon·gi·est
  spon·gi·ness

spon·sor
  spon·sor·ship
spon·ta·ne·i·ty
  spon·ta·ne·i·ties
spon·ta·ne·ous
  spon·ta·ne·ous·ly
  spon·ta·ne·ous·ness
spook
  spook·ish
spooky
  spook·i·er
  spook·i·est
  spook·i·ly
  spook·i·ness
spoon·er·ism
  spoon·er·is·tic
spoon-fed
spoon-feed
  spoon-feed·ing
spoon·ful
  spoon·fuls
spo·rad·ic
  spo·rad·i·cal
  spo·rad·i·cal·ly
spo·ran·gi·um
  spo·ran·gia
spore
  spored
  spor·ing
sport
  sport·er
  sport·ful
  sport·ful·ly
  sport·ful·ness
  sport·ing
  sport·ing·ly
spor·tive
sports·cast
  sports·cast·er
sports·man
  sports·men
  sports·wom·an
  sports·wom·en
  sports·man·like
  sports·man·ly
  sports·man·ship
sports·wear
sports·writ·er
sporty
  sport·i·er
  sport·i·est
  sport·i·ly
  sport·i·ness
spot
  spot·ted
  spot·ting
  spot·less
  spot·less·ly
  spot·less·ness
spot·light
spot·ter
spot·ty
  spot·ti·er
  spot·ti·est
  spot·ti·ly

spot·ti·ness
spouse
spout·er
sprained
sprawl·er
spray
 spray·er
spread
 spread·ing
spread-ea·gle
 spread·ea·gled
 spread·ea·gling
spread·er
sprig
 sprigged
 sprig·ging
spright·ly
 spright·li·er
 spright·li·est
 spright·li·ness
spring
 spring·ing
spring·board
spring-clean·ing
Spring·field
spring·time
springy
 spring·i·er
 spring·i·est
 spring·i·ly
 spring·i·ness
sprin·kle
 sprin·kled
 sprin·kling
 sprink·ler
sprint
 sprint·er
sprock·et
spruce
 spruc·er
 spruc·est
 spruced
 spruc·ing
spry
 spry·er
 spry·est
 spry·ly
 spry·ness
spue
 spued
 spu·ing
spume
 spumed
 spum·ing
 spum·ous
spunky
 spunk·i·er
 spunk·i·est
 spunk·i·ly
 spunk·i·ness
spur
 spurred
 spur·ring
spu·ri·ous
 spu·ri·ous·ness

spurner
spurt
 spurt·er
 spur·tive
sput·nik
sput·ter
 sput·ter·er
spu·tum
 spu·ta
spy
 spies
 spied
 spy·ing
spy·glass
squab·ble
 squab·bled
 squab·bling
squad·ron
squal·id
 squal·id·ly
 squal·id·ness
squall
 squally
 squall·i·er
 squall·i·est
squal·or
squan·der
 squan·der·er
square
 squared
 squar·ing
 square·ly
 square·ness
square-dance
 square-danced
 square-danc·ing
squar·ish
 squar·ish·ly
squash
 squash·er
 squash·es
 squashy
 squash·i·er
 squash·i·est
 squash·i·ly
 squash·i·ness
squat
 squat·ted
 squat·ting
 squat·ly
 squat·ness
 squat·ter
 squat·ty
 squat·ti·er
 squat·ti·est
squawk
 squawk·er
 squawky
 squawk·i·er
 squawk·i·est
squeak
 squeak·er
 squeak·ing·ly
 squeaky
 squeak·i·er

squeak·i·est
squeal
 squeal·er
squeam·ish
 squeam·ish·ly
 squeam·ish·ness
squee·gee
squeeze
 squeezed
 squeez·ing
 squeez·er
squelch
 squelch·er
squib
squid
squig·gle
 squig·gled
 squig·gling
squint
 squint·er
 squint·ing·ly
 squinty
 squint·i·er
 squint·i·est
squint·eyed
squire
 squired
 squir·ing
squirm
 squirmy
 squirm·i·er
 squirm·i·est
squir·rel
squirt
 squirt·er
squish
 squishy
 squish·i·er
 squish·i·est
stab
 stabbed
 stab·bing
 stab·ber
sta·bil·i·ty
 sta·bil·i·ties
sta·bi·lize
 sta·bi·lized
 sta·bi·liz·ing
 sta·bi·li·za·tion
sta·bi·liz·er
sta·ble
 sta·bled
 sta·bling
stac·ca·to
stack·er
sta·di·um
staff·er
Staf·ford
stag
 stagged
 stag·ging
stage
 staged
 stag·ing
stage-coach

stage·hand
stage-struck
stag·ger
 stag·ger·er
 stag·ger·ing
stag·nant
 stag·nan·cy
stag·nate
 stag·nat·ed
 stag·nat·ing
 stag·na·tion
stagy
 stag·i·er
 stag·i·est
 stag·i·ly
 stag·i·ness
staid·ness
stain
 stain·a·ble
 stained
 stain·er
stained-glass
stain·less
stair·case
stair·way
stair·well
stake
 staked
 stak·ing
stake·hold·er
sta·lac·tite
sta·lag·mite
stale
 stal·er
 stal·est
 staled
 stal·ing
 stale·ness
stale·mate
 stale·mat·ed
 stale·mat·ing
Sta·lin
Sta·lin·grad
Sta·lin·ism
stalk
 stalked
 stalky
 stalk·i·er
 stalk·i·est
stalled
stal·lion
stal·wart
 stal·wart·ness
sta·men
 sta·mens
stam·i·na
Stam·ford
stam·i·na
stam·mer
 stam·mer·ing·ly
stam·pede
 stam·ped·ed
 stam·ped·ing
 stam·ped·er
 stam·ped·ing·ly

stamp·er
stance
stand
 stand·ing
 stand·er
stand·ard
stand·ard·ize
 stand·ard·ized
 stand·ard·iz·ing
 stand·ard·i·za·tion
stand·by
stand·ee
stand-in
Stan·dish
stand-off·ish
 stand-off·ish·ness
stand·out
stand·pipe
stand·point
stand·still
sta·nine
Stan·ton
stan·za
 stan·za·ic
sta·pes
 sta·pes
 sta·ped·es
 sta·pe·di·al
staph·y·lo·coc·cus
sta·ple
 sta·pled
 sta·pling
 sta·pler
star
 starred
 star·ring
 star·less
 star·like
star·board
star·dom
stare
 stared
 star·ing
 star·er
star·fish
star·gaze
 star·gazed
 star·gaz·ing
star·let
star·light
star·ling
star·ry
 star·ri·er
 star·ri·est
 star·ri·ly
 star·ri·ness
star·ry-eyed
star-span·gled
start·er
star·tle
 star·tled
 star·tling
 star·tling·ly
star·va·tion
starve

starved
starv·ing
sta·sis
sta·ses
state
 stat·ed
 stat·ing
 stat·a·ble
state·craft
state·hood
state·less
 state·less·ness
state·ly
 state·li·er
 state·li·est
state·ment
Stat·en Is·land
state·room
state·side
states·man
 states·men
 states·man·like
 states·man·ship
stat·ic
stat·ics
sta·tion
 sta·tion·ary
 sta·tion·er
 sta·tion·ery
stat·ism
 stat·ist
sta·tis·tic
 sta·tis·ti·cal
 sta·tis·ti·cal·ly
stat·is·ti·cian
sta·tis·tics
sta·tor
stat·u·ary
 stat·u·ar·ies
stat·ue
 stat·u·esque
 stat·u·ette
stat·ure
sta·tus
stat·ute
staunch
stave
 staved
 stav·ing
stay
 stayed
 stay·ing
 stay·er
stead·fast
 stead·fast·ly
 stead·fast·ness
steady
 stead·i·er
 stead·i·est
 stead·ied
 stead·y·ing
 stead·i·ly
 stead·i·ness
steal
 stol·en

steal·ing
steal·er
stealth
stealthy
stealth·i·er
stealth·i·est
stealth·i·ly
stealth·i·ness
steam·boat
steam·er
steam·fit·ter
steam·fit·ting
steam·roll·er
steam·ship
steamy
steam·i·er
steam·i·est
steam·i·ly
steam·i·ness
ste·a·tite
sted·fast
steel·head
steel·works
steel·work·er
steely
steel·i·er
steel·i·est
steel·i·ness
steel·yard
steep
steep·ly
steep·ness
steep·en
stee·ple
stee·ple·chase
stee·ple·chas·er
stee·ple·jack
steer
steer·a·ble
steer·er
steer·age
stein
stel·lar
Stel·lite
stem
stemmed
stem·ming
stem·less
stem·ware
stem·wind·er
stem·wind·ing
stench
stenchy
stench·i·er
stench·i·est
sten·cil
sten·ciled
sten·cil·ing
ste·nog·ra·pher
ste·nog·ra·phy
sten·o·graph·ic
sten·o·graph·i·cal·ly
sten·to·ri·an
step
stepped

step·ping
step·broth·er
step·child
step·child·ren
step·daugh·ter
step·fa·ther
step·lad·der
step·moth·er
step·par·ent
stepped-up
step·ping·stone
step·sis·ter
step·son
ster·eo
ster·e·os
ster·e·o·phon·ic
ster·e·o·phon·i·cal·ly
ster·e·o·scope
ster·e·o·scop·ic
ster·e·o·type
ster·e·o·typed
ster·e·o·typ·ing
ster·ile
ste·ril·i·ty
ster·i·lize
ster·i·lized
ster·i·liz·ing
ster·i·li·za·tion
ster·i·li·zer
ster·ling
stern
stern·ly
stern·ness
ster·num
ster·na
ster·nums
stern-wheel·er
ster·oid
steth·o·scope
steth·o·scop·ic
Steu·ben
Steu·ben·ville
ste·ve·dore
ste·ve·dored
ste·ve·dor·ing
Ste·ven·son
stew·ard
stew·ard·ess
Stew·art
stick·er
stick·ing
stick-in-the-mud
stick·le·back
stick·ler
stick·pin
stick-up
sticky
stick·i·er
stick·i·est
stick·i·ly
stick·i·ness
stiff
stiff·ly
stiff·ness
stiff·en

stiff·en·er
stiff-necked
sti·fle
  sti·fled
  sti·fling
  sti·fler
  sti·fling·ly
stig·ma
  stig·mas
  stig·ma·ta
  stig·ma·tic
  stig·mat·i·cal·ly
  stig·ma·tize
  stig·ma·tized
  stig·ma·tiz·ing
  stig·ma·ti·za·tion
sti·let·to
  sti·let·tos
  sti·let·toes
still·birth
  still·born
still·ness
stilt·ed
  stilt·ed·ly
stim·u·lant
stim·u·late
  stim·u·lat·ed
  stim·u·lat·ing
  stim·u·la·tion
  stim·u·la·tive
stim·u·lus
stim·u·li
sting
  sting·ing
  sting·er
  sting·ing·ly
stin·gy
  stin·gi·er
  stin·gi·est
  stin·gi·ly
  stin·gi·ness
stink
  stink·ing
  stink·er
  stinky
  stink·i·er
  stink·i·est
stint·er
sti·pend
stip·ple
  stip·pled
  stip·pling
stip·u·late
  stip·u·lat·ed
  stip·u·lat·ing
  stip·u·la·tion
  stip·u·la·to·ry
stir
  stirred
  stir·ring
  stir·ring·ly
Stir·ling
stir·rup
stitch
  stitch·er

stock·ade
  stock·ad·ed
  stock·ad·ing
stock·brok·er
stock·hold·er
Stock·holm
stock·ing
stock·pile
  stock·piled
  stock·pil·ing
Stock·ton
stocky
  stock·i·er
  stock·i·est
  stock·i·ly
  stock·i·ness
stock·yard
stodgy
  stodg·i·er
  stodg·i·est
  stodg·i·ly
  stodg·i·ness
sto·ic
sto·i·cal
stoke
  stoked
  stok·ing
  stok·er
stol·id
  sto·lid·i·ty
  stol·id·ly
sto·ma
  sto·ma·ta
  sto·mas
stom·ach
stom·ach·er
stone
  stoned
  ston·ing
  stone-deaf
  Stone·henge
  stone·ma·son
  stone·ma·son·ry
  stone·wall
stony
  ston·i·er
  ston·i·est
  ston·i·ly
  ston·i·ness
stop
  stopped
  stop·ping
stop·gap
stop·light
stop·o·ver
stop·page
stop·per
stop·watch
stor·age
store
  stored
  stor·ing
store·house
store·keep·er
store·room

sto·ried
stormy
  storm·i·er
  storm·i·est
  storm·i·ly
  storm·i·ness
story
  sto·ries
  sto·ry·ing
sto·ry·book
sto·ry·tell·er
  sto·ry·tell·ing
stout
  stout·ly
  stout·ness
stout-heart·ed
stove
  stoved
  stov·ing
stove·pipe
stow·age
stow·a·way
stra·bis·mus
strad·dle
  strad·dled
  strad·dling
  strad·dler
strafe
  strafed
  straf·ing
strag·gle
  strag·gled
  strag·gling
  strag·gler
strag·gly
  strag·gli·er
  strag·gli·est
straight·a·way
straight-edge
straight·en
  straight·en·er
straight·for·ward
  straight·for·ward·ly
straight·way
strain·er
strait·en
strait·jack·et
strait-laced
strange
  strang·er
  strang·est
  strange·ly
  strange·ness
stran·ger
stran·gle
  stran·gled
  stran·gling
  stran·gler
stran·gu·la·tion
  stran·gu·late
  stran·gu·lat·ed
  stran·gu·lat·ing
strap
  strapped
  strap·ping

strap·less
strat·a·gem
stra·te·gic
  stra·te·gi·cal·ly
strat·e·gy
  strat·e·gies
  strat·e·gist
Strat·ford
strat·i·fi·ca·tion
strat·i·fy
  strat·i·fied
  strat·i·fy·ing
stra·to·cu·mu·lus
strat·o·sphere
  strat·o·spher·ic
stra·tum
  stra·ta
  stra·tums
stra·tus
  stra·ti
straw·ber·ry
  straw·ber·ries
stray·er
  stray·ing
streak
streaky
  streak·i·er
  streak·i·est
stream·er
stream·line
  stream·lined
  stream·lin·ing
street·car
street·walk·er
  street·walk·ing
strength·en
  strength·en·er
stren·u·ous
  stren·u·os·i·ty
  stren·u·ous·ly
strep·to·coc·cus
  strep·to·coc·ci
  strep·to·coc·cal
  strep·to·coc·cic
strep·to·my·cin
stress
  stress·ful
  stress·ful·ly
  stress·less
  stress·less·ness
stretch
  stretch·a·bil·i·ty
  stretch·a·ble
  stretch·er
strew
  strewed
  strew·ing
stria
  stri·ae
stri·ate
  stri·at·ed
  stri·at·ing
strick·en
strict
  strict·ly

strict·ness
stric·ture
stride
strid·den
strid·ing
stri·dent
strid·u·la·tion
strife
strife·ful
strife·less
strike
strick·en
strik·ing
strike·less
string
strung
string·ing
strin·gent
strin·gen·cy
strin·gent·ly
stringy
string·i·er
string·i·est
string·i·ness
strip
stripped
strip·ping
stripe
striped
strip·ing
strip·ling
strip·per
strip·tease
strip·teas·er
strive
strove
striv·en
striv·ing
stro·bo·scope
stro·bo·scop·ic
stro·bo·scop·i·cal·ly
stroke
stroked
strok·ing
stroll·er
strong
strong·ish
strong·ly
strong·ness
strong-arm
strong-box
strong·hold
strong-mind·ed
strong-mind·ed·ly
strong-mind·ed·ness
stron·ti·um
stron·tic
strop
stropped
strop·ping
struc·tural
struc·tur·al·ly
struc·ture
struc·tured
struc·tur·ing

struc·ture·less
strug·gle
strug·gled
strug·g'ing
strug·gler
strum
strum·mer
strum·pet
strut
strut·ted
strut·ting
strych·nine
strych·nia
strych·nic
stub
stubbed
stub·bing
stub·by
stub·bi·er
stub·bi·est
stub·ble
stub·bled
stub·bly
stub·bli·er
stub·bli·est
stub·born
stub·born·ly
stub·born·ness
stuc·co
stuc·coes
stuc·cos
stuc·coed
stuc·co·ing
stuck-up
stud
stud·ded
stud·ding
Stu·de·bak·er
stu·dent
stud·ied
stud·ied·ly
stud·ied·ness
stu·dio
stu·di·os
stu·di·ous
stu·di·ous·ly
stu·di·ous·ness
study
stud·ies
stud·ied
stud·y·ing
stuff·er
stuff·ing
stuffy
stuff·i·er
stuff·i·est
stuff·i·ly
stuff·i·ness
stul·ti·fy
stul·ti·fied
stul·ti·fy·ing
stul·ti·fi·ca·tion
stul·ti·fi·er
stum·ble
stum·bled

stum·bling
stum·bler
stum·bling·ly
stump
stump·er
stumpy
stump·i·er
stump·i·est
stun
stunned
stun·ning
stunt
stunt·ed
stunt·ed·ness
stu·pe·fy
stu·pe·fied
stu·pe·fy·ing
stu·pe·fac·tion
stu·pe·fi·er
stu·pe·fy·ing·ly
stu·pen·dous
stu·pen·dous·ly
stu·pen·dous·ness
stu·pid
stu·pid·i·ty
stu·pid·ly
stu·pid·ness
stu·por
stu·por·ous
stur·dy
stur·di·er
stur·di·est
stur·geon
stut·ter
stut·ter·er
stut·ter·ing·ly
Stutt·gart
Stuy·ve·sant
style
styled
styl·ing
styl·er
styl·ish
styl·ish·ly
styl·ish·ness
styl·ist
sty·lis·tic
sty·lis·ti·cal
sty·lis·ti·cal·ly
styl·ize
styl·ized
styl·iz·ing
styl·i·za·tion
styl·iz·er
sty·lus
sty·lus·es
sty·li
sty·mie
sty·mies
sty·mied
sty·mie·ing
styp·tic
styp·ti·cal
styp·tic·i·ty
Sty·ro·foam

suave
suave·ly
suave·ness
swav·i·ty
sub
subbed
sub·bing
sub·al·tern
sub·arc·tic
sub·as·sem·bly
sub·as·sem·blies
sub·as·sem·bler
sub·base·ment
sub·chas·er
sub·class
sub·com·mit·tee
sub·con·scious
sub·con·scious·ly
sub·con·scious·ness
sub·con·ti·nent
sub·con·ti·nen·tal
sub·con·tract
sub·con·trac·tor
sub·cul·ture
sub·cul·tur·al
sub·cu·ta·ne·ous
sub·cu·ta·ne·ous·ly
sub·deb·u·tante
sub·di·vide
sub·di·vid·ed
sub·di·vid·ing
sub·di·vid·a·ble
sub·di·vid·er
sub·di·vi·sion
sub·di·vi·sion·al
sub·due
sub·dued
sub·du·ing
sub·du·a·ble
sub·du·al
sub·du·er
sub·en·try
sub·en·tries
sub·freez·ing
sub·group
sub·head
sub·hu·man
sub·ject
sub·jec·tion
sub·jec·tive
sub·jec·tive·ly
sub·jec·tive·ness
sub·jec·tiv·i·ty
sub·join
sub·ju·gate
sub·ju·gat·ed
sub·ju·gat·ing
sub·ju·ga·tion
sub·ju·ga·tor
sub·junc·tive
sub·lease
sub·leased
sub·leas·ing
sub·let
sub·let·ting

sub·li·mate
sub·li·mat·ed
sub·li·mat·ing
sub·li·ma·tion
sub·lime
sub·lim·er
sub·lim·est
sub·limed
sub·lim·ing
sub·lime·ly
sub·lime·ness
sub·lim·er
sub·lim·i·nal
sub·lim·i·nal·ly
sub·lim·i·ty
sub·lim·i·ties
sub·ma·chine
sub·mar·gin·al
sub·ma·rine
sub·merge
sub·merged
sub·merg·ing
sub·mer·gence
sub·mer·gi·ble
sub·merse
sub·mersed
sub·mers·ing
sub·mer·sion
sub·mers·i·ble
sub·mi·cro·scop·ic
sub·mis·sion
sub·mis·sive
sub·miss·ive·ly
sub·miss·ive·ness
sub·mit
sub·mit·ted
sub·mit·ting
sub·nor·mal
sub·nor·mal·i·ty
sub·or·di·nate
sub·or·di·nat·ed
sub·or·di·nat·ing
sub·or·di·nate·ly
sub·or·di·nate·ness
sub·or·di·na·tion
sub·or·di·na·tive
sub·orn
sub·or·na·tion
sub·orn·er
sub·poe·na
sub·poe·naed
sub·poe·na·ing
sub·scribe
sub·scribed
sub·scrib·ing
sub·scrib·er
sub·scrip·tion
sub·se·quent
sub·se·quence
sub·se·quent·ly
sub·se·quent·ness
sub·ser·vi·ent
sub·ser·vi·ence
sub·ser·vi·en·cy
sub·ser·vi·ent·ly

sub·side
sub·sid·ed
sub·sid·ing
sub·sid·ence
sub·sid·i·ary
sub·sid·i·ar·ies
sub·si·dize
sub·si·dized
sub·si·diz·ing
sub·si·di·za·tion
sub·si·diz·er
sub·si·dy
sub·si·dies
sub·sist
sub·sist·ence
sub·soil
sub·son·ic
sub·stance
sub·stand·ard
sub·stan·tial
sub·stan·ti·al·i·ty
sub·stan·tial·ly
sub·stan·tial·ness
sub·stan·ti·ate
sub·stan·ti·at·ed
sub·stan·ti·at·ing
sub·stan·ti·a·tion
sub·stan·ti·a·tive
sub·stan·tive
sub·stan·ti·val
sub·stan·ti·val·ly
sub·stan·tive·ly
sub·stan·tive·ness
sub·sti·tute
sub·sti·tut·ed
sub·sti·tut·ing
sub·sti·tut·able
sub·sti·tu·tion
sub·sti·tu·tion·al
sub·sti·tu·tion·al·ly
sub·sti·tu·tion·ary
sub·stra·tum
sub·stra·ta
sub·stra·tums
sub·struc·ture
sub·sume
sub·sumed
sub·sum·ing
sub·sum·a·ble
sub·sump·tive
sub·sump·tion
sub·teen
sub·tend
sub·ter·fuge
sub·ter·ra·ne·an
sub·ter·ra·ne·ous
sub·ter·ra·ne·an·ly
sub·ter·ra·ne·ous·ly
sub·ti·tle
sub·tle
sub·tle·ness
sub·tle·ty
sub·tle·ties
sub·tly
sub·tract

sub·tract·er
sub·trac·tion
sub·trac·tive
sub·tra·hend
sub·trop·i·cal
sub·trop·ic
sub·trop·ics
sub·urb
sub·ur·ban
sur·ur·ban·ite
sub·ur·bia
sub·ver·sion
sub·ver·sion·ary
sub·ver·sive
sub·ver·sive·ly
sub·ver·sive·ness
sub·vert
sub·vert·er
sub·way
suc·ceed
suc·ceed·er
suc·cess
suc·cess·ful·ly
suc·cess·ful·ness
suc·ces·sion
suc·ces·sion·al
suc·ces·sion·al·ly
suc·ces·sive
suc·ces·sive·ly
suc·ces·sive·ness
suc·ces·sor
suc·cinct
suc·cinct·ly
suc·cinct·ness
suc·cor
suc·cor·er
suc·co·tash
suc·cu·bus
suc·cu·bi
suc·cu·lent
suc·cu·lence
suc·cu·len·cy
suc·cu·lent·ly
suc·cumb
suck·er
suck·le
suck·led
suck·ling
Su·cre
su·crose
suc·tion
Su·dan
sud·den
sud·den·ly
sud·den·ness
sudsy
suds·i·er
suds·i·est
sue
sued
su·ing
su·er
suede
su·et
su·ety

Su·ez
suf·fer
suf·fer·a·ble
suf·fer·a·ble·ness
suf·fer·a·bly
suf·fer·er
suf·fer·ing
suf·fer·ing·ly
suf·fer·ance
suf·fice
suf·ficed
suf·fic·ing
suf·fic·er
suf·fi·cien·cy
suf·fi·cien·cies
suf·fi·cient
suf·fi·cient·ly
suf·fix
suf·fo·cate
suf·fo·cat·ed
suf·fo·cat·ing
suf·fo·cat·ing·ly
suf·fo·ca·tion
suf·fo·ca·tive
Suf·folk
suf·frage
suf·fra·gette
suf·fuse
suf·fused
suf·fus·ing
suf·fu·sion
suf·fu·sive
sug·ar
sug·ar·less
sug·ar·like
sug·ary
sug·ar·i·er
sug·ar·i·est
sug·ar·coat
sug·gest
sug·gest·er
sug·gest·i·ble
sug·gest·i·bil·i·ty
sug·ges·tion
sug·ges·tive
sug·ges·tive·ly
sug·ges·tive·ness
su·i·cide
su·i·cid·ed
su·i·cid·ing
su·i·cid·al
suit·a·ble
suit·a·bil·i·ty
suit·a·ble·ness
suit·a·bly
suit·case
suite
suit·ing
suit·or
sul·fa
sul·fa·nil·a·mide
sul·fate
sul·fide
sul·fur
sul·fu·ric

sul·fur·ous
sur·fur·ous·ly
sul·fur·ous·ness
sulky
sulk·i·er
sulk·i·est
sulk·i·ly
sulk·i·ness
sul·len
sul·len·ly
sul·len·ness
Sul·li·van
sul·ly
sul·lied
sul·ly·ing
sul·tan
sul·tan·ic
sul·tana
sul·tan·ess
sul·tan·ate
sul·try
sul·tri·er
sul·tri·est
sul·tri·ly
sul·tri·ness
sum
summed
sum·ming
su·mac
Su·ma·tra
sum·ma·rize
sum·ma·rized
sum·ma·riz·ing
sum·ma·ri·za·tion
sum·ma·riz·er
sum·mar·ist
sum·ma·ry
sum·ma·ries
sum·mar·i·ly
sum·mar·i·ness
sum·ma·tion
sum·ma·tion·al
sum·mer
sum·mery
sum·mer·house
sum·mit
sum·mon
sum·mon·er
sum·mons
sum·mons·es
sump·tu·ary
sump·tu·ous
sump·tu·ous·ly
sump·tu·ous·ness
sun
sunned
sun·ning
sun·bathe
sun·bathed
sun·bath·ing
sun·bath·er
sun·beam
sun·bon·net
sun·burn
sun·burned

sun·burnt
sun·burn·ing
sun·dae
Sun·day
sun·der
sun·der·ance
sun·di·al
sun·down
sun·dries
sun·dry
sun·fish
sun·flow·er
sun·glass·es
sunk·en
sun·light
sun·lit
sun·ny
sun·ni·er
sun·ni·est
sun·ni·ly
sun·ni·ness
sun·rise
sun·set
sun·shine
sun·shiny
sun·spot
sun·stroke
sun·up
sup
supped
sup·ping
su·per
su·per·a·bun·dant
su·per·a·bun·dance
su·per·a·bun·dant·ly
su·per·an·nu·ate
su·per·an·nu·at·ing
su·per·an·nu·at·ed
su·per·an·nu·a·tion
su·perb
su·perb·ly
su·perb·ness
su·per·car·go
su·per·car·goes
su·per·charge
su·per·charged
su·per·charg·ing
su·per·charg·er
su·per·cil·i·ous
su·per·cil·i·ous·ly
su·per·cil·i·ous·ness
su·per·e·go
su·per·e·rog·a·to·ry
su·per·fi·cial
su·per·fi·ci·al·i·ty
su·per·fi·ci·al·i·ties
su·per·fi·cial·ly
su·per·fi·cial·ness
su·per·fine
su·per·flu·ous
su·per·flu·i·ty
su·per·flu·i·ties
su·per·flu·ous·ly
su·per·flu·ous·ness
su·per·high·way

su·per·hu·man
su·per·hu·man·i·ty
su·per·hu·man·ly
su·per·hu·man·ness
su·per·im·pose
su·per·im·posed
su·per·im·pos·ing
su·per·im·po·si·tion
su·per·in·tend
su·per·in·tend·ence
su·per·in·tend·en·cy
su·per·in·tend·ent
su·pe·ri·or
su·pe·ri·or·i·ty
su·pe·ri·or·ly
su·per·la·tive
su·per·la·tive·ly
su·per·la·tive·ness
su·per·man
su·per·mar·ket
su·per·nal
su·per·nal·ly
su·per·nat·u·ral
su·per·nat·u·ral·ism
su·per·nat·u·ral·ly
su·per·nat·u·ral·ness
su·per·nu·mer·ary
su·per·nu·mer·ar·ies
su·per·pow·er
su·per·scribe
su·per·scribed
su·per·scrib·ing
su·per·scrip·tion
su·per·script
su·per·sede
su·per·sed·ed
su·per·sed·ing
su·per·sed·er
su·per·son·ic
su·per·son·i·cal·ly
su·per·star
su·per·sti·tion
su·per·sti·tious
su·per·sti·tious·ly
su·per·sti·tious·ness
su·per·struc·ture
su·per·vene
su·per·vened
su·per·ven·ing
super·ven·tion
su·per·vise
su·per·vised
su·per·vis·ing
su·per·vi·sion
su·per·vi·sor
su·per·vi·so·ry
su·pine
su·pine·ly
su·pine·ness
sup·per
sup·plant
sup·plan·ta·tion
sup·plant·er
sup·ple
sup·pler

sup·plest
sup·ple·ness
sup·ple·ment
sup·ple·men·tal
sup·ple·men·ta·ry
sup·ple·men·ta·tion
sup·pli·ant
sup·pli·ant·ly
sup·pli·cant
sup·pli·cate
sup·pli·cat·ed
sup·pli·cat·ing
sup·pli·ca·tion
sup·pli·ca·to·ry
sup·ply
sup·plied
sup·ply·ing
sup·plies
sup·pli·er
sup·port
sup·port·a·ble
sub·port·a·ble·ness
sup·port·a·bly
sup·port·er
sup·port·ive
sup·pose
sup·posed
sup·pos·ing
sup·pos·a·ble
sup·pos·a·bly
sup·pos·ed·ly
sup·po·si·tion
sup·po·si·tion·al
sup·po·si·tion·al·ly
sup·pos·i·to·ry
sup·press
sup·press·i·ble
sup·pres·sion
sup·pres·sor
sup·pu·rate
sup·pu·rat·ed
sup·pu·rat·ing
sup·pu·ra·tion
sup·pu·ra·tive
su·pra·re·nal
su·prem·a·cy
su·prem·a·cies
su·prem·a·cist
su·preme
su·preme·ly
su·preme·ness
sur·cease
sur·charge
sur·charged
sur·charg·ing
sur·cin·gle
sure
sur·er
sur·est
sure·ly
sure·ness
sure-fire
sure-foot·ed
sure-foot·ed·ly
sure·ty

sure·ties
sure·ty·ship
surf
surfy
surf·i·er
surf·i·est
sur·face
sur·faced
sur·fac·ing
sur·face·less
sur·fac·er
surf·board
surf·board·er
sur·feit
sur·feit·er
surge
surged
surg·ing
sur·geon
sur·gery
sur·ger·ies
sur·gi·cal
sur·gi·cal·ly
Su·ri·nam
sur·ly
sur·li·er
sur·li·est
sur·li·ly
sur·li·ness
sur·mise
sur·mised
sur·mis·ing
sur·mount
sur·mount·a·ble
sur·name
sur·pass
sur·pass·a·ble
sur·pass·ing
sur·pass·ing·ly
sur·plice
sur·plus
sur·plus·age
sur·prise
sur·prised
sur·pris·ing
sur·pris·al
sur·pris·er
sur·pris·ing·ly
sur·re·al·ism
sur·re·al·ist
sur·re·al·is·tic
sur·re·al·is·ti·cal·ly
sur·ren·der
sur·rep·ti·tious
sur·rep·ti·tious·ly
sur·rep·ti·tious·ness
sur·rey
sur·reys
sur·ro·gate
sur·ro·gat·ed
sur·ro·gat·ing
sur·round
sur·round·er
sur·round·ing
sur·tax

sur·veil·lance
sur·veil·lant
sur·vey
sur·vey·ing
sur·vey·or
sur·viv·al
sur·vive
sur·vived
sur·viv·ing
sur·vi·vor
sus·cep·ti·ble
sus·cep·ti·bil·i·ty
sus·cep·ti·ble·ness
sus·cep·ti·bly
sus·pect
sus·pend
sus·pend·er
sus·pense
sus·pense·ful
sus·pen·sion
sus·pi·cion
sus·pi·cious
sus·pi·cious·ly
sus·pi·cious·ness
Sus·que·han·na
Sus·sex
sus·tain
sus·tain·a·ble
sus·tain·er
sus·tain·ment
sus·te·nance
su·ture
su·tured
su·tur·ing
su·tur·al
su·tur·al·ly
Su·va
su·ze·rain
su·ze·rain·ty
svelte
svelte·ly
svelte·ness
swab
swabbed
swab·bing
swab·ber
Swa·bia
swad·dle
swad·dled
swad·dling
swag·ger
swag·ger·er
swag·ger·ing
swag·ger·ing·ly
swain
swain·ish
swain·ish·ness
swal·low
swal·low·er
swal·low·tail
swa·mi
swa·mis
swamp
swampy
swamp·i·er

swamp·i·est
swamp·i·ness
swank
swank·i·ly
swank·i·ness
swanky
swank·i·er
swank·i·est
swan's-down
swap
swapped
swap·ping
sward
swarthy
swarth·i·er
swarth·i·est
swarth·i·ness
swash·buck·ler
swash·buck·ling
swas·ti·ka
swat
swat·ted
swat·ting
swat·ter
swathe
swathed
swath·ing
sway
sway·a·ble
sway·er
sway·back
sway·backed
Swa·zi·land
swear
swore
swear·ing
swear·er
swear·word
sweat
sweat·ed
sweat·ing
sweat·i·ly
sweat·i·ness
sweat·less
sweaty
sweat·i·er
sweat·i·est
sweat·er
sweat·shop
Swe·den
sweep
swept
sweep·ing
sweep·er
sweep·ing·ly
sweep·ing·ness
sweep·stakes
sweet
sweet·ish
sweet·ly
sweet·ness
sweet·bread
sweet·bri·er
sweet·en
sweet·en·er

sweet·en·ing
sweet·heart
sweet·meat
sweet-talk
swell
swelled
swoll·en
swell·ing
swell·head
swel·ter
swel·ter·ing
swel·ter·ing·ly
swerve
swerved
swerv·ing
swift
swift·ly
swift·ness
swig
swigged
swig·ging
swig·ger
swill
swill·er
swim·ming
swim·ming·ly
swin·dle
swin·dled
swin·dling
swin·dler
swine
swin·ish
swing
swing·ing
swing·a·ble
swing·er
swipe
swiped
swip·ing
swirl
swirl·ing·ly
swirly
swirl·i·er
swirl·i·est
swish
swish·er
swish·ing·ly
swishy
swish·i·er
swish·i·est
switch
switch·er
switch·blade
switch·board
switch-hit·ter
Switz·er·land
swiv·el
swiv·eled
swiv·el·ing
swiz·zle
swoon
swoon·er
swoon·ing·ly
swoop·er
swop

swopped
swop·ping
sword
sword·like
sword·fish
sword·play
sword·play·er
swords·man
swords·men
swords·man·ship
syc·a·more
syc·o·phant
syc·o·phan·cy
syc·o·phan·tic
syc·o·phan·ti·cal
syc·o·phan·ti·cal·ly
Syd·ney
syl·lab·ic
syl·lab·i·cate
syl·lab·i·cat·ed
syl·lab·i·cat·ing
syl·lab·i·ca·tion
syl·lab·i·fy
syl·lab·i·fied
syl·lab·i·fy·ing
syl·lab·i·fi·ca·tion
syl·la·ble
syl·la·bled
syl·la·bling
syl·la·bus
syl·la·bus·es
syl·la·bi
syl·lo·gism
syl·lo·gis·tic
sylph·like
syl·van
sym·bi·o·sis
sym·bi·ot·ic
sym·bi·ot·i·cal·ly
sym·bol
sym·bol·ic
sym·bol·i·cal
sym·bol·ism
sym·bol·ist
sym·bol·ize
sym·bol·ized
sym·bol·iz·ing
sym·bol·i·za·tion
sym·bol·iz·er
sym·me·try
sym·me·tries
sym·met·ric
sym·met·ri·cal
sym·pa·thet·ic
sym·pa·thet·i·cal·ly
sym·pa·thize
sym·pa·thized
sym·pa·thiz·ing
sym·pa·thiz·er
sym·pa·thiz·ing·ly
sym·pa·thy
sym·pa·thies
sym·pho·ny
sym·pho·nies
sym·phon·ic

sym·po·si·um
sym·po·sia
sym·po·si·ums
symp·tom
symp·to·mat·ic
symp·to·mat·i·cal
symp·to·mat·i·cal·ly
syn·a·gogue
syn·a·gog·al
syn·a·gog·i·cal
syn·apse
sync
synced
sync·ing
syn·chro·nism
syn·chro·nis·tic
syn·chro·nis·ti·cal
syn·chro·nis·ti·cal·ly
syn·chro·nize
syn·chro·nized
syn·chro·niz·ing
syn·chro·ni·za·tion
syn·chro·niz·er
sny·chro·nous
syn·chro·nous·ly
syn·chro·nous·ness
syn·co·pate
syn·co·pat·ed
syn·co·pat·ing
syn·co·pa·tion
syn·co·pa·tor
syn·di·cate
syn·di·cat·ed
syn·di·cat·ing
syn·di·ca·tion
syn·di·ca·tor
syn·drome
syn·drom·ic
syn·od
syn·od·al
syn·o·nym
syn·o·nym·ic
syn·o·nym·i·cal
syn·o·nym·i·ty
syn·on·y·mous
syn·on·y·mous·ly
syn·on·y·my
syn·on·y·mies
syn·op·sis
syn·op·ses
syn·op·ti·cal
syn·tac·tic
syn·tac·ti·cal
syn·tac·ti·cal·ly
syn·tax
syn·the·sis
syn·the·ses
syn·the·sist
syn·the·size
syn·the·sized
syn·the·siz·ing
syn·thet·ic
syn·thet·i·cal
syn·thet·i·cal·ly
syph·i·lis

syph·i·lit·ic
Syr·a·cuse
Syr·ia
Syr·i·ac
sy·ringe
sy·ringed
sy·ring·ing
syr·up
syr·upy
syr·up·i·er
syr·up·i·est
sys·tem
sys·tem·at·ic
sys·tem·at·i·cal
sys·tem·at·i·cal·ly
sys·tem·at·ic·ness
sys·tem·a·tize
sys·tem·a·tized
sys·tem·a·tiz·ing
sys·tem·a·ti·za·tion
sys·tem·a·tiz·er
sys·tem·ic
sys·tem·i·cal·ly
sys·to·le
sys·tol·ic
tab
tabbed
tab·bing
tab·by
tab·bies
tab·er·na·cle
tab·er·nac·u·lar
ta·ble
ta·bled
ta·bling
tab·leau
tab·leaux
tab·leaus
ta·ble·cloth
ta·ble d'hôte
ta·ble·land
ta·ble·spoon
ta·ble·spoon·ful
ta·ble·spoon·fuls
tab·let
ta·ble·ware
tab·loid
ta·boo
ta·booed
ta·boo·ing
ta·bor
tab·u·lar
tab·u·lar·ly
tab·u·late
tab·u·lat·ed
tab·u·lat·ing
tab·u·la·tion
tab·u·la·tor
ta·chom·e·ter
tac·it
tac·it·ly
tac·it·ness
tac·i·turn
tac·i·tur·ni·ty
tack

tacked
tack·ing
tack·er
tack·le
tack·led
tack·ling
tack·ler
tacky
tack·i·er
tack·i·est
tack·i·ness
ta·co
ta·cos
Ta·co·ma
tact
tact·ful
tact·ful·ly
tact·ful·ness
tact·less
tac·ti·cal
tac·tics
tac·ti·cian
tac·tile
tac·til·i·ty
tad·pole
taf·fe·ta
taf·fy
tag
tagged
tag·ging
Ta·ga·log
Ta·hi·ti
Ta·hoe
tail
tailed
tail·er
tail·less
tail·like
tail·gate
tail·gat·ed
tail·gat·ing
tail·light
tai·lor
tai·lored
tai·lor·ing
tai·lor·made
tail·piece
tail·spin
tail·wind
taint
taint·less
Tai·pei
Tai·wan
take
tak·en
tak·ing
tak·er
take·off
tak·ing
tak·ing·ly
tak·ing·ness
tal·cum
tale·bear·er
tale·bear·ing
tal·ent

tal·ent·ed
tales·man
tales·men
tal·is·man
 tal·is·mans
 tal·is·man·ic
 tal·is·man·i·cal
 tal·is·man·i·cal·ly
talk
 talk·er
talk·a·tive
 talk·a·tive·ly
 talk·a·tive·ness
talk·ie
talk·ing-to
talky
 talk·i·er
 talk·i·est
tall
 tall·ish
 tall·ness
Tal·la·has·see
Tal·ley·rand
tal·low
 tal·lowy
 tal·low·i·er
 tal·low·i·est
tal·ly
 tal·lies
 tal·lied
 tal·ly·ing
tal·ly·ho
Tal·mud
 Tal·mud·ic
 Tal·mud·i·cal
 Tal·mud·ism
 Tal·mud·ist
tal·on
 tal·oned
Ta·los
ta·ma·le
tam·a·rack
tam·a·rind
tam·bou·rine
tame
 tam·er
 tam·est
 tamed
 tam·ing
 tam·a·ble
 tame·ly
 tameness
 tam·er
Tam·ma·ny
tam-o'-shan·ter
Tam·pa
tam·per
 tam·per·er
Tam·pi·co
tan
 tanned
 tan·ning
 tan·nish
tan·a·ger
Tan·a·gra

Ta·nan·a·rive
tan·bark
tan·dem
tang
 tangy
 tang·i·er
 tang·i·est
Tan·gan·yi·ka
tan·gent
 tan·gen·cy
 tan·gen·tial
 tan·ge·rine
 tan·gi·ble
 tan·gi·bil·i·ty
 tan·gi·ble·ness
 tan·gi·bly
Tan·gier
tan·gle
 tan·gled
 tan·gling
 tan·gle·ment
 tan·gly
 tan·gli·er
 tan·gli·est
tan·go
 tan·goed
 tan·go·ing
tank·age
tank·ard
tank·er
tan·nery
 tan·ner·ies
tan·nin
tan·ta·lize
 tan·ta·lized
 tan·ta·liz·ing
 tan·ta·liz·ing·ly
tan·ta·lum
tan·ta·mount
tan·trum
Tan·zan·ia
Tao·ism
 Tao·ist
tap
 tapped
 tap·ping
tape
 taped
 tap·ing
 tap·er
 tape·like
ta·per
 ta·per·er
 ta·per·ing·ly
tape-re·cord
tap·es·try
 tap·es·tries
 tap·es·tried
 tap·es·try·ing
tape·worm
tap·i·o·ca
ta·pir
tap·room
tap·root
tar

tarred
tar·ring
tar·an·tel·la
ta·ran·tu·la
ta·ran·tu·las
ta·ran·tu·lae
tar·dy
tar·di·er
tar·di·est
tar·di·ly
tar·di·ness
tar·get
tar·iff
Tar·king·ton
tar·nish
tar·nish·a·ble
ta·ro
ta·ros
tar·pau·lin
tar·pon
tar·ry
tar·ried
tar·ry·ing
tar·ries
tar·ry
tar·ri·er
tar·ri·est
tar·sal
tar·sus
tar·si
tart
tart·ly
tart·ness
tar·tan
tar·tar
tar·tar·ic
tar·tar·ous
Tar·ta·ry
task·mas·ter
Tas·ma·nia
tas·sel
tas·seled
tas·sel·ing
taste
tast·ed
tast·ing
taste·ful
taste·ful·ly
taste·ful·ness
taste·less
taste·less·ly
taste·less·ness
tast·er
tasty
tast·i·er
tast·i·est
tast·i·ly
tast·i·ness
tat
tat·ted
tat·ting
tat·ter
Ta·tar
tat·tered
tat·tle

tat·tled
tat·tling
tat·tler
tat·tle·tale
tat·too
tat·toos
tat·tooed
tat·too·ing
tat·too·er
tat·too·ist
taunt
taunt·er
taunt·ing·ly
Taun·ton
taupe
Tau·rus
taut
taut·ly
taut·ness
tau·tol·o·gy
tau·to·log·i·cal
tau·to·log·i·cal·ly
tav·ern
taw·dry
taw·dri·er
taw·dri·est
taw·dri·ly
taw·ny
taw·ni·er
taw·ni·est
taw·ni·ness
tax
tax·a·bil·i·ty
tax·a·ble
tax·er
tax·a·tion
taxi
tax·ies
tax·ied
tax·i·ing
tax·i·cab
tax·i·der·my
tax·i·der·mic
tax·i·der·mist
tax·i·me·ter
tax·on·o·my
tax·o·nom·i·cal
tax·o·nom·i·cal·ly
tax·on·o·mist
tax·pay·er
T-bone
Tchai·kov·sky
teach
taught
teach·ing
teach·a·ble
teach·a·ble·ness
teach·a·bil·i·ty
teach·er
tea·cup
teak
teak·wood
tea·ket·tle
team·mate
team·ster

team·work
tea·pot
tear
 teary
 tear·i·er
 tear·i·est
tear·drop
tear·ful
 tear·ful·ly
 tear·ful·ness
tear·gas
tea·room
tease
 teased
 teas·ing
 teas·er
 teas·ing·ly
tea·sel
 tea·seled
 tea·sel·ing
tea·spoon
 tea·spoon·ful
tech·ne·ti·um
tech·ni·cal
 tech·ni·cal·ly
tech·ni·cal·ness
tech·ni·cal·i·ty
tech·ni·cian
Tech·ni·col·or
tech·nique
tech·noc·ra·cy
 tech·noc·ra·cies
 tech·no·crat
 tech·no·crat·ic
tech·nol·o·gy
 tech·no·log·i·cal
 tech·no·log·ic
 tech·nol·o·gist
Te·cum·seh
te·di·ous
 te·di·ous·ly
 te·di·ous·ness
te·di·um
tee
 teed
 tee·ing
teen-ag·er
tee·ny
 tee·ni·er
 tee·ni·est
tee·pee
tee·ter
tee·ter·board
teethe
 teethed
 teeth·ing
tee·to·tal
 tee·to·tal·er
 tee·to·tal·ist
 tee·to·tal·ism
 tee·to·tal·ly
Te·gu·ci·gal·pa
teg·u·ment
Te·he·ran
Teh·ran

Te·huan·te·pec
Tel Aviv
tel·e·cast
 tel·e·cast·ing
 tel·e·cast·er
tel·e·com·mu·ni·ca·tion
tel·e·gram
tel·e·graph
 te·leg·ra·pher
 tel·e·graph·ic
 tel·e·graph·i·cal
te·leg·ra·phy
te·lep·a·thy
 tel·e·path·ic
 tel·e·path·i·cal·ly
 tel·lep·a·thist
tel·e·phone
 tel·e·phoned
 tel·e·phon·ing
 tel·e·phon·er
 tel·e·phon·ic
te·leph·o·ny
tel·e·pho·to
tel·e·pho·tog·ra·phy
 tel·e·pho·to·graph·ic
tel·e·scope
 tel·e·scoped
 tel·e·scop·ing
 tel·e·scop·ic
 tel·e·scop·i·cal
tel·e·thon
Tel·e·type
 tel·e·typed
 tel·e·typ·ing
 tel·e·typ·ist
tel·e·type·writ·er
tel·e·vise
 tel·e·vised
 tel·e·vis·ing
tel·e·vi·sion
tell·er
tell·ing
 tell·ing·ly
tell·tale
tel·lu·ri·um
Tel·star
tem·blor
te·mer·i·ty
tem·per
 tem·per·a·bil·i·ty
 tem·per·a·ble
 tem·per·er
tem·pera
tem·per·a·ment
 tem·per·a·ment·al
tem·per·ance
tem·per·ate
 tem·per·ate·ly
 tem·per·ate·ness
tem·per·a·ture
tem·pered
tem·pest
tem·pes·tu·ous
 tem·pes·tu·ous·ly
 tem·pes·tu·ous·ness

tem·plate
tem·ple
  tem·pled
  tem·ple·like
tem·po
  tem·pos
  tem·pi
tem·po·ral
  tem·po·ral·i·ty
  tem·po·ral·ly
  tem·po·ral·ness
tem·po·rary
  tem·po·rar·i·ly
  tem·po·rar·i·ness
tem·po·rize
  tem·po·ri·za·tion
  tem·po·riz·er
  tem·po·riz·ing·ly
tempt
  tempt·a·ble
  temp·ta·tion
  tempt·er
  tempt·ing
  tempt·ress
ten·a·ble
  ten·a·bil·i·ty
  ten·a·ble·ness
  ten·a·bly
te·na·cious
  te·na·cious·ly
  te·na·cious·ness
  te·nac·i·ty
ten·ant
  ten·an·cy
  ten·an·cies
  ten·ant·a·ble
  ten·ant·less
ten·den·cy
  ten·den·cies
ten·den·tious
  ten·den·tious·ly
  ten·den·tious·ness
ten·der
  ten·der·ly
  ten·der·ness
ten·der·foot
ten·der·ize
  ten·der·ized
  ten·der·iz·ing
  ten·der·iz·er
ten·der·loin
ten·don
ten·dril
Ten·e·brae
ten·e·ment
  ten·e·men·ta·ry
ten·et
Ten·nes·see
ten·nis
Ten·ny·son
ten·on
ten·or
ten·pins
tense
  tens·er

tens·est
tensed
tens·ing
tense·ly
tense·ness
ten·si·ty
ten·sile
  ten·sil·i·ty
ten·sion
  ten·sion·al
  ten·sion·less
ten·sive
ten·ta·cle
  ten·ta·cled
  ten·tac·u·lar
ten·ta·tive
  ten·ta·tive·ly
  ten·ta·tive·ness
ten·ter·hook
tenth·ly
ten·u·ous
  ten·u·ous·ly
  ten·u·ous·ness
ten·ure
  ten·u·ri·al
  ten·u·ri·al·ly
te·pee
tep·id
  te·pid·i·ty
  tep·id·ness
te·qui·la
ter·cen·te·nary
  ter·cen·te·nar·ies
  ter·cen·ten·ni·al
ter·cet
ter·ma·gant
  ter·ma·gant·ly
ter·mi·na·ble
ter·mi·nal
  ter·mi·nal·ly
ter·mi·nate
  ter·mi·nat·ed
  ter·mi·nat·ing
  ter·mi·na·tion
  ter·mi·na·tive
  ter·mi·na·tive·ly
  ter·mi·na·tor
ter·mi·nol·o·gy
  ter·mi·nol·o·gies
  ter·mi·no·log·i·cal
  ter·mi·no·log·i·cal·ly
ter·mi·nus
  ter·mi·nus·es
  ter·mi·ni
ter·mite
ter·race
  ter·raced
  ter·rac·ing
ter·ra cot·ta
ter·ra fir·ma
ter·rain
ter·ra·pin
ter·rar·i·um
  ter·rar·ia
  ter·rar·i·ums

Ter·re Haute
ter·res·tri·al
  ter·res·tri·al·ly
ter·ri·ble
  ter·ri·ble·ness
  ter·ri·bly
ter·ri·er
ter·rif·ic
  ter·rif·i·cal·ly
ter·ri·fy
  ter·ri·fied
  ter·ri·fy·ing
  ter·ri·fy·ing·ly
ter·ri·to·ry
  ter·ri·to·ri·al
ter·ror
  ter·ror·less
  ter·ror·ism
  ter·ror·ist
  ter·ror·is·tic
  ter·ror·less
  ter·ror·ize
  ter·ror·ized
  ter·ror·iz·ing
  ter·ror·i·za·tion
  ter·ror·iz·er
ter·ry
  ter·ries
terse
  ters·er
  ters·est
  terse·ly
  terse·ness
ter·ti·ary
Ter·tul·lian
tes·sel·lat·ed
  tes·sel·late
  tes·sel·lat·ing
  tes·sel·la·tion
tes·ta·ment
tes·tate
  tes·ta·tor
  tes·ta·trix
  tes·ta·tri·ces
tes·ti·cle
  tes·tic·u·lar
tes·ti·fy
  tes·ti·fied
  tes·ti·fy·ing
  tes·ti·fi·er
tes·ti·mo·ni·al
tes·ti·mo·ny
  tes·ti·mo·nies
tes·tis
  tes·tes
tes·tos·ter·one
tes·ty
  tes·ti·er
  tes·ti·est
  tes·ti·ly
  tes·ti·ness
tet·a·nus
te·tan·ic
  te·tan·i·cal
tête-à-tête

teth·er
tet·ra·eth·yl
tet·ra·he·dron
  tet·ra·he·drons
  tet·ra·he·dra
  tet·ra·he·dral
te·tral·o·gy
  te·tral·o·gies
Teu·ton
Teu·ton·ic
Tex·ar·kana
Tex·as
text·book
tex·tile
tex·tu·al
tex·ture
  tex·tur·al
  tex·tur·al·ly
  tex·tured
Thack·er·ay
Thai·land
thal·a·mus
  tha·lam·ic
  tha·lam·i·cal·ly
Tha·les
thal·li·um
thal·lo·phyte
  thal·lo·phyt·ic
thal·lus
  thal·li
  thal·lus·es
thank
  thank·er
  thank·ful
  thank·ful·ly
  thank·ful·ness
  thank·less
  thank·less·ly
  thank·less·ness
thanks·giv·ing
thatch
  thatch·ing
  thatch·er
thaw
the·a·ter
  the·a·tre
the·at·ri·cal
  the·at·ri·cal·ism
  the·at·ri·cal·i·ty
  the·at·ri·cal·ly
the·ism
  the·ist
  the·is·tic
  the·is·ti·cal
  the·is·ti·cal·ly
theme
  the·mat·ic
  the·mat·i·cal·ly
them·selves
thence·forth
the·oc·ra·cy
  the·oc·ra·cies
  the·o·crat
  the·o·crat·ic
  the·o·crat·i·cal

the·o·crat·i·cal·ly
The·oc·ri·tus
the·ol·o·gy
the·ol·o·gies
the·o·lo·gian
the·o·log·ic
the·o·log·i·cal
the·o·log·i·cal·ly
the·o·rem
the·o·re·mat·ic
the·o·re·mat·i·cal·ly
the·o·ret·i·cal
the·o·ret·ic
the·o·ret·i·cal·ly
the·o·rize
the·o·rized
the·o·riz·ing
the·o·re·ti·cian
the·o·rist
the·o·ri·za·tion
the·o·riz·er
the·o·ry
the·o·ries
the·os·o·phy
the·os·o·phies
the·o·soph·ic
the·o·soph·i·cal
the·o·soph·i·cal·ly
the·os·o·phist
ther·a·peu·tic
ther·a·peu·ti·cal
ther·a·peu·ti·cal·ly
ther·a·peu·tics
ther·a·peu·tist
ther·a·py
ther·a·pist
there·a·bout
there·af·ter
there·at
there·by
there·for
there·fore
there·from
there·in
there·of
there·on
there·to
there·to·fore
there·up·on
there·with
ther·mal
ther·mal·ly
ther·mo·dy·nam·ics
ther·mo·dy·nam·ic
ther·mo·dy·nam·i·cal
ther·mo·e·lec·tric·i·ty
ther·mo·e·lec·tric
ther·mo·e·lec·tri·cal
ther·mom·e·ter
ther·mo·met·ric
ther·mo·met·ri·cal
ther·mo·met·ri·cal·ly
ther·mo·nu·cle·ar
ther·mo·plas·tic
ther·mos

ther·mo·stat
ther·mo·stat·ic
ther·mo·stat·i·cal·ly
the·sau·rus
the·sau·ri
the·sau·rus·es
the·sis
the·ses
Thes·pi·an
thi·a·mine
thick
thick·ish
thick·ly
thick·ness
thick·en
thick·en·er
thick·en·ing
thick·et
thick·et·ed
thick-head·ed
thick-head·ed·ness
thick·set
thick-skinned
thief
thieves
thieve
thieved
thiev·ing
thiev·ish
thiev·ish·ly
thiev·ish·ness
thiev·ery
thiev·er·ies
thigh-bone
thim·ble
Thim·bu
thin
thin·ner
thin·nest
thinned
thin·ning
thin·ly
thin·ness
thin·nish
thine
thing
think
thought
think·ing
think·a·ble
think·er
thin-skinned
third·ly
third-rate
third-rat·er
thirsty
thirst·i·er
thirst·i·est
thirst·i·ly
thirst·i·ness
thir·teen
thir·teenth
thir·ti·eth
thirty
thir·ties

this·tle
  this·tly
this·tle·down
thith·er
Thom·as
tho·rax
  tho·rax·es
  tho·ra·ces
  tho·rac·ic
tho·ri·um
thorn
  thorn·less
  thorn·like
thorny
  thorn·i·er
  thorn·i·est
  thorn·i·ness
thor·ough
  thor·ough·ly
  thor·ough·ness
thor·ough·bred
thor·ough·fare
thor·ough·go·ing
thought·ful
  thought·ful·ly
  thought·ful·ness
thought·less
  thought·less·ly
  thought·less·ness
thou·sand
  thou·sandth
thrall
  thrall·dom
thrash·er
thrash·ing
thread
  thread·er
  thread·less
  thread·like
thread·bare
  thread·bare·ness
thready
  thread·i·er
  thread·i·est
  thread·i·ness
threat·en
  threat·en·er
  threat·en·ing·ly
three-deck·er
three-di·men·sion·al
three·fold
three-ring
three·score
three·some
thren·o·dy
  thren·o·dies
  thre·no·di·al
  thren·o·dist
thresh·er
thresh·old
thrift·less
thrift·shop
thrifty
  thrift·i·er
  thrift·i·est

thrift·i·ly
thrift·i·ness
thrill
  thrill·ful
  thrill·ing
  thrill·ing·ly
thril·ler
thrive
  thrived
  thriv·ing
  thriv·er
  thriv·ing·ly
throat
  throat·ed
throaty
  throat·i·er
  throat·i·est
  throat·i·ly
  throat·i·ness
throb
  throbbed
  throb·bing
  throb·ber
throm·bo·sis
  throm·bo·ses
throne
  throned
  thron·ing
  throne·less
throt·tle
  throt·tled
  throt·tling
  throt·tler
through·out
through·way
throw
  throw·ing
  throw·er
throw·a·way
throw·back
thrum
  thrummed
  thrum·ming
  thrum·mer
thrust
  thrust·ing
  thrust·er
thru·way
thud
  thud·ded
  thud·ding
thug
  thug·gery
  thug·gism
  thug·gish
thu·li·um
thumb
  thumb·less
  thumb·like
  thumb·nail
  thumb·screw
  thumb·tack
thump·ing
thun·der
  thun·der·er

thun·der·bolt
thun·der·clap
thun·der·cloud
thun·der·head
thun·der·ous
  thun·der·ous·ly
thun·der·show·er
thun·der·storm
thun·der·struck
Thur·ber
Thurs·day
thwack·er
thwart
thyme
  thym·ic
thy·mus
  thy·mic
thy·roid
  thy·roid·less
thy·self
ti·ara
Ti·ber
Ti·be·ri·as
Ti·bet
tib·ia
  tib·i·ae
  tib·i·as
tick·er
tick·et
tick·ing
tick·le
  tick·led
  tick·ling
tick·ler
tick·lish
  tick·lish·ly
  tick·lish·ness
tick·tack·toe
Ti·con·der·o·ga
ti·dal
tid·bit
tid·dly·winks
tide
  tid·ed
  tid·ing
tide·land
tide·wa·ter
ti·dings
ti·dy
  ti·di·er
  ti·di·est
  ti·di·ly
  ti·di·ness
tie
  tied
  ty·ing
tie-in
tie·pin
tier
Tier·ra del Fue·go
tie-up
ti·ger
  ti·ger·ish
  ti·ger·like
tight

tight·ly
tight·ness
tight·en
  tight·en·er
tight-fist·ed
tight-lipped
tight·rope
tight·wad
ti·gress
Ti·gris
til·de
tile
  tiled
  til·ing
till
  till·a·ble
  till·er
till·age
tilt
  tilt·er
tim·ber
  tim·bered
  tim·ber line
  tim·ber wolf
tim·bre
Tim·buk·tu
time
  timed
  tim·ing
time·card
time-hon·ored
time·keep·er
  time·keep·ing
time·less
  time·less·ly
  time·less·ness
time-out
time·piece
tim·er
time·serv·er
  time·serv·ing
time-share
  time-shared
  time-shar·ing
time·ta·ble
time·worn
tim·id
  tim·id·ly
  tim·id·i·ty
  tim·id·ness
tim·ing
tim·or·ous
  tim·or·ous·ly
  tim·or·ous·ness
tim·o·thy
tim·pa·ni
  tim·pa·nist
tin
  tinned
  tin·ning
tinc·ture
  tinc·tured
  tinc·tur·ing
tin·der
tin·der·box

tin·foil
tinge
  tinged
  tinge·ing
tin·gle
  tin·gled
  tin·gling
  tin·gling·ly
  tin·gly
  tin·gli·er
  tin·gli·est
tink·er
tin·kle
  tin·kled
  tin·kling
tin·ny
  tin·ni·er
  tin·ni·est
  tin·ni·ly
  tin·ni·ness
tin·sel
  tin·seled
  tin·sel·ing
  tin·sel·ly
tint
  tint·er
  tint·ing
  tint·less
tin·tin·nab·u·lar
  tin·tin·nab·u·la·tion
tin·type
ti·ny
  ti·ni·er
  ti·ni·est
  ti·ni·ly
  ti·ni·ness
tip
  tipped
  tip·ping
  tip·less
  tip·pa·ble
  tip·per
tip-off
Tip·pe·ca·noe
Tip·pe·rary
tip·ple
  tip·pled
  tip·pling
  tip·pler
tip·ster
tip·sy
  tip·si·er
  tip·si·est
  tip·si·ly
  tip·si·ness
tip·toe
  tip·toed
  tip·to·ing
tip·top
ti·rade
Ti·ra·ne
tire
  tired
  tir·ing
  tire·less

tire·less·ly
tire·less·ness
tire·some
  tire·some·ly
  tire·some·ness
Tish·chen·ko
tis·sue
ti·tan
ti·tan·ic
  ti·tan·i·cal·ly
ti·ta·ni·um
tithe
  tithed
  tith·ing
  tith·a·ble
  tithe·less
ti·tian
Ti·ti·ca·ca
tit·il·late
  tit·il·lat·ed
  tit·il·lat·ing
  tit·il·la·tion
  tit·il·la·tive
ti·tle
  ti·tled
  ti·tling
tit·mouse
  tit·mice
Ti·to·ism
tit·ter
  tit·ter·er
  tit·ter·ing·ly
tit·tle
tit·u·lar
  tit·u·lar·ly
tiz·zy
  tiz·zies
toad·stool
toady
  toad·ies
  toad·ied
  toad·y·ing
  toad·y·ism
toast·er
toast·mas·ter
  toast·mis·tress
to·bac·co
  to·bac·cos
  to·bac·co·nist
To·ba·go
to·bog·gan
  to·bog·gan·er
  to·bog·gan·ist
Tocque·ville
toc·sin
to·day
tod·dle
  tod·dled
  tod·dling
  tod·dler
tod·dy
  tod·dies
to-do
toed
toe·hold

toe·less
toe·nail
tof·fee
to·ga
  to·gas
  to·gae
to·geth·er
  to·geth·er·ness
tog·gle
  tog·gled
  tog·gling
To·go
toil·er
toi·let
toi·let·ry
toil·some
  toil·some·ly
  toil·some·ness
To·kay
to·ken
To·kyo
To·le·do
tol·er·a·ble
  tol·er·a·ble·ness
  tol·er·a·bil·i·ty
  tol·er·a·bly
tol·er·ance
tol·er·ant
  tol·er·ant·ly
tol·er·ate
  tol·er·at·ed
  tol·er·at·ing
  tol·er·a·tion
  tol·er·a·tive
  tol·er·a·tor
toll·booth
toll·gate
toll·house
toll·way
Tol·stoy
tol·u·ene
tom·a·hawk
to·ma·to
  to·ma·toes
tomb
  tomb·less
  tomb·like
tom·boy
  tom·boy·ish
  tom·boy·ish·ness
tomb·stone
tom·cat
tom·fool·ery
  tom·fool·er·ies
to·mor·row
tom·tit
tom-tom
to·nal·i·ty
  to·nal·i·ties
tone
  ton·al
  ton·al·ly
  tone·less
  tone·less·ly
  tone·less·ness

tone-deaf
Ton·ga
tongue
tongue-in-cheek
tongue-lash
  tongue-lash·ing
tongue-tied
ton·ic
  ton·i·cal·ly
to·night
ton·nage
ton·sil
  ton·sil·lar
  ton·sil·lec·to·my
  ton·sil·lec·to·mies
  ton·sil·li·tis
ton·so·ri·al
ton·sure
  ton·sured
  ton·sur·ing
tool·box
tool·house
tool·mak·er
  tool·mak·ing
tool·room
tooth·ache
tooth·achy
tooth·brush
tooth·less
  tooth·less·ly
  tooth·less·ness
tooth·paste
tooth·pick
tooth·some
  tooth·some·ly
  tooth·some·ness
toothy
  tooth·i·er
  tooth·i·est
  tooth·i·ly
  tooth·i·ness
top
  topped
  top·ping
to·paz
top·coat
tope
  toped
  top·ing
To·pe·ka
top·flight
top-heavy
to·pi
  to·pis
to·pi·ary
  to·pi·ar·ies
top·ic
top·i·cal
top·i·cal·i·ty
  top·i·cal·i·ties
top·knot
top·less
top·most
top·notch
  top·notch·er

to·pog·ra·phy
to·pog·ra·phies
to·pog·ra·pher
top·o·graph·i·cal
top·o·graph·i·cal·ly
top·ping
top·ple
top·pled
top·pling
top-se·cret
top·soil
top·sy-tur·vy
top·sy-tur·vies
top·sy-tur·vi·ly
top·sy-tur·vi·ness
toque
To·rah
torch·bear·er
torch·light
tor·e·a·dor
to·re·ro
to·re·ros
to·rii
tor·ment
tor·ment·ing·ly
tor·men·tor
tor·na·do
tor·na·does
tor·na·dos
tor·nad·ic
To·ron·to
tor·pe·do
tor·pe·does
tor·pe·doed
tor·pe·do·ing
tor·pid
tor·pid·i·ty
tor·pid·ly
tor·por
torque
Tor·rens
tor·rent
tor·ren·tial
tor·ren·tial·ly
tor·rid
tor·rid·i·ty
tor·rid·ness
tor·rid·ly
tor·sion
tor·sion·al
tor·sion·al·ly
tor·so
tor·sos
tor·si
torte
tor·til·la
tor·til·las
tor·tois
tor·toise-shell
tor·to·ni
tor·tu·ous
tor·tu·ous·ly
tor·tu·ous·ness
tor·ture
tor·tured

tor·tur·ing
tor·tur·a·ble
tor·tured·ly
tor·tur·er
tor·ture·some
toss·er
toss·up
to·tal
to·taled
to·tal·ing
to·tal·i·tar·i·an
to·tal·i·tar·i·an·ism
to·tal·i·ty
to·tal·i·ties
to·tal·i·za·tor
to·tal·ly
tote
tot·ed
tot·ing
tot·er
to·tem
to·tem·ic
to·tem·ism
to·tem·ist
to·tem·is·tic
tot·ter
tot·ter·er
tot·ter·ing
tot·ter·ing·ly
tou·can
touch
touch·a·ble
touch·a·ble·ness
touch·er
touch·down
tou·ché
touched
touch·ing
touch·ing·ly
touch·ing·ness
touch·stone
touch-tone
touch-type
touch-typed
touch-typ·ing
touch-typ·ist
touchy
touch·i·er
touch·i·est
touch·i·ly
touch·i·ness
tough
tough·ly
tough·ness
tough·en
tough·en·er
Tou·lon
Tou·louse
tou·pee
tour de force
tours de force
tour·ism
tour·ist
tour·ma·line
tour·na·ment

tour·ni·quet
tou·sle
 tou·sled
 tou·sling
Tous·saint
tout·er
tow·age
to·ward
tow·el
 tow·eled
 tow·el·ing
tow·er
 tow·ered
 tow·er·ing
tow·head
 tow-head·ed
tow·line
town·ship
towns·man
 towns·men
towns·peo·ple
tow·path
tow·rope
tox·e·mia
tox·ic
 tox·i·cal
 tox·i·cal·ly
 tox·ic·i·ty
 tox·ic·i·ties
 tox·i·col·o·gy
 tox·i·co·log·i·cal
 tox·i·co·log·i·cal·ly
 tox·i·col·o·gist
tox·in
tox·oid
toy·like
trace
 traced
 trac·ing
 trace·a·ble
 trace·a·ble·ness
 trace·a·bly
 trace·less
 trac·er
trac·ery
 trac·er·ies
tra·chea
 tra·che·ae
 tra·che·as
 tra·che·al
tra·che·ot·o·my
 tra·che·ot·o·mies
tra·cho·ma
track·age
track·er
trac·ta·ble
 trac·ta·bil·i·ty
 trac·ta·ble·ness
 trac·ta·bly
trac·tion
 trac·tion·al
 trac·tive
trac·tor
trade
 trad·ed

trad·ing
trade-in
trade·mark
trad·er
trades·man
 trades·men
trade·wind
trad·ing post
tra·di·tion
 tra·di·tion·less
tra·di·tion·al
 tra·di·tion·al·ism
 tra·di·tion·al·ist
 tra·di·tion·al·ly
tra·duce
 tra·duced
 tra·duc·ing
 tra·duce·ment
 tra·duc·er
Tra·fal·gar
traf·fic
 traf·ficked
 traf·fick·ing
 traf·fick·er
tra·ge·di·an
trag·e·dy
 trag·e·dies
trag·ic
 trag·i·cal
 trag·i·cal·ly
 trag·i·cal·ness
trail·blaz·er
 trail·blaz·ing
trail·er
trail·er camp
train
 train·a·ble
 train·er
 train·ing
train·man
 train·men
traipse
 traipsed
 traips·ing
trai·tor
 trai·tor·ous
 trai·tor·ous·ly
tra·jec·to·ry
 tra·jec·to·ries
tram·mel
 tram·meled
 tram·mel·ing
 tram·mel·er
tramp·er
tram·ple
 tram·pled
 tram·pling
 tram·pler
tram·po·line
 tram·po·lin·er
 tram·po·lin·ist
trance
tran·quil
 tran·quil·li·ty
 tran·quil·ly

tran·quil·ness
tran·quil·ize
  tran·quil·ized
  tran·quil·iz·ing
tran·quil·iz·er
trans·act
  trans·ac·tor
trans·ac·tion
  trans·ac·tion·al
trans·al·pine
trans·at·lan·tic
trans·ceiv·er
tran·scend
  tran·scend·ent
tran·scen·den·tal
  tran·scen·den·tal·ly
  tran·scen·den·tal·ism
trans·con·ti·nen·tal
tran·scribe
  tran·scribed
  tran·scrib·ing
  tran·scrib·er
tran·script
tran·scrip·tion
  tran·scrip·tion·al
  tran·scrip·tive
tran·sept
  tran·sep·tal
  tran·sep·tal·ly
trans·fer
  trans·ferred
  trans·fer·ring
  trans·fer·al
  trans·fer·a·ble
  trans·fer·ence
trans·fig·ure
  trans·fig·ured
  trans·fig·ur·ing
  trans·fig·ure·ment
  trans·fig·u·ra·tion
trans·fix
  trans·fixed
  trans·fix·ing
  trans·fix·ion
trans·form
  trans·form·a·ble
  trans·for·ma·tion
  trans·form·a·tive
  trans·form·er
trans·fuse
  trans·fused
  trans·fus·ing
  trans·fus·a·ble
  trans·fu·sion
trans·gress
  trans·gres·sive
  trans·gres·sor
  trans·gres·sion
tran·sient
  tran·sient·ly
tran·sis·tor
tran·sis·tor·ize
  tran·sis·tor·ized
  tran·sis·tor·iz·ing
trans·it

tran·si·tion
  tran·si·tion·al
  tran·si·tion·al·ly
tran·si·tive
  tran·si·tive·ly
  tran·si·tive·ness
  tran·si·tiv·i·ty
tran·si·to·ry
  tran·si·to·ri·ly
  tran·si·to·ri·ness
trans·late
  trans·lat·ed
  trans·lat·ing
  trans·lat·a·bil·i·ty
  trans·lat·a·ble
  trans·lat·or
trans·la·tion
  trans·la·tion·al
  trans·la·tive
trans·lit·er·ate
  trans·lit·er·at·ed
  trans·lit·er·at·ing
  trans·lit·er·a·tion
trans·lu·cent
  trans·lu·cence
  trans·lu·cen·cy
  trans·lu·cent·ly
trans·mi·grate
  trans·mi·grat·ed
  trans·mi·grat·ing
  trans·mi·gra·tion
  trans·mi·gra·tor
  trans·mi·gra·to·ry
trans·mis·sion
  trans·mis·si·bil·i·ty
  trans·mis·siv·i·ty
  trans·mis·si·ble
  trans·mis·sive
trans·mit
  trans·mit·ted
  trans·mit·ting
  trans·mit·ta·ble
  trans·mit·tal
trans·mit·ter
trans·mute
  trans·mut·ed
  trans·mut·ing
  trans·mut·er
  trans·mut·a·ble·ness
  trans·mut·a·bil·i·ty
  trans·mut·a·bly
  trans·mu·ta·tion
  trans·mut·a·ble
trans·na·tion·al
trans·o·ce·an·ic
tran·som
  tran·somed
trans·pa·cif·ic
trans·par·ent
  trans·par·en·cy
  trans·par·en·cies
  trans·par·ent·ly
  trans·par·ent·ness
tran·spire
  tran·spired

tran·spir·ing
trans·plant
  trans·plant·a·ble
  trans·plan·ta·tion
  trans·plant·er
tran·spon·der
trans·port
  trans·port·a·bil·i·ty
  trans·port·a·ble
  trans·port·er
trans·por·ta·tion
trans·pose
  trans·posed
  trans·pos·ing
  trans·pos·a·ble
  trans·po·si·tion
Trans·vaal
trans·verse
  trans·verse·ly
trans·ves·tism
  trans·ves·tite
Tran·syl·va·nia
trap
  trapped
  trap·ping
tra·peze
  tra·pez·ist
tra·pe·zi·um
  tra·pe·zi·ums
  tra·pe·zia
trap·e·zoid
  trap·e·zoi·dal
trap·pings
Trap·pist
trap·shoot·ing
  trap·shoot·er
trash
  trash·i·ly
  trash·i·ness
  trashy
  trash·i·er
  trash·i·est
trau·ma
  trau·mas
  trau·ma·ta
  trau·mat·ic
  trau·mat·i·cal·ly
tra·vail
tra·vel
  tra·veled
  tra·vel·ing
  trav·el·er
trav·e·logue
  trav·e·log
trav·erse
  trav·ersed
  trav·ers·ing
  tra·vers·a·ble
  tra·vers·al
  tra·vers·er
trav·es·ty
  trav·es·ties
  trav·es·tied
  trav·es·ty·ing
trawl·er

treach·er·ous
  treach·er·ous·ly
  treach·er·ous·ness
treach·ery
  treach·er·ies
trea·cle
trea·cly
  trea·cli·er
  trea·cli·est
tread
  trod·den
  tread·ing
  tread·er
trea·dle
tread·mill
trea·son
  trea·son·a·ble
  trea·son·ous
  trea·son·a·bly
treas·ure
  treas·ured
  treas·ur·ing
  treas·ur·a·ble
treas·ur·er
  treas·ur·er·ship
treas·ure-trove
treas·ury
  treas·ur·ies
treat
  treat·a·ble
  treat·er
trea·tise
treat·ment
trea·ty
  trea·ties
tre·ble
  tre·bled
  tre·bling
  tre·bly
tre·foil
tre·foiled
trek
  trekked
  trek·king
  trek·ker
trel·lis
trem·ble
  trem·bled
  trem·bling
  trem·bler
  trem·bly
  trem·bli·er
  trem·bli·est
  trem·bling·ly
tre·men·dous
  tre·men·dous·ly
  tre·men·dous·ness
trem·o·lo
  trem·o·los
trem·or
  trem·or·ous
trem·u·lous
  trem·u·lous·ly
  trem·u·lous·ness
trench·ant

trench·an·cy
trench·ant·ly
trench·er·man
trench·er·men
trendy
trend·i·er
trend·i·est
Tren·ton
tre·pan
tre·panned
tre·pan·ning
trep·an·a·tion
tre·phine
tre·phined
tre·phin·ing
treph·i·na·tion
trep·i·da·tion
tres·pass
tres·pass·er
tres·tle
tri·ad
tri·ad·ic
tri·ad·i·cal·ly
tri·al
tri·an·gle
tri·an·gu·lar
tri·an·gu·lar·i·ty
tri·an·gu·lar·ly
tri·an·gu·late
tri·an·gu·lat·ed
tri·an·gu·lat·ing
tri·an·gu·la·tion
tribe
trib·al
tribes·man
tribes·men
trib·u·la·tion
tri·bu·nal
trib·une
trib·une·ship
trib·u·nate
trib·u·tary
trib·u·tar·ies
trib·u·tar·i·ly
trib·ute
tri·ceps
tri·cep·ses
trich·i·no·sis
trick·ery
trick·er·ies
trick·le
trick·led
trick·ling
trick·ster
tricky
trick·i·er
trick·i·est
trick·i·ly
trick·i·ness
tri·col·or
tri·col·ored
tri·cus·pid
tri·cy·cle
tri·dent
tri·den·tate

tri·den·tal
tri·di·men·sion·al
tri·di·men·sion·al·i·ty
tri·en·ni·al
tri·en·ni·al·ly
tri·en·ni·um
tri·en·ni·ums
tri·en·nia
tri·fle
tri·fled
tri·fling
trif·ler
tri·fling·ly
tri·fling·ness
tri·fo·cals
tri·fo·li·ate
trig·ger
trig·ger·less
trig·ger·hap·py
trig·ger·man
trig·ger·men
trig·o·nom·e·try
trig·o·no·met·ric
trig·o·no·met·ri·cal
trig·o·no·met·ri·cal·ly
tril·lion
tril·lionth
tri·lo·bite
tril·o·gy
tril·o·gies
trim
trimmed
trim·ming
trim·mer
trim·mest
trim·ly
trim·ness
tri·mes·ter
tri·mes·tral
tri·mes·tri·al
tri·month·ly
Trin·i·dad
tri·ni·tro·tol·u·ene
Trin·i·ty
Trin·i·ties
trin·ket
trio
tri·os
trip
tripped
trip·ping
trip·ping·ly
tri·par·tite
tri·par·tite·ly
tri·par·ti·tion
trip·ham·mer
tri·ple
tri·pled
tri·pling
tri·ply
trip·let
trip·li·cate
trip·li·cat·ed
trip·li·cat·ing
trip·li·ca·tion

tri·pod
trip·o·dal
tri·pod·ic
Trip·o·li
trip·tych
tri·sect
tri·sec·tion
tri·sec·tor
trite
trite·ly
trite·ness
trit·u·rate
trit·u·rat·ed
trit·u·rat·ing
trit·u·ra·ble
trit·u·ra·tor
tri·umph
tri·um·phal
tri·um·phal·ly
tri·um·phant
tri·um·phant·ly
tri·um·vir
tri·um·vi·ral
tri·um·vi·rate
triv·et
triv·ia
triv·i·al
triv·i·al·i·ty
triv·i·al·i·ties
triv·i·al·i·za·tion
triv·i·al·ly
tri·week·ly
tri·week·lies
tro·che
trog·lo·dyte
trog·lo·dyt·ic
troi·ka
Tro·jan
troll
troll·er
trol·ley
trol·leys
trol·leyed
trol·ley·ing
trol·lop
Trol·lope
trom·bone
trom·bon·ist
troop·er
tro·phy
tro·phies
trop·ic
trop·i·cal
trop·i·cal·ly
tro·pism
tro·pis·tic
trop·o·sphere
trop·o·spher·ic
trot
trot·ted
trot·ting
trot·ter
trou·ba·dour
trou·ble
trou·bled

trou·bling
trou·bler
trou·ble·mak·er
trou·ble·shoot·er
trou·ble·some
trough
trough·like
trounce
trounced
trounc·ing
troupe
trouped
troup·ing
troup·er
trou·sers
trous·seau
trous·seaux
trous·seaus
trow·el
trow·el·er
tru·an·cy
tru·an·cies
tru·ant·ry
tru·ant
truck·age
truck·er
truck·ing
truck·load
truc·u·lent
truc·u·lence
truc·u·lent·ly
trudge
trudged
trudg·ing
trudg·er
true
tru·er
tru·est
true·ness
true-blue
true·love
truf·fle
tru·ism
tru·is·tic
tru·ly
trump
trump·er
trum·pet
trum·pet·like
trum·pet·er
trun·cate
trun·cat·ed
trun·cat·ing
trun·ca·tion
trun·cheon
trun·cheoned
trun·dle
trun·dled
trun·dling
trun·dler
truss·er
trust
trust·er
trust·less
trus·tee

trus·teed
trus·tee·ing
trus·tee·ship
trust·ful
 trust·ful·ly
trust·wor·thy
 trust·wor·thi·ly
 trust·wor·thi·ness
trusty
 trust·i·er
 trust·i·est
 trust·i·ness
truth·ful
 truth·ful·ly
 truth·ful·ness
try
 tried
 try·ing
try·out
tryst
tset·se
T-shirt
Tshom·be
T-square
tsu·na·mi
tub
 tubbed
 tub·bing
tu·ba
 tu·bas
 tu·bae
tu·bal
tub·by
 tub·bi·er
 tub·bi·est
 tub·bi·ness
tube
 tubed
 tub·ing
tube·less
tu·ber
tu·ber·cle
tu·ber·cu·lar
 tu·ber·cu·lar·ly
tu·ber·cu·lin
tu·ber·cu·lo·sis
tu·ber·cu·lous
tu·ber·ous
tu·bu·lar
tu·bule
tuck·er
tuck-point
 tuck-point·er
 tuck-point·ing
Tuc·son
Tu·dor
Tues·day
tuf·fet
tuft
 tuft·er
 tufty
 tuft·i·er
 tuft·i·est
tug·boat
tu·i·tion

tu·i·tion·al
tu·lip
Tul·sa
tum·ble
 tum·bled
 tum·bling
tum·ble-down
tum·bler
tum·ble·weed
tu·mid
 tu·mid·i·ty
tum·my
 tum·mies
tu·mor
 tu·mor·ous
tu·mult
tu·mul·tu·ous
 tu·mul·tu·ous·ly
 tu·mul·tu·ous·ness
tu·na
tun·a·ble
tun·dra
tune
 tuned
 tun·ing
tune·ful
tune·less
tun·er
tune-up
tung·sten
tu·nic
Tu·nis
Tu·ni·sia
tun·nel
 tun·neled
 tun·nel·ing
 tun·nel·er
tur·ban
 tur·baned
tur·bid
 tur·bid·i·ty
 tur·bid·ness
tur·bine
tur·bo
 tur·bos
tur·bo·car
tur·bo·charg·er
tur·bo·fan
tur·bo·jet
tur·bo·pro·pel·ler
tur·bo·su·per·charg·er
tur·bot
tur·bu·lence
 tur·bu·len·cy
tur·bu·lent
tu·reen
tur·gid
 tur·gid·i·ty
 tur·gid·ness
Tu·rin
Tur·ke·stan
tur·key
 tur·keys
Turk·ish
tur·mer·ic

tur·moil
turn·a·bout
turn·a·round
Turn·bull
turn·coat
turn·down
turn·er
turn·ing
tur·nip
turn·key
turn·off
turn·out
turn·o·ver
turn·pike
turn·stile
turn·ta·ble
turn·up
tur·pen·tine
tur·pen·tined
tur·pen·tin·ing
tur·pi·tude
tur·quoise
tur·ret
tur·tle
tur·tle·dove
tur·tle·neck
Tus·ca·loo·sa
Tus·ca·ny
tusk
tusked
tusk·er
Tus·ke·gee
tus·sive
tus·sle
tus·sled
tus·sling
tu·te·lage
tu·tor
tu·tor·ship
tu·tor·age
tu·to·ri·al
tut·ti-frut·ti
tu·tu
tux·e·do
twad·dle
twain
twang
twangy
twang·i·er
twang·i·est
tweed
tweedy
tweed·i·er
tweed·i·est
tweed·i·ness
tweet·er
tweez·ers
tweeze
tweezed
tweez·ing
twelve
twelfth
twen·ty
twen·ties
twen·ti·eth

twen·ty-one
twid·dle
twid·dled
twid·dling
twid·dler
twig
twig·gy
twig·gi·er
twig·gi·est
twi·light
twilled
twin
twinned
twin·ning
twine
twined
twin·ing
twinge
twinged
twing·ing
twin·kle
twin·kled
twin·kling
twin·kler
twirl
twirl·er
twirly
twirl·i·er
twirl·i·est
twist·er
twit
twit·ted
twit·ting
twitch·er
twit·ter
twit·ter·er
twit·tery
two-bit
two-di·men·sion·al
two-faced
two-fac·ed·ly
two-fac·ed·ness
two-fist·ed
two-sid·ed
two-sid·ed·ness
two·some
two-step
two-stepped
two-step·ping
two-time
two-timed
two-tim·ing
two-way
ty·coon
tym·bal
tym·pan·ic
type
typed
typ·ing
typ·a·ble
type·cast
type·face
type·script
type·set·ter
type·set

type·set·ting	ul·nar
type·write	ul·ster
type·wrote	ul·te·ri·or
type·writ·ten	ul·te·ri·or·ly
type·writ·ing	ul·ti·mate
type·writ·er	ul·ti·mate·ly
ty·phoid	ul·ti·mate·ness
ty·phoon	ul·ti·ma·tum
ty·phus	ul·ti·ma·tums
typ·i·cal	ul·ti·ma·ta
typ·ic	ul·tra
typ·i·cal·ly	ul·tra·con·serv·a·tive
typ·i·cal·ness	ul·tra·high
typ·i·cal·i·ty	ul·tra·ma·rine
typ·i·fy	ul·tra·son·ic
typ·i·fied	ul·tra·vi·o·let
typ·i·fy·ing	ul·u·late
typ·i·fi·ca·tion	ul·u·lat·ed
typ·ist	ul·u·lat·ing
ty·po	ul·u·lant
ty·pog·ra·phy	ul·u·la·tion
ty·pog·ra·pher	Ulys·ses
ty·po·graph·ic	um·bel
ty·po·graph·i·cal	um·bel·lar
ty·po·graph·i·cal·ly	um·bel·late
ty·ran·ni·cal	um·bel·lat·ed
ty·ran·nic	um·bel·late·ly
ty·ran·ni·cal·ly	um·ber
tyr·an·nize	um·bil·i·cal
tyr·an·nized	um·bra
tyr·an·niz·ing	um·bras
tyr·an·niz·er	um·brae
tyr·an·ny	um·brage
tyr·an·nies	um·bra·geous
ty·rant	um·bra·geous·ly
ty·ro	um·bra·geous·ness
Ty·ro·le·an	um·brel·la
Uban·gi	Um·bri·an
ubiq·ui·tous	u·mi·ak
ubiq·ui·tary	um·laut
ubiq·ui·tous·ly	um·pire
ubiq·ui·tous·ness	um·pired
ubiq·ui·ty	um·pir·ing
U-boat	ump·teen
ud·der	ump·teenth
Ugan·da	un·a·bashed
ug·ly	un·a·bash·ed·ly
ug·li·er	un·a·ble
ug·li·est	un·a·bridged
ug·li·ly	un·ac·cep·ta·ble
ug·li·ness	un·ac·cept·ed
ukase	un·ac·com·pa·nied
Ukraine	un·ac·count·a·ble
uku·le·le	un·ac·count·a·ble·ness
Ulan Ba·tor	un·ac·count·a·bly
Ul·bricht	un·ac·cus·tomed
ul·cer	un·ac·quaint·ed
ul·cer·ous	un·a·dorned
ul·cer·ate	un·a·dul·ter·at·ed
ul·cer·at·ed	un·a·dul·ter·at·ed·ly
ul·cer·at·ing	un·ad·vised
ul·cer·a·tion	un·ad·vis·ed·ly
ul·na	un·ad·vis·ed·ness
ul·nae	un·af·fect·ed
ul·nas	un·af·fect·ed·ly

un·af·fect·ed·ness
un·a·fraid
un-A·mer·i·can
unan·i·mous
una·nim·i·ty
unan·i·mous·ly
unan·i·mous·ness
un·an·swer·a·ble
un·an·swer·a·bly
un·an·swered
un·ap·pe·tiz·ing
un·ap·pre·ci·at·ed
un·ap·pre·ci·a·tive
un·ap·proach·a·ble
un·ap·proach·a·ble·ness
un·ap·proach·a·bly
un·ap·proached
un·armed
un·a·shamed
un·asked
un·a·spir·ing
un·as·sail·a·ble
un·as·sail·a·ble·ness
un·as·sail·a·bly
un·as·sailed
un·at·tached
un·at·tain·a·ble
un·at·tained
un·at·tend·ed
un·au·thor·ized
un·a·vail·a·ble
un·a·vail·a·bil·i·ty
un·a·vail·a·bly
un·a·void·a·ble
un·a·void·a·bil·i·ty
un·a·void·a·ble·ness
un·a·void·a·bly
un·a·ware
un·a·ware·ness
un·a·wares
un·backed
un·bal·anced
un·bar
un·barred
un·bar·ring
un·bear·a·ble
un·bear·a·ble·ness
un·bear·a·bly
un·beat·en
un·beat·a·ble
un·be·com·ing
un·be·com·ing·ly
un·be·com·ing·ness
un·be·lief
un·be·liev·a·ble
un·be·liev·a·bly
un·be·liev·er
un·be·liev·ing
un·be·liev·ing·ly
un·be·liev·ing·ness
un·bend
un·bend·ed
un·bend·ing
un·bend·ing·ly
un·bend·ing·ness

un·bi·ased
un·bi·ased·ly
un·bid·den
un·bind
un·bound
un·bind·ing
un·blem·ished
un·bolt
un·bolt·ed
un·born
un·bos·om
un·bound
un·bound·ed
un·bound·ed·ly
un·bound·ed·ness
un·bowed
un·break·a·ble
un·bri·dle
un·bri·dled
un·bri·dling
un·bro·ken
un·bro·ken·ly
un·buck·le
un·buck·led
un·buck·ling
un·bur·den
un·but·ton
un·but·toned
un·called-for
un·can·ny
un·can·ni·er
un·can·ni·est
un·can·ni·ly
un·can·ni·ness
un·cap
un·capped
un·cap·ping
un·ceas·ing
un·ceas·ing·ly
un·ceas·ing·ness
un·cer·e·mo·ni·ous
un·cer·e·mo·ni·ous·ly
un·cer·e·mo·ni·ous·ness
un·cer·tain
un·cer·tain·ly
un·cer·tain·ness
un·cer·tain·ty
un·cer·tain·ties
un·chal·lenged
un·change·a·ble
un·change·a·bly
un·changed
un·chang·ing
un·char·i·ta·ble
un·char·i·ta·ble·ness
un·char·i·ta·bly
un·chart·ed
un·chris·tian
un·cir·cum·cised
un·civ·il
un·civ·il·ly
un·civ·i·lized
un·class·i·fi·a·ble
un·clas·si·fied
un·cle

un·clean
  un·clean·ly
  un·clean·ness
un·clear
un·cloak
un·clothe
  un·clothed
  un·cloth·ing
un·clut·tered
un·coil
un·com·fort·a·ble
  un·com·fort·a·ble·ness
  un·com·fort·a·bly
un·com·mit·ted
un·com·mon
  un·com·mon·ly
  un·com·mon·ness
un·com·mu·ni·ca·tive
  un·com·mu·ni·ca·tive·ly
  un·com·mu·ni·ca·tive·ness
un·com·pre·hend·ing
un·com·pro·mis·ing
  un·com·pro·mised
  un·com·pro·mis·ing·ly
  un·com·pro·mis·ing·ness
un·con·cern
un·con·cerned
  un·con·cern·ed·ly
  un·con·cern·ed·ness
un·con·di·tion·al
  un·con·di·tion·al·ly
un·con·firmed
un·con·nect·ed
  un·con·nect·ed·ly
  un·con·nect·ed·ness
un·con·quer·a·ble
un·con·quered
un·con·scion·a·ble
  un·con·scion·a·ble·ness
  un·con·scion·a·bly
un·con·scious
  un·con·scious·ly
  un·con·scious·ness
un·con·sti·tu·tion·al
  un·con·sti·tu·tion·al·i·ty
  un·con·sti·tu·tion·al·ly
un·con·strained
un·con·test·ed
un·con·trol·la·ble
  un·con·trol·la·bly
  un·con·trolled
un·con·ven·tion·al
  un·con·ven·tion·al·i·ty
  un·con·ven·tion·al·ly
un·count·ed
un·cou·ple
  un·cou·pled
  un·cou·pling
un·couth
  un·couth·ly
  un·couth·ness
un·cov·er
  un·cov·ered
unc·tion
unc·tu·ous

unc·tu·os·i·ty
unc·tu·ous·ness
unc·tu·ous·ly
un·curl
un·cut
un·daunt·ed
  un·daunt·ed·ly
  un·daunt·ed·ness
un·de·ceive
  un·de·ceived
  un·de·ceiv·ing
  un·de·ceiv·a·ble
un·de·cid·ed
  un·de·cid·ed·ly
  un·de·cid·ed·ness
un·de·fined
  un·de·fin·a·ble
un·de·mon·stra·tive
  un·de·mon·stra·tive·ly
  un·de·mon·stra·tive·ness
un·de·ni·a·ble
  un·de·ni·a·ble·ness
  un·de·ni·a·bly
  un·de·nied
un·de·pend·a·ble
  un·de·pend·a·bil·i·ty
  un·de·pend·a·ble·ness
un·der
un·der·a·chiev·er
  un·der·a·chiev·ment
un·der·act
un·der·age
un·der·arm
un·der·bel·ly
  un·der·bel·lies
un·der·brush
un·der·car·riage
un·der·charge
  un·der·charged
  un·der·charg·ing
un·der·class·man
  un·der·class·men
un·der·clothes
un·der·coat
un·der·cov·er
un·der·cur·rent
un·der·cut
  un·der·cut·ting
un·der·de·vel·oped
  un·der·de·vel·op·ing
un·der·dog
un·der·done
un·der·es·ti·mate
  un·der·es·ti·mat·ed
  un·der·es·ti·mat·ing
  un·der·es·ti·ma·tion
un·der·foot
un·der·gar·ment
un·der·go
  un·der·went
  un·der·gone
  un·der·go·ing
un·der·grad·u·ate
un·der·ground
un·der·growth

un·der·hand
un·der·hand·ed
  un·der·hand·ed·ly
  un·der·hand·ed·ness
un·der·lie
  un·der·lay
  un·der·lain
  un·der·ly·ing
un·der·line
  un·der·lined
  un·der·lin·ing
un·der·ling
un·der·mine
  un·der·mined
  un·der·min·ing
  un·der·min·er
un·der·most
un·der·neath
un·der·pants
un·der·pass
un·der·pin·ning
un·der·priv·i·leged
un·der·rate
  un·der·rat·ed
  un·der·rat·ing
un·der·score
  un·der·scored
  un·der·scor·ing
un·der·sea
un·der·sec·re·tary
  un·der·sec·re·tar·ies
un·der·sell
  un·der·sold
  un·der·sell·ing
  un·der·sell·er
un·der·shirt
un·der·shot
un·der·side
un·der·signed
un·der·stand
  un·der·stood
  un·der·stand·ing
  un·der·stand·a·bil·i·ty
  un·der·stand·a·ble
  un·der·stand·a·bly
  un·der·stand·ing·ly
un·der·state
  un·der·stat·ed
  un·der·stat·ing
  un·der·state·ment
un·der·stood
un·der·study
  un·der·stud·ied
  un·der·stud·y·ing
  un·der·stud·ies
un·der·take
  un·der·took
  un·der·tak·en
  un·der·tak·ing
un·der·tak·er
un·der-the-coun·ter
un·der·tone
un·der·tow
un·der·wa·ter
un·der·wear

un·der·weight
un·der·world
un·der·write
  un·der·wrote
  un·der·writ·ten
  un·der·writ·ing
  un·der·writ·er
un·de·sir·a·ble
  un·de·sir·a·bil·i·ty
  un·de·sir·a·ble·ness
  un·de·sir·a·bly
un·de·ter·mined
un·dies
un·dip·lo·mat·ic
  un·dip·lo·mat·i·cal·ly
un·dis·ci·plined
un·dis·closed
un·dis·posed
un·dis·tin·guished
un·di·vid·ed
un·do
  un·did
  un·done
  un·do·ing
  un·do·er
un·doubt·ed
  un·doubt·ed·ly
  un·doubt·ing
un·dress
  un·dressed
  un·dress·ing
Und·set
un·due
un·du·lant
un·du·late
  un·du·lat·ed
  un·du·lat·ing
  un·du·la·tion
un·du·ly
un·dy·ing
un·earth
un·earth·ly
  un·earth·li·ness
un·easy
  un·eas·i·er
  un·eas·i·est
  un·ease
  un·eas·i·ly
  un·eas·i·ness
un·em·ployed
  un·em·ploy·ment
un·e·qual
  un·e·qual·ly
  un·e·qualed
un·e·quiv·o·cal
  un·e·quiv·o·cal·ly
un·err·ing
  un·err·ing·ly
un·eth·i·cal
  un·eth·i·cal·ly
un·e·ven
  un·e·ven·ly
  un·e·ven·ness
un·ex·cep·tion·a·ble
  un·ex·cep·tion·a·ble·ness

un·ex·cep·tion·a·bly
un·ex·pect·ed
un·ex·pect·ed·ly
un·ex·pect·ed·ness
un·fail·ing
un·fail·ing·ly
un·fail·ing·ness
un·faith·ful
un·faith·ful·ly
un·faith·ful·ness
un·fa·mil·iar
un·fa·mil·i·ar·i·ty
un·fa·mil·iar·ly
un·fast·en
un·fas·ten·a·ble
un·fas·ten·er
un·fath·om·a·ble
un·fa·vor·a·ble
un·fa·vor·a·ble·ness
un·fa·vor·a·bly
un·feel·ing
un·feel·ing·ly
un·feel·ing·ness
un·feigned
un·feign·ed·ly
un·fet·ter
un·fet·tered
un·fin·ished
un·fit
un·fit·ly
un·fit·ness
un·fit·ting
un·flat·ter·ing
un·flinch·ing
un·flinch·ing·ly
un·fold
un·for·get·ta·ble
un·for·get·ta·bly
un·for·giv·a·ble
un·for·tu·nate
un·for·tu·nate·ly
un·for·tu·nate·ness
un·found·ed
un·found·ed·ness
un·friend·ly
un·friend·li·er
un·friend·li·est
un·friend·li·ness
un·frock
un·furl
un·gain·ly
un·gain·li·ness
un·gird
un·gird·ed
un·gird·ing
un·glazed
un·god·ly
un·god·li·er
un·god·li·est
un·god·li·ness
un·gov·ern·a·able
un·gov·ern·a·ble·ness
un·gov·ern·a·bly
un·gra·cious
un·gra·cious·ly

un·gra·cious·ness
un·gram·mat·i·cal
un·gram·mat·i·cal·ly
un·grate·ful
un·grate·ful·ly
un·grate·ful·ness
un·guard·ed
un·guard·ed·ly
un·guard·ed·ness
un·guent
un·gu·late
un·ham·pered
un·hand
un·handy
un·hand·i·er
un·hand·i·est
un·hap·py
un·hap·pi·er
un·hap·pi·est
un·hap·pi·ly
un·hap·pi·ness
un·harmed
un·healthy
un·health·i·er
un·health·i·est
un·health·i·ly
un·health·i·ness
un·heard
un·heed·ed
un·heed·ful
un·heed·ing
un·hinge
un·hinged
un·hing·ing
un·hitch
un·ho·ly
un·ho·li·er
un·ho·li·est
un·ho·li·ly
un·ho·li·ness
un·hook
un·horse
un·horsed
un·hors·ing
un·hur·ried
un·hurt
uni·cam·er·al
uni·cam·er·al·ly
uni·cel·lu·lar
uni·corn
uni·fi·ca·tion
uni·form
uni·formed
uni·form·i·ty
uni·form·ly
uni·form·ness
uni·fy
uni·fied
uni·fy·ing
uni·fi·er
uni·lat·er·al
uni·lat·er·al·ism
uni·lat·er·al·ly
un·im·ag·i·na·ble
un·im·paired

un·im·peach·a·ble
un·im·peach·a·bly
un·im·por·tance
un·im·por·tant
un·im·proved
un·in·hib·it·ed
un·in·hib·it·ed·ly
un·in·ter·est·ed
un·in·ter·est·ing
un·ion
un·ion·ism
un·ion·ist
un·ion·ize
un·ion·ized
un·ion·iz·ing
un·ion·i·za·tion
unique
unique·ly
unique·ness
uni·son
unit
Uni·tar·i·an
unite
unit·ed
unit·ing
unit·er
uni·ty
uni·ties
uni·valve
uni·valved
uni·val·vu·lar
uni·ver·sal
uni·ver·sal·i·ty
uni·ver·sal·ly
uni·ver·sal·ness
Uni·ver·sal·ist
uni·ver·sal·ize
uni·ver·sal·ized
uni·ver·sal·iz·ing
uni·verse
uni·ver·si·ty
uni·ver·si·ties
un·just
un·just·ly
un·just·ness
un·kempt
un·kind
un·kind·ness
un·kind·ly
un·kind·li·er
un·kind·li·est
un·kind·li·ness
un·known
un·law·ful
un·law·ful·ly
un·law·ful·ness
un·learn
un·learned
un·learn·ing
un·learn·ed
un·learn·ed·ly
un·leash
un·less
un·let·tered
un·like

un·like·ness
un·like·ly
un·like·li·er
un·like·li·est
un·like·li·ness
un·lim·ber
un·lim·it·ed
un·load
un·load·er
un·lock
un·looked-for
un·loose
un·loosed
un·loos·ing
un·loos·en
un·lucky
un·luck·i·er
un·luck·i·est
un·luck·i·ly
un·luck·i·ness
un·make
un·made
un·mak·ing
un·mak·er
un·man
un·manned
un·man·ning
un·mask
un·mean·ing
un·mean·ing·ly
un·mean·ing·ness
un·men·tion·a·ble
un·mer·ci·ful
un·mer·ci·ful·ly
un·mis·tak·a·ble
un·mis·tak·a·bly
un·mit·i·gat·ed
un·mit·i·gat·ed·ly
un·nat·u·ral
un·nat·u·ral·ly
un·nat·u·ral·ness
un·nec·es·sary
un·nec·es·sar·i·ly
un·nerve
un·nerved
un·nerv·ing
un·num·bered
un·ob·jec·tion·a·ble
un·or·gan·ized
un·pack
un·par·al·leled
un·par·don·a·ble
un·pleas·ant
un·pleas·ant·ly
un·pleas·ant·ness
un·plumbed
un·pop·u·lar
un·pop·u·lar·i·ty
un·pop·u·lar·ly
un·prec·e·dent·ed
un·prec·e·dent·ed·ly
un·prin·ci·pled
un·print·a·ble
un·pro·fes·sion·al
un·pro·fes·sion·al·ly

un·qual·i·fied
  un·qual·i·fied·ly
un·ques·tion·a·ble
  un·ques·tion·a·bly
un·ques·tioned
un·quote
  un·quot·ed
  un·quot·ing
un·rav·el
  un·rav·eled
  un·rav·el·ing
  un·rav·el·ment
un·read
un·re·al
un·rea·son·a·ble
  un·rea·son·a·ble·ness
  un·rea·son·a·bly
un·rea·son·ing
un·re·fined
un·re·gen·er·ate
un·re·lat·ed
un·re·lent·ing
  un·re·lent·ing·ly
un·re·mit·ting
un·re·serve
  un·re·served
  un·re·serv·ed·ly
  un·re·serv·ed·ness
un·rest
un·ri·valed
un·roll
un·ruf·fled
un·ru·ly
  un·ru·li·er
  un·ru·li·est
  un·ru·li·ness
un·sad·dle
  un·sad·dled
  un·sad·dling
un·said
un·sa·vory
un·say
  un·say·ing
un·scathed
un·schooled
un·scram·ble
  un·scram·bled
  un·scram·bling
un·screw
un·scru·pu·lous
  un·scru·pu·lous·ly
  un·scru·pu·lous·ness
un·seal
un·sea·son·a·ble
  un·sea·son·a·ble·ness
  un·sea·son·a·bly
un·seat
un·seem·ly
  un·seem·li·ness
un·set·tle
  un·set·tled
  un·set·tling
un·sheathe
  un·sheathed
  un·sheath·ing

un·shod
un·sight·ly
  un·sight·li·er
  un·sight·li·est
  un·sight·li·ness
un·skilled
un·skill·ful
  un·skill·ful·ly
  un·skill·ful·ness
un·snap
  un·snapped
  un·snap·ping
un·snarl
un·so·phis·ti·cat·ed
  un·so·phis·ti·cat·ed·ly
  un·so·phis·ti·cat·ed·ness
  un·so·phis·ti·ca·tion
un·sound
  un·sound·ly
  un·sound·ness
un·spar·ing
  un·spar·ing·ly
  un·spar·ing·ness
un·speak·a·ble
  un·speak·a·bly
un·sta·ble
  un·sta·ble·ness
  un·sta·bly
un·steady
  un·stead·i·er
  un·stead·i·est
  un·stead·i·ly
un·stop
  un·stopped
  un·stop·ping
un·strung
un·stud·ied
un·sung
un·tan·gle
  un·tan·gled
  un·tan·gling
un·taught
Un·ter·mey·er
un·think·a·ble
un·think·ing
  un·think·ing·ly
un·ti·dy
  un·ti·di·er
  un·ti·di·est
  un·ti·di·ly
  un·ti·di·ness
un·tie
  un·tied
  un·ty·ing
un·til
un·time·ly
  un·time·li·ness
un·to
un·told
un·touch·a·ble
  un·touch·a·bly
un·to·ward
  un·to·ward·ly
  un·to·ward·ness
un·truth

un·tu·tored
un·used
un·u·su·al
  un·u·su·al·ly
  un·u·su·al·ness
un·ut·ter·a·ble
  un·ut·ter·a·bly
un·var·nished
un·veil
un·wary
  un·war·i·ly
  un·war·i·ness
un·well
un·whole·some
  un·whole·some·ly
  un·whole·some·ness
un·wieldy
  un·wield·i·ness
un·will·ing
  un·will·ing·ly
  un·will·ing·ness
un·wind
  un·wound
  un·wind·ing
un·wise
  un·wise·ly
un·wit·ting
  un·wit·ting·ly
un·wont·ed
  un·wont·ed·ly
  un·wont·ed·ness
un·wor·thy
  un·wor·thi·ly
  un·wor·thi·ness
un·wrap
  un·wrapped
  un·wrap·ping
un·yield·ing
up-and-com·ing
up-and-down
up·beat
up·braid
  up·braid·er
  up·braid·ing
  up·braid·ing·ly
up·bring·ing
up·com·ing
up·coun·try
up·date
  up·dat·ed
  up·dat·ing
up·end
up·grade
  up·grad·ed
  up·grad·ing
up·heav·al
up·heave
  up·heaved
  up·heav·ing
up·hill
up·hold
  up·held
  up·hold·ing
  up·hold·er
up·hol·ster

up·hol·ster·er
up·hol·stery
up·hol·ster·ies
up·keep
up·land
up·lift
up·most
up·on
up·per
up·per-class
up·per-class·man
  up·per·class·men
up·per·cut
  up·per·cut·ting
up·per·most
up·pish
  up·pish·ly
  up·pish·ness
up·pi·ty
up·raise
  up·raised
  up·rais·ing
up·rear
up·right
  up·right·ly
  up·right·ness
up·ris·ing
up·roar
up·roar·i·ous
  up·roar·i·ous·ly
  up·roar·i·ous·ness
up·root
  up·root·er
up·set
  up·set·ting
up·shot
up·side
up·stage
  up·staged
  up·stag·ing
up·stairs
up·stand·ing
  up·stand·ing·ness
up·start
up·state
up·stream
up·swing
up·take
up-to-date
  up-to-date·ness
up·town
up·trend
up·turn
up·ward
  up·ward·ly
  up·ward·ness
Ural
Ura·nia
ura·ni·um
Ura·nus
ur·ban
ur·bane
  ur·bane·ly
  ur·bane·ness
  ur·ban·i·ty

ur·ban·ize
ur·ban·ized
ur·ban·iz·ing
ur·ban·i·za·tion
ur·chin
urea
ure·al
ure·ic
ure·mia
ure·mic
ure·ter
ure·thra
ure·thrae
ure·thras
ure·thral
urge
urged
urg·ing
urg·er
urg·ing·ly
ur·gent
ur·gen·cy
ur·gen·cies
ur·gent·ly
Uri·ah
uric
uri·nal
uri·nal·y·sis
uri·nal·y·ses
uri·nary
uri·nar·ies
uri·nate
uri·nat·ed
uri·nat·ing
uri·na·tion
urine
urol·o·gy
uro·log·ic
uro·log·i·cal
urol·o·gist
Uru·guay
us·a·ble
us·a·ble·ness
us·a·bly
us·a·bil·i·ty
us·age
use
used
us·ing
us·er
use·ful
use·ful·ly
use·ful·ness
use·less
use·less·ly
use·less·ness
ush·er
usu·al
usu·al·ly
usu·al·ness
usurp
usurp·pa·tion
usurp·er
usu·ry
usu·ries

usu·rer
usu·ri·ous
Utah
uten·sil
uter·us
uteri
Uti·ca
util·i·tar·ian
util·i·ty
util·i·ties
uti·lize
uti·lized
uti·liz·ing
uti·liz·a·ble
uti·li·za·tion
uti·liz·er
ut·most
Uto·pia
Uto·pi·an
ut·ter
ut·ter·a·ble
ut·ter·er
ut·ter·ance
ut·ter·most
uvu·la
uvu·las
uvu·lae
uvu·lar
ux·o·ri·ous
ux·o·ri·ous·ly
ux·o·ri·ous·ness
va·can·cy
va·can·cies
va·cant
va·cant·ly
va·cant·ness
va·cate
va·cat·ed
va·cat·ing
va·ca·tion
va·ca·tion·less
vac·ci·nate
vac·ci·nat·ed
vac·ci·nat·ing
vac·ci·na·tion
vac·cine
vac·il·late
vac·il·lat·ed
vac·il·lat·ing
vac·il·la·tion
vac·il·la·tor
va·cu·i·ty
va·cu·i·ties
vac·u·ous
vac·u·ous·ly
vac·u·ous·ness
vac·u·um
vac·u·ums
vac·ua
vac·u·um-packed
Va·duz
vag·a·bond
vag·a·bond·age
vag·a·bond·ish
vag·a·bond·ism

va·gary
  va·gar·ies
  va·gar·i·ous
  va·gar·i·ous·ly
va·gi·na
  va·gi·nas
  va·gi·nae
  vag·i·nal
va·grant
  va·gran·cy
  va·gran·cies
  va·grant·ly
vague
  vague·ly
  vague·ness
vain
  vain·ly
  vain·ness
vain·glo·ry
  vain·glo·ries
  vain·glo·ri·ous
  vain·glo·ri·ous·ly
  vain·glo·ri·ous·ness
val·ance
  val·anced
val·e·dic·tion
val·e·dic·to·ri·an
val·e·dic·to·ry
  val·e·dic·to·ries
va·lence
  va·len·cy
Va·len·cia
val·en·tine
val·et
Val·hal·la
val·iant
  val·iant·ly
  val·iant·ness
val·id
  val·id·ly
  val·id·ness
val·i·date
  val·i·dat·ed
  val·i·dat·ing
  val·i·da·tion
va·lid·i·ty
  va·lid·i·ties
va·lise
Val·let·ta
val·ley
  val·leys
Val·ois
val·or
  val·or·ous
  val·or·ous·ly
  val·or·ous·ness
Val·pa·rai·so
val·u·a·ble
  val·u·a·ble·ness
  val·u·a·bly
val·u·a·tion
  val·u·a·tion·al
val·ue
  val·ued
  val·u·ing

val·ue·less
  val·ue·less·ness
  val·u·er
valve
  valve·less
  val·vu·lar
va·moose
vam·pire
  vam·pir·ic
  vam·pir·ism
va·na·di·um
Van Bu·ren
Van·cou·ver
van·dal
  van·dal·ism
  van·dal·ize
  van·dal·ized
  van·dal·iz·ing
Van·der·bilt
Van·dyke
vane
  vaned
  vane·less
van·guard
va·nil·la
van·ish
  van·ish·er
van·i·ty
  van·i·ties
van·quish
  van·quish·a·ble
  van·quish·er
van·tage
vap·id
  va·pid·i·ty
  vap·id·ness
  vap·id·ly
va·por
  va·por·er
  va·por·ish
  va·por·ish·ness
  va·por·ize
  va·por·ized
  va·por·iz·ing
  va·por·i·za·tion
  va·por·iz·er
  va·por·ous
  va·por·ous·ly
va·que·ro
  va·que·ros
var·i·a·ble
  var·i·a·bil·i·ty
  var·i·a·ble·ness
  var·i·a·bly
var·i·ance
var·i·ant
var·i·a·tion
  var·i·a·tion·al
  var·i·a·tion·al·ly
var·i·col·ored
var·i·cose
var·ied
  var·ied·ness
var·i·e·gate
  var·i·e·gat·ed

var·i·e·gat·ing
var·i·e·ga·tion
var·i·e·ga·tor
va·ri·e·tal
va·ri·e·tal·ly
va·ri·e·ty
va·ri·e·ties
var·i·ous
var·i·ous·ly
var·i·ous·ness
var·nish
var·nish·er
var·si·ty
var·si·ties
vary
var·ied
var·y·ing
var·i·er
var·y·ing·ly
vas·cu·lar
vas·cu·lar·i·ty
vas·ec·to·my
vas·ec·to·mies
Vas·e·line
vas·o·mo·tor
vas·sal
vas·sal·age
vast·ness
vat
vat·ted
vat·ting
Vat·i·can
vaude·ville
vault
vault·ed
vault·er
vault·ing
vaunt
vaunt·er
vaunt·ing·ly
vec·tor
vec·to·ri·al
veer·ing
veg·e·ta·ble
veg·e·tal
veg·e·tar·i·an
veg·e·tar·i·an·ism
veg·e·tate
veg·e·tat·ed
veg·e·tat·ing
veg·e·ta·tion
veg·e·ta·tion·al
veg·e·ta·tion·less
veg·e·ta·tive
ve·he·ment
ve·he·mence
ve·he·men·cy
ve·hi·cle
ve·hic·u·lar
veil
veiled
veil·ing
vein
veiny
vein·i·er

vein·i·est
vein·ing
Ve·las·quez
vel·lum
ve·loc·i·ty
ve·loc·i·ties
vel·our
ve·lum
ve·la
vel·vet
vel·vet·ed
vel·vet·een
vel·vety
vel·vet·i·er
vel·vet·i·est
ve·nal
ve·nal·i·ty
ve·nal·ly
ve·na·tion
ve·na·tion·al
vend·er
vend·or
ven·det·ta
vend·i·ble
vend·i·bil·i·ty
ve·neer
ve·neer·er
ve·neer·ing
ven·er·a·ble
ven·er·a·bil·i·ty
ven·er·a·ble·ness
ven·er·a·bly
ven·er·ate
ven·er·a·tion
ven·er·a·tor
ve·ne·re·al
Ve·ne·tian
Ven·e·zu·e·la
venge·ance
venge·ful
venge·ful·ness
ve·ni·al
ve·ni·al·i·ty
ve·ni·al·ness
ve·ni·al·ly
Ven·ice
ven·i·son
ven·om
ven·om·ous
ven·om·ous·ness
ve·nous
ve·nous·ly
ve·nous·ness
vent
vent·ed
vent·ing
ven·ti·late
ven·ti·lat·ed
ven·ti·lat·ing
ven·ti·la·tion
ven·ti·la·tor
ven·tral
ven·tral·ly
ven·tri·cle
ven·tril·o·quism

ven·tri·lo·qui·al
ven·tril·o·quist
ven·tril·o·quize
  ven·tril·o·quized
  ven·tril·o·quiz·ing
ven·ture
ven·ture·some
  ven·ture·some·ness
ven·tur·ous
  ven·tur·ous·ness
Ve·nus
ve·ra·cious
  ve·ra·cious·ness
ve·rac·i·ty
  ve·rac·i·ties
Ve·ra·cruz
ve·ran·da
ver·bal
  ver·bal·ly
ver·bal·ize
  ver·bal·ized
  ver·bal·iz·ing
  ver·bal·i·za·tion
  ver·bal·iz·er
ver·ba·tim
ver·bi·age
ver·bose
  ver·bose·ness
  ver·bos·i·ty
ver·bo·ten
ver·dant
  ver·dan·cy
Ver·di
ver·dict
ver·di·gris
Ver·dun
ver·dure
  ver·dured
  ver·dur·ous
verge
  verged
  verg·ing
Ver·gil
ver·i·fi·ca·tion
ver·i·fy
  ver·i·fied
  ver·i·fy·ing
  ver·i·fi·a·bil·i·ty
  ver·i·fi·a·ble·ness
  ver·i·fi·a·ble
  ver·i·fi·er
ver·i·si·mil·i·tude
ver·i·ta·ble
  ver·i·ta·ble·ness
  ver·i·ta·bly
ver·i·ty
  ver·i·ties
Ver·meer
ver·meil
ver·mic·u·lar
ver·mic·u·late
  ver·mic·u·lat·ed
ver·mi·fuge
ver·mil·ion
ver·min

ver·min·ous
Ver·mont
ver·mouth
ver·nac·u·lar
ver·nac·u·lar·ism
ver·nal
  ver·nal·ly
Ver·non
Ver·ra·za·no
Ver·sailles
ver·sa·tile
  ver·sa·tile·ness
  ver·sa·til·i·ty
versed
ver·si·fy
  ver·si·fied
  ver·si·fy·ing
  ver·si·fi·er
  ver·si·fi·ca·tion
ver·sion
  ver·sion·al
ver·sus
ver·te·bra
  ver·te·brae
ver·te·bral
  ver·te·bral·ly
ver·te·brate
ver·tex
  ver·tex·es
  ver·ti·ces
ver·ti·cal
  ver·ti·cal·i·ty
  ver·ti·cal·ness
  ver·ti·cal·ly
ver·ti·go
  ver·ti·goes
  ver·tig·i·nes
ves·i·cant
ves·i·ca·to·ry
  ves·i·ca·to·ries
ves·i·cate
  ves·i·cat·ed
  ves·i·cat·ing
  ves·i·ca·tion
ves·i·cle
ve·sic·u·lar
ves·pers
ves·sel
ves·tal
vest·ed
ves·ti·bule
  ves·ti·buled
  ves·ti·bul·ing
  ves·tib·u·lar
ves·tige
  ves·tig·i·al
  ves·tig·i·al·ly
vest·ment
vest-pock·et
ves·try
  ves·tries
Ve·su·vi·us
vet
  vet·ted
  vet·ting

vet·er·an
vet·er·i·nar·i·an
vet·er·i·nary
ve·to
  ve·toed
  ve·to·ing
  ve·to·er
vex
  vex·er
  vex·ing·ly
vex·a·tion
vex·a·tious
vexed
via
vi·a·ble
  vi·a·bil·i·ty
  vi·a·bly
vi·a·duct
vi·al
vi·and
vi·brant
  vi·bran·cy
vi·brate
  vi·brat·ed
  vi·brat·ing
vi·bra·tion
vi·bra·to
  vi·bra·tos
vi·bra·tor
vi·bra·to·ry
vi·bur·num
vic·ar
  vic·ar·ship
vic·ar·age
vi·car·i·ous
  vi·car·i·ous·ly
  vi·car·i·ous·ness
vice ad·mi·ral
vice con·sul
  vice-con·su·lar
  vice-con·su·late
  vice-con·sul·ship
vice pres·i·dent
  vice-pres·i·den·cy
  vice-pres·i·den·cies
  vice-pres·i·den·tial
vice·roy
  vice·roy·al
vice ver·sa
Vi·chy
vi·cin·i·ty
  vi·cin·i·ties
vi·cious
  vi·cious·ly
  vi·cious·ness
vi·cis·si·tude
Vicks·burg
vic·tim
vic·tim·ize
  vic·tim·ized
  vic·tim·iz·ing
  vic·tim·i·za·tion
  vic·tim·iz·er
vic·tor
Vic·to·ri·an

Vic·to·ri·an·ism
vic·to·ri·ous
  vic·to·ri·ous·ly
  vic·to·ri·ous·ness
vic·to·ry
  vic·to·ries
Vic·tro·la
vict·ual
vi·cu·ña
vid·eo
vid·e·o·tape
  vid·e·o·taped
  vid·e·o·tap·ing
vie
  vied
  vy·ing
  vi·er
Vi·en·na
Vien·tiane
Vi·et Nam
Vi·et·nam·ese
view·er
view·less
view·point
vig·il
vig·i·lance
vig·i·lant
vig·i·lan·te
vi·gnette
vig·or
vig·or·ous
  vig·or·ous·ly
vi·king
vile
  vil·er
  vil·est
vil·i·fy
  vil·i·fied
  vil·i·fy·ing
  vil·i·fi·ca·tion
vil·la
vil·lage
vil·lain
  vil·lain·ous
  vil·lain·ous·ly
  vil·lain·ous·ness
vil·lainy
  vil·lain·ies
vil·lein
vil·lous
vil·lus
  vil·li
Vin·cennes
vin·ci·ble
  vin·ci·bil·i·ty
vin·di·cate
  vin·di·cat·ed
  vin·di·cat·ing
  vin·di·ca·tion
  vin·di·ca·tor
vin·dic·tive
  vin·dic·tive·ly
  vin·dic·tive·ness
vin·e·gar
vin·e·gary

vine·yard
vi·nous
vin·tage
vint·ner
vi·nyl
vi·ol
vi·o·la
vi·o·list
vi·o·la·ble
vi·o·la·bil·i·ty
vi·o·late
vi·o·lat·ed
vi·o·lat·ing
vi·o·la·tor
vi·o·la·tion
vi·o·lence
vi·o·lent
vi·o·let
vi·o·lin
vi·o·lin·ist
vi·o·lon·cel·lo
vi·o·lon·cel·list
vi·per
vi·ra·go
vi·ra·goes
vi·ra·gos
vi·ral
vir·eo
vir·e·os
Vir·gil
vir·gin
vir·gin·al
vir·gin·al·ly
Vir·gin·ia
vir·gin·i·ty
vir·gule
vir·ile
vi·ril·i·ty
vi·rol·o·gy
vi·rol·o·gist
vir·tu·al
vir·tu·al·ly
vir·tue
vir·tu·os·i·ty
vir·tu·os·i·ties
vir·tu·o·so
vir·tu·o·sos
vir·tu·o·si
vir·tu·o·sic
vir·tu·ous
vir·tu·ous·ly
vir·tu·ous·ness
vir·u·lence
vir·u·len·cy
vir·u·lent
vi·rus
vi·rus·es
vi·sa
vis·age
vis·à·vis
vis·cera
vis·cer·al
vis·cid
vis·cid·i·ty
vis·cid·ly

vis·cid·ness
vis·cos·i·ty
vis·cos·i·ties
vis·count
vis·count·cy
vis·count·ship
vis·count·ess
vis·cous
vis·i·bil·i·ty
vis·i·bil·i·ties
vis·i·ble
Vis·i·goth
vi·sion
vi·sion·ary
vi·sion·ar·ies
vis·it
vis·i·tant
vis·it·a·tion
vis·it·ing
vis·i·tor
vi·sor
vis·ta
Vis·tu·la
vis·u·al
vis·u·al·ly
vis·u·al·ize
vis·u·al·ized
vis·u·al·iz·ing
vis·u·al·i·za·tion
vi·tal
vi·tal·i·ty
vi·tal·i·ties
vi·tal·ize
vi·tal·ized
vi·tal·iz·ing
vi·tal·i·za·tion
vi·tals
vi·ta·min
vi·ti·ate
vi·ti·at·ed
vi·ti·at·ing
vi·ti·a·tion
vit·re·ous
vit·re·os·i·ty
vit·ri·fy
vit·ri·fied
vit·ri·fy·ing
vit·ri·fi·a·ble
vit·ri·fi·ca·tion
vit·ri·ol
vit·ri·ol·ic
vi·tu·per·ate
vi·tu·per·at·ed
vi·tu·per·at·ing
vi·tu·per·a·tion
vi·va
vi·va·cious
vi·vac·i·ty
vi·vac·i·ties
viv·id
viv·i·fy
viv·i·fied
viv·i·fy·ing
viv·i·fi·ca·tion
vi·vip·ar·ous

viv·i·sec·tion
vix·en
vi·zier
vi·zor
Vlad·i·vos·tok
vo·cab·u·lar·y
  vo·cab·u·lar·ies
vo·cal
vo·cal·ic
vo·cal·ist
vo·cal·ize
  vo·cal·ized
  vo·cal·iz·ing
  vo·cal·i·za·tion
vo·ca·tion
vo·ca·tion·al
vo·cif·er·ous
vod·ka
voice
  voiced
  voic·ing
voice·less
voice·print
void·a·ble
vol·a·tile
  vol·a·til·i·ty
vol·can·ic
  vol·can·i·cal·ly
vol·ca·no
  vol·ca·noes
  vol·ca·nos
Vol·ga
Vol·go·grad
vo·li·tion
vol·ley
  vol·leys
  vol·leyed
  vol·ley·ing
vol·ley·ball
Vol·ta
volt·age
vol·ta·ic
Vol·taire
volt·me·ter
vol·u·ble
  vol·u·bly
  vol·u·bil·i·ty
vol·ume
vo·lu·mi·nous
  vo·lu·mi·nous·ly
  vo·lu·mi·nous·ness
vol·un·tary
  vol·un·tar·i·ly
vol·un·teer
vo·lup·tu·ary
  vo·lup·tu·ar·ies
vo·lup·tu·ous
vom·it
voo·doo
  voo·doos
voo·doo·ism
  voo·doo·ist
  voo·doo·is·tic
vo·ra·cious
  vo·rac·i·ty

vor·tex
  vor·tex·es
  vor·ti·ces
vo·ta·ry
  vo·ta·ries
vote
  vot·ed
  vot·ing
vot·er
vo·tive
vouch·er
vouch·safe
  vouch·safed
  vouch·saf·ing
vow·el
voy·age
  voy·aged
  voy·ag·ing
  voy·ag·er
vo·ya·geur
vo·yeur
  vo·yeur·ism
  voy·eur·is·tic
Vul·can
vul·can·ite
vul·can·ize
  vul·can·ized
  vul·can·iz·ing
  vul·can·i·za·tion
vul·gar
  vul·gar·ism
vul·gar·i·ty
  vul·gar·i·ties
vul·gar·ize
  vul·gar·ized
  vul·gar·iz·ing
  vul·gar·i·za·tion
vul·gate
vul·ner·a·ble
  vul·ner·a·bil·i·ty
  vul·ner·a·bly
vul·pine
vul·ture
vul·va
  vul·vae
  vul·vas
Wa·bash
wab·ble
  wab·bled
  wab·bling
wacky
  wack·i·er
  wack·i·est
  wack·i·ly
  wack·i·ness
wad
  wad·ded
  wad·ding
wad·dle
  wad·dled
  wad·dling
wad·dler
  wad·dly
  wad·dli·er
  wad·dli·est

wade
  wad·ed
  wad·ing
wad·er
wa·fer
waf·fle
wag
  wagged
  wag·ging
  wag·ger
  wag·gish
wage
  waged
  wag·ing
wa·ger
wag·gery
  wag·ger·ies
wag·gle
  wag·gled
  wag·gling
Wag·ner
wag·on
wag·on·er
Wai·ki·ki
wain·scot
  wain·scot·ing
wain·wright
waist·band
waist·coat
waist·line
wait·er
wait·ing
wait·ress
waive
  waived
  waiv·ing
waiv·er
wake
  waked
  wok·en
  wak·ing
wake·ful
  wake·ful·ly
  wake·ful·ness
wak·en
Wal·den
Wal·do
Wal·dorf
wale
  waled
  wal·ing
walk·a·way
walk·er
walk·ie-talk·ie
walk·out
walk·o·ver
walk·up
walk·way
wal·la·by
  wal·la·bies
Wal·la·chia
wall·board
wal·let
wall·eye
wall·eyed

wall·flow·er
Wal·loon
wal·lop
wall·pa·per
wall-to-wall
wal·nut
Wal·pole
wal·rus
  wal·rus·es
Wal·tham
Wal·ton
wam·pum
wan
  wan·ner
  wan·nest
  wan·ness
wan·der
wan·der·lust
wane
  waned
  wan·ing
wan·gle
  wan·gled
  wan·gling
  wan·gler
want·ing
wan·ton
wap·i·ti
  wap·i·ties
war
  warred
  war·ring
war·ble
  war·bled
  war·bling
  war·bler
war·den
  war·den·ship
ward·er
ward·robe
ware·house
war·fare
war·head
war·horse
war·like
war·lock
warm
  warm·er
  warm·est
warm-blood·ed
warm-heart·ed
war·mong·er
warmth
warn·ing
war·path
war·rant
war·ran·ty
  war·ran·ties
war·ren
war·ri·or
War·saw
war·ship
war·time
War·wick
wary

war·i·er
war·i·est
war·i·ly
war·i·ness
wash·a·ble
wash·ba·sin
wash·board
wash·bowl
wash·cloth
wash·er
wash·ing
Wash·ing·ton
wash·out
wash·room
wash·stand
wash·tub
was·n't
wasp
  wasp·ish
  wasp·ish·ly
  wasp·ish·ness
was·sail
Was·ser·mann test
wast·age
waste
  wast·ed
  wast·ing
  waste·ful
  waste·ful·ly
  waste·ful·ness
waste·bas·ket
waste·land
waste·pa·per
wast·er
wast·rel
watch·dog
watch·ful
watch·man
  watch·men
watch·tow·er
watch·word
wa·ter
wat·er·buck
Wa·ter·bury
wa·ter·col·or
wa·ter·course
wa·ter·cress
wa·ter·fall
wa·ter·fowl
wa·ter·front
wa·ter·less
wa·ter lev·el
wa·ter lily
  wa·ter lil·ies
wa·ter line
wa·ter·logged
Wa·ter·loo
wa·ter main
wa·ter·man
  wa·ter·men
wa·ter·mark
wa·ter·mel·on
wa·ter moc·ca·sin
wa·ter·proof
wa·ter-re·pel·lent

wa·ter·shed
wa·ter·side
wa·ter-ski
  wa·ter-skied
  wa·ter-ski·ing
wa·ter·spout
wa·ter·tight
wa·ter·way
wa·ter·works
wa·tery
watt·age
watt-hour
wat·tle
  wat·tled
  wat·tling
Wau·ke·gan
Wau·sau
wave
  waved
  wav·ing
wave·length
wave·let
wa·ver
Wa·ver·ley
wav·y
  wav·i·er
  wav·i·est
  wav·i·ly
  wav·i·ness
wax
  waxed
  wax·ing
wax·en
wax·wing
wax·work
waxy
  wax·i·er
  wax·i·est
  wax·i·ness
way·far·er
  way·far·ing
way·lay
  way·laid
  way·lay·ing
way·side
way·ward
weak·en
weak-kneed
weak·ling
weak·ly
  weak·li·er
  weak·li·est
  weak·li·ness
weak-mind·ed
weak·ness
wealthy
  wealth·i·er
  wealth·i·est
  wealth·i·ly
  wealth·i·ness
wean
weap·on
weap·on·ry
wear
  wear·ing

wea·ri·some
wea·ry
  wea·ri·er
  wea·ri·est
  wea·ried
  wea·ry·ing
  wea·ri·ly
  wea·ri·ness
wea·sel
weath·er
weath·er-beat·en
weath·er·cock
weath·er·glass
weath·er·ing
weath·er·man
  weath·er·men
weath·er·proof
weath·er·vane
weave
  weaved
  wov·en
  weav·ing
weav·er
web
  webbed
  web·bing
web·foot
  web-foot·ed
Web·ster
wed·ding
wedge
  wedged
  wedg·ing
Wedg·wood ware
wed·lock
Wednes·day
weedy
  weed·i·er
  weed·i·est
week·day
week·end
week·ly
weep·ing
wee·vil
weigh
weight
weighty
  weight·i·er
  weight·i·est
  weight·i·ly
  weight·i·ness
weird
  weird·er
  weird·est
wel·come
  wel·comed
  wel·com·ing
wel·fare
well-be·ing
well-born
well-bred
well-dis·posed
well-done
well-found·ed
well-groomed

well-ground·ed
Wel·ling·ton
well-known
well-mean·ing
well-nigh
well-off
well-read
well-spo·ken
well·spring
well-thought-of
well-timed
well-to-do
well-wish·er
well-worn
Welsh·man
wel·ter
wel·ter·wright
Wen·ces·laus
were·wolf
  were·wolves
Wes·ley
Wes·sex
west·bound
West·ches·ter
west·er·ly
west·ern
west·ern·er
West·ern Hem·i·sphere
west·ern·ize
  west·ern·ized
  west·ern·iz·ing
  west·ern·i·za·tion
west·ern·most
West In·dies
West·ing·house
West·min·ster
West·more·land
West·pha·lia
West Vir·gin·ia
west·ward
wet
  wet·ter
  wet·test
wet·back
Wey·mouth
whale
  whaled
  whal·ing
whale·boat
whale·bone
whal·er
wharf
  wharves
Whar·ton
what·ev·er
what·not
what·so·ev·er
wheal
wheat·en
whee·dle
  whee·dled
  whee·dling
  whee·dler
wheel and ax·le
wheel·bar·row

wheel·chair
wheeled
wheel·house
Wheel·ing
wheel·wright
wheeze
 wheezed
 wheez·ing
wheezy
 wheez·i·er
 wheez·i·est
 wheez·i·ly
 wheez·i·ness
whelm
whelp
whence·so·ev·er
where·a·bouts
where·as
where·by
where·fore
where·in
where·on
where·so·ev·er
where·to
where·up·on
wher·ev·er
where·with
where·with·al
wher·ry
 wher·ries
whet
 whet·ted
 whet·ting
wheth·er
whet·stone
which·ev·er
whim·per
whim·si·cal
whim·sy
 whim·sies
whine
 whined
 whin·ing
whin·ny
 whin·nied
 whin·ny·ing
 whin·nies
whip
 whipped
 whip·ping
whip·lash
whip·per·snap·per
whip·pet
whip·poor·will
whir
 whirred
 whir·ring
whirl·i·gig
whirl·pool
whirl·wind
whisk·er
whis·key
 whis·ky
 whis·keys
 whis·kies

whis·per
whist
whis·tle
 whis·tled
 whis·tling
 whis·tler
white
 whit·er
 whit·est
 whit·ish
white-col·lar
white·fish
whit·en
white·wash
white wa·ter
whith·er
whit·ing
Whit·man
Whit·sun·day
Whit·sun·tide
Whit·ti·er
whit·tle
 whit·tled
 whit·tling
 whit·tler
whiz
 whizzed
 whiz·zing
 whiz·zes
whoa
who·ev·er
whole·heart·ed
whole·sale
 whole·saled
 whole·sal·ing
 whole·sal·er
whole·some
whole-wheat
whol·ly
whom·ev·er
whom·so·ev·er
whoop·ing
whop·per
whop·ping
whorled
whose·so·ev·er
who·so·ev·er
Wich·i·ta
wick·ed
wick·er
wick·er·work
wick·et
wide
 wid·er
 wid·est
wide-a·wake
wide-eyed
wid·en
wide·spread
widg·eon
wid·ow
wid·ow·er
wid·ow·hood
width
wield·er

wieldy
wie·ner
wig·gle
  wig·gled
  wig·gling
  wig·gly
  wig·gli·er
  wig·gli·est
wig·gler
wig·wag
  wig·wagged
  wig·wag·ging
wig·wam
wild·cat
  wild·cat·ted
  wild·cat·ting
  wild·cat strike
Wil·der
wil·der·ness
wild·fire
wild·fowl
wild-goose chase
wild·life
wild·wood
wile
  wiled
  wil·ing
  wil·i·ly
  wil·i·ness
  wily
  wil·i·er
  wil·i·est
Wil·helms·ha·ven
Wilkes-Bar·re
Wil·lam·ette
willed
will·ful
Wil·liams·burg
wil·lies
will·ing
will-o'-the-wisp
wil·low
wil·lowy
wil·ly-nil·ly
Wil·ming·ton
wim·ble
wim·ple
win
  win·ning
wince
  winced
  winc·ing
Win·ches·ter
wind
  wound
  wind·ing
wind·bag
wind·break
wind·ed
Win·der·mere
wind·fall
wind·flow·er
wind·jam·mer
wind·lass
wind·mill

win·dow
win·dow·pane
win·dow-shop
  win·dow-shopped
  win·dow-shop·ping
  win·dow-shop·per
wind·pipe
wind·row
wind·shield
Wind·sor
wind·storm
wind·up
wind·ward
windy
  wind·i·er
  wind·i·est
  wind·i·ly
  wind·i·ness
wine
  wined
  win·ing
win·ery
  win·er·ies
Wine·sap
wine·skin
winged
wing·span
wing·spread
Win·ne·ba·go
win·ner
win·ning
Win·ni·peg
win·now
Wins·low
win·some
Win·ston-Sa·lem
win·ter
win·ter·green
win·ter·ize
  win·ter·ized
  win·ter·iz·ing
  win·ter·i·za·tion
win·try
  win·tri·er
  win·tri·est
  win·ter·y
  win·tri·ly
  win·tri·ness
wipe
  wiped
  wip·ing
wire-haired
wire·less
wire·tap
  wire·tapped
  wire·tap·ping
  wire·tap·per
wir·ing
wiry
  wir·i·er
  wir·i·est
  wir·i·ly
  wir·i·ness
Wis·con·sin
wis·dom

wise
  wis·er
  wis·est
wise·a·cre
wise·crack
wish·bone
wish·ful
wish·y-washy
wisp
  wispy
  wisp·i·er
  wisp·i·est
wis·te·ria
wist·ful
witch·craft
witch·ery
  witch·er·ies
witch·ing
with·draw
  with·drew
  with·drawn
  with·draw·ing
  with·draw·al
with·er
  with·ered
  with·er·ing
with·hold
  with·held
  with·hold·ing
with·in
with·out
with·stand
  with·stood
  with·stand·ing
wit·less
wit·ness
wit·ted
wit·ti·cism
wit·ting
  wit·ting·ly
wit·ty
  wit·ti·er
  wit·ti·est
  wit·ti·ly
  wit·ti·ness
wiz·ard
  wi·zard·ly
  wiz·ard·ry
wiz·en
  wiz·ened
wob·ble
  wob·bled
  wob·bling
  wob·bly
  wob·bli·er
  wob·bli·est
woe·be·gone
woe·ful
wolf·hound
wolf·ram
Wol·sey
wol·ver·ine
wom·an
  wom·en
  wom·an·like

wom·an·ly
wom·an·li·ness
wom·an·hood
wom·an·ish
wom·an·kind
womb
wom·bat
wom·en·folk
won·der
won·der·ful
won·der·land
won·der·ment
won·drous
wont·ed
wood·bine
wood·chuck
wood·cock
wood·craft
wood·cut
wood·cut·ter
wood·ed
wood·en
wood·land
wood·man
  wood·men
wood·peck·er
wood·pile
wood·shed
woods·man
  woods·men
Wood·stock
woodsy
  woods·i·er
  woods·i·est
wood·wind
wood·work
woody
  wood·i·er
  wood·i·est
woo·er
wool·en
wool·gath·er·ing
  wool·gath·er
  wool·gath·er·er
wool·ly
  wool·li·er
  wool·li·est
  wool·li·ness
wool·ly-head·ed
Wool·worth
woozy
  wooz·i·er
  wooz·i·est
  wooz·i·ly
  wooz·i·ness
Worces·ter
Worces·ter·shire
word·book
word·ing
word·less
word·less·ly
word·less·ness
Words·worth
wordy
word·i·er

word·i·est
word·i·ly
word·i·ness
work·a·ble
work·a·bil·i·ty
work·a·day
work·bench
work·book
work·day
worked-up
work·er
work·horse
work·house
work·ing
work·ing·man
work·ing·men
work·man
work·men
work·man·like
work·man·ship
work·out
work·room
work·shop
work·ta·ble
world·ly
world·li·er
world·li·est
world·li·ness
world·ly-wise
world-wea·ry
world-wide
worm-eat·en
worm·wood
wormy
worm·i·er
worm·i·est
worn-out
wor·ri·some
wor·ry
wor·ried
wor·ry·ing
wor·ries
wor·ri·er
wor·ry·wart
wors·en
wor·ship
wor·ship·ful
wor·sted
worth·less
worth·while
wor·thy
wor·thi·er
wor·thi·est
wor·thi·ly
wor·thi·ness
would-be
would·n't
wound·ed
wraith
wran·gle
wran·gled
wran·gling
wran·gler
wrap
wrapped

wrap·ping
wrap·per
wrath·ful
wreak
wreath
wreathe
wreathed
wreath·ing
wreck·age
wreck·er
wrench
wres·tle
wres·tled
wres·tling
wretch·ed
wrig·gle
wrig·gled
wrig·gling
wrig·gly
wrig·gli·er
wrig·gli·est
wrig·gler
wring
wrung
wring·ing
wring·er
wrin·kle
wrin·kled
wrin·kling
wrin·kly
wrin·kli·er
wrin·kli·est
wrist·band
write
wrote
writ·ten
writ·ing
write-in
writ·er
writhe
writhed
writh·ing
wrong·do·er
wrong·do·ing
wronged
wrong·ful
wrong-head·ed
wrought
wry
wri·er
wri·est
wry·ly
Wur·tem·berg
Wyc·liffe
Wy·lie
Wy·o·ming
Xa·ve·ri·an
Xav·i·er
X-chro·mo·some
xe·bec
xe·non
xen·o·pho·bia
Xen·o·phon
Xer·xes
Xmas

X-ray
  x·ray
xy·lem
xy·lo·phone
  xy·lo·phon·ist
Xy·ris
yacht
yacht·ing
yachts·man
  yachts·men
Yah·weh
yak
yam
Yang·tze
yank
Yan·kee
Ya·oun·dé
yap
  yapped
  yap·ping
yard·age
yard·arm
yard·mas·ter
yard·stick
yarn
yar·row
yawn
Y-chro·mo·some
yea
year·book
year·ling
year·long
year·ly
yearn
  yearn·ing
year-round
yeast
yeasty
  yeast·i·er
  yeast·i·est
yel·low
  yel·low·ish
yel·low·bird
yel·low fe·ver
yel·low·ham·mer
yel·low jack·et
Yel·low·stone
yelp
Yem·en
yen
  yenned
  yen·ning
yeo·man
  yeo·men
ye·shi·va
  ye·shi·vas
yes·ter·day
yes·ter·year
yeti
yew
Yid·dish
yield
yield·ing
yip
  yipped

yip·ping
yo·del
  yo·deled
  yo·del·ing
  yo·del·er
yo·ga
  yo·gic
yo·gi
  yo·gis
yo·gurt
yoke
  yoked
  yok·ing
yo·kel
Yo·ko·ha·ma
yolk
Yom Kip·pur
yon·der
Yon·kers
yore
York·shire
Yo·sem·i·te
young
young·ling
young·ster
Youngs·town
your·self
  your·selves
youth·ful
yowl
Yo-Yo
yt·ter·bi·um
yt·tri·um
Yu·ca·tan
yuc·ca
Yu·go·slav·ia
Yu·kon
yule·tide
yum·my
  yum·mi·er
  yum·mi·est
Zach·a·ri·ah
Zam·be·si
Zam·be·zi
Zam·bia
za·ny
  za·nies
  za·ni·er
  za·ni·est
  za·ni·ly
  za·ni·ness
Zan·zi·bar
Zea·land
zeal·ot
zeal·ous
Zeb·e·dee
ze·bra
  ze·bras
ze·bu
Zech·a·ri·ah
Zen·ger
ze·nith
zeph·yr
zep·pe·lin
ze·ro

ze·ros
ze·roes
zest
  zesty
  zest·i·er
  zest·i·est
zig·zag
  zig·zagged
  zig·zag·ging
zinc
Zin·fan·del
zing
zin·nia
Zi·on
Zi·on·ism
  Zi·on·ist
zip
  zipped
  zip·ping
zip·per
zip·py
  zip·pi·er
  zip·pi·est

zir·con
zir·co·ni·um
zith·er
zo·di·ac
  zo·di·a·cal
Zom·ba
zom·bie
  zom·bi
zon·al
zone
  zoned
  zon·ing
zoo
  zoos
zo·ol·o·gy
  zo·o·log·i·cal
  zo·o·log·i·cal·ly
  zo·ol·o·gist
zuc·chi·ni
Zu·rich
zwie·back
Zwing·li
zy·gote